MODERN POLITICS

11727

320.9

Also published by Stanley Thornes (Publishers) Ltd

J.R.S. Whiting   *Politics and Government, a first sourcebook*
Chris Leeds   *Politics in Action, contemporary sources for students of politics and government*

MODERN POLITICS

PAUL DENHAM

what does .

STANLEY THORNES (PUBLISHERS) LTD

First published in 1987 by:
Stanley Thornes (Publishers) Ltd
Old Station Drive
Leckhampton
CHELTENHAM GL53 0DN
England

British Library Cataloguing in Publication Data

Denham, Paul
    Modern politics.
    1. Great Britain — Politics and
    government — 1979–
    I. Title
    320.941   JN231

ISBN 0–85950–648–7

Typeset by Tech-Set, Gateshead, Tyne & Wear in 11/12 Garamond.
Printed and bound in Great Britain at The Bath Press, Avon.

Contents

8 ECONOMIC ISSUES AND NATIONALISATION

9 PRESSURE GROUPS AND POLITICAL INTERESTS

10 POLITICAL PARTIES

11 VOTING BEHAVIOUR

APPENDIX A

APPENDIX B

——————— Documents

Preface

Politics is always in a state of flux, and whatever is put into print will inevitably be dated by the time it reaches the bookshops or the classroom. That, in one way, is why the academic study of politics can be so much fun and a challenge. A good deal of this text has arisen over the past few years in an attempt to cope with the demands of changing A-level syllabuses. However, it is hoped that a judicious balance of description and analysis will make it a useful introductory reader for a variety of politics courses in further and higher education. The political issues upon which this book draws are in the main confined to post-1966, but earlier examples are given where appropriate.

A few words are necessary about the structure of the book. At the end of each chapter there is a summary, which should be useful for class discussion. There is, however, no summary as such at the end of the introductory chapter since Chapter 1 takes a different form from the remainder of the text, nor is there a summary at the end of Chapter 11 since that chapter should be read in conjunction with Chapter 12.

In the first chapter there are two exercises specifically based on the documentary extracts. In the remainder of the book there are no questions on the documentary extracts alone, but at the end of each chapter there are four examination questions mostly from the JMB, the AEB and the London University Board. Like the summaries, the documentary extracts are particularly intended for class discussion or small group work, although they will be of value also to the individual reader.

At the end of the book there is a short reading list, which reflects the author's own views. Also, references are made by way of marginal notes to the two politics source books published by Stanley Thornes – Chris Leeds, *Politics in Action,* 1986, and J.R.S. Whiting, *Politics and Government, a first sourcebook,* 1985.

My particular thanks go to a former colleague, Dr Donald Giles, now Depute Director, SCOTVEC, Glasgow, who has not only given me enormous encouragement, but also read through large parts of the script. I should also like to record the influence of the stimulating thoughts of an early former student, Mr Othman Ghafar (of Brunei). Lastly, I must acknowledge the assistance received from Mr S.J. Patrick of the Public Bill Office of the House of Commons, Mr A.C. McLaren of the Department of Trade and Industry, Mr S. Roberts of the United States Embassy, London and the library staff of Exeter University.

A last word here would be in order if it underlined the point that at A-level and beyond the student must be able to discuss and criticise on the basis of factual knowledge acquired steadily over the whole period of an academic course; mere description, of course, in advanced studies will not suffice. Over the past decade or so such studies have travelled a stage further, towards a deeper analysis of political behaviour, not least in the area of socialisation and voting behaviour, the role of pressure groups and the influence of the mass media, all of which issues are covered in detail in this work.

The political position stated is by and large that which obtained at January 1987. This cut-off point brings us back to the opening paragraph of this preface, and in particular it raises two issues. The first is concerned with local government.

The Widdicombe Report on the conduct of local authority business was published in June 1986; it is a wide-ranging review of local government, especially its political affairs and it makes frequent reference to earlier surveys, from Maud 1967 onwards. For those students paying particular attention to local government, the report should be essential reading. Widdicombe came rather late in the day to be properly incorporated, at every level, in the script. However, a summary is given at the end of Section B in Chapter 7, and further details are to be found in Appendix B.

The second issue is the fast-moving area of privatisation or denationalisation (Chapter 8). Many key industries or services remain in the State's hands – coal, electricity, the railways and steel, for example. The problems discussed in Chapter 8 are therefore still applicable, but as time wears on, increasingly less so, unless, of course, there is a Labour victory at the next general election and widespread renationalisation takes place, as already promised in respect of British Telecom. The table given towards the end of Chapter 8 in respect of Mrs Thatcher's privatisation programme so far is correct to mid-1986, and developments up until mid-January 1987 have also been noted.

At the time of final proof reading a few other points seemed worthy of note. The question of the accountability of ministers and civil servants to the Select Committees of the House of Commons rumbles on (see p. 67); the Government appears to be retreating somewhat and has promised that civil servants may answer more detailed questions than originally envisaged (see 1st Report from the Liaison Committee, HC 100, 1986–7 session). The BBC licence fee is to be index-linked (see p. 372). John Ryman (MP for Blyth Valley) has resigned from the Labour Party (see p. 168). The Education (No. 2) Act 1986 severely restricts the use of corporal punishment in schools.

Finally, I must pay tribute to the skill and forebearance of the staff at Stanley Thornes whose patience with my whims and last minute suggestions has been remarkable.

Paul Denham, February 1987

Acknowledgements

The author and publishers are grateful to the following for permission to reproduce previously published material:

Anthony P. Barker for an extract from *The Listener*, 13.9.84;

Basil Blackwell Ltd. for an extract from *Politics in Everyday Life* by H.V. Wiseman, 1966 and from *Parliamentary Affairs* extracts by W. Plowden and N. Johnson, Winter 1985;

Lord Blake for an extract from *The Sunday Times*, 30.11.75;

A.W. Bradley for an extract from *The Listener*, 5.5.77;

BBC Enterprises Ltd. for an extract from *The Politics of Pressure* by Malcolm Davies, 1985;

David Butler for an extract from *The Sunday Times*, 17.4.77;

Cambridge University Press for extracts from *Decade of Dealignment* by B. Särlvik and I. Crewe, 1983;

Century Hutchinson Ltd. for an extract from *The Government and Politics of Britain* by J.P. Mackintosh, revised and updated by P.G. Richards, 5th edition, 1982, Hutchinson University Library;

Financial Times for extracts from various issues;

The Guardian for extracts from various issues;

The Controller of Her Majesty's Stationary Office for Crown Copyright material;

The Independent for an extract by Peter Kellner, 13.10.86;

David McKie for extracts from issues of *The Guardian*, 22.7.83 and 6.8.85;

Macmillan Publishers Ltd. for extracts from *The British General Election of 1979* and *The British General Election of 1983* by D. Butler and D. Kavanagh;

Colin R. Munro for an extract from *The Times*, 12.2.82;

New Society for extracts including those by J. Gyford, 3.5.84, D. Thomas, 17.1.85, G. Weightman, 23.9.76 and an article 'The present discontents: in defence of deadlock' by S.E. Finer, 5.9.74;

Open University Press for extracts from *How Voters Decide*, 2nd edn., by H. Himmelweit, P. Humphreys and M. Jaeger, 1985;

Oxford University Press for extracts from *Parliamentary Affairs*: 'The Prime Minister and the Appointment of Ministers' by R.K. Alderman, Spring 1971, 'Ministers and Civil Servants; Relations and Responsibilities' by M. Wright, Summer 1977, 'A Mandarin's Duty' by N. Summerton, Autumn 1980, 'The Qualities of Future Civil Servants' by P. Lewis, Autumn 1980, 'Still the era of Party Government' by R. Rose, Summer 1983, 'The House of Lords and the Thatcher Government' by D.R. Shell, Winter 1985, 'The Manifesto as a Mandate' by D. Kavanagh, Winter 1981, 'Whatever is happening to the British Party System?' by A. King, Summer 1982 and 'Culture and Deference' by F.F. Ridley, Winter 1984;

Pergamon Press for an extract from *How Britain Votes* by Heath, Jowell and Curtice, 1985;

Philip Schlesinger for an extract from *The Listener*, 23.6.83;

Times Newspapers Ltd. for extracts from *The Times* and *The Sunday Times,* for an article 'The Consumers' Guide to the Cabinet' by P. Hennessy, *The Times,* 10.2.81; Sir Douglas Wass for an extract from The Reith Lectures, *The Listener,* 24.11.83, also included in *Government and the Governed,* Routledge and Kegan Paul, 1984; Hugo Young for an extract from *The Listener,* 6.6.85.

We would like to acknowledge the following examination boards for permission to reproduce questions from past examination papers:

The Associated Examining Board;
Joint Matriculation Board;
University of London School Examinations Board.

We would also like to thank the following who provided photographs and illustrations and permission to reproduce them:

Associated Press (p. 401);
BBC Enterprises Ltd. (p. 363);
BBC Hulton Picture Library (pp. 24, 42, 45, 57, 106, 116, 173, 238, 268, 285, 290, 293, 312, 383);
Brookes, *The Times* (p. 66);
Central Office of Information (Crown Copyright) (p. 164);
Cummings, Express Newspapers (p. 291);
Garland, Newspaper Publishing PLC (p. 76);
Mac, *The Guardian* (p. 249);
Popperfoto (pp. 8, 10, 20, 65, 192, 207, 257, 319, 341, 387, 399, 404);
Press Association (p. 152);
Sunday People, Mirror Group Newspapers (p. 314);
Syndication International (p. 369);
Times Newspapers Ltd. (p. 211);
Topham Picture Library (p. 380);
Trog, *The Observer* (pp. 195, 276, 343, 358).

Every attempt has been made to contact copyright holders, but we apologise if any have been overlooked.

1 The Political System of the United Kingdom

'For a quarter of a century I have earned my living as a teacher of British government. I have found myself explaining, and in large measure defending, much of
the status quo of the established constitutional machinery. . . . But in the last few
years second thoughts have begun to assert themselves. The system is much less
stable than we used to think.'

David Butler, *The Sunday Times*, 17 April 1977.

The Modern Political System

Without doubt the British parliamentary process is one of the most celebrated in
the Western world, although whether that particular model sufficiently copes with
today's economic problems is entirely another matter; for at times the system has all
the attributes of a beached whale, floundering without clear direction, as some
politicians such as Dr Owen and Mr Steel claim. From a Western point of view,
however, it is *democratic* – the adult population over many decades has acquired the
right to elect its representatives for a maximum period of five years at national
level; governments may come and governments may go, but the democratic system
continues. In the United Kingdom the basis of the system is a Parliament elected by
those over 18 who turn out to vote (about 75 per cent). The party which wins the
most seats, but not necessarily votes, forms a Government for up to five years until
the next general election. That Government frequently has to take controversial
decisions. However, as we shall see throughout this book, the nature of democracy
in an economically developed society is a good deal more complicated than it might
first appear.

So, while Parliament and the Government remain the focal points of the British
system, it is equally important to remember that like other states, especially in the
Western world, Britain is a pluralistic society. Power is dispersed; it rests with the
voter, with political activists, with people in positions of key influence – the so-
called Establishment, with big business, with senior civil servants, trade unionists,
as well as pressure groups and political parties, plus, of course, MPs and ministers.
Moreover, other events, frequently external, will all combine to affect the
workings of government, such as the devaluation of sterling in 1967, the crisis of oil
prices in 1973 and 1979, the coal strike of 1974, the industrial difficulties of 1979,
the Falklands War in 1982.

This book will seek in the remaining 14 chapters to explain and illustrate the main issues in British politics, from those involving the Government (the Executive) and Parliament through to political culture and political change. This will be done principally in the context of the developments that have occurred over approximately the last 15 years. In this introductory note and in the documents below, a number of points will be raised – the gradual, but sometimes violent, development of the British parliamentary process, the unitary, but not entirely centralised, nature of the State, the meaning of politics in terms of British culture, the change in the world status of the United Kingdom since 1945 and the evolution of the Commonwealth as British imperial power inevitably declined, the unique nature of the largely unwritten British constitution, and last, but not least, the growing uncertainties in voting behaviour. Many of these problems, and others, will form a background to what is to follow.

In the next four chapters there is an analysis of Parliament and the central government, including the recent difficulties surrounding official secrecy and the breakdown of consensus politics, together with the problems and politicisation of the Civil Service. The relationship between the Lords and the Commons, increasingly fractious, is examined in Chapter 6. Chapter 7 covers the issues involved in local government, including its difficult relationship with central government, the devolution question and the post-1969 troubles in Northern Ireland. This is followed in Chapter 8 by an analysis of economic problems and the development of the privatisation programme since 1979. After two chapters on pressure groups and the role of political parties, come two other chapters dealing with the growing volatility of the electorate, election results and electoral systems. The final principal chapters conclude with a discussion of the mass media and the concepts of culture and change.

The Nature of Politics

Politics, it is often said, is about choices and the allocation of resources, and as Bismarck, the famous German leader in the nineteenth century, was reputed to have said, politics is the art of the possible. In this country voters consider the success or failure, frequently in economic terms, of the Government of the day and cast their votes accordingly at the next election. However, it should be recalled that it is by no means a majority of the voting electorate, let alone of the total electorate, which votes a Government into or out of office; under the British electoral system, which will be examined later, it is quite likely that a Government will be elected with a large majority of seats on a minority of the votes, as Mrs Thatcher's 'decisive' win in 1983 well illustrated, where the anti-Government votes were almost equally divided between two principal Opposition groupings.

Politics is about how people live and work together, it is about the cohesion of a complicated, technological society. It is concerned with achieving agreed goals, agreeing on the route to realise those goals and, from time to time, reviewing objectives. Equally, political life is about disunity, disagreements, revolts, revolutions and the use of military force. Politics is therefore about government and politicians are directly involved in what governments may be able to bring about. In other words, few governments are universally popular; as will be discussed in Chapter 5 the nature of representative democracy often means that governments must give a lead, must develop policies which will not necessarily, at least initially, meet with widespread approval. However, as an election approaches the governing party has to take greater heed of policies which may win back votes.

Any government will be criticised daily by opposition forces, interest groups and others, as well as up to a point by its own supporters, as illustrated in 1985 by Peter Walker's oblique criticism of his own Cabinet colleagues over economic policy. That is in the nature of a democratic society. Sometimes, however, what a government does will command almost total approval from the electorate; this becomes most obvious in wartime when the nation 'rallies to the flag', although patriotism is, of course, not peculiar to Western democratic countries.

In a political system such as that of the United Kingdom political activity is constant; debates, open arguments and disagreements can be seen nightly on television. Political activity may also be constant in other, less 'democratic' countries, such as in the Eastern bloc; after all, the total membership of political parties in the UK is no greater, proportionately, than that of the Communist Party in the USSR. But here activity is open: opposition is not just tolerated or indeed encouraged, it has been institutionalised, at least since the eighteenth century. Before then the idea of His Majesty's Opposition was a contradiction in terms: how could the Crown be legitimately opposed? Of course, not everything a government does can be scrutinised or is open to the blaze of television lights; there are state secrets, and official secrecy in recent years, as will be seen in Chapter 3, has become an important issue. A popular criticism today is that British government is, in contrast to say, America, unnecessarily secretive.

In the United Kingdom political activity is regulated by a law-making body. As long as there is free debate and a relatively open society, the laws that the representative body passes are usually expected to be obeyed. This poses a problem for those who violently disagree with a particular law, such as coal miners in respect of the laws on picketing during the 1984–5 coal strike. Naturally, a very powerful government with no democratic base, could imprison its most trenchant critics; there are numerous examples, past and present, of dictatorships that do precisely that. In totalitarian systems open political activity is far less; criticism of the Government is regarded as anti-State behaviour and all opposition is, at worst, ruthlessly suppressed or, at best, ignored. Totalitarian and other types of governments will be given separate consideration in the concluding chapter.

In respect of disobeying the law, one former Prime Minister had this to say. Speaking on BBC1's *Panorama* programme, James Callaghan endorsed the TUC's day of illegal, secondary action in support of the National Health Service workers. 'If the law is a bad law, there is always a contingent right to take action that you would otherwise not take.' But ten years before, in 1972, he had said in Parliament:

'The rule of law is upheld and should be upheld by all political parties. Political parties in a democracy live and survive by the acceptance of the law by the nation as a whole. The advice . . . on bad laws is this: accept the law and change the Government, so that the law itself can be changed.'

The Times,
7 September 1982

3

Whether today many in the Labour Party would adhere to the earlier Callaghan line is open to doubt.

A further important point is that in a Western political system, such as Britain's, the concept of democracy is deeply embedded, and has been over the past hundred years or so, at many different levels in society. The most important element remains the election of a Parliament and drawn from that a Government at national level, although as indicated above a Government can often be elected on a minority of the votes. Voters are given some kind of choice and political parties compete for power. But elections also occur at local government level, primarily in counties and districts. And democracy operates in other areas of life, too, such as trade unions and local clubs or associations and at shareholders' meetings in companies; in these organisations it is not always a simple majority that is required. For example, in order to achieve change, such as a constitutional amendment, the rules of the body concerned may demand a weighted majority like two-thirds or three-quarters.

In an economically and socially complex country, such as the United Kingdom, densely populated with 55 million people, there can be no true or moral democracy. Democracy here is indirect, representatives are elected for one reason or another and each voter hopes the promises representatives make, and the way in which representatives use their discretion, will match the voter's own political aspirations. This, however, will never work out fully in practice. Given the size of the population, the difficulty of ascertaining majority opinion on all issues, the fact that governments are there to lead as well as to follow opinion, the problems of detailed technical issues and of unexpected events, such as a run on sterling, or a war, no voter will ever be completely satisfied. Democracy may be about fulfilling people's wishes, or at least the desires of the majority, but politics is concerned with compromise and achieving what appears to those elected sensible, just and proper, and in the case of the central government what is 'in the national interest'. Hence the moral dilemma that arises when the governing party in Parliament passes laws which displease not only the minority but also elements of the majority. On the other hand, the Government governs and Parliament legislates for all parts of the United Kingdom, including since 1972 Northern Ireland. If there were not some degree of social unity and political consensus (if only about the rules of the game), the centralised state, even if the nation is geographically small, would be a political non-starter.

Is it ever possible to satisfy the electoral minority? There are several considerations. Firstly, if special rules are made for minority rights, might not the minority become tyrannical in respect of the majority? Special provision, such as positive discrimination in law on behalf of racial minorities, might deprive the majority of its political wishes. Such positive discrimination in the broadest, American sense (for example, legislating that the Metropolitan Police must have, say, a 15 per cent black quota) does not appear to be on the political agenda, notwithstanding 'race' riots in Bristol (1980), London and Liverpool (1981) and Birmingham (1985) and a judicial inquiry into the London disturbances (Lord Scarman's Report). Equally, a majority can behave tyrannically towards a minority; history is littered with examples, such as the early settlers to America who were forced to emigrate because of religious persecution. These were problems that taxed, for example, the mind of the famous nineteenth-century philosopher, John Stuart Mill. Secondly, as stated

*The Brixton
Disorders
April 1981,
Cmnd 8427,
1981*

4

above, governments in this country can easily be elected, given the nature of the British electoral system, by a minority of the total vote, let alone of the total electorate. A government with around 40 per cent of the votes cast can still gain a huge majority in the Commons, as Mrs Thatcher ably demonstrated in 1983. Under the British electoral system it is mathematically possible, but more than improbable, for Party A to gain more votes in total than Party B, but for Party A to win no seats while Party B becomes the Government. Thirdly, majority public opinion is constantly shifting; it is not easy to identify, despite the frequent use of opinion polls. What may be a 'majority' at election time can, within months, become a clear minority, as far as support for the Government and its policies (or lack of them) is concerned.

Of course, throughout this section the word 'democracy' has been used in a Western, liberal sense. But the concept is much used, or abused, elsewhere in the world. The Eastern communist bloc states also regard themselves as democratic, for example, the DDR – the German Democratic Republic (East Germany). There 'democracy' is used in the sense of higher social goals – democratic centralism means that everyone is working towards the same end, for a united and equal social purpose, in so far as a central political group takes decisions in the interests of the wider movement. But that also denotes little public dissent, and 'democracy' as used in this context is far removed from the Western, liberal definition. In Third World developing countries the notion of democracy is strained as far as Western minds are concerned: there one-party states may be more involved with fostering a sense of nationhood, rather than enjoying the 'luxuries' of competitive party politics. Many leaders of such countries would argue that a multi-party system is incompatible with continuing tribalism and inter-racial conflict. These matters will be touched on again in the final chapter.

An Unwritten Constitution

It is also frequently claimed that the British constitution is unwritten. There are no codes, or sets of rules, as in the American case, no fundamental Bill of Rights to which the Government is answerable, no Supreme Court, again as in the USA, which can strike down actions of the Executive. It is true that apart from Israel and New Zealand we live, alone among the developed nations, by political custom and convention. But it is frequently forgotten that much has been written down; it is more accurate to say that the constitution is partly unwritten.

Even if a constitution is partly written, that may leave the political process in a rather uncertain condition. On the other hand, just because the political rules are neatly set out in a series of documents, it does not mean to say that political life becomes easier or more efficient. In the first place, those rules may be conveniently ignored by the governing power. In the second there is always the problem of interpretation, whether by the Executive (Government) or the judiciary or other

5

institutions. Thirdly, a written constitution may overformalise the political process; the British, it appears, are born pragmatists – it is best, they might say, to deal with problems as they arise, rather than develop a theoretical framework and adopt elaborate solutions for future difficulties that may never materialise.

J.P. Mackintosh, *The Government and Politics of Britain,* revised and updated by P.G. Richards, 6th edn., Hutchinson, 1984, p. 11

The late Professor Mackintosh has written:

'It is often said that Britain has an unwritten Constitution, but this is true only in the sense that rules guiding the system are not set out in a single document with a special procedure required for amending these rules, as was done in the United States. But a great number of these rules are written and embodied in Acts of Parliament such as the Representation of the People Act 1948, which prescribes the arrangements for holding elections, or the Parliament Acts of 1911 and 1949 which set out some of the relations between the House of Lords and the House of Commons. Other aspects of the system which are not laws but are established practices (such as the convention to form a government) are written down in many books on British politics. It is not illegal to break these established practices but if a serious attempt to avoid them occurred, it would indicate that profound changes were taking place in the whole system. Again, there is another category of practices, examples being the way the Cabinet is organized or parliamentary candidates selected, which are neither law nor established conventions but are simple convenient methods of procedure whose change would involve no major shake-up in the process of government. It might even be some time before such changes were noticed.

The difficulty in producing an accurate and comprehensive account of these laws, conventions and practices is partly that they are scattered over the history of the country from the Habeas Corpus Act of 1679 which prevents people being held in prison without trial and the convention that the Queen will not veto legislation, which has been built up since 1708, to recent changes in parliamentary procedure dealing with the control of public expenditure. In part, the difficulty is that situations which call for the application of certain conventions may be few and far between. Thus how far a convention would apply today may not be absolutely clear while some conventions (such as 'the collective responsibility of ministers') may have changed their actual content or meaning though the words used remain the same. As a result, to try and describe the British Constitution is like trying to explain the working of an ancient university with its old statutes, more recent regulations, traditions begun for one purpose but still useful for another where new students and teachers are continually altering current practice.

It is because of the ancient origins of many of the laws and conventions of the Constitution that books on British government often start with an historical section. However, it is not essential to go far back into history because most of the conventions, practices and maxims which have been inherited either date from the late nineteenth century or were in operation then. Also it is important not just to list the various acts or to describe how Parliament or the Civil Service developed, but to show their interconnections. Each part of the machinery of government can only be understood in terms of the other cogwheels with which it must intermesh and many of the maxims or descriptions are only meaningful if they can be seen in relation to the whole system in operation at the time when the conventions became established.'

Stability and History

Certainly, as Mackintosh indicated, the modern British political process has developed over a long period of time; unlike many other systems, it is rooted in history. That makes an academic analysis or description difficult, since the nature of the British system, with its largely unwritten constitution, is circular – begin at one point and the reader may find he has to backtrack.

In many ways the British electorate takes its system for granted. It is often assumed that Westminster is the mother of many parliaments; if it is, it has given birth to some rather embarrassing offspring. Also, to many British people, strangely, and rather cynically, politics is a dirty business. Politicians are assumed to be in the business only for their profit. Conversely, the standards of public life are high, as the Salmon Report found in 1976. Corruption is not endemic as in many developing countries or certain Eastern bloc regimes. That does not mean to say, however, that an 'old boy network', patronage and the Establishment, for want of better words, do not exist, or do not combine to exert powerful political influences. And, if the popular perception is that politics is rather a grubby business, the law, in contrast, pure and simple, is untainted. Judges (as opposed, perhaps, to solicitors) enjoy popular prestige – they, unlike politicians, appear to most people fair and scrupulous. Yet, paradoxically, judges frequently only apply the laws made by politicians. The most important source of law nowadays is parliamentary law – an Act of Parliament. Of course, some Acts are overtly political, like legislation which nationalises an industry; other laws are lawyers' law, not politicians' law as such, a measure which reforms the system of claims for personal injuries, for example, which is not the subject of bitter party dispute.

Royal Commission on Standards of Conduct in Public Life, Cmnd 6524, 1976

The remark by Dr David Butler at the beginning of this chapter pin-points the central feature of British politics – the hitherto assumed stability of the system and its seemingly endless capacity to cope with change in an orderly and gradual manner. Such, it is popularly said, is the traditional and major selling-point of British politics. Indeed gradual change is very much the key phrase in the evolution of the Westminster Parliament itself, and although as stated earlier, it would be futile to deny that there are other important political groups and institutions besides Parliament in a modern industrial society, nevertheless Westminster still plays a crucial part in decision-making. There remains at least some pride among the electorate in the fact that Parliament has survived so many crises in history. The evolution of twentieth-century parliamentary democracy was the result of many challenges, often violent ones, over past centuries. Violence sometimes produced apparently dramatic change, but frequently its effects were limited, a good example being the extension of the franchise under the 1832 'Great Reform' Act.

Parliament as an institution cannot precisely be dated. Some might argue that its origins can be found as far back as the King's Council (Witan) of wise men in Anglo-Saxon times. However, important constitutional developments occurred under Henry II in the twelfth century and in the middle of the thirteenth century there were the anti-baronial Provisions of Westminster (1259) and the faint beginnings of a revenue-raising assembly.

The traditions of Parliament: the House of Commons during the State Opening of Parliament

By 1349 the 'Commons' and 'Lords' had established their individual identities: the bishops associated themselves with the lay magnates (Lords), and the knights of the shires and the burgesses of the boroughs grouped themselves together in the Commons. The Lords assumed the 'higher' function of discussing intricate parts of the law. The Commons merely dealt with problems of taxation, but, as these became more complex, especially under the Tudors and Stuarts, its political importance grew. In the fourteenth century, statute law (that passed by Parliament) vied with the older common or customary law, but by the next century its supremacy was established; moreover, it also became distinguished from the King's decrees made in his own Council.

The system thus slowly developed, through the Civil War of the mid-seventeenth century, the 'Whig' Revolution and the deposing of James II in 1688, to the reforms of the nineteenth century, which included the extensions of the franchise. Who can say, therefore, when the parliamentary democracy of today began – with the 'Great Reform' Act of 1832, with the extension of the vote to skilled town workers and the formation of contemporary political parties in the 1860s, or with universal adult suffrage in 1928?

If, however, history provides a sense of continuity and a degree of social stability, any attempt to bring about political reform may be its prisoner. The guarding of tradition, the upholding of gradual change may militate against looking at the system afresh. By the late 1960s the strains of contemporary society were beginning to look as fundamental as any in the past: the system's inherent stability can never be assured. Economic depression, changes in cultural attitudes, the rise of

8

nationalism and the resurgence of the Irish problem, dramatic shifts in voting behaviour, the growth of pressure groups and the reform of political institutions all pointed towards political unrest, moderate as that unrest might appear when placed on an international scale.

At the end of this chapter there are two documents to examine, and the reader is invited to consider how far they give an accurate, if perhaps oversympathetic account of the British political system in practice. Both, it should be said, are rather conservative views of British politics, and the reader should return to a detailed examination only after he has read the remaining chapters in this book, by which time he should be in a better position to judge. The final section of the chapter is brief and, as will be seen, is largely self-explanatory: it is concerned with the evolution of the Commonwealth in recent times.

See also C. Leeds,
Politics in Action,
Stanley Thornes,
1986 (section A)

Self-questioning and Electoral Change

The loss of the Empire, the difficult role of the Commonwealth, a 'concert of convenience' as Professor J.D. Miller has described it, and Britain's uneasy relationship with its other nine (now 11) partners in the EEC, may have led to a lack of political confidence amongst the electorate. Parallel to this, perhaps even arising from it, has been a sorry catalogue of relative industrial decline and continual economic problems and crises. On the other hand, parts of the Empire have been a drain upon economic resources, for example the Malayan Emergency, 1948–60, the troubles in Aden, 1965–7, the confrontation with Indonesia in Borneo, 1963–6, and not least the cost of the Falklands operation since 1982. It is certainly true that the Empire bred national confidence and international prestige, but it was a relatively short-lived affair (approximately 1880–1960). The post-war period has shown how Britain has become far more dependent upon others than upon its own possessions. In terms of defence it is locked into the Atlantic alliance, dominated by the USA, and in economic terms trade is centred far more nowadays upon Europe and the EEC in particular. And it is economic performance which has been the bane of British political life, at least since the late 1950s. Outstripped by the more successful economic performances of its European neighbours, most notably West Germany, and of more distant allies, like Japan, British Governments have consistently tried, and largely failed, to improve Britain's economic standing relative to other countries. The failure of a host of measures, including various forms of state intervention, incomes policies, industrial relations legislation, and more recently monetarism and tight control of public expenditure, has in turn had political repercussions. This particularly became apparent during the 1960s when consensus politics, or 'Butskellism', appeared to fissure. This term, constructed from the names of R.A. Butler, deputy leader of the Conservative Party in the 1950s and early 1960s, and Hugh Gaitskell, leader of the Labour Party at the same time, implied that few political differences separated the two major parties, except in the areas of defence and the nationalisation of industry. But as the country's economic problems have intensified since the mid-1960s, so the major parties in their never-ending quest for lasting solutions have moved ideologically further

J.D. Miller, The
Commonwealth in
the World,
Duckworth, 1958 apart. The electorate, frustrated, increasingly turned to other parties. Thus the support for the Liberals especially, and the nationalist parties in Scotland and in Wales, rose, fell and rose again. More recently the foundation of the Social Democratic Party (SDP) in 1981, in electoral alliance with the Liberals, has brought a new, and possibly lasting, dimension to the British political scene.

The legacy of Empire: Royal Marines talk to islanders in the aftermath of the Falklands War in 1982

Of course, any crystal ball gazing is politically suspect, but it does seem that as long as the United Kingdom continues to search for a panacea to its economic ills, notwithstanding the mixed blessings of North Sea oil, the electorate will turn more readily to newer political groupings. It is certainly outdated nowadays to talk solely in terms of the two-party system, a practice which derived understandably from the period between 1945 and 1970, when the Liberal Party held on to a presence in Parliament by its political fingernails.

The electorate is now more volatile politically than in any period since the 1920s. Thus a study in 1983 asked:

'Are we witnessing the erosion of the foundations of the Conservative and Labour two-party system which has so decisively put its mark on most of the post-war era? That question has obviously to be asked after the two general elections in February and October 1974 which showed both a remarkable increase in electoral support for the Liberal Party and a new surge towards the nationalist parties in Scotland and Wales.

By the end of the decade – and after the 1979 election – the question had not lost its relevance or importance. Although support for nationalist parties appeared to have subsided in 1979, the Liberals continued to attract substantial electoral support even under circumstances which were especially unfavourable for the party.'

Bo Särlvik and Ivor Crewe, *Decade of dealignment,* Cambridge, 1983, p. 331

At the 1983 General Election the SDP survived its first electoral test and in alliance with the Liberals brought the 'third' party well back to centre stage. Such shifts in voting behaviour, the volatility amongst the electorate, will be considered in detail in Chapters 11 and 12, as will other important issues in recent times, such as central government control of local government, regionalism and devolution (Chapter 7), the state of the economy and nationalisation (Chapter 8).

It should be stressed, however, that whatever the changes are in voting behaviour, the system itself is not, at least yet, under internal threat. The parliamentary process is acknowledged by most, if not all, as the flower of democracy. The representative system of government is not under attack. If, of course, there was a series of 'hung' parliaments, in which no party had an overall majority, then the electoral system might be altered to one based on proportional representation, as used in most Western European countries, but the theories of Western parliamentary democracy and representation would still hold true.

The Liberal/SDP alliance may, or may not, achieve a breakthrough at the general election due before July 1988. It often takes a generation to change political attitudes, although as Harold Wilson said 'a week in politics is a long time'. Yet one change in recent years has been the growth in the fortunes of the third party. Indeed, in the 1970 General Election, the Liberals were reduced to the electoral periphery. As an editorial put it: 'The Liberal battle is not the central issue in this election, which is concerned with the record of the Government and the way that the country should be run in the future. Nevertheless the health of the next Parliament will best be served by increasing Liberal representation, by a strong Liberal voice working with the liberal influences in the main parties.'

The Times, 8 June 1970

British Politics

The distinguishing features of British politics are, then, a Parliament which legislates for the whole of the United Kingdom, including Northern Ireland, whose domestic legislature, Stormont, was suspended in 1972. The British state is thus correctly described as a unitary or centralised one, yet it also possesses a formidable system of local government, although the latter's financial powers have been curbed by Mrs Thatcher's Government.

There is little in the way of regional government, and little public demand for it. However, the question of domestic assemblies for Scotland and Wales – the 'devolution question' – was an important issue in the mid-1970s, but following public referenda in those two countries, the proposed bodies were aborted. Devolution of power away from Westminster, and towards Wales and Scotland in particular, is not entirely off the political map, but it hardly seems to have a high priority. Northern Ireland, however, is a rather different case, with its own special problems since the partition of Ireland in 1922. Parts of the Irish community have never accepted a divided Ireland, and the relentless activity of the IRA since the late 1960s, most notably in 1972, underlines that fact.

Parliament and government

The terms 'Parliament' and 'Government' are frequently used in the same breath, since in Britain there is no true separation of powers as in the USA. The Government is usually and largely formed from the leading figures of the majority party in the House of Commons. But it is the Government which proposes and Parliament which disposes. Most of the legislation that Parliament passes is initiated by the Government. Legislation is, however, the result of many influences. A party's election manifesto gives certain undertakings and these will find their way on to the statute book. But the Government, or Executive, is wider than just ministers. There are some 600 000 civil servants, the most senior of whom will be responsible for shaping the legislative intentions of ministers, as well as floating legislative proposals of their own. Statutory bodies, like the Law Commission, whose task is to suggest reforms in the law, will also come forward with their own ideas, at least in areas that are not politically controversial. Moreover, a whole range of pressure groups (like the National Council for Civil Liberties – NCCL) attempts to persuade the Government and backbench MPs to introduce certain legislation. All these initiatives have to be accommodated within the constraints of the parliamentary timetable, which, given the detailed nature of British Acts of Parliament, is a formidable task.

Parliament is concerned not only with legislation, important though that function is; there is other business to accomplish, such as general debates. Moreover, while Parliament is supposedly supreme, and may achieve whatever it wishes to achieve, there are political limitations. Very often, Parliament allows ministers to fill in the fine print of legislation – ministers are given authority in certain instances to make their own rules (delegated or secondary legislation). Also, by convention Parliament has little say in the conduct of foreign affairs, the Saturday debate on the Falklands Crisis in 1982 being a notable exception. Nor, by custom, does Parliament scrutinise the operations of the secret services. However, whether day-to-day government should be more open is entirely another matter.

Ministers are responsible to Parliament for their actions and those of their civil servants. But whether answerability entails resignation from office is very doubtful nowadays, as will be seen later. Ministers are also responsible to each other for the conduct of policy. This is collective or Cabinet responsibility. If a minister violently disagrees on an issue, then he should either 'shut up' or 'get out'. But the Cabinet is a leaky ship, and many leaks come from the Prime Minister's own Press Secretary. The lobby system, whereby certain accredited journalists have rights of access to ministers and No. 10, ensures that Cabinet government is never totally confidential: journalists once briefed, albeit off the record, are expected to 'leak' or report. There would not be much point to the lobby system if their lips remained permanently sealed.

'Cabinet government' is a phrase invariably associated with the British parliamentary process. Key decisions are taken in Cabinet, collectively, or more likely in a Cabinet committee. But at times the image of government by the Cabinet appears to recede: a strong Prime Minister may become almost presidential in the conduct of affairs.

Further, it is not only Parliament and the Executive whose powers and membership overlap. It is the judiciary too, for the highest court in the land is the Appellate Committee of the House of Lords, the upper Chamber of Parliament.

Moreover, while the Lords is the 'upper chamber' in terms of constitutional tradition, since the passage of the Parliament Acts 1911 and 1949 its powers are quite definitely subordinate to those of the Commons. That two-thirds of its membership are hereditary, a unique enough feature on any political landscape, does not imply that the Conservatives have a majority; strictly speaking, this is no longer the case. Indeed, as we shall see, it can be a Conservative government as well as a Labour one which on occasion finds the House of Lords a thorn in its legislative side.

Three other points are worthy of note. Firstly, since the turn of the century, and in particular since 1945, there has developed the practice of government intervention in certain industries of key importance to the running of the economy. The public corporation is well known if not always well loved. But under Mrs Thatcher the 'frontiers of the State' have been rolled back since 1979 and the Government's interests in such familiar organisations as British Gas, British Airways, British Telecom and the National Bus Company have been, or will be, reduced. On the other hand, the proportion of state spending, that is the proportion of the gross domestic product (GDP) committed to public expenditure, has not substantially altered since Mr Callaghan lost power.

Secondly, the United Kingdom likes to think of itself as a country of free speech, but whether the media are as free as their counterparts in the USA is doubtful. The laws of confidence, libel, contempt and official secrecy are powerful instruments that blunt the otherwise sharp cutting edge of the 'Fourth Estate'. The BBC prides itself on its independence, but being dependent upon the Government

13

to determine its income, via the licence fee, it sometimes runs into difficulties on self-censorship, as the row over a television film on Ulster in 1985 clearly demonstrated (see p. 358).

Thirdly, the British political system is based upon competitive party politics. But the electoral system is another issue. For some years the Liberals have been declaring themselves cheated; they accumulate lots of votes by coming second in a constituency, but under the 'first past the post' or 'winner takes all' method, they are denied, they claim, their true representation in Parliament. Proportional representation is now more actively and publicly discussed, but one electoral swallow does not make a political summer. It will probably need several 'hung' parliaments or lop-sided election results for a change in the voting system to come about.

To sum up so far, we can say that politics is about the rough and tumble of living together and the art of compromise or the holding to and implementation of ideology and belief. In this British politics is no exception. The British political system has developed over the course of many centuries; every Prime Minister, as recent Premiers like Home, Wilson, Macmillan, Heath and Callaghan have said, must have a sense of history. The British guard their parliamentary traditions, if not fiercely at least resolutely.

Parliament and Government may be the centre-piece of politics, yet the United Kingdom lives in an uncertain world. It is no longer a superpower, but rather part of the second league, although it is a leading member of the Commonwealth, NATO and the EEC, as well as a member of the Security Council of the United Nations. But the substantial international clout it once possessed has long since gone. Virtually bankrupted by six years of world war (1939–45), Britain never seems to have made a full economic recovery. As the level of unemployment has risen to over three million in the last few years and as social cohesion seems to become more strained, so there appears to be a restlessness in the political air; three- rather than two-party politics may once more be the norm. It would be a bold person indeed to predict with confidence the future course of political events. Can, in short, the constitution cope?

DOCUMENT

1

Political Democracy

The brief outline given here should show that the British system is not unique, nor indeed infallible. Special it may be, and important certainly as a leading example of the kind of democracy most would wish to preserve and to enhance, as opposed to the 'democracies' of the Eastern bloc or Third World. The late Professor H.V. Wiseman summed up the British system some years ago, but none the worse for that:

'Political Democracy, according to Edward Shils on whose analysis this account is based, presupposes a regime of civilian rule through representative institutions and with public liberties guaranteed. The legislative body is periodically elected by universal suffrage; it is empowered to initiate legislation through private members, committees, or the executive leaders (overwhelmingly the last in Britain), and to enact or repeal legislation initiated by the Executive. The Executive carries out its policies through an hierarchically organized non-political bureaucracy, answerable to its political heads and through them to the legislature. Candidates for the legislature are normally members of contending political parties and the party which wins an overall majority of seats or achieves one in coalition (though, as Disraeli remarked, 'Britain does not love coalitions') dominates the legislature of which its leaders may be members. In Britain they must be members. Executive and legislative action is subject to periodic review through free elections (though in Britain the Prime Minister can, within limits, choose the time to go to the country, as Sir Alec Douglas-Home did in 1964 and Mr Wilson was able to do in 1966). It is also continually scrutinized by the free organs of public opinion, and, in Britain, by a large number of advisory committees. Within the legislature opposition and minority rights are guaranteed by the rules of procedure. An independent judiciary exists to protect the rights of citizens against the Government as well as against each other (though in Britain the courts have for various reasons been frustrated in this, hence the decision in 1965 to establish an Ombudsman or Parliamentary Commissioner). There may be a written constitution (though not in Britain) but in any case traditions and conventions regarding the conduct of the executive, the legislature, the civil service, the army, and the police, as well as the judiciary, are well-known and generally respected.

What are the necessary pre-conditions for this kind of political system? The ruling élite must be stable, coherent, and effective. Governments must receive sufficient support to give them confidence that their policies are likely to be approved and effectively carried out; their authority will in large measure depend upon reasonable effectiveness in the promulgation and execution of policy. Coherence and organization are essential in both the alternative parties or groups, between whom mutual and fundamental trust is also essential. The political leaders must be attached to representative institutions and regard themselves as generally answerable to the electorate. The legitimacy of the élite must be accepted by a very substantial proportion of the population, particularly those sections who are politically conscious. Both competence and integrity in the rulers are essential for this. Nor should the outside party or its bureaucracy be able to turn the parliamentary party into its mouthpiece – a problem of continuous interest in Britain owing to an alleged danger that the Annual Conference, especially of the Labour Party, might be able to dictate to the Parliamentary leaders. The point is that responsibility should be maintained through Parliament, the 'centre of gravity' of the system.

A fairly coherent and responsible opposition must be accepted as a necessary part of the political system; it would appear to follow that too long a period of continuous power for one party is 'not good' for democracy. But opposition criticism should be constructive and not merely obstructive, which, again, is not easy to maintain if opposition appears to be a permanent role; the party should certainly eschew all methods which involve conspiracy and subversion. Together, the majority and the opposition should form a preponderant block against extremists of either right or left.

There must be adequate machinery of authority, which requires a well-trained and organized civil service, detached in its political orientations, loyal to any constitutional government yet independent enough to offer strong and objective advice which politicians feel compelled to take into account. Conversely, the civil servants must never despise politicians. Freedom from corruption is, of course, essential to the 'rule of law', especially that aspect of it which insists upon an independent judiciary. There must be an effective police force, a reliable military force, and other organs of law and order – but all with a binding obligation to the prevailing political authority.

Outside the more formal or 'official' roles there must be a self-confident and self-sustaining set of institutions of public opinion – press, university, civic and independent associations, professional bodies, trade unions, and local government bodies, widely spaced throughout the regions and the classes of the country. Information must be available from sources other than governmental and there must be freedom of expression and association. There should be a 'modern civilian intelligentsia' and a fairly numerous moderately educated and reasonably politically concerned section of the population. There should also be a fairly comprehensive and elaborate system of private and voluntary associations though none should be sufficiently powerful to be able to hold the rest of society to ransom. This ensures an infrastructure of decision and authority which reduces the amount of authority exercized or decisions made by the organs of the State . . . [and] also keeps in check tendencies towards the 'politicization' of life (i.e. the turning of every issue and every relationship into a political matter) which are inimical to a regime of civilian rule, representative institutions and public liberties.

Continuity is essential to civil order. There must be a sense of community, a sufficient degree of interest in public affairs, a general acceptance of the legitimacy of the existing political order, a sense of dignity and rights as well as of obligations on the part of the citizens, and a sufficient degree of consensus regarding existing values, institutions and practices. No part of society must be excluded from access to the policy. On this, it may be added that democracy is basically a political system in which all, or the most significant groups in the population, participate in the political process and have access to effective representation in the process of making government decisions, i.e. of allocating scarce resources. Parties, elections and the rest are more or less reliable symptoms of the existence of democracy rather than factors producing it.'

'Yet there are those who are bored with politics and those who deplore them. The first category may merely represent in the political as in other fields those who lack interest in most things outside their own immediate concern or who just lack the capacity or stimulus to think beyond today and its immediate needs. Or they may feel that the problems are just too difficult and complicated for ordinary understanding. Or they may be the 'deferentials' whom Bagehot found predominant in England in the nineteenth century, who leave these things to their 'betters'; perhaps this is one reason for the large number of working-class Tories, though Karl Marx would have described them less politely as Lumpen-proletariat! The bored are perhaps not as dangerous as those who deplore and denigrate politics; a certain degree of apathy helps to reduce political tension, although too much – particularly if it leads to a feeling of 'alienation' from the society in which one lives – may equally well produce some form of totalitarianism. The denigrators, however, are more dangerous – partly because their dislike of politics may at first sight appear to be based on plausible rational grounds.'

H.V. Wiseman, *Politics in Everyday Life,* Blackwell, 1966

DOCUMENT

2

Kilbrandon's View

A rather more official interpretation has put the unique political qualities of the United Kingdom in a fairly recent context (the Kilbrandon Report), even if the language employed is in places bland:

'What distinguishes the people of the United Kingdom from others who pay homage to the Crown is their representation in the Parliament at Westminster, which is the supreme law-making authority for the whole of the United Kingdom. Even in Northern Ireland, where by the Government of Ireland Act 1920 a separate Parliament was set up to legislate for the province in domestic matters, ultimate authority continued to rest with the United Kingdom Parliament, which created and conferred powers on the Northern Ireland Parliament and was able at any time to change those powers – in 1972 it withdrew them completely – or make laws overriding the laws made in Northern Ireland. Accordingly the people of Northern Ireland have always had representation in the United Kingdom Parliament as well as in their own domestic legislature.

The supremacy of Parliament has the consequence that it is not bound by the acts of its predecessors; equally it cannot bind its successors. No special procedures are required to enact even the most fundamental changes in the constitution. Thus the creation of the Irish Free State in 1922 was made possible by an ordinary Act of Parliament, despite the declared intention of the Act of Union of 1800 that the union of Great Britain and Ireland should last for ever. It is in this sense that the often-repeated statement that the United Kingdom has no written constitution is to be understood. There is no lack of written statutes regulating constitutional institutions and procedures; indeed, the number of statutes of constitutional significance in this country must be at least as great as in most others. But all these are ordinary statutes, having no greater authority than any others (save perhaps what they have acquired by antiquity) and requiring no special procedures for their amendment. Nor are they collected into a single document that can be referred to as "the Constitution".

The United Kingdom is a unitary state in economic as well as in political terms. It has, for example, a single currency and a banking system responsible to a single central bank. Its people enjoy a right of freedom of movement of trade, labour and capital and of settlement and establishment anywhere within the Kingdom (though there is an exception in Northern Ireland in a restriction on employment imposed in the interests of Northern Ireland workers). Similarly, all citizens are free to participate in trading and other concessions obtained by the United Kingdom abroad.

These are the things that are held in common. But there are others that are not. Not all the people of the United Kingdom live under the same system of law, since the separate Scottish legal system which was in existence in 1707 was preserved by the union settlement. Sometimes it is this separate legal system alone which causes the United Kingdom Parliament to pass special Scottish Acts or to include special Scottish provisions in general Acts. In addition, the content of the laws to which people are subject sometimes differs. The particular circumstances of Scotland, producing a requirement for different policies, may lead to separate Scottish legislation. Similarly, special measures applying only to Wales, concerning the Welsh language, for example, are on occasion separately enacted. The content of the law diverges still more in Northern Ireland, which for a period of over fifty years had its own Parliament, with not only its own limited powers of taxation but considerable freedom to differ in some kinds of social legislation. In comparison with the whole body of the law, however, these exceptions, of form and content, even including the variations in Northern Ireland, are relatively minor. For the greater part, the people of the United Kingdom live under the same law.   It is as well, before taking on a task that is necessarily concerned more with the parts of the United Kingdom than with the whole, to take note of its considerable achievements. This country, aided by good fortune but sustained much more by the efforts of its own people, raised itself to a position of unquestioned primacy in the world and used it, on balance, for good. Spread across the world, the areas that have known British rule amount to well over a quarter of the whole; whatever else the British have left, they have endowed these areas with a tradition of Parliamentary democracy and the rule of law. Britain was the first country to transform itself from an agricultural community into a major industrial power. In commerce, in navigation, in banking, in investment, it was British practices that were adopted by the rest of the world.'

Kilbrandon's remarks about the legacy of parliamentary traditions across the world are a highly questionable assumption, as evidenced by the Ugandan experience since 1971. However, the Report continued:

'These achievements have owed much to the union. The United Kingdom has been greater than the sum of its constituent parts. While, for example, Scotland's desire to participate in England's overseas markets may have been a major factor in her decision to agree to the union, the benefits were by no means one-sided. The removal of the threat of internal strife allowed the energies and talents of all the British people to be directed to peaceful pursuits at home and to expansion abroad.   The story of the United Kingdom has thus been, at least in the larger island, a success story. But this is not to say that the union has brought unalloyed advantage to the constituent parts. It can be argued that in Scotland, Wales and parts of England, as well as in Ireland, a price in political, social and economic terms has had to be paid for progress; that the interests of the majority have been fostered partly at the expense of national and regional minorities; that traditional ways of life have been disrupted by the exploitation and then the abandonment of local resources; that the resultant social distress has not been adequately recognised by governments which have seemed physically and psychologically remote; and that the minorities most concerned with these problems have not been allowed the power or the means to alleviate them. Nevertheless, outside Northern Ireland, there has been little general disposition to question the maintenance of the union, particularly in times of political crisis and when the security of the United Kingdom has been threatened. At such times, indeed, all sections of the British people have never failed to re-assert their loyalty to the wider entity.

It would nevertheless be idle to pretend that nothing is happening to the old spirit of unquestioning unity. With the British Empire – in the sense of wide territories for whose rule these islands were responsible – so largely relinquished, and with the manifest diminution of Britain's role on the international stage, the necessity for a tight union at home as a base for external expansion has passed. For both defence and economic welfare it is to outside groupings rather than to our own unaided strength that we now look. These changes have, by an inevitable process, caused people to question what has for so long been taken for granted.'

The Kilbrandon Report: Royal Commission on the Constitution, Cmnd 5460, 1973

Changes Since 1945

As the Kilbrandon Report noted, it should not go without a passing mention that in terms of external relations the position of the United Kingdom has radically shifted since 1945. It may have won the Second World War, with a great deal of help, but in so doing it was made nearly bankrupt. It was now a second division power, not a superpower. The foreign policy of Ernest Bevin under the Labour Government of 1945–51, the triple theme, has dominated external relations to this day – a close relationship to the USA through NATO, a growing role in Europe (Britain joined the EEC in 1973) and decolonisation. In respect of the latter, Britain soon lost control of a quarter of the world; first with the independence of the Indian sub-continent and Burma in 1947–8, then with a further rapid period of decolonisation in the late 1950s and early 1960s after the debacle of the Suez Crisis in 1956. The United Kingdom did not extricate itself painlessly, even after the partition of India in 1947, as shown by the Malayan Emergency 1948–60, the Mau-Mau rebellion in Kenya 1954–9, plus the troubles in Cyprus (1955–60) and Aden (1965–7), the confrontation with Indonesia in Borneo between 1963 and 1966 and last, but not least, the interminable problem of Southern Rhodesia (1965–79). Even then colonial left-overs could threaten to blow up in Britain's face, or actually did, as in the Falklands (1982).

The rapid process of decolonisation has been officially recorded as follows:

'The present Commonwealth as a free association of sovereign nations is the outcome of the development of self-government in the older British Dominions and, more immediately, of their demand during the First World War for an equally full control of their own foreign policy. Recognition was given to this in the resolution of the Imperial War Conference 1917, that 'the constitutional relations of the component parts of the Empire . . . should be based upon a full recognition of the Dominions as autonomous nations of an Imperial Commonwealth'.

A Year Book of the Commonwealth 1986, HMSO

Accordingly, the Dominions and India signed the Versailles Peace Treaty individually, and had their own representation in the League of Nations. The Inter-Imperial Relations Committee of the 1926 Imperial Conference, under the chairmanship of Lord Balfour, made the first formal attempt to describe the resultant status and mutual relationship of the members in what came to be

19

known as the 'Balfour formula'. The Committee's report declared that they are autonomous communities within the British Empire, equal in status, in no way subordinate one to another in any aspect of their domestic or external affairs, though united by a common allegiance to the Crown and freely associated as Members of the British Commonwealth of Nations.

This principle was legally formulated in the Stature of Westminster of 1931 which gave effect to this fully independent status of the Dominions in relation to Great Britain and, by implication, in relation to each other'.

The process which India had already made towards a similar status was completed in 1947 when India and Pakistan became independent and members of the Commonwealth. The Second World War had hastened this development with the remaining dependencies and by 1983 the total membership had reached 49, the current figure. Now, since 1973, the European dimension, via the EEC, has assumed an equal, if not predominant, role in Britain's international affairs. The European Communities (Amendment) Act 1986 (the 'Single European Act') foreshadows the further integration of parliamentary into EEC law.

Mrs Thatcher with Prime Ministers Rajiv Gandhi of India and Bob Hawke of Australia at the mini-summit of Commonwealth leaders in August 1986

Exercises

1. What do you consider to be the distinguishing features of the British political system? In what ways are they deficient?

2. Study documents 1 and 2. Do they convey a fair view of British politics?

(Both these exercises, especially 2, can be treated as revision tasks, after a complete reading of the book.)

2 — The Executive

'The Chancellor himself, with his leader beside him, was not at his scintillating best, and adopted his recently introduced technique of keeping the angry Left quiet by being very boring indeed. Sometimes the Left sit and seethe. Sometimes they just sit. Yesterday they did the latter.'

Peter Cole in *The Guardian*, 3 August 1976.

The Executive in the United Kingdom is not directly elected as is the President of the USA. A vote in a British parliamentary election is not only for an area representative but also for a Prime Minister and his team. However, as Anthony King has remarked, it is strange that there are so few studies on the office of the British Prime Minister and on the Cabinet system, few at least when compared to the enormous range on the American federal system.

J.P. Mackintosh in *The British Prime Minister* (ed. Anthony King), Macmillan, 1969 p. 3

The Prime Minister is a vital focal point in the British system, and although his exact relationship with the rest of the Cabinet has been difficult to quantify, it is clear that he is enormously influential as the person who guides the most important organs of the Executive – the Cabinet and its committees. The Prime Minister is the one who becomes most identified with the image, and the success or otherwise, of the governing party. Not only must he bring coherence and team loyalty and a sense of purpose to his ministers, but, if he is to get anywhere at all – if he is to stay in charge – he must also make sure that there is no one who can, 'so to speak, steer the bus from the back seat.'

New Society, 25 March 1976

As W.J.M. MacKenzie has remarked: 'The strings must be in his [the Prime Minister's] hands; he is the chief dispenser of patronage, First Lord of the Treasury, Lord of the armed men, Lord of diplomacy, Lord of the parliamentary majority, Lord of the Cabinet's agenda.'

Prime Ministerial Crises

Party unity

Any British Prime Minister is as sure of his informal political power as any US President is of his very formalised position of authority (accidents like Watergate notwithstanding). Indeed, it is remarkable how few British Prime Ministers have been removed or driven from office during this century. This in itself is a measure of the stability and continuity of the system. That is not to say, however, that other developed, industrialised societies do not rival that position, and not just in Western Europe either. For example, despite the enormous differences in the socio-political culture of the country, Japan's Prime Minister, Takeo Miki, in 1976, resisted strong pressure from his Cabinet colleagues to curtail his anti-corruption campaign and certain other measures and almost threatened to bring down the whole of the Liberal-Democratic Party with him if necessary. The struggle lasted for over 18 months before he finally resigned in order to preserve party unity.

Party unity in the Western capitalist system is a key point; when a Prime Minister on the British model fails to give a lead there is almost no political lead at all, for it is unlikely his Cabinet colleagues will step in. The modern Prime Minister undoubtedly owes much of his power to the tradition of party loyalty. This tradition stems from the 1870s–90s when disciplined party voting was introduced in the Commons to help Prime Ministers and their colleagues to push legislation through. (Balfour's reforms of Commons procedure in 1902 were a further step in this direction.)

Asquith, Lloyd George and Chamberlain

In the strictest sense only three Prime Ministers have been forced out of office this century – the first being Asquith in 1916, owing to his handling of the war effort and personality differences with other Liberals, notably Lloyd George. The other major instance also occurred in wartime – involving Neville Chamberlain in 1940, after the disastrous Norwegian campaign and his failure to secure a meaningful vote of confidence. Even the third instance was indirectly connected with war: in 1922 the Tory back-benchers simply refused to remain part of a wartime coalition government perpetuating itself into peacetime under Lloyd George, nominally still a Liberal. Once that decision had been taken, Lloyd George immediately resigned.

Suez and Profumo

Certain other Prime Ministers, while not being forced out of office by Parliament or their party, have chosen to resign under pressure. Two post-war instances of this might be mentioned. The Suez Affair in 1956 caused a deep split not only within the country generally but also within the Conservative Party. Although no minister of consequence actually resigned, the episode certainly influenced Eden's eventual decision to stand down because of ill health in January 1957. In doing so he pre-empted action that might otherwise have been instigated by the Conservative Party. The other example involved Eden's successor, Harold Macmillan. In the autumn of 1963 Macmillan decided to resign on health grounds, although his condition turned out to be less serious than Eden's. His decision came after his Government, which had previously enjoyed some popularity, reached an economic low point. It also coincided with a vigorous anti-Government, and, by implication, anti-Macmillan, press campaign over the breaking of the Profumo scandal. Macmillan's resignation thus, like Eden's, anticipated a period when his power might seriously have been called to question. However, even when Prime Ministers are under considerable pressure, there is still a basic desire, in the British political culture at least, for self-preservation in the party. As J.P. Mackintosh has said, the lesson for students of British government is that even at times of maximum weakness the *office* of Prime Minister (if not necessarily its occupant) is still

Sir Anthony Eden at the time of the Suez Crisis

enormously strong. Overall direction can come from no other source, 'no junta can take command, powers that are circumscribed are not taken by others, but merely fall into abeyance, and the only way out of the impasse is a recovery of the authority of the Prime Minister.'

As for Prime Ministers themselves, the length of service they have given as an ordinary Cabinet member before reaching No. 10 varies. Mr Callaghan entered Parliament at the age of 33, Mrs Thatcher at 34. Mrs Thatcher became Prime Minister at 54, having held only one Cabinet post, Secretary of State for Education, for less than four years. Mr Callaghan became Premier at 64, having held three Cabinet posts over eight years. Both these Prime Ministers (and Heath, Wilson and Lloyd George) could be said to have experienced a lower middle-class/skilled worker environment, with only Ramsay MacDonald coming from a truly manual, working-class background. The others this century either fall into an aristocratic category (Balfour, Churchill, Eden and Home) or a middle-class, professional one (Campbell-Bannerman, Bonar Law, Baldwin, Asquith, Macmillan, Attlee and Chamberlain).

Other crisis points

It is worth mentioning at this stage the various other severe difficulties which Prime Ministers, and often their Cabinet colleagues, have faced since 1945. There have been moments when prime ministerial authority has clearly been challenged, when party loyalty has been miscalculated in some way or other by a Premier. This usually happens only when the Government is well established; very few ministers care to challenge prime ministerial actions when a general election appears to be approaching, since in the first place no one wants a divided party, and in the second most wish to retain their posts in Government should their party be returned to office.

The principal post-1945 crises include the fuel emergency and general post-war austerity in 1946–8 under Attlee, the 1956 Suez crisis under Eden and the economic difficulties of 1966–8 under the Wilson Government. The latter included a ministerial 'plot' (greatly exaggerated by the press) against Mr Wilson while he was visiting the USSR in 1966 at the beginning of a sterling crisis. Mr Heath, too, faced a severe test of his leadership, which resulted in defeat at the polls and a subsequent change in Conservative leadership. This took place during the winter of 1973–4, and was to a large extent the result of an economic crisis which centred around the miners' strike and the three-day working week in industry. The latter was imposed by the Government in an effort to conserve energy, after its failure to reach agreement with the National Union of Mineworkers. Just as war has ruined the political lives of some Premiers, such as Asquith in 1916 and Chamberlain in 1940, so it has enhanced the reputation of others, such as Lord Salisbury in the early stages of the Boer War when he held the General Election of 1900. Mrs Thatcher, according to the polls, was not a particularly popular Prime Minister, in fact in 1981 the most unpopular post-war Premier; yet the successful military outcome of the Falklands War in 1982 more or less ensured her return to office when she called an early election in 1983. But by the time of the Brecon and Radnor by-election in 1985, the popularity was wearing thin again.

A Prime Minister's Powers

Constructing a government

The power of appointing members of the Cabinet and junior ministers is often ranked as one of the most significant at the disposal of the Prime Minister, but in fact it should be realised that he is very much circumscribed (more so than the American President) by the factor of 'party seniority'. He is bound, especially in his first Cabinet, to include a large number of senior MPs who have been in the party for a long time and who have probably been members of the shadow Cabinet. It is often not so much a question of whom the Premier is going to include, as of which few he may dare to leave out of his team and in particular out of the Cabinet.

See also C. Leeds, *Politics in Action*, Stanley Thornes, 1986, (section B)

As time goes by, the Prime Minister may enjoy a little more flexibility in the construction of his Government. Nevertheless, as J.P. Mackintosh observed, Richard Crossman in the draft of his introduction to a new edition of Bagehot's *English Constitution* included a sentence which implied that the British Prime Minister could liquidate the political career of any of his colleagues almost as effectively as Russian leaders can remove potential rivals. He deleted these controversial words only after objections from his publisher.

25

R.K. Alderman,
*Parliamentary
Affairs,* Spring 1976

In fact ministers often lay down their own conditions for joining the team, and some (for example, Enoch Powell and Iain Macleod under Sir Alec Douglas-Home in 1963) will even refuse to serve when there is a sudden change of Premier. R.K. Alderman, in a survey of Cabinet appointments over the last 80 years or so, has remarked that it is easy to find instances of politicians making acceptance of office dependent upon exclusion of certain others from office, or from particular posts, and 'indeed, Lloyd George claimed that every Ministry suffered from such misfortunes.' More recently, in a Cabinet reshuffle by Harold Wilson in 1975, Reg Prentice, on being moved from the Department of Education, insisted that as Minister for Overseas Aid and Development he should retain Cabinet rank. With probably some justification from his evidence, Alderman has remarked, 'J.P. Mackintosh's assertion that only two politicians have refused Cabinet office since 1918 is very wide of the mark.' He calculated that on hard evidence the figure is at least ten times that, and probably considerably more. This is particularly likely when account is taken of the very delicate state of parliamentary government in most of the inter-war period. Even in more recent times there have been several occasions when Prime Ministers have had to include in their Cabinet very close rivals for the leadership. For example, Macmillan in 1957 and Alec Douglas-Home in 1963 both had to make sure of R.A. Butler's support and, despite a rift later, so it was with George Brown when Wilson formed his first Ministry in 1964.

The personality of individual MPs is a further factor that the Premier must consider when constructing his Government. As Alderman has said, 'A Prime Minister's strategy must, inevitably, be guided in part by what he has reason to expect particular individuals to accept, or to insist upon.' He concluded: 'A Prime Minister cannot automatically assume that all politicians desire political advancement above all else,' and illustrated this by the fact that during the Labour Government of 1964–70 there were at least seven known instances of posts being refused, two of Cabinet rank. Similarly, in 1981, Norman St John Stevas refused to be demoted to non-Cabinet rank, preferring instead the wilderness of the backbenches.

DOCUMENT

3

The Prime Minister and His Team

A Prime Minister may, sometimes, have no clear preference as between two or more rivals for a particular office. In such circumstances, he may do no more than act as an arbitrator between them. It is not unknown for a Prime Minister to play an even less active role, and leave the disputants to resolve the matter between themselves: when both Churchill and Haldane insistently demanded the Admiralty, in 1912, Asquith resorted to the expedient of shutting them up in a room together to argue it out. So passive a course of action can be adopted only very rarely, however. Even a Prime Minister genuinely indifferent as between aspirants for a particular post has an interest in averting friction and enmity between his ministers. In 1929, MacDonald allowed Henderson and Thomas to come face to face, during the course of discussions as to which office each should have. The acrimonious dispute which ensued should be a clear warning to any Prime Minister that such direct confrontations are fraught with danger. There is the obvious risk that any ill-feeling thereby engendered will render extremely difficult the subsequent welding of ministers into an effective and harmonious team. It may have the additional effect of increasing the Prime Minister's own vulnerability to bargaining pressures over appointments. Ambitious politicians tend to be highly competitive; they are prone to take exception to any disposition of offices which appears to place them at a disadvantage to, or in an inferior position to, others whom they regard as their peers or rivals. The greater the information available about other appointments, the greater is their capacity both to make such comparisons and, in consequence, to aggravate the problems with which the Prime Minister has to contend. It is, therefore, not surprising that most Prime Ministers endeavour, in so far as is possible, to restrict communication of such information until appointments have been finalised. Baldwin had politicians to whom he had offered appointments ushered out of his office by a route designed to prevent them meeting others on the way in. In 1924, MacDonald enjoined his senior appointees not to divulge information as to which posts they had been given, even to men whom they knew must, inevitably, be future Cabinet colleagues, until all appointments had been made.

Whether he be one of the parties in a bargaining process or merely an arbitrator, successful performance of the Prime Minister's role in the appointment of ministers calls for considerable acumen, a high degree of negotiating skill, and a keen insight into human nature. By no means all Prime Ministers are endowed with these qualities. The right to appoint all other ministers undoubtedly constitutes a very significant aspect of Prime Ministerial power. If, as has sometimes been suggested, it actually were an attribute of the "thoroughly professional politician" that he should display an "invariable readiness to serve wherever his services were thought appropriate by the captain of the team", then the Prime Minister's lot would, indeed, be a happy and relatively simple one. But the psychology with which men enter the political market-place is much more complex than this, and so, too, are the confines within the Prime Minister exercises his prerogative. It is not the *right* to appoint all other ministers *per se* which confers power upon the Prime Minister. It is, rather, the freedom to *choose* whom to appoint (or not to appoint, as the case may be). Whatever tends to limit that freedom of choice constitutes a constraint upon his power, and such constraints are more numerous and more restrictive than is generally allowed. The balance of advantage certainly does not always lie with the Prime Minister. Indeed, he may, at times, be at a distinct disadvantage. It is not as unusual as is commonly assumed for a Prime Minister to meet the demands of prospective ministers. The much-vaunted right to appoint can, on occasion, become an irksome responsibility, neither easy nor particularly pleasurable. Patronage can be a source of power, but only if it is dispensed sensitively and judiciously. Handled carelessly, it can actually create problems for a Prime Minister, antagonizing even those upon whom he has bestowed office.

R.K. Alderman, 'The Prime Minister and the Appointment of Ministers,' *Parliamentary Affairs,* Spring 1976

Dissolving Parliament

The other important power which is often written about in rather hallowed terms is the Prime Minister's right to seek the dissolution of Parliament at any time he chooses. Usually, however, Prime Ministers are obliged by force of circumstances to consult their ministerial colleagues, and on occasion they may consult a wider party grouping as well. The Prime Minister's decision is also influenced by the state of the economy both at home and abroad. The freedom to choose the best economic opportunity to go to the country was clearly apparent in the 1950s and early 1960s, as can be seen by the circumstances in which the Elections of 1955, 1959 and 1964 were called. This freedom, however, has become much more restricted since the late 1960s, as the economic upswings have been even fewer and further between.

J.P. Mackintosh noted that when Baldwin was a relatively unknown quantity as Prime Minister in the autumn of 1923 (having succeeded Bonar Law only a few months before), there was a distinct possibility that the old practice of consulting the Cabinet about the dissolution date could have been revived. But when he was faced with the decision again, in 1929 and 1935, everyone accepted that it was his alone. In fact, Baldwin had left the Cabinet little choice in 1923, since his announcement of a policy of 'protective tariffs' took his own party as much by surprise as it took the country generally. However, Alderman and Cross argued that Baldwin called an election in 1929 'only after considerable discussion of the matter in the Cabinet, and in 1935 opinions were invited even from such relatively junior members of the Cabinet as Anthony Eden.' The termination of the minority Labour Governments, however, were very much in the hands of the Cabinet as a whole – in 1924 because of the Liberal and Conservative attitudes towards the Campbell Case and in 1931 because of the extreme economic position.

R.K. Alderman and J.A. Cross, *Parliamentary Affairs*, Autumn 1975

In the post-1945 period senior colleagues have invariably been consulted about the proposed election date, although, in Alderman and Cross's phrase, Wilson seems to have played it close to his chest on the occasion of the 1970 General Election, when the June date came as a complete surprise to his own party headquarters and to many of his more junior colleagues. Similarly, with Attlee, the full Cabinet was not consulted about the 1950 and 1951 Election dates.

It is generally accepted that in 1966 Wilson took his cue from the favourable result of the Hull (North) by-election two months previously. In the case of the 1970 Election it is fairly clear that Wilson had been greatly persuaded by the favourable evidence then being presented by the most influential opinion polls; it takes a hard calculation by any Prime Minister to move an election forward to the early summer, interrupting the parliamentary session and thus risking the loss of important legislation.

In recent years such tactical considerations of timing have been given considerable emphasis by political scientists. They are particularly important in the context of the floating votes (although usually relatively small) that determine each party's majority. In a 'photo-finish', such as both 1974 elections, timing may be crucial. Any Prime Minister, however, who ignores the consultation process completely, for the sake of a gamble whose tactical advantages for his Government are poorly calculated, does so at his peril. As Alderman and Cross say, 'tactical considerations . . . inevitably have a distracting and disruptive effect upon the general conduct of government business.'

In 1945, 1955 and 1959, consultations were limited to senior Cabinet ministers, the Chief Whip and the party chairman. In 1964 they were more extensive. Sir Alec Douglas-Home, who had been the compromise successor to Macmillan for only a matter of months, appears to have been heavily influenced by Conservative Central Office about the precise timing of the General Election of that year, although Lord Home later remarked: 'One of the decisions which cannot be taken by anyone other than the Prime Minister is the date of an election. That is for him, and him alone.' In 1974, Heath appears to have taken the advice of Robert Carr, the Home Secretary, as opposed to that of Anthony Barber, Chancellor of the Exchequer, and Lord Carrington, who was Chairman of the party and Defence Secretary, not to call an election on 7 February. How far it was Mr Heath's own decision eventually to call an election on 28 February, after it appeared that the miners' talks had broken down, is an open question.

The Sunday Times,
10 October 1976

In September 1978 Mr Callaghan, contrary to the expectations of the public, the media, and nearly all of his Cabinet, broadcast to the nation that he had decided not to call a general election until 1979. Of course, when 1979 came Mr Callaghan was left with no choice, since in March of that year a motion of no confidence in his Government was passed in the Commons by a majority of one vote. The general election followed automatically on 3 May. In 1983 Mrs Thatcher chose wisely but not entirely alone. A key figure in helping her to make up her mind was Cecil Parkinson, the Chairman of the party, who was influenced by the relatively favourable result of the Birmingham Northfield by-election in October 1982. He was in favour of calling an early election, although Mrs Thatcher let it widely be known that her natural inclination was to allow Parliament to run its full five-year term until the early summer of 1984. But with the Labour Party engaged in internecine strife and the Liberal/SDP Alliance losing political momentum since the Falklands conflict, the opportunity to go to the country in early 1983 rather than late 1983 or early 1984 was too much to resist.

Of course, it has been known for Prime Ministers to use dissolution as a threat with which to rally the more dissident parts of their party, as Harold Wilson well illustrated when he was at a politically low ebb in early 1968. But in a sense the threat is an idle one, since no Prime Minister or Cabinet particularly relishes the prospect of an election when it is fairly evident to the electorate that the Government is not united.

The media and question time

Although some have been more adept than others at extracting maximum advantage from television, for example, Wilson compared with Heath and Douglas-Home, all political leaders appreciate its power in affecting the Government's standing between elections. In Macmillan's time there was the parallel development in importance of Prime Minister's question time in the Commons. The session provides the leader of the Government with the opportunity to take up a public stance on a variety of current issues in the sure knowledge that his replies will be picked up both by the press and, more recently, by live radio transmission. It is an opportunity however, which demands considerable political tact. As G.W. Jones points out, 'as difficulties befell his government in its declining years, Mr Wilson tried to fend off the Opposition . . . by giving lengthy replies, full of statistics, so as to avoid reaching later embarrassing questions, an argument to which Wilson might have replied that he had to educate the Commons and the country with the facts.'

G.W. Jones,
*Parliamentary
Affairs,*
Summer 1973

The Cabinet Structure

It is, however, the relationship between a Prime Minister and his Cabinet which has come to occupy considerable attention in recent years. While the Cabinet's structure is secret, its composition must, according to J.P. Mackintosh, be a 'national microcosm', reflecting both left and right as well as the various geographical parts of the UK and, in Labour's case, links with the TUC.

The composition of the Cabinet

All Cabinets will be bound to include most of the party's senior MPs, if only on account of their very length of service in the Commons. It is notable that the Labour Party leader in Opposition is obliged to include in the shadow Cabinet (and since 1981 in the first Cabinet proper) the 15 MPs elected as the 'Parliamentary Committee' by the party in the Commons.

Some Cabinet ministers, though, are more important than others: by tradition the voices of the Chancellor of the Exchequer, the Foreign Secretary and the Home Secretary carry more weight than others. For example, Edward Heath has commented that during the whole of his Cabinet experience (1955–64, 1970–4) not a single vote was taken, but rather voices were counted or opinions noted.

Size is an important consideration. Open discussions in a large body become unwieldy and mitigate against an efficient decision-making process. It would appear that most Prime Ministers attempt to limit their Cabinet to about 20, but usually, and especially in the last 15 years, the actual membership has been rather higher than this. The sense of continuity is weakened further on those occasions when restructuring of departments takes place, or Cabinet reshuffles occur. Reshuffles and administrative restructuring are very much in the hands of the Prime Minister himself, and are usually undertaken for party convenience. The number of Cabinet reshuffles since Macmillan took office in 1957 has steadily grown, and was especially large under Wilson in the late 1960s. Edward Heath's Cabinet also saw several major rearrangements, notably in 1973 when there was a three-way change involving the Secretaries of State for Trade and Industry and the Environment and the Chancellor of the Duchy of Lancaster (European affairs) – John Davies, Geoffrey Rippon and Peter Walker. However, the trend towards 'super' Ministries under Heath helped him to keep the size of the Cabinet at a manageable level (for example, by the creation of the Department of the Environment and the Department of Trade and Industry – DTI).

The subsequent Labour Government found size even more of a problem; after the February 1974 Election the DTI was split into two, the Department for Prices and Consumer Protection (DPCP) was added, and the Department for Overseas Development was given Cabinet status. In late 1976 Callaghan, whose antipathy towards big government departments was self-evident in Whitehall, hived off the Department of Transport from the Environment Department; both kept Cabinet status. Under Mrs Thatcher Trade and Industry were remerged into the DTI; the Prices Department no longer exists, and Overseas Development is part of the Foreign Office, but Transport survives intact. The Heath Cabinet initially, in 1970, numbered 18, but the Wilson Cabinet following the October 1974 Election was 22 and the Callaghan Cabinet by 1976 had reached 24, with Mrs Thatcher falling back to 21 by 1983. During the Falklands War of 1982 Mrs Thatcher adopted a War Cabinet of four other key ministers, including the Foreign and Defence Secretaries, plus, rather surprisingly, the Chairman of the Conservative Party who was Paymaster-General. The fourth member was William Whitelaw, the Home Secretary, who was Deputy Leader of the party.

The functions of the Cabinet

The operation of the Cabinet system is, as Colin Seymour-Ure has said, 'one of the great unstudied questions of the last decade. Practically every other institution of government has come under discussion. . . . Alone the structure of the Cabinet and its relation to Parliament have been ignored.'

C. Seymour-Ure, *Parliamentary Affairs,* Summer 1971

While Mr Heath has maintained that the Cabinet is not just a 'committee of cyphers, ministers at most levels do not find sufficient time to deal with matters at departmental level, let alone with constituency problems.' Andrew Roth has quoted one minister as saying,

BBC Radio 3 discussion, 26 March 1976

'When you represent a seat 200 miles from London you are under tremendous pressure. When you get there on Friday, you feel that you have done a good week's work. But the people in the constituency act as though your parliamentary and ministerial work are an irrelevance and your only meaningful work is that done specifically for your constituents.'

New Society, 29 April 1976

Even if it is true that Prime Ministers have increased their individual power relative to ordinary ministers, who have become more and more overshadowed by the sheer complexity and size of their departments, the Cabinet cannot be dismissed lightly. It is still the place above all others where ministers fight for their departmental resources and where political issues are discussed. One 'Think-Tank' member is reported to have remarked that the Prime Minister 'has enormous initiative in dealing with things locked in equilibrium' – but on the other hand, the office of Prime Minister has a certain weakness, in the sense that its occupant, not enjoying the back-up in terms of research that is available to, for example, the President of the United States, is presented with issues solely in terms of sectional interests. The scale and volume of Cabinet work is, at least, a means of bringing party dissidents into the Government machine, rather than leaving them outside

J. Gretton, *New Society,* 1 March 1973

31

where they might cause more embarrassment to the Prime Minister. One example was Aneurin Bevan, who was given the very wide responsibilities of housing, health and local government during Attlee's 1945–51 administration.

The Cabinet can, however, be said to have two principal overall functions: firstly, that of dealing with day-to-day matters of importance, especially those raised by changes in international or economic circumstances. Secondly, it must at the same time try to put party policies and principles into practice. On occasion these two functions may conflict. The second function, for example may well have to be modified or abandoned in favour of the first. An instance of this occurred in 1975, when the Labour Government limited pay rises to £6 per week; this policy to a great extent compromised general Labour principles on free collective bargaining. Within the scope of its two main functions, the Cabinet operates in various ways. The full Cabinet can act as a clearing-house for inter-departmental reports and matters of national and international urgency. On more specific matters decisions may often be made by the Prime Minister and the relevant Cabinet minister acting together or by the minister himself in his capacity as head of department. The majority of the routine business, however, is dealt with in Cabinet committees.

DOCUMENT

4

Policy-making and the Cabinet

The private sector, certainly if it's operating in a competitive environment, can gauge its efficiency by its profit performance. Although the output of government is something successive administrations have tried to measure, it has eluded capture except in some small areas. So judgments about efficiency in government become very subjective. Of course, if a given standard of service can be supplied by new techniques at lower cost, efficiency is improved. But most reductions in costs – the saving of staff for instance – involve some deterioration of service, some exposure to fraud or loss, or, and this is something which isn't always realised, some increase in cost to the people for whom the service is provided. Putting personal taxation on a self-assessment basis would not necessarily be an efficient step if the taxpayer had to expend more effort making his return than the Inland Revenue did when making the assessment for him. We would have reduced the number of civil servants, but we would not be a more efficient society. However, difficulties like this must not stand in the way of a continuing effort both to judge the efficacy of administration and to improve it.

But if efficiency is an elusive concept to translate to the administration of individual departments, how much more difficult it is at the level of government policy as a whole. Even if each individual department is operating at peak efficiency, how can we be sure that the balance of effort between departments is right? I ask this question because the functions that government undertakes are both wide-ranging and disparate, far more so than those performed by any other entity in our society. When a business firm, even a conglomerate, has to decide which activities to pursue, it can reduce its options to a common form, to the rate of return on assets for instance, and an efficient decision becomes possible. But governments are not only undertaking widely divergent functions, ranging, for example, from immigration control to the provision of advice to exporters and judgments about the amount of effort to put into each service cannot be founded on any standard or uniform basis of comparison, so difficult is it to compare the contribution each makes to the social good.

Before I come to the conceptual difficulties which complicate the making of choices between such unrelated and incommensurable issues as those I have instanced, it is worth looking at the conventions which apply to collective decisions. Governments, here as elsewhere, are organised on a functional basis, each department being headed by a Minister whose personal responsibilities are usually defined by statute. But overriding almost all the individual responsibilities of Ministers and departments runs the doctrine of the collective responsibility of the Cabinet. The Cabinet, some would say in formal terms though I would say in real terms as well, is the ultimate embodiment of the executive government in this country. A Minister may have statutory responsibilities peculiar to himself, but if the exercise of those responsibilities affects his colleagues – if, for example, he exposes the whole government to criticism and attack, or if he imposes costs on his fellow Ministers – he must expect to submit his decision to collective endorsement.

The way issues are presented to Cabinet, indeed, the way issues are settled between departments, is crucially affected not only by these conventions but also by the organisation of government. An issue which is brought to Cabinet for approval or resolution is always presented by the Minister whose business it is. If it impinges other than tangentially on another Minister, he, too, may make a presentation to Cabinet, supporting or opposing the case of the Minister who is principally concerned. But the essence of any collective Cabinet discussion is that it takes place on the basis of statements by interested parties, and they can always be relied on to do their best by argument and presentation to secure approval for what they want to do. Where the proposals are contested by a colleague whose departmental interests are adversely affected, the discussion assumes an adversarial character and the Cabinet acts in what amounts to a judicial role. But where, as so often happens, there's no adversary, the Cabinet simply hears the case which the Minister concerned presents, and this case is inevitably put in terms which suit the Minister himself.

Now, it may be that in ideal circumstances the Minister will present the issue with the same objectivity that his own officials have employed in presenting it to him. The Cabinet will then, as a minimum, have the same information as the Minister, and its decision can be presumed to be an efficient one. But if, for any reason, the Minister does not present all the relevant information to his colleagues, how then can the Cabinet be said to be taking an efficient decision?

In no area of policy-making does this problem arise more acutely than in the management of the economy and, in particular, the Budget. The Minister who brings these issues to Cabinet is, of course, the Chancellor of the Exchequer. No other Minister has at his command the back-up of analytical support that the Chancellor receives from his Treasury and Revenue Department officials and from the Bank of England. How can his colleagues be assured that they're getting the whole story and not just the one which the Chancellor wishes them to hear? They have no independent staff. They have indeed no direct access to the official advice which the Treasury provides. Yet they are obliged to come

33

to a view on the basis of what one of their colleagues, a committed party, is telling them.

Decisions in this area are governed by two well-entrenched, if rather arbitrary, principles. Number one: 'as things have been, so, broadly, shall they remain'; and number two: 'he who has the muscle gets the money'. Let me explain what I mean. Principle number one stems from the Annual Public Expenditure Survey when departments make bids for future allocations of money on the basis of their existing plans and programmes. The implicit assumption is that these plans are 'right', in the sense that they were accepted in the past and that the only question is how rapidly or how slowly they should develop. Principle number two manifests itself in the process by which the individual bids for expenditure are settled. The essence of this process, given that the aggregate of bids invariably exceeds the agreed total, is that Treasury Ministers have to do battle with all the spending Ministers in turn. And the outcome of each battle is determined less by rational argument than by a judgment each party makes of the way the Cabinet would adjudicate in the event of continuing hostilities between the parties. Sometimes the Treasury will yield, knowing that the spending Minister has a strong political case. Sometimes it is the Minister who concedes, by not pressing his bid, perhaps through lack of conviction in the strength of his case. Unresolved conflicts are finally settled in full Cabinet.

Now, there are a number of criticisms which can be made of this system, but, first, a word in its defence. The principle that programmes should develop much as they have in the past is not simply evidence of inertia on Whitehall's part. It is a reflection of political reality; the reality that in a pluralist society significant shifts in policies and programmes are liable to encounter strong opposition. And the principle of settling differences between the Treasury and the spenders on the basis of political strength, while crude and pragmatic, may well lead to a series of decisions which somehow reflect rational choice. A spending Minister who lacks conviction in his programme may be expressing the implicit view of his colleagues and his party. If he concedes readily to the Treasury, he may be doing so not out of weakness but in recognition that his programme does not command high priority. He may feel he can deal with the beneficiaries of his spending programme more easily than his colleagues can with theirs, and this, in turn, may reflect the political strength of the interest groups affected. So, at the end of the day, the distribution may take quite a lot of account, albeit implicitly, of political preferences.

But it is clearly not a very scientific process, and most theorists of collective decision-taking would find it unsatisfactory. Now the system could be made a bit more rational and efficient if it incorporated some feature for giving Ministers a 'feel' for the relative value to them of different parts of their whole programme. (I mentioned earlier the difficulty of comparing the value of the immigration service and the provision of advice to exporters.) Let no one imagine that such comparisons are easy. But I believe that more could be done by sophisticated cost-benefit analysis to give Ministers a sounder basis than they have at present for exercising choice about where to expand and where to contract government services, and to help them away from the inefficient and indiscriminate approach, where cuts have to be made uniformly and across the board. Another feature I would like to see would be one for regularly evaluating the expenditure incurred on each programme against the objectives it was designed to achieve. The world is a changing place: administrative techniques, social habits, industrial performance, are not static, and government programmes should respond flexibly to changes like this in the environment. I do not doubt that many government departments do periodically ask themselves whether an entire programme should be redesigned to reflect changing circumstances. But the system as it operates today does not encourage this. It is far easier to get the Treasury and the Cabinet to agree to unchanged programmes than to persuade them that programmes should be modified as circumstances change, especially if the variations involve temporary increases in expenditure. The Treasury's proper concern to limit the total claims of the public sector sometimes leads it to resist any increase in programmes, whatever the benefits may be in terms of improved efficiency.

It would be possible to counter these 'inertial' features of the present system by making two specific changes. The first would be to make the spending departments think what they would do if the money available to them were drastically cut. Just as the ordinary person or the ordinary business has, from time to time, to face a sharp reduction in income, so departments would have to think, either of different, cheaper ways of realising their objectives or of scrapping some objectives altogether. This system, which is known in the jargon as zero-based budgeting, has often been considered in the past, but it has always been rejected, either because the programme managers have convinced themselves that alternative ways of carrying out their policies were simply not available or because Ministers were not prepared to abandon some aims altogether. These are understandable reactions, but the arguments against change do not really convince me. I would therefore like to see zero-based budgeting tried out, in the first place on a selective basis, to see whether it is as unworkable as the spenders have always argued in the past.

The second change, which would have something like the same effect, would be to reinstate a regime which Mr Heath's administration introduced over ten years ago, the regime of policy analysis and review, 'PAR' for short. This system required Whitehall to comb over its programmes and find out whether they were working in the way they had been intended to. Take transport, for instance. The idea of 'PAR' would be to mount a searching review of the government's various policies towards public and private transport, to see whether they were contributing to the creation of a coherent system of roads, railways, canals, airports and so on, which matched the users' requirements. The instruments used to bring about these policy aims, for instance the taxation of cars, investment-spending on the railways, the licensing of civil air routes and so on, would be examined to see how effective they were, and if the policies were not producing the desired results, they would become candidates for change. The concept was admirable, but in practice it did not come off. Why not? In part, the answer is that each 'PAR' imposed a heavy burden on officials and many of the reviews led to no perceptible change in policy. The effort seemed pointless. The cost of each radical review was the neglect of some part of the continuing job of administration. But another reason why the system fell into disuse was that many departments chose to offer relatively unimportant programmes for analysis and kept their major policies out of the area of review.

The experience of the 1970s should give anyone pause before recommending the reinstatement of 'PAR'. But I believe its demise was not due to any inherent flaw or defect – and a new generation of officials, and a firm commitment by Ministers, could make it a success. The effort it would involve could be amply repaid by the substantial rewards to be gained in even a few programmes. The Treasury has made a start in this direction by calling for departmental reviews at the conclusion of each annual expenditure survey. This needs to be given strong ministerial support.

Sir Douglas Wass, The Reith Lectures, *The Listener,* 24 November 1983

Cabinet committees

Little is known about the committees of the Cabinet, although in 1961 there was some mention in the press of a Public Expenditure Control Committee. Michael Davie of *The Observer,* in trying to establish the names of Cabinet committees, met with considerable resistance from various departments and the Cabinet Secretary, Sir John Hunt, even though he was able to quote Peter Walker, the Conservative minister, as saying that the secrecy was 'crazy'. Davie, however, concluded that at the end of 1976 the following Cabinet committees existed:

1   Overseas Policy and Defence

2   Two (or three) Economic Committees (macro and micro)

3   Home Affairs

4   Social Services

5   Legislation

6   PESC (Public Expenditure Survey Committee). (PESC usually refers to the Treasury Committee of 40–50 officials. Davie was unsure about the inclusion of PESC as a Cabinet Committee.)

7   Energy

8   Queen's Speech

9   Devolution

10   Northern Ireland (9 and 10 were responses to recent developments)

11   Agriculture

12   Transport

13   Urban Aid

On occasion very important decisions are taken at Cabinet committee level only; an example is the decision of the committee (GEN 163) in 1947 to authorise the manufacture of the atomic bomb (the Commons was told 14 months later). Decisions on the mounting of the Suez operation in 1956 might well fall into a similar category. Whether in either case the full Cabinet was made aware of the decision has been unclear; Hennessy certainly denies that in the former case it was. In respect of Suez, much of the detailed work was carried out in the Egypt Committee over a period of several months. The Cabinet did not know anything about the secret meeting at Sèvres where it was agreed among the three powers that Britain and France should 'intervene' to stop Israel's 'attack' on Egypt. But otherwise claims Rhodes James '... the decision had been made, and had been ratified by the Cabinet. The doubters did not press their doubts ... even to the threat of resignation'.

The Times in 1978 (21 July) listed the following Cabinet committees (being, it said, of two types – standing, about 25, and *'ad hoc'* – General/GEN committees, about 130).

P. Hennessy,
Cabinet, Blackwell,
1986, p. 125

R. Rhodes James,
Anthony Eden,
Weidenfeld and
Nicolson, 1986,
p. 538

Standing

EI	Industrial Strategy
EY	Economic Strategy (chairman: PM)
EY/P	Pay Policy Progress
HS	Home and social policy
DOP	Defence and foreign affairs (chairman: PM)
LG	Legislative Programme (chairman: deputy PM)
QF	Queen's Speech
DVY/DVI	Devolution
TRM	Terrorism
RD	Overseas Aid (chairman: Foreign Secretary)
IN	Ulster

General included GEN 12 on South African affairs, GEN 38 on inner cities, GEN 91 on the press, and GEN 112 on British Steel.

In 1981 *The Times* took up the issue again and published the following 'consumers guide' chart. Mr Callaghan said in an apparently confidential document of guidance to ministers in 1978:

> 'the principle of the collective responsibility of ministers, upon the maintenance of which the Cabinet and Cabinet committee system depends, requires opportunities for free and frank discussion between ministers . . . and such discussion will be hampered if the processes by which it is carried on are laid bare.'

DOCUMENT

5

The 'Consumers' Guide' to the Cabinet

In the immediate aftermath of the killing at the first opportunity last Friday afternoon of Mr Frank Hooley's Freedom of Information Bill by the Government's "payroll" vote, it is difficult to see the Thatcher Cabinet as anything but totally dedicated to that all-concealing administrative secrecy which has helped to produce an almost unbroken string of policy disasters for Britain since 1945.

But such a judgment would be unfair. In her first month of office Mrs Margaret Thatcher went farther than any prime minister before her in disclosing the existence, in a   37 parliamentary written answer, of four Cabinet committees, on economic strategy, defence and overseas policy, home and social affairs and legislation.

Encouraged by her openness, and that of another Commonwealth prime minister operating in a parliamentary system modelled on our own, Mr Pierre Trudeau of Canada, who published the titles and membership of all his Cabinet committees last summer, I wrote to Mrs Thatcher last month asking her to go farther, and enclosing the Trudeau list I had been given in Ottawa.

Last week I received a courteous reply from Mr Bernard Ingham, her Chief Press Secretary, saying that the Prime Minister was interested to learn of Mr Trudeau's action but was not prepared to "alter her view of what is appropriate here". To go farther than her answer of May, 1979, Mrs Thatcher believes "would not be consistent with the principle of collective responsibility as it has developed in this country".

So, as a contribution to the spirit of openness to which the Prime Minister has yet to be fully converted, and as a service to the consumers of their product, the general public, "Whitehall brief" would like to present a tabular guide to those Cabinet committees, both ministerial and official, whose existence has become known since May, 1979, despite the fog of secrecy in which the Government has enshrouded them. A word of explanation is needed. The committees are divided into two main types: standing, or permanent bodies such as H, E and OD (these terms are explained in the accompanying table); and ad hoc, or miscellaneous groups, such as MISC 7. Most, but not all, ministerial gatherings are shadowed by official committees of civil servants such as E(OCS), under Mr Angus Fraser, of the Civil Service Department, which works to E(CS).

One of the most secret is the steering committee on intelligence, chaired by Sir Robert Armstrong, Secretary of the Cabinet. It supervizes the work of the JIC and advises the Prime Minister's very select ministerial group.

Mrs Thatcher has managed to govern with a much leaner committee structure than any of her predecessors since 1945.

The list published in the table is far from complete. Any public-spirited minister or civil servant inclined to the view that the Government's attitude towards Cabinet committee secrecy is excessive could fill the gaps by supplying details in an unsigned, typed message, slipped in the traditional brown envelope favoured by "moles" and addressed to *The Times,* taking care, naturally, to remove any incriminating trademarks that might provide clues for his or her departmental security officer and MI5.

CONSUMERS' GUIDE TO MRS THATCHER'S CABINET COMMITTEES

Initials	Chairman	Functions
E	Mrs Thatcher	Economic strategy, energy, the most important EEC matters.
E (PSP)	Sir Keith Joseph	Public sector pay policy.
E (EA)	Sir Keith Joseph	Micro-economic affairs and aspects of industrial policy.
E (CS)	Lord Soames	Civil Service pay and contingency planning for public service strikes.
E (DL)	Sir Geoffrey Howe	Disposing of state industries and assets.
PESC	Mr Geoffrey Littler	Annual public expenditure survey round plus any special cuts exercises commissioned by the Cabinet.

Initials	Chairman	Functions
OD	Mrs Thatcher	Foreign affairs, defence and Northern Ireland.
OD (E)	Lord Carrington	EEC policy.
Ministerial group on N Ireland	Mr William Whitelaw	Preparation of new initiatives.
Ministerial group on Intelligence	Mrs Thatcher	Supervision of the clandestine agencies.
JIC	Sir Anthony Acland	Joint intelligence committee scrutinizing the product from all sources.
TWC	Sir Robert Armstrong	Transition to War Committee planning the mobilization of the Armed Forces and the home front should war break out between Nato and the Warsaw Pact countries.
HD	Mr Robert Wade-Gery	Civil Defence.
SPM	Sir Anthony Duff	Security and policy methods of the Civil and Diplomatic services, including positive vetting.
H	Mr Whitelaw	Home and social affairs, including education.
CCU	Mr Whitelaw	Civil Contingencies Unit which plans to break strikes and keep essential industries and services going.
NIP	Sir William Ryrie	Nationalized industries policy
QL	Mr Francis Pym	Future legislation and preparation of the Queen's Speech.
MISC 7	Mrs Thatcher	Replacement of Polaris with a new nuclear deterrent.
MISC 14	Sir Geoffrey Howe	Innovations.
MISC 15	Mr Robin Ibbs	Civil Service group servicing MISC 14.
MISC 21	Mr Whitelaw	Fixing level of rate support grant.
MIO	Mr Pym	Meeting of information officers to manage government news.
MIO (E)	Mr Bernard Ingham	Management of government economic news; now meets irregularly because of persistent leaking.
EOM	Mr Angus Fraser	Meeting of Whitehall establishment officers on personnel and industrial relations. Recently commissioned to fight off threat of freedom of information.

Peter Hennessy, *The Times*, 10 February 1981

In a BBC radio interview in 1976 with Professor Robert McKenzie, Edward Heath commented that government work was so complex that it was automatic that senior Cabinet members chaired the most important committees of the Cabinet, among which was the Home Affairs Committee. Mr Heath also commented that it was disagreement in Cabinet committees which usually produced a full Cabinet agenda item, and that in his experience as Prime Minister between 1970 and 1974 too many of such disagreements found their way to full Cabinet meetings. In the same radio discussion Lord Trend (a former Secretary to the Cabinet) observed that it was the difficult, sensitive matters which were inevitably referred to Cabinet.

Heath's remark about giving senior Cabinet members the important committee jobs raises the question of to what extent there exists an 'inner Cabinet'. There was a great deal of comment in the press about the possible operation of such a body under the 1966–70 Wilson Government. However, some political scientists, such as J.P. Mackintosh, have held that it is extremely misleading to talk in such terms. Some ministers are always more important than others and some are personally close to the Prime Minister. It should be emphasised that the Cabinet does not always have to meet as a full body if some specialised matter occurs suddenly; there are such things as partial Cabinet meetings. But that is not the same as identifying a special 'inner circle'.

The operation of the 1966–70 Wilson Cabinet was of particular interest since it was often held (for example, by Robert McKenzie) that Wilson introduced a rule which stated that no matters could go before the full Cabinet unless the permission of the appropriate Cabinet committee chairman was received. Mr Heath, however, has clearly stated that his Cabinet operated upon no such lines; indeed, he has said that any minister, in consultation with the Secretary to the Cabinet, could place an item on the full Cabinet agenda. In his time as Prime Minister there were usually four fixed agenda items before departmental business was taken – Parliamentary Business, Foreign and International Affairs, Europe/EEC and the Irish question. The control of the Cabinet agenda is often seen as one of the Prime Minister's most important powers, but in view of Heath's comments it could well be dangerous to be too emphatic about that.

BBC Radio 3,
26 March 1976

The Secretary to the Cabinet has a major influence in the shaping of the Cabinet agenda and ministerial briefs. As its name implies, the Secretariat is the Cabinet's property, not the Prime Minister's. Indeed, Heath has remarked that his only criticism of the Cabinet Secretariat system is that it is a Rolls-Royce of a machine; it operates so perfectly that you obtain constant compromise. The Prime Minister has no central back-up department, although some Prime Ministers, including Harold Wilson, have given consideration to setting up a small organisation. To some extent the establishment of the Central Policy Review Staff – CPRS (the 'Think-Tank') by Heath provided a means of keeping the Prime Minister better informed about complex departmental activities. Lord Trend commented that the CPRS was the first real attempt to institute a major part of the 1918 Haldane Report on the Machinery of Central Government. The CPRS crossed departmental boundaries to rationalise different ministerial claims and facts, and brought more logic to the compromise system of Cabinet committees. In addition it took a longer-term view of Government strategy (as opposed to fundamental policy).

The doctrine and the suspension of the doctrine

Lord Trend also made the somewhat remarkable statement that if a member of the Cabinet was not 'intellectually convinced' of the arguments advanced for a particular policy he would resign from the Cabinet. However, there must have been many an occasion when a Cabinet minister has not been intellectually convinced yet has decided instead to swallow his political pride. This illustrates the unofficial principle of the Cabinet's 'collective responsibility' which each Prime Minister strives to uphold in order to help keep up Government morale and maintain a team effort.

It is only on rare occasions that the doctrine is suspended. One instance of this occurred during the EEC referendum campaign in 1975. During that period ministers were officially allowed to dissent from the Government's recommended line on EEC membership. The suspension was repeated in 1977, when ministers were allowed a free vote on the second reading of the Government's own Bill on direct elections to the European Parliament. In answer to a question in the Commons in June 1977 the Prime Minister, Mr Callaghan, stated blandly that the doctrine of Cabinet collective responsibility continued to operate, except where he said it would not apply.

Few ministerial resignations

British Cabinet resignations or sackings on policy grounds, as opposed to those for mainly personal or departmental failure, are relatively few nowadays. Professor Mackintosh suggested that this was because a minister's job was now far more concerned with complex, technical matters – in other words the burden of routine administration drove out dissension. There were a few difficulties in Macmillan's Government, and several resignations from the first Wilson Governments. Under Macmillan the most celebrated case was Peter Thorneycroft's resignation in 1958 as Chancellor of the Exchequer. He left the Cabinet because of the Prime Minister's refusal to cut public expenditure. The Prime Minister himself was able to shrug this off as just 'a little local difficulty'. In 1962 there occurred the famous dismissal of one-third of the Cabinet (the 'jaded third', according to Macmillan) before they had a chance to contemplate resignation at all; among the seven was Selwyn Lloyd, the Chancellor of the Exchequer. This example is often referred to as a demonstration of prime ministerial strength, but it is probably more important to see it as a sign of weakness, a sign that Macmillan was conscious of the poor image his Government had by then acquired. And he could hardly have repeated such an exercise very often.

The Wilson Governments of 1964–70 included the short-lived tenure of Frank Cousins, who, having been specially brought in from the trade union movement in 1964, resigned as Minister of Technology in 1966 on account of the Government's pay policies. In 1967 a senior non-Cabinet Minister, Margaret Herbison, resigned from her post at the Ministry of Social Security because of dissatisfaction with what she regarded as the meagre level by which old-age pensions were to be raised. During the previous year another important non-Cabinet minister, Christopher Mayhew, the Navy Minister, had resigned on account of the Government's determination not to build any more aircraft carriers, a decision related to Britain's withdrawal from east of Suez. Also in 1967 Douglas Jay was sacked as President of the Board of Trade on account of his continued opposition to membership of the EEC. In 1968 Lord Longford, a lesser-known member of the Cabinet, resigned over the Government's decision to postpone until 1972 the raising of the school-

41

Harold Macmillan as Prime Minister (1957–63)

leaving age to 16. In the same year George Brown resigned as Foreign Secretary over a crisis in sterling and Ray Gunter quit as Minister of Power after a two-month tenure (he had served as Minister of Labour from 1964 to 1968). In 1969 several Cabinet ministers found themselves demoted, ostensibly as part of a major departmental reorganisation. They included Richard Marsh, the Minister of Transport (who by one of the ironies of the British political system was later appointed Chairman of British Rail). Marsh lost all ministerial rank, although the reason for this, apart from his general dissatisfaction with Government economic policy, was not entirely clear. However, Marsh and the others involved (Peter Shore, Judith Hart and Anthony Crosland) had been part of a Cabinet team that had noticeably failed to give support to the Prime Minister over the Industrial Relations Bill of that year.

There were only a few minor resignations during the Heath administration, but in the Labour Government elected in October 1974 there were a few more 'local difficulties'. Among these was Eric Heffer, (a non-Cabinet) Minister of State for Industry, who was sacked in 1975. He had already pursued a difficult course by his public statements about the Government's decision in 1974 to honour a contract for supplying warships to Chile, despite the overthrow of Salvador Allende's parliamentary regime in October 1973; but more important was the position he adopted publicly in 1975 over the nature of the EEC referendum (as an ardent left-wing Labour MP, he was much opposed to EEC membership). It should be noted that only a year before the 'agreement to differ' on the question of membership of the EEC, Wilson had stressed the importance of Cabinet collective responsibility.

Shortly after the referendum Wilson showed the tactical adroitness that many a Prime Minister has displayed by moving his outspoken critic on the EEC and many other matters, Tony Wedgwood Benn, from Industry to Energy (in a straight switch with Eric Varley). At the same time Judith Hart left the Government altogether, refusing to accept a junior post, after having been replaced by Reg Prentice as Minister for Overseas Development, and having made impassioned but unsuccessful pleas for the level of overseas aid to be at least maintained, if not increased, in what were difficult economic circumstances. Mrs Hart subsequently returned to her old post in 1977, two months after Mr Prentice's resignation.

In 1974 the Government allowed a joint naval exercise to take place between the UK and South Africa (this was related to the renewal of British naval facilities at the South African port of Simonstown). Labour's National Executive Committee (NEC) soon passed a motion declaring that this decision was a 'gross error'. Three members of the Labour Party NEC who voted for the motion also happened to be Government ministers (Mr Benn, of Cabinet rank, and the junior ministers Mrs Hart and Miss Lestor). It was reported that Mr Wilson sought assurances that the ministers concerned would not again vote against Government policy at NEC meetings, and it appeared the assurances were forthcoming. The incident underlined the often precarious relationship of certain members of the Parliamentary Labour Party (especially Government members) with the NEC.

Mrs Thatcher's Cabinet

Mrs Thatcher's Government of 1979–83 saw a number of ministerial casualties. Most notable were those that occurred in 1981. Firstly, Norman St John Stevas, Leader of the House and Chancellor of the Duchy of Lancaster was dismissed. Mr Stevas was regarded as a 'wet' or liberal in respect of the Government's economic policy, and it subsequently became clear that he was unhappy about certain aspects of Thatcherism, notably tight fiscal control whose effect might be to increase unemployment whilst lowering the inflation rate. Later in 1981 other 'wets' were dismissed – Lord Soames, Lord President and Leader of the House of Lords, Mark Carlisle, Education Secretary, and Sir Ian Gilmour, Lord Privy Seal (Deputy Foreign Secretary). Sir Ian later said that the country was heading for the rocks as a result of the Government's economic policy. Lord Thorneycroft was also sacked as Party Chairman in the same year. In some ways the dismissal of Lord Soames was the most surprising, since he had been identified with the successful Lancaster House negotiations in 1979 that paved the way for the independence of Zimbabwe in 1980, and he had acted as Rhodesia's last Governor in the transitional period. But he was seen to have acted ineptly over the prolonged Civil Service strike in 1981, the strike having the effect of Mrs Thatcher changing her mind over preserving the Civil Service Department (CSD). Also, in 1981 a senior non-Cabinet figure, Keith Speed, resigned as Navy Minister over defence cuts in the Navy.

Despite the 1981 'purge' other 'wets' survived, notably Peter Walker as Minister of Agriculture. But James Prior was removed from the Department of Employment, where he had adopted a 'softly softly' approach in respect of trade union reform, and exiled to Belfast as Northern Ireland Secretary. He resigned from the Government in 1984, having made it clear publicly that he disagreed with major aspects of Government economic policy.

In 1982 the surprise attack upon the Falkland Islands by Argentina brought more ministerial casualties. The liberal Conservative Lord Carrington resigned as Foreign Secretary, a post to which he had brought colour and prestige world-wide. Humphrey Atkins, Lord Privy Seal (Lord Carrington's deputy) also resigned and a junior Foreign Office minister, Richard Luce, who had been directly responsible for the Falklands. Mr Luce returned to the Government in 1984. Francis Pym succeeded Lord Carrington as Foreign Secretary but on the day after the result of the 1983 General Election Mrs Thatcher sacked him too. The departure of Pym, Carrington and Soames marked the end of the patrician element in the Tory Cabinet and with it attitudes which might be termed enlightened paternalism. Radical Toryism, as exemplified by the self-made Tory businessman, now predominated.

While the Falklands could well have been Mrs Thatcher's political and military Waterloo, the successful outcome of the war consolidated her position to such an extent that it could be argued she adopted an almost presidential, or at least headmistressy, approach to Cabinet affairs and the principle of collective responsibility. Her 'no nonsense' approach, not least in respect of economic arguments within the Cabinet, had been presaged in 1980 when she publicly stated that her Employment Secretary, James Prior, had made a mistake, for which he was 'very, very sorry indeed', regarding his remarks about the difficult future the Chairman of British Steel, Sir Charles Villiers, might face as a result of a national strike within the industry. But sometimes the 'presidential' approach rebounded. In 1981 there was a major row after the liberal (or 'wet') members of the Cabinet felt thoroughly unhappy with the monetarist policy of Sir Geoffrey Howe's Budget. It is not usual for the Cabinet to discuss Budget details much in advance anyway, but such was the strength of feeling on the 'left-wing' that the 'wets' won a concession in so far as the Budget would no longer be presented as a *fait accompli* a few hours before the Chancellor made his statement to the Commons.

Eric Varley and the Chrysler Case

It was Eric Varley who was involved in another episode which serves as an interesting example of the tension between prime ministerial and Cabinet government. At the end of November 1975 the Labour Government issued a White Paper on its new industrial strategy, which largely concentrated on giving aid to

Lord Carrington as Foreign Secretary, accompanying Mrs Thatcher

companies which showed promise and initiative. This was not a new idea, and it even bore some resemblance to the celebrated policy of giving no aid to 'lame-duck' industries, pursued by John Davies, Conservative Minister for Trade and Industry between 1970 and 1973. Unfortunately, only days after the publication of the White Paper, it became apparent that the UK section of the Chrysler car company was on the very brink of financial collapse; this implied the loss of many jobs in the Midlands and Scotland, as well as of an important contract with an oil country (Iran).

Mr Varley undertook direct negotiations with Chrysler, but the position was complicated by the fact that Harold Lever, Chancellor of the Duchy of Lancaster, was also negotiating, as the head of a special economic advisory unit to the Prime Minister. This to some extent undermined Varley's position as Industry Secretary. The new industrial strategy, which had primarily been the work of Varley and Wilson, now, in the light of the Chrysler debacle, became the concern of the whole Cabinet. But the Cabinet was deeply divided over the extent to which the Government should commit itself to a rescue operation.

45

According to *The Sunday Times* (14 December 1975) the Prime Minister and four other leading Cabinet members favoured a large subsidy not only to the Chrysler plant in Coventry but also to the firm's Scottish plant (because of the Scottish nationalist electoral factor). Yet Varley and the Chancellor of the Exchequer, Denis Healey, favoured upholding the basic approach of the White Paper. Mr Wedgwood Benn favoured total nationalisation through the National Enterprise Board.

It appeared that Healey shifted his position to that of the first, larger group, because of the implications for jobs and exports, and it was that view which carried the day. It is doubtful to what extent this was due to the forcefulness of the Prime Minister; rather it appears that most of the Cabinet was convinced there was little alternative anyway. It also appears that Wilson personally persuaded Varley to stay on as Industry Secretary; in the 1950s such a *volte-face* could well have been taken as a resignation issue.

Crossman's views on Cabinet versus prime ministerial government

Maybe Crossman, had he been alive and in the Cabinet at the time, would have claimed the Chrysler episode as one more piece of evidence for his theory of prime ministerial government. Maybe he would have counted Chrysler alongside other examples of Prime Ministers in the post-war era handling certain issues personally – as illustrated by Wilson and the Rhodesian negotiations of 1965–8 and Heath and EEC entry in 1970–2. The publication in 1975 of the first volume of *The Crossman Diaries* (despite *The Sunday Times'* battle with a Government arguing that publication was not in the 'national interest') was an important landmark. The diaries, highly personalised as they are, are inconclusive about the extent to which prime ministerial government has increased, if at all. Yet some of Crossman's observations do give credence to the idea that it was the Prime Minister and one or two important ministers who ran the Cabinet. So, for example, for 12 July 1966 Crossman wrote: 'the long-announced Cabinet discussion on productivity. All the papers were desultory and of no interest. However, at the last moment the Chancellor circulated a sensational *Top Secret* document.'

The Observer,
27 June 1976

But the Crossman memoirs must be treated with some circumspection. As Lord Goodman remarked in 1976, Harold Evans (the Editor of *The Sunday Times*) 'by brilliant techniques managed to create the impression . . . that *The Sunday Times* would reveal to the world secrets of fascinating allure.' Dick Crossman was a 'remarkable man of great intellectual power'; but such a quality 'gave him his reputation, by no means wholly deserved, for indecision.' In a BBC Radio 3 broadcast (1 January 1978) Harold Wilson refuted all aspects of Crossman's 'prime ministerial' (as opposed to 'Cabinet') thesis of central Government. He remarked that Crossman was 'not so much a minister as the Cabinet's educational conscience. . . . He did not understand Cabinet government.'

However, despite substantial qualifications, a number of Crossman's observations upon Cabinet operations cannot be lightly dismissed; for example, during a long entry for 18 April 1965, he remarked:

'This means that very often the whole job is pre-cooked in the official committee to a point from which it is extremely difficult to reach any other conclusion than that already determined by the officials in advance . . . only formal approval is needed from the full Cabinet. This is the way in which Whitehall ensures that the Cabinet system is relatively harmless.'

Richard Crossman, *The Diaries of a Cabinet Minister,* Hamish Hamilton and Jonathan Cape, 1975, vol. 1, p. 198

In the same entry he also stated,

'I have yet to see a minister prevail against an inter-departmental paper without the backing of the Prime Minister . . . or the Chancellor. And this is where one's relations with the PM are so all-important. If one doesn't have his backing, or at least the Chancellor's . . . the chance of winning against the official view is absolutely nil.'

It may well be that the most we can conclude is that prime ministerial power tends to be cyclical and that at certain times the pendulum does swing more in the direction of collective Cabinet government. But under Mr Wilson from 1966–70 and Mrs Thatcher since 1979 the emphasis was on the prime ministerial-presidential theme. Mrs Thatcher's constant use of the personal pronoun, 'I' and less often 'We' in television and radio interviews has been in marked contrast to the use of the phrase 'the Government' by former Prime Ministers.

DOCUMENT

6

Mrs Thatcher's Style of Government

On one level Mrs Thatcher's reluctance to question the conventional wisdoms of Cabinet government is surprising. She is a very unconventional PM in thought and method. And it was she, after all, who, in her first few weeks of office, brought in Lord Rayner from Marks and Spencer to send teams of young efficiency scrutineers up and down the corridors of Whitehall in search of sacred cows and armed with a set of lethal questions penned by Sir Derek (as he then was). Those questions are custom-made for application to the performance of Cabinet government: Why do we do this at all? What value does it add? If it has to be done, does it have to be done this way?

Yet, Rayner's Raiders will not be unleashed on the Cabinet system. It has become the plumpest sacred cow in Whitehall. Why? According to Whitehall intelligence, the Prime Minister does not regard her personal bit of the system as a problem. It is one of the parts that Raynerism cannot reach.

Ironically, it is Mrs Thatcher's style which has made Cabinet government an issue once more. She has worked a minor miracle and made the study of public administration interesting again. Her instincts are more presidential than prime ministerial. 'Collective' is a tarnished adjective in her political vocabulary, whether it be applied to Cabinet discussion, pay-bargaining or the organisation of industry. Her preferred procedure is to invite a Secretary of State to prepare a policy paper for her rather than for the full Cabinet (the postwar Cabinets of Attlee and Churchill often considered over 400 papers a year; last year's tally was between 60 and 70).

The Minister is summoned to No 10 with his back-up team of civil servants for an *ad hoc* meeting. He sits across the table from Mrs Thatcher and her team, which can be a mixture of people from the Downing Street Private Office, her Policy Unit, the Cabinet Office and the Treasury (if public spending is involved), plus one or two personal advisers. She then proceeds, after an opening statement by the accused (the Minister), to 'act as judge and jury in her own cause', as one insider put it. It is this method more than any other which has led observers to speak of the decay of traditional Cabinet government, since these groups fall outside the formal Cabinet Committee structure as well. But, as even its detractors admit, it is a quicker and more efficient way (in the short term) of dispatching business than consultation and collective discussion. And we were warned. Three months before becoming PM, Mrs Thatcher told Kenneth Harris of *The Observer* that: 'It must be a conviction government. As Prime Minister I could not waste time having any internal arguments.'

A highly personal style of government may work well enough for a Prime Minister with a 'conviction' administration, like Mrs Thatcher. Aneurin Bevan once said: 'There are only two ways of getting into the Cabinet. One way is to crawl up the staircase of preferment on your belly; the other way is to kick them in the teeth.' Most of the personalities around Mrs Thatcher's Cabinet table are staircase men.

When the Prime Minister wrote in her letter accepting the resignation last year of Mr Jim Prior: 'I take your point about frankness! That's what Cabinets are for, and lively discussions usually lead to good decisions', it aroused a good deal of ironical, harmless amusement in Whitehall. Though the mirth was lost on some, like David Howell, her former Energy and Transport Minister. It struck him, as he says on Radio 3 on 11 July, in the third of a series of conversations on Cabinet government: 'With some foreboding because I felt that the word "lively" discussions is a codeword for "argument" and I don't regard high-pitched argument as the best means of reaching decisions.'

P. Hennessy, *The Listener*, 27 June 1985

7

David Howell's View of Cabinet Government

A conversation between Peter Hennessy of *The Times* and David Howell, who was Secretary of State for Transport in Mrs Thatcher's Cabinet until his dismissal in 1983. BBC Radio 3, 11 July 1985 (abridged version).

Hennessy: Former Cabinet ministers are obliged by convention to keep quiet about the secrets of the Cabinet Room for 15 years. There is, however, nothing to prevent them talking about the style of Government as soon as they relinquish the seals of office. David Howell left Mrs Thatcher's Cabinet after the 1983 General Election having served as

Secretary of State for Energy and later Transport. A trained economist and an authority on public administration, he is that rare thing – a technocrat with long personal experience of the political process. He is also an expert on Government, having played a prominent part in Mr Heath's efforts to introduce a new and more managerial style into the Cabinet system. Edward Heath was the first Prime Minister since David Lloyd George to attempt a fundamental reform of the machinery of Cabinet Government. In the late 1960s David Howell was a member of the Public Sector Research Unit, the body established by Mr Heath as Leader of the Opposition with a brief to produce new techniques to bring bite to policy-making at the highest levels.

Howell: We reached the conclusion that there were fundamental weaknesses in the way that decisions were reached, policy formulated and the management of public programmes was carried out. We thought there were fundamental weaknesses in the relationship with Parliament and the control of public spending. Remember we were also caught up in a stream of thought which was much more political. We had to get a grip on the eternal growth of public spending generally, both for reasons of economic policy and for reasons of Tory political philosophy; so all these things combined together to give our work a terrific political drive, a personal drive and as it were a technical and managerial drive.

Hennessy: The outcome of the exercise in the White Paper, I think, had three main parts: one was a new Think Tank, the central policy review staff which presumably reflected some of the stuff you had seen in the United States at Rand and so on. The other was a new system, I suppose you would call it, of zero based budgeting where you would look at long-standing government commitments and see if they should stagger on – that was programme analysis review, and to reduce the weight in Cabinet there were to be big conglomerate departments which led to the Department of Trade and Industry and the Department of the Environment and so on. It seems to me, however, that the 1970 White Paper was the only attempt since Lloyd George in 1916 actually to tackle head-on problems of central government organisation and the Cabinet above all, and there has been nothing like it since. It does seem to have been a one-off thing.

Howell: Well, except, I think, it was the planting of some seeds. I agree it was very radical. We were saying not merely what we wanted to do but asking ourselves and the machine how it was to be done. That was the single new radical question and we wanted that questioning spirit to go right through the entire Whitehall system. We also wanted it to go through the nationalised industry and local government systems as well, but in fact the Heath Government never really got round to that and there again weaknesses, I think, developed because those two vast areas that are now being tackled weren't tackled then.

Hennessy: By the late '70s after the change of Government the original concept of programme analysis and review had withered to near disappearance though it wasn't formally killed until Mrs Thatcher was Prime Minister and also the Think Tank changed its nature very substantially after Rothschild had departed, so when you'd left Government it unravelled even further. Did you notice these changes with concern from the back-benches?

Howell: I noted the changes with concern but there is one thing you said there that is not quite right. After 1979, of course, we came on to the scene and programme analysis and review had been largely lost, not completely and I think what remained was then greatly reactivated. Derek Rayner and others were in Government and in some senses they weren't familiar with what had gone on in the early '70s, well, Derek Rayner was but 49 others weren't. They did in some sense re-invent the wheel – they said, why don't we have a more questioning programmatic approach to Government business, so after '79 that aspect was reactivated because it was very consistent with Mrs Thatcher's desire and the Treasury's passionate desire to restrain and reduce public spending and to bring efficiency on a far greater level into Whitehall, and indeed into local government as well. The CPRS is a different ball game. By the time we got back in 1979 the CPRS had already changed beyond recognition . . .

. . . You need to have vast access to information at least as good as that of all the departments who are putting forward their voices and you need to have the time and the staff; I don't think they always had that and as a result occasionally papers would fly round of, I'm afraid, rather a shallow kind – you know, a rather last minute dash by some bright brain on a subject which very able people in departments and outside advisers might have worked on for months and months and months and that created a slight canary hopping attitude to policy-making, which I don't think was very good. In the end I think Mrs Thatcher felt the same – what's the point of having this body she must have felt – she much rather wanted a real policy research unit, which, of course, she has now got.

Hennessy: Mrs Thatcher was very keen on a more efficient and economical public service and she very certainly did something about it when she became Prime Minister, but it looks as though you couldn't interest her in a systematic look at the quality of Cabinet government.

Howell: No, I think she was much more concerned with policies and aims, and also she reached a view which in a sense we had all reached by the end of the '70s, that without very tight control of public spending it wasn't going to be possible to reform very much inside or outside government, so she was looking for parliamentary and political activity as well which would be driving in the direction of retrenchment, which is why, I think, she quite welcomed another development we haven't talked about – that's the growth of the parliamentary select committees. She was anxious to see emerge a retrenchment parliament instead of a 'spend more' parliament.

Hennessy: She has a great virtue of candour and just before she became Prime Minister she announced in a newspaper interview how she was going to run her Cabinet and she said it must be a conviction government, as Prime Minister she couldn't waste time having internal arguments. Now this remark implied that she was going to mount a substantial assault on the traditional nature of Cabinet government which is collective discussion, free ranging before decisions are reached. Did it turn out like that? You were Secretary of State for Energy in '79 when the Government was first formed. Was it actually like that?

Howell: It is very hard to say. On some issues there was a good deal of discussion, but if by conviction government Mrs Thatcher meant that certain slogans were going to be elevated and written in tablets of stone and used as the sort of put-down of every argument then, of course, that is indeed what happened. I mean certain things were asserted beyond per-adventure, namely that we had to get the public sector borrowing requirement down because if it went up or stayed up it would keep interest rates up. Now it happens that is a very controversial and highly questionable political economic proposition, but as a political shibboleth it was raised to all-powerful heights and was used as a battering ram to silence any suggestion by anybody that one might ever spend more on anything, even if the aim of spending more immediately was to spend less later.

Hennessy: That rather vitiates the traditional nature of Cabinet government, if you have a strong minded figure who just happens to be Prime Minister, ending discussions in this way; presumably it meant that after a while you ceased to bring things to the Cabinet that you knew would produce the put-down?

Howell: Of course, there is a deterring effect if one knows that one is going not into a discussion where various points of view will be weighed and gradually a view may be achieved, but into a huge argument where tremendous battle lines will be drawn up and everyone who doesn't fall in line will be hit on the head. Of course it deters you and, I think, that element of deterrence did take place. I don't want to exaggerate it, because on the complex issues however determined or single minded a Prime Minister is he has to discuss things with an inner group of colleagues. You are talking now to someone who certainly worked very closely with Mrs Thatcher and was a member of the Cabinet, but I wasn't of the seniority to be one of the inner group of ministers which all Prime Ministers tend to work most closely with. . . . The country really since the 16th century has basically been run by five or six people.

Hennessy: This suggests, does it not, that having 22 people in the Cabinet is exactly the wrong number, that you can't run an efficient system with that many people sitting round a table, and yet every Prime Minister wants a smaller Cabinet and they nearly all are forced up to 20 and above?

Howell: Well, wait a minute; we are now talking about Cabinet as a body running things, but Cabinet isn't that at all. Cabinet is a clearing house, an exchange market where different inter-departmental clashes are sorted out and where also, it always used to be the theory although that is long since gone I think under this Government, clashes between the Treasury and the Department – is it right to cut something or not – are sorted out. I say that's gone because I have already described to you . . . the spirit of the '79 Government, and indeed as far as I can make out the '83 Government's view is: 'No, don't bother with the facts, the Treasury's figures are settled; good afternoon.' So that part of the argument hasn't come very much to Cabinet I suspect, although certainly it occasionally comes and there were terrific rows, but the Cabinet is not a place where discussions can be formulated; it is bound to be a place where decisions have [already] been formulated by smaller groups, may be of ministers, may be of minister and party people together, may be parliamentary groups and then put to ministers, or may be the Prime Minister and her advisers, and quite separately are then tested and validated.

Hennessy: You mention that there is a great degree of toughness since 1979 on Treasury targets and public expenditure and so on; the word goes down the line and there is no argument and yet the process for fixing expenditure allocation seems to be as much of a shambles as ever it was when you and Mr Heath were so concerned about it in the late 1960s. Every September we have the small ad hoc Cabinet Committee known as the Star Chamber in which Lord Whitelaw sits down and tries to bang heads together, and then the Prime Minister comes in at the last minute and bangs heads together even more and it seems that the money, in so far as it emerges in budgets, clearly is determined by crude political muscle and nothing to do with reason and analysis, all the things that you stood for in the '60s and '70s. Don't you find that depressing?

Howell: A bit depressing, but not entirely, because even in a more refined system there is going to be a stage where issues cannot be resolved by analysis or delicate agreement and can only be resolved by crude political battering. So I am not totally depressed. If I'm depressed at all, it is that I think you could make this process slightly less obtrusive and violent and spark generating if there was more systematic analysis and discussion beforehand. You have got to stand back a long way before you get to the final decisions on costs and budget. So more programme analysis and discussion, and less argument and assertion, would make the whole thing less fraught on the one side. On the other side, of course, the fraught quality is greatly heightened and increased by this feeling I have already described that the Treasury's figures are there and absolute and that to transgress beyond them will be beyond civilisation as we know it, [that] interest rates will go sky high and hyper-inflation will return. Therefore the argument is of people whose backs are pinned to the wall before they are questioned and that doesn't make for a very sober and calm discussion, especially as there is some doubt, I suspect in the minds of ministers but certainly in the minds of many people in the Conservative Party, about whether these great absolutes – this wall against which ministers and departments are nailed – really need exist in quite the form it has been constructed, or whether the whole issue couldn't be handled in a rather more sensitive and relaxed way.

Hennessy: Some observers thought that the Falklands crisis of 1982 actually saw a revival, albeit briefly, of classic Cabinet government. I know you weren't in the War Cabinet, the small group that ran it operationally, but you were in the full Cabinet at all the big decisions, like sending a task force, landing at San Carlos before they could actually take any decisions to move in, and that this was a restoration of almost 19th century Cabinet government. Do you think that is right?

Howell: Well, I can't discuss what went on on the specific issues in the Cabinet and I don't wish to do so, but I think it is reasonable to observe that the major issues of the Falklands War were more or less written in the stars. There wasn't actually a great sense of option or choice. It was there: the task force had to go; having gone it was clear that, if it reached there before any serious and sensible peace proposal was offered, the task force then had to do something. It was clear that fudge proposals from the Argentinians which amounted to saying, 'we've done what we've done, now let's negotiate', were quite unacceptable, and it was clear that the task force had to land and do its bit. So I think, of course, it was right and proper that these things came to Cabinet, but I think it would be glorifying things a bit to say that re-created Cabinet government in its full glory, if it ever existed in its full glory in the 19th century which I, frankly, rather doubt!

Hennessy: Mrs Thatcher wrote a letter in 1984 accepting Mr James Prior's resignation from the Northern Ireland Office and she said in it, 'I take your point about frankness – that's what Cabinets are for and lively discussions usually lead to good decisions.' How did that remark strike you?

Howell: It struck me with some foreboding, because I feel that the words 'lively discussion' were a code word for argument and I don't regard high pitched argument as the best means of reaching decisions.

Hennessy: Finally, Mr Howell is it fun being a Cabinet minister?

Howell: It has good moments and very bad moments. I don't think I was on the same wave-length as the Prime Minister almost from the start, although I did work for her beforehand, so I think if you are asking me, I can only speak of my personal experience. Yes, I enjoyed certain moments very much indeed and other moments were most certainly not fun. And Parliament can be a very demanding mistress indeed; and there we are, Parliament a demanding mistress, the Prime Minister a demanding mistress – how much fun can you have with so many demanding mistresses?

The Executive and the Courts

Before leaving the question of the Executive, there is one further topic which it is convenient to examine at this point. It has been implied in this chapter that governments in modern, industrialised societies have become big, complex businesses, affecting the daily lives of people in a number of different ways, and that this has been especially so in the post-war period; there is also the difficulty that elected representatives have in controlling the day-to-day actions of the Executive. In that situation an individual, or a group of individuals, may be compelled to rely more and more upon his or their own political defences and organisational skill; and perhaps, in the last resort, on what the Courts provide. One or two examples will illustrate this last point later on in this section.

Firstly, though, it is important to emphasise that on rare occasions the Executive can display the extremely forceful side of its powers. A notable case occurred in 1965 when the Burmah Oil Company pursued a lengthy and complicated claim against the Crown for compensation for the destruction of oil installations by the British Army, done to hinder the Japanese occupation of Burma during the Second World War. The Government warned the oil company that if it won its legal battle, retrospective legislation would be introduced into Parliament to safeguard the taxpayer from similar claims. This was duly carried out. The 1965 War Damage Act annulled the House of Lords' judgment in favour of Burmah. The whole question of retrospective legislation is always one that is highly controversial: the point was again underlined by the semi-retrospective nature of Labour's Housing Finance (Special Provisions) Act 1975, a measure which precluded the possibility of future sanctions against those councillors who had refused to implement the provisions of the Housing Finance Act 1972 (a Conservative measure). A Tory back-bench rebellion arose in 1980 at the time of the passage of the Iran (Temporary Powers) Act. The Government had led the Commons to believe that the 1980 Act's provisions could not be used retrospectively against existing trading contracts with Iran. However, a few days later the Government admitted that it was prepared to use such powers under an existing statute (Import, Export and Customs Powers (Defence) Act 1939).

The Crown (that is the Government) has exercised considerable powers, too, under English common law. It can, for instance, legally resist the production of documents whose release it considers not to be in the interests of Parliament and the public. This was very evident in the case of *Duncan* v. *Cammell, Laird and Co* in 1942, which concerned the loss of a submarine on sea trials. In *Ellis* v. *Home Office* in 1953, the defendant successfully claimed Crown privilege to withhold certain medical reports about an inmate of Winchester Prison, which meant, in effect, that the plaintiff was unable to substantiate his claims. The case of *Burmah Oil Co Ltd* v. *Governor and Company of the Bank of England* in 1979 raised similar problems in respect of Crown privilege, or public interest immunity as the courts now prefer to call it. In this instance the Bank refused, at the Government's prompting, to release certain commercial documents. In 1984 the courts upheld the Government's decision to withdraw the rights of employees at GCHQ at Cheltenham to belong to a trade union, on grounds of national security.

However, a string of other cases, in the 1970s, appeared to suggest that the courts were prepared to challenge strongly the nature of ministerial action when requested to do so. The first instance occurred in 1975 in relation to the Home Office. In January 1974 the Government announced that the price of colour television licences would rise from £12 to £18 on 1 April that year. However, several newspapers were quick to point out that holders of licences due to expire after 1 April could save themselves money by taking out a new licence at the old price before the changeover date, and by 1 April over a quarter of a million such licences had been issued. In June the Home Secretary, Roy Jenkins, announced that their holders would have to pay an excess charge. A report by the Ombudsman censured him for bungling the issue from the start, 'by muddle, inefficiency and lack of foresight'. Mr Jenkins accepted the Commissioner's findings and apologised to the Commons. Later, when the Home Office was still trying to recover the extra licence fees, the matter became the subject of a Court of Appeal case, *Congreve* v. *Home Office*, which the Government lost and which led to another Commons apology from the Home Secretary.

The Tameside Case

The Tameside Case in 1976 involved not so much one individual as a group of individuals, elected representatives at the local level. Tameside, a metropolitan borough of Greater Manchester, had been Labour-controlled until the spring of 1976. Arrangements were under way for comprehensive secondary schools to be introduced from the beginning of the new school year. The Conservatives, however, gained control of the Council after the local elections and immediately in May announced a return to a selective system of secondary education. The Labour Education Minister, Fred Mulley, soon intervened, and in July 1976 the Queen's Bench Division of the High Court, presided over by Lord Chief Justice Widgery, granted the Minister an order of *mandamus* directing Tameside Council to keep to the previous arrangements for secondary schooling. The Court thus agreed with Mr Mulley, who had argued that under section 68 of the 1944 Education Act Tameside Borough was behaving 'unreasonably' in changing the plans at such short notice. The Court agreed that it was difficult to see how, given the likely non-co-operation of the teachers, all the children under the council's aegis could have been allocated to appropriate secondary schools in time for the new autumn term. But Tameside Borough appealed and the Court of Appeal reversed the ruling of the High Court. In late July 1976 the House of Lords, sitting over a weekend for the first time in its history, upheld the Court of Appeal's verdict.

At almost the same time the High Court ruled that Mr Shore, in his former capacity as Secretary of State for Trade, had acted beyond the powers vested in him by statute in refusing permission for Laker Airways' non-advance booking 'Skytrain' to join the North Atlantic crossings.

The Laker case was followed in 1977 by one of considerable constitutional complexity. At the beginning of that year the Union of Post Office Workers had agreed to instruct its members to take part in an international boycott of South African mail and telephone services. However, John Gouriet, a representative of the National Association for Freedom, sought permission from the Attorney-

General to obtain an injunction to restrain this boycott (chiefly on the grounds of the Post Office's statutory obligations under the 1953 Post Office Act).

It is normally held that the Attorney-General's consent must be obtained by an individual member of the public (like Gouriet) who seeks civil injunctive relief in order to prevent a criminal action taking place. This area of the law is complex, to say the least. If, however, a criminal action has already been committed then any private individual may prosecute, although certain prosecutions (about 138 offences) may be commenced only by, or with the consent of, the Attorney-General, the Director of Public Prosecutions (DPP) or, exceptionally, a Government minister. Moreover, the DPP may (under the Prosecution of Offences Act 1985) take over any prosecution where it appears appropriate because of the importance or difficulty of the case.

The Attorney-General is in an unique position: although he is a Minister of the Crown, he is not bound by the theory of collective responsibility since he is also a Law Officer. In the Gouriet case the Attorney-General maintained that when it came to threatened breaches of the law, in other words where no crime had hitherto been committed, it was up to him, and him alone, to decide what to do. As an MP and a Minister of the Crown he was still answerable to Parliament for his decision.

The Court of Appeal, however, threw doubt upon the nature of that answerability to Parliament within the context of common law. Counsel for the Attorney remarked, 'what the court is suggesting is that power should be taken away by saying: 'We will say to the Crown "You are wrong" ' '; Lord Denning retorted, 'in the last resort it is for the court to protect the individual', thus putting the issue into a broader context of conflict between the individual and the State (the Crown). The Appeal judges were not totally in agreement in their assessment of the Attorney-General's authority, Lord Denning questioning it most fundamentally: 'the law does not stand still', he said. The case subsequently went to the House of Lords.

In July 1977 five Law Lords unequivocally reversed the Court of Appeal's ruling. The Lords held that the Attorney-General, and the Attorney-General alone, was the person to decide whether or not to initiate litigation to prevent a breach of the law. In such circumstances no private individual could commence proceedings.

All this led some experienced commentators to make fairly sweeping speculations about the new political weight of judges *vis-à-vis* the Executive. *The Observer* (1 August 1976) commented: 'one great theme' was whether Lord Denning and the Court of Appeal had 'extended' or merely 'reformulated' judicial power over ministers. And *The Sunday Times* (1 August 1976), more loudly, demanded:

> 'Will the Law Lords vindicate or demolish their own political prejudices? What political and social bias attaches to Lord Wilberforce, Lord Diplock and the rest? . . . Yet there is no reason to think that the judges are incapable of changing. Their impulse is invariably legal conservatism not ideological prejudice . . .'

It almost seemed that certain judges, like some MPs, were determined that in the mid-1970s, the Executive should not fulfil its political will too easily.

55

*: The
Constitution under
Crisis', Parliamentary
Affairs,
October 1986

In 1980 the courts ruled that the Secretary of State for Social Services (Patrick Jenkin) had acted unlawfully in suspending the members of the Lambeth Area Health Authority the previous year. And a number of other cases in the early 1980s (frequently involving the Social Services, Transport and Environment Secretaries) illustrated how the courts have continued to 'challenge' Executive actions. For example, in 1985 the court said that Nicholas Ridley, the Transport Secretary, had behaved 'irrationally and improperly' over the transfer of London Transport, while in 1984 it was held that it was no argument for the DHSS to say that the cost of identifying a group of claimants outweighed the amount of underpayment.

Ministerial Responsibility

Ministers of the Crown may be exercising real power when they decide to give so many millions of pounds to industry or when they decide to reduce defence spending over a period of years. But power in a pluralistic society is never concentrated for long in any one place, and there are many occasions when members of the Government merely exercise authority rather than real power. The minister's name might be used in a legal, technical sense, but often power lies to all intents and purposes with bureaucrats locally and centrally – as, for instance, in matters of planning. An Education minister, for example, may well wish to pursue a particular policy, but be unable to do so because of the independence of a local education authority – he may use his own authority, his political status, to persuade, but he may have no power to compel.

New Society,
12 October 1972

The increasing influence of television has added a highly visual dimension to the modern concept of authority. As Michael Banton has said, it is not enough now simply to hear or read that a minister has embarked upon a particular course of action. Instead he must be seen to be convincing, he must be totally articulate and apparently in control of the situation, he must make the television audience feel not just that he has acted justifiably within his legal powers but that, if they had been in his position, they would have come to the same conclusion. The citizen has to identify positively with those in office – if a minister is to exercise total authority and not just political power, he has to battle successfully with the probings of the television interviewer. In a sense, the last of the old school of pre-television era Premiers was Sir Alec Douglas-Home. He performed poorly on television, although, of course, that had very little to do with his professional competence. But it was enough that Conservative Central Office was aware of his liability in that direction.

Whatever the nature of power and authority, whatever the exact definition chosen, all forms of authority raise the question as to how it can be exercised with a degree of *responsibility* acceptable to the general community. A.H. Birch has given us a by now standard definition of the responsibilities of power.

Sir Alec Douglas-Home as Prime Minister in 1963. He later reckoned that his poor television performances cost him the 1964 election, which he narrowly lost. As a make-up girl remarked to him, there was nothing that could be done for the shape of his skull, while Lady Home told him that his constant use of half-moon glasses only reinforced his patrician and 'out of touch' image

57

Birch's definition

Responsibility, according to Birch, can be divided three ways. Firstly, the word can be used to indicate that a regime should be responsive to public opinion and demands. This, it can be argued, is one of the major differences between Eastern Europe and the West. Secondly, there is a kind of 'higher' responsibility that a government has to the whole country – that of maintaining its overall moral welfare and protecting 'the national interest'. Thirdly, there is ministerial authority which is dealt with below.

The limits to which a government can legitimately claim to be acting in the national interest are not clearly defined. Anthony Eden argued that Britain should intervene at Suez to protect her national interests in the canal and throughout the Middle East. Others felt that his proposals threatened higher national interests, such as the need for peace and an uncontroversial foreign policy at a time of very poor relations between the superpowers.

A.H. Birch,
*Representative and
Responsible
Government,*
Allen and Unwin,
1964, p. 19

Birch has given an example of the terms being used in much the same way: a Government spokesman said in 1955 that everyone would like to reduce the period of National Service but it would be irresponsible to pretend that the country could afford to do it. The same concept could be applied to the actions of President Nixon in 1973 and 1974. Commentators talked about Nixon having lost his 'moral authority' and about the lost authority of the Presidential Office; in other words saying that throughout the Watergate Affair he was behaving irresponsibly, for example in his dismissal of Special Prosecutor Archibald Cox, in his causing Elliot Richardson, the Attorney-General, to resign, and in his evasive replies to the many questions that were asked about his own involvement in that particular but sensational scandal. (The 'Watergate Affair', which led to Nixon's downfall, was concerned with the Republican burglary of the Democratic Party headquarters.)

Departmental responsibility

The third sense of responsibility is the narrow but very important one of ministerial departmental authority; collective ministerial responsibility has already been discussed. In fact 'ministerial responsibility' is something of a political myth, but perhaps its perpetuation has been useful. There has been a long-standing tradition that British ministers should never overestimate their own authority, that when serious mistakes occur within their departments they should resign. Experience, as A.H. Birch has suggested, shows the penalty of resignation is rarely paid. Nevertheless the idea has not only continued to be held by some MPs, but also featured in writings – including textbooks – of the 1950s and 1960s. The belief that a minister in the United Kingdom resigns when a departmental mistake is discovered is a relic from the old Liberal nineteenth-century view of the constitution. As A.H. Birch has said, 'the statement that ministers are responsible to Parliament for the work of their department conveys the important truth that ministers have to appear in Parliament and explain, and, if possible, justify what their departments have done. But it also conveys the impression that ministers have to pay the penalty of resignation if departmental blunders are revealed, and this is hardly borne out by experience.'

As the political head of a department, a minister is meant to be responsible not only for his own actions but also for those of his 'agents' – principally, in other words, departmental civil servants. If he fails to satisfy Parliament in the exercise of such responsibilities, he might well face the possibilities of censure and resignation. At least, that is the theory. But in practice the principle of individual responsibility has lost much of its real meaning. Of course, ministers do still resign for *personal* failures, such as Hugh Dalton in 1947 for leaking certain details of his proposed Budget to the press; John Profumo, Minister of War, following the sex scandal of 1963; Anthony Lambton (a junior Defence Minister, for the RAF) and Lord Jellicoe (Leader of the Lords) in 1973 for involvement in sex scandals; Reginald Maudling, Home Secretary, in 1972 for tenuous links with the Poulson affair and the consequent corruption trial. (The Profumo, Lambton and Jellicoe scandals involved questions of national security.) Nicholas Fairbairn resigned as Solicitor-General for Scotland in 1982, for committing Dalton's sin and talking to the press before speaking to the Commons about a controversial rape case in Glasgow. Cecil Parkinson, the Trade and Industry Secretary, resigned in 1983, following revelations about his private life.

In contrast, there have been very few examples of ministerial resignations for *departmental* failures. The one notable exception was Sir Thomas Dugdale, the former Minister for Agriculture, who in 1954 resigned as a result of the Crichel Down affair, involving the irregular use of a piece of Dorset land. (The land in question had been requisitioned for military purposes before the Second World War. The correct procedures for putting it back on the market after the War were not followed by the civil servants concerned.) But Dugdale is almost the only real example since the War, although it would be patently absurd to believe that Crichel Down has been the only serious administrative blunder made during the last 30 years or so.

Indeed, there are many examples of ministers who have quite deliberately held on to power, perhaps even saving their moral and political authority in the process, such as John Strachey (Minister of Food) after the Groundnuts Scandal in Tanganyika in 1950, or Alan Lennox-Boyd (Colonial Secretary) in 1959 following the very critical Devlin report on the Nyasaland disturbances.

Ferranti and the Spies Scandal

Two memorable cases occurred during the Macmillan era. Firstly, Julian Amery was attacked as Minister for Aviation, in 1964, for the excessive profits made by Ferranti Ltd on a contract to supply Bloodhound missiles. Harold Wilson, then Leader of the Opposition, criticised Amery in the House for appearing to allow the blame to be laid on the officials of the technical cost section within his department. In the Commons Amery would neither confirm nor deny that disciplinary action would be taken against the civil servants involved, who had been criticised by the committee inquiring into the affair (the Lang Report). As far as his own position was concerned, Amery believed that as the minister he had defended the taxpayers' interest perfectly adequately.

The other case, in 1961, involved Lord Carrington, who as First Lord of the

Admiralty was responsible for naval security. Following the revelations about the Portland spy ring and the critical report of the Romer Committee which had been set up to investigate the affair, Lord Carrington offered his resignation to the Prime Minister, Harold Macmillan, who, however, refused to accept it. Macmillan told the Commons, in reply to a question from the Leader of the Opposition, that no one could avoid their responsibilities, but that, in the modern conditions of an extremely complicated organisation, it would not be reasonable to have applied the principle in quite the same way. George Brown was to remark that this indicated a considerable deterioration from the standards applied in the Crichel Down affair. Mr Brown, however, refused to resign over the Sachsenhausen Case in 1967–8 (see p. 90).

As noted earlier, Lord Carrington resigned in 1982 as Foreign Secretary because of the failure by the Foreign Office to anticipate the invasion of the Falkland Islands by Argentina. Later in the same year John Nott resigned as Defence Secretary, although he maintained he would have resigned at that time in any case. The resignations of Mr Brittan (individual responsibility) and Mr Heseltine (collective responsibility) over the Westland Affair in 1986 are examined below.

Other cases

Michael Heseltine, who was Minister for Aerospace and Shipping in the Heath Government, refused to resign in 1973 over the question of abandoning the tracked hovercraft scheme, although he did later apologise to the House for mis-leading one of its Select Committees of inquiry earlier. Nor did Mr Jenkins resign over the colour television licences fiasco in 1975 or Mr Benn in 1974 over the Court Line scandal or Mr Shore over the Laker affair in 1976 or Mr Jenkin in 1980 over the Lambeth Health Authority case. Indeed S.E. Finer in 1956 placed Dugdale with 15 other ministers from the previous 100 years in what he called the 'plain unlucky category' – 'not for these sixteen the honourable exchange of offices, or the silent and not dishonourable exit. Their lot is public penance in the white sheet of resignation speech or letter.' Moreover, in the Dugdale case it was only the wealth and the political connections of the interested party concerned that led to a special enquiry, and even after the results of the inquiry, Dugdale did not resign at once. But Mr Brittan's resignation in 1986 may well put the over-quoted Dugdale case into the constitutional shade.

S.E. Finer, *Public Administration*, Winter 1956

The effect of the PCA

It could be argued that the recent arrival of the Parliamentary Commissioner (the Ombudsman) has given the minister added protection: his powers and authority are even less assailable, since the Commissioner is commenting directly about the behaviour of civil servants. Ironically, George Brown said that the Sachsenhausen Case was responsible for his very grave doubts about the office of the Parliamentary Commissioner, since when things went wrong it was ministers, not officials, who should be attacked, although one might add that Mr Brown himself withstood such attacks very nicely. Indeed the very introduction of the ombudsman was delayed on the grounds that it would interfere with the inviolable doctrine of ministerial responsibility.

A Prime Minister's attitude

While Mr Macmillan's statement in respect of the Naval Spies Scandal was not altogether clear, it did give some indication of the causes of the decline in the principle of departmental ministerial responsibility. In the first place no Prime Minister wishes to be publicly embarrassed by an open admission of incompetence by a central department; such an admission would not only tarnish the general image of the Government but also affect his own personal standing as head of that Government. In fact the Prime Minister might well go as far as insisting that the rest of the Cabinet supports the errant minister: in this way individual responsibility can become confused with Cabinet (collective) responsibility, as illustrated by the Westland Affair in 1986. But a Prime Minister will not save a minister if he appears particularly weak. For example, although his department had not actually made any mistakes, its sheer lack of activity in producing an overall national strategy led to the resignation of the Minister of Transport, Tom Fraser, in 1965.

The almost total abandonment of the principle has produced little reaction in the Commons itself, probably because most MPs at heart agree that it is no longer applicable to modern conditions – and because the authority of the House is better served by not saying so too openly. As Macmillan said, the fact that many government departments are of great size and complexity and that many policy and administrative issues are highly technical in nature means it is neither realistic nor reasonable to expect the minister to know about everything that is taking place within his own particular organisation.

DOCUMENT

8

The 'Lack' of Ministerial Responsibility

Crichel Down wasn't surplus land. The new demonstration farm unit was to arise from the investment of a good deal of public money. Two policies were being applied here, both inherited from wartime and confirmed by the Labour government which held office until October 1951. One was a food policy, promoting home production and thus requiring some investment by the taxpayer. The other was a presumption against reducing or releasing state assets and thus a tendency also favouring direct expenditure and control.

Pursuing these twin policies led these officials to behave very badly towards Marten and other local farmers who wanted a chance to lease Crichel Down and farm it themselves, at much less cost to the taxpayer. The officials took against Marten, who was being a nuisance, and arbitrarily excluded him and the other locals from consideration as possible tenants of the land. Worst of all, they deceived the local farmers into thinking that their offer to rent the land would be properly considered when in fact it had been decided to rule them out.

Although almost infinitely more serious than Crichel Down, the Maze escape of last autumn was a more simple matter, at least on its face. Slack management and supervision reduced this maximum-security prison to a tragic farce. With guard towers and gates unmanned, with certain doors unlocked and certain prisoners holding keys in their role as prison orderlies, the mass escape was easily achieved, supported by the use of violence and terror against prison officers. A massive failure of routine administration had occurred, and it was on this basis that Prior and Scott have declined to accept any blame, and thus any responsibility, which might require either to offer to resign. Only prison service heads should roll if any roll at all.

A tragic case occurred in 1959, when 11 Kenyan detainees were beaten to death by Kenyan guards in the Hola prison camp of the British colonial government. Neither the colony's governor nor the British Minister resigned: no one in Kenya was either prosecuted or even sacked, (only disciplined).

No one now believes in the individual responsibility doctrine. The only conclusion, both before and since Crichel Down, is the cynical one that Ministers will stay or go, following these various affairs and scandals, according to the political convenience of the Prime Minister and the governing party. So we should long since have added to Mill's dictum that the Minister should take the blame for what is ill in his department the saving phrase: '... unless it suits his Prime Minister and party to ignore the matter'. This seems a cynical conclusion but it might be politically realistic. Mill's absolutist view suits neither modern conditions of massive government administration nor the modern pragmatic temperament.

The major difficulty with this conclusion, however, is that we end up with no one in government plainly responsible for anything. As in Kenya in 1959 or Northern Ireland last winter, nothing much actually happens after a tragic and hugely damaging failure. John Stuart Mill had another comment on this effect which has worn better than his prescription on the actual form of ministerial responsibility. He wrote: 'Responsibility is null when no one knows who is responsible.'

The public interest is to insist that someone must be held responsible and to refuse to be drawn into detailed arguments between officials and their ministerial superiors, each distinguishing the so-called 'policy' and 'administrative' elements of whatever has gone wrong in a way which suits them, and each trying to edge away from the scaffold.

Thirty years after the Crichel Down affair we've finally lost the tradition of Ministers resigning because of civil servants' mistakes or misconduct, but to try to revive it would be both very difficult and unattractive. To modern eyes the merely symbolic sacrifice of a competent Minister because of the faults of others seems pointless – and also unfair.

It seems to me, therefore, that we need consciously to move forward to a new doctrine or accepted practice on public accountability and this must involve moving away from the 19th-century idea that officials and their work can or should remain without identity or public form as part of their Ministers' theoretical blanket responsibility to Parliament for everything which officials do or fail to do. In its place, carefully limited elements of administration, practice and policy should be designated as the tasks of individual senior officials and their personal answerability to Parliament and the public, through the press and broadcasting, clearly established.

Officials wouldn't accept this role unless their policy framework were pretty clearly given them by the government of the day. Some types of Civil Service work would be easy to set up on this basis. MPs in their select committees or other activities would move easily between these officials, other, more conventionally based, officials and Ministers themselves, as they probe policy and management matters. Journalists, organised interests and the public at large would do the same. Ministers would draw back from practical detail, in order to encourage direct official responses, while the officials in these designated positions would no more get pulled into controversial policy questions than they do today. Most of what Whitehall does is non-partisan and these officials are likely to be operating in non-partisan fields.

A. Barker, *The Listener,* 13 September 1984

Answerability, not responsibility?

It seems since the 1960s to have been tacitly, if not explicitly, agreed that a minister cannot be held responsible to the point of resignation in cases with which he was not directly involved or indeed where the actions of his civil servants were contrary to his known instructions. In a similar vein in 1976 a Commons Select Committee commented that the Department of Industry had not adequately anticipated the scale of economic collapse facing the Chrysler UK car company in 1975, but that given the circumstances the minister concerned (Mr Varley) had had little alternative but to give the cash grants he authorised.

Nevertheless what we can say is that the minister is still answerable – if only in a narrow sense – for what has gone wrong: he must, at least, offer to Parliament a reasonable explanation, and he alone can say what is proposed to rectify the situation. If he does accept culpability personally, he will probably feel morally obliged to resign. In the nineteenth century culpability was automatically thought to be an essential part of responsibility, of both moral and political authority, but nowadays there is a distinction between *answerability* and *culpability*. This may simply be the best and only practical way of facing up to political reality, but it can also be regarded as the loss of one of the traditional safeguards for the electorate.

It is notable that there is no real parallel in local government – councillors who chair departmental committees will be far more willing to expose the mistakes of a chief officer or senior official, although the scope for administrative error may be less than in Whitehall. Ironically, that may reflect the fact that council officials rule elected local representatives even more effectively than civil servants rule their ministerial masters.

The Westland Affair

The political row that broke in 1986 must rank as one worthy of a constitutional footnote, and probably more than that, for it neatly illustrated several facets of the British political system.

It became apparent towards the end of 1985 that there were divisions within the Government over the way the ailing Yeovil-based helicopter firm, Westland, should be rescued. General Government policy was that it was for the board of Westland to decide, but the Trade and Industry Secretary, Leon Brittan, appeared to favour an American-led rescue bid, while the Defence Secretary, Michael Heseltine, argued strongly for the plan proposed by a consortium of European companies.

That might have been the end of the matter had not Mr Heseltine accused Mrs Thatcher of stifling Cabinet debate on the issue, not allowing him sufficient time to prepare his case fully, cancelling a Cabinet meeting arranged to discuss the Westland options, and via the Cabinet Secretary, distorting Cabinet minutes. All these charges Mrs Thatcher subsequently denied. Mr Heseltine saw Mrs Thatcher's allegedly presidential and ill-tempered style of government as undercutting the traditions of collective Cabinet decision-making and he resigned.

The Guardian,
10 January 1986

'Such detailed and damaging criticism of Mrs Thatcher's handling of ministers is unprecedented from such a senior figure. His version of events accuses the Prime Minister of manipulating the Cabinet for her own policy purposes, limiting discussion in an autocratic way and using the Cabinet Office as an instrument of harsh discipline.'

Mrs Thatcher claimed that on the contrary she had been too generous in allowing Cabinet discussion to continue over the problems of a minor manufacturing company; instead, she should have exercised collective discipline in Cabinet, thus challenging Mr Heseltine to resign on a point of policy disagreement earlier rather than later. What this curious episode illustrated was that the Prime Minister's political awareness was not as keen as it should have been: it is often issues that at first appear comparatively trivial which can grow into political disasters.

There are, in fact, Cabinet Office guidelines, called *Questions of Procedure for Ministers.* The relevant section on collective responsibility reads:

The Times,
10 January 1986

'Decisions reached by the Cabinet or Cabinet committee are normally announced and defended by the minister concerned as his own decisions. There may be rare occasions when it is desirable to emphasise the importance of some decisions by stating specifically that it is the decision of Her Majesty's government. This, however, should be the exception rather than the rule. The growth of any general practice whereby decisions of the Cabinet or of Cabinet committee were announced as such would lead to the embarrassing result that some decisions of government would be regarded as less authoritative than others. Critics of a decision reached by a particular committee could press for its review by some other committee or by the Cabinet, and the constitutional right of individual ministers to speak in the name of the government as a whole would be impaired.'

For his part, it was revealed that Mr Brittan had had an argumentative meeting with Sir Raymond Lygo, the managing director of British Aerospace, to the effect that the European rescue operation was 'against the national interest' (British Aerospace being part of the European consortium). In addition, Heseltine claimed that Brittan had tried to prevent the BBC from putting out a radio interview. There, the hapless Mr Brittan might have been left to pick up the pieces. However, during the course of the Affair, part of a letter Sir Patrick Mayhew, the Solicitor-General, had written at the behest of the Prime Minister to Mr Heseltine was leaked to the press. The letter drew Mr Heseltine's attention to certain material facts which the Solicitor-General felt the Defence Secretary had misrepresented to Lloyds Merchant Bank, advisers to the European consortium.

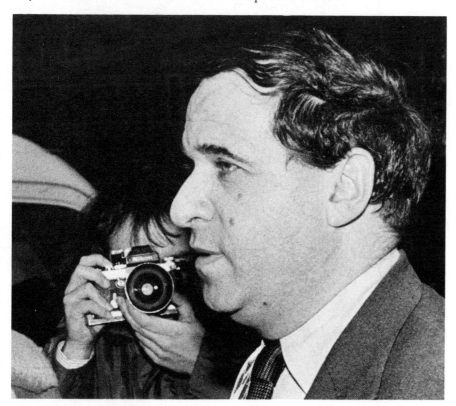

Leon Brittan

The release of the extract was damaging to Mr Heseltine, who saw behind it the hand of No. 10. Mrs Thatcher ordered an inquiry into the manner of the leak, and it was this aspect of the Affair which led to a furious parliamentary row. Sir Robert Armstrong, the Secretary to the Cabinet, who conducted the inquiry, came to the conclusion that it was Mr Brittan who personally authorised the leak. This Brittan did not deny, although he regretted the way it had been carried out by DTI civil servants. The role of the Prime Minister's press secretary and private office, let alone that of the Prime Minister herself, was less than clear.

Once Brittan had made his admission, there was little the Prime Minister could do to save him, although she asked him not to resign. Other members of the Cabinet, however, noticeably distanced themselves when faced with questioning on television or on the radio. In this instance the doctrine of collective Cabinet responsibility could not be invoked in order to subsume individual ministerial responsibility. It was too late: had Brittan announced some two weeks earlier that he had been the person who had authorised the leak, it is possible that he might have escaped. As a well-established lawyer Brittan, it might be argued, should have

Mr Heseltine walks out of the Cabinet, *The Times*, 10 January 1986

appreciated that the advice of the Law Officers to Government ministers is, by and large, confidential. It was reported that both the Solicitor-General and the Attorney-General, who had been ill in the early stages of the Affair, had contemplated resignation too, as a mark of protest. If one or both had resigned, Mrs Thatcher's own position would have been vulnerable. Mr Brittan's resignation does not belong so much to the category of individual ministerial responsibility, although the civil servants concerned did make mistakes in the way the letter was leaked, as to the division of personal failure, for it was clearly politically inadvisable to have released the Solicitor-General's letter wholly or partially in the first place, especially since his permission had not been sought. Throughout the Affair, questions were raised on official secrecy and section 2 of the 1911 Act (see Chapter 3).

> '. . . Section 2 of the Official Secrets Act 1911 should be abolished. It is that ridiculous Act that repeatedly leads to either prosecutions or embarrassments. It is designed to protect all official information regardless of its value and makes both the donor and recipient technically guilty of an offence. In the Westland Affair it even led to the Government not knowing how to leak information it wanted made public. In the end it makes all governments look ham-handed.'

Financial Times, 25 January 1986

Moreover, was the leaking of the letter, and in this particular manner, something civil servants should be involved in at all? Did it not show how politicised the Civil Service had become under Mrs Thatcher? These were questions that the Defence Select Committee had in mind when it sought, probably outside its 'terms of reference', to investigate this aspect of the whole Affair. This part of the Committee's enquiries was challenged by Mr Brittan himself, but he was sharply rebuked by Sir Humphrey Atkins, the Conservative chairman of the Committee:

> 'It is an ancient rule of this House that the interpretation and the terms of reference of a select committee are a matter only for that committee. It follows that we alone will judge what is and what is not relevant to our inquiry.'

The Guardian, 31 January 1986

The Committee interviewed both Sir Robert Armstrong and Mr Brittan, among others, but the Government prevented the questioning of the civil servants directly involved in the leak, a matter which annoyed the Conservative as much as the Labour members of the Committee and which led to a major row between it and the Government. Later, in evidence to the Treasury and Civil Service Select Committee, Sir Robert admitted that the civil servants involved had indeed behaved incorrectly.

The Treasury Committee suggested that it was poor policy for Sir Robert to occupy two posts, that of Secretary to the Cabinet and Head of the Home Civil Service, but the Government thought otherwise. At the same time, the Defence Select Committee, in its report, strongly criticised Sir Robert's role in the Westland Affair. 'We do not doubt that Sir Robert accurately reported what he was told in his inquiry but we do hope that his credulity was as sorely taxed as ours'. The Committee said that Sir Robert had not given a clear lead to his civil servants. The Government, however, conceded that any civil servant faced with an issue of conscience could, in the future, appeal directly to the Head of the Civil Service.

Civil Servants and Ministers: duties and responsibilities, Government response to the 7th Report from the Treasury and Civil Service Select Committee, Cmnd 9841, 1986

The Government subsequently made it plain that civil servants appearing before select committees should refuse to answer questions about their own conduct or that of other civil servants. 'The Government does not believe that a select committee is a suitable instrument for inquiring into or passing judgement upon the actions or conduct of an individual civil servant'. Civil servants were ultimately responsible to ministers, it said. As for the dual position of Sir Robert, the Government thought that this posed no particular problem.

Westland PLC: the Government's decision-making: 4th Report from the Defence Committee, HC 519, 1985-6

Westland PLC:
Government
response to the
Defence
Committee,
HC 518 and
HC 519, Cmnd
9916, 1986

See Appendix A

It should also be added that the mass media played a prominent role in keeping the Affair headline news, perhaps reflecting the fact that in the British political culture, the public enjoys nothing better than the occasional ministerial embarrassment. Certainly the Westland crisis inflicted considerable political damage upon Mrs Thatcher herself, at a time when the Conservatives were appearing to climb slightly in the opinion polls, not least because of the manner of Mr Heseltine's departure – he was the first minister to walk out of a Cabinet meeting since Joseph Chamberlain in 1886. Moreover, to lose a second Cabinet minister within a couple of weeks was even more serious, and with Brittan's resignation, Mrs Thatcher had, since entering office in 1979, replaced the virtual equivalent of an entire Cabinet.

Popular Power: Referenda

A rather different debate about the concepts of power, authority and responsibility emerged in 1974 and 1975 over the holding of the referendum on the issue of the United Kingdom's membership of the EEC. Many saw it as a question of the power of parliament *vis-à-vis* the authority of the people. The experiment, novel in the UK (but not so novel in other countries, such as France), caused a great deal of anxiety amongst MPs and academics alike. Some leading political scientists, for example, J.P. Mackintosh and Anthony King, thought that it would do irreparable damage to the traditions of the political system, even if at the time it was a successful device for holding the Labour party together. Although it was not until 1975 that the United Kingdom used a referendum on a national scale, it had been suggested on many previous occasions – for example, in 1893 over Irish Home Rule, in 1910 and in 1917 over the reform of the House of Lords, in 1932 (by Baldwin) to overcome the problem of tariff reforms, and in 1945 (by Churchill) over whether to prolong the life of Parliament still further in the period of immediate post-war reconstruction.

Criticism of the referendum

Mackintosh argued that a referendum on the EEC would imply that referenda should be held on other major issues of constitutional importance, such as membership of NATO and the devolution proposals for Wales and Scotland (on which the Government initially refused to hold a referendum). Further, he said that opinion polls could do a better job on complex issues than simple Yes/No ballots – although, given the record of some opinion polls at general elections and by-elections, perhaps that suggestion was a little suspect. But most of all, he said, a referendum would strike at the very nature of parliamentary power, from which is derived a system of representative government; MPs are elected to give a lead, not to be delegates. If they were delegates, the argument goes, murderers would still hang – perhaps witches would be burned at the stake. Moreover, the holding of referenda would make Britain look uncertain and hesitant in the eyes of other countries; and in any case a referendum only tests public opinion at one particular

The Observer,
15 September
1974

point in time, although the same could perhaps also be said of parliamentary elections.

Anthony King extended the argument by commenting that a referendum would almost destroy the traditions of Westminster power; it would lessen Cabinet responsibility. He remarked that in 1974 the political élite in Switzerland (a nation which regularly holds referenda) was very apprehensive that a suggestion for the deportation of 500 000 foreign workers and their families might in fact be adopted: 'one imagines the reaction of Gladstone instructed to coerce Ireland, or Churchill told that it was his duty to appease Germany.'

The Observer,
16 March 1975

In this particular instance the Prime Minister suspended the doctrine of collective Cabinet responsibility, allowing the 'antis' (such as Shore, Benn, Foot and Castle) to have free reign in public speeches. There was a precedent in the 'agreement to differ' suggested by Baldwin in 1932 over the question of protective tariffs, but that was a tactic to keep the Liberals in the coalition National Government. Whether the collective team management of the Cabinet could ever resume after 1975 was a pertinent question, but all the indications, first under Wilson and then even more under Callaghan and Thatcher have been that it has.

Anthony King's assertion that Governments will be tempted to pass the buck to the electorate rather than risk resignation and demand: 'Will you the people please get us out of this mess?', remains as yet entirely unproven. It may not have been right therefore for some academics to view the 1975 referendum, as two writers put it, as a Trojan horse which 'has been smuggled into the constitutional citadel in preparation for its overthrow.'

Parliamentary Affairs,
Summer 1975

Precedents for calculating the effects of referenda in the UK were virtually non-existent. It is true that Wales under the provisions of the 1964 Licensing Act is granted the opportunity at periodic intervals of holding district polls on the question of the Sunday opening of public houses – a subject which, given the nonconformist culture of Wales, usually generates some political heat, but this was hardly a useful precedent when it came to holding a national referendum on an issue of international importance. In a similar way, under the Northern Ireland (Border Poll) Act 1972, provision has been made for a referendum to be held periodically in Ulster on the question of the province's future within the United Kingdom. Nevertheless the academic argument that regular referenda would wreck the British political system needs to be put far more convincingly. When De Gaulle in 1969 used the tactic unsuccessfully and was forced to resign, did that seriously damage the French political system? On the contrary, was it not positively healthy for it?

Should, however, the results of a referendum merely advise the legislative body? When the Labour Government in 1977 changed its mind and agreed to hold referenda in Scotland and Wales over their proposed assemblies, it made it clear that the results would be binding upon Parliament. Under a storm of protest from back-benchers on both sides of the House, the Government retreated and agreed that they would be advisory only. Sweden has provided an excellent example in this area: in 1955 a national referendum showed that most people wished to continue driving on the left; but in 1963 the Swedish Government and Parliament reversed that decision.

BBC Radio 3,
16 March 1977

69

Elections as referenda

Of course, general elections themselves have on occasion almost acted as referenda, putting one major question to the electorate. The 1886 Election was fought on Home Rule for Ireland, the 1906 Election principally over the question of free trade, the 1910 Elections on the powers of the House of Lords, and to a limited extent the February 1974 Election on the powers of the big trade unions. On the other hand, however, Gladstone's first Irish Home Rule Bill in 1886 was brought in with little electoral warning, as indeed were Asquith's social reforms of the 1906–10 Parliament. There was really no mandate for the adoption of tariff preferences by the National Government in 1932, nor for an application to join the EEC under Macmillan in 1961. David Watts has commented:

Financial Times,
4 November 1977

> 'The point is that for the last 140-odd years the political parties have operated under the following, admittedly loose, set of rules: (a) they have normally submitted major constitutional changes to some test of electoral opinion; (b) where they have not done so they have recognised the risk and have been, in almost every instance, excoriated by their opponents for unconstitutional behaviour; (c) they have in any case felt it necessary to put forward the main points of their normal legislative programme in election manifestos and (d) when they have varied them substantially they have, again, been effectively roasted.'

Some of the problems raised by the organisation and relationships of the Executive have been demonstrated above. Many of these will help to form underlying themes of the following two chapters. What can be said now is that British central government was in a state of flux during the 1960s and 1970s – over the relationship between Government and ordinary MPs, over the operation of Cabinet procedures, over the power of the Prime Minister, over the structure of the Commons, even over the Executive's relationship with the courts. But whether such changes, such shifts in the common perspective of Westminster tradition, are so dramatic or revolutionary in a European or an international context is very much another question.

Summary

However fashionable it may be talk about Mrs Thatcher's presidential style of government, not least in the light of the Westland Affair in 1986, both in constitutional and in practical terms it is still correct to talk of 'Cabinet government'. Government by Cabinet has been the cornerstone of British politics during the whole period of modern, competitive party politics since the 1870s.

As long ago as 1918 the Haldane Committee on the Machinery of Government made it clear that the Cabinet fulfilled a tripartite role – the final determination of policy as submitted to Parliament, the control of the Executive in accordance with parliamentary policies, and the co-ordination of the Departments of State. That is still true, but today the Haldane definition appears a shade bland. The most important function of the Cabinet is to initiate and manage party and Government policy – the policy of the Government being, in the main, the programme of the dominant party in the House of Commons. In that context the Cabinet plans the annual legislative programme. But, in addition, it must deal with unanticipated national crises (for example, the Falklands in 1982) as well as resolve inter-departmental claims and conflicts, especially when the estimates for public expenditure are prepared. A great deal of this work, as noted above, will be done not in a full Cabinet but through the complex network of Cabinet committees.

Both at committees of the Cabinet and at the weekly meetings of the full Cabinet, business is conducted in a very formal and serious atmosphere. Some ministers will always be regarded as more senior to others, chiefly the Foreign Secretary, the Chancellor of the Exchequer, the Leader of the House of Commons and the Home Secretary. For a minister to gain backing for a particular proposal he must have canvassed the support of other key ministers beforehand, and perhaps that of the Prime Minister himself. Votes on issues are not taken, it would appear, but voices or heads counted in the sense that a Prime Minister, acting as the chairman of the Cabinet, must sum up the feeling of the meeting. The Prime Minister, together with the Secretary to the Cabinet, has control of the Cabinet agenda, and to a lesser extent the minutes and briefing papers, but there is a danger of overstating the extent of this power.

Despite the formality, meetings will be conducted in different ways, according to the personality of the Premier. The first post-war Prime Minister, Attlee, was well known for keeping meetings to the point. Mrs Thatcher also, it seems, prefers to proceed with business at a brisk pace, and does not appear as fond of full Cabinet sessions as most other Prime Ministers since 1945.

Once decisions are made by the Cabinet, each member is bound by them – the doctrine of collective ministerial responsibility. In practice, collective responsibility has been weakened by 'leaks' to the press, not least from Downing Street itself. However, if a minister feels passionately about an issue to the point of resigning in disagreement, then sometimes he does go, as Harold Wilson and Aneurin Bevan did in 1951 over proposed cuts in health expenditure and Michael Heseltine did in 1986 over the handling of the Westland Affair. The principle of collective Cabinet responsibility has not been applied consistently, particularly under recent Labour governments, and even less has that of individual (departmental) ministerial responsibility as outlined earlier.

'Individual ministerial responsibility' embraces those occasions where a minister resigns on account of some serious mistake occurring within his department (Dugdale in 1954, Carrington in 1982, perhaps Brittan in 1986), but in the wider sense it may include resignations for personal reasons or failures (Profumo in 1963, Parkinson in 1983, perhaps Brittan in 1986). The conventions of both collective and individual responsibility appear to have been weakened during the post-war period, but they are still part of the constitutional network, and certainly were thrust into the political limelight in 1986 during the Westland Affair.

Lord Salisbury's statement in 1878 about the operation of collective responsibility is still therefore pertinent:

> 'For all that passes in Cabinet every member of it who does not resign is absolutely and irretrievably responsible and he has no right afterwards to say that he agreed in one case to a compromise, while in another he was persuaded by

his colleagues. It is only on the principle that absolute responsibility is undertaken by every member of the Cabinet, who, after a decision is arrived at, remains a member of it, that the joint responsibility of ministers to Parliament can be upheld and one of the most essential principles of parliamentary responsibility established.'

The British system of government is primarily Cabinet government, but nevertheless, as Mackintosh and Crossman showed, Prime Ministers are powerful figures. Party support is usually assured; indeed only three premiers have been driven out of office this century – Asquith in 1916, Lloyd George in 1922 and Chamberlain in 1940. However, a number of Prime Ministers have come under considerable criticism within their respective parties, for example, Eden in 1956, Macmillan in 1963, Wilson in 1968 and Mrs Thatcher in 1986.

Each Premier has a different style of approaching Cabinet proceedings, from Attlee's succinct and concise approach to Churchill's often unstructured meetings (in his post-1951 Cabinet) that apparently indulged in war-time reminiscences. Nearly all post-war Prime Ministers have been forced to concentrate upon economic problems on the one hand, except for a brief interlude from about 1952 to 1960, and foreign affairs on the other (the manufacturing of the atomic bomb in 1947, the partition of India in 1947 and subsequent decolonisation together with the Malayan Emergency of 1948–60, the Korean War 1950–3, Suez 1956, the Cuban missile crisis 1962, the Borneo confrontation 1963–6, the involvement in Aden 1965–7, Southern Rhodesia 1965–79 and the Falklands 1982, as well as membership of NATO and entry into the EEC).

In the end every Prime Minister in the post-war period and, up to a point, his senior ministers also, has been overwhelmed by the sheer scale of economic problems, and to a lesser extent, international crises. Every Premier in the end becomes stale, as in many other occupations. It is notable that in the broad popular perception no Prime Minister since 1945 is regarded with great affection. Macmillan (1957–63) is probably the nearest exception, and Callaghan (1976–9) started off with a common sure touch, but ended badly. Mrs Thatcher has been widely admired, even by the leaders of the Opposition parties, as a tough, single-minded leader; she is respected, but not loved.

Since 1945 every Prime Minister has fulfilled the role of *primus inter pares* (first among equals) and some have exercised rather greater power. But each Premier's powers are circumscribed by party philosophy, back-bench feelings, advice and warnings from civil servants and opposition from Cabinet colleagues. Even Mrs Thatcher has by no means achieved all she set out to do in Cabinet and has been forced to retreat by her ministers on a number of issues since 1979, including MPs' pay, public expenditure cuts, the Zimbabwe Settlement, the EEC budget and trade union reform.

Questions

1. To what extent do the records of recent governments support the view that the power of the Prime Minister is determined by the unity of the Cabinet? (AEB specimen question 1986)

2. Assess the impact of Mrs Thatcher's tenure of office upon the role of Prime Minister. (Joint Matriculation Board)

3. 'Individual ministerial responsibility has become a device which can be used at times, and in ways that are convenient.' Discuss this statement in the light of recent cases. (Joint Matriculation Board)

4. Lord Hailsham once referred to the British parliamentary process as an 'elective dictatorship'. How far do you agree?

3 Openness, Privacy and ─ the Government

'We think that the administrative process is surrounded by too much secrecy. The public interest would be better served if there were a greater amount of openness.'

Report of the Committee on the Civil Service, Cmnd 3638, 1968

─────── Privacy and the Individual

The reference quoted above made by the Fulton Committee (the Committee on the Civil Service) about the secrecy that surrounds the British Civil Service underlines the difficulties of keeping a close guard, in an increasingly technological and bureaucratic age, both on the rights of access to official information and, almost paradoxically, on the privacy that organisations and individuals expect to enjoy. The Fulton Committee's short examination of these questions reflected the growing public concern in the 1960s about the citizen's right to privacy on the one hand and open government on the other, and it formed the background to two Government reports in 1972, that of the Younger Committee on Privacy, and that of the Franks Committee on a more specific but extremely important subject, the 1911 Official Secrets Act. It is these two problems that are examined first below.

Report of the Committee on Privacy, Cmnd 5012, 1972

The Younger Committee set out to consider whether any additional legislation was necessary to protect the private citizen, commercial organisations and interests, against intrusion into privacy by other individuals. Its report, which was restricted to England and Wales, as Scottish civil law tends to give rather greater coverage to questions of individual privacy, clearly reflected the difficulty in arriving at any precise definition of privacy. It commented that any law which stated that privacy meant the right to be let alone would have to be qualified in so many ways that the 'generality of the concept would be destroyed.' Although it suggested a number of ways in which the current situation might be improved, comparatively little radical political action resulted from the Report.

Nevertheless Younger can be said to have created a new climate of opinion towards the use of personal records and technological devices. Furthermore the Report was influential in respect of part of the Consumer Credit Act 1974 – that which stipulates that a person is entitled to discover from any creditor or owner to whom he has applied to enter into a regulated agreement the name of any credit reference agency consulted, and from the agency, for a nominal sum, he can demand a copy of the file made out on him. It is also fair to point out that the Committee's recommendations did filter through to other areas of public life. The Press Council, for example, in 1973 doubled the lay element of its membership, the BBC revised its complaints procedure in 1974 (the Broadcasting Complaints Commission followed in 1981) and local education authorities in a few areas opened up pupil records for inspection (contrast the extremely open access to education reports in the USA under its Family Educational Rights and Privacy Act 1974). The Report also had some limited influence upon the Employment Protection Act 1975. In 1975 the Government published a White Paper on computers and privacy: a Data Protection Committee was established to advise the Government as to how the White Paper's principles should be put into operation. The Committee (the Lindop Report) confirmed in 1978 to the Home Secretary the need to establish a Data Protection Authority, which would draw up rules for opening most medical, social work, credit rating and employment history records to those concerned. After much hesitation by the Government, the Data Protection Act 1984 was eventually passed. This Act, to be phased in during 1985–7, gives all individuals a general right of access to computer records concerning them, and a duty is imposed upon those who store such information to abide by seven principles laid down in the Act as to accuracy, security and the purpose of storage, and disclosure. But there are certain exemptions (principally medical records). The job of safeguarding the individual's privacy rests with the computer ombudsman, the Data Protection Registrar.

Report of the Committee on Data Protection, Cmnd 7341, 1978

> 'Critics argued that the Bill's safeguards could be circumvented easily by arranging for sensitive information to be stored manually. But evidence from other countries argues against that, Home Office officials maintain. They say that data legislation has not brought about any important transfer of data from computers to manual files.'

The Times, 4 June 1984

The Younger Committee also looked at the position on individual privacy in other countries in Europe and North America (as did Franks on secrecy). In France, for example, it had become clear in the 1960s that invasion of privacy by the press was increasing – 80 per cent of cases in that period involving the two leading 'popular' newspapers, *France Dimanche* and *Ici Paris*. In West Germany the basic provisions for defending the rights of 'personalities' are covered by the 1949 Constitution; of course, the 'right of individual personality' in Germany has been especially important in view of the Nazi era. In 1973 the West German Government introduced legislation covering data banks and the electronic means of recording personal information, but it took the United Kingdom another 11 years to follow suit.

Official Secrecy

The Franks Report on official secrecy appeared just a few months after the Younger Report, and again partly owed its origins to the Committee on the Civil Service a few years earlier. The 1911 Official Secrets Act had been passed at a time

Departmental
Committee on
Section 2 of the
Official Secrets Act
1911, Cmnd 5104,
1972

of tense Anglo-German relations but, curiously, continued to serve as the basis for Britain's security laws.

The 1911 Act: section 2

The Franks Committee's terms of reference were largely confined to section 2 of the Act, which relates principally to the internal as opposed to external security of the State. Section 1 deals with external factors – espionage and spying – and is not the subject of as much political dispute as section 2. Nevertheless, the distinction between sections 1 and 2 is by no means clear in practice. Section 2, simple and straightforward, has been criticised for being too broad in scope. It makes no distinction whatever between different kinds of information, having been designed with a 'catch-all' quality. 'All information which a Crown servant learns in the course of his duty is "official" for the purposes of section 2, whatever its nature, whatever the importance, whatever its original source,' Franks said. The 'catch-all' nature of the 1911 Act has been well illustrated in recent years, most notably in the failure of prosecutions in the 'ABC trial' in 1978 and the Ponting case in 1985. In the former the three defendants had written about the work of GCHQ (Government Communication Headquarters) at Cheltenham. In the latter the accused, a senior civil servant, had sent two Ministry of Defence documents relating to parliamentary enquiries about the sinking of the Argentine vessel, the *General Belgrano*, during the Falklands conflict, to the MP, Tam Dalyell. The first document was unclassified and the second was marked confidential.

See also C. Leeds,
Politics in Action,
Stanley Thornes,
1986, (section H)

Sir Robert Armstrong, Secretary to the Cabinet, finds himself in difficulties while giving evidence for the Government in a court case in Australia to prevent the publication of the memoirs of a former MI5 officer.

In addition, section 2 has applied not merely to civil servants and other public officials but also to private citizens, as in the 'ABC' case. This has meant that Government contractors can be bound by the Act in the same way as civil servants. Similarly, it has applied to any member of the public entrusted with confidential information by civil servants as well as to any person in possession of official but unauthorised information (rather in the way the handling of stolen goods is treated). In other words the minister or his agent, probably a senior civil servant, will decide whether to authorise the release of certain official information for public consumption. Thus section 2 of the 1911 Act is used to prosecute those responsible for the unauthorised dissemination of official information. Moreover, the mere receipt of information may be illegal, even if the recipient does not make use of it – the defendant has to show that the information was communicated to him contrary to all his desires. Under section 2 it is also an offence to communicate secret codes or passwords to any person or to any foreign power in a manner 'prejudicial to the safety and interests of the state.'

The Franks Committee recognised that while progress in education and technology had increased the possibility of circulating information on a wide scale and in considerable detail, by the same token it was also possible to see an increase in effective propaganda which was centrally controlled.

In 1977 the Prime Minister instructed all Government departments to release more of the information and statistics that formed the basis of various departmental policy options, so that the public could participate more closely in the Whitehall decision-making process – in other words, to publish even 'Greener' Papers. The Government and the then Head of the Home Civil Service, Sir Douglas Allen (later Lord Croham) claimed that a great deal of background material was released. However, *The Times,* which kept a close watch for the first year or so on the flow of such information, remained highly sceptical. The main point is that any greater release of material is still at the private discretion of departmental ministers.

In the United States, as Franks found, the position is largely governed by the first amendment to the Constitution, which says, 'Congress shall make no law . . . abridging the freedom of speech or of the press.' Moreover, the 1966 Public Information Act – amended in 1974 and known popularly as the 'Freedom of Information' Act – requires all US Government agencies to publish details of their organisations, policies and decisions, as well as making certain documents available to the public for inspection. However, there are exceptions to this, including defence and foreign policy secrets specified by Executive Order, matters excluded by other laws, confidential trade secrets or intra-governmental documents, and reports relating to the supervision of financial institutions.

A new Information Act?

'Open government' is not necessarily a question of persuading a minister to make up his mind in a new way but rather of showing a wide audience why a particular decision has in fact been made, and sometimes of allaying fears and anxieties. 'Openness' is not always as radical as it might sound – to many politicians at Westminister it has a fairly restricted meaning: removing the more absurd features from the decision-making process, and by definition reducing the number of Cabinet leaks as well.

It was the greater openness of public information in countries like Sweden that led the Franks Committee to recommend the repeal of section 2 of the 1911 Act and its replacement by a new Official Information Act which would remove criminal sanctions from the unauthorised disclosure of all official information with the following main exceptions: defence; aspects of foreign affairs which overlap with defence – such as negotiations for treaties with other countries; sterling matters, currency reserves and certain matters relating to trade; Cabinet papers – the 30-year rule under the Public Records Act 1967, thus maintaining the principle of collective responsibility; confidences of the private citizen, as Younger had indicated – for example, medical information, personal job information; the armed forces of the Crown; the maintenance of law and order (e.g. prison security, methods of crime prevention and detection). Franks also recommended that the mere receipt of information should no longer be an offence.

DOCUMENT

9

The Background to Official Secrecy

Government secrecy and democratic control

1   The Official Secrets Acts have been in existence in this country for only eighty years. Section 2 of the Official Secrets Act 1911, which is our concern, has been in force for sixty-one years. But from the earliest times governments of all types have been anxious to preserve secrecy for matters affecting the safety or tactical advantage of the State. It is, however, the concern of democratic governments to see that information is widely diffused, for this enables citizens to play in controlling their common affairs. There is an inevitable tension between the democratic requirement of openness, and the continuing need to keep some matters secret.

2   This tension has been increasing in recent years. In part this is because the dangers to the State have changed in character and become more complex, and have come to seem internal as well as external. The processes of government have become more sophisticated; the activities of a government increasingly affect all the affairs of the citizen. Its economic manoeuvres have come to be considered no less vital to the basis of the life of the community than the movement of its troops. Many new advances in science have both peace-time and military applications. Rapid changes in society, and the increased influence of centralised institutions, further complicate the issue. More and more information about the private affairs of citizens comes into the possession of the Government: there is a feeling that the Government should safeguard the confidences of the citizen almost as strictly as it guards information of use to an enemy.

3   Such developments have increased the pull towards secrecy. They have at the same

time made more obvious the need to improve the effectiveness of democratic control. This must mean more information to enable citizens to make rational decisions about matters which affect so much of their lives. Progress in education and in technology has increased the possibility of circulating information on a wide scale and in considerable detail. It has also increased the possibility of effective propaganda, centrally controlled. Those concerned with the mass media of communications in Britain have felt the need not just for more openness in government but for a loosening of control of information at all levels in the machinery of government. Only thus, they have argued, could they play a developing part in the operation of a modern democracy. We are faced, therefore, with an increased area in which considerations of secrecy may arise, and at the same time with an increased need for the diffusion of information together with the technical capacity to supply this need.

4   It is against this background that we have investigated the operation of section 2 of the Official Secrets Act 1911. This section is part of the criminal law, aimed at preventing unauthorised disclosures of official information. In the changing circumstances we have indicated it would be very unlikely that legislation passed two generations ago would not require reconsideration.

The reasons for our appointment

5   There has, however, been misunderstanding about the more immediate reasons for our appointment in 1971. It is important to make clear what these reasons were, if the scope of our investigation is to be appreciated. Our appointment can be traced directly to the Report, published in 1968, of the Fulton Committee on the Civil Service. It was there suggested that the administrative process was "surrounded by too much secrecy" and that "the public interest would be better served if there were a greater amount of openness". The Report welcomed recent trends in this direction but stated that "there must always be an element of secrecy (not simply on grounds of national security) in administration and policy making". It then went on to propose that "the Government should set up an enquiry to make recommendations for getting rid of unnecessary secrecy in this country. Clearly, the Official Secrets Acts would need to be included in such a review".

6   The Labour Government of 1966–70 published in June 1969 a White Paper on this subject "Information and the Public Interest". This stated that the Government had carried out the enquiry recommended by the Fulton Committee "on a wide inter-departmental basis, studying comprehensively both the existing trend and its possible further development". It referred to the increasing amount of information published by governments in recent years and the trend towards wider and more open consultation before decisions are taken. Towards the end the White Paper contained a passage on the Official Secrets Acts which said that there was a case for protecting much official information from unauthorised disclosure, and that a criminal sanction was needed for the protection of some official material. It then argued that the Official Secrets Acts as such were not a barrier to greater openness in government since they did not inhibit the *authorised* release of information in any way. The Conservative Party manifesto at the 1970 General Election promised to eliminate unnecessary secrecy concerning the workings of government, and to review the operation of the Official Secrets Acts. We were appointed in fulfilment of that undertaking.

The case of the Nigerian Report

7   It is nevertheless commonly supposed that our appointment was the result of a recent prosecution under section 2. This is not so. Our appointment was announced

shortly after the conclusion of the case. This was because the Government had deferred its announcement while the case was being tried. The case was not the cause of our appointment but the cause of our appointment being deferred. We should, however, make some reference to it.

8   The case involved four defendants, who were charged under section 2 in connection with the communication and receipt of a confidential assessment of the situation in Nigeria written by the Defence Adviser at the British High Commission in Lagos. A copy of this report passed through a number of hands and eventually came to the *Sunday Telegraph,* which published it. As a result, the newspaper, its editor, and two of those along the chain of communication, were prosecuted. In February 1971 all four defendants were acquitted. In the course of his summing up Mr Justice Caulfield made the suggestion that section 2 should be "pensioned off". This dictum was widely reported and was widely represented as a call for the simple repeal of section 2. The full text of the summing up shows that Mr Justice Caulfield was in fact suggesting the replacement of section 2 by new provisions which would, as he put it, enable people like the four defendants to determine without great difficulty in what circumstances the communication of official information would put them in peril of prosecution.

9   Even without these remarks by the Judge, the case of the Nigerian Report would have occasioned much public interest for two reasons. First, it related to a matter of political controversy on which strong opinions were held. Secondly, a case which involves those who work in the communications media appearing in the dock to face a criminal charge for publishing information will rightly attract close attention. These two factors, followed by the remarks by the Judge and the acquittal of the defendants, made this a *cause célèbre.* The case, the summing up, the verdict, were much discussed in the press. A common theme was the need to do something about section 2.

10   It is not surprising in these circumstances that some of the evidence presented to us was influenced by the Nigerian case. It was difficult to avoid the feeling that a few witnesses were inviting us to draw conclusions on the basis of this one case alone. The case was indeed important and we did give it proper attention. It was nevertheless but one case out of a number of cases over the years. Though it happens to be the most recent, undue concentration upon it would give a misleading picture of the way in which section 2 has operated and would shut out other issues of great significance.

General issues underlying our work

11   We have so far indicated these wider issues in the most general terms. But they can be more simply expressed. Even a democratic government requires a measure of secrecy for some of its functions, as a means whereby it can better carry out its duties on behalf of the people. Among the primary tasks of government are the defence of the nation from external threats, the maintenance of relations with the rest of the world and the preservation of law and order. Defence against external attack would be severely prejudiced if potential enemies had access, directly or indirectly, to the details of our plans and weapons. It would be impossible to negotiate with other countries if all discussion, however delicate, was conducted completely in the open. Some measures for the prevention or detection of crime would be ineffective if they were known to criminals. Some of the internal processes of government should be conducted in confidence if they are to result in effective policies. The presentation of clear issues to Parliament and to the electorate depends upon Ministers and administrators being able, in some instances and

at some stages, to argue out all possibilities with complete frankness and free from the temptation to strike public attitudes.

12   A totalitarian government finds it easy to maintain secrecy. It does not come into the open until it chooses to declare its settled intentions and demand support for them. A democratic government, however, though it must compete with these other types of organisation, has a task which is complicated by its obligations to the people. It needs the trust of the governed. It cannot use the plea of secrecy to hide from the people its basic aims. On the contrary it must explain these aims: it must provide the justification for them and give the facts both for and against a selected course of action. Nor must such information be provided only at one level and through one means of communication. A government which pursues secret aims, or which operates in greater secrecy than the effective conduct of its proper functions requires, or which turns information services into propaganda agencies, will lose the trust.of the people. It will be countered by ill-informed and destructive criticism. Its critics will try to break down all barriers erected to preserve secrecy, and they will disclose all that they can, by whatever means, discover. As a result matters will be revealed when they ought to remain secret in the interests of the nation.

13   The means of preserving secrecy in any operation are various. The need for keeping some discussions confidential is felt in private undertakings and in business as it is in public affairs. Not all discussions can be carried on at noon in the market place any more than at midnight in a debating chamber. The discipline of a service, the penalty of dismissal, may often be enough to maintain the confidences of private concerns. But the affairs of government are of a different order of difficulty and importance from those of ordinary business. They affect the whole community, for good or ill, and special measures are needed both to inform the public and to protect the public against damaging breaches of trust in a dangerous world. There is, therefore, a justification for using the criminal law as well as professional discipline to protect secrets of the State.

14   Our direct concern is the part which the criminal law should play in the protection of official information. In this context we have had to consider how the demands of Parliamentary democracy for the fullest information and for efficiency in operation can be reconciled. The present law, contained in section 2, is notable for its extreme width and for the considerable uncertainty attaching to its interpretation and enforcement. It does not carry public confidence. We propose its replacement by provisions reduced in scope and less uncertain in operation. We believe that these provisions provide the necessary minimum of criminal law required for the security of the nation and the safety of the people, and for the constructive operation of our democracy in the conditions which obtain today.

15   To determine the right point of balance between these interests we have had to sift a great deal of material and weigh many opinions. The considerations are complex. Although in the course of more than a year's intensive study we have familiarised ourselves with them, we do not pretend that they make for easy reading. Nor can the solutions we have preferred be quite as simplistic as some protagonists on both sides of the argument desire. The issues touch the heart of government in a Parliamentary democracy too closely. We think it prudent to say as much at the outset.

Report of the Departmental Committee on Section 2 of the Official Secrets Act
1911, Cmnd 5104, 1972

The Labour Government's response

Reform of Section
2 of the Official
Secrets Act 1911,
Cmnd 7285, 1978
For several years the Franks Report collected dust, but in 1978 a White Paper was issued. The Paper reflected the perennial question once posed by Sir Burke Trend (a former Cabinet Secretary and subsequently Lord Trend): 'Once you embark on the strip-tease of Government, where do you stop?' It was a very cautious document. Although it stated that introducing more openness into British government along Swedish or American lines was still a matter for discussion it also said that those countries' systems were not necessarily correct for the UK; further, to adopt the US model would be extremely expensive.

But the Paper underlined the fact that, like the Franks Report, it was solely concerned with section 2 of the 1911 Act, no more and no less. Most of its recommendations followed Franks and it agreed that the mere receipt of information should no longer be a criminal offence.

Royal Commission
on Standards of
Conduct in Public
Life, Cmnd 6524,
1976
In three important respects the Paper did differ from Franks. Firstly, it saw no need for a specific excepted category for Cabinet documents, since such material could be covered by the other excepted categories. In any case the Paper noted that the Government preferred to rely on well-practised, 'ad hoc' methods of distributing Cabinet information – presumably a veiled reference to press leaks and the like. Secondly, the Paper said that criminal sanctions need no longer apply to the disclosure of economic information, since distinctions between different types of such activity were impossible to draw. How far, exactly, the Government believed in this statement is hard to say, since on the face of it this was an important concession to the liberalisation of information. Thirdly, while it agreed with Franks that it should be an offence for a public servant to use official information for private gain (and here it also agreed that a redefinition of the term 'Crown servant' was long overdue), it thought it best to consider the matter separately in the light of the Salmon Commission recommendations.

The Paper was not warmly received by pressure groups and MPs alike. The Paper's weaknesses were principally the following:

(a) it failed to consider the question of open government in the widest sense; instead it restricted itself to the relatively narrow confines of section 2 of the 1911 Act, that is the criminal penalties that apply in respect of the unauthorised disclosure of official information – in other words it followed the very terms of reference of Franks itself, from which it quoted approvingly and at length;

(b) it barely considered the overlap between sections 1 and 2: where the Paper did make a reference, it was, it could be argued, a confused one.

Open Government,
Cmnd 7520, 1979
The Labour Government fell before any legislation on secrecy could be introduced. But just before it did, it issued a Green Paper on the wider question of open government generally. It, again, was a cautious document, but it did recommend a Code of Practice for public access to official information.

In 1979 the Thatcher administration introduced its Protection of Information Bill. The Bill began its life in the Lords where it immediately ran into difficulties. Both MPs and peers felt that the legislation as drafted was even more restrictive than the 1911 Act. At the same time the Anthony Blunt spy scandal broke and some of the media suggested that under the proposed measure public discussion of the scandal would not have been allowed. As a consequence Mrs Thatcher, whose enthusiasm for reform of section 2 was not much greater than Mr Callaghan's, withdrew the Bill. Since that episode there have been no further developments, at least in legislative terms, in respect of the 1911 Act or openness generally.

DOCUMENT

10

Openness in Government

1.   This Green Paper is concerned with proposals for greater openness in government. It examines existing practices and recent developments, and considers the broad issues entailed in further measures to promote openness, taking account of the political and constitutional arrangements in this country. It also refers to the experience of other countries in the field of open government, especially in the establishment of a statutory right of access to official records.

2.   The Paper notes the evidence of the steady increase of public interest in knowing how and why Government decisions are taken and it discusses some of the reasons for the demands which have been made for a public right of access to information. There is however no consensus of view on the means which should be adopted to provide more information and this is well illustrated by the differences between the various schemes for access which have been published over the last year or so. In the Government's judgement further steps designed to achieve greater openness must be fully in accord with our constitutional tradition and practice which have developed in this country. Nothing must be allowed to detract from the basic principle of Ministerial accountability to Parliament; and the prime aim of any new measures must be to strengthen Parliamentary democracy and public confidence in it. The Government believes that these objectives will best be achieved by gradual developments, which build on existing arrangements, and which are capable of adjustment and modification in the light of experience. The wisdom of adopting such a policy appears to be amply borne out by the experience of those countries which have introduced public rights of access to information. Moreover that experience also shows the need for clarity in setting out precisely what any proposals for providing a right of access are designed to achieve.

The Main Themes of Openness

8.   The debate on what is entailed in "openness of government" extends across a wide and varied spectrum. Those arguing for greater openness have various objectives; to secure more information to assist debate on national issues; to explain government decisions affecting groups of citizens; to assist interest groups in urging particular priorities within an area of policy; or to amplify the grounds on which decisions affecting individuals have been taken. There is also concern about decisions taken by government in the allocation and management of resources. These issues for the most part do not include those affecting the way of life of groups of people in a local community, where   83

there have, in recent years, been considerable developments in the rights of people to obtain information on decisions in the built environment, such as proposals on roads, town plans, power station sites, etc. This Green Paper assumes that the development of these arrangements will continue in ways which respond to the expressed needs of affected parties. While all of these are aspects of the pressure for greater openness in government, this Green Paper is concerned primarily with the need for more openness in the wide range of issues and decisions which affect the nation as a whole, or large sections of it.

9.   There is no fixed or agreed definition even of the "national" aspects in "open government". The demand to know about national policies and decisions can range from wanting increased explanations of official policy and a different style of government to a general public legal right of access to all official documents, including Cabinet and Cabinet Committee papers, departmental working papers and raw files. It can mean greater access to documents and records or greater readiness among Ministers and officials to argue individually and publicly about what they think, or have thought, about particular policies and decisions.

10.   Nor is it possible to establish, precisely and for all time, how much official information should be published, what sort of material this should be, and at what point it should be revealed. In the same way, it is impossible to fix, exactly and for ever, what categories of material should remain confidential, and for how long. Rules and guidelines will need periodic revision. How rules and guidelines should be drawn and how they should be enforced is a matter of judgement on which opinion will always vary. Even among those who argue for a public right of access there is no unanimity on how these issues should be resolved.

What the United Kingdom has done already

11.   The British system of Parliamentary democracy has had a long and complex evolution, impossible to summarise here in all its conventions. One feature, however, stands out as a key doctrine, subject itself to gradual modification and refinement – individual and collective Ministerial responsibility and accountability to Parliament. This doctrine is the hub around which so much of our administrative and political life revolves, and lies behind our existing practices of disclosure of official information. In essence it means that Ministers have to provide information about the exercise of their responsibilities in order that an account can be rendered to Parliament. Over the years, different mechanisms have been developed for the disclosure of information including Parliamentary Questions, Adjournment and Supply Day Debates, Command Papers presented to Parliament, evidence to Select Committees and the legislative process. There are too the reports to Parliament of the Comptroller and Auditor General and Parliamentary Commissioner for Administration, independent office-holders who, in the discharge of their responsibilities have special access to Departmental information.

12.   Parliamentary conventions have been established governing the disclosure of information by Government to Parliament which have recognised that a balance must be struck between the legitimate requirements of Government, as of any other organisation, to have a certain degree of privacy for the proper and effective conduct of its business and the need to ensure that Parliament has the information which it requires to scrutinise the Executive and to hold Ministers to account. These conventions are under continuous development and in recent years governments have made much more

information available than previously through the Parliamentary mechanisms mentioned above. In particular an increasing amount of information has been provided by Government in written and oral evidence to Select Committees.

13.   One of the most significant recent developments has been the creation of the Parliamentary Commissioner for Administration in 1967 (and subsequently the National Health Service Commissioner and the Local Government Commissions). The Parliamentary Commissioner was created as an independent office holder to assist members of Parliament in performing one of their traditional tasks, that of assisting the individual citizen in redress of a grievance against the Government. Because complaints of an injustice caused by maladministration must come through an MP, the Parliamentary Commissioner in no way supplants the MP. Nor does he have separate powers to enforce his findings, after investigation of a complaint. He does, however, have complete powers to call for persons and papers. He reports his findings to the MP who sent in the complaint, to the department or authority concerned, and to Parliament. Any failure or reluctance to agree with a finding of maladministration on the part of the executive is subject to the usual methods of Parliamentary criticism and censure.

The 1976 Initiative by the Prime Minister

18.   The most significant recent initiative in this direction, however, was built on the undertakings given to Parliament by the Prime Minister in November 1976. A letter was sent on 6 July 1977 by Lord Croham (then Sir Douglas Allen, Head of the Civil Service) to Heads of Departments intended to secure the release of background material wherever possible (subsequently referred to as "the Information Directive").

19.   This Information Directive said that the working assumption in future should be that background material relating to policy studies and reports would be published unless Ministers decided that it would not be; that the aim normally would be to publish as much as possible of the background material, subject to Ministerial decision, once they had seen the study and reached their conclusions on it; and that when policy studies were being undertaken in future the background material should as far as possible be written in a form which would permit it to be published separately, with the minimum of alteration, once a Ministerial decision to do so had been taken. The effects to date of this policy initiative by the Government have been detailed in replies to Parliamentary Questions and more material will be released as work in hand in Departments is completed.

49.   The question how far papers relevant to the formulation of policy should be open to disclosure raises difficult issues. A great deal of such information is already published in the form of Green Papers, discussion documents, evidence to inquiries and the like. It is argued however that public participation in the formulation of government policy requires a much greater readiness to disclose the considerations, opinions and arguments which were canvassed in reaching a particular decision. It is sometimes held that information about internal disagreements amongst Ministers or between Ministers and their advisers, since they must inevitably occur in any case, is necessary for full public understanding of the reasons why certain policies were adopted, and certain courses followed.

50.   Against this, there is the more compelling argument that those who come together and act jointly in pursuit of a common purpose need the assurance of privacy in their deliberations. This is true of any walk of life and in any organisation, be it social, commercial or political; and Government is no exception. Unless the participants can talk   85

freely among themselves, possibilities and opinions which may be unpopular or embarrassing may not be adequately explored and discussed. The private conversation would tend to assume importance at the expense of thorough discussion by the whole body, to the detriment of sound decision-taking and the orderly conduct of business. Moreover under our constitutional conventions civil servants have for the most part been anonymous, offering advice in the assurance of confidence and hence free to express their views frankly. It is their duty to expose even uncomfortable facts or aspects of a question in order to present as full a picture as possible of the issues which Ministers have to decide and for which they are accountable to Parliament. The alteration of the conventions within which they at present proffer advice could well affect adversely the value of that advice.

51.   Another important category which should be considered for exemption is commercial information, whether disclosed voluntarily or not, or whether received by, or generated by, the Government. Disclosure of such information, without the consent of those who supplied it, could undermine the government's relations with industry and could jeopardise competitive positions. Where Government is itself trading or exploiting information it owns, it would give an advantage to its competitors, including those overseas, and allow opportunities for the results of research which had been financed from public funds to be exploited for private gain.

52.   The exceptions to the obligation to disclosure must clearly include information whose unauthorised disclosure would be an offence under a revision of the Official Secrets Act, but they should also encompass certain other categories, including financial and economic matters whose publication could be damaging (eg to the reserves or the exchange rate).

53.   Rather different considerations arise in dealing with proposals for the publication of manuals and guides dealing with the administration of major areas of legislation, particularly in the taxation and social security fields. Much of this information of course should be available to the general public and indeed is already provided in other publications. But there is also material which offers guidance and advice to officials on such matters as the detection of fraudulent claims for benefits and the evasion of taxes and duties. To make these parts of the internal manuals generally available would clearly be contrary to the best interests of the community at large.

59.   In the Government's view the essential requirements of any scheme of access to official information is that it should satisfy public demand so far as is reasonable and practicable; that it should be fully compatible with the constitutional and Parliamentary systems of this country; and that the costs should be commensurate with the public benefit.

A Code of Practice

65.   A Code of Practice on access to official information, which the Government was fully committed to observe, would be a major step forward. Such a scheme could be devised to meet the essential requirements set out in paragraph 59 above. Access would be given to official documents and information other than in fields which were specifically exempted from the operation of the Code. The initiative in the release of material would no longer rest exclusively with the Government. But accountability to Parliament would be retained and the jurisdiction of the courts excluded. There would be no retrospective application.

70.   The detailed provisions of such a Code; the question of whether or not it should,

from its introduction, be put on a statutory footing, and if so, in what form; and the appropriate choice of machinery for monitoring the Code's application, are matters for further detailed examination. It would be the Government's intention to recommend to Parliament that a Select Committee of the House of Commons should be appointed for this purpose.

Open Government, Cmnd 7520, 1979

Crown Privilege and other Matters

In addition to the laws on secrecy there are a number of other ways in which the Government can restrict the individual's access to official information and these can now be briefly discussed.

Crown privilege

In legal proceedings application may be made to the court for 'discovery' – that is for the production of certain documents that will assist one or both parties in their case. As already outlined in the previous chapter, the doctrine of 'Crown privilege' means quite simply that the Government intercedes in that case: it claims that it would be against the public interest to produce those documents. The Government itself does not have to be a party to the proceedings (the doctrine more often than not applies to civil cases), and while the documents need not be Government ones, they will invariably be of an official or quasi-official nature if the question of injury to the 'national interest' is to be raised at all.

The courts now prefer to call Crown privilege the doctrine of 'public interest immunity'. (Certain examples under this section have been cited briefly, in Chapter 2.)

Cases which have illustrated the doctrine in practice have been:

(a) *Duncan* v. *Cammell, Laird and Co* (1942) A submarine sank on sea trials; in an action for compensation for the victims' relatives the Government refused to release the submarine's design plans.

(b) *Ellis* v. *Home Office* (1953) The Government refused to release medical reports about an inmate of Winchester Prison.

(c) *Conway* v. *Rimmer* (1968) A probationary police officer was cleared of theft but nevertheless dismissed from the force. The Government objected to the release of certain documents in an action the officer brought for malicious prosecution.

(d) *Burmah Oil Co Ltd* v. *Governor and Company of the Bank of England* (1979) The oil company brought an action that challenged the fairness of a commercial agreement made with the Bank; the Government objected to the publication of certain documents, a number of which related to Treasury matters.

87

(e) *Lonrho Ltd* v. *Shell Petroleum Co Ltd* (1980) Essentially the company brought an action against Shell for loss of profits occasioned by Shell's breach of the economic sanctions imposed by the British Government and the United Nations once the Southern Rhodesian Government had illegally declared independence in 1965. The Foreign Office supported Shell in its refusal to release certain confidential material.

The 30-year rule

Cabinet documents and the files of the various Government departments are not released until 30 years have elapsed (50 until the Public Records Act 1967). Certain sensitive material – for example the records of MI5 and MI6 – may be kept secret for much longer periods.

An incident of note in this area occurred in 1976, when details of how the Cabinet had decided to postpone the new Child Benefit scheme (under the Child Benefit Act 1975) were published anonymously by the weekly periodical *New Society.* The magazine commented that the Cabinet decision was a clear example of a potentially radical Government becoming managers rather than reformers. The Prime Minister, Mr Callaghan, ordered the Head of the Civil Service, Sir Douglas Allen, to conduct an internal inquiry into the leak, but his report was inconclusive and no prosecutions were forthcoming under section 2 of the 1911 Act. In the House of Commons Callaghan told MPs that leaks were a very grave matter, saying that, if there were to be good relations between members of the Government, there must be absolute confidence that papers and discussions were kept within the circle for which they were intended: the 'honourable thing' was for the culprit responsible for the leaks to resign.

D-Notices

The D-Notice (or Defence notice) system is a voluntary one only, it does not have the force of law. It is the process whereby advisory warnings are issued to the press by a minister not to publish certain material in the interests of 'state security'. In 1967 there were allegations that the *Daily Express* had breached the usual form of mutual trust and as a result the Radcliffe Committee considered the system (it recommended no change). At the same time the Secretary to the non-statutory Services, Press and Broadcasting Committee (the body responsible for D-Notices), Colonel Sammy Lohan, resigned after what he regarded as undue questioning by senior civil servants about his professional conduct.

In 1980 the *New Statesman* deliberately breached the D-Notice system by publishing material on telephone tapping. It was then revealed that 12 different types of D-Notice were in existence. The new Commons Defence Committee held an investigation but decided that very limited reform of the system was preferable to abolition (at least until the Official Secrets laws were reformed). The Government not surprisingly agreed. The number of notices was reduced to eight in 1982.

The Law of Confidence

The legal position of confidential documents is by no means clear in English law: in short, the doctrine of confidence is ill-developed as the Younger Report pointed out in 1972. However, in 1975 the Attorney-General, on behalf of the Government, attempted under the guise of the law of confidence to prevent the serialisation of the *Crossman Diaries* on the grounds that Crossman's record revealed Cabinet discussions that were less than 30 years old. The Lord Chief Justice took the view that while confidence may have been broken, publication did not harm the national interest and that in any case Crossman's account was not an official record of Cabinet proceedings and thus not covered by the 30-year rule. Had the Government decided to use the full might of the Official Secrets Act 1911, as suggested by some organs of the press, things might have taken a different course. The Attorney-General, though, conceded at the start of the case that it was not, in his opinion, a matter for the 1911 Act (*Attorney-General* v. *Jonathan Cape Ltd*).

The Ombudsman

The Whyatt Report

A certain increase in the openness of British government, again following overseas experiences, began in 1967, with the institution of the Ombudsman (the Parliamentary Commissioner for Administration – PCA). This arose out of the Whyatt Report (of the Justice committee) in 1961, which had itself come into existence against the background of the Crichel Down Affair and the Franks recommendations on administrative tribunals in 1957. The Report made the point that public complaints fall into two main categories – complaints against discretionary decisions of public servants for which there is no formal method of challenging, and complaints against serious errors of bureaucracy (maladministration). It was for the second type of complaint that it recommended the Government appoint a parliamentary commissioner.

The most established ombudsman systems are that of Sweden and Denmark. However, more recently a large number of Commonwealth states have introduced PCAs, so much so that it can now be said that the ombudsman system is almost a Commonwealth institution.

In the United Kingdom access to the Ombudsman is only possible through Members of the Commons, a fact which reflects MPs' fears that the traditional authority of the House could be undermined. Members of the Lords are excluded from dealing with complaints. Originally many MPs were dubious about the whole idea of an Ombudsman: it would encourage 'grievance collectors', said one. Yet, although it was left to the Ombudsman to decide the definition of 'maladministration', he was hindered by a number of considerable restrictions. He was not given the power to investigate complaints about the police, local government, administrative tribunals, the National Health Service, the armed forces, nationalised industries or personnel matters in the Civil Service. Moreover, he could not disclose any information from his investigation if the minister concerned thought that it would be prejudicial to the safety of the state or contrary to the public interest. In 1981, however, Parliament agreed to extend his powers to cover complaints about the activities of British consuls overseas. The PCA's jurisdiction was extended to Northern Ireland in 1969. Also, as from 1987 it is planned to extend the PCA's powers to cover about 50 or so non-departmental public bodies or quangos.

In early 1977 the Government agreed that future Parliamentary Commissioners would be drawn from professions outside the Civil Service. The fourth Ombudsman, appointed in 1979, was a lawyer, Sir Cecil Clothier. In other countries ombudsmen are not ex-civil servants but politicians, businessmen or lawyers; one Danish ombudsman, Nordskov Nielsen, was reported in 1976 as saying that if civil servants said he was a good ombudsman he knew he must be a bad one. But in Britain it seems to be accepted that roles can be switched without too much difficulty; for example, Sir Alan Marre found himself investigating an issue (invalid tricycles) for which he had been largely responsible in his previous capacity. Similarly, the vexed matter of the escalating expense of the centralised Driving and Vehicle Licensing Centre at Swansea was one which came to the attention of Sir Idwal Pugh although he had been responsible for it while at the Department of the Environment. (Sir Alan was PCA 1971–6 and Sir Idwal 1976–9.)

Year	Number of MPs referring complaints	Number of complaints referred by MPs	Number of written enquiries received directly from members of the public	% of cases examined for jurisdiction accepted for investigation	% of investigated cases where maladministration was found to some degree
1979	368	758	822	27	56
1980	401	1031	1194	29	64
1981	387	917	870	24	64
1982	389	838	1002	27	65
1983	492	751	952	24	78
1984	386	837	901	22	86
1985	373	759	935	26	87

Source: *Annual Reports of the Parliamentary Commissioner for Administration*

The Parliamentary Commissioner has, over the years, been involved in several *causes célèbres*. The first was the Sachsenhausen Case in 1968. The Foreign Office had rejected the claims of certain survivors of the Sachsenhausen concentration camp under the terms of the Anglo-German compensation agreement. Under pressure from the PCA the Foreign Office awarded *ex gratia* payments. (The Ombudsman cannot enforce the awarding of compensation.) The second and third both occurred in 1975 – the Court Line affair and the Congreve case. In the former the PCA criticised the Government for misleading the public over the financial security of the holiday company, Court Line, which subsequently collapsed. In the second case the Home Office bungled an attempt to claw back money from those people who had taken out colour television licences well ahead of renewal time in order to avoid projected increases in the fee.

DOCUMENT

11

The Role of the PCA

3.   As the years passed I came to realise that the distribution between departments of the complaints referred to me was a reflection of the importance of those departments to the citizen. Thus nearly half of all the work of my Office has consistently been devoted to complaints about tax and social security. The extent to which a citizen contributes to the common purse in good times and the extent to which he or she draws upon it when in trouble or in old age, are accurate reflections of what seems most important in the regulation of the community. The services rendered by the two departments principally concerned, the Inland Revenue and the Department of Health and Social Security, are therefore probably those most valued by the thoughtful citizen and those he would least like to see reduced in scale or efficiency. This is not to say that numerous other Departments of State do not provide services which every civilised community needs. But it is to say that there is a discernible order of priority of services, at any rate in the mind of the ordinary citizen. And although good organisation and leadership can effect great economies in the provision of a public service there comes a point at which these services cannot be maintained or improved without the application of funds. The number of complaints I receive is tiny in relation to both Departments' caseloads, and in some of the cases I investigate I find Departments blameless. But there is no escaping the fact that in these two spheres of fiscal administration, it more often than not turns out that a citizen's affairs are found to be out of order on my causing them to be examined at a high level.

4.   I am far from saying that the provision of more money will of itself tend to reduce errors in administration. Much of the trouble in these two areas of government springs from the dilemma that equity and efficiency are mutually antagonistic abstractions. Both our tax and our social security laws are now very complex. They have become so because successive governments have tried to make them more sensitive to the circumstances of the individual and thus more equitable as between one citizen and another. The resultant complexity, compounded each year by one or more Finance Acts, creates enormous difficulties for the administrator and adds to the probability of error in applying the law. Fewer mistakes would be made if our arrangements were much simpler: but there is no doubt that more individual hardship would be suffered. I see no practicable escape from the dilemma thus presented. One can only try to balance the opposing forces, to contain

the inevitable mistakes and to have a good system for investigating allegations of error and providing a remedy when the allegations are well-founded.

5.   Consideration of equity and efficiency leads me to another recurrent problem in administration. This arises from the urgent desire which every citizen feels to have some personal contact with those who govern him. It is very evident in my work that lack of the personal touch is a common cause of dissatisfaction with administration. For example, the printed stock letter from which unwanted parts are deleted by a stroke seems to the average man or woman to be the archetype of all that is bureaucratic and remote in government. Yet the cost of personal correspondence between Departments of State and the citizen on all matters would be unacceptably great. Again a balance must be sought. Accessibility of senior administrators is important in this connection, costly though it may be in terms of time. Many a taxpayer finds relief in seeking out his tax inspector to put his plea to him personally and very often is delighted with the personality he finds and with whom he is thereafter on good terms. People may well prefer to deal with human beings who make mistakes than with machines who cannot be addressed. So if a contented society is one aim of good administration, money may be as well spent on personal relations as on computers.

6.   Yet another intractable problem in administration is delay. There are few services, public or private, which are instantly available on demand. Tolerable delay varies according to whether one is waiting for an ambulance, a bus or the outcome of an inquiry into the location of a new airport. Nevertheless, there are areas of the public service where unreasonable delay is seen as a denial of justice. It may become more common for departments to say that greater delays are inevitable if resources are limited. I have been troubled about the validity of this argument. Taken literally, it seems to say that because of shortage of staff the volume of demand at a particular point in the public service exceeds the output which that point is capable of delivering. If this is what is meant, the position can only grow steadily worse, to the point where delays become intolerable. The proper corollary, it seems to me, is that if resources have to be reduced, some of the functions of the public service must be correspondingly reduced either in quantity or in quality. It cannot always be the case that by working harder a shrinking Civil Service can maintain both. Here again it is a matter of balance.

7.   Accessibility of officials puts me in mind of access to my own office. It is often said that I am not sufficiently accessible to the public and that access to me should be direct instead of through Members of Parliament. To my knowledge, the only other national ombudsman to whom access is indirect is the Médiateur in France. I have often deployed the familiar arguments in defence of our system, chief of which is that every Member of Parliament is an ombudsman for his constituents and that the body of Members makes a natural and valuable filter for discriminating between simple and complex cases, the worthy and the unworthy. But five years' experience has led me to doubt the validity of these arguments, at any rate in opposition to some modification of our arrangements. At present the Member may, and often does, ask the Minister for the appropriate Department to let him have, in the familiar phrase, "an answer which I can send to my constituent" about his grievance. But on receipt of that reply, the Member has neither the time, nor the resources, nor the powers to verify by examination of departmental papers or witness the explanations offered, which must of necessity be composed on the basis of facts and opinions advanced by those against whom the complaint is laid. When Members do send me their files, it sometimes happens that the Minister's letter of response is the starting point of an investigation which shows that

there is more to the case than the letter might be thought to suggest. It has occurred to me that without resorting to either extreme about access to this office, it would be possible to provide that the citizen must first invite his Member of Parliament to attend to his grievance and if he, the citizen, is dissatisfied with the ultimate response then he should have a right to invite me to examine the progress made upon his complaint. This would be unlikely I think to result in any great increase of acceptable complaints. But it seems to me that it would be an improvement on our present arrangements if the citizen had a right to have my personal judgement on the standing of his complaint before he was finally, and without appeal, dismissed.

8.   So far as I know I am alone among the hundred or so national ombudsmen of the world in having no powers to investigate on my own initiative apparent maladministration which has come or been brought to my notice. Only occasionally have I felt a particular wish to investigate something of my own accord and the ability to do so would have added no more than three or four cases to my workload in the five years about which I write. Yet I have felt it a reflection on a parliamentary democracy which prides itself on its considerate attitude towards its citizens that this country alone should impose such a restriction on its Parliamentary Commissioner. If it were felt that my discretion was not to be trusted, I would be glad to share the right to initiate an investigation with the chairman of the Select Committee of the House of Commons on the Parliamentary Commissioner or with the whole Committee, to whom I might on occasion suggest that an investigation without a specific complainant would be in the public interest.

9.   It is often urged that my jurisdiction be extended to include various other bodies discharging public functions whose operations have a direct impact on the citizen, such as the police, the service industries and the wider field of so-called quangos. The inspiration for these suggestions is entirely understandable. But such proposals need the most careful evaluation. The first and most obvious difficulty is that the personal involvement of the Parliamentary Commissioner, an identifiable figure, with the complaint seems important to the acceptance of the ombudsman system both by the citizen and by the government. As matters stand, the jurisdiction, which involves some 50 Departments of State, public offices and even a quango or two, yields a sufficient volume of complaints to make it hard work for one man to be able to take a personal interest in each of them. A larger office with a wider jurisdiction and a much greater volume of work would quickly develop into and be seen as the Department of Complaints with all those disadvantages which need no rehearsal. On the other hand, there remain two kinds of complaint which both the Select Committee on the Parliamentary Commissioner and I have thought that I ought to be able to examine. These are personnel and contractual or commercial matters. I remain of the opinion that complaints of these two types ought to be brought within my jurisdiction, at any rate within certain limits and I regret that no Government has acceded to the strong recommendations of successive Select Committees in favour of that liberalisation of this Office's functions. Again, this restriction is, so far as I know, peculiar to this country: and indeed peculiar in part to England, Wales and Scotland since the Parliamentary Commissioner in Northern Ireland does examine complaints about personnel matters.

Annual Report of the Parliamentary Commissioner for Administration, 1983

In 1973 the Offices of Health Service Commissioners for England, Wales and Scotland were established. The Parliamentary Commissioner holds all three posts. People may complain directly to him in matters alleging injustice caused by either failure or maladministration on the part of a health authority, although the complainant must notify the health authority of his or her grievance in the first instance. Thus in health matters (unlike issues that concern the PCA) an individual may complain directly to the Commissioner, whose terms of reference, by including 'failure' as well as 'maladministration', are wider than those of the Parliamentary Commissioner. The Health Service Ombudsman may not investigate matters involving the clinical judgement of medical staff nor can he investigate complaints against doctors, dentists, pharmacists and opticians, whose professional standards are covered by various administrative tribunals. The Health Service Commissioner receives about 500 complaints a year, of which approximately half are rejected on jurisdictional grounds (primarily because they involve issues of clinical judgement). The Commissioner completes full investigations into about 100–50 complaints a year of which about half are found to be justified.

Local ombudsmen

The Local Government Act 1974 established three commissioners for local government in England and one in Wales. They may investigate complaints about local government and regional water authorities, as well as local authorities in their capacity as police authorities (except that of London, which is responsible in police matters directly to the Home Secretary). Again the definition of maladministration was left to the Commissioners to decide, but the Commissioners have followed the practice of the central government Ombudsman in making it clear to complainants that maladministration means neglect, unjustifiable delay and incompetence, but not the actual merits of decisions.

Case-Load for the English Local Commission for Administration

Year	Total number of complaints received directly	% of directly received complaints referred correctly at later stage	Total number of complaints properly referred	% of referred complaints relating to housing/ planning	% of cases investigated where maladministration causing injustice was found
1978/79	1899	44	2116	61	58
1979/80	1598	43	2181	67	54
1980/81	1765	47	2434	66	53
1981/82	1953	50	2706	63	57
1982/83	2045	50	2753	65	54
1983/84	2145	50	3034	68	63
1984/85	2050	50	3389	68	66
1985/86	2007	50+	3502	70	67

Source: *Annual Reports of the Local Commission for Administration in England*

In the first instance complaints have to be directed (as in the case of central government via MPs) through a local councillor or to the local authority concerned, but there is a degree of flexibility in so far as if a satisfactory reply is not received, reference may then be made directly to the Local Commissioner. Under the Local Government Act 1978 councils have powers to compensate complainants.

Annual reports from the Commissions for Local Administration show that most complaints concern decisions on planning, housing and education. Four types of matter are excluded from investigation: (a) certain education matters, including the internal organisation of schools and colleges; (b) personnel matters, including dismissals and pay; (c) the commencement or conduct of civil or criminal proceedings before any court of law; and (d) the investigation or prevention of crime, including all such actions taken by the police forces. The revised procedure for complaints about police officers is now covered by the Police and Criminal Evidence Act 1984.

See also J.R.S. Whiting, Politics and Government, Stanley Thornes, 1985, (sections D and E)

The 1984 Act came into force in 1986; it is therefore too early to determine whether certain public fears that the police have become too powerful are grounded. Worries about the role of the modern, technologically equipped police force were accentuated during the miners' strike of 1984–5, not least in respect of the use of centralised computers and the apparent lack of detailed accountability to local police committees.

DOCUMENT

12

The Work of the Local Commissioner

80.   Complaints must be referred through a Member of the authority complained against, unless there is evidence that a Member has been asked to refer the complaint but has not done so. In the year ended 31 March 1985 the three Local Ombudsmen in England received 3,389 complaints, including 395 accepted because members had been asked to refer them but had not done so. The total compared with 3,034 in the previous year, an increase of 12%. The main subjects of complaints continued to be housing (38%) and planning (30%).

81.   Consideration of 3,284 complaints was completed in that year. The figure includes 857 complaints on which work was in progress at the start of the year.

897 (27%) – were examined but investigation was not pursued because the complaints were outside jurisdiction, or plainly contained no element of maladministration, or because the complaint was settled locally. The average time to consider a complaint to this stage was four weeks.   95

1,997 (61%) – investigation was terminated after consideration of the complaint as submitted and of comments obtained from the authority, or because the complaint was settled locally. The average time to consider a complaint to this stage was 15 weeks.

98 (3%) – investigation was discontinued at a later stage either because it became clear there had been no maladministration or because the complaint was settled locally. The average time for these investigations was 34 weeks.

292 (9%) – investigation continued to the issue of a formal report. The average time for these investigations was 41 weeks.

82. The number of complaints settled locally in the year was 483 or 15% of all complaints considered. [. . .] apart from local settlements, 2,459 complaints were not investigated to the issue of a formal report.

83. In the year ended 31 March 1985 there were 2,050 complaints received direct compared with 2,145 in the previous year, a decrease of 4%. Prior to 1 June 1984, people making a complaint direct were advised of the correct procedure. About half of these complaints later came back properly referred. Some others were satisfactorily settled when taken to a Member, but some did not come back to the Local Ombudsman even though they would have justified investigation.

88. When injustice caused by maladministration is found the authority have to consider the formal report issued and say within a reasonable time what action they have taken or propose to take.

89. The table below shows the number of cases where injustice through mal-administration was found and how many of these had been settled to the satisfaction of the Local Ombudsman by 31 March 1985.

Year	Report Finding M & I	Satisfactory settlement	Unsatisfactory outcome	Awaiting settlement
1974/81	896	831	65	–
1981/82	158	147	11	–
1982/83	170	158	10	2
1983/84	202	186	5	11
1984/85	193	120	1	72
Totals	1,619	1,442	92	85

90. The Commission record their concern, as in previous years, at the time taken in many cases before an authority provide a satisfactory remedy for injustice.

91. The figures given in paragraph 89 show that at 31 March 1985 the outcome was known for 1,534 cases where injustice was found. In only 92 (6%) of those cases did the authority not take action satisfactory to the local Ombudsman. This figure may not seem high, but each case represents 100% failure for the person involved.

92. If a Local Ombudsman is not satisfied with an authority's response to a critical report, he must issue a further report setting out the facts. In practice that report records the action which the authority should, in his view, take to remedy the injustice. Because a further report is the last formal action that a Local Ombudsman can take to help a complainant, the Commission naturally hope that such reports will produce remedies. Unfortunately, to date, only one in five further reports has had the desired effect. Since

the local Ombudsmen started work in 1974, they have issued 128 further reports but satisfactory remedies followed in only 27 of these cases.

FINDINGS OF MALADMINISTRATION

93. The following are illustrations of actions (or inactions) which the Local Ombudsmen found in 1984/85 as maladministration following investigation of complaints:

Housing

- delay in dealing with an application for a repairs grant
- misleading advice given about eligibility of certain items for an improvement grant
- inadequate inspection of work carried out with the aid of an improvement grant
- delay in dealing with the completion of the sale of a Council house
- misleading advice given to Council tenants about the proposed purchase of their homes and failure to compensate them in the same way as other tenants who had been similarly misled
- delay in processing claims for housing benefit
- failure to carry out essential repairs to a Council house
- failure to provide satisfactory temporary accommodation during modernisation of a Council house
- failure to respond adequately to complaints about damp
- shortcomings in the way a Council dealt with rehousing a homeless family
- failure to deal effectively with Council tenants' complaints about the unsocial behaviour of a neighbouring tenant

Planning

- failure to ensure that a house was constructed in accordance with the approved plans
- failure to refer a planning application to the Planning Committee
- failure to notify the complainants, contrary to the Council's policy, of a planning application to construct a block of flats on a site adjoining their property
- failure to take action to prevent a complainant's neighbour using his house in connection with a second-hand car business
- failure to inform an applicant of the conditions attached to the granting of planning permission
- failure to take adequate action to deal with the problems caused by dust and noise from a saw mill near the complainants' home
- failure to take due account of the effect of a proposed development on neighbouring properties
- failure to prevent or terminate the unauthorised use of Council owned land
- failure to take action when a temporary planning permission expired
- failure to implement a Planning Committee's decision to take enforcement action against the unauthorised use of a site

Education

- failure of an Education Appeal Committee to follow its publicised policy
- failure to provide the correct information about fees for a course at a College of Further Education
- failure to give the reasons for the refusal of an application for assistance towards the cost of boarding education for a gifted child
- consideration of an application for a grant on the basis of incomplete information
- misleading information given about eligibility for the reimbursement of travelling costs incurred when attending university interviews

Social Services

- shortcomings in the way a Council considered an application for a free travel pass under a disabled persons' concessionary fares scheme
- delay in notifying the complainants of the withdrawal of their registration as foster parents under the Special Foster Parent Scheme
- failure to deal adequately with a complaint about the care of a resident in an old people's home

Highways

- delay in taking effective action to prevent the unauthorised parking of vehicles on common land and on a public highway
- failure to take due account of objections to a Traffic Regulation Order
- delay in the making-up of a grass verge prior to the adoption of a highway
- failure to keep a footpath and bridleway free from obstructions

Land

- failure to obtain the necessary deemed planning consent to remove a fence and establish a footpath
- use of a site for waste disposal without the necessary licence required under the Control of Pollution Act 1974
- failure to take effective steps to remedy the unsightly state of a piece of derelict land

Drainage

- failure to take into account the effect of additional development on existing drainage facilities
- failure to safeguard water supplies when granting a waste disposal licence

Environmental Health

- failure to take effective action to prevent nuisance to residents from the operation of a nearby business
- failure to prevent unauthorised tipping of waste and to control emissions of smoke and smell from a nearby site

Rating

- shortcomings in dealing with an application for rate relief

Leisure and Recreation

- imposition of an unjustified ban on the complainant preventing him hiring or entering one of the Council's halls

Commercial
- failure to observe a Code of Practice relating to the drawing up of lists of approved contractors
- shortcomings in the way of a Council awarded a contract for micro-filming some of their records
- shortcomings in the administration of street trading in a high street

The Local Ombudsmen: *Annual Report, 1984–5*

A Bill of Rights

One line of thought presupposes that the whole problem of openness in government, redress of grievances and individual privacy could be more rationally dealt with if there were established a national and comprehensive Bill of Rights which would set out clearly the fundamental rights and freedoms of each citizen. A further step would be to set down all the rules of the political system – in short, to have a completely written constitution. The parallel, of course, is the United States of America. There the first ten amendments to the constitution form its Bill of Rights and it is the Supreme Court which, although political rather than strictly judicial in composition, is the lynch-pin of the American view of liberty. This was shown in the famous Brown judgment in 1954 (about the question of racial segregation in schools), in its upholding of the Civil Rights Act 1964 (discrimination generally) and the Voting Rights Act 1965 (which outlawed such things as literacy tests), and in 1974 in its judgment forcing President Nixon to hand over the secret Watergate tapes.

Equally, it can be argued that the mere existence of a new document does not guarantee anything. If a Bill of Rights were introduced in the United Kingdom what would happen to the notion of parliamentary supremacy? Moreover, although a Bill of Rights might, for example, limit the all-embracing powers of the 1911 Official Secrets Act, it has by no means limited the US Government in many of its executive actions, such as the restrictions on immigration from 1919 and Roosevelt's detention of thousands of Japanese-Americans in concentration camps during the Second World War. Similarly, although a Bill of Rights might have been useful in the Crossman Diaries case, it made little difference in the closest American analogy, the Pentagon Papers case in 1971. Determined legislative majorities have not as a rule been unduly deterred by it either.

In the United Kingdom would the House of Lords be turned into a US-style Supreme Court, the guardian of a written constitution? Secondly, who enforces a Bill of Rights? A Bill of Rights does little by itself to change social attitudes such as those on race.

The argument for a Bill of Rights has more often than not come from the Conservative wing of British politics. For instance, Sir Keith Joseph has suggested that such a Bill would prevent episodes like the Clay Cross Urban District Council's defiance of the Housing Finance Act 1972, the campaign in 1974–5 for the release of the Shrewsbury building pickets, and the threat to editorial press freedom under the trade unions Bill in 1975–6. (Clay Cross UDC refused to introduce 'market rents' for their own tenants. The Shrewsbury case involved dimensions of criminal damage and conspiracy in relation to organised protests against certain provisions of the Industrial Relations Act 1971.)

The lack of a political consensus in the UK about a Bill of Rights was illustrated in 1978 and 1979 when attempts in the House of Lords to introduce a Bill of Rights were defeated. A short cut would be to enact the European Convention on Human Rights. The United Kingdom has in fact ratified the European Convention for the Protection of Human Rights and Fundamental Freedoms – it did so in 1951 – but Parliament has never adopted it in legislative form. Appealing to the European Commission on Human Rights at Strasbourg is a laborious process, although quite a few Britons undertake it. When all efforts at reconciliation have failed the European Commission sends a report to the Committee of Ministers of the Council of Europe. That report may be published, providing there is no objection and providing two-thirds of the Committee have found a breach of the Convention. Alternatively, the case can be referred from the Committee to the Court on Human Rights for a public hearing and a legal decision. In 1979 the European Court of Human Rights ruled (by 11–9) that the English law of contempt was incompatible with the Convention (article 10). The ruling was related to an appeal from *The Sunday Times,* which in 1972 had been prevented by the House of Lords from publishing an article about the thalidomide tragedy in view of the fact that the drug company (Distillers) was already involved in protracted litigation with the parents of deformed children. Prior to *The Sunday Times* case, prison rules were changed after the European Court's ruling in the Golder case in 1975 when the applicant was detained in a prison where serious disturbances broke out, leading to his seeking to bring defamation proceedings against a prison officer who had accused him of assault. Similarly there was a change in the way prisoners were questioned in the Maze prison in Northern Ireland as a result of another judgment against the British Government (1978). The Court also ruled against birching in the Isle of Man (1978), and corporal punishment in Scottish schools (1982). In 1985 certain immigration rules were judged as unlawful.

A Bill of Rights might at least provide the individual with a basic reference point to use, if necessary, against slow-moving bureaucratic machines, and it would mean that more senior officials, as well as ministers and councillors, would be answerable in public. Even so, most advocates of such a Bill recognise that it would only mean a small shift of power away from the Government towards the judges – who, in many left-wing eyes, appear in any case to be too pro-Establishment or conservative. These alleged conservative leanings on the part of many judges are, however, almost impossible to analyse objectively, and it should be pointed out that it was the judges who refused the Attorney-General his injunction to stop the publication of the Crossman Diaries in 1975, and who also resisted the recommendations of the Criminal Law Revision Committee in 1972 aimed at strengthening the powers of the prosecution in the rules for criminal evidence. No Bill of Rights is perfect; the value of such a Bill can only be determined in practice.

See M. Zander, *A Bill of Rights?*, 3rd edn., Sweet and Maxwell, 1985

But, whatever the provenance of a Bill of Rights, there remains the question of its relationship with legislation passed after its establishment. Ordinary legislation could conflict with a Bill, either deliberately or unconsciously. Two possible solutions have been suggested. Firstly, such legislation could become automatically invalid, a stipulation which, as already indicated, would conflict with the traditional rights of Parliament. Secondly, following the practice under the Canadian Bill of Rights of 1960, the legislation could be interpreted by the courts as being consistent with the Bill, unless it expressly stated otherwise.

Either way it is clear that the course would be full of parliamentary land-mines, particularly as the Westminster Parliament, if it adopted the European Convention, would still keep the right to withdraw from it any time, just as it was made clear in 1972 that Westminster could always reverse the Act binding the UK to membership of the EEC. The pathway towards the introduction of a Bill of Rights would be a stony one indeed.

Summary

Since 1972 and the publication of the Younger Report on Privacy and the Franks Report on official secrecy, there has been a growing public debate as to how confidences can be kept in a computerised age on the one hand, and how much more open government and official information should be on the other. These are not necessarily mutually exclusive aims, as was well illustrated by the Westland Affair in 1986, where as seen elsewhere (see Chapter 2) various confidences were broken, most notably the Solicitor-General's letter to the Defence Secretary, parts of which were deliberately released or 'leaked' by another government department (the Department of Trade and Industry) to the Press Association.

Franks recommended reform of section 2 (the 'catch-all' clause) of the 1911 Act in 1972, but it still survives, although for how much longer is a matter of speculation. To date the Campaign for Freedom of Information is still campaigning, but with the support of the Alliance and the Labour Party, and Sir Douglas Wass, former Permanent Secretary to the Treasury. All governments have used the system of unattributable briefings to accredited political correspondents from newspapers, television and radio, but whether the 'lobby system' is healthy for democracy or not is an issue on which senior political journalists and the lobby correspondents themselves are not totally united. Some take the view that if governments did not operate in this way, even less official information would be available. Others view it as a kind of government propaganda machine, which would disappear were section 2 reformed or abolished, or open government more liberally practised or a Bill of Rights enacted. Under the first seven years of Mrs Thatcher's Government there have been 34 inquiries into leaks of unauthorised information. In 1986 two newspapers, *The Guardian* and *The Independent*, decided to withdraw from the lobby system.

In recent years it has been the judges who have sometimes taken a minister to task. The courts have been more inclined to question ministerial decisions or discretion when challenged by an aggrieved person, and in this way the policy-making process has been liberalised or 'opened up' to some degree. But this is inevitably haphazard and unsatisfactory since it depends solely upon those who are prepared to embark on what may be a lengthy battle in court. Some of these cases, such as Tameside, have been examined earlier. In Britain there is no Supreme Court in the American sense that can interpret a written constitution and politically challenge the Government. Its absence, however, is not necessarily to be deplored, for in the last three decades or so the judges of the US Supreme Court have sometimes found themselves entering into fierce political debate as a result of their judgments.

Other issues concerned with civil liberties in recent years have centred upon the role of the police and the redress of grievances. In respect of the former the police have found themselves drawn into industrial and political disputes (for example, the miners' disputes in 1972 and 1984 and their role in relation to certain inner-city areas such as Liverpool (Toxteth) and Brixton in London in 1981). The Police and Criminal Evidence Act 1984 (effective from 1986) has introduced new machinery for public complaints about police action. In respect of public complaints about maladministration by civil servants and local government officers there have existed commissioners since 1967 and 1974 respectively, but the extent of public awareness about the national and local ombudsmen must be questioned.

Questions

1. 'The opportunities for individual citizens to gain redress for their grievances are many but still inadequate.'

(a) Describe *two* of the opportunities open to the individual.

(b) Evaluate the effectiveness of these two opportunities and suggest improvements. (AEB specimen question 1986)

2. Discuss the assertion that there is too much secrecy in British politics. (AEB specimen question 1986)

3. What did the Fulton Report mean by 'Open Government'? (London)

4. Critically appraise the role performed by Ombudsmen in the British system of government and politics. (Joint Matriculation Board)

4   Policy and the Civil Service

"I am very much against opposition parties having detailed policies for everything.'

The Conservative parliamentary spokesman for Trade.

The above quotation from *The Guardian* (14 August 1978) reflects the ritual of Parliament. While the House of Commons possesses collective power, its policies are essentially the decisions of the Government, although on occasion MPs may influence what is usually accepted as the predestined course of legislative debate. Initially, of course, it is the Commons' role to produce a Government after an election, or possibly between elections should a Government, lacking an effective majority in the House, fall. However, policy is formulated and executed not just beyond the immediate precincts of the Palace of Westminster, but even outside of the Cabinet Room and Whitehall itself.

Government ministers produce policies and civil servants administer them. That is the simplistic theory. But many individuals and groups have a say, large or small, in the shaping of a particular proposal. Some, but by no means all, of these interested parties, from the public generally to the highly specialised Central Policy Review Staff, and some of the problems their involvement brings, are examined below.

Two of these problems recur constantly. Firstly, it is virtually impossible to make a clearly satisfactory distinction between policy and its administration for, as senior civil servants well know, the execution of a scheme can often become, in a complex world, a policy in itself. Secondly, as the above quotation again illustrates, policy is by no means always planned. The ability to solve problems on a *pragmatic* basis is often described as a British cultural trait. In that context the political parties are good examples with which to start.

The Political Parties

Richard Crossman once remarked that he viewed the annual conferences, comprising the constituency activists, as one of the most important elements in the political process. To a limited extent he was right, not least in the cases of the Labour and Liberal parties. Also, in both of those parties a National Executive Committee (NEC) fulfils an important role between the conferences. In the SDP policy is in the hands of the National Committee, on which there is strong parliamentary representation. The party activists, as more broadly represented in the Council for Social Democracy and the Annual Conference (the Consultative Assembly) only 'discuss' policy.

103

The Conservative Party Conference tends to be less of an in-depth debate over party philosophy and more a spiritual and political recharging for the party hierarchy. Nor in the Tory case is there an exact equivalent of a National Executive, although the committees of the National Union of Conservative Associations (NUCA) are important, as is the role of the Area Chairmen.

The Tory NUCA has a narrower brief than the NECs of the Labour and Liberal parties. Its main purpose is to provide administrative co-ordination between the various geographical parts of the Conservative organisation. This is not unlike the Liberal NEC, whose functions, however, do touch upon policy-making; in the Liberal party policy resolutions are more the province of the quarterly Party Council. For the Labour NEC, policy-making between annual conferences is a crucial activity. The NUCA, the Liberal Party Council/NEC and Labour's NEC consist of senior party activists from various parts of the country and on the two NECs there is some form of parliamentary representation, as there is on the Central Council, and its Executive Committee, of the NUCA.

The annual conferences

However, it is the party conferences themselves which face the real difficulties in controlling policy once formulated. In 1976, for example, both the Liberal and Labour conferences proved something of an embarrassment to their leaderships. The Liberal Assembly produced a

The Guardian,
18 September
1976

'nasty surprise for the party's leadership . . . when it tossed out the main plank in the Liberal economic platform . . . John Pardoe (the Liberal parliamentary economic spokesman) asked bitterly: "Since when is it a major purpose of the party to defeat a major section of itself? Is that the sum total of your contribution to defeating unemployment? We are not going to defeat it by going back to the laws of the jungle." '

And, interviewed on television later, Mr Pardoe commented that the parliamentary party would ignore such antics by the annual conference. Similarly, when interviewed by Sir Robin Day of the BBC at the beginning of the 1979 Assembly, the Liberal leader, David Steel, stated that the parliamentary party would take little heed of a motion (if passed) urging British military withdrawal from Northern Ireland. In 1986 the Assembly rejected the leadership's proposals for nuclear defence, but Mr Steel, with Dr Owen, immediately embarked on a 'damage limitation' exercise.

Financial Times,
10 October 1978

Sir Charles Johnston, chairman of the Executive Committee of the NUCA, was reported a short while before the Conservative Conference in 1978 as saying: 'Nothing the representatives say or do in Brighton will have any direct effect on the party's manifesto.'

In the case of the Labour party the position is rather more serious, since from a *governmental* point of view the party conference is that much more important. The 1976 Conference occurred at a time when sterling was under severe financial pressure on the international money markets; yet despite some dire warnings from the Prime Minister and the Chancellor of the Exchequer, the Conference succeeded in passing a motion to nationalise the banks and another motion against the holding of direct elections for the European Parliament, as well as one which resisted its own Government's proposals for public expenditure cuts and positively urged local authorities to spend to their previously planned targets. As L.J. Sharpe has commented,

> 'Unlike the situation in the Conservative Party, the leadership is given much less leeway, and if it gets too far out of step it must either face a revolt or compromise. In short, as Samuel Beer has shown, conflict over policy is the Labour Party's very pith and substance.'

New Society, 13 July 1972

Beer's point was never better illustrated than by the occasion of Hugh Gaitskell's defeat (over his pro-nuclear arms policy) at the 1960 Labour Conference. Gaitskell's authority as party leader was soon reasserted, and the Conference of 1961 reversed the decision of the previous year. In 1979 the Conference voted to give the NEC the sole right to draw up the party's election manifesto: no longer would the PLP share that task, it would merely be consulted by the NEC; but this policy was reversed at the 1980 Conference.

Moreover, the trade unions affiliated to the Labour Party, with their block votes at the annual conference, have frequently played an important role. Yet they cannot be identified with either the left- or right-wing of the party, for two reasons: firstly, when Labour is in Opposition the trade unions will at conference time rally very much to the middle ground of the movement in attacking the seemingly negative policies of the Conservative Government, with united pleas for the repeal of particularly 'reactionary' pieces of Tory legislation (such as the Housing Finance Act in 1972, the Industrial Relations Act of the year before and the Employment Acts 1980 and 1982). Secondly, when the party is in power the trade unions may agree to an economic policy which does not necessarily come from the left of the party. For example, they upheld at Conference the £6 and £4 a week policies for limiting wage increases under the Social Contract, from 1975 to 1977. This took place despite the fact that the unions' inclination was to maintain free collective bargaining, which had been used to such good effect in 1974. The four largest unions exercising the block vote are the TGWU, AUEW, GMBATU and NUPE.

In addition to the trade union influence on Labour policy there has been, as L.J. Sharpe has pointed out, a strong university contribution (notably from the London School of Economics). This has included people such as Richard Titmuss, Peter Townsend and Brian Abel-Smith in respect of policies on poverty and social services, while other academics (such as Nicholas Kaldor, Stuart Holland and Thomas Balogh between 1964 and 1977) have acted as special economic advisers to Labour Governments. Ex-academics became involved in the party leadership itself, notably R.H.S. Crossman but also Patrick Gordon Walker, Anthony Crosland and Douglas Jay, as well as Gaitskell and Wilson themselves.

Furthermore, there exist policy committees of the Parliamentary Labour Party, although they are weak in comparison with their Conservative opposites, and the more important and influential trade unions in any case have their own research departments. But in one particular sense none of this detracts from the prestige attached to the policy-making role of the annual party conference, even if in all parties that function tends to be symbolic rather than politically meaningful. Party leaders, however, have to take heed of the mood and direction of the conference, even if they frequently ignore the fine print.

The constituency and regional organisations certainly take their party conferences seriously. In the 1976 Conservative Conference handbook, for example, there were no less than 1529 resolutions, three times as many as ten years before. But the Labour party forms a contrast in being much more prepared to disagree internally and in public in its examination of policy motions, and if necessary to rebuff its parliamentary hierarchy, most of whom will not be members of the conference platform if they are not also NEC members. As Ian Aitken has put it,

The Guardian,
24 September
1976

'even the most cursory reading of the rules of the two parties suggest that, whereas the Conservative conference is designed as a rally of the faithful, Labour's week by the seaside is the genuine article in terms of democratic policy-forming. All you have to do, according to the rule book, is to get a two-thirds majority and your opinions become part of Labour's election platform.'

In fact choosing which motions will be discussed is a delicate business, and in all four major parties this is to some extent left in the hands of the party's hierarchy or one of its committees, although in the case of the Liberals, constituencies are given the chance to ballot for their preferences on the preliminary conference agenda.

A party conference: the Conservatives in 1969

The Guardian, in the middle of 1976 (21 July), commented upon how the 1976 Labour Conference agenda had been 'fixed'. It revealed, for instance, that although more than 30 constituencies had submitted motions concerning the re-selection of MPs (in view of the constituency difficulties of Reg Prentice and some other MPs at that time), none had been called, since the five-member conference committee had used its discretion under the 'three-year rule'; this meant that motions might not be allowed if similar ones had occurred within the previous three years. Yet, as Professor Anthony King has remarked the Conservatives have 'nothing remotely comparable to Labour's quasi-democratic procedures, with their formally constituted committees all responsible to the National Executive and ultimately to annual conference. As many individuals may participate on the Tory side, sometimes more; but they work in private.'

The Guardian,
24 September
1976

Labour's NEC

In the Labour Party the position of its National Executive Committee, elected annually by the Conference, with the Leader and Deputy Leader of the party as ex-officio members, becomes crucial when a Labour Government is in office, since Labour ministers have frequently appeared to the NEC to depart from party philosophy. The trade unions, with 12 seats, form the largest group.

Following Wilson's retirement as party leader in 1976, Mr Callaghan clearly wished to avoid the problems that had been created because of the way Wilson had treated the NEC (and therefore the party conference) in his last years as party leader. He was not successful. In 1972 a new TUC-Labour Party Liaison Committee was set up, consisting of the front-bench team, members of the TUC general council, officers of the Parliamentary Party, and, almost as an afterthought, representatives of the NEC. It was this body which cemented the alliance between the Labour Government and the TUC in the form of the Social Contract of 1974–7 on prices and wages.

The Labour NEC consists of two main committees, the Home Policy and International Committees on domestic and foreign affairs respectively. These committees since 1985 have been serviced by the Policy Development department. The streamlining of Labour Party headquarters has reduced the number of departments to three – the other two being the Organisation department and the Campaigns and Communications department. The third policy committee is the Local Government Committee; two other NEC sub-committees are Organisation and Campaign Strategy.

There is often greater tension between Labour ministers and the party's research groups than between their Conservative counterparts. This tension 'seems to be reinforced by a deep suspicion of civil servants who, the [research] department feels, are always more accommodating to their opposite numbers in the Conservative party when the Conservatives are in power' (L.J. Sharpe). The Research Department was reduced to

'complaining, in Labour's evidence to the Fulton committee, that some ministers were just 'tools' of their civil servants. It may be that Labour's leaders find the party's policy-making machinery so inadequate in Opposition that they resolve half-consciously to have nothing to do with it in government' (Anthony King).

The Conservative machine

In the Conservative case an important development under Heath between 1965 and 1970, when in Opposition, was the setting up of some 30 different policy groups. These were usually chaired by the appropriate shadow minister and consisted mainly of a mixture of MPs and outside experts; such groups helped the Tories fill in the details of their policies for the General Election of 1970.

Besides the permanent and important influence of the Research Department at Conservative Central Office, another vital element in Tory policy-making has been the Advisory Committee on Policy. This has principally consisted of representatives from the parliamentary party (usually two peers and five MPs elected by the parliamentary party, separately, in both Houses) and from the party in the constituencies (eight members from the National Union Executive Committee), as well as a number of ex-officio members, including the party Chairman. 'Unlike Labour's NEC, the Advisory Committee on Policy has no formal policy-making status; but it does have a traditional claim to be consulted, to advise and warn.' Since Professor King made that remark, however, the Conservative picture has been complicated a little further by the establishment in 1975 of the Centre for Policy Studies (CPS), initially under Sir Keith Joseph. It appears to serve as a kind of miniature 'think-tank' within the party machine. It is, however, the Conservative Research Department which has serviced the Advisory Committee on Policy as well as the 20 or so back-bench subject groups in the House of Commons. The role of the Conservative Research Department should not be underestimated; it has been at the heart of many a manifesto commitment. The Advisory Committee on Policy is still very much in existence, although in a less vigorous manner than formerly. It meets about four or five times a year and its current membership is: one peer, six MPs, eight members from the NUEC, four ex-officio members and seven co-opted ones.

New Society,
20 July 1972

See J. Ramsden,
*The Making of
Conservative Party
Policy: The Con-
servative Research
Department since
1929,* Longman,
1980

Both the party conferences and the permanent party machinery, whether in the shape of a national executive committee, a research department or an advisory policy committee, play a part in the policy formulation of the major parties. That part is often understated; nevertheless, like many things in political science, it is difficult to quantify precisely. It is possible to argue that since 1945 the parliamentary parties have increasingly ignored the party activists. Certainly in Labour's case many younger, left-wing party workers came to feel that Mr Wilson as Prime Minister had consistently disregarded the resolutions passed by the annual conference and the NEC. Sometimes genuine attempts are made to counteract this trend; for example, in 1970, working on an idea of the Swedish Social Democrats, the Labour Party asked its constituency associations to send in comments on some two dozen possible 'areas of study': '543 local parties responded and it is estimated that about 10 000 party members took part in the discussions on the questionnaire' (L.J. Sharpe). But perhaps in the final analysis the role of party conferences only amounts to that described by a journalist in *The Guardian* (24 September 1976) – 'the party workers enjoy rubbing shoulders with the leaders. For the rest of the year they slave away, addressing envelopes in the constituencies.'

Ten years later, Peter Kellner has taken the same line, posing two questions about the annual gatherings of the political activists:

The Independent,
13 October 1986

'The first is do they determine party policy? Hardly ever. They *make* policy in the sense that resolutions are passed. But they have little or no leverage on their party leaderships. The Liberal Assembly "decided" last month that Polaris should not be replaced, yet if Mr Steel wishes to write a pro-nuclear defence policy into the Alliance's next election manifesto, he can and will.

Even resolutions that achieve a two-thirds majority at Labour conferences do not bind the party leader. As long as he commands a majority at the "Clause V" meeting of shadow cabinet and national executive members before each election, he decides what goes in the manifesto and, more significantly, what is left out.

Do conferences expose alternative views to rigorous examination? On the contrary: their very format excludes serious debate. Real political choices are complex, their consequences uncertain. A hall containing three thousand activists looking for heroes to cheer and dragons to slay is the last place for rational examination.

A Labour conference could never explore rationally the alternative risks of nuclear power and coal-burning power stations. No Conservative conference could unravel the case for or against joining the European Monetary System. The real arguments take place elsewhere, away from constituency delegates and television cameras.

The SDP has a better record than the other parties of holding candid, reasoned debates. This has something to do with its size: should it ever grow large enough to pull the levers of power, the SDP's conferences are likely to lose their seminar-like quality.

At least the Conservative conference has the merit of not pretending to have any democratic purpose. It is, technically, a gathering of the National Union of Conservative Associations. The union is legally separate from the party leadership. Norman Tebbit is "Chairman of the Conservative Party Organisation" and answers directly to Mrs Thatcher rather than the union and its members.

The conference has no chance to elect or depose the union's officers, or to approve its accounts or discuss the executive's decisions. The union's equivalent of an annual general meeting does not take place in October, but at its Central Council meeting each March.

Conferences do not, in fact, exist principally for those who attend them at all. True, many delegates enjoy their week by the sea. They rub shoulders with the famous; they talk and drink and socialise with each other; many of them go home inspired to work harder for their party's success. But these are secondary purposes. The main function of conference delegates is to act as a loyal stage army, visibly serving the leadership for the benefit of the television-viewing public. Party conferences have as much to do with real politics as Cecil B. de Mille's epics have to do with real history.'

Whitehall, the CPRS and Special Advisers

In 1970 it was the Heath Government which, from a ministerial as opposed to a more general party point of view, introduced an important addition to the policy-forming process, in the shape of the CPRS (the Central Policy Review Staff). The CPRS, popularly known as the 'Think-Tank', to some extent gave the Civil Service a new stimulus in the way policy suggestions were presented and in the way performance was reviewed; but on the other hand it did little to lift the cloud of secrecy which usually shrouds most of the central bureaucracy. As Robert Taylor has said, 'everyone, from the permanent secretary to cleaners, is sheltered behind the hallowed dogma of ministerial responsibility.'

New Society
14 March 1974

See Appendix A

The functions of the erstwhile CPRS are discussed below. But first, what is the nature of the ministerial-civil servant relationship in the policy-making process?

It should be noted that some civil servants do not refrain from speaking their minds, when they think a wrong policy is being pursued. For example, in late 1973 the Permanent Secretary at the Department of Trade and Industry (Sir Robert Marshall), viewing the attitude of his minister (Peter Walker) towards the oil crisis as complacent, called for conservation measures, including petrol rationing, to be taken as quickly as possible. As a result Sir Robert was moved from his post to another department (Environment) – a rare occurrence – but in the longer term Mr Walker lost that particular battle.

Sir Jack Rampton (Permanent Secretary at the Department of Energy 1974–80) emphasised in 1976 that a Permanent Secretary must have a good working relationship with his minister. Civil servants in Britain must be very careful to know what ministers want done. Equally, a senior official must be able to tell the minister what, in the civil servants' view, should be done:

The Guardian,
12 October 1977

'Sir Jack talks about the tension between what is politically attractive and what is "practical" . . . Sir Peter Carey, Permanent Secretary at the Department of Industry, had to face Mr Benn at a time when, as Minister for Industry, he was actively trying to encourage the setting up of industrial co-operatives supported by public funds. Sir Peter went so far as to send Mr Benn what is known as "a permanent secretary's note", dissenting from the decision to give aid to the Kirby Co-operative. . . . But it was, and is, left to the Cabinet, and in the last resort the Prime Minister, to decide how and when to change the direction of policies and when to assert the convention of collective responsibility. . . .'

The need, Richard Norton-Taylor observed, for greater political control over the Civil Service was highlighted by Alex Lyon's dismissal from his job as Minister of State at the Home Office in 1976 for liberal views on immigration policy.

'As with DHSS officials, Home Office civil servants become case-hardened . . . Whitehall mandarins persistently give the impression when they talk about Ministers as though they see themselves rather like housemasters, cautious guardians of the establishment, talking to new prefects. From the top table, they look on the temporary tenants of political office with an air of scepticism. . . . Civil servants resent MPs blaming them for being coy during Select Committee hearings. "It is not our job to defend policies," says one, "all we can do is to explain them." '

The CPRS, as a kind of counter-civil service, did little to challenge the traditional nature of the relationship between senior civil servants and their political masters.

The CPRS

The most immediate criticism of the CPRS, however, was that the longer a Government had been in office, the more the CPRS seemed to become involved in day-to-day policy-making and the less in forward planning, and the less was there a clear distinction between it and the rest of the Cabinet Office. In fact, when Lord Rothschild was appointed as the first head of the Think-Tank in 1970, the Prime Minister told him that his job was to stimulate, 'not irritate'. Sir Richard Clarke (a former Permanent Secretary) in a series of lectures to the Civil Service College in 1971 warned that if three separate bodies, the Treasury, the Civil Service Department and the CPRS, started to pull in different directions then there would be 'a critical weakening of the centre.' *New Trends in Government, HMSO, 1971*

The CPRS was both an advisory body for the Prime Minister and a kind of supplementary organisation to the Cabinet, acting as a horizontal link between Government departments where the Cabinet could not be expected in modern circumstances to resolve satisfactorily every issue of significance.

Lord Rothschild himself wrote in *The Times* (5 September 1977) that one senior member of his team had observed that the functions of the Think-Tank were

> 'sabotaging the ever-smooth functioning of the machinery of government; providing a central department which has no departmental axe to grind but does have overt policy status and which can attempt a synoptic view of policy; providing a central reinforcement for those civil servants in Whitehall who are trying to retain their creativity and not be totally submerged in the bureaucracy; trying to devise a more rational system of decision-making between competing programmes; advising the Cabinet collectively, and the Prime Minister on major issues of policy relating to the Government's strategy; focusing the attention of ministers on the right questions to ask about their own colleagues' business; bringing in ideas from the outside world.'

Lord Rothschild also commented that in his view central departments had been

> 'quite allergic to our briefs because they provided an independent analysis, by a group of people uncontaminated by years of Whitehall experience, of the subject under consideration.'

John Gretton interpreted the role of the Think-Tank as three-fold. In the first place it reviewed critically every six months the performance of the Government's main policies; secondly, in the short- to medium-term it looked at various policy alternatives, some of which had already been given as semi-commitments, such as those on the future of Concorde or the British computer industry, or on the deployment of oil resources – in other words it examined methods, rather than decisions to do something. Thirdly, part of the CPRS looked at longer-term policies and options, especially economic ones. *New Society, 1 March 1973*

Mrs Thatcher, however, was not enamoured by the existence of too many separate organisations within Whitehall, even if the CPRS may have been an interesting experiment in government strategy. Thus in 1979 she abolished the system of PAR – the long-term Programme Analysis Review committees which assessed departmental objectives and priorities and reassessed performance in the light of those objectives. In 1981 she abolished the Civil Service Department, its principal functions returning to the Treasury, and in 1983 the CPRS itself.

In 1977 the CPRS examined the role of the highly-competitive Diplomatic Service (in 1978 there were 1185 applicants for just 20 graduate jobs), with a view to slimming down the number of diplomats and attachés overseas. It was this investigation – the so-called Berrill Report – together with another, on the UK's overseas representation (principally by the Foreign Office, but also through the BBC, the British Council and other bodies), which received considerable media attention, and which perhaps signed the CPRS's own death warrant. In fact, the final version of the CPRS's report on the Diplomatic Service in 1977 was much milder than that originally envisaged by press reports, owing to internal pressure from the Foreign Office; a proposal to merge the Diplomatic Civil Service with the Home Civil Service was quietly dropped. At about the same time Think-Tank suggestions to reorganise the Treasury into two or three separate departments, concentrating respectively on accounting procedures and long-term economic strategy, were shelved after strong opposition from the Treasury itself.

The first head of the Think-Tank had been very much the Prime Minister's personal adviser, and was credited with being particularly influential in bringing about the change of attitude on incomes policy in 1972 and in persuading Mr Heath to open tripartite talks with the TUC and CBI. This all changed following the return of Harold Wilson in March 1974. Wilson also established a Policy Unit in No. 10, initially under Lord Donoughue, that works only for the Prime Minister, but more on short- rather than on long-term projects.

Shortly after the General Election in 1983 Mrs Thatcher decided that the CPRS had outlived its usefulness, not least because many departments had by then developed their own mini-Think-Tanks. It is probably true to say that the CPRS had the greatest effect upon government policy and the Whitehall machine during the Rothschild period (1971–4).

Political advisers

Mr Wilson, in his Governments of 1964–70, introduced into the administrative system various advisers from the universities – the so-called 'Whitehall irregulars'. This trend was encouraged again by Wilson upon his return to office in 1974, and appears to have caused some consternation in the Civil Service. The appointments in 1974 were of 'special advisers' (almost like the French ministerial *cabinets* or teams of advisers), many of whom had been undertaking research for the Labour Party in Opposition. Their number rose as high as 38.

By the end of 1976 most of the really significant advisers had left. Their position had not been helped by the leakage of Cabinet papers about the Child Benefit Scheme earlier in that year, and the new Prime Minister, Mr Callaghan, gave his full approval to the tightening up of Cabinet security by Sir John Hunt, the Cabinet Secretary. One of the difficulties for the special advisers appears to have been that they were hemmed in by Civil Service working conditions. For example, it seems that a request for Jack Straw, an adviser to Barbara Castle at the DHSS from 1974 to 1975, to be allowed to remain an Islington borough councillor in London had to be taken by Mrs Castle to Wilson personally.

A White Paper of 1978 indicated that the normal rule of two advisers per minister (usually a Secretary of State) was 'not immutable'. Mr Callaghan in the same year decided to change the rules and give the 'special advisers' greater security in employment. Initially they had been appointed as 'temporary' civil servants for a period of five years from April 1974, a requirement dropped in 1978. When Mrs Thatcher succeeded Mr Callaghan, the new Conservative Government cut back the number of political advisers and those it did employ were paid for out of party funds, as had been the case under Mr Heath's Government. Of Callaghan's Government 13 Cabinet and one non-Cabinet ministers had one or more special advisers. Callaghan himself had six special advisers (the Policy Unit). Labour's advisers were technically paid for by the Rowntree Trust. Mrs Thatcher's administration has 22 special advisers, mostly on five-year contracts.

The Civil Service: Government Observations on the 11th Report from the Expenditure Committee, 1976–7, Cmnd 7117, 1978

Professor G.W. Jones described the political adviser's role in this way:

'The special adviser examines policy papers for politically sensitive items; briefs the minister on political aspects; handles his political correspondence; chases up the minister's political requests, thinks about policy in political terms, links the minister to his party; contacts pressure groups on political issues; helps prepare speeches and statements for political occasions with a special concern for political presentation; and generally acts as aide, confidant, and dogsbody.

The Guardian, 22 June 1978

'He has no other master, unlike the civil servant, who has a commitment to the department, the service, and his official superiors. The adviser stays with his minister and leaves with him when he departs from office, whereas civil servants are moved around to suit the needs of the service.

'He enables the Minister to be more responsive to currents of opinion, outside the Civil Service and, indeed, strengthens the Minister's political control over his department.

'The special adviser is an *alter ego* for the busy Minister who lacks time and expertise to master alone the many problems that come before him, and helps him to be more effective and to do what he would do if he had an extra brain or pair of hands.'

However, although Mrs Thatcher reduced the number of political advisers, it was clear that she attached considerable importance to strengthening the Prime Minister's Office with the appointment of key expert advisers. These included Professor Alan Walters as an economic adviser, from 1981, and Sir Michael Palliser as a special adviser on foreign affairs, from 1982. Sir John Hoskyns proved to be a robust head of the Policy Unit from 1979 to 1982, but his aim to 'deprivilege' the Civil Service appeared thwarted by the Cabinet Office; after his departure he became a leading critic of the Whitehall machinery. Lord Rayner headed the Prime Minister's efficiency unit from 1979 to 1982. Its aim was to root out procedures and tasks in the Civil Service that were incompetent or redundant.

The Times, 24 March 1986

Efficiency units, policy advisers, the CPRS, political advisers, the Cabinet Office, whose head has been sole Head of the Home Civil Service since 1983, the CSD – all tended to suggest a patchwork quilt of a Prime Minister's Department. But Mrs Thatcher maintained there was no such intention to create a separate department of State at No. 10. Be that as it may, the separation of the Cabinet Office, policy advisers, the Policy Unit and the Management and Personnel Office (MPO) indicate something of a fragmented approach to policy making in prime ministerial quarters.

There was, however, a widespread feeling among the mandarins that the Civil Service under Mrs Thatcher had been brutalised, in the sense that it was perceived that Downing Street did not always feel that it and the Service were riding in the same political direction. In 1985 Sir Douglas Wass, former Permanent Secretary at the Treasury and joint head of the Home Civil Service from 1981 to 1983, suggested that the Head of the Civil Service should have the right to complain to MPs about undue political interference in appointments to senior Whitehall jobs, and officials who found ministers lying or falsifying records should also be able to report to a new Whitehall ombudsman (this was in the wake of the unsuccessful prosecution in 1985 under the Official Secrets Act of Clive Ponting, a senior civil servant, in respect of the *Belgrano* affair).

*The Political
Quarterly,
July–September
1985*

Public Consultation

Green Papers, White Papers

The introduction of the Think-Tank in 1970 was linked to the process of making central government a little more open and accessible to the general community. This development can also be seen in the introduction of the system of Green Papers and Consultative Documents. The first Green Paper was issued in early 1967, on the Development Areas (Regional Employment Premiums). Although the distinction between Green Papers and Consultative Documents is not always clear, the former appear to be addressed to as wide a selection of the public as possible for comments and views, while the latter are usually referred to particular organisations, for example that issued in February 1971 by the Welsh Office on the Reform of Local Government in Wales. The second White Paper on Devolution (November 1975) was described by Edward Short, Lord President of the Council, and then in charge of devolution plans, as a 'White Paper with green edges'. The same phrase was used by Douglas Hurd, the Home Secretary, in respect of the White Paper on Criminal Justice ten years later (March 1986). Arthur Silkin has remarked,

*Public
Administration,
Winter 1973*

'In some instances Green Papers have done no more than set out a list of possible alternatives. . . . In such cases it is reasonable to assume that the final decision, when it has been taken, has, at least to some extent, been influenced by comments from organisations or individuals. In other instances, Governments have themselves admitted that they have dropped some of their proposals because they have been unfavourably received either by organised groups or by informed opinion.'

Royal Commissions

Mention should also be made in passing of Royal Commissions and departmental committees of inquiry. Nowadays there is little practical difference between the two, although a Royal Commission has slightly grander status and usually a wider-ranging brief. Few of such Commissions and committees ever see their recommendations adopted in full, although some can nevertheless be extremely influential, for example, the Kilbrandon Commission on the Constitution in 1973.

Some departmental committees of inquiry receive greater attention by the media than Royal Commissions. Understandably the Annan Report (1977) on the future of broadcasting fell into such a category. Its main recommendation – that the fourth television channel should be allocated neither to the BBC nor to the IBA but to an independent OBA (Open Broadcasting Authority) – was accepted by the Labour Government in 1978. On the other hand, the Government refused to bring local radio under one roof and going beyond Annan's recommendations it proposed three new managing boards for the BBC (radio, television, external services). The Conservative Government elected in 1979 dropped the OBA scheme and decided instead to allocate ITV a second channel – Channel 4. Such was the Annan Report's influence upon policy-making.

It could also be suggested that committees of inquiry, because of the length of their deliberations, fail to attract members of the highest calibre who can ill-afford to give up large amounts of time. As a legal correspondent once wrote,

> 'the trouble with Royal Commissions is that they are unwieldy in numbers; contain too many people involved with particular interest groups; do their job on only a part-time basis, and, to put it bluntly, too often contain members of inferior ability and intellectual calibre. The combined effect of those factors is greatly to increase the time taken to produce a report, while diluting its quality, thus making it easier for a government to ignore its recommendations.'

The Times, 11 July 1978

Moreover, they are extremely costly operations to maintain.

Nevertheless, all Royal Commissions and departmental committees of inquiry are bound to give greatest emphasis not to their own opinions but to the evidence they receive from the witnesses that appear before them – organisations and individual members of the public. That being so, it might be thought that commissions and committees, with the concomitant interest of the media, do go some way towards making public consultation more of a reality than of a fiction.

⎯⎯⎯ The Nature of the Civil Service

The Crossman and Wolff viewpoints

R.G.S. Brown has said that a government department is only part of a larger social and policy-making system with which it merges at the edges; the larger system includes ministers, Parliament and the electorate. But the Whitehall organisation is an extremely powerful machine. As Richard Crossman wrote in his diaries,

R.G.S. Brown and D.R. Steel, The Administrative Process in Britain, 2nd edn., Methuen, 1979, p. 209

> 'the whole Department is there to support the Minister. Into his in-tray come hour by hour notes with suggestions as to what he should do. Everything is done

Richard Crossman,
*The Diaries of a
Cabinet Minister*,
Vol. 1, Hamish
Hamilton and
Jonathan Cape,
1975, vol. 1, p. 31

to sustain him in the line which officials think he should take. But if one is very careful and conscious, one is aware that this supporting soft framework of recommendations is the result of a great deal of secret discussion between the civil servants below.'

The controversial *New Society* account in 1976 (17 June) of the postponement of the Child Benefit Scheme also revealed how influential the hand of the Treasury was, and again Crossman (admittedly writing some years before the establishment of the new Civil Service Department) spoke of a relationship which

'makes so many higher civil servants willing to spy for the Treasury and to align themselves with the Treasury view even against their own Minister.'

Similarly, on another occasion he wrote in his diaries that at the end of a particular day a senior official had pushed into his hand a draft paper on the Rent Bill (1965) to approve:

'I took one glance. Practically everything we had achieved in that late-night meeting . . . had been removed from what was now a civil servants' document. It wasn't only written in Civil Service style: we had slipped back four-fifths of the way to the policy the *Ministry* wanted.'

Crossman was not the only one with suspicions about the workings of the Civil Service. The late Michael Wolff (who was Director-General of the Conservative Party Organisation from 1974 to 1975) in a series of articles in *The Times* (in 1976)

Richard Crossman

quoted Sir Eric Roll, a former Under-Secretary at the Treasury, as saying that the tradition that civil servants only carry out policy – that is, administer – had long been 'over-taken by reality'; and Wolff himself seemed to think that it was senior civil servants who were chiefly responsible for the excited debate about the change in industrial tactics at the time of the Chrysler Affair in 1975. Wolff remarked that Eric Heffer, a leading left-wing Labour MP, was of the opinion that civil servants had lots of 'potty ideas' which they attempted to get approved by some minister or other over the course of time. On the other hand, Sir Eric Roll commented that the Civil Service examined election manifestos very closely and tried to anticipate political events. During an election campaign civil servants may be forced to face both philosophical ways; as *The Guardian* (12 April) said during the 1979 campaign,

> 'In co-operation with the Cabinet Office, they are also preparing contingency briefs – one for the Tories and one in the event of Labour being returned to office.'

Equally valid was Lord Marsh's and Sir Monty Finniston's view that, while civil servants should not fail in their programmes and administration, they did not necessarily have to succeed – a stark contrast to the industrial situation. (Sir Monty Finniston was Chairman of the British Steel Corporation, 1973–6, Sir Richard Marsh Chairman of the British Railways Board, 1971–6.) Mr Heath, too, thought that civil servants were still well suited to running the Empire of 80 years ago, without corruption, but not totally geared to running a 'great industrial nation'. Lord Marsh thought that Civil Service control of policy could be seen in the fact that the nationalised industries had not really become more accountable to Parliament, but only the departments concerned.

The Times, 27 May 1976

One senior civil servant interviewed by Wolff commented that ministers who had never run anything in their lives were fascinated by the machine. 'They love to take it to pieces to see how it works and play with it.' But Sir Eric Roll commented, 'The machinery is so cumbersome and weighty that it is very difficult for an average minister to raise his head above the flood of paper that descends on him.'

The Times, 25 May 1976

However, in one sense all crucial aspects of national policy and its implementation come back to the office of the Prime Minister, since overall strategy rests with Downing Street. In key situations the Prime Minister cannot stand aside. Yet there may be occasions when he wishes to utilise an 'anti-machine'. This could take the form of special policy advisers or academic recruits (such as the 'Whitehall irregulars') or perhaps the CPRS, but the Prime Minister's best 'anti-machine' is the mass media. Michael Wolff concluded that no British Prime Minister would ever have the powers of the French or American President, or even of the German Chancellor. 'But he can determine the style and strategy of his administration by the company he chooses.'

The Times, 24 May 1976

Discussion of policy and its administration poses certain other questions. For instance, is it healthy for senior civil servants to be recruited from the middle- and upper-classes and from a public school background? Is there too much of a left-wing or right-wing bias amongst senior civil servants? Certainly the Labour Party has long been suspicious of 'establishment, conservative' leanings – but it is probably true to say that the main 'bias' is a departmental one; 'departmental identities' rather than Government ones, are paramount amongst senior civil

See also C. Leeds, Politics in Action, Stanley Thornes, 1986 (section C)

117

servants. Finally, is the Civil Service view too London-dominated? In fact only about 20 per cent of the 600 000 civil servants are based in London, but, judging by the extreme resistance that proposals to move some 31 000 staff from the capital to the regions (for example, to Glasgow) met in 1974 and 1975, the answer must be yes. (In 1979 the new Conservative Government largely abandoned these plans; less than 40 per cent of the original figure were in fact moved.) There has, however, been a slow trend during the last 20 years towards regional decentralisation, although most senior figures remain in London.

The Effects of Fulton

Report of the Committee on the Civil Service, Cmnd 3638, 1968

The Fulton Committee (1966–8) on the Civil Service did not mince words. Its first volume opened with the remarks that the Home Civil Service was still fundamentally the product of the nineteenth-century philosophy of the Northcote-Trevelyan Report. 'The tasks it faces are those of the second half of the twentieth century. This is what we have found and it is what we seek to remedy.'

One of the cornerstones of the Fulton Report's recommendations was the creation of a single unified grading structure to replace the separate departmental classes within the general administrative staff, and also to reduce the number of different grades within the service. The Treasury itself had proposed in its evidence to the Fulton Committee that the administrative and executive classes (of the general administrative branches) should be replaced by a single General Management Group of eight grades. The proposal to merge the clerical, executive and administrative class (or caste) systems was accepted without hesitation by the Government in 1968, but was a lengthy process and open to interpretation, as discussed below. The second Fulton proposal was that the professional and scientific classes ought to have a much better chance of reaching the top levels of the service. Lord Fulton, in evidence to a sub-committee of the Commons Expenditure Committee, in late 1976, spoke of the model French civil servant as 'the super technocrat born and bred out of the scientist', while Lord Crowther-Hunt, in his evidence said that what was needed were young people with knowledge of economics and international affairs, able to understand the problems of modern Britain, rather than those of ancient Greece or Rome.

At the time of the Report the distinction between 'administration' and 'experts' was a closely guarded one, although in 1969 the Davies Report found no special evidence of positive discrimination towards the holders of classics and history degrees from Oxford and Cambridge. The 'amateur tradition' of the British Civil Service has been one very hard to break, being based on the idea that administration is not so much a skill as an art which is best learned through experience, and which requires (at least until American thinking in management techniques crossed the Atlantic in the early 1960s) little, if any, formal post-entry training.

In this way the Permanent Secretaries and other leading figures of a government department do not have to be academically or professionally qualified in that particular department's work.

In contrast the chief officers of each department in local government (especially at county level) are invariably specialists in their own fields. The Chief Education Officer is always an ex-teacher, the County Architect an architect by previous profession, the County Surveyor, a qualified engineer, the County Treasurer, an accountant, and so on. Perhaps the reason is that as local authorities tend to be agencies of central government, the chief officers have, by tradition, been required to be specialists within their own local area. The Clerk or Chief Executive is more often than not a lawyer still, despite attempts to break out of that tradition, although a precedent was created in 1971, when Essex County Council appointed its County Planning Officer as its new Clerk, when the latter post fell vacant.

The 'enlightened amateur' argument, that is the argument of specialists versus generalists as top civil servants, is an on-going one, and one which certainly refuses to lie down very easily. For example, *The Guardian* ran an interesting, if somewhat provocative, series of articles on the Civil Service, and a comparison with France, between 18 and 22 April 1977. An opening article by Lord Crowther-Hunt on the higher eschelons of the Civil Service led to several postscripts in the newspaper: Sir Basil Engholm, a retired senior civil servant, commented that as he saw it the job of senior civil servants was to take and understand the advice of the experts in the different disciplines on any particular problem, to analyse and assess that advice, and to reach a balanced view on the pros and cons of different possible courses of action. Their job was also to manage staff and to organise the flow of work. They were 'general' managers who had, through experience, acquired a considerable skill as professional administrators.

'Indeed, the man who has practised and graduated in a particular discipline, and turns to general management, has to be especially careful not to use any expertise he may have, which will rapidly get out of date. If a general manager, for example, has started life as a vet, and still thinks and behaves like a vet, he will not be a very good general manager, and will not have the confidence of his staff to reach impartial decisions in which veterinary questions are involved. I have also known this to work the other way. For example, a general manager with an agricultural background may underplay the agricultural factors in a problem for fear he would be considered biased in their favour. The professional administrator whose original degree was not 'relevant', but 'educational', is sometimes better placed to become a good professional administrator because he has no biased 'relevance' to overcome. . . .'

Lord Crowther-Hunt's riposte to Sir Basil's included the following statement:

'First, take Sir Basil's business analogy. In so far as it is true that British business managers are, like top civil servants, generalists with irrelevant arts degrees topped up by management training and experience, this is one of the reasons why British industry is having such difficulty in matching our European competitors. In Western Germany, by way of contrast, engineers (not Sir Basil's generalists) are the biggest and most important single group among their top industrial managers while arts graduates (our form of generalists *par excellence*) play an insignificant role. So not much support there for Sir Basil's generalist thesis.' [The number of specialists getting top administrative jobs had risen from 38 per cent in 1970 to just 41 per cent in 1978.]

'Secondly, our civil service concept of the generalist plays a major role in producing the rapid movement of administrators between different jobs – to give them breadth of administrative experience rather than depth of knowledge about one area of issues and problems. Here the situation seems to have deteriorated in the last ten years . . .'

The third major recommendation that Fulton made was the creation of a Civil Service College to develop a whole range of post-entry training schemes, a recommendation which was also quickly adopted. The local government service, in contrast, was ahead of the Civil Service, as a result of the Mallaby Committee reporting some two years prior to Fulton, by which the Local Government Training Board was established for the purpose of providing standardised training schemes for all local authorities, although the amount of training provision will still vary from one local authority to another.

The Civil Service was therefore, in a sense, catching up with local government when it established the Civil Service College, although local authorities tend, instead of having one central college, to take advantage directly of the resources of universities, polytechnics and local colleges.

The fourth proposal of Fulton was that departments should establish planning units, ensuring that current policy decisions were taken with the fullest possible recognition of likely future developments. But the development of such planning units was spasmodic, since the creation in 1970 of a central 'Think-Tank' (to look at longer-term programmes and review Government efficiency) under the new Conservative Government to a large extent overtook events.

The fifth proposal of significance was that there should be far greater career mobility between the Civil Service and other employment. 'We therefore recommend the expansion of late-entry facilities, temporary appointments for fixed periods, short-term interchanges of staff and freer movement out of the service. These proposals involve substantial changes in the pension scheme and the replacement of "established" status by new terms of employment.' But the scheme, particularly in relation to private industry, was fraught with difficulty, for while there might be some incentive for civil servants to move across to the freer atmosphere of industry for a period, what inducement was there for industrialists to enter the Civil Service?

The sixth proposal of the Committee was that 'accountable units' should be established in the service with a clear chain of command, a rather vague managerial recommendation it might be thought, but it was part of the trends that were at work in local government and the nationalised industries too: the Report was merely saying, in no uncertain terms, that it found within the service too many muddled lines of communication, and these needed to be uncrossed; each official should be able to identify himself with a particular team and know to whom he was immediately responsible.

Other proposals

Other main proposals included one that there should be closer contact between the Civil Service and the community it serves, which could be achieved by going some way towards reducing the secrecy and anonymity surrounding civil servants. (This recommendation led to the appointment of the Franks Committee in 1972, on official secrecy.) The Report also said that a new Civil Service Department should be established having wider functions than the pay and management division of the Treasury (responsible for overall recruitment and conditions of service), and absorbing the latter as well as the Civil Service Commission (examinations and recruitment). The traditional Treasury dominance of the Civil Service, the report said, should be ended and responsibility for the service as a whole should pass to the Civil Service Department, responsible directly to the Prime Minister. As noted above, the CSD was abolished in 1981 and many of its functions (manpower and pay) returned to the Treasury; the Civil Service Commission became responsible to a Management and Personnel Office, itself answerable to the Cabinet Office.

The Fulton Committee was not without its critics, and although for a while it seemed to strike a very radical posture, a number of observers suspected that it was nothing better than a sheep in wolf's clothing. Lord Simey, a member of the Committee and Professor of Social Science at Liverpool University, wrote a dissenting note which suggested that part of the Report was 'unfair to the Civil Service. . . . Necessary reforms could be obtained by encouraging the evolution of what is basically the present situation, given the necessary amendments in direction and emphasis.' J.P. Mackintosh remarked, 'in general, the Fulton Committee's critique was overdone, in that it is attacking a caricature of the service which was never wholly true and certainly underestimates the changes that had taken place since the late 1950s.' Professor Mackintosh considered that the Civil Service was moulded chiefly by the doctrine of ministerial responsibility and all that flowed from it, including secrecy, anonymity, and isolation from the wider community, and he concluded that the Fulton Committee was not by its references allowed to look at relationships with Parliament but as a result it blamed the service itself for many characteristics imposed upon it by virtue of this relationship.

J.P. Mackintosh, *The Government and Politics of Britain,* revised and updated by P.G. Richards, 6th edn., Hutchinson, 1984, p. 190

Implementing Fulton

However, the implementation of the Fulton proposals in some instances was fairly rapid; the Civil Service Department came into operation in 1968, and a Civil Service College was opened in 1970, with a greatly extended programme introduced throughout the service. A merger of the administrative, executive and clerical classes (up to and including assistant secretary level) was announced with effect from 1971.

Simey and Mackintosh were not alone in their suspicions, and other criticisms have been more trenchant. For example, R.J.S. Baker (following the lines of R.G.S. Brown's critique) remarked that 'for all its pose of modernity, [Fulton's] basic thinking retained a considerably classical character.' In a *New Society* article G.W. Jones was moved to say, 'the champions of Fulton are disappointed. They accuse the mandarins of the civil service, the administrative class, of subtly sabotaging the working-out of the Fulton proposals so as to preserve their own existence and influence. Appearances and titles may have changed, but little of significance has altered.' Jones considered that part of the trouble was due to the fact that while

R.J.S. Baker, *Administrative Theory and Public Administration,* Hutchinson, 1972, p. 117

New Society, 17 August 1972

121

politicians call for general reform they have neither time nor inclination to consider the details of administering it. Furthermore given their numerical strength and their collective experience the 'generalists', the enlightened amateurs, could hardly all be discarded.

Jones also drew attention to the fact that although the administrative classes had now been merged, the graduate entrants could take advantage of a 'fast' stream (through Higher Executive Officer class A, as opposed to ordinary Higher Executive Officer), deliberately created after the Fulton Report for the promising young administrator of two to four years standing, since it was feared that with 'the dilution of standards required for the administration trainee compared with assistant principal, the really able graduate would no longer come forward'.

A few years later, in 1975, a report from the Society of Civil and Public Servants (SCPS) claimed that the system was still prone to 'class distinction and élitism'. What had happened, the report said, was that after the Fulton Report in 1968 it had been intended that 40 per cent of administration trainees (around 100 of whom are recruited annually) would be appointed from within the ranks of the Civil Service, while some 60 per cent would be appointed by direct recruitment. But in fact it appeared that direct graduate recruitment was about 80 per cent, with in-service appointments accounting for only 20 per cent: these proportions are borne out by the figures of the Civil Service Commission. Gerry Gillman, the General Secretary of SCPS, said that he would have expected to have seen more breaking down of barriers seven years after the Fulton Report had been published. 'We are beginning to think that the HEO(A) fast stream is really the old class distinction of assistant principal writ large and a cloak for disguising the old élitist approach.' On the other hand, senior civil servants were doubtful about the wisdom of postponing or diluting the selection of 'high-fliers' who were destined for early promotion to important responsible positions.

	Internal candidates	Total ATs appointed
1977	32	140
1978	52	149
1979	37	121
1980	31	94
1981	14	55
1982	3	24
1983	2	47
1984	8	59
1985	7	63

Numbers of internal candidates appointed as Administration Trainees; source: *Annual Reports of the Civil Service Commission*, 1977–85

The declining numbers reflect the fact that the Thatcher administration on entering office in 1979 was determined to reduce the size of the Civil Service from 730 000 to 630 000 by 1984, 594 365 being the figure reached at April 1986. Also, from 1982 it has been Commission policy to recruit a smaller number of fast stream

Administration Trainees who would be expected to reach HEO(D) grade after two years. Existing staff might be appointed to HEO(Development) where appropriate; thus HEO(D) replaced the HEO(A) grade. This was the result of the Moore Report (Report of the Administration Review Committee, Civil Service Department 1978).

One of the important elements in the Moore Committee's thinking was the increasing proportion of Executive Officer recruits from graduates (5 per cent in 1965 to 28 per cent in 1973).

1977	45%
1978	48%
1979	45%
1980	52%
1981	53%
1982	55%
1983	47%
1984	57%
1985	59%

Source: *Annual Reports of the Civil Service Commission*

Another issue that has been examined several times in recent years by the Civil Service is the alleged bias towards Oxbridge amongst the senior ranks.

1977	56%
1978	48%
1979	46%
1980	52%
1981	49%
1982	71%
1983	66%
1984	68%
1985	50%

Proportion of AT graduate entrants who attended Oxford/Cambridge; source: *Annual Reports of the Civil Service Commission*

A review in 1983 by Sir Alec Atkinson did not find that the Civil Service Selection Board demonstrated a pro-Oxbridge and pro-Arts bias, but it did suggest a greater effort should be made to attract non-Oxbridge graduates (*Selection of Fast-Stream Graduates to the Home Civil Service, Diplomatic Service and the Tax Inspectorate, and of Candidates from within the Service*, MPO, 1983).

The Fulton Report did not, it appears, lead to a more egalitarian climate within the Civil Service, despite the fact that many critics of Whitehall practices in the 1960s hoped that it would. The post-Fulton problems may have been exacerbated by frequent government policy changes, and by continual administrative reorganisation, for example the splitting up of the Department of Trade and Industry after the February 1974 Election, which meant civil servants became tired of being moved around.

This all culminated in a Civil Service Department report in 1975, which noted that there was widespread discontent, especially among the lower and middle grades which made up the bulk of the 500 000 non-industrial staff. The report, *Civil Servants and Change* from the CSD's Wider Issues Review Team, concentrated upon pay and working conditions, the service's decline in status relative to the private sector, poor career prospects and the monotony of routine office work. Amongst the remedies suggested were a greater degree of decision making at the local level (so much, it seems for Fulton's accountable units), a systematic review of personnel procedures, increased opportunity for interdepartmental promotion, improved catering and health facilities, and greater attention to size and identity in the larger ministries. 'Civil servants feel that they have been mucked about a lot in the last five or ten years', the report graphically said; 'so there is an atmosphere of sourness in many parts of the service, and we have found it at every level'.

The report suggested that poor office accommodation was the single biggest cause of dissatisfaction, but recognised that there had been many improvements since Fulton in 1968. However, it expressed considerable dissatisfaction that many of the lower grades, such as messengerial and paper-keeping, had hardly been affected at all by improvements in personnel management systems, besides the promotion prospects of the scientific and technical grades being far from satisfactory. The Whitehall response was generally lukewarm: Anthony Christopher, General Secretary of the Inland Revenue Staff Federation, welcomed the report, but remarked on the gap between theory and practice, while another official, Mr Gillman, said, 'I do not think the report comes up with anything new.'

The Times,
20 February 1975

DOCUMENT

13

Civil Service Recruitment

We have already referred to the significant increase in the volume of our recruitment business in 1984. As far as we can foresee, the scale of our recruitment work, whether measured by the number of competitions, vacancies or applications, will remain at a high level. We are, however, apprehensive about the continued ability of the Civil Service to attract candidates of very high quality at a time of increasing competition from other employers. Our recruitment experience suggests (and this is reinforced by what we have learnt from our contacts with universities and other institutions of higher education) that, nowadays, a smaller proportion of the most able undergraduates than in the past regard the Civil Service as an attractive form of employment. There are undoubtedly a variety of reasons for this change in attitude. It is impossible to be precise about how significant immediate remuneration is in the success of a recruitment scheme; that it is a factor can, however, be asserted with confidence. Other important considerations are the intrinsic interest of the job, its location, promotion prospects and, not least, how well-regarded the employment is seen to be by the community as a whole. While recognising the reservations that increasing numbers of students and others appear to have about the Civil Service, we are concerned about the effect because it is in the national interest that the Civil Service should be able to take its share of the talent that exists in the universities, institutions of higher education and the employment market more generally. A major effort will be needed to reverse the trend; but the Commission can make only a contribution to solving the problem. This is something to which we shall particularly direct our publicity efforts, notably during our discussions with the staff and students in the universities and other institutions in the course of 1985.

There is a wide range of appointments, mainly but not solely of a specialist nature, to which we experience particularly serious difficulty in recruiting enough candidates of sufficient quality. Examples of this problem are scientists in the physical and mathematical sciences and 'new technology' disciplines; accountants; statisticians; lawyers; and engineers in a variety of disciplines. There is no doubt that in some problem areas, there is a national shortage of those with the qualifications and experience which we require (a situation on which the Commissioners have found it necessary to comment frequently since the mid-1970s): in such cases we are competing with other employers for a very limited pool of talent, and the response to our recruitment schemes reflects the Civil Service's lack of attractiveness. In other cases our advertisements attract a reasonable field of applicants, in terms of both quality and quantity, but we find that our efforts are frustrated towards the end of the recruitment process as a result of a significant proportion of successful candidates – including, very often, some of the best – declining the offer of appointment. Our follow-up research reveals that candidates have a variety of reasons for rejecting an appointment in the Civil Service, including those mentioned above. In the case of a number of recruitment schemes, however, uncompetitive pay features as the most commonly-given reason.

Civil Service Commission, *Annual Report*, 1984

Training

Earlier on, in late 1974, yet another report showed that despite Fulton there were considerable variations in both the quality and quantity of training offered by the principal Government departments. The Heaton/Williams Report (from the CSD) thought that a clearer system for the budgeting of training requirements was needed; it showed that in 1972–3 69 per cent of civil service training was carried out within departments, which took some £26m out of a total budget for training of £34m. The Report had some harsh criticism for the Civil Service College as set up by Fulton, to replace the Centre for Administrative Studies, established in 1963. The Report commented not only upon the poor quality of teaching at the College, the over-academic nature of some of the courses and the irrelevance of the work to the main business of civil service life, but also upon truancy amongst the young graduate entrants.

The Report said,

'They have their own ways and means of showing their opinion of a lecturer, of which completing *The Times* crossword puzzle is perhaps the least conspicious. Bad time-keeping and absenteeism are not unknown, as evidenced by the remark reportedly made to a visiting lecturer, "This is not a bad turn-out for 9.30 a.m."'

Doubtless the College noted some of the more severe criticisms, but there was no intention to alter the basic character of the College envisaged by Fulton, as a broad-based, non-élitist institution, by, for example, imitating the very intensive, specialist training courses provided by the more élitist French equivalent, the École Nationale d'Administration (ENA), once very much admired and envied amongst British senior civil servants.

A three-year improvement of the CSD's training facilities and the Civil Service College started in 1977, beginning with an internal reorganisation of the CSD and the appointment of a civil servant as a new head of the College. The longer-term aim appears to be to follow the best of the French ENA, concentrating on training those in their middle-thirties who had already proved their capacity, and preparing them for further analytical difficulties: 'teaching would be provided by the men and women who had already experienced such demands rather than outside academics'. But to date (1987) the objectives of rivalling the ENA seem as remote and ill-considered as ever.

The Times,
18 January 1977

The training review produced by the Heaton/Williams document was the first major review since Fulton; training was seen as having grown 30 per cent over the six years between 1967 and 1973, although it was still considered as in the development stage. The Civil Service has not acquired a completely bad image, however, although the public perception of it has been affected by adverse economic circumstances.

Applications to the Civil Service in open and limited competitions

1977	119 824
1978	114 960
1979	98 137
1980	76 990
1981	91 556
1982	119 434
1983	108 402
1984	105 803
1985	102 716

Source: Annual Reports of the Civil Service Commission

Size of the Civil Service

Numbers in the Civil Service have certainly increased dramatically since the inter-war period, and although the Conservatives hoped to reduce the number when they won the election in 1970, they found it very difficult to do so. In 1972 there were just over 100 000 in an executive grade, 36 000 who were classified as professionals and technologists, with 16 000 scientists, 200 000 clerical personnel and nearly 11 000 messengers and paper-keepers. 'The term "civil servant" covers wardens of the Tower of London, driving examiners, industrial accident inspectors, prison officers, and vets.'

New Society,
14 March 1974

The Civil Service pyramid is thus very broad at the bottom. It is the clerical staff who carry the organisation, and this was indeed one of the principal factors behind what has been dubbed the 'post-Fulton malaise'; the clerical grades were left out by Fulton and although the 1955 Priestley Report laid down the principle of fair comparison for wage reviews, the high rate of inflation in the 1970s took its toll, and it is doubtful whether the Civil Service will ever be quite the same again. One survey quoted one executive officer as saying, 'the dedication in the service has gone;' and an assistant secretary of the Civil and Public Services Association commented, 'we were sandwiched between lavatories and office machines under the general heading of working environment in the Fulton Report's index.'

In 1976 the total size of the Civil Service peaked at 744 000. By 1980 under the new Conservative Government the figure had fallen to nearly 700 000, and by 1984, 630 000. Mrs Thatcher appointed Sir Derek Rayner, Managing Director of Marks and Spencer, as the head of a small internal unit (in the Cabinet Office) whose brief it was to examine efficiency and waste in the Civil Service. The Rayner Unit continued until the end of 1982, when upon Sir Derek's departure it was attached to the Management and Personnel Office (part of the Cabinet Office) which had been created out of the CSD after its abolition in 1981.

DOCUMENT

14

The Size of the Civil Service

The big question is whether the reforms could survive a new government. Once considerations of quality of service are introduced, you can glimpse an opening that might satisfy civil servants, taxpayers and claimants alike, as well as people of all ideological persuasions. For Mrs Thatcher hasn't really been a radical when it comes to the machinery of government. She hasn't built a new edifice which an opponent will feel honour-bound to knock down. She's been cautious, for instance, about importing political appointees. The most ideological element has been the drive to privatise, but this has mainly affected humble folk like cleaners and messengers; it has left the core of the civil service untouched.

127

Even the efficiency reforms can be seen as the final acceptance, more than a decade later, of some central themes from the Fulton report, which had been fought off by the civil service in a heroic defensive action. Efficiency should be a partly-neutral objective, if it is interpreted in a broad enough sense to include quality of service. It is even arguable that a party wanting to *expand* public services has more to gain from the efficient use of resources. By the end of Mrs Thatcher's administration, if the civil service has an effective system for measuring performance as well as costs, then in retrospect the reforms may seem more substantial than an exercise in giving intellectual respectability to manpower cuts.

How the Civil Service has (mostly) shrunk

	1 April 1979	1 April 1984	% change 1979–84	target 1 April 1988	% change 1984–88
Defence	247 000	200 000	−19	170 000	−15
Energy	1300	1100	−15	1000	−9
Treasury, Inland Revenue, Customs & Excise, etc	126 900	113 000	−11	104 200	−8
Employment, Manpower Services Commission, etc	53 700	57 700	+7	54 000	−6
Environment	56 000	37 000	−34	34 600	−6
Foreign Office	12 000	11 200	−7	10 500	−6
Health & Social Security	98 400	90 700	−8	87 900	−3
Scottish Office	10 900	9800	−10	9500	−3
Agriculture	14 000	11 500	−18	11 300	−2
Education	2600	2400	−8	2400	nil
Trade & Industry	19 500	14 900	−24	14 900	nil
Transport	13 900	14 200	+2	14 200	nil
Welsh Office	2600	2200	−15	2200	nil
Courts, etc	16 500	17 300	+5	17 400	+1
Home Office	33 500	35 800	+7	41 100	+15
All civil service	732 300	624 000	−15	592 700	−6

NB: Total includes small departments not listed separately

D Thomas, *New Society*, 17 January 1985

The 'Freedoms' of Civil Servants

By tradition civil servants, via their trade unions and staff associations, used to maintain a low profile in respect of industrial action. But this convention probably came to an end in 1973, when large numbers, some at relatively senior level, took to protest marches and strikes, following the announcement of salary increases for higher civil servants at special rates in contrast to the modest rises for other grades. Further difficulties came in 1976, when civil servants were becoming particularly restive over a possible loss of between 26 000 and 30 000 jobs as part of the Government's medium-term economy drives, with some staff in the more important departments swiftly banning overtime. Civil servants were also beginning to drop their non-political, impartial mask. In 1981 there was a prolonged strike which culminated in the disbanding of the CSD.

In 1976 the Civil Service unions were seeking greater freedom for half a million white collar staff to play an active part in politics outside office hours. The Armitage Committee was set up by the Prime Minister to examine the issue. The existing rules established in 1953 after investigation by the Masterman Committee had divided civil servants into three categories, the first two dealing with mainly the clerical groups, but the third category applying to executive officer grade upwards, who were 'politically restricted', which meant effective disqualification from active party politics, nationally or in the constituencies (all categories of civil servants are subject to the general provisions of the 1911 Official Secrets Act). The Civil Service unions sought a simple proviso that a civil servant would notify his department before taking an active role in politics, the department then being given one month in which to object, and the civil servant in his turn being able to seek redress against any departmental objection. The Armitage Report of 1978 recommended that 173 000 or so middle (executive) to senior grade civil servants should be allowed to take an active part in politics, like the clerical grades, provided the agreement of the appropriate department was obtained beforehand. This was done. The 23 000 or so officials in the most senior grades would remain subject to the traditional restrictions. In 1983 the Government whilst reiterating that all staff were free to belong to a political party stated that staff in local offices (clerical and executive grades in other words) should not take an active part in politics in the locality served by the office, and that where staff were allowed to take part in political activities, discretion should be exercised by avoiding personal attacks, expressing comment with moderation, and avoiding embarrassment to ministers or to their department.

Report of the Committee on Political Activities of Civil Servants, Cmnd 7057, 1978

There has, therefore, been a large and varied number of problems affecting the Civil Service in the post-Fulton era. Whether they were caused by the Report itself or would have happened anyway is a difficult question to answer, but it is likely that they flowed from the very existence of Fulton: it was the Fulton shake-up which provided a suitable climate to test opinion and which triggered off subsequent events. However, as a deputy general secretary of the Civil Service Union, Len Moody, commented, it would need at least ten years for the Fulton Report's recommendations to work their way through the system. 'You cannot legislate prejudice out of people's minds.'

The Guardian, 30 October 1973

Parliamentary reactions

It is interesting to note that the 11th Report from the Expenditure Committee of the House of Commons, on the subject of the Civil Service, in 1977, a report which was not without controversy over some of the recommendations made, was

129

11th Report of the
Expenditure
Committee,
HC 535, 1976–7

sharply critical of the original Fulton proposals: there was no consideration of the problems created by the separation of expenditure from manpower and efficiency, for expenditure problems could not really be divorced from the efficient use of manpower, particularly in labour-intensive departments like the DHSS and the Inland Revenue, the report stated.

The Commons Report also had some other very strong things to say, and one of the Committee's members (the Labour MP, Brian Sedgemore) issued his own damning critique of the Civil Service, within the Report, concluding, as an ex-civil servant himself, that whereas the French Civil Service had been efficient, if not always democratic, since 1945 the British Civil Service had been neither.

The Committee stressed that ministers should be seen more clearly as the people in charge of central government departments, and that a minister's wishes to reorganise his department in whatever way he wished should be complied with, although removal of a permanent secretary would still require the Prime Minister's permission. Ministerial policies should not be subject to the delay and obstruction that was quite commonplace in the post-war period, the Report claimed. Similarly, if a minister wished to have his own private team of advisers within the department (on the lines of the French ministerial *cabinets*) he should be allowed to do so. Ministers should also be able to see papers relating to previous Governments of different political complexions.

The Times,
5 April 1977

The French state, however, does not just sponsor the École Polytechnique for its top public service scientists and engineers, it also sets aside a 'reserved graduate occupation', for each candidate winning a place there. As Dr Sally Jenkinson and Dr Guy Neave have pointed out, the fully-fledged engineer-civil servant is soon at the top of his profession. 'Moreover the technological orientation of the entrance examination he sits is reflected throughout the education system. Though some *polytechniciens* are bought out by industry, it must be assumed the attraction was not industry itself, but the challenge of the competition and the possibility of a secure and brilliant future whether in government or in industry throughout the administrator's career.' Jenkinson and Neave remarked that the British Civil Service could do much to emulate the French in respect of the career structure of its scientists and engineers, if only by reserving a number of high prestige places in its ranks for such graduates; meanwhile students would continue to opt for arts and social science courses.

The Times,
3 June 1977

However, Jenkinson and Neave, writing a little later, argued that it did not follow that the other side of the French coin, that of the general administrator trained through the ENA, mentioned above, was equally applicable to Britain. Indeed, they pointed out that in the mid-1970s the French Minister of Education, M Haby, was broadening out the role of the École Nationale d'Administration in particular, away from its original task of being solely a Civil Service recruiting shop.

Jenkinson and Neave commented: 'the differing values of the French and British societies are well reflected in these contemporary debates on their administrative élites. Here, government and Parliament are discussing the training of a social science background. The French – taking the values of Maths and Science for granted – are weighing the relative merits of pure versus applied sciences as the proper curriculum for tens of thousands of young people throughout the country staying on at school both at 16 as well as at 19 plus.' It is clear, they wrote, that the demands made by the French system of civil service recruitment actually encourage 'large numbers of students to prepare energetically for . . . mathematical and philosophical-based examinations. Second, the proposals show that notwithstanding the attraction of reforming the British Civil Service "along French lines", in practice this would require a uniformly spread reform over the whole secondary and higher education curriculum. Current administrative thinking in Britain about what a society *ought* to demand of its education system does not quite run to that. The question is: *should* it?'

DOCUMENT

15

Ministers and their Civil Servants

That conflict between a Minister and his civil servants can arise is hardly surprising, but even tough, intelligent, determined Ministers may find it very difficult, and sometimes impossible, to overcome the resistance of their civil servants. Now, it is well understood that constitutionally the civil servant's role includes a responsibility to tell a Minister unpalatable truths, to argue the case against what he wants to do if the facts do not point in that direction, if what he intends seems to be "politically" unacceptable, to protect the Minister from the danger that his own optimism will move him into a scheme which will be seen to fail. But how far can and should a civil servant press his case, where the Minister, supported by his Cabinet colleagues, is bent on his course of action? Where does concern for the continuity of government override his paramount duty to serve his Minister? When does legitimate pressure on a Minister to convince his civil servants become obstruction? Much, of course, depends upon the way that it is done. Pressure may be exerted subtly from any quarters within the administration, making it difficult for the Minister to proceed. For example, his senior civil servants may not press his case quite as hard in discussion and negotiation with colleagues in other departments; the Treasury might be appraised of the weakness in the departmental case; an interest group might be "encouraged" to petition the Minister or "fed" useful information for a campaign against a proposed policy. The Minister may find his room for manoeuvre circumscribed by such pressures.

However, a civil servant could not individually, or with like-minded colleagues, publicly campaign for a policy contrary to that of his Minister or the Cabinet; even anonymous criticism of government policy may be held inconsistent with loyalty to the Minister. To do so would compromise the civil servant's claim to impartiality and limit his potential usefulness, not only to his Minister, but to the Minister's successors. To be seen publicly to challenge the existing policy of his Minister or the Cabinet, or publicly promoting an alternative policy, is to assume an identity separate from that of the 131

Minister and the department. Such a challenge, if it is to be made, must come from within the department and remain private and confidential.

In recent years some civil servants have argued that there is, or ought to be, a recognition that they have a duty which goes beyond that of undivided loyalty to Ministers, a duty to the "public interest". They feel that the civil service should accept the need for an ethic based on the public interest, by which they mean "a collection of factors other than Ministerial intentions which may legitimately influence judgements". Part of the civil servant's professional task would then be to ascertain objectively what the public interest was in a particular context. Leaving aside the formidable difficulties of doing that accurately and acceptably, two conditions must be met if such an interpretation of the civil servant's duty is to prove acceptable to those outside as well as inside the service. First, the anonymity of the civil servant would have to be eroded even further to enable him to take part in a much more open discussion of policy making at the formative stage when ends and means are not foreclosed. Second, following from the first condition, it would require much less emphasis on the traditional practice of protecting Ministers from possible criticism, both parliamentary and extra-parliamentary.

To some extent, in some departments for some policy areas, some progress has been made in recent years towards meeting the first condition. Whether they like it or not, civil servants find themselves increasingly obliged to discuss departmental activities in public, at moments not always of their choosing: before Select Committees, in explanation to the Parliamentary Commissioners for Administration, and in cross-examination by counsel before courts and tribunals of inquiry. Their difficulty is that in so doing they have still a duty to protect their Minister and the actions taken in his name.

In the present climate of opinion further progress towards a more public debate at the policy-formulation stage seems doubtful. On the strength of their evidence to the Franks Committee, Permanent Secretaries are firmly opposed to any such move. The current orthodoxy, to which they all subscribe, is that Ministers and civil servants must be able to exchange views frankly and fully among themselves without the risk that details of their discussions will be made public. The conventions governing the confidentiality of these discussions, threatened by the judgment of the Lord Chief Justice in the High Court to allow publication of the first volume of the Crossman Diaries, have been reaffirmed and strengthened by the Government's acceptance of the recommendations of the Radcliffe Committee of Privy Counsellors on Ministerial Memoirs in January 1976. Ministers will now incur an "obligation of honour" to observe working-rules on the reticence due from them when leaving office. They undertake not to reveal the advice given to them by their civil servants and advisers, nor make public their assessment of those who served under them. "The Minister must observe a scrupulous reticence with regard to the attitudes and personalities of those who have served him in office." It seemed to the Committee "wholly repugnant that he should at a later date regard himself as free to record this material and to discuss it in the course of a public account of his Ministerial experience". These and other working-rules relating to the disclosure of discussions with colleagues in Cabinet and its committees, are not backed by statutory sanctions; there are to be no new offences. The obligations of reticence are "public duties" which Ministers assume on taking office. Where a Minister chooses to disavow his obligation, existing law provides no protection for his colleagues and civil servants.

The Lord Chief Justice's ruling in the Crossman case has been used by his publishers to vindicate the decision to publish the second volume, which is more revealing still. No doubt Prime Ministers and their colleagues hope that the embarrassment of the publication of Crossman's Diaries will not be repeated. By reiterating the need for collective responsibility in the Cabinet and its committees, and by underlining the disadvantages to both Ministers and civil servants if their relationships are not to be based on confidentiality, Governments will hope through the Radcliffe rules to emphasize the need for Ministerial reticence. As before, former Ministers will be expected to submit their manuscripts to the Secretary of the Cabinet, with a right of appeal to the Prime Minister.

M. Wright, 'Ministers and Civil Servants: Relations and Responsibilities',
Parliamentary Affairs, Summer 1977

To return to the Commons report, the Expenditure Committee, impressed by US and European practices, stressed that the Commons should not just conduct financial audits but also undertake wide-ranging efficiency audits, while the Comptroller and Auditor-General's Department should become staff of the House of Commons, rather than Treasury staff. In 1986 the Comptroller himself rebuked Members of Parliament for voting through vast sums of money without adequate discussion. The Government's expenditure plans, as presented to Parliament, gave inadequate information, he said. (See Chapter 5 for the 1983 audit reforms.)

The Guardian,
14 February 1986

The Committee was concerned, too, about the old question of recruitment patterns (in other words the dominance of public school Oxbridge graduates) in the upper levels of general administrative staff, as discussed above. This so-called question of Oxbridge 'bias' was rebutted by a special enquiry undertaken by the Civil Service Commission in 1979, and by the Commission in its Annual Report for 1978, and again in 1983 in the MPO report as noted earlier. The Annual Report observed: 'We would wish to emphasise most strongly that we have no preference for graduates of Oxford and Cambridge as such; our only preference is for the ablest candidates, whatever their origin. We hope that the imbalance in favour of Oxord and Cambridge which this analysis has confirmed will not discourage, but will serve as a challenge to more of the best graduates from other universities.'

The Allen enquiry came to the following conclusion:

'Oxford and Cambridge . . . attract a disproportionately large number of the ablest school-leavers and it can be argued that their collegiate and tutorial system of education does much to develop, not only the intellectual but also the personal qualities that are desirable in a sound administrator.'

The Commons Report also recommended the abolition of the Civil Service College, and proposed that training should be shared by the departments themselves and outside educational institutions. Graduate trainees would be sent on certain courses only after they had proved themselves 'on the job', and recruitment should at least be widened to include young administrators in the NHS and local government. Working in local government, civil service regional offices or industry for short periods would widen the experience of civil servants; high-powered seminars in specialist subjects should be held more frequently, on the lines of the French ENA.

The Report stressed again the importance of the transfer of jobs between the Service and other occupations, but at the same time expressed its surprise that there were no legal sanctions against ex-civil servants taking jobs within two years of leaving the Service in companies having close links with the Government, and without Government permission. Concern amongst MPs about this matter has again been noticeable since 1979. The rule that a civil servant must obtain official permission if, within two years of leaving the Civil Service, he intends to take a job with a firm that he has dealt with in his official capacity or that has had a close relationship with Whitehall dates from 1937. In 1975 the Prime Minister, Harold Wilson, laid down a further rule that three months should normally elapse between resignation and the date of the new appointment. He also set up a committee to look at individual cases. These amendments followed public concern in 1974 when Lord Armstrong, then Head of the Home Civil Service, resigned to become Chairman of the Midland Bank. Although this movement of labour poses less of a problem in France and the USA, it was a subject the Treasury and Civil Service Select Committee returned to in 1981, saying that the rules were biased too much in favour of freedom of movement and too little in the direction of removing the suspicion of impropriety. Between 1979 and 1983 there were 1942 applications from senior civil servants applying to take up jobs in the private sector, 90 per cent of them for jobs in related industries, mostly in defence.

Acceptance of Outside Appointments by Crown Servants, 4th Report from the Treasury and Civil Service Committee, HC 216, 1980–1 session

The Report concluded by arguing that close scrutiny by the Commons must always be maintained in order to ensure as many Government departments practised as much administrative simplicity as possible; it recommended a 'programme of regular surveys' of major departments, but at the same time it was suspicious of the practice of 'hiving off' certain departmental functions to separate, *'ad hoc'* Government agencies, like the Property Services Agency, or quangos (quasi-autonomous non-governmental organisations). A decade later, however, Mrs Thatcher's intention to privatise wide areas of civil service work was underlined by Government guidelines which insisted that there were 'no limits' to Whitehall activities that might be candidates for competitive tendering.

The Independent, 27 December 1986

DOCUMENT

16

The Duties of Senior Civil Servants

[There] is, however, an area of uncertainty in the conventions delimiting the civil servant's duty. Difficult choices on this question are the common lot of those giving advice on policy, at least down to the level of Principal. Requests to check party documents and speeches for accuracy are frequently made and present no real difficulty. Nor does the provision of raw information. But does the provision of information in the form of words which the minister might use fall within the definition of the provision of information? Is it legitimate to advise him on the practicality of proposals which are being canvassed by others in Party circles: ministers are, of course, often anxious to have such advice because they are only too conscious that party activists are not subject to the constraints of office. Nor is it easy sometimes to judge whether a minister is attending a meeting *qua* minister or as a party politician: for example, if he is a regular member of the Labour Party–TUC liaison committee and it is to discuss matters falling within his area of ministerial responsibility, or (more difficult) relevant to it, what is his status and to what extent would it be right to assist him?

In fact, the civil servant habitually takes counsel with his conscience when he is asked to do work which is manifestly party political even though his master is clearly acting in a ministerial capacity. Sir William Armstrong was acknowledging this when he told the Select Committee that he would have regarded it as improper for civil servants without an express ministerial instruction to have initiated a campaign to bring "greater balance" to the Questions on the Order Paper; and when he implied that the Department of the Environment officials concerned showed what they thought of the instruction by the apolitical and trivial character of the draft Questions which they submitted – were the Questions about the facilities in the Strangers' Bar and about pigeon nuisance in public buildings a twit?

Different practices are discernible among civil servants as regards the extent to which material of a distinctly political character should be provided for ministerial occasions. Some would see no great difficulty on the grounds that it is entirely a matter for the minister to decide what words to use, and if he chooses to use the words offered to him he takes complete responsibility for them. Those who follow this line would, of course, take it for granted that they should offer this service to whatever minister was in office: they might indeed take some pride in their professional ability to provide acceptable words (to be used on ministerial as distinct from party occasions), say, both for a minister who was known to be associated with the Monday Club and for a Minister who identified himself with the left of the Tribune Group. A second group would not have any strong scruples against such a practice, but would doubt its prudence; they would agree with Dr Jeremy Bray that the political touch of civil servants is not always as good as most of them think it is. The third group would take the line, that while they will supply basic material and speeches which are of a judicious governmental character, it is for ministers and party men to provide political words. For the latter two groups at least, the advent of political advisers has had distinct advantages in this respect. Whatever a civil servant's stance on the question of providing material of a more or less political character for ministerial occasions, there would be little if any dissent from the proposition that such material should be faithful to the drafter's conception of the truth in terms of the substance of the matters to which it refers; and it would be considered mandatory to point out where the minister's own material is misleading.

The civil servant's duty to ministers as a body rather than to his own minister presents difficulties as great as those just considered. It has long been accepted that the civil servant's duty is to the political head of his department so that the decisions of junior ministers may be referred higher if they seem to civil servants to be unsatisfactory. But how far may civil servants expose their disagreements with their departmental heads to other ministers? And what are a civil servant's obligations if his minister wishes to refuse cooperation with his colleagues and to conceal information from them which might in due course be used in inter-departmental discussion, whether at the official or political levels? Criticism from politicians and in the press has been particularly trenchant on this score. The complaint made by the Labour Party to the Fulton Committee was specifically that civil servants used the network of official committees and contacts to frustrate proposals with which they disagreed, and the report of the Select Committee on 135

Expenditure referred to "briefing ministers in other departments to oppose the initiative in Cabinet or Cabinet committee". The minority were particularly outraged by this tactic. Both Mr Meacher and Mr Benn have recently reiterated the charge.

In the terms often described the practice is currently unacceptable, while on the other hand cherished schemes have often been frustrated by opposition among ministers, not the civil service. The Select Committee report was clear enough on the point: "The civil service has a duty to preserve the overall consistency of Government policy when a minister embarks on a course conflicting with that of a minister in another department. It may be right for one minister to be frustrated, and the other (or the Prime Minister) alerted, until such time as the two have met and argued the matter out to a decision, either in or out of Cabinet. In addition, when a Permanent Secretary considers that his minister is acting improperly he has a right to appeal to the Prime Minister and should do so". The underlying principle presumably derives from collective responsibility and the implication is that the civil servant has a duty to ministers as a whole which in some circumstances ought to prevail over his duty to his own. In that sense, Whitehall is a unity.

N. Summerton, 'A Mandarin's Duty', *Parliamentary Affairs*, Autumn 1980

The Nature of Bureaucracy

It is not necessarily true that government by bureaucracy is efficient. Certainly as both central and local government staffs have become progressively larger during the post-war period, there has been increasing public doubt that even the minimum standards of efficiency are being met. In fact the bureaucratic practices that are introduced as an organisation grows are often efficient, not inefficient. 'Red-tape' by its very nature has to be standardised; forms may appear irrelevant to a particular person in a particular situation, but a modern complex society can hardly allow for individual forms or amendments. In addition, bureaucracy has an important psychological function in any Western society, since feelings of anger, dissatisfaction, and then perhaps redress of an administrative grievance, fulfil important, supplementary, participatory roles for the public. But in some Eastern European societies that psychological function may be far more enhanced. It could be argued that since there is no deviation in the USSR because there can be no deviation from the true socialist goal, criticisms of bureaucratic inefficiency occupy an even greater political plane in society, and indeed criticisms are indirectly encouraged by the authorities since inefficiency itself is opposed to the interests of the State and must consequently be rooted out.

Of course, the very word 'bureaucracy' has been given many different shades of meaning, although the most celebrated was probably Weber's 'continuous organisation of official functions bound by rules.'

R.G.S. Brown has observed that there have been many suggestions over the past few years to try and find ways to improve the administration of large organisations, and such suggestions have chiefly centred around the 'relationship between the structure and function in various parts of the administrative machine and such factors as recruitment and training, which are thought to influence the quality of major decisions.' Such suggestions would probably all change the balance of force within public administration by 'strengthening one element in it and so causing a shift in priorities.'

R.G.S. Brown and D.R. Steel, *The Administrative Process in Britain*, 2nd edn., Methuen, 1979, p. 170 and 189

Most administrators will be plagued by the temptation at some time or other to concentrate upon the matters which are there to be dealt with, even if not urgent, rather than engage in the more difficult, abstract task of planning and programming. Brown has commented that in one of the Carnegie projects in the United States the subjects involved were obliged to draw up an inventory control system, and they were told that all tasks were equally important. But it was found that as the flow of information increased so the amount of time spent on planning was gradually reduced until none virtually was done at all. As Brown said, 'this is Gresham's law of planning – that daily routine drives out planning,' something which has often characterised the general administrator or senior civil servant level.

What is perhaps rather more fundamental, however, is the extent to which the whole Weberian model of bureaucracy became discredited by developments in management and administrative theory during the 1960s and early 1970s. For Weber there had to be an organised hierarchy for any bureaucracy to be at its rational best. Such a model carries with it the implicit assumption that one or two persons are at the administrative apex and are completely responsible for the methods the organisation employs in order to function in accordance with its aims, which may have been decreed in another place. Weber in fact placed the prime ministerial-cabinet organisation in a bureaucratic setting, a point graphically illustrated by the Westland Affair in 1986 (see Chapter 2).

The Weberian model, which has been so dominant in administrative thinking in the past half-century or so, is also suspect in the sense that it does not allow for the fact that it is often the junior staff who determine what problems will be transmitted upwards. A senior civil servant might also not be aware of a particular problem, which nevertheless could have fairly serious administrative implications, had not, for instance, a Member of Parliament been in a position to furnish information; or, for example, the same is true in local government, where an MP or councillor, or both, might bring pressure to bear upon a chief officer of a local authority to solve a problem 'buried' at a lower level.

However, it is dangerous to generalise too freely about the 'management revolution' of a decade or so ago. For example, Brown quotes one writer (N.P. Mouzelis) in the following way, 'it is possible to doubt whether statements of any value can be made that will apply equally to organisations as diverse as a Soviet kolkhoz, General Motors, the British Medical Association, the Roman Catholic Church, a handful of grocery stores in Iceland, the University of Rome, a Japanese shipping line, a Swiss mountain hotel, the Police Department of a Swedish town, or a government department in the Sudan'. In short, national cultures will often either hinder or defy adequate definition of administrative theory when applied in its broad international context.

137

Nevertheless in the British context the Ombudsman (the PCA) has often taken exception to the manner in which discretionary decisions are reached. Officials have been criticised for:

New Society,
11 January 1973

'taking into account irrelevant information; basing decisions on inaccurate information, erroneous assumptions and unsound advice, not taking into account relevant information already in the possession of their department, failing to appreciate the significance of such information, failing to collect all the relevant evidence, and not taking into account all the relevant arguments and not adopting procedures . . . that would have ensured that they were in possession of all the information required for reaching a decision.'

That comment in itself is quite damning enough criticism of the central bureaucracy.

M. Albrow,
Bureaucracy,
Macmillan, 1970,
p. 89ff

Martin Albrow has suggested that bureaucracy in the wider definition can be viewed in seven different ways if the various writings of leading sociologists and political scientists in this field are examined. In the first place bureaucracy is a rational organisation, a view put forward by Peter Blau, in the sense that bureaucracy is large and complex nowadays (and can be applied to all sorts of groups in society), and is in fact a method of organising while maintaining efficiency and stability. On the other hand, the more popular view of bureaucracy is that of organisational inefficiency, implying that bureaucrats actually gain some element of satisfaction from delay and muddle. There have been few academic writers to support this view, although Michael Crozier is a notable exception, perhaps indicating some dissatisfaction with French 'over-centralisation'. Thirdly, bureaucracy may be viewed as 'rule by officials', in which a large amount of day to day matters has fallen into the hands of officials, away from the elected representatives and thus threatening the lives of the individual citizen. This is akin to the viewpoint of Harold Laski in the inter-war period. Alternatively, bureaucracy may be seen as an art in itself, that is bureaucracy as public administration, as essential community functions in a kind of politically neutral sense. Such was at the heart of Michels' thinking, which later became subsumed in the political organisation of Mussolini's fascist Italy. Fifthly, there is bureaucracy in the sense of administration by officials – this is the classic Weberian view of bureaucracy as an organised, efficient hierarchy, in which orders are both clearly given and clearly obeyed. Sixthly, some contemporary social scientists, such as Talcott Parsons and Etzioni, have drawn attention to bureaucracy in the broader context, that bureaucracy can almost be equated with organisation in the sense that the college or the school, or the trade union or powerful pressure group, is as much a bureaucracy as the civil service itself. Finally, bureaucracy can be seen as modern society itself, as a governmental equivalent to democracy, aristocracy, or communism; such a viewpoint again owes something to the Italian fascist background and to Mosca's ruling class thesis, but has largely been developed by Marxist heretics, such as Djilas in Yugoslavia.

There have sometimes been responses to the various theories about bureaucracy, especially from those politicians who see it as a form of creeping organisation encroaching on the individual rights of the citizen. In France there has long been an elaborate system of administrative law which governs the relationship between officials and the public, while in the United States there has been the development of Congressional committees of inquiry, perhaps reaching its most dramatic as well as its most absurd point in the Watergate Senate hearings. In the UK there has been the introduction of the ombudsman system from 1967 and the development of select committees since 1979.

As Albrow himself has said, the term bureaucracy is useful for identifying a range of related problems, but 'we cannot expect this name to tell us anything more than the fact of relationship, of historical and logical connection between these problems. But that single piece of information is important enough, for academics and citizens alike.'

DOCUMENT

17

The Functions of Senior Civil Servants

To sum up, tomorrow's civil servants will be required to have the ability to use resources efficiently (in the sense of using as few resources as possible to carry out any given task) and economically (in the sense of taking steps to eliminate tasks and activities which are not, on a close analysis, necessary). Their ability to do this will depend partly on the nature of the structure within which they are working, in that these structures may provide either built-in incentives or built-in disincentives to economy and efficiency. But it will also depend crucially on their own abilities and (even more important) on their attitudes. It is also desirable that they should show an equal concern about the incidental demands they can impose on the resources of members of the public or of companies, for example by requiring extensive information or statistics.

Finally there are the challenges civil servants face as a result of *new styles of management*. These are by no means confined to the civil service, but they are certainly having a major impact there, and the processes of adjustment are by no means complete. The traditional notion of civil servants as (in the main) operatives making marks on pieces of paper and passing them to the next person in the chain is already obsolete in human and operational terms; with the rapid spread of electronic systems, it will very soon be obsolete even in terms of the basic technology. There will have to be a much greater emphasis on motivating staff and welding them into an effective team. There will have to be a much greater emphasis on participative systems of management and, within these systems, on the exercise of leadership by senior staff. In part these new demands reflect changes in the nature of the work, in part they reflect changes in the characteristics of public servants themselves.

The young people who are now entering the civil service are more highly educated and more articulate. They do not display the kind of deference to authority that was expected in the past. The changing nature of civil service trade unions [the last decade has seen the first strikes] is certainly linked with this change in attitudes, whether as cause or effect. Young people also have a greater expectation that their work will be not only interesting, but also responsible. These are not features of one passing generation (for example, those who experienced the period of student revolt in the late 1960s), but represent long-term 139 trends which are unlikely to be reversed. The changes will be accelerated by the "retirement bulge": the fact that, because of the pattern of recruitment at the end of the second world war, a disproportionately high number of older civil servants will reach retirement age in the next few years.

Staff at management levels have the vital task of trying to mobilise and deploy the efforts and abilities of the more junior staff for whom they are responsible. This will mean giving them greater discretion, so that they can think critically and constructively about the purposes of the particular unit within which they are working and how these can best be fulfilled; so that, where appropriate, they can explore, devise and implement new and better methods of working. Irrespective of other considerations, the new methods of working may be superior simply because the staff involved have thought them out for themselves. This can release energy and enthusiasm which was previously unsuspected and produce a much higher level of commitment. It will also create an organisation which is more flexible, and thus better equipped to cope with changes in its technology or its environment.

However, there is a paradox here. Deference is a traditional characteristic of the servant, and a paramount requirement of the civil service is that (within the given constitutional conventions) he should be responsive to the duly constituted government. It will be apparent that a policy of giving greater discretion and autonomy to more junior staff within the civil service is in potential conflict with this requirement. I do not want to exaggerate the conflict. In practice it may be possible to obtain the best of both worlds, in that the more participative organisation is also likely to be more effective. But it is a major challenge to civil servants in management positions to ensure that this is in fact the outcome.

To the four basic qualities already identified (integrity, expertness, the ability to use resources efficiently and economically, and the ability to adopt a participative style of management), we can add qualities which are even more personal. Tomorrow's civil servants will be expected by the government and public (or, at least, by different groups within the government and public) to show contrary qualities at different times, or even contrary qualities at one and the same time. No doubt they will be expected, from time to time, to provide a greatly improved service at a greatly reduced cost, or to boost the job satisfaction and morale of their staff while at the same time responding instantaneously to all the instructions received from ministers. To survive, and cope with the demands made on them, they will have to be patient and resilient. Their more traditional realism will have to be heavily spiced with optimism. They will need to have, and display, a proper humility. In these and other ways they will have to try to keep alive human feeling, individuality and sensitivity, even in the hostile and alienating environment of large and technocratic organisations.

It may be argued that this list of requirements is so utopian as to be ridiculous. It might be impossible to find all these qualities in any substantial measure in a single individual, or even as general characteristics of any one system. But, if they are regarded as ideals, they do provide us with some guidelines in taking the more mundane decisions we can take in order to ensure that future civil servants at least begin to meet the demands made upon them.

First, there is the possibility of doing something more to develop and maintain public confidence and trust. This is partly a matter of how well civil servants do their jobs. Confidence and trust have to be earned. But it may also be a matter of fostering clearer and more realistic views about their role. A good deal of informed public discussion may be necessary, both to resolve conflicting views of this role (so that they have a clearly understood job to do) and to improve understanding of what can in practice be achieved and at what cost (so that the job they are required to do is a realistic one).

The second, and more important, question is one of personnel management, how best to produce the civil servants we need. The process will obviously start with selection and recruitment, especially so far as personal qualities are concerned. Expertness will be built up through a combination of intellectual training and practical experience. The ability to use resources efficiently and economically, and to adopt participative styles of management, will depend partly on training, but also on practical experience at an early stage in the individual's career. It may be an equally important factor that the structures within which civil servants work should encourage these characteristics and that, when they are displayed, the system of promotion should reward them. The task of producing and moulding tomorrows's civil servants will certainly not be a once-for-all task undertaken at the beginning of their careers. Rather, it will continue throughout their working lives, blending such techniques as career development and post-experience training with the crucial contribution to the process that must be made, in the last resort, by the civil servant himself.

D. Lewis, 'The Qualities of Future Civil Servants', *Parliamentary Affairs,* Autumn 1980

The Future of the Civil Service

A number of the problems currently affecting the Civil Service, as outlined above have been recently discussed by William Plowden (a former senior civil servant and now Director-General of the Royal Institute for Public Administration) and Nevil Johnson (of Oxford University) in two thought-provoking articles.

Plowden has argued that widespread criticisms of the senior levels of the Civil Service point in the direction of a reformed Treasury or a recreated CPRS, or possibly an enlarged Prime Minister's department. This would also entail the departmental select committees of the House of Commons (post 1979) adopting an even greater scrutinising role than is presently exercised. But that was not all.

Special issue on the Civil Service: *Public Administration,* Winter 1985

'The efficiency strategy is relatively unconcentious. Not so a rather different line of argument about how best to get things done in government which is now starting to emerge from the closet. This is the belief that if ministers are to develop a more effective organization they should have more control over key postings within it; or, more strongly, that they should ensure that key posts are held by civil servants enthusiastic about the policies projected or actually in hand; or, more strongly still, that some posts should be held not by career officials but by outside appointees. The Prime Minister's undoubted personal influence on a few recent senior appointments is seen as a portent.

See also the series of articles on the Civil Service in *Parliamentary Affairs,* October 1986

A portent, that is, variously of a more rational approach to the manning of government or of an irreversible slide towards a replica of the situation in the United States.

It is not at all obvious that practices in Whitehall have in fact changed greatly in the past decade. Some of those most closely involved argue that for years determined ministers have successfully influenced at least key appointments. But, in a curious conspiracy of double-bluff, others prefer to pretend that although the formal rules acknowledge the possibility of ministerial influence none is actually exercised. This, they say, is quite right: acknowledging ministerial influence in this context would mean abandoning a tradition justified by years of practice, whereby impartial officials offer neutral advice to ministers of any persuasion and carry out, with unemotional efficiency, the instructions which they receive.

The straw man of the US federal civil service is fetched out and vigorously pummelled yet again. A recent public talk by the Secretary of the Cabinet contained not only a reference to the USA but also the dire words: 'There is an overall pattern and logic about the (constitutional and administrative) system as a whole; and it would be difficult to change particular conventions without putting the stability of other parts of the framework at risk'.

Others argue, rather differently, that in the absence of a British Bill of Rights or constitutional court the civil service is our best available check on arbitrary behaviour by ministers.

My own belief is that recent events are indeed a portent of a long-term trend towards greater political control – using that phrase very loosely to cover both the strong and the weak senses outlined above – of the civil service. I also believe that such a trend is necessary and desirable. What C.H. Sisson called the 'non-entity of the administrator' seems to me a psychological nonsense. That is to say, I do not believe that thoughtful individuals, with their own established practices and values, can, in fact, support with equal enthusiasm governments with totally dissimilar ideologies; or that they can prevent the relative intensity of their enthusiasms from influencing their behaviour. Alternatively, an intolerable strain can be placed on conscientious officials compelled to implement policies with which they personally disagree. Whatever the theoretical right of civil servants to ask to be moved if they find themselves in this unhappy situation, the actual conventions are pretty clear: you get on with the job. The individual who successfully insists on a move is likely to be marked down as unsound. What is needed is a system, and a change of attitudes, which would make it relatively normal for individual officials to be moved, at their own request or at their minister's, out of (and into) sensitive jobs without loss of face.

Many jobs, of course, are not affected by changes in government complexion; there is no need for wholesale politicization of the civil service and there are strong arguments against this. I am thinking of the relatively few posts whose responsibilities closely touch the ideology of the governing party, or which bring them into close personal contact with ministers.

My reasons for arguing this are partly pragmatic. The relationship between politicians and bureaucrats is always liable to be problematic; I believe that in Whitehall it has for long been unsatisfactory, and that it is deteriorating. It is partly a question of the balance between politicians and officials. This may be more a psychological than a managerial issue. I suspect that some ministers' aggressive attitude towards officials derives from their feeling of insecurity when faced with these serried ranks who may not be on their side. They believe that only the brutal approach will carry them through; or, more moderately, that it is prudent not to consult the mandarins for fear of becoming engulfed in a treacly consensus. Whatever the explanations, it is no use civil servants claiming that the traditional relationship works well if politicians feel that it does not. Some account must be taken of the facts of life.

I am also uneasy at the line which seems to be gaining currency in the present government, that all these problems can be avoided if the proper distinctions are made between policy and administration (or implementation): the former should be reserved for elected politicians and political advisers, and the latter left to civil servants. Attempts to enforce this kind of distinction can do only harm. If ministers do not trust their officials' involvement in policy, they would do better to change at least some of their officials.

I am unmoved by the plausible counter-argument that if ministers are served and advised by sympathisers they will never hear the frank dissent which from time to time they need. Plain speaking is surely much more likely – and likely to be acceptable – between people who believe that they are on the same side.

Finally, the claim that a neutral civil service is the best guarantee of an Englishman's liberty seems to me a wholly undesirable argument for an increasingly undemocratic status quo. Politicians in power should be able to carry out the policies to which they are pledged, and then judged by their electorate on the effectiveness or ineffectiveness of these. They should not be obstructed by unaccountable permanent officials guided by some inexplicit private conception of the national interest.'

Plowden continued: 'This brings me to reflect briefly on management, and on change.' He argued that the Whitehall 'mandarins' should not think of themselves as 'mere administrators'. They were managers, just as they would have been in the private sector.

'In my view the main failings of the civil service include those identified by Lord Curzon and Mr Heath: caution, lack of creativity, scepticism towards new ideas. To these I would add its insularity, and the lack of sensitivity towards other institutions – including the public at large – that flows from this. These faults are not peculiar to the British civil service; indeed it compares pretty well with other bureaucracies.'

Johnson has also argued for change in the upper echelons of Whitehall and sees the problems in constitutional terms.

'The fashionable criticism of the present government's approach to the civil service is that it has come near to demanding from civil servants a degree of commitment incompatible with their duty to offer equal support to whatever government is in power. More specifically the government has at least shown signs of exercising a discretion in the making of top appointments which is, formally speaking, its by right, but which by custom and practice had come to be vested for the most part in the Head of the civil service. In other words, the government's inclination not to treat the civil service as a closed corporation, hermetically sealed against external interference, has been seen by some as a serious breach of constitutional convention.

The issue of political influences on senior appointments is, however, not at the heart of the constitutional difficulty. The fundamental constitutional problem arises in relation to those familiar principles, ministerial responsibility and parliamentary accountability. Both in law and in the popular imagination ministers remain responsible for a formidable range of decisions: the policy responsibility remains theirs because policy is what involves an exercise of political discretion and for that reason is a matter of political controversy. Sustaining the theory and practice of ministerial responsibility is Parliament's insistence on the accountability of ministers before it. There is little to be gained from an attempt to assess the effectiveness and range of parliamentary accounta-bility. What matters is that the House of Commons still focuses its attention on ministers and the new departmental select committees notwithstanding, generally refuses to accept officials as surrogates for ministers.

The prejudice in society and in Parliament in favour of being able to get at ministers remains strong, and it must be admitted that so far no adequate methods of enforcing the accountability of managers in the public services have been devised. The outlines of a solution to the problem can, however, be discerned, even though it would in turn produce other difficulties. This would be to draw a sharper distinction between officials specialising in policy advice and political support functions, and those (in the majority) with managerial functions. For the former the principle of subordination to ministers would continue to apply, whilst for the latter it would be necessary to define their duties in terms of executive functions for which they would owe a greater degree of public accountability to appropriate controlling or supervisory agencies. Perhaps such bodies as the National Audit Office and select committees of the Commons could be the means through which the public accountability of this more independent public service manager for the performance of his organization and services would be ensured, though it is likely that supplementary arrangements would also need to be developed. No doubt too a clearer separation between political administration and management of the kind envisaged would be reinforced by a continuing tendency to take executive tasks out of central departments and to give them a distinctive organizational form. It is very doubtful whether a development going as far as this is yet seriously envisaged either by ministers or by the few senior officials who can be expected to advise on such matters. But a careful examination of the implications of much that is now being done to improve management practices might well suggest that to gain substantial benefits from such action more far-reaching structural changes in the civil service will be required than have so far been envisaged.'

See Appendix A

Johnson concluded that there remained much uncertainty and ambiguity about the type of Civil Service which would emerge as a result of the commitment to a managerial role, and that strong attachments to traditional doctrines remained, as illustrated by the Cabinet Secretary's memorandum issued in 1985 after the Ponting Case. Above all, Johnson thought, the management, and by implication morale, of the Civil Service would continue to be affected by a long-term depressed economy, compared with the favourable rates of growth from 1950 to 1970. That would mean that by the end of the century the Civil Service would be qualitatively different in decisive respects from that which was created by the great reforms of the last century, and the pursuit of them to completion in the early decades of this.

144

'Perhaps Parliament and the parties will modify some of their deeply-rooted prejudices in order to recognise the limits of ministerial responsibility and the need to acknowledge the accountability of the managers; and in all probability the civil service will continue to shed those characteristics, institutional, social and operational, which traditionally have been held to distinguish it as a world apart, an estate of the realm. If and when such an evolution has been completed, the inheritance of the Victorian civil service will have been subsumed in a new ethos of public service which may, paradoxically and without premeditation, attach more importance to efficient service to the public than to deference to the transitory demands of politicians.'

Summary

The Civil Service has been tested on a number of issues since the late 1960s including the report by the Fulton Committee. In more recent years it appears that some of the senior ranks in Whitehall have been politicised under Mrs Thatcher's Government, as illustrated by the Westland Affair in 1986 (see p. 63).

As we have seen, most senior civil servants are based in London, and it is their task to shape policy, including legislative proposals, as well as to implement it as efficiently as possible. Of course, there are other policy inputs, most notably from the political parties, as well as from interest groups and other organisations.

Despite possible politicisation under Mrs Thatcher, the Civil Service is permanent and politically impartial. The most senior staff, the Permanent Secretaries who head each department of State, are not replaced when a government of a different political persuasion takes office, as in the USA. Impartially and continuity are the twin themes of 'good government', but how good or efficient that government has proved to be in recent years must be open to question.

Civil servants are also, by and large, anonymous. In the last resort ministers are responsible – the doctrine of ministerial responsibility is not quite dead, as seen by Dugdale in 1954, Carrington in 1982 and Brittan in 1986.

Various developments have, however, brought the Civil Service more into the public eye – poor morale and industrial action coupled with the growing influence of television. In addition, the probing functions of the departmental select committees since 1979 have ensured that many civil servants have had to give evidence in public, and under some very close questioning by MPs, the like of which had not been heard before. The general trend towards openness in government since 1970 has also increased the pressure on senior civil servants, as have investigations by the Ombudsman and the effect of the Crossman Diaries. Rarely, civil servants who have made serious mistakes will be named, as was the case with the 1972 inquiry into the collapse of the Vehicle and General Insurance Company the previous year.

One of the most important points covered in this chapter has been the recommendations of the Fulton Committee and the extent to which the opportunity for real reform in the Civil Service has been missed. This charge is a difficult one to answer, but the general conclusion must be that it was unsatisfactory to allow civil servants virtually total control of implementing a report which was pointedly critical of the same people. Moreover, the method of recruitment to the senior general administrative posts, including some extremely dated examination techniques such as very old and highly questionable intelligence tests, remains a cause for serious concern. Another charge, that of Oxbridge bias, has been consistently defended by the Civil Service Commission on the grounds that those universities produce the ablest students among those who apply to join the Civil Service. That may be so, but its critics would argue that such recruitment may not be socially desirable, and, moreover, while the Civil Service is full of able administrators, it is not well endowed with problem solvers, initiators or risk-takers, hence the economic muddle of the last 20 years or so. Senior civil servants would defend themselves by claiming that they must not go beyond the bounds of implementing (as opposed to formulating) Government policies. In some ways it is right that a major function of civil servants should be negative rather than positive; they can warn ministers of the pitfalls of a policy, but it is not always advice that is heeded, sometimes with disastrous results, as illustrated by the failure of the Industrial Relations Act 1971.

It should also be observed that within the Whitehall machine there is a degree of both departmentalism and interdepartmentalism. Senior civil servants will respond to ministers who keep on top of their briefs, the red boxes, who initiate policy, and, most importantly, who fight for the interests of the department, particularly when it comes to the allocation of resources. Equally, senior civil servants, a highly-knit profession, do co-operate with each other to solve inter-departmental disputes – Cabinet committees are 'shadowed' by committees consisting entirely of officials. In addition, because the Whitehall community is relatively small at the top, senior officials soon learn what is politically fashionable or what is not, which minister's star is in the ascendant and whose is in decline.

Finally, as economic problems since the mid-1960s have increasingly taxed the minds of civil servants and ministers, so there has been a parallel search for greater efficiency and more appropriate structures within government departments, such as PAR and the CPRS, which have been described earlier. Others are of more recent pedigree, including FMI and MINIS. The latter, Management Information for Ministers, was introduced by Mr Heseltine at the Department of the Environment, and subsequently at the Ministry of Defence, until his resignation as Defence Secretary in 1986. It was an information evaluation system to let the ministers know what the department was doing, by enabling ministers and senior civil servants to review work, compare priorities and allocate resources. It has been concerned with administrative rather than policy matters and placed a strong emphasis on staff costs and numbers.

See *Efficiency and Effectiveness in the Civil Service*: Government Observations on the 3rd Report from the Treasury and Civil Service Committee, HC 236, 1981–2 session, Cmnd 8616, 1982.

From the Government's White Paper of 1982 on efficiency in the Civil Service, has emerged FMI (Financial Management Initiative) which is not unlike MINIS but has a different emphasis. FMI's aim was to force managers (civil servants in this context) to develop a clear view of objectives and performance and of how to make

146

the best use of resources 'including a critical scrutiny of output and value for money'. The language of the 1982 White Paper is unsettlingly vague in places and it remains to be seen whether MINIS/FMI join PAR, CPRS and family in the museum of 'management techniques'.

See A. Gray and W.I. Jenkins, *Administrative Politics in British Government*, Wheatsheaf, 1985.

Questions

1. Consider the arguments for and against the widespread introduction of politically-committed academics or businessmen into government departments. (Joint Matriculation Board)

2. Compare and contrast the attempts of recent governments to tackle the problems of central government organisation. (Joint Matriculation Board)

3. What factors limit the ability of ministers to control the actions of civil servants? (London)

4. Is it true to say that the Civil Service merely carries out Government or parliamentary policy?

5 The House of Commons

'Politics is all one big fairy tale, none of them do what they say. We can argue about it, but it's meaningless because we have no say in what happens. I'll vote for anybody who looks after me, whether they're nudists or Chinese or what have you. But if they say they'll give us striped paint, then we should have the right to kick them out if they don't.'

A voter from Gloucester interviewed during the February 1974 General Election
(*New Society*, 28 February 1974)

Representatives

The voter from Gloucester was expressing – if in a very individual way – the problem of 'democratic' representation that is at the root of any political system, and which in the United Kingdom has been a recurring theme in politics ever since Edmund Burke's celebrated address to the electors of Bristol some two centuries ago. (Edmund Burke was an acknowledged philosopher of Whig conservatism in the eighteenth century. The point of his Bristol speech in 1774 was that representatives (MPs), once elected, were free agents.) How political representatives are chosen and how they behave are puzzling questions that belong as much to modern as to ancient times. Before looking at the House of Commons in detail, therefore, it is appropriate to examine briefly the general nature of the representative process.

See also C. Leeds, *Politics in Action*, Stanley Thornes, 1986, (section D)

Birch's definitions

A.H. Birch has given us three very useful definitions of the term 'representative'. In one sense it can be used, he has observed, to indicate that someone or something is the symbol of a certain abstract identity or quality. Thus it might be said that the Russian leader is the most important representative of the communist world in Eastern Europe, or that the hammer and sickle represents communism.

A.H. Birch, *Representation*, Macmillan, 1971, p. 17

Secondly, the term can be used to mean 'being typical of'. Labour Members of the Commons might be thought to represent the working class and Conservative MPs the middle class. But, given the social background of Labour MPs, most Members of the Commons are very much middle-class people, whichever party they belong to.

Some research by R.W. Johnson proves the point. He has shown that three-quarters of Labour MPs in the inter-war period were working class, with solely an elementary school background, but that by 1970 the proportion had fallen to one-

148

quarter. He also calculated that two-thirds of Tory MPs and 44 per cent of the total Commons membership had business backgrounds. Perhaps this means that 'we shall return to the situation which last took place in the late nineteenth century, when the two major parties, led by upper- and middle-class élites, vied for the votes of a working class which was effectively excluded from representation at élite level.' *New Society, 24 January 1974*

The point is well illustrated by looking at the figures for the House of Commons after the General Elections of October 1974, 1979 and 1983.

Occupational and educational background of Members of Parliament	Labour 1974	Labour 1979	Conservative 1974	Conservative 1979
1. Barristers or Solicitors	43	31	59	70
2. Journalists, Publishers (including Public Relations)	37	19	36	38
3. Teachers or Lecturers	75	53	8	14
4. Farmers or Landowners	0	2	21	25
5. Company Directors or Management Executives	57	34	114	134
6. Trade Union Officials	19	27	0	1
7. Party Officials	3	5	4	12
8. Manual Workers	28	32	0	0
9. Others	57	65	34	45
10. Oxford University	60	38	80	94
11. Cambridge University	24	20	73	75
12. Other Universities	106	107	56	87
13. Eton	1	1	48	50
14. Harrow	0	0	10	9
15. Winchester	24	2	116	7
16. Other Public Schools		18		138
17. Grammar or Equivalent	161	108	58	90
(Figures 10–17 exceed totals of MPs elected because of pro-gressive nature of education)				
Number of Members elected	319	268	276	339

Source: *The Times Guides to the House of Commons, October 1974 and May 1979*
In respect of the 1983 House of Commons about one-third of all MPs had attended Oxford or Cambridge; about 60 per cent of Conservative MPs had been to private school but only approximately 15 per cent of Labour MPs. Virtually all the Conservative MPs had pursued a professional or similar career while the figure for Labour was about two-thirds.

Professor Birch has emphasised that the word 'representative', defined as 'typical', tells us little about a person's functions, intentions or perhaps even behaviour, but is rather a comment on his personal and social characteristics, and he has underlined his argument by providing the example of a lecturer in international relations at an American university conducting a seminar on the problems in the Middle East. The lecturer might call on an Arab student (if present) to put forward the 'Arab view-point', and perhaps introduce him as a 'representative of the Arab world'. Yet, Birch says, the student in question might not hold views typical of Arabs in general, and might well put up a less adequate defence of Arab politics than an American student. 'As a spokesman for the Arab world he might be a complete failure. But a special significance would probably be attached to his contribution because of his nationality, and subsequent speakers might weigh their words more carefully than they would if no 'representative of the Arab world' were present.'

If a legislature or a government (or both) were reasonably typical of the whole community, if it were a cross-section of the various constituent parts of a nation or state, then it could be described as a genuine social microcosm. But things rarely turn out as simply as that, as has been observed in respect of the educational and occupational background of Members of Parliament. Sometimes, however, custom may ensure – up to a point – that self-correcting mechanisms are built into the political process, so that identifiable minorities are guaranteed a fair hearing. In Canada history and tradition dictate that a reasonable number of places in the federal Cabinet shall be reserved for French Canadians. In Wales, for instance, parliamentary candidates are invariably of Welsh extraction. In a similar way American campaign managers will feel obliged to go for the balanced ticket, especially in city elections. A party which put forward in Boston no candidate with an Irish background would commit local political suicide.

Custom and convention may prove inadequate, however, and may mean the passage of special, and possibly discriminatory, legislation. Social engineering by political means can frequently be found in countries, often developing ones, that are faced with acute ethnic or religious problems.

'Positive discrimination' can, though, work in reverse; it is not always a matter of guaranteeing adequate representation to regional, ethnic, or religious minorities. The majority itself may take protective measures if it feels potentially threatened by a minority that is either substantial or likely to become so. Such problems can be observed in Malaysia, and to a lesser extent in its ethnically similar neighbour – Indonesia. In Malaysia it is the Chinese who, constituting some 40 per cent of the population, dominate commercial life. Apparently overwhelmed by the scale of Chinese entrepreneurial activity, the indigenous Malays – the *bumiputra* – have been determined to keep their hands on the levers of political power – particularly as they constitute 50 per cent of the population (Indians and others form the remaining 10 per cent). In effect this had led to compensatory overrepresentation for Malays in parliament. Furthermore, since the end of the Malayan Emergency in 1960 special laws have been passed. Based initially on previous British practice in the Malay states, these have been designed to give the *bumiputra* a head start not just politically but also economically. Looked at in a negative sense, through European eyes, such a policy might be judged as a milder form of apartheid; in a more positive sense it could be seen as part of a careful long-term plan to carve a harmonious multi-racial nation out of a country whose extremely diverse ethnicity had been brought about largely through the actions of its former colonial master. The policy of 'Malayanisation' was considered necessary in order to give Malays (as opposed to Chinese and other non-Malays) 'the capability to overcome their initial inadequacies, both material and environmental. . . . Malays cling to the belief that the upliftment of their economic status is a *sine qua non* for communal harmony and national integration.' The party groupings in the Malaysian Parliament have long reflected this crucial political dilemma.

Tham Seong Chee, *Malays and Modernization*, Singapore University Press, 1977, pp. 146 and 293

Delegates or free agents?

The third meaning of 'representative' is the most important, and it is that which refers to an agent or spokesman acting on behalf of a person or group. It is a vital, but unwritten, rule in Western systems that the electorate must be given a meaningful choice of two or more party programmes; the one-party state, in whatever form it may appear, is unacceptable. (The electorate, it is believed, knows best, even if in some instances its wishes result in a confused election outcome.) Members of the House of Commons are representatives of the mass electorate, constituency by constituency, elected along party lines for the sake of educational and logical convenience in a socially mobile and complex industrial society. But, following Burke, they would invariably claim that once elected they must, within the constraints of the party platform on which they stood, be given reasonable freedom of action to vote and to do as they think best. Although they are identified with a stated party programme, they are not mandated to vote in a particular way upon every parliamentary detail. Individual MPs do not regard themselves as delegates – Parliament is not a 'Westminster Conference' at which they have been instructed, either by their constituency parties or by the wider electorate, to vote in one direction or another on the fine print of the governing party's election manifesto.

That MPs regard themselves as free agents was well illustrated during the Falklands Crisis in 1982. Following the unexpected invasion of the islands by Argentina an emergency debate was held on a Saturday in the Commons. (The Lords also met that day.) MPs were in a bellicose mood and the few who wanted the Government and the House to pause before it despatched the Navy to this remote 'outpost of Empire', 8000 miles away and with a population the size of an English village, were shouted down. At that stage public opinion was not particularly in favour of despatching the armed forces, although once the conflict was underway traditional patriotism came to the fore.

The House of Commons, we can argue, enshrines the representative system, for its role is crucial in the country's adherence to a political system which says that the people can, and should, choose their own representatives. But representation takes place in all countries and at a variety of levels, as a series of what might be called horizontal layers of political activity. It may play a part in 'such varied phenomena as the selection of trade union leaders, the resolution of disputes in a nomadic tribe, the government of a modern industrial state, diplomatic relations between states, and the activities of the Vietcong or the Palestine Liberation Front' (A.H. Birch). The House of Commons may be the most important representative body in the

151

Clement Attlee, Prime Minister 1945–51

UK, but it is by no means the only one. The United Kingdom, like most other societies, even the semi-traditional, less-developed ones, is a pluralistic country. In addition, since the objectives of a society, a group or a national government are often all-embracing, representatives, whether chosen or elected, assign either themselves or others a variety of roles which the electors may never have had specifically in mind at the time of choosing them. Such roles can include intervention in the economy, intervention in the internal politics of local government at home, or intervention in the policies of other states – either surreptitiously, as with the CIA's involvement in President Allende's Chile from 1971 to 1973, or in Nicaragua since 1982, or more formally, for example through representation at the United Nations or on such bodies as the Namibian Settlement Conference since 1978.

In Britain today it may appear that the system of parliamentary representation is limited and inadequate; it is not Parliament but the Government which succeeds or fails in the eyes of most electors. Whatever the particular model of representation may be, or however it may develop, modern Western society is dominated by large bureaucracies, big international business and powerful sectional and interest groups, such as trade unions and City financiers. Parliamentary representatives are reduced to the role of legislative checks and political safety-valves. But that, it is argued, and as we shall see later, is perhaps too pessimistic, if not simplistic, a view. In the end, albeit rarely, a parliamentary vote may bring down a

Government, as happened to Chamberlain in 1940 and Callaghan in 1979. Peter Jenkins offered the following apposite observation in *The Guardian* in 1977 (2 March):

> 'Representative Democracy does not depend upon political parties – still less upon trade unions or other interest groups – being themselves democratic in the same form or to the same degree. Representative Democracy is in its essence a system of government judged by results. . . . Only through consent, resting upon the satisfactory performance of government, can the legitimacy of Representative Democracy be assured. How to obtain it in an arena of competing groups, and how to exercise the authority necessary for obtaining the results, are among the conundrums of our times.'

Parliament and Government: the Constitutional Position

The relationship of the Legislature to the Executive (Government) has been a familiar enough theme in British political history. Parliament is supreme; it can make whatever laws it likes, the Executive must implement them, and the judiciary – whatever its doubts or whatever its powers of interpretation and legal commentary – must enforce them. Ministers of the Crown are responsible to Parliament for their conduct of departmental affairs. That, at least, is the theoretical position. In practice the Government will usually succeed in what it wants to achieve, if only because virtually all MPs are party people. Given the nature of parliamentary elections and the traditions of fairly rigid party discipline, most legislation introduced into Parliament by the Executive will obtain a majority vote. Nevertheless, back-benchers can – and do – rebel; they will demonstrate that they are still in command, even if that command over the Executive seems rather passive at times. In the summer of 1969, for example, there was a threat of widespread revolt among Labour back-benchers against their Government's proposed Industrial Relations Bill. A similar, although less dramatic, scene occurred in the Commons in 1976 after the Government's proposals to defer the new Child Benefit Scheme had been leaked to the public by a weekly periodical. In 1979 a number of Conservative back-benchers forced Mrs Thatcher's Government to reduce the proposed cuts in the BBC's External Services. Between 1966 and 1970 there were Labour back-bench revolts covering most major areas of the Labour Government's activity, including prices and incomes, Rhodesia, social services, defence, the EEC, Vietnam, Northern Ireland, the House of Lords, the Nigerian civil war, immigration, the IMF and taxes.

See also J.R.S. Whiting, Politics and Government, Stanley Thornes, 1985, (sections B and C)

> 'Altogether, there are records of open revolts involving at least 15 Labour MPs on 33 divisions in the House of Commons during the 1966–70 period. However, undoubtedly the traditions of British party government played a part in setting limits on both the size of the Labour rebellions and the actions of the rebels, particularly in that most Labour MPs possessed ingrained loyalties to their party and, indirectly, to the Government placed in office by that party.'

Parliamentary Affairs, Autumn 1974

153

Twice within the space of a dozen years the Government responded to the unrest by introducing a system of specialist select committees.

One important qualification must be added here. As Valentine Herman has judged (in a study of post-war Queen's Speeches), there is in any case a physical limit to the number of important things the governing party can get through Parliament. To take two examples, 1967–8 and 1968–9 were both sessions when the Government faced particular difficulties over its policy intentions, even though there was a large Government majority in the Commons at that time.

Parliamentary Affairs, Winter 1974–75

'The reason why the Labour administration failed in these sessions, and why other governments have failed in the past, is because an attempt was made to pass too many important measures through Parliament in too short a time, and, in drawing up the relevant Queen's Speeches, misjudgements of the effects of various constraining legislative and extra-legislative forces were made.'

Mrs Thatcher faced not dissimilar problems in the 1979–80 session, for example over the Housing Act 1980 which had to be supplemented by further legislation in 1984 and 1986.

Sometimes the Government may misjudge the mood of the whole House. This was apparent when the Commons expressed its collective dissatisfaction that the 1977 Fay Report enquiring into the financial irregularities of the Crown Agents was too narrow in scope. The Government established a tribunal of inquiry which reported in 1982, the Croom-Johnson Report, whose publication was totally overshadowed by the outbreak of the Falklands War.

BBC Radio 3, 26 March 1976

Whether the relationship of the House of Commons to Government policy and administration – including the problems of financial scrutiny – would be assisted at all by some form of pre-legislative committee (as opposed to standing committees, which examine the details of legislation without regard to the merits or demerits of having it in the the first place) is very much an open question. In a radio discussion Edward Heath recalled one occasion in the 1950s when both a committee of civil servants and another in the Commons considered the advisability of reforming the Army and Navy Acts, and thus effectively assumed the role of a pre-legislative committee, but that was a rare instance. Nowadays Government has become big business, and the growth and variety of administrative 'ad hoc' bodies have added to the already increasing pressure on MPs. And although in the late 1960s the Civil Service in a drive towards greater efficiency and internal accountability, employed a large number of new management techniques (such as Organisation and Methods, Operational Research, Discounted Cash Flow), that development did not remove the problem of gaining adequate parliamentary control over the Executive and its bureaucracy. These were difficulties that were reflected in two major periods of back-bench unrest – from 1965 to 1971 and from 1975 to 1980. In the first period (1965–71) there was some development in the role of select committees under Richard Crossman, Leader of the House between 1966 and 1968, but the experiment was by no means a success.

Demand from the back-benchers for a revitalised committee system began in 1975, but this time MPs were far more concerned with the financial accountability of the Government to Parliament. This debate owed its origins to the 1961

Plowden Report on the management of public expenditure. Despite increasing 'co-operation between ministries', the Report had found that in general most public expenditure decisions were made in a piecemeal fashion. In the meantime the Commons had learnt several things from the Crossman experiment, notably that it had provided an opportunity to put ministers and civil servants on the spot. One minister who had been grilled for two hours by a select committee is reported to have said, 'it's terribly disturbing because there is nowhere to run for cover.' Nevertheless that remark needs to be qualified in the sense that experienced members of the Cabinet may find the going less rough. In his review of the Crossman committees, Shell remarked, 'appearances by ministers before Select Committees may be chiefly noted for their uneventfulness.' Many MPs have certainly suspected that civil servants are reluctant to spend too much energy on supplying information to select committees. The Agriculture Committee found a large number of obstacles put in its way, and encountered almost total silence when it asked for details of how the Annual Farm Price Review was calculated. To some extent perhaps the specialist select committees have not always been fully trusted because of a tendency to develop, in Professor Crick's phrase, 'a shocking habit of regarding the Executive as guilty until it is proven innocent.'

Control of Public Expenditure, Cmnd 1432, 1961

D.R. Shell, Parliamentary Affairs, Autumn 1970

The Guardian, 12 June 1973

Edmund Dell, chairman of the Public Accounts Committee from 1972 to 1974, and Trade Secretary from 1975 to 1978, complained that the committees often wasted their influence by 'writing essays' about what policy ought to be, rather than accepting it and scrutinising the way it was being implemented. Crossman himself thought that the changes of the late 1960s and early 1970s had not succeeded in shifting the balance against the Government and, in typically Crossman fashion, posed the question: 'Are you quite sure that you haven't denuded the floor and strengthened the Executive after all?'

The referendum debate about membership of the EEC in 1975, the European Assembly elections issue in 1977, the devolution question in 1978 and a number of other problems (such as the inquiry into the financial collapse of the Crown Agents in 1977) again placed in question the power of Parliament itself and its position in a pluralistic society of pressure groups and industrial trade unions.

As stated earlier, one of the most serious points of contention in the second half of the 1970s was the degree to which the Commons exercised effective power in the area of financial scrutiny. This area was critical because of the huge sums of money involved. Public expenditure as a proportion of GDP reached a peak of 47 per cent in 1975, compared with just a few per cent at the turn of the century. The Commons' committee watchdogs – the select committees on Expenditure and Public Accounts – attempted to keep some back-bench track of Government expenditure, but with increasing difficulty, although from time to time major Government blunders were discovered, for example that of Ferranti's overcharging for missiles in 1964.

See Parliamentary Affairs, Spring 1980 for an assessment of the PAC.

Du Cann's views

Edward du Cann, chairman of the Expenditure Committee from 1971 to 1972 and chairman of the Public Accounts Committee from 1974 to 1979, told the Commons in 1975 that he doubted whether the House set about the task of

155

examining expenditure as skilfully as it might have done. He urged the amalgamation of the two committees, and remarked that perhaps the British Parliament could learn from the experience of the United States. In 1976 he remarked, on a television programme, 'there is an irony that never is there greater interest in the subject and never is expenditure more out of control.' Parliament was simply not doing its job, he said; in Britain 'we elect dictatorships'. He wanted to restore to the back-benches 'the authority they once had'. Du Cann said that all Governments should keep to their [three]-year plans, subject to special appeal to Parliament, instead of the parliamentary scenes being 'littered with open-ended commitments'; ministers should be obliged to surrender a large part of their authority to Parliament, he added.

BBC 2,
31 July 1976

Even allowing for party views, these were pretty damning criticisms of the Executive, and they underline the fact that any legislature in a modern, technocratic and probably inflationary society will experience considerable practical difficulty in maintaining its *authority* over ministerial-executive *power*. In the United Kingdom this is illustrated by the fact that traditionally every year, usually in November and February, Parliament is asked to vote Winter and Spring Supplementary Estimates for the current year's Supply Estimates. The main Supply Estimates consist, broadly speaking, of immensely detailed breakdowns of departmental expenditure. As such they are usually too complex for MPs to examine in depth. (The Supply Estimates form the basis of the annual Consolidated Fund Act.) They are agreed in May, and subsequently prove deficient in some way – hence the need for Supplementary Estimates. In 1985 MPs complained that the Government allowed them insufficient time to discuss the main (Winter) Supplementary Estimates: 'it cannot be in the best interest of the House for its business to be conducted in such haste.'

First Report,
Liaison Committee,
HC 363,1984–5
session

A New System

HC 588, 1977–8
session

Somewhat unexpectedly the newly-elected Conservative Government, in 1979, proposed that the most notable recommendation of the 1978 Report from the Select Committee on Procedure should be put into effect, and the Commons readily agreed. Thus the existing patchwork system of select committees was largely swept away. The Expenditure, Nationalised Industries, Race Relations and Immigration, Science and Technology and Overseas Development committees were all abolished. Instead 12 new committees were established to examine the expenditure, administration and policies of the major Government departments. They were: Agriculture; Defence; Education; Science and Arts; Employment; Energy; the Environment; Foreign Affairs; Home Affairs; Trade and Industry; Social Services; Transport; and the Treasury and Civil Service. Later in the same year two further committees were added – one on Scottish Affairs (to monitor the Scottish Office) and one on Welsh Affairs (to monitor the Welsh Office).

The Commons approved the Government's suggestion that a separate select committee should still continue to examine the reports of the Parliamentary

Commissioner for Administration and where appropriate those of the Health Service Commissioner. The Public Accounts Committee also survived. In addition, any two or more of the Energy, Environment, Trade and Industry, Transport and Treasury select committees might, from time to time, establish a sub-committee to consider any matter common to two or more nationalised industries.

The new departmental committees have the power to demand (but not, in practice, to compel) the attendance of ministers and the production of necessary papers at their hearings, a number of which are held in public. Whether, during the course of the 1980s, the select committees will develop inquisitorial characteristics in the manner of American congressional committees is another matter. As one political correspondent commented, writing before the Westland inquiries,

'Over a period they could transform the relationships between back-bench and front-bench MPs, between Whitehall and Westminster and, ultimately, between civil servants and their political masters. . . . It is up to MPs to make of the reforms what they will'.

Financial Times, 29 June 1979

One other important point should be noted: the appointment of MPs to the select committees is in the hands of the Commons' own Committee of Selection, not, as before, in those of the party Whips. (The Whips, however, nominate the members of the Selection Committee.) Moreover, the Government agreed that the committee chairmen could form their own Liaison Committee.

In the Commons debate on the new committees, the shadow Home Secretary, Merlyn Rees, remarked: 'These committees will require thoroughness on the part of the members, otherwise they will fail,' and the Leader of the House, Norman St John Stevas, observed:

'I give the House this pledge on the part of the Government, that every minister, from the most senior Cabinet minister to the most junior Parliamentary Under-Secretary, will do all in his or her power to co-operate with the new system of committees and make it a success.'

It remains to be seen how far the select committees introduced in 1979 can maintain an effective bipartisan approach in their examination of Government policies. In other words, what is the maximum point to which both Government and Opposition back-benchers can travel in their critical analysis of Whitehall forecasts before the traditions of competitive party philosophy negate the committee's initially united front? Having dubbed the system of estimates 'a farce', the new Treasury and Civil Service Committee (chaired by du Cann) launched a blistering attack on the Government's forecasts for industrial output, unemployment and the PSBR (Public Sector Borrowing Requirement). Du Cann said, 'If the House of Commons is to decide whether it supports the Government, it must have all the forecasts and assumptions with which to make up its mind.' One comment on the episode was as follows:

1st Special Report, HC 503, 1979–80 session: Consideration of Spring Supplementary Estimates

3rd Report, HC163, 1980–1 session

'Treasury civil servants, accustomed to running rings round ill-briefed parliamentarians, have had to reconsider how in future to let out information without sounding like stones wrung from blood. And the eleven committee members themselves have to decide whether they and their professional advisers have the time and stamina to keep up the pressure on Whitehall or whether the system will drive them back as it has done with so many reforming initiatives.'

The Sunday Times, 4 May 1980

157

In 1982 two Conservative members of the Transport Committee abstained on the second reading of the Transport Bill because of the Government's insistence upon selling off HGV testing stations to the private sector, although the committee, fearing that the sale could endanger safety, had taken the opposite view.

There is no doubt the new system of departmental committees has produced a wealth of useful information about the governmental and legislative process since 1980. But the crux of the matter is: how far has the Government taken notice? This is a difficult point, but it does appear the Government is no more influenced by highly critical reports than it is by those which are argued less harshly.

Under the National Audit Act 1983 the Public Accounts Committee (PAC) has greater powers to oversee 'value for money' investigations into the spending departments: these are undertaken by the Comptroller and Auditor-General, now an officer of the House. The Comptroller may take into account any proposals made by the PAC to investigate the economy, efficiency and effectiveness of any department or relevant authority. Nationalised industries and local government are not subject to his authority. Financial scrutiny of the Comptroller's department, the National Audit Office, is undertaken by the Public Accounts Commission, made up of the Leader of the House, the PAC's chairman and seven non-ministerial MPs.

DOCUMENT

18

The New Select Committees

The reconstituted system of Commons select committees, which was described as "major, successful parliamentary reform" by a monitoring committee of MPs early in June, is looking rather less healthy today after a series of setbacks in the closing weeks before the recess.

A select committee examining the Government's conduct of the Falklands war divided irreconcilably along party lines and delivered two rival reports. A select committee report on the NCB's treatment of miners dismissed during the pit dispute was dismissed with open contempt by the Prime Minister, other senior ministers, and most Conservative MPs.

The Defence Secretary, Mr Michael Heseltine pushed on with plans to put naval dockyards under private management despite strong reservations from two select committees. And a joint committee of the Lords and Commons, which came out against the building of a by-pass at Okehampton, Devon, because it would pass through a national park was briskly overruled by the Transport Secretary, Mr Nicholas Ridley.

The SDP leader, Dr David Owen, said that Mr Heseltine's decision to press on with his chosen course for the dockyards without even publishing a response to the strictures of two select committees was such a serious affront that there ought to be an emergency debate on it. The Speaker disagreed.

Earlier in the session there had been complaints in the Commons from some Conservative MPs, as well as from the opposition parties, when the government fixed the second reading debate on the Transport Bill before the relevant select committee had completed its report on the issue. Government sources said the trouble lay with the select committee for not completing its work earlier.

Some MPs sympathetic to the select committee system think the fate of the foreign affairs committee report on the Falklands and the employment committee report on the NCB demonstrate the need for these committees to steer clear of mainstream issues on which the parties are divided.

In the employment committee, chaired by the Labour MP, Mr Ron Leighton, a split along party lines was averted only because Mr John Gorst, the maverick Conservative backbencher joined Labour MPs in criticising the NCB's treatment of dismissed miners.

When the committee's report appeared it was greeted by ministers without even the formal courtesies usually accorded even to those select committee reports, which ministers most dislike. The tone was set by the Prime Minister, who when asked to comment at question time, said that the select committee had completely failed to condemn the violence and intimidation which had been used against working miners.

The Energy Secretary, Mr Peter Walker, and the Employment Secretary, Mr Tom King, were equally contemptuous when questioned about the report later, using the same formula – the report's failure to condemn violence – as a reason to dismiss its findings entirely.

Mr Gorst was denounced by Conservative backbench colleagues on the committee during the press conference called to launch the report.

Divisions on party lines have often occurred before in select committees. But opponents of the system have usually hoped to keep them to a minimum, since it is when committees challenge government decisions on a cross-party basis that these committees are usually regarded as working most effectively as a curb on the executive.

In the case of the dockyards, the public accounts and defence committees were united across party lines in their criticism of Mr Heseltine's handling of the issue. The public accounts committee, one of the most senior and respected of all parliamentary select committees, expressed "severe misgivings" about Ministry of Defence costings for the scheme and said the department had not provided Parliament with enough evidence to enable it to take an informed decision. The committee suggested that savings of £40 million might be bought at a cost of £60 million. But these reservations were brushed aside by Mr Heseltine when he announced his decision to the Commons on July 2.

Some advocates of the select committee system see evidence that the Government is simply unwilling to listen to select committees when its own ideological preferences are threatened. They fear that ministers are attempting to relegate the committees to a minor commentating role. When Mr Ridley was attacked in the Commons by Mr Peter Rost, the Conservative backbencher who chaired the joint select committee on Oke-hampton, for disregarding its findings he told the House: "Committees do not make decisions, they make recommendations to Parliament, which in the end has to decide one way or another."

A further test of the Government's attitude will come after the recess, when it will have to respond to a report published at the end of July by the social services select committee.

Uniting across party lines, this committee had some severe criticisms of Mr Norman   159

Fowler's social security review. Condemning the absence of figures from the proposals, the committee said it was practically impossible to judge the plan without them. And it recommended that any legislation to abolish Serps (the state earnings-related pensions scheme) should be delayed until proper consultation had taken place.

David McKie, *The Guardian,* 6 August 1985

The Back-bencher's Powers

Private Members' Bills

One of an MP's cherished rights is that of introducing legislation of his own in the form of a Private Member's Bill. It should be remembered, however, that Government business takes up half the Commons' time each session, while Private Members' Bills (and motions) account for something like 8½ per cent. Back-bench MPs may use the ten-minute rule (Standing Order 19) by which during that space of time they will try to convince their colleagues that their legislative proposals are worth a second reading. The majority fail. An alternative is to introduce a Bill directly into the House under SO58, which is only marginally more successful than the ten-minute procedure. A SO19 Bill that survives the ten-minute hurdle must then follow the same route as one introduced under SO58. Some MPs can be very enterprising about the way in which Commons procedure may be adapted to their own party's advantage. For example, in November 1969, the Conservative Member for Tiverton, Robin Maxwell-Hyslop, queued all night outside the Public Bill Office and so obtained for himself and his back-bench party colleagues all the available time for introducing ten-minute rule Bills until December 1970.

But the best chance of success for a Private Member's Bill is by a third method, the annual ballot (SO13) at the beginning of each parliamentary session – each year some 20 MPs will draw a place, which gives them leave to introduce their own particular piece of legislation. The important thing that an MP who is lucky enough to draw a place in the ballot must remember is, in the first instance, to begin negotiations with the appropriate Government department (whichever side of the House he sits on), since it is only with Government backing that he stands any real chance of his own idea being placed on the statute book. The effects of the main points of the Bill must be calculated as closely as possible – will it offend certain vested interests in the community, and will it cause a significant number of other MPs to try to wreck it? The Public Bill Office will usually give a certain amount of free advice and help towards the drafting of a Bill, and nowadays an MP receives a grant towards the expenses involved.

The annual number of days for debate of Private Members' Bills is normally ten, of which six are generally reserved for second readings. This means in theory that it is usually the top six of the 20 balloted places who have by far the best chance of success, especially if the Bill chosen promotes useful but not controversial reform.

It is the debate on the second reading which will show what attitude the Government is taking. If the MP is clever and skilful enough to organise a strong cross-party alliance, he may be able to fight on without Government support, but the lower down the ballot he is the more difficult it becomes to succeed owing to lack of time. One of the best examples, of course, of a Private Member's Bill receiving fairly strong Government support (the Government did not want to introduce legislation itself on what was a sensitive moral issue) was the 1967 Abortion Act, piloted by David Steel. In contrast John Corrie's attempt to amend Mr Steel's Act failed in 1980 through lack of even indirect Government support. But Executive objections should not be seen as purely destructive, since in all fairness, Governments sometimes have more expertise at hand to judge what the results might be if a poorly constructed piece of legislation became law.

Emergency debates

There are many other tactics whereby back-benchers can make their influence felt. For example, motions for emergency debates under SO20 suspend the normal business of the House. Back-benchers of both major parties are equally frequent users of early day motions. These motions can cover any topic, and are, theoretically, meant to be debated at the earliest opportunity although the Speaker will usually give Government business first priority. It is sufficient, therefore, for the protest to have been made, even if the House spends no time debating it.

It is through emergency debates that Parliament as a whole can occasionally exert direct influence or control over the Executive, when it has the political will to do so. The Commons possesses considerable powers if it wishes to utilise them. A very good example occurred in 1977 when the Commons forced the Government to hold a public inquiry into the financial fiasco of the Crown Agents' activities between 1970 and 1976, although the Commons had itself failed to make the relevant ministers openly accountable in the first place.

The Parliamentary Commissioner for Administration (PCA)

Since 1967 MPs have had the added facility of the Parliamentary Commissioner, through whom attention may be drawn to certain issues. One study in 1972 showed, however, that 81 per cent of MPs used the PCA rarely or very rarely, 11 per cent never and only 8 per cent often or very often. However, since about 1977 the position appears to have improved, as shown by the statistics in Chapter 3. (The same survey showed that 4 per cent of MPs never asked a parliamentary question, 60 per cent rarely and 36 per cent often. All MPs approached ministers personally or by letter on various problems.)

Public Administration, Spring 1973

Adjournment debates

There are also adjournment debates, normally at the end of each day's business. Although Richard Crossman once referred to adjournment debates as 'lonely little affairs often related to parochial issues', Valentine Herman has observed that, like questions to ministers, they are one of the few devices which the back-bencher can use to control the timetable of the House in the face of Executive power. In his study of the 1966–7 session he found that the range of topics discussed in them was considerable, from a flooded street in a northern constituency, to the Banaban Islands, from a constituent's pension appeal, to the work of the United Nations.

Parliamentary Affairs, Winter 1972–73

Adjournment debates, although usually occurring late at night, can shift attention from national to local level. They are a kind of safety-valve to be used by MPs when letters and questions to ministers have failed to produce a satisfactory response. Through such debates, however unglamorous they may be, MPs can raise specialised interests and can go some way towards keeping government open. Up to a certain point adjournment debates have to be balloted for like Private Members' Bills.

Question time

Of course, the opportunity afforded to every back-bencher several times a week to ask ministers and the Prime Minister questions has been regarded as sacrosanct by parliamentarians – although the well-briefed replies of ministers have something of a hollow ring about them, and it is often the supplementary question which is the more devastating.

One survey found that there were few 'generalists' in either major party, both Conservative and Labour back-benchers preferring for the most part to ask questions, apart from constituency ones, only according to their own specialist interests – although this varied by party and by age. The survey, which analysed the 1970–1 session, found that in the Labour Party the ten most important categories of parliamentary questions, in order, were: constituency, Scotland, welfare, aviation, economics and finance, health, housing, employment, industry and agriculture, while the Conservative back-benchers produced the following ranking: constituency, EEC, aviation, economics and finance, agriculture, housing, transport, industry, welfare and foreign affairs.

Parliamentary Affairs, Spring 1974

Committee participation

Back-benchers have a vital part to play in committees in the Commons. The committees fall into three types; firstly, (the standing committees (which deal largely with the fine print of most Bills) and the specialist select committees of enquiry. Both perform an obvious and extremely important role in back-bench participation. The whole House is itself a committee on occasion, usually to discuss the details of an important piece of legislation.)

Secondly, there are a number of largely informal, almost non-political all-party committees. In the latter category fall such strange bedfellows as the Anglo-Malaysian Parliamentary Committee, the Deserted Families Group, the Houses of Parliament Swimming Club and the Parliamentary Migraine Group. One survey, by Kimber and Richardson, during the first half of 1971 showed that the most active all-party groups were, in this order: the Mental Health Parliamentary Group, the Third London Airport Group, the Commonwealth Parliamentary Association (UK), the Inter-Parliamentary Association (UK), the Parliamentary Disablement Group, the Anglo-Hong Kong Parliamentary Group, the Pollution of the Environment Group, the Anglo-German Parliamentary Group, the Parliamentary and Scientific Committee and the Tourist Committee.

Many of these groups (as J.D. Stewart had previously recognised) are logical extensions of outside pressure groups. Kimber and Richardson concluded that although only a small proportion of such all-party committees was really active, their work should not be undervalued, since

Parliamentary Affairs, Autumn 1972

> 'more than a handful of outside bodies have reason to be grateful for the fact that back-benchers are capable of co-operating with each other across party lines. Indeed all-party committees could become the focus for greater back-bench influence providing the back-benchers can develop an issue before the party lines have had a chance to harden.'

The third category of committee embraces purely party groups. The 1922 Committee is a body of Tory back-benchers; on the Labour side more emphasis is placed upon meetings of the whole parliamentary party (PLP). Both operate fairly secretly. When the Conservatives are in power, ministers attend meetings of the 1922 Committee only by invitation. Labour ministers, on the other hand, frequently attend meetings of the PLP, although it is chaired by a back-bencher.

The 1922 Committee has played a very significant role on at least three occasions: in 1922 (hence its title), when Conservative back-benchers decided to withdraw their support from Lloyd George's coalition Government; in 1940, when Chamberlain was virtually forced to resign from the premiership; and in 1951, when it drove Attlee's Labour Government (with its very slim majority) into a general election. The 1922 Committee, which appears to meet rather more frequently on average than the PLP, seems to be more successful in containing intra-party dissidence within the Conservative back-bench ranks; but then loyalty to the party leadership is generally more of a Conservative trait anyhow. The PLP meetings are probably less organised and disciplined than the 1922 Committee, with little in the shape of an agenda, and, in Michael Foot's words, 'on occasion the procedure may resemble a kind of liberal form of lynch law.'

The 1922 Committee and the PLP are not the only party committees in the House, but they are the most important and well-publicised. The Labour Party for instance, has House committees on employment, energy and other domestic affairs, while among the committees on the Tory side are those on the arts, foreign and Commonwealth affairs, Europe and finance. The structures of both parties' committees are similar.

Legislative amendments

One further important power at the disposal of MPs is that of putting down amendments to legislation. (See note on legislative procedure on p. 171.) These frequently come from the Government's own supporters. In the period Lynskey was studying up to the late 1960s, he observed that during the 1945–51 Attlee

Parliamentary
Affairs,
Winter 1973–74

administration two embarrassing amendments were moved in the Address (debate) replying to the King's Speech in 1946, as well as several motions and amendments to reject Government Bills. On the Conservative side there have been far fewer attempts to embarrass the Government, although in 1956 a notable one occurred in the shape of an amendment by Gerald Nabarro aimed at ruining the Coal Industry Bill.

Herman, in a study of most of the legislation in the 1968–9 session, noted that 533 amendments came from the Government side, while 225 came from the Opposition. (He was referring to amendments taken at report stage or in a Committee of the Whole House in the 45 (out of 51) Government Bills he considered.) Of the Opposition amendments only 12 were passed, but he pointed out that it is dangerous to consider that figure in isolation. In fact a certain number of Opposition suggestions were adopted by the Government, so that for that year, counted on a less strictly technical basis, the number of successful Opposition amendments went up to one major, eight important and 41 minor. Many amendments (emanating from pressure group activity) were withdrawn on explanations given by the minister, and a further significant number were withdrawn on Government assurances that the problems would be met when the Act was implemented. Thus

New Society,
27 April 1972

'only amendments which contain policy differences that basically separate the Government from the Opposition are unlikely to be accepted. . . . All other

The House of Commons in session: the debate on the Queen's Speech, 1986

amendments the Government is likely to . . . accommodate in one way or another into its legislation. Although the Government draws up the details of its legislation without consultation . . . and exerts tight control over what amendments are accepted, the Opposition is able to make its mark on both the principles and details of legislation in the committee and report stages.'

In committee most amendments, about 70 per cent, are moved by Opposition members, about 10 per cent by Government back-benchers and 20 per cent by ministers (to improve their own Bills).

It should perhaps be added to all this that MPs will, of course, specialise in the variety of roles and functions that they can fulfil in Parliament. For instance, some will attach more importance to a watchdog, educative function, attempting to safeguard individual liberties from government action, than to legislative functions.

DOCUMENT

19

The Attitude of Back-benchers

The question thus arises: why do a majority of MPs in the governing party accept discipline from the minority who are government ministers? Party is the answer; it is the tie that binds frontbench and backbench MPs together to control British government. All members of the governing party share some collective goals, both ideological and instrumental. Much as they may differ among themselves, almost all are united in wishing to maintain their party in government, and to secure their own and their party's victory at the next general election. For this reason, sharp disagreements are likely to be differences about means. The end is common: electoral victory.

Frontbench ministers win a vote in the House of Commons by making it a vote of confidence. If a government lost a vote of confidence because of a split within its own ranks, it would be expected to call a general election and risk loss of control of government. A backbench MP in the majority party will almost invariably vote for the frontbench position, no matter how much he objects to a given proposal, when the alternative is the party losing a vote of confidence, losing office, and the MP in question perhaps losing his seat. No governing party with a majority in the House of Commons has lost a vote of confidence on an Opposition censure vote in more than a century. In 1940, Neville Chamberlain resigned as Prime Minister, even though he had the support of a majority in a crucial Commons confidence vote, because the size of the majority dropped. In March 1979, James Callaghan lost a vote of confidence, but the Labour government did not have a majority of seats in the Commons. No Labour MP abstained or voted against the government in this division, notwithstanding the intra-party differences that quickly became evident as soon as Labour went into Opposition in 1979.

Government ministers are favourably placed to secure support by their own backbenchers. First of all, they are party leaders; many gain office because they have a following among backbenchers and, as the most successful members of the governing 165 party, enjoy a degree of confidence from backbenchers. Secondly, the individual minister responsible for a contentious bill will be personally committed to carrying backbenchers with him. Thirdly, ministers can claim superior knowledge, by virtue of their position as heads of major government departments. Last and not least, there are a large number of backbench MPs who want to become ministers and believe that consistent opposition to the government in the Commons will damage their chances of promotion to the front bench. Anticipatory socialisation to a ministerial post is formalised by the appointment of several dozen unpaid parliamentary private secretaries (PPSs) to ministers, who are expected to vote with the government on virtually all occasions.

Because ministers are politicians, they usually use their authority with regard for the sensitivity of their backbenchers. A good minister will wear a velvet glove, albeit having a mailed fist within it. Cultivating good relations with backbenchers in the governing party gains support for a department's policies in party meetings, in interdepartmental negotiations and on the floor of the House of Commons. Ministers spent more time conciliating others than riding roughshod over opposition. One indicator is that 78% of all government legislation introduced in the House of Commons is consensual; it is not voted against by the Opposition party, let alone the governing party's own backbenchers, at the second reading debate on principle.

Backbench MPs are strategically weak. To challenge the policies of the governing party is to start with very great disadvantages. Much of British government is literally an official secret to backbench MPs in the governing party. The Official Secrets Act precludes the publication of documents circulated within Whitehall ministries. It also prevents the publication of a great mass of information that would be useful in the Commons to critics (or, for that matter, supporters) of the government. The doctrine of collective responsibility inhibits Cabinet ministers from publicly challenging positions taken by their colleagues. Civil servants, who know far more about the weaknesses of policies than ministers, are debarred from commenting publicly on policy matters. Collectively, backbench MPs in the governing party are followers not leaders.

The votes of backbench MPs are a weak resource. Yet because the expectation of party loyalty is so strong, any deviation therefrom appears disproportionatly important: abstention or a vote against the government by half a dozen or by a dozen MPs in the governing party can make headline news, and backbenchers can sometimes use the threat of public rebellion to secure ministerial modification of a policy. Debate within the governing party in private meeting rooms in the Palace of Westminster is tending to replace inter-party debate between government and Opposition as the chief mechanism for influencing the government of the day. But there remain strict limits on the extent to which backbench MPs can criticise their leaders in government. Ministers can accept criticism from their own extremists, whose ideological principles will differentiate them from the Opposition even more than from their own party leaders. To defeat a government measure, backbenchers in the governing party must be prepared to combine with the whole of the Opposition to secure a majority of votes. In the 1974–79 Parliament, the minority Labour government benefited because the votes of at least four different Opposition parties were required to form a majority against it.

Overall, the evidence of the postwar era shows that individual MPs' behaviour is changing, but its collective effect upon the House of Commons is slight. The small scale of change must be emphasised. Otherwise, any departure from 100% unanimity, both the norm and the actuality at recent points in British parliamentary history, can be misinterpreted as a breakdown of the iron cage of party discipline. Moreover, misinterpretation is encouraged by specific facts of the 1974–79 Parliament. Because the Labour government lacked an overall majority, it was ready to tolerate defeat in the Commons by its opponents, and therefore to tolerate defeat by its own dissenters as well. By parliamentary standards of the past half-century, the 1974–79 period was an aberration.

R. Rose, 'Still the era of Party Government', *Parliamentary Affairs,* Summer 1983

Voting

Naturally the most significant way any MP can make his presence felt – although it is one which needs careful prior consideration – is in the division lobbies, either by abstaining or by voting with the other side. Despite considerable party loyalty in the British political culture, there have been a reasonable number of 'rebellions' since 1945. For example, Nabarro's 1956 motion on the Coal Industry Bill attracted 22 other dissidents, and on one of the Suez Canal motions in the same year 15 Conservatives abstained. In 1947, 72 Labour MPs voted against the Labour Government's National Service Bill and 35 others abstained. The abolition of the resale price maintenance Bill, under Sir Alec Douglas-Home's Government, came under strong Conservative attack in 1963–4. In 1972 a considerable minority on both sides of the House did not follow their parties' instructions on the EEC votes, so that the Conservative Government found the European Communities Bill passed its second reading by a majority of only eight. As mentioned earlier, between 1966 and 1970 there were widespread revolts (chiefly involving left-wing Labour back-benchers) over such matters as prices and incomes legislation, designed to give the Government considerable power to freeze wages, and EEC negotiations.

Under Mrs Thatcher's first Government the principal back-bench rebellions occurred in respect of the proposed cuts to the BBC's External Services in 1979 and 1981, changes in the immigration rules in 1980 and 1982, and the increase in heavy lorry weights in 1981. The Government was also forced to drop two Local Government Bills in 1979 and 1981; new legislation was, however, reintroduced and passed successfully. Moreover, in 1980 the Government retreated on the retro-spective parts of emergency legislation dealing with commercial contracts made with the post-Shah regime in Iran. It also made significant concessions on the Nationality Bill in 1981 as a result of pressure from back-benchers and other interested parties. In 1982 there was a revolt on the Finance Bill – the majority fell to eight – concerning cuts in unemployment benefits. In 1983 71 Tory MPs voted with the Opposition to defeat the Government over the pay awards for MPs, so as to link their salaries to Civil Service pay. Between 1945 and 1972 no government lost a vote of the full House, although Wilson withdrew two major pieces of legislation in 1969 – House of Lords reform and industrial relations. The Heath Government (1970–4) was defeated on six major occasions the most significant of which was on the immigration rules in 1972. The comparable figure for the Wilson/Callaghan administration of 1974 (October)–9 was 23, exclusive of 19 defeats on account of its position as a minority government.

P. Norton, *The Commons in Perspective,* Martin Robertson, 1981, p. 230

Another serious rebellion during Mrs Thatcher's administration came in 1985 following the announcement of pay increases for senior figures in the public sector by the Top Salaries Review Body, which gave increases of up to 46 per cent for the Head of the Home Civil Service, judges, the Lord Chancellor and military figures; 50 Conservatives abstained and 48 voted against in the Commons (on the Lord Chancellor's increase, the only one requiring parliamentary approval). The House of Lords, by a majority of five votes passed a motion criticising the Government's insensibility on this issue.

But worse was to come: the following year saw a major parliamentary revolt against the Shops Bill, legislation designed to relax the Sunday trading laws, and the measure was dropped. The Government also climbed down over a suggestion that General Motors should take over the Land-Rover division of the ailing Rover Group. Large government majorities can be as much trouble as wafer-thin ones, as Mr Pym observed during the 1983 General Election campaign, to the evident irritation of the Prime Minister.

Of course, in order to discipline its members the party concerned can apply the final sanction, withdrawal of party privileges – that is, withdrawal of the whip in the Commons, so that the MP becomes an Independent Conservative or Labour Member. The MP, on the other hand, may leave the party altogether, either to join a not totally dissimilar group (as, for example, Enoch Powell joined the United Ulster Unionists in 1974, and Dick Taverne formed his Democratic Labour group in 1973, and John Robertson and Jim Sillars their Scottish Labour Party in 1976), or to cross the floor of the House (as, for example, Christopher Mayhew, a former Labour Navy Minister, joined the Liberals in 1974, Reg Prentice went from Labour to Tory in 1977 and John Stonehouse, having sat for Labour, became the sole English National Party representative in 1976). 1981 saw the formation of the SDP (Social Democratic Party) by the 'Gang of Four', two of whom were Labour MPs and former members of the Cabinet under the 1974–9 Labour Government, plus one former Labour MP and Cabinet minister, Shirley Williams. (The fourth member of the 'Gang' was Roy Jenkins, former President of the European Commission and also a former Labour Cabinet member.) By the following year another 28 Labour MPs had joined the SDP, plus one Conservative member, Christopher Brocklebank-Fowler being the first Tory since 1906 to cross the floor of the House. One Labour defector subsequently sought to rejoin the Labour Party and stood as an Independent Labour candidate in the 1983 General Election.

The Conservatives usually resign the whip voluntarily, that is a Member acts first, before the parliamentary party itself has a chance to withdraw the whip. Nine did so in 1956 over the Suez Canal conflict. (Two years before, Major Legge-Bourke had resigned the whip in protest over the Government's decision to withdraw from Suez in the first place.) In no case did the step seem to harm the MPs' longer term interests in the party. In fact, it appears that in this century the Conservative parliamentary party has withdrawn the whip on just four occasions – from Rowland Hunt in 1907, from Sir Robert Newman in 1927, from Sir Basil Peto in 1928 and from Captain A.S. Cunningham-Reid in 1942. In the Labour Party the whip, perhaps not surprisingly, has been withdrawn more often: between 1945 and 1963 34 dissidents were involved.

Since 1963 the whip has not been withdrawn from any MP in the major parties. However, policy disagreements led the Labour MPs Reginald Paget and Desmond

Donnelly to resign it, the former in 1966 and the latter in 1968 (Mr Donnelly was expelled from the party in the same year). Neither withdrawal nor resignation of the whip occurred in either party during the 1970s; that did not, however, exclude the changes in political allegiance mentioned above, or S.O. Davies and Eddie Milne being returned as Independent Labour members in, respectively, the 1970 and February 1974 General Elections, or Edward Griffiths standing unsuccessfully as an Independent Labour candidate in Sheffield Brightside in October 1974. Ben Ford stood as an Independent Labour candidate in Bradford North in 1983, as did Michael O'Halloran in Islington North having left the SDP. George Cunningham briefly sat as an Independent Labour MP before joining the SDP (Islington South), as did Bob Mellish in Bermondsey, before forcing a by-election there in 1982.

DOCUMENT

20

Rebellion by the Back-benchers

Since any government last experienced a large parliamentary majority (1966–70), major changes in parliamentary behaviour had taken place, notably the greater readiness of MPs to express dissidence openly and to vote against their party whip. In part, this may be thought of as simply a change in the style of parliamentary politics. The former inhibitions on voting against the whip have diminished. Everybody is doing it, so it no longer matters. And if government defeat is the result, everyone knows that need only mean the disappearance of a bill or clause or whatever, and not the disappearance of the government. But something more fundamental underlies this change. MPs in general are more professional about the business of politics, less content to be simple lobby fodder, readier to develop their own views on issues and stand by them. The major parties, too, are less cohesive and more fragmented than they used to be. The changed patterns of behaviour, alterations in the rules of the game and the decline in party cohesion have all had an effect.

In 1984 the most effective parliamentary opposition to government policies came from within the Conservative ranks. Policies towards local government were regularly contested. On the second reading of the Rates Bill (17 January) 13 Conservatives voted against the government (including Mr Heath and five other former ministers), while at least 25 abstained; at report stage on the same bill (28 March) 24 Conservative MPs had put their names to an amendment upon which the government decided to allow a significant compromise, though despite this 14 still cross-voted in the lobby. Legislation to implement the 1983 manifesto commitment to abolish the Greater London Council and the metro-counties was keenly contested. In the 1983–4 session a paving bill provoked Conservative rebellion in the Commons (on 11 April and 9 May especially), though in this case the government's most serious reverse was inflicted by the Lords (see below). In the 1984–85 session a dozen or so Conservatives abstained at second reading on the bill dealing with abolition (4 December), but then most remarkable was a vote on the first day in committee of the whole house, when a Conservative backbench amend- 169 ment to ensure that the GLC was replaced by a directly-elected authority of some kind was rejected by only 23 votes (233 to 210, 12 December). So large a loss of support so early in the parliamentary stages of this bill was a serious blow to the government and an encouragement to the bill's opponents, not least in the House of Lords.

The frequency of significant rebellion appeared to quicken as the year proceeded. The Chancellor's autumn statement triggered off two examples. The first was due to the suggestion that overseas aid might be cut, which caused a fair row in the party and brought 8 Conservative MPs into the opposition lobby, while a further 40 or so abstained (22 November). More notable was the rebellion on student grants, though in this case the government gave way (4 December) before any parliamentary vote had taken place. This story deserves telling more fully for it illustrates much about the character of internal party opposition.

A Treasury statement issued on 12 November, the day of the Chancellor's autumn economic statement, indicated that parental contributions for the living costs of students from better-off families (those with residual incomes of over £12,000 per year) would be increased, while families at the top end of the income scale (residual incomes over £20,000) would henceforth be obliged to contribute towards tuition costs also. The total sum involved was about £39 million. Apparently this proposal had been made by Department of Education ministers, agreed by the Treasury, and then not discussed by Cabinet, despite its obvious political sensitivity. Two days later, more precise details were spelt out in a parliamentary written answer by Peter Brooke, the junior minister responsible for higher education. The money thus saved was in part to be spent under another head in the Education budget, namely scientific research.

Over the next few days political pressure began to built up. On 23 November it was announced that Mr Brooke would attend a meeting of the Conservative backbench Education Committee to discuss these proposals on 5 December. But by 29 November a motion put down by Conservative backbenchers critical of the increased charges had attracted over 100 signatures; it was announced that the Secretary of State, Sir Keith Joseph, would himself meet the committee a day earlier on 4 December. By 30 November 130 MPs had signed the critical motion, including nine of the 18 officers and executive members of the 1922 Committee, 18 former ministers and six Parliamentary Private Secretaries, though by the following day the six PPS's had been obliged to remove their names. By December 2, 180 Conservative MPs – about half the parliamentary party – had signed one or other of two motions critical of the changes. It was suggested that the party Whips would work intensively over the weekend (December 1–2) to turn around MPs opinions, but on Monday it was reported that no special activity by the Whips had taken place. Question time on 4 December saw the Education Secretary at the despatch box, with over 50 Conservative MPs on their feet attempting to put questions. The same evening Sir Keith attended a meeting of the Conservative Education Committee at which over 250 MPs were present, with only three out of 33 speakers offering even guarded support for his decision. The following morning a ten-minute meeting took place in Downing Street between the Prime Minister, Chancellor of the Exchequer and Education Secretary, and later that day all were present in the House when Sir Keith made a statement announcing a compromise under which parental cost-of-living contributions would be increased less steeply (raising £18 m instead of £39m), with no tuition charges being imposed; a review of student finances would also take place, which would include the possibility of introducing student loans. The inclusion of

170 this latter point meant that Sir Keith had salvaged something from the furore.

Two points are significant about the whole episode. First, the anger of backbench MPs was as much because of the government's high-handedness and lack of political sensitivity as over the issue itself. There were many calls for more consultation, especially with backbench committees. MPs were showing that they were simply not prepared to tolerate a situation where government refused to give them any input on sensitive policy issues. Secondly, the government's capitulation on this issue, which directly effected the more prosperous sections of the community (typically staunch party supporters in constituencies) needs to be contrasted with its resolute stand on other issues, where the Conservative party's kith and kin were not directly affected. If the most effective opposition was coming from within the governing party, did this mean that the Thatcher government need only concern itself with the well-off? Was there any political incentive to do otherwise? It was doubtful in 1984 whether such incentive was provided, at least through parliamentary politics.

D.R. Shell, 'The British Constitution in 1984', *Parliamentary Affairs*, Spring 1985

Legislative Procedure
in the Commons

The Commons normally sits from 2.30 to 10.30 on Mondays to Thursdays and 9.30 to 3 on Fridays. From Mondays to Thursdays much of the committee work on legislation is undertaken in the mornings. The legislative process starts with the First Reading (formal announcement) of a Bill, and proceeds to a Second Reading which is the discussion of the main principles. After this comes the committee stage, dealt with by a Standing Committee, which reflects the political balance of the Commons as a whole. It is at this point that a large number of amendments to the Bill may be made. (It is the custom for important constitutional measures to be dealt with by a Committee of the Whole House; this occurred with the Scotland and Wales Acts 1978 and the European Communities Act 1972.) The committee's work is reported – the Report Stage, where further amendments may be taken. There will, of course, be no Report Stage where a Committee of the Whole House has sat, providing the Bill was unamended; but if amendments were accepted, then a Report Stage will still occur. Final votes are taken at the Third Reading. Standing Committees include the Welsh and Scottish Grand Committees. The former is primarily deliberative, but the latter has important legislative powers, since it takes the Second Reading of exclusively Scottish Bills, having regard to the fact that the Scottish system of law is distinct from that in the rest of the United Kingdom. In the Lords all business is dealt with on the floor of the House, although an experiment with Standing Committees was commenced at the end of 1986.

(For a useful guide see *The Committee System of the House of Commons*, Committee Office, House of Commons, 4th edn., 1982.)

The Back-bencher and Minority Government

The British tradition has been one of one-party majority government, supposedly strong and stable, whether the political emphasis in that government has been more on the Prime Minister than on the Cabinet or vice versa. The General Election of February 1974 produced the first minority Government in the UK for some 43 years and many feared stability would be threatened. Was the experience so strange and how does Britain's experience compare with other parliamentary countries which have faced the same problem?

The 1974–9 Government

In some ways the minority Labour Government of February 1974 to May 1979 (between October 1974 and April 1976 the Government in fact operated with knife-edge overall majorities) achieved much far-reaching legislation, including drastic alterations to existing laws on housing and industrial relations. The 1975 Industry Act established the National Enterprise Board; the 1976 Education Act made comprehensive secondary education compulsory in all local authority areas; the 1977 Aircraft and Shipbuilding Industries Act brought further nationalisation; and the 1976 Health Services Act phased out private beds in state hospitals. The Aircraft and Shipbuilding Bill probably had the roughest legislative ride: it underwent 'prolonged scrutiny in 58 sittings in standing committee where there were 105 divisions and three government defeats'.

I. Burton and G. Drewry, *Parliamentary Affairs*, Spring 1978

The position of the back-benchers

The power of the individual back-bencher certainly increases in proportion to the smallness of a Government's Commons majority (or indeed the size of its minority). It was two right-wing Labour back-benchers, Professor J.P. Mackintosh and Brian Walden, who in 1976 were primarily responsible for emasculating the main provisions of the Dock Work Regulation Bill; and it was two left-wing Labour back-benchers, Jeff Rooker and Audrey Wise, who in 1977 voted with Conservative MPs in committee against some very fundamental provisions of the Labour Government's Finance Bill. Their action resulted in the indexation of personal tax allowances with the rate of inflation. In 1974 Anthony King went as far as to remark: 'the private member has come into his own again. The politics of the second Wilson age may well be strangely reminiscent of the age of Palmerston.'

New Society, 14 March 1974

It was not just Commons back-benchers who sensed increased political power at a time of minority government. The Upper House, too, was ever watchful. It was the Lords which prolonged the 1975–6 parliamentary session in November 1976 and which was responsible for the Bill for the nationalisation of the aircraft and shipbuilding industries having to be reintroduced in the 1976–7 session, in accordance with the provisions of the Parliament Acts.

172

James Callaghan, Prime Minister 1976–9

Overseas experience

In 1973 the minority Government of Lars Korvald in Norway succeeded in two controversial areas – negotiating special trading terms with the EEC (after a national referendum had narrowly resulted in rejection of full membership), and extending the State's interest in Norway's share of North Sea Oil. (The Government, although in a minority, was nevertheless a coalition one, Mr Korvald's

173

Christian People's Party being the dominant partner. After a general election in the same year Mr Korvald was succeeded by a minority Labour administration.)

The Guardian,
6 March 1974

As Mark Arnold-Foster wrote in 1974, commenting on the Norwegian experience, 'the arts of minority government may be complicated, but they can be effective. The fact that no one has practised them in Britain since 1929 does not mean that no one could.'

In West Germany, since the foundation of the state in 1949, there has been only one one-party majority Government (1957–61). Most federal administrations are coalitions in which one of the two major parties, the SPD (Social Democrats) and the CDU/CSU (Christian Democrats) is supported by the Liberals, the FDP (Free Democrats). But one, from 1966–9, included both the SPD and the CDU, a 'grand' Government which pursued rigorous measures to deal with economic recession. Coalition majority government (as opposed to one-party or coalition minority government, neither of which usually occurs in Germany) is not always popular. For example, in the early 1970s many SPD members of the Government led first by Brandt and then by Schmidt saw the FDP, which in 1969 had become the junior partner, acting as a brake upon SPD economic strategies – a view held with some justification.

The Guardian,
6 March 1974

Perhaps, however, it is Canada that has provided the most stimulating example of minority Government, especially since the Canadian political system is a 'carbon copy' of Westminster. Patrick Keatley has argued that minority government in Canada since 1962 has meant increased power to the ordinary back-bench MP, a higher standard of parliamentary debate, some influence being given to the Opposition in policy-making and an all-round increase in the efficiency and openness of Government. 'Minority administrations in Canada, under Pearson and Trudeau, have put through an impressive list of reform', including a pension plan, manpower training schemes, regional development, family allowances and reform of the criminal law. 'Overall, the experience in Canada, as in Denmark, Norway and Sweden, shows there is a pronounced swing towards consensus and moderation.' Pierre Trudeau's minority Liberal Government lasted from 1972 to 1974. But the experiences of Joe Clark's minority Conservative administration of 1979–80 were less than salutary.

The Lib-Lab Pact, 1977–8

BBC Radio 3,
24 September
1976

Not all of this corresponds with the British one-party tradition of 'legislate and be damned', but the 1974 Elections threw up many political doubters. In a House of Lords debate on 'the state of the nation', no less a figure than Lord Home was moved to remark that perhaps the adversary nature of one-party majority government in the United Kingdom had been a caricature of what parliamentary democracy should be. Lord Home probably had little idea how relevant his words would be to the political condition of the UK in the years to come. In the spring of 1977 the Labour Government, once again in a parliamentary minority, faced a crucial vote of no confidence from the Conservative Opposition. Callaghan could no longer count upon the votes of the Welsh and Scottish Nationalists, since the Scotland and Wales Bill (the devolution Bill) had ground to a halt through the

THE HOUSE OF COMMONS

failure of the Commons to pass a debating guillotine (a timetable programme). Nor were the Ulster Unionists to be wholly relied upon, since they felt the Government was negligent towards the security and devolution problems of Northern Ireland. It was only the votes of the Liberals that could, and did, save Labour.

Mr Callaghan and his ministers reluctantly entered into a parliamentary agreement with David Steel and his Liberal colleagues. The Liberals agreed to give general support to the Labour Government in return for something of a common understanding on new devolution Bills, on the Bill for direct elections to the new European Parliament which included an option of proportional representation, on the fight against inflation, and to a lesser extent on worker participation; the Government also gave its official backing to a Liberal Private Member's Bill on homelessness.

Although the arrangements (which lasted until the end of summer 1978) meant that Mr Steel and others saw a mass of official Whitehall documents, the like of which they had never seen before, the Liberals were in no way helping to form a coalition Government, but merely providing continued support for a minority one. Although Mr Steel called the agreement a 'novel and historic constitutional arrangement' (it was indeed strange in the context of British politics since 1945), in terms of earlier history it was nothing of the sort.

Summary

The House of Commons is in essence parliamentary government. Since the advent of disciplined, modern political parties in the late nineteenth century, coupled with greater Executive control of the legislative process since 1902 (Balfour's 'parliamentary or railway timetable'), governments are assured of support. In particular, legislation will rarely be opposed, although governments with small majorities may defer controversial proposals, for instance, the nationalisation of the steel industry under Mr Wilson between 1964 and 1966. Since 1945 there have been only two periods of minority (Labour) government: 1974 (March–October) and 1976-9. Nevertheless a Government may misjudge the mood of its own back-benchers; thus industrial relations legislation and reform of the House of Lords were dropped in 1969, and local government bills in 1979 and 1981 (different Acts were passed in 1980 and 1982). Also, legislation may not be dropped, but amended in a way thoroughly distasteful to the Government, for instance the 40 per cent rule in respect of the devolution referenda in 1978 (see Chapter 7). Or the Government may suffer defeat in terms of secondary legislation (the immigration rules in 1982). Some proposals may arouse hostility in the constituency parties and be withdrawn even before they reach the Commons or at least shortly afterwards (the increased parental contributions to higher education student grants and the question of student loans in 1984 or the GM/Ford 'takeover' of British Leyland in 1986).

Moreover, by convention Parliament leaves many matters within the discretion of the Government, primarily the conduct of foreign affairs, declaring war or the making of treaties, being prerogatives of the Crown. Although there was a stormy debate about the invasion of the Falkland Islands in 1982, it was the Government's decision to despatch the Navy. (It could be argued, though, that the tenor of the debate left the Government little choice.) Similarly, it was the Government which signed the Anglo-Irish Treaty in 1921 and the Anglo-Irish Agreement in 1985, without reference, initially at least, to Parliament.

A further point is that although British legislation is by tradition immensely detailed, and parliamentary sessions are much longer and more concentrated than the other major comparable Western examples, nevertheless government ministers, or rather civil servants, still fill in the details, through delegated legislation. Such secondary legislation may be subject to an affirmative vote of the House. Most delegated legislation takes the form of 'statutory instruments', which like Acts of Parliament, must be printed and published.

Committee work is also crucially important to the life of the Commons through the system of Select Committees, and most noticeably in the new system of departmental committees established in 1979, as discussed at length earlier.

The individual MP has a number of opportunities to make his voice heard, apart from participation in a standing or select committee. There are adjournment debates and limited occasions to introduce private members' legislation. But the most crucial is the vote. Voting against the party or abstaining seems to have increased in regularity since 1970, as seen earlier, and has certainly not abated under Mrs Thatcher's Government since 1983 with its large, and at times restless, three-figure majority. Most notably, the Labour Government of 1974 (October)–1979 suffered a total of 42 defeats; although the Government either had a knife-edge majority or was in a minority. Government ministers bluffed out the defeats, in marked contrast to certain examples from history, such as the treatment of a defeat on a minor matter (the 'cordite vote') as a matter of confidence and resignation by the idiosyncratic Liberal Prime Minister, Lord Rosebery, in 1895.

As for the Opposition their role remains to oppose, as Disraeli once said. But opposition must be constructive, and frequently it is. It must be remembered that much of the annual legislative programme is not controversial and will not be opposed for party reasons. Moreover, where amendments are made to 'party' or 'political' legislation, many are frequently accepted if the overall purpose of the legislation remains intact. Often such amendments are minor; other amendments will be withdrawn, upon assurances from Government ministers. In a normal parliamentary session the Opposition usually has 19 days (Opposition Days, or formerly Supply Days) which it may utilise as it sees fit. But the main point is that both in the Commons and through the media the Opposition parties must present themselves as an alternative government in waiting, seizing upon the mistakes that every government inevitably makes, not least the longer the ministerial team has been in office.

Questions

1. To what extent is the House of Commons representative of:
(a) the opinions;
(b) the social composition
of the electorate? (AEB specimen question 1986)

2. To what extent has the present select committee system strengthened the power of MPs to control the Executive? (AEB specimen question 1986)

3. 'MPs are overworked and ill-equipped.' Discuss in relation to their work in Parliament. (Joint Matriculation Board)

4. What major changes have occurred during the twentieth century in the relative powers of the Executive and Parliament? (London)

6 The House of Lords and the Monarchy

The Nature of the House of Lords

The gradual restriction of the political power of the House of Lords is marked by well-known turning-points in British history. The 1911 Parliament Act ensured that the upper House could not veto or amend finance Bills (having been declared as such by the Speaker of the Commons) and that such Bills would become law anyway, if the Lords failed to pass them, after a period of one month. Other Public Bill legislation could be delayed for up to two years (over three parliamentary sessions). This provision was reduced to one year (over two parliamentary sessions) by the 1949 Parliament Act, principally because of the threat to the social and nationalisation programmes of Attlee's Government.

But this has still left the 'Upper' Chamber with some powers: it can introduce legislation of its own, it can put down any amendments to non-money Bills, and it can reject provisions relating to delegated legislation (ministerial regulations made within the framework of an Act of Parliament). If the House of Commons does not accept a Lords' amendment, and the Lords insists on amendment, then any such amendment is deemed a rejection of the Bill under the 1911 Act.

Debates about the reform of the House of Lords recur from time to time, depending on political difficulties or sometimes upon the interests of members: for instance, in 1976 Lord Carrington, a former Chairman of the Conservative Party, put forward some discussion points for modifying the Lords' membership.

The main arguments for reform, however are, firstly, that the hereditary principle is out of date with modern needs – it is one tradition that is no longer necessary in the political system and members should rather be elected or nominated for life. Secondly, the apparent built-in Conservative bias needs to be eliminated because of the problems that arise when the Labour Party forms the Government. This could be seen, for example, in September 1976 when the Lords was recalled early to deal with unfinished business from the 1975–6 session, left by the Commons in the previous month. The Conservative peers decided to assert their 'moral' right (which they saw as strengthened by Conservative wins in by-elections in the two 'safe' Labour seats of Walsall North and Workington on 4 November 1976) and cover five controversial Bills of the Labour Government with equally controversial amendments, thus delaying the State opening of Parliament for the 1976–7 session. The five Bills concerned were those dealing with agricultural tied cottages, education (nationwide comprehensive secondary schooling), NHS private pay beds (phasing out of), docks labour, and aircraft and shipbuilding nationalisation. It was the first and last two Bills upon which the Lords, from the Government's point of view, caused most damage. In the ship-building case, the Bill was reintroduced into the following parliamentary session (the controversial clauses nationalising ship-repair yards having been dropped by the Government) and it passed safely through the Lords. The provisions of the 1949 Parliament Act were almost used for the first time. The provisions of the 1911 Act that give the Commons the power to override rejection of a Bill by the Lords have been used on only three occasions – the Welsh Church Act 1914, the Government of Ireland Act 1914 and the Parliament Act itself of 1949.

Thirdly, there is the problem of participation; the membership of the Lords is now over 1170, although only a fairly small minority is active, leading to the suspicion that attendance allowances (£52 a day) are collected but ill-deserved. There are about 150 peers taking the Labour whip, but only 90 are active, while on the Tory side about 200 are regular attenders, out of a nucleus of solid supporters of approximately 450. There are approximately 40 Liberal members, and 40 SDP peers, and 220 cross-benchers (independents), plus 26 bishops and ten Law Lords. The Conservatives effectively, therefore, no longer have a majority.

Yet there are counter-arguments as well. The hereditary principle can be defended, if only in a negative fashion: it is not a totally unreasonable way of representing a cross-section of society, since elected members would merely duplicate the House of Commons.

Some members, such as Lord Boothby, have argued that without a considerable smattering of younger hereditary peers, the average age of the Lords would be even higher, since life peerages are not usually awarded to people under the 55–60 age range, for most people will not have achieved 'great things' in the public eye before that time.

BBC Radio 4, 7 September 1973

In addition, with the Lords' powers in practice having been reduced, the Conservative bias is relatively harmless. And that bias can be embarrassing to both Labour and Conservative governments, for example, Labour's Transport Bill in 1968 ran into continual difficulty in the upper House, but equally the Conservatives' National Health Service Bill was dissected in great detail in 1972, not least over the question of free family planning. Similarly, in 1980 a majority in the Lords voted out a controversial clause, introducing charges for school transport, from the Conservative Government's Education Bill. And in the same year the Lords excluded council housing built specifically for the elderly from the 'right to buy' provisions of the Housing Act. In 1983 the Lords deleted a clause from the Housing and Building Control Bill extending the right to buy to tenants of charitable housing associations. In 1985 the Government shelved the Education (Corporal Punishment) Bill which gave parents the option of refusing permission for their children to be subjected to corporal punishment in schools. The Bill had been introduced to comply with a judgment in the European Court of Human Rights in 1982, but the Lords amended the bill to ban corporal punishment in all schools. (The United Kingdom has been a party to the European Convention for the Protection of Human Rights and Fundamental Freedoms since 1951 and since 1966 has largely complied with judgments of the European Court, although its decisions have no binding force in British Law, until, that is, new legislation is passed by Parliament or a minister takes the required action.) In 1986 the Government suffered several sharp reverses in the Lords to its Social Security Bill.

DOCUMENT

21

The House of Lords Against the Government

Comparative Party Strength

A. Attending the House once or more in session.
B. Attending over one-third of sittings in session.

	1967/68		1975/76		1981/82	
	A	B	A	B	A	B
Cons	314	125	292	140	366	153
Lab	113	95	149	105	121	77
Lib/SDP	37	19	30	22	67	44
Crossbench	215	52	281	63	221	57
Total	679	291	752	330	775	331

(*Sources:* 1967–68: Cmnd 3799, House of Lords Reform; 1975-6, 1981–2: Author's calculation based on information provided by Clerks)

Major Government Defeats 1983–4

Date	Bill/Motion/Subject	Mover of Amendment or Motion	Outcome
1. 15.12.83	Equal Pay Regulations	McCarthy (Lab)	Compromise
2. 21.2.84	Telecommunications Bill – telephone tapping	Mishcon (Lab)	Compromise
3. 28.2.84	Housing and Building Control Bill	Selkirk (Cons)	Compromise
4. 28.2.84	Housing & Building Control Bill – accommodation for disabled	Ingleby (Cross-bench)	Accepted

5.	28.2.84	Housing & Building Control Bill – accommodation for elderly	Birk (Lab)	Rejected*
6.	10.5.84	Housing & Building Control Bill – accommodation for elderly	Birk (Lab)	Accepted
7.	19.6.84	Trade Union Bill – postal ballots	Beloff (Cons)	Compromise
8.	26.6.84	Police & Criminal Evidence Bill – stop and search in uniform	Elwyn-Jones (Lab)	Rejected
9.	28.6.84	Local Government (Interim Provision) Bill – timing of elections	Elwyn-Jones (Lab)	Accepted
10.	19.7.84	Ordnance Factories and Military Services Bill	Graham of Edmonton (Lab)	Rejected
11.	19.7.84	Ordnance Factories and Military Services Bill – sale to be single unit	Graham of Edmonton (Lab)	Accepted
12.	31.7.84	Police & Criminal Evidence Bill – collection of evidence	Scarman (Cross-bench)	Rejected

(*Initially rejected by government, but accepted after second defeat.)

In all, ten major defeats have been identified in the 1979–83 parliament. In most cases the government accepted the defeat, or at least the principle involved. An exception occurred on the British Nationality Bill, which received a good deal of anxious scrutiny in both Houses. The Lords sent this bill back to the Commons with 90 amendments, several involving government concessions, and two as a result of government defeats. On one of these, concerning the status of Gibraltarians (on which the Government was under considerable pressure from its backbenchers in the Commons), the Lords' view was conceded. On the other, which was designed to make discretionary decisions taken by the Home Secretary subject to appeal to the courts if an applicant alleged discrimination, the government obtained a convincing Commons majority (259–203) overturning the Lords' view. When the matter came back to the upper House, Lord Elwyn-Jones urged peers to insist on their amendment despite its rejection by the Commons; in the ensuing division the government won, by 116 votes to 96. Interestingly, 13 of the 22 Conservative peers who had voted against the government in July voted for it in October, and the remainder stayed away.

Later in the same session the government suffered five defeats on its Housing Bill, and indeed nowhere has the Lords' impact been more decisive since 1979 than on the government's 'right to buy' legislation. In 1980 one Lords' amendment exempted accommodation designed or specifically adapted for the elderly, thus excluding some 220,000 dwellings from those covered by the bill. The government gave way on this, but only after initially saying it would not and with obvious reluctance. A further amendment regarding option mortgages for the elderly was accepted by the government, but three others which all involved government defeats in the Lords were ultimately rejected; one of these would have reduced the discount for purchasers in certain circumstances, and the other two concerned the designation of rural areas. In the 1982–3 session the House 181 voted by a two to one majority to delete from the Housing and Building Control Bill a clause which extended the right to buy to tenants of charitable housing associations. The government announced that it would not attempt to restore that provision, but the whole bill was lost in any case because of the early dissolution.

In two cases the government resisted motions which called upon it to take some specified action. The first of these was Lord Byers' motion urging reconsideration of cuts imposed on the BBC's external services. The government did make some alteration in these cuts, though Lord Byers – then Liberal leader in the House – clearly did not feel these went far enough, and in any case they were certainly not simply the result of pressure exerted through the Lords. In the second case Lord Shackleton (a former Labour leader of the House) called on the government to submit its plans for the 'privatisation' of the Ordnance Survey to an independent review board, which it did and subsequently changed its policy.

In the 1979–83 parliament whenever a Lords' amendment was rejected by the Commons, the Lords gave way (though sometimes not without a further vote) save in one instance, notable only for its triviality. This exception occurred on the 1981 Wildlife and Countryside Bill when peers insisted that protection be extended for certain foreshore waders (partly because it was hard to distinguish them from other protected birds) despite the disagreement of MPs. The flavour of much debate on his bill in the Lords is captured by quoting Lord Chelwood speaking on this amendment, "Which of your lordships could put his hand on his heart and say that in the half-light or even good light they are sure of the difference overhead between a curlew, a whimbrel and a bar-tailed godwit?"

As already indicated, in the new (1983–) parliament the frequency of defeat, especially serious defeat, increased. At least twelve of the 19 defeats of the first session (until August 1984) were major.

The most notable defeat took place on the Local Government (Interim Provisions) Bill, a 'paving' bill concerned with transitional arrangements for the abolition of the Greater London Council and the metropolitan counties, (due to take place in 1986 providing parliament approves the necessary legislation in the 1984–5 session). As part of the transitional arrangements, the government proposed to cancel elections due in 1985 and to set up bodies nominated by the lower-tier authorities to run the affairs of these doomed authorities during their final year. This proposal was heavily criticised in the Commons, partly because in London at least it would involve the replacement of a Labour authority by a Conservative one. In the Lords the government was decisively defeated (by 191 votes to 143) on an amendment which would prevent the cancellation of elections until the main abolition legislation had received royal assent. This would almost certainly have been too tight a timetable, and the government offered a compromise which allowed the existing councils to run on for an extra year, thus still cancelling the election due in 1985. Peers accepted this compromise by 248 votes to 155 (16 July). The whole issue was widely perceived as "constitutional": it was not merely that the government proposed to cancel elections, but also to substitute for an elected authority of one party a nominated authority of another.

When peers voted to include safeguards on telephone tapping in the Telecommunications Bill, the government argued that the subject was inappropriate to a privatisation bill from the Industry Department but that in the following session a bill dealing with the subject would be introduced. With that promise publicly made, peers allowed their amendment to be overturned. On another privatisation measure, the Ordnance Factories and Military Services Bill, peers made two important amendments imposing restrictions on the proposed sale of factories; on the Police and Criminal Evidence Bill amendments of a liberal kind were passed against government resistance. All these examples were amendments moved by Labour or cross-bench peers, though almost always with some Conservative support in the division lobbies, as the table shows. In one instance, however, a Conservative peer, Lord Beloff, moved an amendment which was carried against the government, despite the fact that most Labour peers who voted supported the government. On this occasion – concerning the extension of secret ballots for trades union elections – Lord Beloff had the support of the Alliance, and most Conservative peers who voted disobeyed their party whip.

On Housing further major defeats were suffered by the government. In a new Housing and Building Control Bill the right to buy elderly persons accommodation was again included (albeit only at report stage in the Commons), but the Lords again rejected the proposal. Back in the Commons (12 April) the government secured the re-inclusion of elderly persons accommodation, along with a few changes designed to meet objections expressed by some peers. But the Lords refused to accept this compromise, and on 10 May voted narrowly to insist on the exclusion of elderly persons accommodation. After a four week interval the government announced its acquiescence. The Lords also secured the removal from the bill of accommodation specially built or adapted in major ways for the disabled, a change accepted reluctantly by the government. The bill sought to extend the 'right to buy' to tenants of those public sector landlords who owned the leasehold but not the freehold of the properties concerned. This was a complex matter, but peers were again especially concerned to safeguard charitable trusts which owned the freehold of such properties. On this the government was heavily defeated; in the Commons it overturned this amendment, but again back in the Lords peers insisted that at least where universities were owners of freehold, their position should be protected, and this the government eventually accepted.

Notable in all this was the determination, indeed the intransigence, of peers, including Conservative backbenchers. The general principle of selling public sector housing was not in question, but what the House of Lords did from 1980 to 1984 was to insist on definite limits and exceptions to that principle. Lord Simon of Glaisdale, a former Lord of Appeal and also a former Conservative MP and minister, expressed well the tensions felt between the House and the government on this matter; during a powerful speech in the debate which culminated in the government's compromise on elderly persons accommodation being rejected by a single vote, he expressed support for the general principle of the right to buy policy, but disagreement with the "passionate logic" which sought to carry that "good principle into every corner of our social and legal life in the face of commonsense, humanity and all experience". Many peers would like to feel that when their views collided with the government's, they were champions of commonsense and human experience.

Whipping in the Lords remains essentially low-key. It may be possible to persuade peers, but they cannot be coerced, commanded or bullied. In attempting persuasion, appeals to party loyalty may be used and may be effective in some quarters, but in general such appeals are probably less effective than reasoned arguments. Whereas MPs are mainly professional politicians, elected on a party manifesto, mostly with considerable ambition for promotion to office, possibly with constituency reselection to think about (to say nothing of re-election as MPs), none of these characteristics apply to peers. Apart from a handful of office-holders, they receive no salaries; the vast majority are part- 183 timers in the House, and very few can have ambitions for office. In such circumstances heavy whipping is unlikely to be effective. Lord Denham, government Chief Whip remembers the very considerable pressure put on Conservative peers to prevent any amendment being made to the European Communities Bill in 1972. This he felt had a devastating effect on the morale of peers, and he determined to avoid the repetition of such pressure. Thus on the Local Government (Interim Provisions) Bill, a three line whip was used by the Conservatives at second reading to fend off a critical motion. This succeeded with 455 peers altogether voting (238 to 217), but to use a three line whip again a fortnight later to safeguard the committee stage of the bill was not so much thought unnecessary as quite simply inappropriate and possibly counterproductive. One should not put excessive pressure on volunteers otherwise they may cease to be volunteers.

D.R. Shell, 'The House of Lords and the Thatcher Government',
Parliamentary Affairs, Winter 1985

Bicameralism

All the various debates about the House of Lords reveal a somewhat wider dilemma, about the nature of bicameralism generally. Most parliamentary systems are bicameral, although the nature of the system will vary considerably. Israel is one of the few significant examples in the Western world of a unicameral system. Other examples include Norway, New Zealand, Denmark, and more recently Sweden.

The terms 'upper' and 'lower' chambers are also misleading in the liberal-democratic world. The upper house in the USA, the Senate, through cultural tradition and the organisation of its committee system, tends to be the distinctly more powerful part of Congress. In Italy it was intended after the Second World War that both the Senate and the Chamber of Deputies should be in a state of political equilibrium, but by the early 1950s, the balance was moving towards the lower house (the Deputies).

In other countries, the situation may be different again; the ratio of power between the upper and lower houses may have remained more consistent either because of the political and geographical nature of the country or because of the special powers of the Head of State. In the latter category, France, since 1958, is a good example. The President's political programme can dominate both sections of parliament, although this too could always change if the nature of party support shifts, as illustrated by President Mitterrand's recent political difficulties: in the 1986 elections to the National Assembly the Socialists remained the largest party, but lost overall control, with the result that a new government was formed under the conservative Jacques Chirac as Prime Minister. Chirac headed the Gaullist party (RPR – Rassemblement pour la République) supported by the UDF (Union pour la démocratie française). Later in 1986 President Mitterrand announced that he might not seek re-election at the expiry of his term of office in 1988.

In the former category, West Germany is a leading case: although the powers of the federal Bundestag (lower house) together with the Chief Executive (the Federal Chancellor) are of extreme importance, the upper house (Bundesrat) also has considerable significance because it is linked directly through the electoral system to the *Länder,* the provincial or state parliaments.

It may well be that major reform of the House of Lords, although probably still in the long-term, is linked to the political relationship between central and local government, perhaps in the context of the devolution debate in the late 1960s and the 1970s. It is possible to visualise a reformed system of local and provincial government acting as an electoral college which determines the membership of the House of Lords, without the hereditary element of course, either for a fixed term of office, or, if the nature of 'peerage' was to be continued, for life. The West German model might well be able to offer a few political hints in how to deal with a recurrent problem within the 'mother of Parliaments'.

The Lords as a Second Chamber

There are a number of arguments in favour of the House of Lords continuing as a second chamber. One of the principal reasons advanced is that a revising chamber is always politically desirable, for it can act as a constitutional balance *vis-à-vis* the House of Commons. Furthermore, it is a convenient political refuge for members of the Commons who no longer wish or are unable to stand for the lower House in an election.

Thirdly, because of the constant pressure upon the House of Commons' legislative timetable, the Lords can act as a safety-valve by introducing legislation of its own. This has been particularly true in recent years. Indeed the increasing legislative pressure on the Lords, as well as the Commons, has raised the question of how far the second chamber needs to develop a system of Public Bill Committees comparable to the Standing Committees of the House of Commons; hitherto most business in the Lords is taken on the floor of the House. In the 1977–8 session, for example, the Lords made 525 amendments to 11 Government Bills; interestingly 70 per cent of these were accepted when the legislation returned to the Commons for further consideration. The Lords commenced an experiment with Standing Committees in December 1986.

These are not the only arguments for the Lords surviving as the second chamber. A fourth factor justifying its continued existence is the contention that debating standards are 'higher' because of the greater availability of specialist knowledge in the Lords, compared with the Commons, and because of the fact that the Lords has generally (except, towards the end of a parliamentary session) rather more opportunity to study the details of a particular proposal. Another argument, and probably a more valid one, is that the House of Lords represents 'social' interests as opposed to the 650 geographical units in the Commons: free of constituency responsibilities, the members of the Lords can pursue their own individual political philosophies within existing party loyalties. They may be able to put forward more effectively the views of various pressure groups than the House of Commons, whether of the CBI, the TUC, or the Church. Another virtue claimed for the Lords is that there is more scope for introducing Private Members' Bills, there being no need for a ballot as in the House of Commons. In addition, there is more opportunity for individual initiative, since 'cross-benches' exist in the upper House to accommodate 'independent' members who do not wish to take a party whip. And finally, the House of Lords is said, often by its own members, to be more socially advanced in areas of sensitive concern, for example, as seen in its attitude in the late 1960s towards the Wolfenden Report (1958) on the reform of the law relating to homosexuality, and towards proposals to reform the law on divorce: in such areas of public interest the fact that the Lords is not directly answerable to the electorate can be a political advantage.

Counter-arguments

Of course, there are equally valid arguments against all of these so-called political virtues. Firstly, the Lords as a revising chamber is a contradiction in terms, for the Commons is the only true body which is directly responsible to the electorate, although, of course, in practice that answerability is very complex: if there is a need for a revising chamber at all, at least some principle other than the hereditary one should be devised for choosing it.

As for the Lords being a place of reward for public service within the Commons or outside, the Prime Minister's powers of patronage are already very extensive, and the ending of the award of peerages for 'public service' would drastically curtail a considerable power, or, as some might see it, abuse of power.

The argument about the Lords relieving pressure upon the Commons begs another question: if the political system was not so centralised, the directly elected chamber could organise its procedure more effectively and the control of parliamentary business would be less like a railway timetable. Devolution of power to the English regions or counties, as well as to Scotland and Wales, would be one answer; the more effective use of the specialist committee system that was established in 1979 would be another.

The 'quality of debate' argument is also perhaps overrated: it might be more accurate to say that the style of debate in the Commons is more 'extreme', whereas the style in the Lords is more consistently polite. And although, the counter-argument runs, the Lords is expected to produce specialist debate, nevertheless if the Lords were abolished the loss of debating quality would not be particularly noticed. The argument about the value of the Lords as a political chamber without any constituency responsibilities is one which can be equally reversed: while the Lords may well be able to represent interests outside the mainstream of party politics, pressure group activity, largely conducted through the mass media and professional lobbyists, is sufficiently well-organised nowadays to influence members of the House of Commons. Back-bench opinion in the Commons will make itself felt on particular occasions.

These, then, are the main 'pros' and 'cons' for the House of Lords as presently constituted. It should be noted that at the present time the Conservative Party does not appear to regard reform of the Lords as a priority, while the Alliance parties are committed to reform and Labour is in favour of outright abolition (i.e. a unicameral system). One further point should be added here: the very recent televising of the Lords' proceedings appears to have given the upper House a new lease of life, for when their lordships so wish, the most thoughtful debates – more considered perhaps than those in the Commons – do indeed take place.

The House of Lords is the most anachronistic part of the British constitution, particularly when compared with the upper houses of other Western-type political systems, and yet it survives in a remarkable way. This does not mean to say, however, that the House of Lords is inefficient. Indeed, always mindful of the need to conduct business expeditiously, the peers decided in 1976 to embark upon some reforms of their own parliamentary procedures. Lord Shepherd, then Lord Privy Seal and Leader of the House, commented that the country received excellent value from the Lords, since its total annual cost was £3.6m., compared, he said, with the estimated cost of £20m. for the proposed Scottish and Welsh Assemblies. The Lords has survived the crises of the 1832 Reform Act (under Lord Grey), of 1909–11 and the rejection of Lloyd George's budget, and of Attlee's reforming programme in 1947–9. From time to time the Lords will come under fresh scrutiny, and further reform is not only likely but inevitable. On 6 July 1976 the Prime Minister, Mr Callaghan, in a reply to a question in the House of Commons, indicated that he would be ready to consider any proposals to reform the House of Lords: 'I have never felt the House of Lords was truly representative of the fine flower of democracy in this country. But having attempted to pluck it once in 1968, I found it stung rather, and I would be careful before putting my hand there again.'

Later that same year, on 22 November 1976, a BBC1 television survey elicited the following interesting replies to half a dozen questions from members of the House of Lords itself. (779 questionnaires were sent out, and 418 peers responded wholly or in part.)

(i)   Should the new House of Lords be:

	Hereditary Peers	Life Peers
elected	12%	6%
appointed	34%	46%
both	49%	48%

(ii)   Who should appoint members (if members are appointed)?
All peers:

Queen and party leaders	70%
special committee	15%
interest groups	14%

(iii)   What powers should the Upper House have in respect of Commons' legislation?
All peers:

delay	75%
amend	84%
reject	20%

		Hereditary	Life
(iv)	Should hereditary peers be totally abolished?	21%	40%
(v)	Should the Lords be abolished?	2%	2%
(vi)	Should hereditary peers stay, but as non-voting members?	31%	37%

In 1983 a Marplan poll showed only 17 per cent of the public, in its sample, were opposed to any second chamber.

DOCUMENT

22

Public Attitudes Towards the House of Lords

This is how the 1,502 Marplan sample divided on a series of questions on the future of a second chamber and the position of hereditary peers in such a chamber.

Percentages saying that the second chamber should include

Hereditary peers alone	4
Hereditary plus life peers	15
Hereditary plus directly elected	4
Hereditary plus life plus directly elected	11
Total favouring inclusion of hereditary peers	34

Percentages saying that the second chamber should include

Life peers alone	6
Life peers plus hereditary peers	15
Life plus directly elected	11
Life plus hereditary plus directly elected	11
Total favouring inclusion of life peers	43

Percentages saying that the second chamber should include

Directly elected peers alone	27
Directly elected plus hereditary peers	4
Directly elected plus life peers	11
Directly elected plus hereditary plus life	11
Total favouring inclusion of directly elected peers	53

Percentages saying that the second chamber should exclude hereditary peers	
In favour of life peers alone	6
In favour of directly elected peers alone	27
In favour of life plus directly elected peers alone	11
Total	44
Opposed to any second chamber	17
Total opposed to hereditary peers in Parliament	61

Percentages saying that the second chamber should exclude life peers	
In favour of hereditary peers alone	4
In favour of directly elected peers alone	27
In favour of hereditary plus directly elected peers only	4
Total	35
Opposed to any second chamber	17
Total opposed to life peers in Parliament	52

Percentages saying that the second chamber should not include directly elected peers	
In favour of hereditary peers only	4
In favour of life peers only	6
In favour of life plus hereditary peers only	15
Total	25
Opposed to any second chamber	17
Total opposed to directly elected peers in Parliament	42
Don't know/won't say/no indication	7

The Guardian, 22 July 1983

A Constitutional Crisis

This concerned the Government's proposals for the reform of the Lords itself. Reform of the upper chamber had been part of the Labour Party manifesto in 1966 and an all-party committee of the Commons was given the task of producing a plan. However, the proposed plan for consultations between the two chambers was upset by the Lords' rejection (by 193 to 184 votes) of the Order in Council renewing United Nations sanctions against the illegal Smith Government in Southern Rhodesia. (A second Order was subsequently passed.) The episode, however, gave the Government the opportunity to use its large Commons majority to produce its own solution to the problem. The proposals in the reform package included reducing the delaying power of the Lords (for Bills) to six months, by-passing the rejection of a statutory instrument (delegated legislation) in view of the Rhodesian sanctions Order, by its becoming law automatically if a vote was taken for the second time in the House of Commons, and, most important of all, dividing the peerage into non-voters, who would be principally the remaining hereditary

189

Lords, and voters (with a minimum 30 per cent attendance record) who would be specially created peers for life, although some hereditary peers might become life peers instead.

The compromise was in line with the age-old pragmatism of the British political culture. It appeared to tackle the problem of the idiosyncracy of an upper house second to none in Western bicameral systems in the pecularity of its com-position. The Parliament (no. 2) Bill passed both first and second readings in the Commons, and then, in accordance with convention for a Bill of constitutional importance, it went to the Committee of the Whole House. It was here that both left-wing Labour MPs and right-wing Conservatives, although for different reasons, formed an unofficial and unholy alliance.

Because the package of reform was clearly going to please neither the defenders of the 'status quo' nor those who wanted more radical change, if not outright abolition, the Bill became trapped in the committee machine; the Government lost interest (the moment of crisis over Rhodesian sanctions having passed) and so after some 80 hours in committee spent on just a few clauses, the Bill was aborted in April 1969.

At present the upper House continues largely on party lines, although with two hundred or so 'cross-benchers'; it includes over 790 hereditary peers, nearly 300 life peers, some 18 law lords and former law lords, and 26 bishops of the established Church. Very few hereditary peerages have been created since life peers were first introduced in 1958, and clearly the ratio of life to hereditary peers will increase in favour of the former. Mrs Thatcher has created most new hereditary peers recently: Viscount Tonypandy (George Thomas, the former Speaker of the House of Commons), Viscount Whitelaw, and the Earl of Stockton (Harold Macmillan). But it is always possible that when some political issue develops into a confrontation between the two Houses, a fresh attempt at 'modernising' the Lords will be made, if only to bring it more in line with the current practice of other Western parliamentary systems.

The Guardian,
28 March
1978

The Guardian, in a 'Green Paper' of its own in early 1978, suggested that one simple method to reform the Lords would be to limit the membership to 243, elected on a multi-member basis or through regional lists and based on the 81 constituencies for the European Assembly (Parliament). A further 121 members would then be elected by the directly elected 243 so as to preserve the traditional 'influence' element in the House, such as trade union and industrial leaders, or academics – people who would normally not find their way up through the party system.

The House of Lords would remain subordinate to the Commons except on matters of constitutional change. Here any deadlock that might occur would have to be resolved by a joint session of both Houses or by a popular referendum.

The Guardian also pointed out that most other upper chambers were in part indirectly elected. Belgium, for example, has a senate of 184 of which 51 are indirectly elected by provincial councils, 26 are co-opted by the senate itself, and one is a member of the royal family. The remaining 106 are directly elected.

In France 309 of the 317 members of the Senate (13 of whom represent overseas possessions) are indirectly elected by an electoral college comprised of deputies of the National Assembly, representatives of the council of each department, and a representative group of municipal councillors. In West Germany the Bundesrat has 45 members of whom 41 represent the governments of the *Länder* (states) which mandate them. In Ireland there is a senate of 60: 11 are nominated by the Prime Minister (Taoiseach), 3 each chosen from the two universities, with 43 chosen by an electoral college of the incoming Dáil (Parliament's 'lower house'), the outgoing senate, and members of every county and county borough council. In the Netherlands the upper chamber of 75 is elected by the members of the eleven provincial councils.

On the other hand, as one elderly peer was once reported as saying, 'The nice thing about this place is that there's not too much damned politics' (*The Guardian*, 1 March 1979).

The Monarchy: Controversial Issues

The monarch has evolved in the United Kingdom as a constitutional Head of State, a symbolic figurehead in the political system, but also at times a political referee. There are not many monarchies left in the world. Following General Franco's death in 1975, the Spanish monarchy was restored and although the new King, Juan Carlos, at first inherited formidable powers, his authority is now strictly limited, following the rapid development of a parliamentary democracy. But Spain is the exception to the rule; elsewhere the drift away from royal Heads of State continues. In Europe, the monarchy in Greece was abolished in the plebiscite of 1974, which heralded the return to parliamentary government. In 1975 a turning point in 400 years of Swedish history came when for the first time Parliament opened its new session itself – King Carl Gustaf merely declaring the new session open while it was now the Prime Minister who read the Government's programme: no longer did Parliament go to the King's palace to hear him read the Government's Speech – he went instead to Parliament to listen.

But not so in the United Kingdom. Although the monarch is for the most part undeniably a constitutional one, the ceremony of tradition and history very much remains – it is still the Queen's Speech at the beginning of each parliamentary session. The monarchy, which in modern constitutional form dates from at least Victorian times, has also played significant roles in the twentieth century. Most of the monarch's political power can be perceived largely in the symbolic sense, and that symbolic sense is transmitted all the more readily in an age of mass communication. But it is not solely ceremonial and symbolic; the monarch in a negative sense has 'guardian' powers, even if they are rarely used.

George V (1911–36) faced a number of constitutional problems of which the most controversial was the formation of the National Government in August

'The Guardian of the Constitution': the Queen arrives for the State opening of Parliament

1931. The idea of a coalition Government to deal with the very pressing economic difficulties was one which came not from the King but from the acting Liberal leader, Sir Herbert Samuel, who appeared to have arrived at the Palace first, for an all-party meeting with MacDonald, Baldwin and the King. The degree of George V's intervention should not, however, be overstated, for the formation of a rare peacetime coalition government was largely dependent upon the agreement of the three party leaders, an agreement which was later regretted by Samuel and MacDonald.

Things may have gone more smoothly for Elizabeth II, but there is no guarantee that this will continue in the future. 'There are really no precedents for the present situation. I must use my own judgement as each case arises', George V wrote in 1924, upon the formation of the first minority Labour Government. The fact that George V had to be acutely aware of the various political possibilities that general elections produced during the 1920s, when the three main parties were in a state of equilibrium, is in marked contrast to the post-1945 period. Until the General Election of February 1974, one party, either Labour or Conservative, always secured, often by a very safe margin, a majority over all other parties. As the two major parties suffer a decline in their combined share of the total national vote, there is an increasing possibility that the Head of State could be deeply involved in the discussions leading up to the formation of a new Government.

Some other European countries, however, of necessity experience such consultations, particularly where, as in Belgium or the Netherlands, a multi-party system exists.

In some cases the involvement of the Head of State in the formation of a new Government is constant, as in the case of Italy during frequent crises in the post-Fascist era, and particularly in relation to the support given by the Communists (PCI) for Christian Democratic administrations between 1974 and 1980.

The British Head of State has, so far, largely avoided this kind of political involvement. The symbolic role for the British monarch is therefore almost paramount, although Bagehot's 'right to warn' clearly remains.

The right to warn, even if the nineteenth-century 'right to advise' has grown weak, can be illustrated by a few examples from the reign of George VI. Although not faced with as many constitutional issues as his father, George VI inevitably encountered during the Second World War and its immediate aftermath several political problems. One incident involved the membership of Attlee's Cabinet after the Labour victory in the 1945 General Election. The account is that it was the King who suggested that it would be preferable, in view of what he had achieved during the War, to make Ernest Bevin Foreign Secretary and give the Chancellorship of the Exchequer (originally destined for Bevin) to Hugh Dalton. This odd, yet widely accepted episode, may be partly myth, as Attlee's version plays down the influence of the King, but at least it is clear that the King conveyed his feelings directly to the Prime Minister.

Another interesting example under George VI happened in a rather oblique way. Between 1950 and 1951 Attlee's Government had only a small overall majority, and after the 1950 General Election results, the question of a further dissolution of Parliament was much discussed in the press. However, in May 1950, Sir Alan Lascelles, the King's Private Secretary, wrote under a pseudonym in *The Times,* making it clear that the King maintained the constitutional right to refuse a dissolution of Parliament if he was convinced that the existing Parliament should carry on in the 'national interest', if in fact a general election would be detrimental to the national economy, or if he could find another Prime Minister who would continue the Government for a reasonable period with a working majority in the House of Commons. Whether such a refusal to dissolve Parliament would arise in practice is a highly dubious question, in view of the enormous implications such usage would have upon parliamentary conventions; it is also extremely difficult to define exactly what might be meant by the 'national interest', a term of great political convenience in many systems throughout the world.

Commenting upon the situation immediately after the February 1974 General Election, Lord Blake has written:

The Sunday Times, 30 November 1975

'Mr Wilson behaved as if he was confident that it would be granted, and the Conservatives at the last moment seemed to have become convinced that it would. [Lord Blake was referring to the possibility of the Queen's Speech in March 1974 being defeated in Parliament, with Mr Wilson thus requesting an immediate dissolution.] There is at present no means of knowing for certain what was the truth, but it is quite clear that in those circumstances the Queen was not obliged to grant a dissolution even if not obliged to refuse. The determining factor may well have been the failure of the overture already made by Mr Heath to the Liberals, which must have made it seem unlikely that a stable majority could be formed out of any other ingredients; in that case having refused a dissolution to Mr Wilson she might have had to grant it to his successor. To take a more extreme case, suppose Mr Heath had himself decided to meet Parliament, as he was entitled to do, and suppose that opinion polls or some other cause led him to believe that a quick election would reverse the previous one, could he have claimed a dissolution if he had been beaten on the Queen's Speech? Surely this would have been a case where the Crown would have had a strong argument for refusing.'

The Guardian of the Constitution

The monarch has several different symbolic functions to perform, such as Head of the Established Church and Head of the Commonwealth. In the latter function, there is sometimes rather more involved than mere political symbolism, particularly in the case of the 'old' dominions such as Australia, Canada and New Zealand, where the Queen is Head of State. In Australia a complex and extraordinary situation arose in 1975 concerning the Queen's representative, the Governor-General who is appointed by the Queen but nominated by the Australian Prime Minister. The Governor-General, Sir John Kerr, telephoned Buckingham Palace to inform the Queen that he had dismissed Mr Whitlam from the office of Prime Minister. (Sir John had formed the opinion that dissolution of both houses of Parliament was necessary as the Senate had refused the Whitlam Government finance or, as it is technically known, supply.) In the subsequent general election against a background of financial scandals, Whitlam's Government was clearly defeated. Nevertheless, although Mr Whitlam was defeated at the polls, there were widespread public demonstrations against the Governor-General throughout 1976 and 1977, culminating in Sir John's resignation. Although the British monarch was only indirectly involved, the monarchy and the British Government were embarrassed, for it appeared that the Governor-General had acted too quickly by forestalling Mr Whitlam from asking the Queen to replace Sir John himself, with a new Governor-General. It also appears that Sir John had not exhausted all possible alternatives in solving the crisis, in accordance with the usual Westminster traditions, although constitutionally he had not infringed the Australian system.

Prince Charles publicly expresses his fears about the United Kingdom's considerable economic problems and deplores the lack of entrepreneurial spirit

The Observer, 1 December 1985

The monarch is important as the guardian of the constitution, and it should never be taken for granted that constitutional challenges only take place overseas; the parliamentary system of government is not necessarily sacrosanct. Indeed it cannot be assumed that the Queen or her successors will remain indefinitely free from the kind of constitutional issues that faced her grandfather. Walter Bagehot, the nineteenth-century constitutional theorist, once remarked that Queen Victoria would be obliged to sign her own death-warrant if the two Houses sent it up to her: now the power of veto is dead, apart from perhaps extreme political circumstances which are almost impossible to define under a largely unwritten constitution.

Summary

The House of Lords, for many years, had not been on equal political terms with the Commons, and that position was formalised by the Parliament Acts 1911 and 1949. However, that does not mean to say that the upper chamber (so-called) cannot threaten the House of Commons. Debates may be calmer and more considered in the Lords, but when their lordships feel strongly about a legislative matter, the Government, whether Labour or Conservative, must respond positively, as has been seen earlier.

While the Conservative peers form the largest group in the Lords, and therefore a Labour Government will always feel under greater pressure than a Conservative one (compare the difficulties on legislation in 1975–7 with those during 1982–4 for example), it is no longer true to say that there is a Conservative majority in the Lords, implying that a Conservative Government will always achieve its ends. Indeed, the present Government Chief Whip in the Lords, Lord Denham, has on several occasions made it clear that to persuade many Tory peers to attend on vital votes demands very much the art of gentle persuasion.

The Conservative in-built hereditary majority has, therefore, disappeared. This was particularly the result of the Life Peerage Act of 1958. Life peers now account for about one-third of the total membership of the Lords. The other major reform was the Peerage Act 1963 which enabled hereditary peers to disclaim their titles. This Act was the result of a campaign by Lord Stansgate (Anthony Wedgwood Benn).

Outside of its judicial functions as the most senior appellate court, the constitutional future of the House remains controversial. But to date, since the abortive attempt in 1969, the parties have not been able to arrive at a compromise over reform.

The role of twentieth-century constitutional monarchy is less fraught with argument. While Queen Victoria was the last of the 'old style' monarchs and the first of the new, she was not above expressing political preferences, at least when it came to the choice of Prime Minister. Since 1901, monarchs have sometimes had to face political dilemmas, for instance, over the formation of the National Government in 1931; but by remaining 'above politics', by eschewing involvement in day to day matters, the popularity of the monarchy, which Queen Victoria did much to revive, has continued. There remains the residual role of political referee, a function that could be very important where there was no clear result after a general election, given the complex nature of the unwritten constitution.

Questions

1. Discuss the role of the monarchy in the contemporary British system of government and politics. (Joint Matriculation Board)

2. Can the existence of the House of Lords and the Monarchy be justified when both are based upon hereditary principles?

3. Is there a case for further reform of the House of Lords? What political difficulties have recent attempts at reform encountered? (London)

4. Is it not the Civil Service rather than the Crown which now gives a sense of continuity to the British State? (London)

7 Local Government — and Regionalism

' "Keep your feet out of Marsham Street", Mr Page (Minister for Local Government) said. "You come to us too many times. We give you matters to decide at the local level, and many of you keep coming running to us".'

The Guardian, 7 August 1973

A. The Local–Central Government Relationship

Although the tradition of local government in the United Kingdom has been a strong one for at least the last hundred years, compared with that of France for example, it has also been one frequently fraught with difficulties. Graham Page, the Minister for Local Government and Development under the Heath Government, addressed the annual conference of Town Clerks in the summer of 1973 in terms which well illustrated the difficulties involved in allowing local government sufficient freedom of action and political manoeuvre but, at the same time, ensuring that services are standardised over the whole of the country and under the direction of Whitehall (in other words the Department of the Environment in Marsham Street).

See also C. Leeds, *Politics in Action,* Stanley Thornes, 1986, (section G)

In fact at that particular conference Mr Page went on to accuse one Town Clerk (John Elven of Cambridge) of 'extraordinary acrobatics' in asking in the same breath for less Government interference and more Government help and guidance. He commented that he was 'horror-struck' at one speaker's implication in local government.' As we shall see, the subsequent Conservative Government in local government'. As we shall see, the subsequent Conservative Government of Mrs Thatcher from 1979, seemed to lose almost complete confidence, at least in respect of local authorities' financial self-discipline, or rather lack of it.

These lively exchanges in 1973 arose from a debate about co-operation and agency agreements (especially in relation to planning matters) between the then new county and district councils. Mr Page stated that it was up to the councils in question to agree among themselves on what areas of work they might do on behalf

197

of one another, although when in dispute they could appeal to the Secretary of State for the Environment, but, at the same time, local authorities should not use the Secretary of State as a method of settling disputes on details; appeals should be made only in exceptional circumstances.

Not every Minister for Local Government might have addressed such a conference in the words Mr Page used, but nevertheless what he did say shows that the relationship between the political centre and a system of local government that prides itself on something like semi-autonomy is always a finely balanced one.

The nature of that central–local relationship will alter if a government decides upon a change of direction in accordance with its party philosophy. So, for example, it has often been a Conservative government which has been prepared to see a greater freedom of local action, and therefore consequently a greater variation in standards and range of services provided, while Labour Governments have frequently been conscious of the standardisation of services implicit in the centralism of a socialist ideal. But this does not always hold true, as the experiences of the Thatcher administration amply testify.

In this context is the famous circular 10/65 of Labour (in 1965) which attempted to induce local education authorities to draw up complete plans for comprehensive secondary schooling, while five years later the Tories' circular 10/70 informed local authorities that they were free to pursue secondary schooling in their areas according to how they perceived local needs, and both comprehensive and selective schemes of secondary education would be considered by the Department of Education and Science on their merits.

Similarly the Conservatives under Mr Heath in 1970 restored to local government the choice of whether to sell council houses or not by circular 54/70. But just ten years later Mrs Thatcher's Government, under the provisions of the Housing Act 1980, said that it was not a matter of local discretion and every council tenant (and others) should have a statutory right to buy the property he occupied.

R.J. Buxton,
Local Government,
2nd edn., Penguin,
1973, pp. 58–9

At the same time, some governments can use the legislation of its predecessor to centralise or decentralise as the case may be; for instance, there is the example of the compulsory amalgamations of county and county borough police forces introduced in 1966 by the then Labour Home Secretary under a clause in section 21 of the Conservative-passed Police Act of 1964, Buxton commenting that it was quite clear that whatever the local representations may have been the Home Secretary was absolutely determined to carry out such changes.

Of course, it is also important to realise that it is Parliament, and no one else, who imposes on and disposes of local authorities' functions. Thus under the Attlee Government, control over trunk roads (and thus motorways) was handed to central government, and gas, electricity, and (except in Scotland) water functions to nominated area or regional boards, as well as control of hospitals, which meant that overnight London County Council, the largest hospital authority in the world, ceased being such an authority at all.

In 1974 those local authorities which still had some control over water resources lost that control when a massive reorganisation of the water industry established new regional authorities (replacing the large number of river authorities and area boards); at the same time control of further health functions (principally the ambulance service) was lost when the tripartite divisions of the NHS were merged in another large-scale administrative reorganisation. Given such losses it might be thought that the local government service is in a parlous state, but the decline has been only relative to a situation that might have been; local government has remained a powerful force in the British political system since the services it has retained have grown and expanded considerably since 1945.

Furthermore, some other services have been transferred. For example, the Transport (London) Act of 1969 gave strategic control of the London Transport Board to the Greater London Council, while the provisions of the 1968 Transport Act meant that provincial local authorities, especially the county councils, were more and more involved in the operation of road transport by their permissive powers to subsidise bus companies, especially subsidiaries of the state-owned National Bus Company. Under the 1972 Local Government Act county councils were given a general 'co-ordinating' role for public transport in their area, and, as far as bus subsidies were concerned, by the mid-1970s these had grown considerably, thus giving local authorities a measure of influence in public transport which they had not enjoyed before. From 1973 local authorities were also given wider authority in the field of consumer protection. However, what is added may be taken away later. In anticipation of the abolition of the Greater London Council, London Transport (or London Regional Transport as it was now renamed) was placed under the direct control of the Department of Transport in 1984. The deregulation of provincial bus services has also reduced the role of local councils in granting subsidies.

Statutory Authority

Local councils must have and must show statutory authority from Parliament for all their actions; if they cannot they may be judged to have acted *ultra vires* (beyond their powers). Some Acts of Parliament give local government general authority regarding financial loans and grants (such as the 1933 and 1966 Local Government Acts, and that of 1974 giving the reorganised authorities their financial base), although these Acts may not cover every eventuality: for example, when Derbyshire County Council wished to raise loans on the European money markets, it had to promote a private Bill (the Derbyshire County Council Act 1969) through Parliament. Other Acts will give the authorities their legal form, so the 1963 Local Government Act established the new GLC and London Boroughs, while the 1972 Act reorganised local government county and district boundaries in the rest of England and Wales. Other Acts give local authorities their powers in a particular field: thus the 1944 and 1986 Education Acts are the principal pieces of legislation which govern the operation of educational services, the 1971 Town and Country Planning Act that of planning. The greater part of such legislation is mandatory upon local government, although there is often a wide measure of

199

interpretation within the broad principles laid down by Parliament, but some provisions are permissive – local authorities may use their discretion whether to use certain powers or not. An example can be given by the fact it has long been mandatory for local education authorities to give grants for students on first degree courses in higher education, that is a duty, but grants for certain other courses are discretionary.

Under the 1972 Local Government Act, local authorities were given the power to spend how they wished, but within reason, the product of a two new pence rate. This, of course, amounts to only a very small fraction of their total expenditure. The 1967 Maud Committee on Management (and to some extent the 1969 Redcliffe-Maud Royal Commission on Local Government) argued that local authorities were responsible enough, and it would thus make for 'better' management for them to be given a 'general competence' to provide what services they saw fit in their particular areas, within a statutory framework. In a strongly argued chapter in its report which drew upon German, Swedish and Dutch experiences, the Maud Committee recommended that local authorities should

> 'have a "general competence" enabling them to undertake at their discretion services for the community additional to those provided for by specific legislation. We believe that this extension of power would in due time induce a much less negative outlook in those concerned with local government both at central and local levels, whilst at the same time the citizens' needs would be better catered for.'

The Report said that if few people in central government believed in John Stuart Mill's dictum that 'local representatives and their officers are almost certain to be of a much lower grade of intelligence than Parliament and the national executive' (which may have been true in the nineteenth century when Mill was writing) then local government in the twentieth century should be allowed to prove itself. Maud's passionately worded reasoning perhaps contradicted another remark made almost in the same paragraph, when the Report stated that central government control over local authorities' capital investment and of their borrowing was necessary as part of central control of the national economy. Much as Committee members admired the seemingly greater flexibility of local government systems in some other European countries, there were distinct British centralist strains in many parts of the Maud Report.

Report of the Committee on the Management of Local Government, 1967

In a succinct survey of local–central relations, the Government's Think-Tank (the CPRS) made the following observations in 1977:

Report by the Central Policy Review Staff: Relations between Central Government and Local Authorities, 1977

> 'Central government needs to accept that its attempts to influence the precise content of local authority services are often liable to be ineffective in the short run, and in the long run to weaken (or not to strengthen) local authorities' ability to deal effectively with local problems. The point is not that intervention is always bad, any more than it is always desirable. The relevant questions here are ones of degree. Central government's roles *vis-a-vis* the many activities of local authorities extend along a continuum; at one extreme is the neutral proferring of information on questions of detail, at the other are centralised decisions on major questions of local authority policy.'

23

Political Relationship between Central and Local Government

276. The central government must have an overall responsibility for the promotion of the national interest, but the extent to which the central government should, in practice, carry this responsibility by invading the sphere of local government activity is of some importance to our enquiry. The central government plays an increasing part in the ordering of society, and the public is conditioned to look at it as the only source of power and authority. The Boundary Commission in 1947 said that there was an increasing tendency of Parliament to hold ministers and their departments responsible for every act or omission on the part of a local authority. It seems to us that no minister is willing to disclaim responsibility for an issue relating to his portfolio even though it is within the province of a local authority; there is a notable tendency for ministers to claim credit for achievements which in fact result from local authorities' schemes or proposals and from local authorities' energies in their execution.

277. Nationalised industries are operated and administered by public corporations and their relative independence from direction by the central government and from scrutiny by Parliament is a matter of continuous and, periodically, critical discussion. Those national services which are the responsibilities of local authorities reflect the policies of the central government. These policies may represent party political aims. Local authorities which are run on party political lines may be in sympathy with, or opposed to, certain of these aims. The interests of central and local government may not always coincide; they may be in conflict because of different views on priorities, or on methods or techniques quite unrelated to party political aims. Even where party political views are common, local interests may still run counter to those of the central government. Local authorities vary in the range and quality of their resources; the central government may consider that in the national interest there must be a standard of adequacy for a service which all local authorities must observe; this pursuit of common standards involves the central government in the affairs of local authorities.

278. The present climate of opinion which expects the central government to concern itself deeply in the affairs of society, the concern of the national political parties for their reputation, a social conscience which demands that the standard of services should not for any reason be lower in some areas than in others, the need to control national resources of money and manpower, all contribute to a centralising process which weakens the effectiveness of local authorities, magnifies their subordinate role and reduces them in the eyes of the public to the status of mere agents of the central government. Their legal and constitutional position, their financial dependence and their administrative subordination all reflect political attitudes. We do not consider that people of calibre will be attracted to the service of local authorities when the realities of power and influence are concentrated at the centre, nor do we see local authorities being responsive to the 201

needs of their electorate, when an excess of responsibility is assumed by the central government.

279. Our conclusions are:-

(a) That a fresh approach is required by the central government which ought to acknowledge openly that local authorities are not only responsible for the administration of such services as are conferred upon them by Parliament within the framework of national policy, but are also competent to administer them. This approach should allow local authorities freedom to provide other services which they believe are necessary.

(b) That local authorities should be seen to be responsible to their electorates for the adequacy of the services which they provide.

(c) That unless local authorities are seen to have a greater measure of responsibility, they are unlikely to continue to attract people of high ability to their service to share in it.

Report of the Committee on the Management of Local Government, HMSO, 1967

The Financial Relationship

In many ways it is the financial relationship which is at the core of that delicate balance between a powerful Whitehall and a centralist, unitary Parliament on the one hand, and a traditionally strong and independent-minded local government service on the other.

Central government exercises financial control. For example, in 1976 Mr Shore, the Environment Secretary, made it clear to a meeting of the Consultative Council on Local Government Finance (a joint committee of local and central government representatives) that any overspending in excess of the agreed reductions in targets would be reduced from the amount of rate support grant Whitehall was prepared to give local government in the following year (in this case 1977–8). Such periods of economic difficulties invariably awake fears among the leaders of local government that its autonomy is once more under further pressure. The legislation of the Conservative Government from 1979 is discussed below.

One considerable difficulty for local government has been caused by its inability to speak with a united voice in the face of closer Whitehall control. Although the authorities which had been more stringent financially in 1974–6 wanted preferential treatment for 1977–8, the national local government associations (such as the ACC, the Association of County Councils) saw the dangers in such a tactic, fearing that the Department of the Environment would undertake a much closer inspection and audit of local authority accounts. As one Association spokesman put it, 'We, the associations, are trying to seek a consensus among ourselves on some answer that will prevent local government from being killed off before Layfield [the 1976 Report on Local Government Finance] comes to the rescue.' Although fewer since the reorganisation of local government in 1974, the national bodies which represent the main types of council units, principally three associations in

England and Wales, still have different interests. The Association of Metropolitan Authorities (AMA), in contrast to the ACC and ADC (Association of District Councils), strives to ensure that as large a share as possible of central government grants (the rate support grant) is given to the city authorities for a variety of programmes of urban renewal. Moreover, the AMA has tended to be Labour controlled, while the ACC, like the ADC, has been dominated by the Conservatives. Nevertheless, that does not imply that local government cannot lecture central government, even if a totally united voice can only be achieved when there is one national association representing all different types of local authorities.

Rate Support Grant

The question of financial control centres on the basic question of how much the Government is prepared to provide in way of grants. In the late 1960s the ratio of grants to rates was approximately 50:50, but by 1971 it had reached the ratio of 60:40, and by 1975 a peak of 66:33. By 1985 it was down to 55:45. In short, the way in which central government grants operate and the degree to which local government financially depends upon them, has become politically very significant. Income from charges (principally council house rents) accounts for about 12 per cent of all local authority revenue. To a lesser extent the method of allocating such central grants is also important – these have varied over the years, usually between grants for specific services and grants of a more general nature giving local authorities greater flexibility, relatively, to allocate grants according to the particular priorities given to the various services operated.

The new 'rate support grant', which was introduced in 1958 and reformed in 1966, fell approximately into the latter category. A number of important specific grants outside the rate support grant have continued or developed, notably in the area of the police and education. The Home Office funds 50 per cent of the police budget. There is also the Transport Supplementary Grant (TSG), a special block grant payable with rate support grant. Since 1985, however, the significance of the TSG has been reduced – expenditure on buses is no longer eligible and the grant is payable only for capital expenditure on roads and traffic management.

But even more important now is that when a local authority embarks upon a major 'capital' project (such as the building of a new school), the expenditure involved will normally have to be financed by borrowing so that the cost of the asset can be spread over a number of years, the repayment of the loan and the interest charged on it being debited to current income (revenue) – this gives Whitehall additional political leverage since central government departments may disapprove of certain capital proposals put up to them. As a general principle sanction for loans is only given if the local authority shows that it can stay within its limit of block-borrowing as determined annually by Whitehall. The Local Government, Planning and Land Act 1980 enables the Government to set ceilings on local government capital expenditure, whether by borrowing or from revenue.

J.G. Greenwood and D. Wilson, Public Administration in Britain, Allen and Unwin, 1984, pp. 156–8

The powers of the 1980 Act should not be underestimated, since approval by the Government is now principally given to annual programmes rather than individual projects, loan sanction being directly related to capital expenditure under the broad headings of housing, education, transport, personal social services and other services; virement may, though, take place between those categories. Overspending on loan allocations is subject to penalties, if it is in excess of 10 per cent (a 10 per cent underspending is also allowable). One of the major criticisms of the 1980 Act in this context is that it has made forward planning by local authorities increasingly difficult. It is therefore still no exaggeration, as R.J. Buxton has commented, to say that a wide range of capital projects, the essential means of policy changes, are frequently controlled by Whitehall by use of its power to prevent the borrowing of money. The 1980 legislation was severely criticised by the Commons' Public Accounts Committee. It said that the Act had had 'adverse effects' on the performance of local authorities. The legislation was so complex that many councils did not understand it while others had exploited its complexity by 'abuses of controls'. The Rate Support Grants Act 1986 was designed to clarify the law relating to the RSG, but the necessity to pass the Local Government Finance Act 1987 would appear to make this wishful thinking.

Control of Local Authorities' Capital Expenditure, 51st Report of the Committee of Public Accounts, HC 444, 1985–6 session

Alternative Methods of Financing Local Government

Local Government Finance, Report of the Committee of Inquiry, Cmnd 6453, 1976

The Layfield Committee mentioned above was a much-heralded report on the broader issues of local government finance, although it was by no means the first attempt to suggest alternative sources of revenue. For example, in 1971 a Green Paper was issued by the Government, which considered various financial possibilities, such as a local sales/VAT tax, a local income tax, a local employment (payroll) tax, diverting motor fuel and licence duties to local government, super rating (additional to domestic rating), and site (as opposed to property) value rating, but the Government came to the conclusion that ordinary property rating was the lesser of several evils.

Certainly the rating system is cheap and simple in both the assessment of rateable values and the collection of revenue, and although major rate 'revaluations' have to take place from time to time, it does give local government some measure of independence. Major rating revaluations, often leading to higher rate demands, can be electorally extremely unpopular, as the Conservative Government found after the Scottish revaluation in 1985, hence the planned replacement of rates in Scotland by a community charge (poll tax) from 1989.

Rates, though, are regressive in nature, in that they will take a larger share of a poorer person's income, and, in addition this regressive quality adds to the reluctance of local government to raise rates substantially in periods of inflation. In a general sense it can also be argued that the rating system produces an unequal distribution in the burden of providing local services across the country.

The financial structure for the new local authorities was considered separately, and, it could be argued, very unwisely, from the general processes of reorganisation (under the 1972 Act), and was not put into legislative form until 1974. Professor P.G. Richards has commented, 'the lack of attention given to finance is the most unsatisfactory feature of the 1972 Act'.

P.G. Richards,
*The Local Govern-
ment Act 1972:
Problems of
Implementation,*
Allen and Unwin
1975, p. 193

The Layfield Report

It was against this background that the Layfield Committee made its report in 1976. In one sense Layfield can be said to have discussed more problems than it found answers to; it reiterated the old claim that local government finance was confused and no longer had any clear objectives. Among its main recommendations it said that local government should be made more accountable to the electorate by introducing local income tax. Layfield estimated that a system of local income tax would imply 12–13 000 extra Inland Revenue staff, a proposal not well received in the economically lean years of the 1970s and 1980s. It should be added here that in 1982 the national Audit Commission was established; the right of local authorities to opt for audit by a district auditor or a private 'approved auditor' was abolished. The Audit Commission has considerable powers, including that of questioning whether local authorities are achieving value for money in the way they implement their policies. This body is likely to play an increasingly important part in local government finance.

Changes in local finance

The Layfield Report, although dealing with a vital subject affecting an important political institution, did not receive an enthusiastic reception in any political quarter, partly because the Committee failed to argue convincingly enough on behalf of local government itself.

In 1977 the Labour Government issued a Green Paper which clearly rejected the idea of formally defining central and local responsibilities, and thus rejected Layfield's idea for a local income tax system. The Paper stated that the Government faced the dilemma of securing and promoting an effective local democracy with genuine political choice while at the same time fulfilling its responsibilities for the management of the economy and for the standards of public services. The Government accepted that the dividing line between local and central responsibilities was not always clear, and that it could change because national economic and social conditions could alter rapidly. But such changes still remained compatible with a well understood and accepted constitutional relationship.

Local Government
Finance, Cmnd
6813, 1977

The Green Paper also added that the Government had been impressed by the way local authorities' spending, by and large, had been kept within public expenditure cuts, in planned growth, between 1975 and 1977. Much of this the Government felt was due to the co-operation received from the Consultative Council on Local Government Finance set up in 1975, and whose work the Government wished to expand. In addition, the Government made it clear that local rates would be retained, although they would be assessed on property market

205

values, rather than the old, notional, annual rental value of a property, which bears little relation to capital values and can lead to bizarre variations in rate demands. Business premises (which carry no vote nowadays) pay about 55 per cent of all rates.

Mrs Thatcher's administration from 1979 also had something to say about the central–local financial relationship. Like Labour the Conservative Government issued a Green Paper on rate reform in 1981. Mrs Thatcher was (and still is) particularly committed to rate reform, but like other Prime Ministers found the matter more intractable than appeared at first sight. The Green Paper came to no firm conclusions but indicated that if the domestic rating system were to be reformed then the most likely alternative, apart from pure reform, would be a local sales tax, a local income tax or a poll tax.

Alternatives to
Domestic Rates,
Cmnd 8449, 1981

Under Mrs Thatcher's Government three important pieces of legislation were passed. Firstly, the Local Government, Planning and Land Act 1980 replaced the existing rate support grant by a new block grant which had as its aim an objective measurement of how much each local authority needed to spend – GREA (Grant Related Expenditure Assessment). Central government would decide what each authority 'ought' to spend, rather than top up by way of grant past expenditure (which, it was argued, encouraged the big spenders). The effect of the Act was to give more discretion to the Secretary of State, and a former Conservative Environment Secretary, Geoffrey Rippon, remarked that a Labour Government would have hesitated to give the minister such draconian powers. By way of GREA, which assesses what an authority needs to spend in relation to other councils and which calculates the amount of block grant to be allocated to that council, and in particular via the tapering of grant above the 'target' expenditure for each council, there operates a system of penalties. Indeed since 1984 it has been possible for an authority to lose all its grant in this way, although this would be rare.

The Local Government Finance Act 1982 prohibited the levying of all supplementary rates by local authorities, and in that regard contained retrospective provisions, by making lawful earlier grant penalties. The Audit Commission was set up to scrutinise the finances of local authorities.

Professors G.W. Jones and J.D. Stewart argued about these centralising tendencies as follows:

The Times,
14 August 1981

'Local authorities have had up to now the right to determine their own level of expenditure within a financial framework set by Central Government. The relative independence of local government from direct governmental control over the expenditure levels of particular authorities, which can be seen by central government as a challenge, can also be seen as an essential part of the diffusion of political power in our society.'

The formulae under both the 1980 and 1982 Acts, but particularly the former, were very complex and the new rate support grant and GREs proved extremely difficult and, in some instances, impossible to administer. But the main thrust of the legislation was clear: local authorities' grant aid would be tightly controlled and councils which refused to conform to spending targets would be severely penalised. Nor could they seek refuge in setting high rates – the third side of the legislative triangle was completed by the Rates Act 1984. Under the Act the Secretary of State

THE GLC ON BEHALF OF LONDONERS
Rates Bill resulting from withdrawal of Government Grant
April 1981-March 1983

MRS MARGARET THATCHER
10 DOWNING STREET
SW1

REFERENCE NUMBER

MONEY OWED TO:	RATE IN £	AMOUNT NOW DUE
2,671,000 HOUSEHOLDERS		
148,000 SHOPS AND OFFICES		
397,000 OTHER COMMERCIAL USERS	**31p**	**£600,000,000**
16,000 INDUSTRIAL USERS		
115,000 OTHER PREMISES		

Ken Livingstone, Leader of the Greater London Council, and Iltydd Harrington, Deputy Leader, outside No. 10 Downing Street in April 1983 to protest at the reductions in grants to local government

can set a ceiling to the rates raised locally, and if local councils again refuse to conform they will be financially penalised or 'rate-capped'. As a consequence the Conservative Government found itself in conflict with a number of Labour controlled local authorities, notably Liverpool City Council and the London Borough of Lambeth. One Conservative controlled council, Portsmouth, also found itself briefly at odds with the Government. The full effect of of the legislation will probably not be felt until 1988 (20 local authorities were rate-capped in early 1987), but the overall objective is clear enough – tighter control than ever before of local government spending by a Government determined to restrict the growth of total public expenditure. Indeed, under the 1984 Act the Secretary of State has a reserve general power to cap the rates of all local authorities. In 1986 the Conservative Government published another Green Paper on rates reform. This suggested a flat-rate community or poll tax, phased in from 1990, linked with the freezing of domestic rate bills and a 10-year phasing out of domestic rates, together with a simplification of the central government grants system. A national business rate would also be introduced, whose proceeds would be re-distributed amongst all local authorities. At the end of 1986, in view of its Scottish rate reforms, the Government decided to extend the new scheme to the rest of the United Kingdom.

Paying for Local Government, Cmnd 9714, 1986

207

Political Conflicts

In the central–local relationship, however, there are not just financial balances to be taken account of, but there is also purely political conflict. There have been three recent examples, two concerned with education, and one with housing. In one of the educational battles the conflict was an institutions-community one (the Enfield case), but the other examples were inter-institutional.

In 1967 the London Borough of Enfield was proceeding with plans for comprehensive secondary school reorganisation, but various objectors in the local community opposed the scheme, and successfully contested its introduction. The local council was shown, despite having accepted contrary advice from the Department of Education in good faith, and despite a number of ministerial interventions, not to have followed the correct administrative procedures in several instances. However, as Professor Richards has pointed out, the Enfield case showed that the courts can insist that the law be respected and procedures for changing regulations be operated in a reasonable way, even if in policy terms the minister may well achieve his aim in the end (although this particular case largely put an end to the ministerial career of the then Education Secretary, Patrick Gordon Walker).

P.G. Richards,
The Reformed Local Government System, Allen and Unwin,
1974, pp. 93–7

Another educational conflict over comprehensive education in secondary schools was a simple but fundamental dispute between Whitehall and a local authority – the Tameside case in 1976. Tameside, a metropolitan borough in Greater Manchester, had been Labour controlled until the spring of 1976, when district elections took place. Arrangements were under way for comprehensive secondary schools to be introduced from the beginning of the new school year. The Conservatives, however, gained control of the council after the local elections, and immediately announced, in May 1976, a return to a selective system, in effect a continuation of the existing system.

It might be noted here that this attitude seems to confirm that the working-class Toryism of the towns is more right-wing than the 'enlightened paternalism' of the Conservative middle-classes of the rural or semi-rural counties. The Secretary of State for Education soon intervened, and in July 1976 the High Court, presided over by Lord Chief Justice Widgery, granted the Minister an order of *mandamus,* directing Tameside Council to adopt a comprehensive system of education, and thus agreeing with the Education Secretary (Mr Mulley) who argued that under section 68 of the 1944 Education Act, Tameside Borough was behaving 'unreasonably' in changing the plans at such short notice. (Section 1 of the 1944 Education Act states that the Minister for Education has a duty 'to secure the effective execution by local authorities, under his control and direction, of the national policy for providing a varied and comprehensive educational service in every area'.)

The Court agreed that without the co-operation of the teachers it was difficult to see how all the children under the council's aegis could have been allocated to appropriate secondary schools in time for the new term. But Tameside Council appealed, the Court of Appeal reversed the High Court ruling, and the House of Lords (sitting over a weekend for the first time in history) upheld the Court of

Appeal's verdict. As noted in Chapter 2, this led some experienced commentators to make some fairly sweeping speculations about the new political weight of the judges, especially as almost at the same time the High Court ruled that Mr Shore in his former capacity as Secretary of State for Trade had acted beyond the powers vested in him by statute in refusing permission for Laker Airlines' 'Skytrain' to join the North Atlantic crossings.

Professor Anthony Bradley, in a talk on BBC Radio 3 offered the following observations on the Tameside affair:

> 'For most of the time the relationship between local and central government is doubtless one of partnership and co-operation. Central government has the resources to give expert advice to local councils, and often this advice is backed by powerful sanctions; for example, in relation to finance. But when a local council does not wish to follow the central government's lead, the ensuing dispute may have to be settled in the courts. General rules of law governing such disputes are strangely difficult to find, except for the principle that a local authority is free to make its own decisions unless Parliament has provided to the contrary. But detailed rules may be found in many Acts of Parliament. For example, under planning law, most local decisions are subject to an appeal to central government. . . .
>
> 'The Tameside case was not the first time that the courts have had to decide disputes arising from the 1944 Act. More than once parents have come to court to seek a remedy against local decisions with which they disagree. But never before had the minister come to the court to enforce an order under section 68 of the Act.
>
> 'The judges evidently did not regard the minister as having the monopoly of educational expertise. Assisted solely by the evidence given for the two parties to the dispute, and by the arguments of the barristers, they were prepared to evaluate the educational issues in the case against the yardstick of unreasonableness. As an editorial in *The Times* commented, "the courts do not profess any expert knowledge of education, but they do claim to know what is, and what is not, unreasonable".'

The Listener,
5 May 1977

Clay Cross

The third affair, the Clay Cross dispute, has, however, become the most legendary of central–local disputes – this time a Labour authority in conflict with a Conservative Government. Gavin Weightman has written:

> 'as it has passed into the language, the term 'Clay Cross' means something less romantic: simply the defiance of central government by a local authority.'

New Society,
23 September 1976

Clay Cross Urban District Council defied the Conservative Housing Finance Act of 1972 concerning the raising of all council house rents (with a new rebate system). The Act was subsequently repealed by the Labour Government. In fact the Clay Cross councillors were disqualified from holding office only a month or so before the UDC was swallowed up by the new larger district council (North East Derbyshire) in the reorganisation of local government in 1974. Clay Cross, however, was not the only authority to resist the 1972 Act, and some councils in Labour areas of Wales and Scotland (including Glasgow) only implemented the Act after much delay.

Weightman and others have suggested that Clay Cross may well have been picked out by the Conservative Government as a special public example, a warning to other local authorities. Eventually the housing services of Clay Cross were suspended in 1973, with the rare step of a central commissioner being appointed to run the services in place of the council. Later, various Labour-controlled local authorities were opposed to the 'right to buy' provisions of the Housing Act 1980 and consequently deliberately processed applications slowly. In the case of Norwich City Council the Environment Secretary appointed a commissioner to take over the city's housing service, an action upheld by the courts in 1982. The council decided to comply.

The whole Clay Cross episode placed the Labour Party and the new Government of 1974 in something of a moral dilemma – should retrospective legislation be passed (as the Labour left-wing wanted) which would completely cancel all prosecutions and surcharges arising out of the 1972 Act? The result was something of a compromise, since the then Environment Secretary, Mr Crosland, made it clear to Parliament that legal cases already under way or completed could hardly be reversed (the Conservative Opposition, of course, accused the Government of upholding law-breakers, and MPs on both sides were quick to offer various definitions of the 'rule of law').

The Housing (Special Provisions) Act 1975 was semi-retrospective in nature in the sense that any possibility of future prosecutions arising under the 1972 Act was now struck down, and the 1975 Act also put the responsibility for collecting the 'lost' rents upon the new local authorities rather than upon the councillors who refused to raise the rents in the first place. In the Clay Cross case an 'extraordinary' inspection by the District Auditor found a number of other irregularities in the last few years of the old Urban District Council, and by the beginning of 1976 it was clear that the original 11 Labour councillors at Clay Cross were bankrupt on the surcharge (*ultra vires*) debts they were still facing.

See also
Appendix B

In fact the Clay Cross councillors had taken their case to the High Court and Court of Appeal, but no court, however much it may have doubted the ethics of the 1972 Act, had any alternative but to rule in favour of the provisions of the Act (such is the 'supremacy' of statutory authority). During the passage of the 1975 Act the Labour Government was defeated on its proposal to lift from surcharged councillors the bar of disqualification of holding political office. The Clay Cross Affair in one way highlighted the suggestions that have occasionally been put forward by political scientists for a general local inspectorate responsible to Whitehall, since communication at present tends to be one-way – it is local councillors and senior officials who visit London to canvas civil servants and ministers, but it is only 'technical' civil servants, such as surveyors and engineers, or those connected with planning inquiries, who visit local authorities. Yet it is by no means certain that local authorities would welcome a greater number of visits from central officials: they are quite understandably jealous of their 'quasi-independence' and in present circumstances would resent anything that seemed to be a new type of Whitehall general inspector, French style.

The Clay Cross councillors

There were echoes of the Clay Cross affair in 1986 when 80 Labour councillors in Lambeth and Liverpool faced heavy surcharges as a consequence of planned overspending.

Reorganisation

The reorganisation of local government in 1974–5 should have strengthened the local–central relationship, in as much as by the reduction of units authorities are now larger and implicitly stronger; but if local government had been reorganised along 'unitary' (one-tier) lines as the Redcliffe-Maud Royal Commission proposed in 1969 (the basis of Labour's Local Government Bill in early 1970) it may well have found itself as something more than the junior partner in its relationship with central government. Whether in terms of geographical remoteness such larger units would have been wise is a difficult question to answer, but on the other hand in view of the Welsh and Scottish devolution proposals made soon after reorganisation, and in view of the widespread criticism in the press of the staffing costs of a two-tier reorganisation, the problems of 'political balance' in the central–local relationship were not really solved.

Royal Commission on Local Government in England, Cmnd 4040, 1969

211

In 1978 the Secretary of State for the Environment (Peter Shore) announced the Government's intention of transferring certain services (wholly or in part), such as education and social services, to about a dozen large district councils (formerly county boroughs) as part of a process of 'organic change' in local government. A White Paper at the beginning of 1979, a few months before the Government fell, formalised the position. Nine former County Boroughs (Bristol, Derby, Hull,

The Local Government Structure between 1974 and 1986

ENGLAND	Responsibilities
London	
Greater London Council (GLC)	– Overall planning, transport, fire services, some housing, waste disposal
Inner London Education Authority (ILEA)	– Education in Inner London (12 boroughs plus City of London)
32 London borough councils and City of London	– Housing, local planning, environmental health, personal social services, waste collection, education (in 20 Outer London boroughs)
Metropolitan areas	
6 metropolitan county councils	– Overall planning, transport, fire services, police, waste disposal
36 district councils	– Education, personal social services, housing, local planning, leisure, waste collection, environmental health
Non-metropolitan areas	
39 shire county councils	– Overall planning, transport, police, fire services, education, personal social services, waste disposal
296 district councils	– Housing, local planning, leisure, waste collection, environmental health
Over 8000 local councils (i.e. parish and town)	– Local amenities
WALES	
8 county councils	⎫ Similar to responsibilities of non-metropolitan
37 district councils	⎬ areas in England
About 500 community councils	– Local amenities
SCOTLAND	
9 regional councils	– Overall planning, transport, police, fire services, education, personal social services, water, waste disposal, drains
53 district councils	– Housing, local planning, environmental health, leisure, tourism, waste collection
Over 1200 community councils	– Local amenities
3 island councils	– All regional and district powers

212

Leicester, Nottingham, Plymouth, Portsmouth, Southampton and Stoke-on-Trent) were to receive back their responsibilities for education if they so desired, and districts with a population of over 100 000 could apply for the transfer of social services and traffic management. The Conservative-dominated Association of County Councils fought a strong and successful rearguard action against the proposals. The new Conservative Government was intent upon more radical surgery, but in a different area, as seen below.

Organic Change in Local Government, Cmnd 7457, 1979

Finally, here, it should also be noted that in 1967 the Maud Committee stated that local authorities in North America and continental Europe undertook many of their tasks in co-operation with outside agencies, while in the UK the difficulties of 'inducing local authorities to act together, or to combine with outside agencies, reinforces the central government's liking for provisions which allow little latitude.' The Maud Committee's thesis was that the *ultra vires* rule, the central government audit with the power to surcharge members and officers for expenditure that did not have legal authority, not only affected the internal freedom of local government but also severely limited any degree of enterprise that might be shown in its relations with central government, making long-term financial planning in respect of capital expenditure difficult.

Report of the Committee on the Management of Local Government, 1967

Certainly the last point has considerable validity, but financial difficulties can often be caused not by the system of planning and central control but by sudden turns in the national economy; whether such turns in the national economy could be better dealt with in a system which involved a less demanding degree of responsibility of local to central government is another, but probably rather doubtful, question.

Further Reorganisation

The reorganisation of local government in England and Wales in 1974 (Scotland was similarly reorganised in 1975) was a massive undertaking, and the general structure, between 1974 and 1986, is illustrated in the table on page 212. Unitary authorities, that is county boroughs such as Bristol or Birmingham that were in control of all local services, were abolished. Everywhere a two-tier system was introduced, although the allocation of functions differed in metropolitan and non-metropolitan areas, district councils in the former having more power than those in the latter. Local government in London had been reorganised earlier, in 1965, but the division of functions between the GLC (Greater London Council) and the London boroughs was broadly similar to the new metropolitan areas a decade later. The six metropolitan areas established in 1974 were West Midlands, Merseyside, West Yorkshire, South Yorkshire, Greater Manchester and Tyne and Wear.

The 1974 reorganisation led to larger district councils, thereby abolishing many small councils. County boundaries were also redrawn, so that some new counties appeared, for example, Avon and Humberside, and others disappeared, for example, Huntingdonshire and Rutland.

213

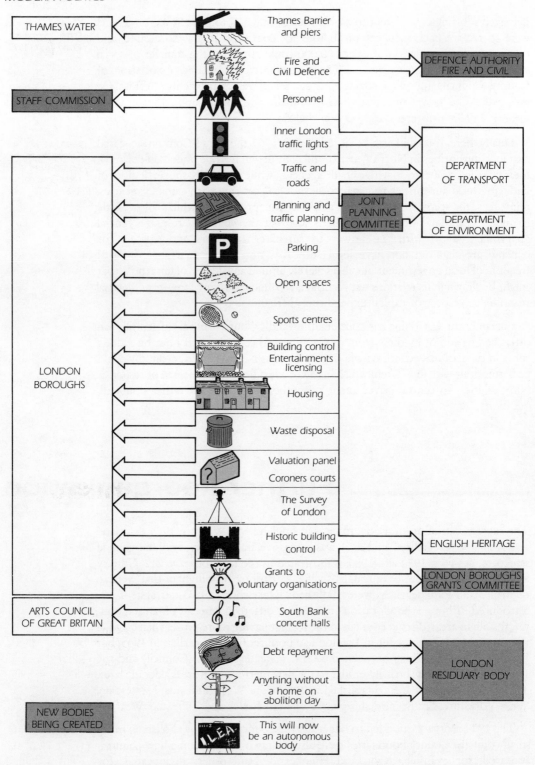

The redistribution of GLC services after the abolition of the GLC on 1 April 1986

In the 1983 General Election the Conservatives made a manifesto commitment to abolish the six metropolitan county councils and the GLC. Their argument was that they constituted an unnecessary tier of government and some of the county councils had been financially irresponsible, in particular the GLC and South Yorkshire, the latter, for instance, in respect of its heavy subsidies to public transport. Whether abolition will bring the savings promised is probably doubtful, since the services have been redistributed rather cumbersomely to the district councils, joint boards of district councils or *ad hoc* agencies. Many leading Conservatives have had severe doubts about the merits of a major reorganisation without the opportunity for widespread public consultation, perhaps through the medium of a Royal Commission. Edward Heath, for one, thought the exercise constitutionally dubious. Other critics thought the measure purely politically partisan, in that it stemmed from the Government's determination to rid itself of certain left-wing Labour-controlled councils. The GLC and the metropolitan county councils were abolished in April 1986.

B.   Management and Politics in Local Government

In the 1960s and the early 1970s the term 'environment' became a very fashionable one to deploy, but not just in the sense of polluted rivers or countryside. In the context of public services it could also be taken to mean that elected representatives and their officials, particularly at the local level, should examine the services which they were providing in their area, as a whole, and see the relationship of one service to another. In other words they should develop a 'corporate' approach to management, in the way the Bains Report outlined in 1972, following the Maud recommendations of 1967.

The New Local Authorities: Management and Structure, HMSO, 1972

The Maud Committee on Management observed that a local authority, in addition to providing a wide range of public services on a scale and to standards prescribed by Parliament or a minister, must necessarily study the physical and social environment of the area it serves, and assess its future needs and developments. The Maud Report went on to comment that following from this each local authority must draw up conclusions on what its objectives were to be and how these objectives were to be achieved. Key decisions had to be taken on the means and plans to reach those aims. 'It is necessary to ensure that resources are available to do what is wanted when it is wanted, and to do it effectively and efficiently. Action needs to be co-ordinated, performance watched and timing and costs reviewed, so that corrective action can be taken when necessary.'

Report of the Committee on the Management of Local Government, 1967

Perhaps the need to relate one service to another was put most succinctly by the Cullingworth Report on new and expanding towns, *The Needs of New Communities*. It said, towards the end of its survey, that the Committee could not end its observations without recording its absolute conviction that to build houses without the parallel provision of community facilities and amenities would result in the 'unnecessary creation of social problems. This short-term saving in local authority expenditure may well turn out to be a false economy. What is saved and more may have to be spent by the personal social services in the rescue of families in distress.'

Report of a sub-committee of the Central Housing Advisory Committee, HMSO, 1967

215

Mallaby and Staffing

See Appendix B

Much of the discussion about the management and party politics of local government has centred around four Government committees of enquiry – Mallaby, on staffing trends, in 1967; the controversial Maud Report on management by chief officers and councillors, also in 1967; plus the less controversial Bains Report on the management of the new local authorities in 1972, and Widdicombe in 1986.

Report of the Committee on the Staffing of Local Government, 1967

The Mallaby Committee's brief was to consider the existing methods of recruiting local government officers and of using them, and to recommend what changes might help local authorities to 'get the best possible service and help their officers to give it.' The Report was dull and made uncontroversial recommendations, although it was the first of several important landmarks in local government.

Mallaby said that the Clerk of each authority should be in overall charge of establishment work, including post-entry training facilities, while nationally a Local Government Training Board should be set up to provide a proper central organisation to cover most aspects of training (and thus pool the costs fairly between the richer and the poorer, smaller authorities), and to supersede the Local Government Examinations Board. This recommendation the local authority associations agreed to readily in 1968.

Less successful recommendations put forward by Mallaby included one that all education posts should be open to general administrative officers, except the post of Chief Education Officer, and that there should be more mobility of staff between local government and the Civil Service and industry – a recommendation to be echoed by Fulton a year later. A more realistic suggestion was that senior officers should be trained more adequately in management techniques, and thus sent on more 'refresher' courses. One important point was that Mallaby, while underlining the fact that the Clerk of a local authority should be the undisputed head of the paid local govenrment service, said he should not necessarily be a solicitor as had been customary, since top management skills were not the same as top legal skills, a point picked up by both the Maud and Bains Reports.

One criticism of Mallaby was that it was élitist in character – it talked about the bulk of clerical staff in a couple of paragraphs, while largely concentrating upon graduates and senior officers. In short, the Mallaby Report was a rather disappointing affair on an important subject, virtually on the eve of local government reorganisation.

Maud on Management

The Maud Report on Management, which leaned on the experience of foreign countries, especially Germany and Sweden, as well as experiments at home in a few authorities such as Newcastle and Basildon, stressed even more firmly the position of the Clerk of the Council. It was around the Clerk that Maud's new management scheme revolved – he was to be the pivot of the new administrative structure.

The Report was both controversial and influential, and its opening sentences were clear enough:

> 'excellent work is being done by many of the 43 000 men and women members of the councils elected to govern our towns, counties and rural districts. . . . But the country is not getting full value in terms of human happiness for the time spent. . . . The result is often both inefficient and undemocratic',

a style rather like the opening paragraphs of the Fulton Report a year later. It can be seen that both the Management Report of Maud as well as the Royal Commission on Local Government which he chaired (1969), were committees which stressed the term 'efficiency', possibly at the expense of local democracy.

The main point of the Report was that the Clerk of the Council should be the undisputed head of the paid service, and that in relation to his position there should be created in each authority a 'management board'. The board should comprise five to nine (depending upon the size of the council) of the more senior members of the authority, and would chiefly be responsible for working out the major policies which would have to be approved or rejected or amended by the full council. The board would also undertake some element of programme review, to see that the Council's major schemes were being carried out effectively. The Clerk would be the full-time official responsible for the organisation, management and policies of the board.

Other chief officers would be directly answerable to the Clerk (or through him to the Board and Council), rather than to any other body. This meant two major things: firstly, greatly enhanced power for the Clerk (or Chief Executive) in each authority, and secondly, and correspondingly, a reduction in the number of the committees, whether departmental or cross-departmental committees.

The committee system in local government, with most full council meetings occurring only quarterly, was almost sacrosanct. Its tradition has been to provide a degree of participation for both elected and co-opted members, who are able to bring their particular specialist knowledge to the committees on which they wish to serve, while at the same time reducing the work-load of the full council, since councillors are often engaged in full-time occupations elsewhere. The Maud proposal also meant in effect the down-grading of the role of the chief officers, other than the Clerk, of course. In essence the attempt was to introduce Cabinet style government into local authorities, something totally alien to them.

The main proposal was ill-received by councillors and officers alike. Most elected representatives could not stomach the drastic reduction in the role of the council committees to a purely advisory function, while a few selected councillors would be privileged enough to serve upon the new management board.

A Government report in 1977 put the spotlight upon the personal role of local councillors. The Robinson Committee on the Remuneration of Councillors recommended that the £11 (now £16) a day attendance allowance for councillors should be abolished. (Attendance allowance is taxable; the optional maximum financial loss allowance of £24 is not.) Instead all district and county (or the equivalent representatives in Scotland) councillors throughout the country should receive a part-time salary of £1000 per annum, together with additional payments of up to £3000 to leaders and some committee chairmen with special responsibilities. The basic scale recommended for those having such special tasks on a council (which would be from three to eight on most councils) would vary according to populations: £750 for areas below 50 000; £1000 for 50 000–100 000; £1500 for 100 000–400 000, and £3000 for over that figure thus putting a small country like Somerset on a par with the GLC (401 000 compared with over 7 million). A statistical survey revealed that ordinary members spent an average of 79 hours a month on council activities, a 50 per cent increase on 1964. Committee chairmen, party leaders and mayors might spend anything up to 122 hours a month.

The Report commented:

Report of the
Committee on
Remuneration of
Councillors,
Cmnd 7010, 1977

'the role of councillors is not easy. There are occasions when they have to take unpopular decisions. They have often to be free to discuss electors' problems at times when others are enjoying some leisure; and, above all, in recent years, their motives have frequently been regarded with suspicion by the community at large. This cannot be good for either their morale or the general health of local government. We believe that councillors deserve better recognition and appreciation of the part they play in public affairs.'

The Maud Committee also made some other points, such as the recommendation that the office of alderman should be abolished (which was under the 1972 Act, except for London which had been reorganised earlier in 1965). It asked, with some success, for the repeal of legislation which required the creation of particular committees and officers (for example, the 1970 Social Services Act stipulates that every appropriate local authority must appoint a Director of Social Services and set up a corresponding committee). Each council should be able to determine its own management structure, internally. With Sweden in mind the Committee felt that there was a need for local government to involve itself more closely in the community by co-opting rather more members of the public on to its committees, and that co-operation should be sought from schools and the mass media, both of which should make themselves more aware of the processes of local democracy.

Bains on Management

The Bains Report, whose Chairman was the Clerk to Kent County Council, was therefore a second attempt to produce a more acceptable management structure for the new local authorities, but still within the climate which the Maud Report had created.

Public
Administration,
Summer 1973

Bains' keynote was the 'corporate approach' to management: as one observer put it, 'where Maud was suspicious of committees in local government, Bains is enthusiastic. He notes that where members have been deprived of participating in committee work they have felt frustrated at having little to do', exactly the point Maud missed. The Bains Report was not, however, about one single type of structure for all local authorities, although a common feature, it said, should be a policy and resources committee, supported by four sub-committees and a chief executive supported by a management team of chief officers.

The spending committees would be responsible for the preparation and submission of major policies to the council, but on the other hand the corporate approach would be underlined by the fact that all important matters of policy and expenditure would also go to the policy and resources committee which would have the opportunity of reporting at the same time to the full council. The policy and resources committee in each authority would be a kind of monitoring committee, but it would not be the powerful decision-making body that the Maud Management Board would have been even if in some authorities the resources committees did evolve into more Maud-type creations than originally envisaged.

The Bains Report was therefore following the note of dissent that one member of the Maud Committee, Sir Andrew Wheatley (the Chairman of the Royal Commission on Scottish Local Government), recorded in the 1967 Report. Sir Andrew had feared that the Maud Management Board could easily become too autocratic, too remote, and by excluding most of the elected representatives from active policy-making decisions, recruitment of local government candidates might be adversely affected.

The Bains Report would have none of that; as P.G. Richards has remarked, the Policy Committee should not consist solely of the Chairmen of other committees,

> 'there would be less of a distinction between inner-group councillors who serve on the Policy Committee and those who do not. The pattern of other committees should be related to the objectives of a council rather than to the organisation of particular services.'

P.G. Richards, *The Reformed Local Government System*, Allen and Unwin, 1974, pp. 155–6

As another writer has remarked, 'Bains approached the problem of committee structure by pointing out what is overlooked in discussions of local government management, that the ultimate decision-making body of any local authority is the Council itself', that the full council would therefore be assisted in its broad policy-making decisions by the advice and information put forward by the central policy committee. In fact such a committee had been envisaged by the second Maud Report, the Royal Commission on Local Government itself, in 1969, when it remarked that it believed that each of the new authorities should work out for itself the precise position of a central committee and the division of duties between that committee and the service committees, but that the central committee 'must be at the core of the administration, and the profileration of committees must be ended', phraseology that was somewhat muted when compared with the Maud Management Report of two years earlier.

R. Buxton, *Local Government*, 2nd edn. 1973, p. 257

Royal Commission on Local Government in England, Cmnd 4040, 1969

Although the Bains central policy and resources committee may have turned out more powerful than anticipated in some authorities, the Bains Committee

> 'expected each committee to undertake systematic reviews of progress. An additional proposal was that the performance review sub-committee should also be able to investigate in detail any project, department, or area of activity.'

Lord Redcliffe-Maud and B. Wood, *English Local Government Reformed*, 1974, p. 85

For better or worse the Bains Report's management structure suggestions have been very influential upon most of the new local authorities since 1974.

Bains and Chief Officers

The more controversial part of Bains in relation to its corporate approach was at officer level. The chief executive, who did not need to be a lawyer or accountant, but have 'across the board' experience, should not carry departmental responsibilities (legal functions would in future be carried out by a chief secretary or solicitor).

The report suggested that the corporate function of the management team, comprised of chief officers, would be part of the formal management structure, while it would be the responsibility of the chief executive, plus the team, to set up the necessary working groups to serve committees. Chief officers should be given an annual appraisal of their performance, perhaps by the review sub-committee, advised by the chief executive, who in turn should be appraised annually by the policy and resources committee. This kind of proposal opened up a new relationship, and perhaps potential dangers, between principal officers on the one hand and the chief executive with his enhanced status on the other.

However, the chief executive was a creature that belonged to the county authorities and the larger districts; by 1976, mainly through their own managerial 'successes', several chief executives of predominantly rural district councils had, in effect, made themselves redundant, and in 1977 the Chief Executive of Exeter was dismissed, while in 1980 Stafford Borough Council abolished the post of Chief Executive. In addition, Bains did nothing to remove, in its definition of the role of the Chief Executive, the suspicions of the elected representatives that senior officers had enough power as it was, or as one chief officer, in a candid moment, put it to the Maud Management Committee in 1967, 'the members like to think they are doing something, that they are running the place, but in reality the services they perform amount to nothing'. That may have been the case in 1967, but by the 1980s most of the counties and all of the city districts were thoroughly politicised; councillors of the party in power, often younger than in the past, were closely involved in the policy-making process, and not always in the major areas. (See p. 410 for the Widdicombe Report on this.)

Although the principal recommendations of the Bains Report were adopted there are considerable local variations in the interpretation of 'corporate management', especially as personalities play a large role in management, not least that of the Chief Executive himself.

A personality clash seems to have been behind the dismissal of the new Chief Executive of Somerset County Council, Maurice Gaffney, in 1974, just a few months after the new county had come into operation. Gaffney had been recruited from private industry and had had little previous local government experience. It was perhaps the difficulty of applying experience gained in a different environment to the bureaucratised world of a county council that led to the very rare instance of a local government principal officer being dismissed by his employers, the elected representatives. The attitude of Gaffney's senior colleagues, in the summer of 1974, was probably a crucial factor in the case.

Bains left unanswered the question of whether the Chief Executive was to be thought of as American-style presidential or 'city-boss' figure, or whether he should behave more in the style of a British Prime Minister as a kind of chairman of a Cabinet, and if so were members of the management team expected to show a measure of 'collective responsibility'? As P.G. Richards remarked, 'over the past months I have talked to a variety of chief officers about the question of corporate management. I can only report that I have no clear idea of how it works. No doubt this is partly because there are variations in practices.'

P. G. Richards, *The Local Government Act 1972*: Problems of Implementation, Allen and Unwin, 1975, pp. 185–6

The surprise resignation of Derrick Williams in 1976 as Chief Education Officer of Avon was interpreted as a protest against the Council's management system, although it may well have had far more to do with a particular style of political leadership in a newly created county. However, one comment, in *The Guardian* (6 and 7 December 1976), was as follows:

> 'Mr Williams' complaint is that, in Avon corporate management has come to mean centralised control of the basic resources – money, manpower, buildings – by a handful of managers and committees whose rule extends to the farthest reaches of the various services departments. They are taking important decisions about priorities in spending, the use of buildings and personnel, to the point where, Mr Williams says, there is little left in education for the chief officer and his staff to manage. . . . Corporate management – on which there exists a mountain of literature – is not something which uniformly exists in local government, nor is it capable of uniform application. It is part philosophy, part style, part a variable bundle of organisational structures and management controls and techniques which should be designed to meet the particular purposes and characteristics of an individual authority. Corporate management aims to reduce the mess to a coherent and cohesive pattern in the interests of greater efficiency and effectiveness and better service to the public. Its critics see the aim as a pipe dream. One senior officer encapsulated what many seem to feel: "it's good in theory, but it's a waste of time".'

Corporate management does not run on strictly party lines.

> 'It has been embraced with equal fervour in Tory shires, in Labour and Conservative metropolitan districts, but it has been noticeable that many of the moans have come from the small metropolitan districts in the north.'

The chairman of the AMA (Association of Metropolitan Authorities) observed:

> 'Corporate management can become an old-style dictatorship in the hands of the chairman and leader. With the help of one or two others he can put things through whatever committees he chooses, however much education and social services officers and back-bench politicians may oppose.'

The Times Educational Supplement, 18 March 1977

Party Politics

There was one other way in which the Bains Report might be said to have failed, in that the committee did not really consider the relationship between the new management structure it was proposing and the extension of party politics into local government after the 1974–5 reorganisations.

The pre-1974 situation can be amply illustrated by the fact that the 1967 Maud Committee found that a party political system in the fullest sense operated only in 34 per cent of counties, 93 per cent of the then county boroughs, 78 per cent of urban districts, 86 per cent of municipal (non-county) boroughs, and just 23 per cent of rural districts, with counties with a population of over 600 000 operating a completely party system. Maud also found that only 63 per cent of all local councillors thought the political party system in local government was necessary (but 66 per cent of then county borough councillors and 74 per cent of London borough councillors thought it was).

The Committee's Social Survey abroad found that in none of the other countries studied were the parties 'permanently embattled in the same way as in many English industrial authorities', while in Sweden party disagreements were kept to major matters of party ideology. In the Netherlands a large number of parties was encouraged but 'parties having usually to govern in alliance with others, do not press their tenets too far', while in West Germany although political parties were encouraged, the relations between the local parties and central headquarters were weak, and 'this contributes to an absence of ideological difference in local government matters'. Following the county elections in 1985 only Powys and Gwynedd in Wales were upper-tier authorities organised along purely non-political lines. A very large number of district council elections are now contested also along strictly party political lines.

If the Bains Report did not consider the inevitable extension of party politics in local government sufficiently, part of the problem centred upon the relations between the new Bains-type chief executive and the political leadership of the new authorities. It is to the chief executive that the leader of the majority party will turn as his dependable guide and adviser, and, of course, in respect of major policy issues the chief executive can always say that he will seek the advice of his management team. However, as one Chief Executive of the London Borough of Camden, has pointed out, if often comes back to that old problem – the fact that nine-tenths of the time the Leader of the Council will be wanting quick answers to seemingly trivial questions –

Public
Administration,
Autumn 1975

'why a particular development is not progressing more rapidly; should a particular voluntary body receive more financial assistance; why somebody's claim against the council has not been allowed; should a council tenant who is physically disabled but who is also a councillor be moved to a ground floor flat? Perhaps the press have got a story critical of the council – what should be done about it?'

In respect of the national parties' attitudes, all the major organisations have been more involved in local government elections since 1974.

The Widdicombe Report noted:

The Conduct of
Local Authority
Business,
Cmnd 9797,
1986

'Councillors of the same political party on an authority invariably organise through a party group, normally with their own standing orders. The Conservative, Labour and Liberal party national organisations all issue model standing orders for party groups. These cover matters such as links between the group and the local party (including attendance of party representatives at group meetings), election of officers (such as chairman, secretary and whip), procedure at meetings, and group discipline. The models are more marked for their similarities of content than their differences. They do however differ in status. The Conservative and Liberal models are for guidance and have no binding force. Labour groups must however either follow the model standing orders or have their own standing orders ratified by the party's national executive committee; their own standing orders must not conflict with the model.'

In this newer, more politicised situation, it might be argued that local government is providing a competitive training ground for potential members of parliament. In both the Labour and Conservative parties in the 40 years since the end of the Second World War, the number of MPs who served on local councils has more than doubled. Approximately one-half of all MPs fall into this category. In the Liberal Party the ALC (Association of Liberal Councillors) is an influential group. The SDP is too new yet to have achieved extensive local government experience.

Types of Councillors

In local government there are probably about three types of councillors, irrespective of the degree of party politicisation. The first type might be called the 'purist', who will be content to speak for and defend certain areas, groups and individuals.

The second type is the specialist who is interested in one or two particular services of the council, maybe because of his previous or continuing professional occupation. On the other hand, the third type is the broad policy-maker who is interested in almost the whole business of the council, and it is this latter type of councillor, concerned with sorting out aims and priorities, who has become more prevalent, in contrast to the more traditional, if old-fashioned, specialist approach. This slow change is partly due to the greater role of party politics itself, to the desire to attract younger members, and to the continuing emphasis upon proper management of the council's business through its elected representatives.

Of course, the more councillors who are elected on a political basis, the more power and influence lies in the hands of the local constituency party. Or does it? The frequent complaint of constituency parties is that once their local government candidates are elected, they become so busy and committed that they are lost to the local party machine and have insufficient time for other political activity. The powers the constituency party officers have is frequently only an initial one, in the control of their selection and in the publication of their election manifestos. But like MPs, if rather less so, since there is always greater competition to be selected as a parliamentary candidate, councillors have to behave themselves 'reasonably', politically, otherwise there is the danger of the party ticket being forfeited at the next election. Members of a council usually meet regularly as a party group to decide how they should act prior to a full council meeting or a key committee meeting. The importance of party group meetings has been particularly highlighted since the Conservative Government came into office in 1979, as the financial squeeze on local government has concentrated the local mind wonderfully and widened the difference between the political parties at every level.

K. Newton,
Second City Politics,
Oxford, 1976,
p. 137

Newton in his study of Birmingham City Council, discerned five role types for councillors – the parochial (those who concentrated upon ward issues), people's agents (taking up individual problems rather than developing policy issues), policy advocates (the shapers of party programmes), the policy brokers (similar to the advocates, but the brokers were mediators trying to reconcile party differences over certain issues or policy), and the party spokesmen (those who saw themselves as mere delegates, implementing policy once decided). But Newton also found that community organisations, when they wanted to achieve action, would more frequently approach the officers rather than council members.

On party differences, the Conservatives invariably regard themselves as the trustees of the ratepayers' money, and their concern is largely with economy, being reluctant to commit monies on extending services to those who could afford to pay privately; thus the keynote is low rates and self-help, while Labour usually welcomes expanding public services as a method of raising standards – they are therefore willing to increase public expenditure and prefer to rely wholly on council employees for the provision of public services. The major clashes between Liverpool City Council and the Conservative Government in 1985–6 well illustrate this point. However, in recent years even some Conservative controlled councils have been heard to protest at the scale of financial cutbacks imposed by Whitehall, for example, Buckinghamshire County Council in 1984–5.

DOCUMENT

24

The Politicisation of Local Government

"Younger, better-educated, often from the professions, and often full-time politicians." This description would seem to do fair justice to many of the councillors I have been describing. In fact, it is how Henry Drucker described contemporary MPs, with Conservative MPs coming from the private sector professions and Labour MPs being more likely to come from the state-employed professions.

These similarities between national and local politicians may reflect the further spread of party politics into local government since reorganisation. The three main national party groupings now account for 98 per cent of the seats in metropolitan districts and counties, for 90 per cent in shire counties, for 77 per cent in shire districts, and for 64 per cent in Scotland. Party activists may be seeking the same qualities and backgrounds in both parliamentary and council candidates. Moreover, local government seems to have become increasingly important as a recruiting ground for MPs. The 1979 parliament had more ex-councillor MPs (44 per cent) than any parliament since 1945.

It is easy to see why there has been talk of the "nationalisation" of local politics, with councillors and MPs being much the same sort of people, with the national parties dominating local authorities, and with local idiosyncrasies being increasingly smoothed away. But is that true? Do the generalisations obscure local diversity?

There is the regional disparity over women and black councillors; and inner London evidently has very different local politics from the rest of the country. The spread of party throughout local government has happened at the same time as an ideological polarisation and the emergence of a putative three-party system. This complicates matters and creates scope for local divergencies.

The MORI study found, for example, that Labour councillors identified themselves as being on the left more often in London and Liverpool than in Newcastle and Norwich. In turn, left-wing politics in Liverpool are different from those of London. There is the stronger manual-worker representation in the Liverpool Labour group. The locally dominant Militant Tendency concentrates on class politics, leaving the life style politics of race and sex to the London left.

There are differences, too, on the Conservative side. Tory councils show varying degrees of enthusiasm for privatisation. Even the most cost-conscious of Conservative authorities, like Essex, sometimes find they have to step out of line and overshoot Patrick Jenkin's spending targets. Other ruling Conservative groups are grievously divided, as Hertfordshire is over school meals.

The political parties themselves, as their grip on local government has tightened, have proved to be less than monolithic. Conservative and Labour councillors dispute vigorously among themselves and with their own national party leaders about how best to respond to the Thatcher government's local government legislation. Even local elections, once generally regarded as almost national referendums on the government of the day, have begun to show deviations from the national swing. This was already noticeable when the local elections and the general election took place on the same day in 1979. But later years have produced more instances of national trends being modified by local factors. Electoral behaviour is now characterised by volatility and party "de-alignment." Both the Labour and the Conservative parties have more and more come to recognise the electoral rewards of doorstep community politics. It may be that local factors will now take on a new significance.

This is no bad thing. A plural society holds many differences within it. It is surely right that councils and their councillors should mirror some of the variations of geography, local social and economic circumstances, ethnic and cultural mix, and political traditions.

The left-wing politics of Sheffield's David Blunkett, and the right-wing politics of Westminster's Lady Porter, may not be everybody's cup of tea. But neither may they be the pattern of everybody's future. They may, instead, reflect the interplay of particular local circumstances with broader national trends. We may applaud more diversity in local politics. But can such diversity survive the rigours of a centralising government?

J. Gyford, *New Society*, 3 May 1984

The Widdicombe Report

The Widdicombe inquiry has recently conducted a wide-ranging survey of local authority practice, against a background of Conservative centralisation of local government finance and growing 'politicisation' of the council chamber.

The Conduct of
Local Authority
Business, Cmnd
9797, 1986

A. Parker, A. Rose
and J. Taylor,
*The Administration
of Standards of
Conduct in Local
Government,*
Charles Knight
Publishing, 1986

Prime Minister's
Committee on
Local Government
Rules of Conduct,
Cmnd 5636, 1974

Royal Commission
on Standards of
Conduct in Public
Life, Cmnd 6524,
1976

Widdicombe's research demolished a few popular myths. The report showed that councillors are not younger, indeed there are fewer councillors under 35 than ten years ago. The workload was not greater, and few councillors received substantial expenses. One-half of the larger authorities had at least one full-time elected member.

As for financial interest, a parallel survey found that about only half of the councils kept a register of members' interests, despite the recommendations for a national code of conduct as suggested by the Redcliffe-Maud and Salmon Reports in 1974 and 1976.

The main thrust of Widdicombe was about the so-called politicisation of local government. The committee found evidence of certain abuses. The report said that at its worst, politics could be a malign influence. It could operate as a means of distributing the spoils rather than serving the community through the appointment of political allies, misuse of planning powers, or channelling services to supportive groups. The committee also found, in an opinion poll, that most people would prefer politics not to enter local government matters.

The report recommended enhanced powers for the local ombudsmen. Where councillors have authorised an illegal decision or action and this was legally unreasonable in the court's view, then the court should have a discretion to disqualify councillors for a period of time. Chief executives could be disqualified from their posts under the same rules.

Senior council officers should be debarred from standing for election to another authority. A flat rate allowance should replace the current system of attendance and financial loss allowances. There should be a statutory requirement for party balance on key council committees and protection for minority groups. Also, all councils should keep a public register of pecuniary and non-pecuniary interests of members. Moreover, the report recommended that there should be a statutory code of practice on appointments to ensure that they were made on merit and not for political reasons, as well as additional powers for the Audit Commission to restrain councils from incurring illegal expenditure. Widdicombe's more detailed observations are listed in Appendix B.

C.   Regionalism and Devolution in the United Kingdom

Elements of regionalism

The United Kingdom, as we have seen before, can generally be classed as a unitary state. That is, it is largely governed from the centre – from London, from Westminster, from Whitehall, from Downing Street. On the other hand, the United Kingdom's political process has long been more decentralised than, for example, that of France. A vigorous local government system does indeed exist, as noted above, notwithstanding financial stringency since 1980. But by the same token there is no structure of regional governments or parliaments; certainly among the English electorate there is no sense of passionate regional identification.

Scotland, Wales and Northern Ireland each present a politically special picture, Ulster most of all (Northern Ireland is examined separately at the end of this chapter). Both Scotland and Wales are ancient nations; to them the term 'region' is hardly flattering: it does little for their national pride. That in turn begs the question 'what is an English region?' Can we, in fact, think in such broad terms as the West Country, the Home Counties, Greater London, the Midlands, East Anglia, the North-West, Yorkshire and the North-East? There are eight Standard Regions as defined by the Registrar-General – South-East, South-West, East Anglia, East Midlands, West Midlands, Yorkshire and Humberside, North-West and Northern.

Perhaps what we can say is that outside of Northern Ireland, in other words in Great Britain, the demand for regional autonomy pales into insignificance when compared internationally – with that in the Basque Region of north-east Spain, Corsica (France), Mindanao (the southern Muslim islands of the largely Catholic Philippines) and in the past the 'Deep South' of the USA.

There is, however, a sort of regionalism and it is manifested in a number of ways, including the following:

1. Both BBC television (BBC1) and ITV are organised in regions, and this tends to encourage interest in the areas concerned. The commercial network is made up of regional television companies. However, some of the Independent Broadcasting Authority's franchises are geographically a little peculiar. HTV, for instance, serves both part of the West of England, part of Wales and part of Merseyside. The Borders company serves part of North-West England, part of North-East England and part of southern Scotland.

2. Under the National Health Service Reorganisation Act 1973 14 Regional Health Authorities were established in England. They are responsible for the strategic planning of the NHS; the board of each RHA is nominated by the Secretary of State for Social Services and includes representatives from local government.

3. Under the Water Act 1973 nine regional water authorities were established in England. Again local authorities are represented on them. (In Scotland water is the responsibility of the regional councils, the upper-tier of local government – the equivalent of Welsh and English county councils.)

4. Eight Regional Economic Planning Councils and Boards in England were created in 1964. The Boards consisted primarily of senior civil servants from the regions. The Councils were appointed by the Secretary of State for the Environment and included local government representatives. Charged with the task of developing a corporate regional economic strategy, the Councils started off with a

227

flourish, but lacking political clout, they soon fell from favour. They were abolished by the Thatcher administration in 1979 as part of the Prime Minister's drive to reduce the number of Government agencies (quangos).

5. Public transport run by the State has traditionally been organised regionally or on an area basis. This has been true of the railways, although since British Railways was slimmed down in the 1960s, this is less meaningful. The National Bus Company has been run by means of regional operating companies although recently the trend has been towards smaller, local companies in anticipation of deregulation and privatisation in 1986–7. Gas and electricity are also regionally organised.

6. Central government is regionalised administratively. Many of the Departments of State have regional offices. Most notable are the Welsh Office, the Scottish Office and the Northern Ireland Office.

The Scottish Office in its current form dates from 1939 and under the control of the Secretary of State for Scotland deals, *inter alia,* with six main services (agriculture and fisheries, environment, industrial planning, education, health and law and order) which in England would come under separate departments in Whitehall. The Scottish Office is therefore multi-functional and most of its staff are located in Edinburgh.

The Welsh Office dates from 1964 but is smaller. Its functions include primary and secondary education, water, social services and health, environmental matters and industrial assistance. The main offices are in Cardiff.

Scotland and Wales at the House of Commons

Politically, although the Westminster Parliament has recognised the special historical culture of both Scotland and Wales, it has hitherto given that history only mild institutional expression. For the committee stage of Scottish Bills the House has two Standing Committees. One was formed in 1957 and consists of 30 MPs and up to 20 others if necessary. This committee considers matters relating to most Scottish public Bills which, in the normal course of events, would be considered by Standing Committees, A, B, C and so on. In 1968 there was added the second committee, which was to deal mainly with Scottish Private Members' Bills. (It should be noted here that Standing Committees for Ulster and the English regions were introduced in 1975. Despite their categorisation both committees are merely advisory. The correct titles of the two Standing Committees are the Northern Ireland Committee and the Standing Committee on Regional Affairs. The former consists of all Ulster MPs plus 25 others, the latter of all English constituency MPs plus five others.)

A third Standing Committee – the Scottish Grand Committee – found its powers strengthened in 1957. This committee is by far the most important of the three. Its main task is to undertake the second reading of Scottish legislation and, theoretically, it may also undertake the report stage. It may also consider estimates and other matters. What is referred to the Grand Committee, however, largely rests in the Government's hands. Its membership is composed of all 72 Scottish MPs. The Grand Committee has thus dealt with a wide range of Scottish issues in the House of Commons, and indeed it is of some significance that many leading Conservatives, including at one stage the former Prime Minister, Lord Home, have favoured a Scottish Assembly which in effect would merely transfer the Grand Committee to Edinburgh. (Sometimes special Scottish – and Welsh – debates also take place in the House of Commons as a whole.) But the Grand Committee has not provided a complete opportunity for detailed examination of Government administration and policy in Scotland.

Partly in response to nationalist electoral success, a fourth Commons Scottish committee, the Select Committee on Scottish Affairs, was established in 1969. In view of the growth of SNP strength it was perhaps rather surprising that the Committee was allowed to lapse in 1972 but it had been unpopular in many parts of the House, and the Committee had not considered matters of Scottish administration which were controversial or of great public concern. In 1979 a new Select Committee on Scottish Affairs was established – to monitor the activities of the Scottish Office.

Wales, on the other hand, has had special Commons representation only in very limited form. The Welsh Grand Committee was introduced in 1960. It consists of all 36 Welsh members, plus not more than five others. The subjects it discusses are chosen by the Government in consultation with the Opposition. The issues are perennial ones: employment and industry, rural Wales, education, broadcasting and the status of the Welsh language, transport, housing and agriculture. The Committee was therefore intended to be purely advisory, a Welsh debating chamber which would try to involve the specialist interests of the Welsh MPs.

But both Welsh and Scottish provisions at Westminster graphically illustrate the fact that while they may have been useful up to a point, they were never – especially in the 1970s – really in tune with the growth of Welsh and Scottish national consciousness. It should also be noted that in 1974 the Welsh Grand Committee was empowered to discuss the principle of any Bill relating to Wales alone – that is, to take in effect its second reading – although 20 MPs rising in their places (objecting) can prevent this (20 MPs also in the case of the Scottish Grand Committee). In 1979 the Select Committee on Welsh Affairs, whose primary function was to shadow the activities of the Welsh Office, was introduced. Although the Committees on Scottish and Welsh Affairs have as their strict task the examination of the policy and administration of the Scottish and Welsh Offices, clearly they can also examine Scottish and Welsh problems generally, in so far as they impinge upon the two Offices. In short, the Welsh and Scottish Grand Committees are now effectively limited to the job of considering the main principles of Welsh and Scottish legislation as and when appropriate.

Elections and Nationalism

The devolving of political power to Scotland and Wales became significant in the late 1960s, when the Welsh and Scottish national parties each won a parliamentary by-election (Plaid Cymru in 1966 at Carmarthen, the SNP in 1967 at Hamilton). These victories led the major parties at Westminster to make a hasty and partly erroneous diagnosis of the new political scene. It can be argued that the political developments in Wales and Scotland were not great uprisings in nationalist sentiment, but an approximation to the Liberal protest vote in England against the economic conditions of the day. Nevertheless, in pure pragmatic style, the Royal Commission on the Constitution was quickly assembled in 1969, just as the Royal Commission on Local Government reform – the Redcliffe-Maud Report – was finishing its work. If ever there was a case of 'pragmatic confusion', that was surely it: reform local government first, then examine the entire constitution immediately afterwards!

Certainly Scotland's economic situation has been poor particularly between the wars; some 30 per cent of the Scottish workforce was out of work in 1932, including 76 per cent of shipbuilding workers. In the 1960s the average rate of unemployment in Scotland was double that for the country as a whole, and unemployment has again become acute in the 1980s. The dissolution of the British Empire in the 1950s and 1960s also closed opportunities to the many Scots who had served overseas in various capacities. The discovery and exploitation of North Sea oil thus came as a crucial electoral weapon to the Scottish National Party (SNP) – offering the chance, at least in theory, of cutting what until then had seemed the inevitable economic bond between Scotland and the South. Even if the reason for the support of nationalist parties outside England has often been less than clear, the electoral trends have been dramatic. In 1966 the SNP and Plaid Cymru took just 5 per cent of the combined vote in Scotland and Wales, but by October 1974 this had risen to 21 per cent, returning 14 MPs to Parliament.

In Ulster, parties peculiar to Northern Ireland since 1974 have taken around 97 per cent of the vote in the province. In the October 1974 Election Ulster returned ten Unionists among its 12 seats – the UUUC, the United Ulster Unionist Coalition, which fell apart in 1977. Ten Unionists were again returned at the 1979 Election – three Democratic Unionists, five Official Unionists, one Ulster Unionist and one United Ulster Unionist (none of these were from the Unionist wing of the Conservative Party, except the sole Ulster Unionist, who by 1980 had left to become leader of the Ulster Popular Unionist Party). In 1983 there were now 17 seats which divided Official Unionists 11, Democratic Unionists three, Independent Unionist one, SDLP one, Provisional Sinn Fein one.

Percentage share of total Scottish or Welsh vote at general elections

General Election	1970	Feb. 1974	Oct. 1974	1979	1983
SNP	11.4	21.9	30.4	17.3	11.8
Plaid Cymru	11.5	10.7	10.8	8.1	7.8

Aims of the Nationalist Parties

The aims and support of Welsh and Scottish nationalism, as opposed to the very special religious divisions of Ulster, are by no means easy to analyse. SNP literature has consistently contained denunciations of 'monopolies' and the concentration of economic power, while Plaid Cymru's plan for a new Wales once referred to the selfish greed of the capitalist and the inhuman planning and direction of the bureaucratic state.

Support for Welsh nationalism seems to come principally from farmers, middle-class professional people, lawyers and teachers, a number of the latter being active in the Welsh Language Society, Cymdeithas yr Iaith Gymraeg. In Wales concern about material and economic status has become interwoven with a sense of cultural insecurity – a not unfamiliar combination in distinctive regions or sub-groups in many countries around the world. SNP literature has contained more references to the economic deprivation of Scotland than Plaid Cymru's to that of Wales, but the SNP has also made references to the threat to the cultural fabric of Scotland – a threat which might now be termed almost unreal, in view of the distinctively Scottish literary and artistic renaissance that took place during the 1970s. Scotland's Gaelic language society, An Comunn Gaidhealach, is more of a literary and cultural organisation than the more overtly political Welsh Language Society.

The SNP (founded in 1934) has argued for complete self-government, while the Plaid Cymru (founded in 1925) has argued for 'national freedom' with recognition at the United Nations. Plaid Cymru's October 1974 Election manifesto said, 'our ultimate aim is full freedom within the Commonwealth', but in 1981 'self-government' or 'independence' was abandoned, it appeared, in favour of a decentralised socialist state. The 1983 manifesto stated that Wales should accept the responsibility of self-government. SNP's 1979 Election manifesto said that the party stood for 'a new relationship under the Crown'. The 1983 manifesto referred to the need for an independent Scottish Parliament and Government. Nevertheless it is clear that by and large both parties would 'settle' for a substantial measure of home rule.

It is difficult to place either the SNP or Plaid Cymru on an ideological left-right line in terms of attitudes to social and economic policy. But even if the policies of the SNP and Plaid Cymru seem like those of modern liberalism, it would be extremely foolhardy to draw more than the most tentative conclusions from those published so far. It is notable, however, that at their 1979 Annual Conference the Scottish National Party did appear to become ideologically divided. The arguments, for instance, of Mrs Margo MacDonald (a former senior Vice-Chairman of the SNP) and the 79 Group for a socialist independent Scotland were roundly defeated. Similarly, later on in the same year a row broke out between Plaid Cymru's socialists and non-socialists at its Annual Conference. By 1985 the differences between Plaid Cymru's two MPs had become very plain, Dafydd Thomas, the member for Meirionnydd Nant Conwy clearly being a committed socialist whilst the same could hardly be said of Dafydd Wigley, the member for Caernarfon.

231

Most nationalist candidates appear to come from the middle, professional classes as indeed do most other parliamentary candidates. In the House of Commons elected in October 1974, one Plaid Cymru MP was a farmer, the second was a financial executive and the third a university lecturer. Among the SNP members teachers and lecturers predominated heavily, five out of its 11 members falling into that category; of the others three could be described as company directors or management executives, one was a lawyer and one was a journalist, and the eleventh was a farmer and company director who had fought a seat for the Conservatives in the north of Scotland in 1966. In the 1979 General Election Plaid Cymru lost its farmer, and of the two SNP members who held their seats, one was the lawyer and the other was one of the company directors. The same four SNP/Plaid MPs held their seats at the 1983 Election.

The Kilbrandon Report

Given the fluid electoral situation – at least between 1966 and 1974 – both Conservative and Labour administrations were faced with four options, some more theoretical than others: firstly, to do nothing; secondly, to give independence or semi-independence to Scotland or Wales or both; thirdly, to establish a German-type federal system for the whole of the United Kingdom; and fourthly, to provide some kind of special domestic arrangements for Scotland and Wales. It was around the last two options that the debate largely centred.

Royal Commission on the Constitution, Cmnd 5460, 1973

The Kilbrandon Report noted that the necessary will for complete separation did not exist. The Report found a number of areas in which power might be devolved, the largest being those of the environment, health, education and personal social services. Secondly, it said Scotland and Wales should have freedom of expenditure, under the authority of ministers drawn from elected domestic assemblies and appointed by the Crown. Thirdly, the numbers of Welsh and Scottish MPs at Westminster could probably be reduced (to 31 and 57 respectively) in view of the new elected regional assemblies; the continued positions of Secretary of State for Scotland and for Wales would be difficult to justify. However, two members of the Commission (Lord Foot and Sir James Steel) favoured not legislative but executive assemblies for Scotland and Wales, and also for eight English regions, while three supported a directly elected Welsh advisory council and one favoured a similar Scottish advisory council. Eight members suggested – as successors to the Regional Economic Planning Councils – regional co-ordinating and advisory councils for England, consisting of indirectly elected representatives from local authorities.

Devolution: the English Dimension, A Consultative Document, 1976

The Government's own Paper on the English Regions in 1976 came to no firm conclusions, merely formulating various options, in particular for strengthening regional economic planning. Its main argument was that there was very little public demand for regional government in most parts of the country.

The Commission found three main areas of discontent. Firstly, the distinctive cultural backgrounds of Scotland and Wales had not been given sufficient recognition by England; the Commission took particular note of the fact that in Wales discontent was as much cultural as economic. Secondly, there was the old question of centralisation – the Report said that the evidence it had received contained widespread criticism of junior civil servants in the regions. Lastly, there was the problem of remoteness; while the Scottish and Welsh Offices may have been effective administratively, they had appeared to make little impression on a public which, the Report claimed, was losing confidence in the democratic process.

In addition, the members of the Commission found considerable difficulty in defining the British 'regions'; this included the problem of finding a satisfactory course for the English–Welsh border.

Its proposals were far-reaching, at least by the standards of what had gone before, and they form – together with the Government's reactions – an absorbing case-study for any country with substantial problems of regional autonomy. The Commission remarked that it thought its proposals would strike the right political balance; most people in Scotland and Wales, it said, would not accept anything less than what it was offering. But the Government took a rather different view.

The Government's reaction

It was a newly elected Labour Government that had to face Kilbrandon's recommendations, and the Labour Party in Scotland was hardly – to start with – a willing supporter of devolution. A few Scottish Labour MPs, however, were impatient for power to be devolved. In 1976 Jim Sillars and John Robertson set up their own breakaway Scottish Labour Party; it was disbanded in 1980.

The Government correctly detected that there was even less enthusiasm for an Assembly in Wales than in Scotland. Lengthy public consultations followed; four White Papers were issued between 1974 and 1977. The Government's legislative proposals departed significantly in certain respects from the Kilbrandon Report. In the first place while the Scottish Assembly would be given substantial legislative powers for domestic matters, the Assembly for Wales (partly because Welsh law was the same as English) was to be limited to powers delegated to it within Acts of Parliament passed at Westminster – in other words an executive Assembly, not a legislative one. Proportional representation would not be used for the assemblies, but rather the simple majority system since it was, said the 1974 White Paper, 'simple to operate [and] easily understood'. Proportional representation was in any case voted out by the Commons in 1977 for Scotland and in 1978 for Wales.

Democracy and Devolution: Proposals for Scotland and Wales, Cmnd 5782, 1974

The Secretary of State for Scotland would be responsible for inviting 'a prospective Chief Executive' to form an administration which would receive the support of the majority of the Assembly; in the normal course of events this would be the leader of the majority party (as at Westminster). (A troublesome point must have filled the Government's mind: if under a first-past-the-post – simple majority – voting system the SNP were to do well, it might result in their capture of a large majority of seats in the Assembly, albeit by small individual majorities, thus producing an Assembly which would be constantly at odds with the UK Parliament and Government.) In Wales the Government did not see the need to operate the same procedure, because the Welsh Assembly was not to be a legislative one, but in essence a series of committees.

Our Changing Democracy: Devolution to Scotland and Wales, Cmnd 5782, 1975

Devolution to Scotland and Wales: Supplementary Statement, Cmnd 6585, 1976

233

The financial allocation would be in the form of a block grant voted by the Westminster Parliament – there would not be an intermediary agent of a regional Exchequer Board as Kilbrandon had recommended.

The number of Scottish and Welsh MPs at Westminster would not, after all, be reduced. Moreover, Westminster would retain a power of veto over Scottish Assembly Acts; the technical details of the veto were intricate and would have involved judges in the shape of the Judicial Committee of the Privy Council. Neither would the Civil Service be split up.

The devolution legislation was, however, something of a botched effort. MPs could not agree on a parliamentary timetable for the 1977 Scotland and Wales Bill and it quickly foundered. Following the parliamentary pact with the Liberal Party, the Labour Government introduced separate Bills which became law in 1978. This legislation, too, was not without its difficulties as it was heavily amended.

Such alterations arose from three sources: 'militant' back-bench feeling in the Commons – MPs on both sides of the House being acutely aware how important their votes had become for a struggling minority Government; the House of Lords, which spent many a painstaking session on the fine print of the Bills as they went to and fro between the chambers; and the Government itself, which, in the rush to get the legislation on the statute book, was compelled to suggest alterations too.

Two amendments greatly irritated the Government. The first was carried by a majority of just one vote and it related to any Bill which affected part or the whole of the non-Scottish sections of the United Kingdom. Such a Bill was to embrace some aspect of domestic policy, the Scottish equivalent of which was devolved to the Edinburgh Assembly. If it was clear that the Bill's second reading had been achieved only on account of the way Scottish MPs had voted, then, subject to an affirmative resolution of the Commons, a gap of two weeks would ensue and the vote on second reading would be taken again. Although the amendment was one which emanated from the Lords, this issue was popularly known as the 'West Lothian Question', after Tam Dalyell, Labour MP for that constituency and a passionate anti-devolutionist, since he had been among the first to highlight the problem of Scottish MPs voting on non-Scottish matters.

Secondly, the Commons voted for a dramatic referendum provision in both Bills. MPs insisted that unless 40 per cent of the *total electorates* in Scotland and Wales respectively voted in favour of the Government's proposals for the country concerned, the assemblies would not proceed, with the likely outcome that the Acts would be repealed by Parliament. It was this last provision that led to the deaths of the Scotland and Wales Acts, and of the Government that had been – ironically – the rather reluctant sponsor of the legislation in the first place.

A majority in the Commons also forced the Government to agree that the Secretary of State for Scotland should, if necessary, make special provision for the Orkneys and Shetlands, both island groups being opposed to participating in the devolution scheme.

In March 1979 the Scottish and Welsh electorates delivered their verdicts. In Scotland the turn-out was 62.9 per cent and in Wales 58.3 per cent. In Wales not one county voted for the proposals – the highest 'yes' vote (at 34.4 per cent) was in Gwynedd. In Scotland the pattern was rather more uneven – six regions voted 'yes' and six 'no'. There the overall 'yes' vote was 32.5 per cent (of the entire electorate) – not a decisive rejection of the Government's scheme, but well short of 40 per cent. (The 'no' vote was 30.4 per cent, with 37.1 per cent thus not voting; among those who voted, the 'yes' vote was 51.6 per cent and the 'no' 48.4 per cent. The five corresponding figures for Wales were 11.8 per cent, 46.5 per cent, 41.7 per cent, 20.3 per cent and 79.7 per cent.)

The Scottish result took ministers by surprise. In a nationwide broadcast Mr Callaghan, the Prime Minister, admitted that his Government's plans, on which much legislative time had been spent, had been rebuffed, and that the Commons would, as required under the Acts, be given the chance of repealing the devolution legislation. He also proposed spending a further few weeks on political reflection and all-party talks. However, what otherwise might have passed for eminently sensible suggestions also appeared to contain a distinct element of ministerial procrastination. Before long the SNP had tabled a motion of no confidence in the Government and it was adopted by the Tories, as the senior Opposition group. Labour lost the vote (by just one vote) and a general election automatically ensued. The Conservatives under Mrs Thatcher, pledged to repeal the Scotland and Wales Acts, swept to power – although it is perhaps interesting to note that they captured one-third of the votes of the total electorate, just a fraction more than the overall 'yes' vote in Scotland.

It could perhaps be said that a Government that was already in its death-throes had been brought down by constitutional mismanagement. Nearly all sections of the mass media reported that this was the first time a Government had been driven out of office by defeat on a confidence vote in the Commons since Ramsay MacDonald's first minority Labour administration in 1924. Technically speaking, this is not true – it would be more accurate to say that the Callaghan example was the first this century. In MacDonald's case, the Prime Minister chose to treat as a matter of confidence what was in fact not necessarily a resignation issue – defeat on a Liberal amendment (designed, paradoxically, by Asquith to save MacDonald's political skin) to a Tory motion of censure over the Government's mishandling of the prosecution of the acting editor of *Worker's Weekly* (the Campbell case).

The Problems of Autonomy

Devolution north of the English border was therefore the subject of the most acute disagreement among the public. Certainly both major United Kingdom political parties in the early 1970s had realised that the Scottish nationalist movement was far removed from the heady romantic nationalism of the 1930s and 1940s and had more of machine party politics about it; and it is always important to distinguish between nationalism and what may be termed national economic self-consciousness. Kedourie has said that nationalism looks inwardly, away from and beyond the imperfect world; but Scottish self-consciousness may well have far more to do with

E. Kedourie, *Nationalism*, Hutchinson, 3rd edn., 1966, p. 87

235

the fact that some 60 per cent of the Scottish workforce nowadays works for non-Scottish employers. Given the general conservatism of the United Kingdom as a whole, it is possible to see Scottish economic nationalism as an alternative to left-wing socialism as it manifests itself, for example, in France and Italy. (The very institution of a Scottish Assembly would, in fact, have led to a rationalisation of the half-dozen or so agencies which deal with industrial planning and growth.) And as for Scottish public opinion itself, in the pre-referendum days no totally firm conclusions could be drawn, although one System 3 poll conducted for the BBC was of some help. System 3 found in 1976 that 18 per cent wanted no change and 31 per cent wanted an Assembly for Scottish affairs on the lines of the Government's proposals, while 33 per cent wanted an Assembly with wider powers on trade and industry (points the Government did make concessions on) and 18 per cent wanted complete independence.

In Wales, culture has been more important than economics for a long time. Despite signs of political volatility, the Labour vote in Wales is usually not far short of an absolute majority and its size is still the dominant feature of Welsh politics. But those in receipt of the Welsh radical vote (with its nineteenth-century heritage of being anti-Church) cannot live for ever off this kind of political capital. The 1979 General Election result bore eloquent testimony to that fact – the Conservatives advanced deeply into rural areas, their most notable wins being Anglesey (from Labour) and Montgomery. The latter returned to the Liberals in the 1983 Election. The existence of the Welsh language (spoken by barely 20 per cent of the Welsh population) has been a divisive rather than a unifying force, there being a suspicion among the middle class that Welsh speakers take too many of the top jobs in Wales. It is important to appreciate that in Wales, with its very special cultural background in religion and the arts, nationalism – or national self-consciousness – has not been the exclusive property of the nationalist party, as it has been in Scotland. It exists almost as much within the Welsh Labour and Liberal parties as in Plaid Cymru.

As far as Welsh public opinion about the devolution proposals was concerned, a Marplan survey for the BBC in 1975 reflected significantly less enthusiasm for an Assembly than among the Scottish electorate. The survey showed that 51 per cent of those sampled favoured retaining the status quo, while 27 per cent wanted a Welsh Assembly as proposed by the Government, 12 per cent would have supported an Assembly with much wider powers and only 10 per cent would have opted for Welsh independence.

The Kilbrandon Report, and the legislation flowing from it, may have had the political diagnosis roughly right, but, it can be argued, a political cure is still wanting. Conversely, it must not be assumed that the 1970s found devolution on the lips of every Welsh and Scottish elector. As one newspaper put it, it could not be said that 'in the bars of Glasgow, the streets of Aberdeen, the Highland hills and valleys, people nowadays talk of little else. The conversation in Glasgow trains and buses last weekend seemed to rate devolution as a poor runner-up to Motherwell's prospects at Celtic.'

The Guardian,
21 November
1975

The devolution question has provided the most fascinating constitutional case-study in British post-war political history. The question is what its next chapter will be, if there is one at all.

Northern Ireland

It is not proposed to examine here the immensely detailed history of Northern Ireland and the relationship between the Irish Republic and the United Kingdom, but a brief outline is required. Suffice it to say that the conflict between the north and south of Ireland can be dated at least to 1688 – the year of the 'Whig' Revolution, the deposing of the Catholic James II and the arrival of the Protestant William III (of the Dutch House of Orange). The conflict is partly religious, partly socio-economic and cultural, but it is there. Those who defend the Protestant traditions, are the Orangemen who maintain the memory of 'King Billy'. Those who defend the union of Ulster with Great Britain are the Unionists, loyal to the British Crown. If necessary Ulster 'will fight and Ulster will be right'.

At the end of the last century Gladstone attempted to establish a domestic parliament in Dublin, to bring 'Home Rule' to Ireland. Another Liberal Prime Minister, Asquith, achieved this in legislative form in 1914. But the First World War interrupted the process of constitutional change. The Orangemen, under their leaders Craig and Carson, would have none of it. The Government of Ireland Act 1920 envisaged separate domestic parliaments for Ulster (at Belfast) and southern Ireland (in Dublin).

Under the Anglo-Irish Treaty of 1921 Ireland was partitioned. The six counties of the north-east of Ireland remained within the United Kingdom. On domestic matters they had their own Prime Minister and Parliament (Stormont). The 26 counties of the south and west achieved complete independence and became the Irish Free State – a dominion of the British Empire.

From 1921 to 1972 the Protestant majority in Ulster (two-thirds of the population) ruled, and by the gerrymandering of constituency boundaries for Stormont, and in particular ward boundaries for local government, the 'Loyalists' were able effectively to exclude the Catholics from political power and to practise discrimination against them (most notably in council housing).

In 1949 the Free State left the Commonwealth and the Irish Republic was established. An unsuccessful IRA campaign was conducted in Ulster from 1956 to 1962. In 1968, in line with student protest movements in both America and Europe, a civil rights organisation was established: its objective was to end all anti-Catholic discrimination.

Violence quickly ensued and the British Army was despatched to Northern Ireland in 1969. Although the Kilbrandon Commission considered the difficulties of Ulster, the province's political future continued to be dealt with by Westminster as a separate issue. Since 1969 about 2500 people have been killed in the 'troubles'. The increase in the level of violence since 1969 has in the main been the work of the Provisional IRA, a splinter group of the Official IRA (the Marxist wing of the Irish Republican Army). The Officials have been more prepared to achieve their aims through the ballot box, fighting elections under the banner of the Republican Clubs, while the Provisionals are far more committed to violence. There are also several Protestant paramilitary organisations, including the Ulster Defence

237

Association – UDA. The Catholic dominated SDLP (Social Democratic and Labour Party) has sought the reunification of Ulster and the Republic only through peaceful methods. Sinn Fein, the political wing of the IRA, advocates reunification through violent means. In recent years Sinn Fein has contested elections and has one MP, Gerry Adams; but as with early Sinn Fein MPs he boycotts the Westminister Parliament.

British troops patrol the streets of Belfast in 1969

In 1972 Stormont was suspended and direct rule imposed from London. Since then Northern Ireland has been governed by *ad hoc* agencies and Government departments; there is a separate Northern Ireland Civil Service. All these are answerable to the Secretary of State for Northern Ireland and the Northern Ireland Office. Centralised Boards under the Northern Ireland Office deal with such matters as housing, police, fire and electricity. Area Boards deal with health, education and libraries, and social services. The Northern Ireland Office deals directly with planning, water and roads. Since 1973 the only local government unit has been 26 District Councils. While district councillors sit on various Area Boards, the functions of the district councils themselves (especially since 1977) are negligible – markets, recreation and street cleaning.

In 1973 the so-called Sunningdale Agreement, between the UK, Northern Ireland and the Irish Republic, provided for the establishment of a new Northern Ireland Assembly (and from it the Executive), to be elected by proportional representation. In other words Catholics and Protestants would at last share power. Under the Northern Ireland (Border Poll) Act 1972 referenda are held periodically in Ulster to determine whether it wishes to remain part of the United Kingdom.

Sunningdale was effectively a disaster: the new political structure lasted just a few months at the beginning of 1974. A general strike organised by Protestants opposed to the whole concept of power-sharing, ensured its collapse. The Northern Ireland Constitutional Convention of 1975 also ended in failure.

In 1979 the Government issued a Consultative Document which, following Kilbrandon principles, outlined six possible schemes for devolving power to the province. Three of the options were weighted towards a reformed local government structure. This document formed the basis for discussion between the political parties of Northern Ireland at another Constitutional Conference; the discussions collapsed in 1980. This, however, did not prevent the Government from issuing another abortive White Paper during the same year. The Paper proposed two models for a future single house legislature of 80 seats, to be elected by proportional representation. The Assembly was to have an Executive and it would control most domestic matters, while Westminster retained control over foreign affairs, defence, law and order and finance. Once again the Protestants refused to contemplate the idea of power-sharing.

The Government of Northern Ireland, Cmnd 7950, 1980

By the Northern Ireland Act in 1982 the Government tried again. A 78-member Assembly elected by proportional representation (STV) was established. The principal task of the Assembly was to reach agreement amongst its members on how devolved functions might in the future be exercised, subject to the approval of the Secretary of State for Northern Ireland and Parliament. No such agreement was reached and indeed some political groups boycotted the Assembly. This latest version of Stormont proved to be yet another political failure in Northern Irish affairs: the Government dissolved the Assembly in 1986 and direct rule from London remains. Without the support of the SDLP the Assembly was doomed from the start. The 1982 initiative was in some measure a response to the difficulties of the previous three years, although in terms of the scale of violence since the 'troubles' began in 1969 the number of people killed by the late 1970s was declining. However, in 1979 Lord Mountbatten was assassinated and in 1981 an Official Unionist MP (the Revd Robert Bradford). Also, in 1981 a number of IRA prisoners at the Maze H-block cells in Belfast went on hunger strike. Ten died before the protest, which was about prison conditions, was called off, including Bobby Sands who, while still a prisoner, was elected as MP for Fermanagh and South Tyrone in a by-election.

Northern Ireland: A Framework for Devolution, Cmnd 8541, 1982

In 1985 Mrs Thatcher gravely disappointed the Unionists by signing the Anglo-Irish Agreement with Dr Garret FitzGerald, the Prime Minister (Taoiseach) of the Irish Republic. This agreement gives Irish ministers a consultative say in Ulster affairs, through the establishment of an Anglo-Irish Secretariat in Belfast. All Northern Ireland's Unionist MPs (15 out of 17) resigned their parliamentary seats and forced by-elections in 1986, on the policy of total opposition to any Republican involvement in Ulster's affairs. They lost one seat to the SDLP, but retained the other 14. Ulster Unionists are determined to bring the Anglo-Irish Agreement to an end, by force if necessary.

Summary

Local government has always played some kind of role in British political affairs, and consistently so in the form we know it since the establishment of county councils by Lord Salisbury's Government in 1888.

Local government, it can be said, allows people to decide their own problems, within their particular community. Excessive centralisation leads to large bureaucracies, overmanning and inefficiency. The more cogent argument is that it maximises democracy, it allows greater participation, but the low turn-out in many local elections is not entirely conducive to this argument. Nevertheless the United Kingdom is a centralised, unitary State. Local authorities have no legislative powers, they must work within the parliamentary framework. How tightly that framework is drawn depends upon the government of the day. Traditionally, the Conservatives have favoured a greater degree of local accountability than Labour, since equality of opportunity and equitable standards nationally applied are a socialist concept. Traditionally, also, the Liberals have been the most decentralist minded of all the major parties, although the last Liberal Government (1905–15) operated on noticeably centralised lines.

Recently, however, Labour has moved a little in the direction of decentralisation, through its espousal, albeit on fleeting occasions, of workers' co-operatives and more starkly through the independent minded policies of some Labour controlled local authorities, notably Liverpool and Sheffield. But this is insignificant when compared with the increased central control over local government finance that has grown since the Conservatives took power in 1979, even if both Labour and Conservative governments have used the rate support grant as an effective centralising mechanism.

Perhaps even more dramatic has been the way in which the Conservatives have abolished certain local councils, from 1986 – the GLC and the six metropolitan county councils, an acknowledgement, at least in Tory eyes, that the massive local government reorganisation in 1974 (under Mr Heath's 1972 Local Government Act) was faulty.

There has also been much discussion on the internal structure of local government, as evidenced by the Mallaby and Maud Committees (1967) and the Bains Report (1972). It was Bains which had the greatest influence, but overall the way in which the reformed local authorities and their committees are organised and function has not changed dramatically from the pre-1974 councils.

While Labour set up the Redcliffe-Maud Commission in 1965 (reporting in 1969), which led to the 1974 reorganisation, although in a different form under the Conservatives, it has avoided becoming embroiled in local government reform. But it could not avoid the challenge posed to Westminster by the growth of Scottish and Welsh nationalism. The Labour Government effectively wasted two parliamentary sessions (1976–7 and 1977–8) on the Scotland and Wales Acts, but it was not an issue which at the time could be easily avoided, as outlined earlier on.

Governments of either political complexion have not been able to devolve power satisfactorily to Northern Ireland. Although there is a Secretary of State for Northern Ireland, he alone, via the Northern Ireland Office, cannot expect to meet the political demands on all sides of the Ulster community. In contrast, given the fact the proposed Assemblies for Scotland and Wales were rejected in referendums in 1979, decisively in Wales, the Secretaries of State for Scotland and Wales, through the Scottish and Welsh Offices, do act as some kind of unifying force. They can argue a case in Cabinet, although they are not its most senior members, in a way that might not be done were Cabinet ministers to have nationwide domestic responsibilities. Of the two the Office of the Scottish Secretary is the more powerful, and older, dating from the late nineteenth century.

Questions

1. Is it healthy for local democracy for the majority of a local council's policy to be determined by officers?

2. 'The battle of the parties within local authorities is not a mere charade.' Discuss. (Joint Matriculation Board)

3. Assess the means possessed by local authorities of exerting pressure on central government and resisting pressure by central government. (Joint Matriculation Board)

4. Analyse the problems of the devolution issue, following the Kilbrandon Report of 1973.

8 Economic Issues and Nationalisation

'But by now the CBI and the city were in a near hysterical state, egged on by Conservative suggestions that the whole of industry was about to be nationalised. When the White Paper finally appeared in August reportedly after twenty-five redrafts, the policy had been emasculated.'

The Guardian, 3 November 1975

The Problem Economy

All British governments in modern times, and all governments in the Western world, have been buffeted by financial storms of one kind or another, and all have sought to ride them out. A good illustration of this was Baldwin's success in breaking the General Strike of 1926, less successful in the inter-war period were various government responses (or lack of them) to the depression years of the 1930s.

Since 1945 most governments have been committed to a wide measure of state intervention in the economy and to maintaining full employment. Programmes of public works have been accelerated. This was Keynesian economics in its barest form. The United Kingdom's economic problems, however, appear to have been greater than those of comparable Western, industrial nations, and the government's handling of the economy has been at the centre of nearly every general election since 1959. A succession of economic crises and industrial difficulties, during the late 1960s culminated in the devaluation of sterling in 1967 (this was the era of the Bretton Woods system of fixed exchange rates).

Although we now live in a world of freely floating exchange rates, that does not prevent governments from exercising influence over the value of the pound. High interest rates, although determined largely by the market and the Bank of England, may be encouraged by the Government if it wishes to attract overseas capital, or restrict the growth in the money supply. Equally, a government can impose or lift exchange controls; Mrs Thatcher's Government suspended such controls in 1979.

Then, too, there are various other methods by which the Government can control or manipulate the economy. In the first place it may introduce price and wages controls (usually by legislation), as has happened on a number of occasions

242

under both Labour and Conservative administrations. Secondly, the Government may attempt to control the 'money supply' (M3), the amount of actual money in circulation (notes, coinage and the like), as, perhaps, a tool to keep down inflation. Much has been heard of this during Mrs Thatcher's term of office since 1979. Thirdly, a government may restrict public expenditure (currently about 44 per cent of the GDP) in an effort to liberate market forces, remove 'artificial' restraints and allow the economy to grow. This is the so-called monetarist school of thought, as opposed to the Keynesians who see public expenditure as a way of stimulating the economy and reducing unemployment.

Allied to the monetarists, are the 'supply-siders', those members of the Government or economists who believe that if taxes are reduced, people will, apart perhaps from working harder, have more money to spend (supplied that is), which in turn will boost demand and force the economy to expand.

See 'Mrs Thatcher's Approach to Leadership in Government, 1979–83', Parliamentary Affairs, Autumn 1983

This philosophy has dominated Conservative thinking since 1979 and at the heart of this programme has been the Government's Medium Term Financial Strategy (MTFS) and its increasingly strict control over local government finance; in respect of the latter, this has been achieved through extensive legislation in 1980, 1982 and 1984. The amount of central government grants (the Rate Support Grant and certain specialist grants) to local authorities is currently highly controlled via the GREA (Grant Related Expenditure Assessment). There are stiff and complicated penalties which may be imposed upon local authorities if they spend above the grant targets, whereby grants are severely and progressively reduced. Nor may local authorities make up short-falls by raising rates – the amount that can be raised in this way is also strictly controlled, authorities could find themselves 'rate-capped'. The natural driving force behind the long process that produces the annual Public Expenditure White Paper is the Treasury. It is the Treasury which dominates the inter-departmental committee, composed of 40 to 50 officials, which attempts to ensure that public spending in the medium-term bears some relation to the general trends in the economy as a whole. PESC (the Public Expenditure Survey Committee) is primarily a creation of the 1961 Plowden Report.

DOCUMENT

25

The UK's Economic Problems

Historically, Britain's post-war rate of economic growth compared favourably with that earlier in the twentieth century. What fuelled the sense of disappointment was partly the promises of politicians, partly the expectations of voters and partly the much better performance of other countries. The vast foreign investments and the imperial structure which had cushioned undulations earlier in the century were no longer there. It could always be said that GNP was not everything, but the fact remained that any indicators of 243 the quality of life, such as education and health care, depended upon economic growth. The recession, following the five-fold increase in oil prices in 1973/4, heightened perceptions of Britain's economic weaknesses. Whereas Britain's record on most economic indicators had been poor before the oil crisis, the uncomfortable fact remained that in the recession she continued to perform worse than other countries. Between 1973 and 1976, for example, output per head grew by only 1.2% compared with 9% in France and 10% in West Germany. The pound lost over one-third of its value against a basket of international currencies between 1972 and 1978. The inflation record was markedly worse than that in other leading Western countries, except Italy. The increase in real wages, averaging 1.5% in the years between 1963 and 1973, had been less than half that in the rest of the European Community. There was a fall of 1.4% in living standards between the middle of 1975 and the middle of 1977 (though this was followed by a 6% increase in the twelve months to October 1978).

The 1970s also saw a sharp challenge to the neo-Keynesian assumptions which had long prevailed among leading civil servants, front-bench spokesmen and most economists. That consensus assumed that policy-makers would and could keep the economy roughly in balance by increasing demand when economic activity and unemployment fell below the 'natural' levels, and restricting demand when inflationary tendencies appeared. Prices, interest rates, wages and unemployment were thought to be related in a predictable manner. Inflation and unemployment had been seen as competing elements, with an increase in one being traded off against a decline in other. In the 1970s, however, unemployment and inflation increased in tandem, and it was widely acknowledged that governments could not spend their way out of a recession without producing a further increase in inflation. By the first quarter of 1972 unemployment had reached 4%, or nearly 900,000, and the Heath government was panicked into reflation. Unemployment passed a million in the third quarter of 1975 and the powers that be came to accept the new high level as more or less inevitable. Inflation, which had averaged a little over 3% annually between 1952 and 1957, averaged 20% for the first three years of the Labour government.

Economists fashioned new theories, and the politicians developed their own 'alternative' right- and left-wing strategies. A growing body of opinion, influenced by commentators such as Samuel Brittan, Peter Jay and Alan Walters, insisted on the importance of money supply in creating inflation. Before 1974 the money supply figures had not even been published. After 1975, Mr Healey's strict control of the money supply and the intellectual ascendancy among Conservatives of Sir Keith Joseph and Sir Geoffrey Howe created a new front bench consensus on the importance of money supply as an instrument for combating inflation. It became even more important for the government when the incomes policy broke down in 1978. There was of course a big distinction between the pragmatism of monetarists like Mr Healey and the almost theological advocacy of free market economics by certain Conservatives who drew on Hayek and Friedman for inspiration. But strict Conservative monetarists such as Sir Keith Joseph, John Biffen and Nicholas Ridley could feel more sympathy with the economic management of Mr Callaghan and Mr Healey than with that of the Heath–Barber regime.

There was also a growing debate over the role of public expenditure. As in other countries public expenditure had grown steadily as a proportion of GNP since 1945, with particularly steep surges in the first years of the Labour governments in 1964 and 1974. If transfer payments are included, public expenditure as a proportion of gross domestic product increased from 44% in 1965 to 60% in 1976 – a level that the Nobel-prize winner Milton Friedman and his disciples stigmatised as a threat to freedom. The contrast between Labour as a party of high public expenditure and commitment to the social services on the one hand, and the Conservatives as a party of restricted public expenditure and lower rates of income tax had been muted in the past. As a result of economic growth the Conservative governments after 1951 had maintained the Welfare State, and sustained a high level of public expenditure, while actually cutting direct taxation.

By 1975, however, Labour itself moved some way to checking public spending. In the spring of 1975 cuts were made and cash limits imposed on government departments; further cuts followed in July 1976 and, after the sterling collapse and the intervention of the IMF, still more cuts were made. The public sector deficit, though not appreciably out of line with that of other countries hit by the recession, required overseas loans for its funding, and its size was a target of criticism. Labour's left wing exaggerated these events, describing them as a betrayal of the Labour commitment to a high level of public expenditure. But the real take-home pay of the average worker was influenced by public policy, and levels of direct taxation were biting at a lower level. The inevitably escalating claims of the welfare state, combined with the workers' pressures to increase their take-home pay, were overloading the economy at a time when there was little or no growth in national wealth.

D. Butler and D. Kavanagh, *The British General Election of 1979,* Macmillan, 1980

Controlling public spending at central or local level did not, it should be emphasised, arrive in 1979 with the advent of Mrs Thatcher. Elements of the present system were already in existence, although it is true to say that local government finance is nowadays much more tightly controlled. For example, 'cash limits' were introduced in 1976 and then progressively extended. The system of cash limits is a ceiling, applied to the actual cash spent by most public bodies, and is designed to overcome the problems of adjusting expenditure for reasons of inflation. If a department 'overspends', it has either to find more money from the Treasury or, more likely, to delay projects to the following year.

Cash Limits on Public Expenditure, Cmnd 6440, 1976

Such are just a few of the ways governments exercise economic influence and fiscal control. One other major route is how far the State controls, acquires and disposes of capital assets, in other words, to nationalise or privatise, or not as the case may be.

State Intervention

The politics of the control of the means of economic production has been consistently explosive, and in the post-war period has been at the root of the political differences between the two major parties, although at times the philosophical gulf between Labour and Conservative has been less distinct than on other occasions. State intervention in the economy is not new, and the trends have been developing since the earlier part of the century. Nor is it an issue confined to the United Kingdom. Bismarck, in the imperial Germany of the 1880s, in an effort to stem the tide of socialism, embarked upon a programme which extended the state's role in what we would recognise today as 'public services'. Italy during the inter-war era, under Mussolini, became the model of the corporativist state, which developed the closest of links between state and industry, although in fact for various reasons the scheme was never really successful.

In the United Kingdom the peak of the nationalisation programme was reached in 1945–50 under the Labour Government, which was intent on carrying out a radical programme of reform. But there had in reality been a gradual increase in the level of state intervention before the Second World War. For example, in 1908 the Liberal Government created the Port of London Authority in order to establish control over what was then the vast complex of London docks. In 1926 the Conservative Government under Baldwin set up the Central Electricity Generating Board, to ensure some measure of standardisation in the production of electricity, and in the same year the British Broadcasting Corporation was established as a public body, although not subject to direct ministerial control. In 1933 the coalition National Government created the London Passenger Transport Board, to end the notorious competition between London's bus companies, while in 1939 the same Government established the British Overseas Airways Corporation (BOAC). Thus the precedent had been established, albeit a weak one, of public ownership based on what might be termed pragmatic convenience.

The post-war Labour Government, however, extended the programme much further. One of the nationalisation acts which raised little controversy was that of the Bank of England in 1946. Indeed the Bank of England is a good example of the problems of definition involved with 'nationalised industries'. In fact the Bank was established by Royal Charter in 1694 and the 1946 Act simply transferred its assets to be held on behalf of the Treasury. In evidence to a Commons committee, the Governor, Sir Leslie O'Brien remarked that 'we are not a nationalised industry; we are a nationalised institution.' And in his evidence, the then Chancellor of the Exchequer, Roy Jenkins, commented, 'it is a system which on the whole works very well and one has always to be a little concerned as to whether there is a good argument for overturning a system which works well.' The position of the Bank, although perhaps more accurately described as a semi-nationalised industry, is important, since it illustrates the difficulties in the relationship between central government departments and any state 'agency' or '*ad hoc*' body. While both Government and Parliament must have the last word (as has been illustrated in several disputes in the 1970s and 1980s in state undertakings) nationalised industries are powerful pressure groups within the political system. In the Bank of England's own case, the Permanent Secretary to the Treasury usually has a weekly meeting with the Governor, and the Bank is represented on more than 20 committees in Whitehall; Lord Balogh has commented on the nature of this apparently one-way process: 'I must say from this point of view, I think the civil servants are not much better off than outsiders to know how Bank opinion . . . is shaped.' In the light of the Johnson Matthey banking scandal in 1985, this observation has much truth in it.

First Report from the Select Committee on Nationalised Industries, Bank of England, HC 258, 1969–70 session

246

Ian Mikardo MP, in his evidence to the same Select Committee said, 'Nobody can know whether to condemn or commend because nobody knows.' The enquiry of the 1969–70 Select Committee on Nationalised Industries clearly raised questions of public accountability about not only the Bank of England but also all nationalised undertakings. In the Bank's case, since it publishes no accounts and few financial statistics, the degree of accountability is very low; on occasion the Governor of the Bank of England may find himself being under scrutiny from the media for controversial statements in public which might embarrass the Government. As one writer has put it, 'It is quite remarkable that the nationalisation of the Bank seems to have prevented publication of the Bank's activities.' And the same writer commented upon the secrecy which surrounds the recruitment of staff, noting that the Governor of the Bank has often been a non-expert, a situation, which Lord Balogh has pointed out, would be unacceptable in countries like Germany, Italy, France, Australia and Canada.

Parliamentary Affairs, Summer 1971

Long-term economic strategy, especially in the public sector, is always subject to the vagaries of a change in government, but is this not part of the price to pay for a parliamentary democracy? Also, it would be dangerous to overemphasise the extent to which one government will completely reverse the programme of its predecessors, for in fact (despite the transport or iron and steel industries) that is simply not the case on past record, at least until Mrs Thatcher's Government arrived in 1979. Privatisation was not high on the Conservative agenda in 1979, but by 1984 it had become a key political issue.

In the case of iron and steel it was simply a Labour commitment to take over the means of production of one of the most basic industries in the country, and this it did by the 1949 Iron and Steel Act. Perhaps more than the control or decontrol of transport, this particular piece of nationalisation reasserted the great divide between Labour and Conservative in a way no other issue did in the post-1945 period. By 1953 the Conservative Government had denationalised the bulk of the industry, but in 1967, under Labour, 13 major steel firms were brought back into public ownership, these 13 firms accounting for something like three-quarters of the industry's manpower, and nearly 85 per cent of the basic steel output. The British Steel Corporation survived the Conservative Government that was returned in 1970.

Although strong party feelings have been aroused, the Conservative Party has not been altogether opposed to public ownership, at least on pragmatic, 'non-ideological' grounds, as illustrated by its record in the inter-war period.

The Conservatives in 1970 encountered a certain amount of Civil Service resistance, to the effect that undoing vast organisations was more difficult than creating them in the first place. In this instance Butskellism triumphed once more, and the Conservative Government, making at least a placatory gesture towards the party faithful, sold the state-owned pubs in Carlisle and the nationalised travel firm of Thomas Cook and Son. On the contrary, the Heath Government found itself effectively taking over not only Upper Clyde Shipbuilders, but also Rolls-Royce, the symbol of Britain's industrial 'best', both of which were in desperate financial straits between 1971 and 1972. No such inhibitions about denationalisation were apparent in Mrs Thatcher's Government from 1979; her wide-ranging privatisation programme is dealt with at the end of this chapter. It is this Conservative administration that in the past few years has changed the whole nature of the state sector.

Accountability

How to maximise the accountability of public corporations to Parliament is a perennial problem, and one to which successive governments have found no easy solution.

One medium was the Commons Select Committee on Nationalised Industries which existed in various guises between 1945 and 1979. In 1955 a permanent committee was established, but defining what was meant by nationalised industries proved something of a puzzle, as its terms of reference amply demonstrated: 'to examine the reports and accounts of the nationalised industries as established by statute whose controlling boards are wholly appointed by ministers of the Crown and whose annual receipts are not wholly or mainly derived from monies provided by Parliament or advanced from the Exchequer.'

The 1955 Committee touched a sensitive political point when it resolved not to engage itself in matters which either clearly fell within the ambit of ministerial responsibility, or concerned wages and conditions of employment and other questions which were normally decided by collective bargaining arrangements, or which were matters of day-to-day administration (something not very easy to categorise). In fact the committee was replaced by yet another in 1956, with broader powers.

Ministerial Control of Nationalised Industries, HC 371, 1968–9 session

The next committee usually looked at one industry year by year, but in the late 1960s it became part of Crossman's experimental specialist committees, and in the 1967–8 session it considered the problems of nationalised industries as a whole.

The 1968 committee attempted, with some degree of difficulty, to define what was meant by the 'public interest'. It commented that the public interest included wider issues which could be ignored if commercial success was the sole criterion of nationalised industries. At the same time the committee attempted to define what commercial success meant, but it found it an equally exacting task. It said that the purposes of ministerial control were several: the public sector enabled the Government to use it as an instrument of economic policy, to regulate investment and to ensure some conformity of price movement. Ministers also had to formulate long-term policy (for example, the future size of the railways), as well as to establish good employment practices, such as in the payment of 'fair' wages. At the same time ministers had both to respond to political and parliamentary pressures, and to ensure that industries operated reasonably efficiently, two aims which could come into conflict with each other.

It was also clear that different aims lay behind ministerial control; the Minister for Energy might emphasise the efficient deployment of resources, while the

248

Minister for Transport would probably emphasise the integration of transport into the Government's economic planning, if such existed. The committee recommended that the minister should continue to select, appoint, and if necessary dismiss, the chairman and his board, a rather conservative proposal in view of the discussion for 'opening up' central government, but that the industries should nevertheless be left free to carry out policies independently, once established; in other words there should be less day-to-day interference by Government departments. The latter recommendation was probably the most politically sensitive of all.

The NCB's financial plight after the national coal strike 1984–5.
The Guardian, 10 July 1985

It also observed that more information should be published about the performance of each industry, and in that context the minister should be more accountable to parliamentary scrutiny.

In addition, the 1968 Report darkly stated that ministers should be given powers to give directions on any matter which would appear to them in the 'national interest', a recommendation which it could be argued contradicted its plea for less interference. At the same time an attempt was made to arrive at a definition of a service which was run for a social obligation. The reasons for unremunerative services might vary, such as the very nature of postal or telegraph services; other charges, such as the fares of London Transport, might be kept deliberately low in

249

the consumer's interest. Furthermore, a social obligation might be imposed by the minister, such as the retention of a very unprofitable railway line, or imposed by statute, such as the supply to rural areas of electricity. The committee said that in future the minister himself should decide the nature and extent of a particular industry's social obligations, and that his decision should be made public.

Although the financial and accounting procedures of many of the nationalised concerns have been tightened up, two decades after the Report there is still ample confusion over exactly what constitutes a 'social obligation', and more to the point, over the scale of ministerial interference or intervention. One leading newspaper commented ruefully about the 1967–8 Report: 'It recommends separating these industries from political influences by detaching them from their present controlling ministers. The effect of this is to create independent corporations which can pursue normal commercial policies. The principle is to commercialise industries which have been damaged by political interference. This in itself makes a strong case for denationalisation. If what we want to do is to make the State undertakings resemble private corporations as closely as possible, then the obvious way to do it is to turn them into private corporations by disposing of the equity.' There is no doubt that in the last few years this is precisely what Mrs Thatcher has done by, in her own phrase, 'rolling back the frontiers of the State'.

The Times,
14 September,
1968

As it has been put by one writer, Lord Marsh (former Chairman of British Railways) was right when he said he personally could not be held responsible for much of what the railways did.

The Guardian,
15 December,
1976

'This is because successive governments interfere so much with strategic decisions (capital investment, size of network, fare structure) that the resulting losses often follow directly from Government [decisions] rather than executive decisions by the railway authorities. By the time losses are made, of course, the minister concerned has moved on to pastures new so that there is no one individual who can be personally held accountable for the consequences of previous policies.'

Social Aims and Financial Conflicts

One of the fundamental problems, therefore, for nationalised industries is not so much the question of their internal efficiency, something which has been steadily improving over the past 20 years or so, as the maintenance of a coherent policy on a national basis. The careful Treasury rules from the late 1960s that the public sector should operate on financial and investment criteria similar to the private sector, have frequently been overturned. Fluctuations in the economy upset long-term planning. For example, at the end of 1974, only a few months after winning the general election, the Chancellor of the Exchequer, Denis Healey, was obliged to announce that price restraint in the public sector would have to be phased out, simply because it was draining away some £1000m. in deficit financing.

The system of financial control can be traced to the 1961 White Paper on the structure of the public sector. Consequently the Government introduced a series of specific annual financial targets for each of the public corporations, after consulting the board of each industry, and taking into account all the particular factors likely to affect the performance of each undertaking. The White Paper defined taking an average of good and bad years as being over a five-year period. The White Paper also suggested that in future a much bigger share of a nationalised industry's capital investment should come from its own reserves.

Financial and Economic Obligations of Nationalised Industries, Cmnd 1337, 1961

The same theme of financial and ministerial accountability can be seen in the 1978 White Paper on the future role of nationalised undertakings. While stressing the need for each industry to maintain a vigorous, independent role, it also recommended the need for strengthening the minister's hand in certain instances: 'in the absence of powers to give specific directives, governments have had to rely on a process of persuasion. Because this has been informal, accountability for decisions has on occasion been blurred and this has caused friction and resentment.' The Paper therefore proposed that a minister should have the power to give specific directions to a nationalised board on matters 'which appeared to him to affect the national interest.' But such directions would have to take the form of statutory instruments, which Parliament would at least have the chance of debating. Nor could a specific direction extend or curtail the existing statutory powers of an industry.

The Nationalised Industries, Cmnd 7131, 1978

The White Paper of 1978 also added: 'The Government will be prepared, on occasion, to appoint special committees of inquiry to examine the structure, performance and plans of particular industries where it appears that there is a need for a far ranging review.'

The growing application of cash limits did not help the problem. In the strict sense cash limits apply to local and central government, but nationalised industries have not escaped, for in recent years both Labour and Conservative administrations have controlled the investment programme of each industry via what are known as EFLs (External Financing Limits) which effectively constitute a strict financial ceiling in every state-owned concern. EFLs are comprehensive limits, they embrace both grants and borrowing, but are not always adhered to, as in 1984–5 when the nationalised industries exceeded their EFLs by 100 per cent, partly because of the effects of the miners' strike. For 1985–6 the EFL target was £2200m but for 1987–8 the target, originally a mere £67m, is £692m.

Cash Limits 1984–5: Provisional Out-turn, Cmnd 9569, 1985

The Government's Expenditure Plans, 1986–7 to 1988–9, Cmnd 9702, 1986; Autumn Statement, Cmnd 14, 1986

The Labour philosophy is that nationalisation is a method of keeping prices down, but whether it is the cheapest way to achieve that aim is entirely another matter. There has also been Labour's viewpoint that nationalisation is a method of increasing capital investment, and achieving certain economies of scale by knitting together different kinds of companies, and introducing enlightened labour and social policies. It could be argued that in this there has been considerable success. The Conservative philosophy, as seen below, is to privatise extensively.

251

26

Finance and the Public Sector

THE PLANS FOR 1986–87 and 1987–88

34. The White Paper proposes EFLs for the Nationalised Industries falling from an estimated £3,211 million in the current year to a negative £110 million by 1987–88. If these plans are to be realised these industries as a whole would need to be earning sufficient profits to cover their investment needs, and over and above that, they would be making a contribution of £110 million towards reducing the PSBR. This scenario is reminiscent of the unfulfilled plans made in 1980.

35. Officials expressed confidence in the extent to which improved efficiency, greater cost control, and better trading conditions will transform the Nationalised Industries' financial position:

> "I think the chances of this being borne out are reasonably good. The nationalised industries as trading bodies are greatly affected by the trading environment and it is, therefore, not surprising that ... a forecast that was made some years ago did not come about ... There is a steady improvement in cost performance. The trading environment has improved. The improvement ... over the next few years is not confined to one or two industries but spread quite widely ... the chances of succeeding this time, therefore, are really good."

The Chief Secretary seemed to put particular emphasis on potential efficiency gains. We concede that the trading environment for the nationalised industries for the early years of the decade was particularly difficult. Nevertheless, moderate growth has been occurring for some time now, and though the nationalised industries have reduced their need to resort to Government finance (after adjustment for the effects of the miners' strike), the present plans imply a sharp acceleration in this trend. The MTFS growth assumption made at the time of the 1984 Budget was for average GDP growth of slightly over 2 per cent per year over the next three years – that is, no higher than in the past three years.

36. Our other particular doubts about the viability of the White Paper plans concern pay, local authorities and unemployment benefits:

(a) Although a pay assumption for these years is not given, clearly the plans are tight, and we see little hope of their being achieved, for the same reasons as apply to 1985–86.

(b) Though local authorities have been a persistent source of overspending since 1979–80, this reflects the tight allocations individual authorities have been set. In fact over the past five years current direct spending has increased in total by less than 10 per cent. But as local authorities' gross investment has declined by 23 per cent, their total expenditure has increased by only ½ per cent per year. The White Paper plans imply a reduction in their cost-term expenditure by around 7 per cent by 1987–88, to be enforced by a combination of rate-capping and higher penalties for overspending. No doubt these measures will have some impact; but lesser penalties imposed in past years allow some room for doubts as to the full efficacy of the recent proposals. Estimated local authority expenditure for 1984–85 now seems to have been revised upwards by around £2 billion – of this £1,200 million relates to current expenditure, and £700 million relates to capital expenditure.

(c) Benefit expenditure on the unemployed is forecast to rise by 9 per cent to £6,970 million by 1987–88. This is £230 million lower than the level implied by full price indexation over the survey period. Officials were unable to explain the apparent inconsistency. In a subsequent written answer the Treasury said: "This reflects the fact that means tested benefits which account for the greater part of benefits for unemployed people are not uprated directly in line with the RPI; and changes, such as those proposed in board and lodging payments". Nonetheless, we draw attention to the fact that the figures are based on a stylised assumption about a flat rate of unemployment, rather than one based on economic growth rates.

LOCAL AUTHORITY ASSET RECEIPTS [AND EFL TARGETS]

37. To contain overspending on capital account the Government has proposed restricting the extent to which capital receipts, such as the proceeds from council-house sales, can be used to finance capital spending over and above individual authorities' allocations. In the case of council housing it is intended that only 20 per cent of the proceeds, instead of the previous 40 per cent, should be so used in future. This sharply contrasts with the situation in Autumn 1982 when the Prime Minister was exhorting local authorities to spend more on capital projects.

38. We questioned the Chief Secretary and officials about this in the light of the statement by the Secretary of State for the Environment in the House on 18 December 1984 and the subsequent debate on the following day. The effect of treating the proceeds of council house sales as negative expenditure has been to reduce the Government's published figure for public expenditure and the PSBR in previous years when the sales took place.

39. We have suggested earlier that it would be better to regard the proceeds as a means of funding the PSBR rather than reducing it. In the case of some of the proceeds of council house sales, we should perhaps have said *temporary* funding of the PSBR since it has always been apparent that the local authorities would wish to use the money received – and the Secretary of State for the Environment has conceded that the funds belong to the local authorities.

40. We find it strange that the Government did not forsee the problems inherent in this accounting treatment for these transactions, or its scale. We are left with the impression that the rationale for the existing arrangements has had everything to do with the Government's desire to reduce the apparent size of the PSBR, and too little to do with the rational use of local authority assets.

47. We are also concerned at the Government's insistence on using the nationalised industries' finances to offset public expenditure. Manipulation of EFLs and target rates of return can lead to distortions in both pricing and investment. Moreover, while monies lodged in the National Loans Fund can still be considered as part of the nationalised industries' assets the fact is that, unlike funds lodged in conventional bank accounts, these cannot be used to finance investment programmes. They look very much like forced loans.

253

48. If these targets are to be realised, it seems likely that the nationalised industries will resort to using their monopolistic power to raise prices. It appears that the Government's intention, as exemplified by its recent statements on the water industry, is that industries should be expected to pay off debt and finance all future investments from current earnings rather than borrowing, so that effectively the whole burden of paying for long-term assets will fall entirely on the present generation.

Sixth Report from the Treasury and Civil Service Committee
of the House of Commons, HC 213, 1984–5 session.

Public Representation

One other point on control is worth mentioning at this stage. In order to avoid parliamentary questions on matters of great detail, and to provide for some measure of direct representation from the public, area and national 'consumer councils' have been established for some of the nationalised undertakings – gas, electricity, coal and transport. They usually are comprised of about 20–30 unpaid members, appointed in the majority of cases by the minister himself. Nominations are made by various bodies to the minister concerned – by local government authorities, professional associations, trade unions and commercial organisations. Whether this is an entirely satisfactory procedure is highly speculative; it is not only the method of recruitment that is very much a 'grey' area: the degree of effectiveness with which the consumer councils do their job is also questionable. Their public image is a very poor one, little known and little publicised, although that does not mean to say that behind the scenes valuable work is not done.

This raises questions about the openness of the governmental process. Watchdogs over nationalised industries are not to be disputed: the state industries spend an enormous amount of money each year, and in view of the fact that the Ombudsman's powers do not include the public corporations, some kind of popular voice at community level is highly desirable, but whether the present, rather obscure method of consumer councils and area 'users' committees', whose nominations are effectively controlled by Whitehall, is the best form of representation is a highly doubtful point. There is a case, in this context, for giving some voice over nationalised industries directly to local government, at least at county level.

Another issue was that at the time when most of the industries were being established (the late 1940s) it was thought that high standards in public ownership could only be achieved if the administrative structure in each industry was highly centralised. In the 1950s, under the Conservatives, the trend was in the opposite direction, with a large measure of administrative decentralisation, in the case of the railways (1955) and electricity (1957) for example. In the case of the coal industry it is true that the Fleck Committee in 1955 reported that the existing NCB structure was too decentralised but in 1969 the National Coal Board was subdivided into 17 new areas, the consequences of which were well seen in the 1984–5 miners' strike when workers and management adopted differing attitudes across the country.

It appears that the fashions of administrative organisation have come and gone in equal proportions. In later years the trend, under both parties, has been back towards centralisation, and with buses and railways after 1968 (partly because there was simply less of them), and gas and airways from 1973.

The National Enterprise Board

A brief word should be said about the developments under the Industry Act of 1975. The National Enterprise Board which was established by the Act as an instrument to extend the State's interests into industry, by 'partnership agreements', had its roots in the failure of the National Plan of 1966, and the relatively poor track-record of the IRC (Industrial Reorganisation Corporation) under the Labour Government in the late 1960s. The National Enterprise Board could also be said to bear some resemblance to the now well-established Italian state industrial holding company Instituto per la Ricostruzione Industriale (IRI).

The new plan was perhaps one of the most controversial to come out of any party while in Opposition, in the post-war period. The Labour Government envisaged the NEB not as a kind of politico-industrial safety-net, coming to the aid of the 'lame ducks' of industry, but as a positive organisation, which would give the State considerable influence in the pricing, investment and production pro-grammes of the most important manufacturing industries in the UK, many of which were now very large multinational concerns, accountable to neither Government nor Parliament. The aim was not to set up a Soviet-style Gosplan, a massive central planning bureaucracy, but to concentrate attention upon a few, but economically important, companies.

Under the 1975 Act, the NEB was to have no compulsory purchase powers (except on order to prevent foreign take-overs), planning agreements were to be voluntary, and there was no list of major firms to be taken over, although more by accident than economic design, British Leyland soon fell 'victim' in 1975 to the Enterprise Board. One left-wing Labour MP called the NEB 'not a genuine instrument of socialist transformation', although the Conservative Opposition in the Commons viewed the watered-down proposals in the Industry Bill, theatri-cally if not with genuine belief, as a great trap for unlimited state take-overs. Although in fact the scheme as originally proposed envisaged the NEB's role as one of giving the State a new say in the running of the principal firms in the country, and not as a dumping ground for companies in distress, the early days of the Board seemed to confirm its lame duck role: for instance, British Leyland and Norton Villiers Triumph (the ailing motor-cycle firm).

The background to the evolution of the Industry Act and the NEB, in rather different form than was envisaged by many of the party hierarchy when Labour was in Opposition in 1972–3, illustrates graphically the problem of a party trying to compromise with itself. But it also illustrates the realities of a social democratic or socialist party (and the difference in the labels is important) trying to live within the confines of the capitalist world, of pressure from the City not to go too far too fast, especially in an economic system in which the extension of nationalisation since 1945 had already played a significant role.

Perhaps the greatest controversy concerning the NEB occurred in 1979 when the entire Board resigned as a result of Rolls-Royce being removed from their control. The NEB's residual activities were merged with those of the National Research Development Council in 1981, now reformed as the British Technology Group.

The nationalised industries have, it seems, a curious dual obligation to society; on the one hand they must always be mindful of the public interest (whatever that interest may exactly be), but on the other they have been required, at some times more than others, to operate upon efficient commercial lines. Nationalisation is a comparatively new political development in the twentieth century, although with roots in Marxism and the earlier part of the previous century. What can be said, even if it does sound like a truism, is that the experiences of the UK, since 1945, have amply demonstrated that there is no one form of effective management or organisation that can be applied with equal ministerial vigour to each of the nationalised undertakings. Its difficulty, as well as its challenge, is for nationalisation to combine the acceptable face of capitalism with public accountability and social obligations.

Privatisation since 1979

Under the Thatcher administration, since 1979, the key word has been privatisation, a policy which again raised the question of the nature of the relationship between political ministers and commercial bosses. This was particularly noticeable in the fields of energy and transport. In 1982 the Chairman of the CEGB, Glyn England, was sacked. The Chairman of British Gas, Sir Denis Rooke, opposed attempts to sell off oil-fields and gas showrooms, and the equally colourful Sir Peter Parker, the Chairman of British Rail, ran into difficulty over the future shape of the railway network.

Privatisation strictly means partial denationalisation, leading to the BP model whereby the State and the private sector are joint shareholders in a company. By 1983 the Conservative Government was committed to privatising a whole range of industries. Outlined below are the achievements virtually to date, as listed by the Department of Trade and Industry to July 1986. The programme of privatisation, as can be seen, now amounts to a formidable list. By the latter part of 1985 the Government had also announced its intention to sell assets of the British Gas Corporation and the British Airports Authority, and to sell the remaining ordinary shareholding in Britoil. It also by then had sold off the remaining shareholding in British Aerospace, save for one 'special share'.

The avowed aim of the Conservative administration has been to reverse the trend of share ownership, in other words back to the individual shareholder and away from the large institutional investors, such as the pension funds, and the sale of the assets of some of the nationalised industries has been the route to such an objective. There have been mixed results, but the sale of shares in British Telecom in 1984 was heavily and popularly oversubscribed.

British Telecom shares go on sale to the public

In 1979 the nationalised industries in the UK accounted for about 10 per cent of gross domestic product, a seventh of total investment in the economy and about 10 per cent of the Retail Price Index. They employed about 1½ million people. By the end of 1985, 12 major companies had been privatised, representing over 20 per cent of the 1979 State sector and 400 000 jobs. The mechanics of privatisation are complex, and each individual case raised its own problems. The principal options are: a trade sale, where a company is sold to a single firm or consortium; a placing with a group of investors, a public flotation on the Stock Exchange, either by a fixed price offer or by a tender offer with a minimum price; a management/employee buy-out.

257

One thing, however, has not been mentioned here, which while not concerned with industry, was clearly by far the most popular act of privatisation with the electorate and played a significant part in Mrs Thatcher's victory in the 1983 General Election. This was the introduction of the 'right to buy' for council house tenants in every local authority district, under the Housing Act 1980, as since extended by the Housing and Building Control Act 1984 and the Housing and Planning Act 1986. The purchase price was the market value substantially discounted. Other groups, including various housing association tenants, were also given comparable rights to purchase, although defeats in the House of Lords (see Chapter 6) led to some exemptions from the scope of the legislation.

DOCUMENT

27

Privatisation 1979–86

TABLE 1

SALES SO FAR	(Proceeds net of costs £ million)				
SALE	1979–80	1980–81	1981–82	1982–83	G
Amersham International			64		S
Associated British Ports				46	
British Aerospace		43			
British Petroleum*	276		8		
British Sugar Corporation			44		nil
Britoil				334	
Cable and Wireless			182		
National Enterprise Board Holdings***	37	83	2		
National Freight Consortium			5		nil
North Sea Oil Licences		195		33	
Miscellaneous	57	84	189	75	
TOTAL[2]	370[1]	405[1]	494[1]	488	

(1)   Excludes certain advance oil payments which net out to zero over the three years 1979–82.

(2)   Excludes proceeds from sales of subsidiaries; these are retained by parent industry. The main sales in this category were:

		£ million
1982–83	International Aeradio (British Airways)	60
	British Rail Hotels	30

TABLE 2

SALES SO FAR	(Proceeds net of costs £ million)				
SALE	1983–84	1984–85	1985–86	1986–87 (so far)	G
Associated British Ports		51			nil
British Aerospace			346		S
British Petroleum*	543				31.7%
British Telecom		1357	1246[1]	1090	49.8% S
BT Loan Stock			44	61	
Britoil	293		426		S
Cable and Wireless	263		571	9[2]	S
Enterprise Oil**		380			S
National Enterprise Board Holdings***		142	28		
North Sea Oil Licences		121			
Miscellaneous	43	40	23		
TOTAL[3]	1142	2091	2684	1160	

(1)   Includes some third instalments (worth £87 million approx.) paid early.
(2)   Some late payments in 1986–87.
(3)   Excludes proceeds from sales of subsidiaries; these are retained by parent industry. The main sales in this category were:

		£ million
1983–84	British Rail Hotels	15
1984–85	Jaguar (Rover Group)	297
	Sealink (British Rail)	40
	Wytch Farm (British Gas)	82
1985–86	Warship yards (British Shipbuilders)	75
	Sealink (British Rail)	26

Notes for both tables

G = residual Government shareholding; S = Government retains one special share
*The first sale of BP shares was in 1977 under the Labour Government when the State holding was reduced from 68.3% to 51%
**formed from British Gas Corporation's North Sea oil production and exploration interests
***Sales by BTG (British Technology Group), formerly the NEB, include:
ICL (computers) (1979) – 25% NEB holding sold to institutional investors
Fairey (engineering) (1980) – 100% NEB holding sold to Doulton (S. Pearson & Co)
Ferranti (electronics) (1980) – 50% NEB holding sold to institutional investors
Inmos (silicon chips) (1984) – 75% BTG holding sold to Thorn EMI

NATIONALISED INDUSTRIES

National Coal Board
Electricity (England and Wales)
North of Scotland Hydro-Electric Board
South of Scotland Electricity Board
British Gas Corporation
British Steel Corporation
Post Office
National Girobank
British Airways Board
British Airports Authority
British Railways Board

British Waterways Board
National Bus Company
Scottish Transport Group
British Shipbuilders
Civil Aviation Authority
Water (England and Wales)
London Regional Transport

OTHER PUBLIC CORPORATIONS

Audit Commission
Bank of England
British Broadcasting Corporation
British Technology Group
Cable Authority
Commonwealth Development Corporation
Covent Garden Market Authority
Crown Agents
Crown Agents Holding and Realisation Board
Crown Suppliers
Development Board for Rural Wales
English Industrial Estates Commission
General Practice Finance Corporation
Highlands and Islands Development Board
Housing Corporation
Independent Broadcasting Authority
National Dock Labour Board
National Film Finance Corporation
New Town Development Corporations and Commission
Northern Ireland Development Agency
Northern Ireland Electricity Service
Northern Ireland Housing Executive
Northern Ireland Public Trust Port
Northern Ireland Transport Holding Company
Oil and Pipelines Agency
Local Authority Passenger Transport Companies
Pilotage Commission
Property Services Agency (supplies)
Royal Mint
Scottish Development Agency
Scottish Special Housing Group
HM Stationery Office
Trust Ports
United Kingdom Atomic Energy Authority
Urban Development Corporations
Welsh Development Agency
Welsh Fourth Channel Authority

Department of Trade and Industry, July 1986

Note: The Government sold off British Gas, almost in its entirety, at the end of 1986. This was just after the total sale of the Trustee Savings Bank Group (TSB), strictly speaking not a flotation or a public corporation. In the early part of 1987 British Airways and the British Airports Authority (BAA) will be completely sold. The Government also controls Rolls-Royce and the Rover Group (formerly British Leyland). Privatisation of these two companies is scheduled for 1987; 80 per cent of Austin Rover's spare parts division, Unipart, is to be sold as UGC, while the Leyland Bus division was subject to a management buy-out at the beginning of 1987. In respect of the National Bus Company, its operating companies have been broken up into smaller units to enable deregulation and privatisation to proceed more rapidly. By the beginning of 1987 only 12 of more than 50 operating companies had been sold, almost exclusively to management buy-outs. The management of the naval dockyards will also be privatised in 1987.

Summary

British governments, like many others in the Western world, have come to intervene in a capitalist economy more and more during the course of this century. In the nineteenth century the prevailing doctrine was *laissez-faire:* the government's first duty was the defence of the realm, intervention in the market place was best left alone. But by the 1870s this philosophy was under attack, as newly enfranchised voters looked to central government to solve social ills. The introduction of a welfare state and the first act of nationalisation under the Liberal Government immediately before the First World War marked the real beginnings of interventionism. Consequently the central bureaucracy, that is government departments and the Civil Service, grew apace. This trend was continued under Attlee's Labour Government (1945–51) with the extension of public ownership and the implementation of the Beveridge plan on social security. The Second World War had changed public attitudes fundamentally; the desire not to repeat experiences of the depression years of the 1930s came high on the political agenda. The maintenance of full employment was a stated policy.

Both Labour and Conservative governments in the post-war period have intervened in the economy in a variety of ways, both 'positively' (for example, raising public expenditure) or 'negatively' (cutting public expenditure). Even under Mrs Thatcher's Government, with its commitment to keep tight controls on public spending and the money supply, public expenditure in 1986 amounted to 44 per cent of GDP (Gross Domestic Product).

Nationalisation has proved to be something of a political football, especially in recent years. After Labour lost power in 1951, the Conservatives did not denationalise to a great extent; the real shift has come with Mrs Thatcher's massive 'privatisation' programme as seen earlier in this chapter. In the past, at least, Conservative as well as Labour governments have felt forced to come to the rescue of ailing industries, which have employed large numbers of workers and whose demise would have had significant political and social consequences, for example,

261

Rolls-Royce and Upper Clyde Shipbuilders (UCS) under Mr Heath (1971–2), Chrysler under Mr Wilson (1975) and in the same year British Leyland (via the National Enterprise Board).

By the late 1970s the nationalised industries accounted for about 10 per cent of the GDP and employed nearly as a great percentage of the working population. But nationalisation, as perhaps Mrs Thatcher realised, was never overwhelmingly popular, not as much as a national health service and social security system, the criticism of the public corporations being that they have been inefficient and unproductive compared with the private sector, an argument not always justified since many were responsible for operating 'social services', such as rural train or bus services. The sale of British Telecom under the Conservative Government in 1984 attracted wide public attention; this was just part of a determined policy to reduce the State's role in the economy, and not simply in the nationalised sector

Sale of Government Shareholding in British Tele-communications, 3rd Report from the Committee of Public Accounts, HC 36, 1985–6 session

alone. The Conservative privatisation and monetary policies have been directed towards giving the individual greater freedom and encouraging more self-reliance. Labour argues that this has been achieved only at immense cost to the community as a whole. In 1985 the Commons Public Accounts Committee reported that the Government's £3900m sale of shares in British Telecom did not raise as much money for the taxpayer as it might have done.

Third Report from the Treasury and Civil Service, Monetary Policy, HC 163-1, 1980–1 session

However, even if Mrs Thatcher has touched on popular economic issues, or even if the nationalised industries were not highly regarded, that does not mean to say that the electorate favours unbridled capitalism; in contrast to Americans, British people, by and large, see far more faults in the free enterprise economy and remain concerned about gross unfairness in the distribution of income and wealth. The Keynesian, social democratic philosophy of the 1950s is by no means extinct, a point implicitly recognised by a Commons Select Committee in 1981 which claimed that the Government's medium-term financial strategy was not soundly based either in theory or in practice.

Questions

1. How are modern governments affected by economic matters.

2. 'The relations between the public corporations and Whitehall are unsatisfactory and in need of change.' Discuss. (Joint Matriculation Board)

3. Has the public corporation proved to be an effective form of organisation for state enterprises? (London)

4. Choose *either* the Post Office *or* British Rail and consider whether it should be run as a public service or as a self-financing economic enterprise. (London)

9 Pressure Groups and Political Interests

'We've knocked on doors and said, "we represent the Labour Party," and they've said, "where the hell have you been?" It all boils down to contact . . .'

Wife of a Labour councillor, *The Guardian*, 26 September 1973

Participation and Involvement

Political parties

Although political parties may be viewed as an essential part of any liberal-democracy, it can be argued that in the United Kingdom and other European countries popular participation has been in steady decline since 1950. Pressure and interest groups have partly displaced political parties, because they provide quicker action and direct involvement in issues. Good examples of such organisations are the Child Poverty Action Group and Shelter (the campaign for the homeless). Since the 1950s there has been an overall decrease in the paid-up membership of political parties; but while the parties have lost some of their active support in the past 30 years that does not prevent them from serving as the basis of 'capitalist democracy' and providing competing teams for government office. Membership of the Labour Party has fallen from about 900 000 in 1950 to approximately 300 000 in 1984, while membership of the Conservative Party has declined from 1.5 million to 1.1 million between 1974 and 1984. The Liberals' membership has fluctuated since 1945 in line with their changing electoral fortunes, but in recent years has been about 150 000 (twice the SDP membership).

See also C. Leeds, *Politics in Action*, Stanley Thornes, 1986, (section E)

Choosing the parliamentary candidate

On the other hand, the party officers and other activists in each constituency party do have very formidable power when it comes to the selection of parliamentary candidates. Since there are no primary elections in the UK, local party members in effect choose at least one-half of all MPs, if that approximate figure is taken as representing the proportion of 'safe' seats in the country. The first rule of political survival for any MP is to cultivate and maintain the support not of the local electorate, but of his constituency association. (In the late nineteenth century

263

Joseph Chamberlain – who later, in 1886, defected from the Liberal to the Conservative Party, over Ireland among other things – once suggested that there should be a Liberal Party Parliament, composed of the party faithful and activists, to 'shadow' the elected Parliament at Westminster.)

Constituency parties

British politics is lacking in studies of how the political parties operate locally. In 1959 Birch undertook a study of part of the High Peak constituency – the small market-town of Glossop in Derbyshire. There he found that the Labour group still clung to the idea that the local party was something like a band of comrades, a 'crusading movement', whereas the Conservatives had never adopted this attitude, tending to look upon local party associations merely as a means of bringing like- and right-minded people together.

Birch's findings illustrate the difference beween the historical backgrounds of the two major parties. Conservative (and Liberal) party organisations grew out of the parliamentary groupings of the 1860s and 1870s, when party competition was becoming more fierce with the extensions of the franchise in 1867 and 1884. In Labour's case the parliamentary party came much later, growing out of a loose unit of several political movements in the country at large. In High Peak, Birch found that real party activism was on a small scale. In Glossop alone, although the Conservatives claimed more than 1000 members, most took little interest in the party machine and the local Conservative club. Nevertheless, it was from this group that local council candidates were usually drawn ('we try to get businessmen every time', one party worker remarked). The recruitment of local council candidates is always difficult. Even though the local government reforms of 1974–5 reduced the number of local authorities and introduced an improved expenses allowance, all political parties face difficulty in finding enough local candidates of a reasonable calibre, the SDP and Liberal plight usually being the worst and the Conservative the least. Birch also found in High Peak that there were social divisions within the Conservative party, the shopkeepers and small businessmen finding their interests and outlooks did not always match those of the other type of Conservative, which was dominant in the constituency – retired army officers, the country gentry and professional people. As for the working-class Conservative, there did exist a certain deferential attitude towards the local leaders coupled with a notable reluctance to contribute financially: one such supporter commented crisply that, if the constituency leaders were not wealthy and powerful enough, it was so much the worse for them.

A.H. Birch,
Small Town Politics,
OUP, 1959, p. 74

In contrast, the Labour Party was not so well placed financially, although at that time the constituency did have a union (AEU) sponsored parliamentary candidate. Among its party activists there was an older group, a younger, more 'moderate' group and a left-wing group – a not untypical structure in Labour Party associations. The divisions were apparently not so much over policy (possibly that is now far from true in many constituency parties) as over tactics, and covered at that time an old problem – should party politics enter into local government? (Since 1974 this question has become increasingly irrelevant as local government has become more politicised.) Birch recorded a low level of Labour party activity. About three-quarters of Labour members were industrial workers, the rest being drawn from shops or offices. He also made the comment that, although the party activists realised that the personality of the parliamentary candidate had little effect upon the way people voted, election organisation was a 'ritual to which a great deal of importance is attached.'

W.J.M. Mackenzie has also remarked: 'both major parties in England depend on rather small numbers of combative activists. These are needed to "get out the vote", and their rewards in cash terms are remarkably small' (in fact not so much small as totally non-existent). 'But they require symbolic satisfaction, and must be spoken to like an American football team or a Shakespearean army on the eve of battle. In other words, politicians must talk a lot of nonsense to constituency workers and in party conferences; and if they fail to do so, the militants exact penalties, as from Nigel Nicolson and Reg Prentice.' Nicolson, Conservative MP for Bournemouth East from 1955, was forced to stand down as candidate for the 1959 General Election, after a long and well-publicised quarrel with his local association. In 1976 Prentice (MP for Newham NE in London) and Frank Tomney (MP for Hammersmith North in London) lost their appeals to the Labour Party's NEC and Annual Conference to overturn the rulings by their constituency parties that they would not be invited to stand at the next general election.

New Society,
25 March 1976

One other significant study (that of Bealey, Blondel and McCann in the early 1960s) came to conclusions not totally dissimilar to Birch's in High Peak. Bealey, Blondel and McCann examined the political interests and knowledge of the voters in the constituency of Newcastle-under-Lyme, 84 per cent of whom had voted in the 1959 General Election and 38 per cent in the 1960 local government elections. Only 25 per cent of them could be counted as knowledgeable about at least three current policies of one party. Only 2056 people (3.2 per cent of the electorate) were party members, although the national average at that time was nearly 9 per cent. Only 1 in 4 voters in that constituency could name one local councillor, only 1 in 400 was a party activist and only 1 in 2000+ was a party 'stalwart' (a very active worker). (The low level of membership in that area was partly explained by the continuing traditional influence of one large family, the Wedgwoods.)

F. Bealey, J. Blondel
and W.J. McCann,
*Constituency
Politics,*
Faber, 1965, p. 407

Bealey also found that the people at the top of the local party machines came from a 'high' social class. It was estimated that half those who usually voted Conservative were manual workers, but that only 18 per cent of Conservative members came from that social group and that no manual worker had held office in the constituency party. Manual workers comprised 90 per cent of Labour voters and 77 per cent of Labour members, but only 44 per cent of Labour local councillors.

Bealey and Blondel came to the conclusion that the peak of mass party involvement, in this Staffordshire constituency as elsewhere in Britain, had been in the late 1940s – in the immediate post-war period, when the urge for social change was strong. They remarked that the Labour membership figure was 2000 in 1945 (five times the 1960 figure) and the Conservative figure more than 5000+ in 1949 (about three times the 1960 estimate). The study concluded that by the late 1950s television was making a greater impact – most of all upon those seemingly least interested in politics. Gradually the party organisations had been deprived of their educating and 'agitating' roles, being left with 'the humdrum task of getting out the vote.'

R.T. McKenzie,
*British Political
Parties,*
Heinemann, 1963,
p. 648

As Robert McKenzie remarked two years before Bealey's survey, in retrospect it is more than apparent that party interests and organisations saw their heyday when the various extensions of the franchise had created a mass electorate with whom there had hitherto been no effective means of communicating in their own home.

In Britain there is a considerable difference between rural and urban areas in terms of political interest and participation. It may well be that in some of the remoter, rural constituencies political activity performs a social function, the fund-raising bingo session or jumble sale serving as a political equivalent of the cinema or theatre. In urban areas, most markedly in some of the inner-city constituencies, local party organisation has invariably gone to seed, with pressure groups filling the gap in respect of such things as housing waiting lists or slum clearance and re-development. The results of this process are sometimes dramatically reflected in a by-election, such as that in November 1973 when Margo MacDonald won Glasgow Govan for the SNP. One left-wing Labour MP's reaction was: 'It was suicide to select that candidate. He was 60, not even young. The bird [the winning Nationalist candidate] was a knockout, highly articulate and young. We got what we deserved.' He commented that while personalities had not necessarily come into it, the Labour candidate had been identified with the local party, with a 'council which hasn't rehoused them, which hasn't swept the streets or emptied the dustbins, which has kept them crammed in tenements.'

The Guardian,
10 November
1973

The parties thus differ considerably in their history, in their membership and in classes to which they appeal. The gulf is wider than that between the Democrats and the Republicans in the USA. But while their internal tensions may be different, and while the level of support a party enjoys will vary from one area of the country to another, the way in which the parties respond to pressures at both local and national level is often remarkably similar.

In his study of Birmingham, Newton observed:

K. Newton,
*Second City
Politics,*
Oxford, 1976,
p. 101

'In many ways the two organisations are strikingly similar. . . . Both parties put their main emphasis on organisation at the ward level, and both make ward organisations subordinate to constituency organisations. Both make special provision for youth, womens' and trade union groups. Both give agents an important and central role in running party business, select their local election candidates in a rather similar manner, give their constituency organisations considerable autonomy in running their own affairs, and make the local councillor responsible to his ward and not to the constituency.'

The Labour Party was, however, more policy-minded than the Conservatives; its public representatives were more 'tightly integrated into the mass party'.

Pressure Groups

Many different terms have been used to describe the non-party forces. Some of those forces have been very prominent in recent years, not least the trade unions, but such organisations wield widely varying degrees of economic power and influence.

Finer's definitions

The most widely used labels are 'pressure groups', 'interest groups' and 'lobbies'. S.E. Finer has preferred the latter two terms, since he claims 'pressure' implies the application of force to the Government if demands are not met. However, whatever the overall label, two types of groups can usually be identified – sectional and promotional. The former represents a section or class of people, and is more likely to be permanent, whereas promotional groups lobby for a particular cause and anyone who is motivated and interested may join them. Trade unions represent a *section* of the community; the campaign to abolish capital punishment in the late 1950s was *promoting* a particular cause. What is not always sufficiently appreciated is that management of a pressure group, which may subsequently become very bureaucratised, can, as time passes, cease to run parallel to the requirements of its members. Original aims become lost in institutionalised growth.

For example, the reason most people join the Automobile Association is to be rescued in the event of a mechanical failure in their vehicle – but where does that place the AA's peripheral, but important, tourist interests and pro-roads campaign? Similarly, the RSPCA's aims are indicated in its very name, but it has not always been clear whether its membership has wanted hunting included under that banner or not, as the society's public difficulties over the last ten years have clearly illustrated.

Some interests may be both sectional and promotional; the European Movement in 1974 and 1975 had the obvious aim of keeping the UK within the EEC, but it could also be said (as indeed it was by many anti-EEC left-wingers) that its real aim was to further the financial interests of businessmen on the continent. Similarly, the Road Haulage Association may believe that in addition to defending the interests of its members it is also promoting a cause for the common good – in this instance that of private enterprise. Teachers' unions would claim to be concerned not merely with the interests, economic and otherwise, of the teaching profession, but also with the standards of public education, as was underlined during the 1985–6 industrial action by teachers.

The growth of pressure groups

What cannot be disputed is the considerable growth in the number of interest and pressure groups since 1945 in the USA and Western Europe. For example, in the UK there are over 1000 active employers' associations. Moreover, pressure group activity does not direct its attention solely to central government. It is true that the lobbying of MPs and ministers is a powerful process and that access to civil servants

R. Kimber and J.J. Richardson (eds), *Pressure Groups in Britain*, Dent, 1974, p. 10

has become equally important – for the National Farmers' Union, for instance, in being consulted every year by the Ministry of Agriculture about farm subsidies. But there is also almost daily lobbying – often equally determined – in the corridors of local authorities.

Protesters opposing cuts in public spending lobby Mrs Thatcher in Salisbury in 1980

The roles of pressure groups

What should also be appreciated are the subtle forces at work within pressure groups and institutions. For instance, the staff of a school or college, through their teaching union, may be continually lobbying their headmaster or principal (who is, in effect an agent of the education authority) over some aspect of working conditions, while at the same time the principal or headmaster may be a member of the same union as them, requiring its services on another occasion and in a different capacity. This may lead to conflicts of interest.

In the same way there may be pressure group activity within a university *vis-à-vis* the Vice-Chancellor, or, indeed, between the university's departments, but the whole institution itself becomes a pressure group in relation to the Department of Education and Science and the Universities Grants Committee when the Government threatens to alter established financial quotas (as in 1975 and 1981). The same model of 'interest-organisation' could be applied to a large commercial undertaking. At least one more generalisation may be made about interest groups, in that in any liberal-democracy it would be foolish to underestimate the complexity of group behaviour. That cannot be explained simply by examining the structure of both the group and political system, but must also be seen in the light of the tactical positions that pressure groups find themselves in, or by the success or failure of their public relations efforts.

Interest groups sometimes oppose the Government, as, for example, between 1970 and 1974, when the Conservatives were faced with strong, organised opposition both over the Industrial Relations Act and over their refusal to hold a referendum on the question of entry into the EEC. Groups may also act as substitutes for government – a situation which in its extreme form would mean anarchy. In liberal-democracies, or indeed in developed Communist systems, this is a practical impossibility, although in the latter case it is worth remembering that strict Marxist philosophy holds that communism, the goal of socialism, is the final state of human existence in which government and state bureaucracy will 'wither away'. And to some extent countries in turmoil, or undergoing difficult transitions, find government replaced by various groups – for example, Portugal for the first year or so after the overthrow of Caetano in 1974, and Cambodia in 1975–80 with the shrinkage of the Lon Nol Government, the rise of the Khmer Rouge and the subsequent de-urbanisation programme, and then the Vietnamese-inspired coup.

Groups, as S.E. Finer has defined them, may also be seen as extensions of government. No doubt many Conservatives would say precisely this of the TUC, in view of the Labour Government's Social Contract of 1974–7, but in a liberal-democratic context such statements need to be carefully qualified. A more extreme example occurred in Nazi Germany, where various professions were invited to express opinions about their particular fields of interest, although it amounted to no more than that; and a more extreme one still was in Mussolini's 'corporativist' state, where in the late 1920s the government attempted, although not always successfully, to organise industry and other economic groups in society according to special political criteria. To some extent the second Peronist regime in Argentina (1973–6) had similar characteristics; the difficulty there was that so many competing groups, of either an industrial or a semi-military character, were seen as extensions of the Government that the Government itself could not control them, and there followed the inevitable military take-over.

In the UK, and the West generally, most interest and pressure groups are either intermediaries or participants in the relationship between the Government and the public.

Effective participation

S.E. Finer in
Participation
in Politics,
ed. G. Parry, 1972,
pp. 59–79

S.E. Finer has argued that there are four fundamental conditions which need to be met if effective participation in a pressure group is to take place, although they may not all be fulfilled. Firstly, there must be unlimited freedom of speech, association and access to the government. Most writers besides Finer would claim that, while all governments impose restraints upon groups, the Western liberal-democracies impose the least number. The USA grants virtually complete freedom to groups, whereas in Eastern Europe groups must be officially approved. The growth, for example, of the civil rights and anti-Vietnam war movements in the late 1960s seemed to underline the fundamental strengths of American democracy. In contrast, the 'free' trade union organisation in Poland, Solidarity, has been suppressed by the Polish Government. On the other hand, the American movements had to fight hard to be heard; even the liberal-minded administration of President Johnson scarcely welcomed the growth of such groups and access to official information was not always granted. The expansion of federal agencies under President Nixon from 1969 to 1973, together with the practice of covert operations, wire-tapping and unlawful 'slush' funds, culminating in the Watergate scandal itself, hardly suggested an administration that trusted its own citizens.

It is also dangerous to make too many generalisations about Eastern Europe, where the situation is not necessarily the same as in the USSR. In Poland the Catholic Church and agricultural organisations are extremely significant political groups, as are the literary circles in Hungary. There is, however, one feature common to both East and West; it is probable (although difficult to document exactly) that élites of most groups are of a somewhat higher social class than the bulk of their membership, in the same way that élites of local political parties come from those who have had less restricted educational opportunity.

Secondly, Finer has said, groups ought to give individuals unlimited freedom both to join and to leave; yet, although this freedom may be more common in Western societies than Eastern European ones, there are always subtle pressures at work (perhaps more in political parties than in pressure groups) to make sure that only the 'right' type of member is recruited. And, of course, many groups impose moral or religious restrictions, even if these are somewhat discreet, as shown, for example, by the attitude of the Church of England's Mothers Union towards separated or divorced mothers, even in comparatively recent times.

Thirdly, Finer has suggested that there should be a degree of mutual responsiveness between leaders and members within groups; this may be difficult in Eastern Europe, where group leaders are usually appointed directly by governments, like trade union leaders in the USSR. But we should be cautious of over-emphasising this factor in Western societies. After all, although their views often differ, no national leaders of British trade unions are members of the Conservative Party, yet looking at the numbers of working-class Conservative voters alone, some 20–30 per cent of their followers must vote Conservative. Sometimes a union leadership is divorced from popular feeling – in 1966, for example, the 'doctors charter' on pay and conditions was the direct result of the fact that almost half the general practitioners belonging to the British Medical Association had broken away in order to make it clear to their leaders that they should negotiate a better pay settlement. The National Farmers' Union has, on various occasions, provided parallel examples. In 1985, after a catastrophic coal strike, Nottinghamshire miners left the NUM, and founded their own group, the Union of Democratic Miners (UDM).

Fourthly, there should ideally be an active membership. But interest is hard to cultivate. As the extensive survey by Almond and Verba showed, 76 per cent of Americans were not even passive members of a political group (other than a party); the figures were 81 per cent in the UK, 82 per cent in Germany, 94 per cent in Italy and 89 per cent in Mexico, the latter being not strictly a liberal-democracy. Only 12 per cent of Americans were found to have been officers of non-party political groups, 6 per cent of Britons, 3 per cent of Germans, 4 per cent of Mexicans and 1½ per cent of Italians. (The latter figures are those extrapolated by Professor S.E. Finer from Almond and Verba's survey.) Even though it is the liberal-democracies which proclaim most loudly their long traditions of democratic participation, the figures (whether presented by Almond and Verba or by Butler and Stokes) often reveal an appallingly low level of activism.

G. Almond and S. Verba, *The Civic Culture*, Princeton, 1963, Chapter 14

Finer concluded that the scope for participation via interest groups was still higher in Western societies than elsewhere, but that the number of genuine active groups was small, like the number of activists. Activism is essential to the success of a group, as is the belief that a particular issue should be taken account of in the policy of the Government. If both are present, results may be achieved – as they were, for example, by the British Road Haulage Association, which campaigned during the late 1940s against the nationalisation of the road haulage industry (only partial nationalisation was finally implemented).

Groups as safety-valves

Robert McKenzie noted that while the basic function of British political parties was to 'select, organise and sustain teams of parliamentarians between whom the general body of citizens may choose at elections', pressure groups differed from parties 'in that they seek to influence the policy decisions of politicians (and administrators) without themselves seeking to assume direct responsibility for governing the country'. Indeed, the heated debates over 'closed shop' arrangements in industry has been a case in point. McKenzie also pointed out that there are always 'potential interest groups', just beneath the political surface. A good illustration of this in the United Kingdom was the lengthy correspondence in 1974 in *The Times*, from people like Sir Walter Walker, at a stage when some sections of the

R.T. McKenzie, *The Political Quarterly*, No. 1, 1958 and D.B. Truman, *The Governmental Process*, Knopf, 1962, p. 37

271

community, including former military men, thought that the relatively left-wing programme of the new Labour Government posed a real threat to Britain's democratic system. Another was the spontaneous reaction in 1972 when the BBC announced that it would abolish Radio 3 (the Third Programme); if the BBC had not quickly dropped its plans a formal pressure group would have been started somewhere. A similar situation occurred in 1979 when the new Conservative Government announced plans to reduce the output of the BBC's External Services, although by 1982 further cuts were implemented, but not on the scale the Government had envisaged.

As J.D. Stewart has remarked, interest and pressure groups are at the core of the government of any complex society, and it is important that the political system allows them a responsible role. 'The coherent expression of opinion they render possible is vital. . . . Without them discontent would grow and knowledge be lost.' Some promotional groups have had marked successes with comparatively small memberships, such as those which campaigned for the abolition of hanging and for the reform of the divorce and abortion laws during the 1960s. Others with much larger memberships have been notable failures – sometimes perhaps because the aim has been too grandiose, as with the CND movement (Campaign for Nuclear Disarmament). Those whose aims have been relatively confined (such as the CPAG) have been particularly helped by television exposure. Nowhere was this better illustrated than in the civil and racial rights movements in the United States during the 1960s, for television coverage was critical to success.

J.D. Stewart,
British Pressure
Groups: their role
in relation to the
House of Commons,
OUP, 1958, p. 244

DOCUMENT

28

Pressure Group Tactics

Some groups, like the Animal Liberation Front, prefer direct action and are prepared to use violence. Ten thousand elderly citizens, on the other hand, opted to attend a peaceful rally at County Hall in London (in support of the Pensioners' Action Day) on 29 September 1983. One month after the rally more than two million people took part in a series of co-ordinated demonstrations against nuclear weapons throughout Europe. The oil industry prefers to misinform: in September 1983 *The Sunday Times* reported that the oil industry has misled the Government during private consultation earlier that year by not revealing the existence of a refinery in Britain which could already produce lead-free petrol suitable for all cars. The Government's acceptance of the continued use of lead in petrol until the next century was based on the oil industry's claim that it would cost too much to produce lead-free petrol for both old and new cars, and that a long phasing-out period was essential on economic grounds.

What factors determine the strategies chosen? Basically it is a case of internal organisational factors, the external political context within which the groups operate, 272 and the inter-relationship between these two.

The internal organisation features of lobby groups can be analysed in terms of quantitative and qualitative factors. The quantitative factors are:

1   Resources (money and manpower).
2   Size and scope (how many employees, how many offices, how wide a network of contacts and organisers).

The qualitative factors are:

1   Clarity and singleness of purpose.
2   Commitment of membership and leadership to this purpose.
3   The level of cohesion within the organisation and the consequences of internal divisions.
4   The effectiveness and astuteness of organisational leaders and representatives.
5   Organisational efficiency.
6   The willingness of the leadership and the membership to adopt alternative strategies and tactics when necessary, and the extent to which this may involve illicit, illegal, or illegitimate methods of lobbying.

An examination of these internal features of an organisation concerned with lobbying alone is insufficient if we wish to understand the impact that it can have on decisions made by the Government. Lobbying does not take place in a political, economic or cultural vacuum. As David Truman, an American academic who wrote the influential pluralist book *The Governmental Process*, points out, there is a need for pressure groups to operate with cohesive and appropriate organisations relevant to the governmental form. But it is not only the form of government – in terms of the system of elections and the relationship between the executive and legislative branches of government – which provides the context in which lobbies operate. There are also economic constraints which impose practical limitations on what can be achieved; as can the less concrete but no less real ideological and cultural factors which help to shape our political demands and define our notions of the legitimate and the desirable, and deflect our vision from what we conceive to be impractical, unethical and impossible.

In any political system, there are two basic types of constraint which an effective lobby group must heed. Firstly, there are those which result from the socio-economic structures of society with its in-built prejudices and taken-for-granted practices that underpin everyday life. These prejudices and practices involve the system of production and its corresponding interests, which, because of their strategic significance in the economy, are unlikely to be challenged or even questioned by normal lobbying techniques. These socio-economic interests are not static; change can occur in a number of ways, not least through technological innovation. This frequently has ramifications for protectional interest groups.

The second fundamental constraint emanates from the political process within which lobbying operates. Four factors are relevant: a group's access to the decision-makers; ideological factors; the system of elections; and a group's relationship with other agencies and lobby groups.

Some groups have ready access to the political decision-makers. They enjoy a privileged relationship with government. They have been incorporated into the decision-making process, or have been granted a deliberate representational monopoly. Some groups are seen to have the status of playing a legitimate role in policy formation. The most influential receive unsolicited notice of policy discussions at which their attendance is automatic and their advice is listened to with deference. Access will be affected by the 273 ideological concurrence between the Government and the lobby groups concerned. Sometimes it will be established by the permanent officials in a government department rather than by the minister. Regular negotiations over a long period establish a group's position so that it becomes, in the eyes of a department, the natural expression and representative of a given sectional interest.

Formal liaison between the Government and such lobby organisations is established for consultative discussion and inquiries. This 'insider status' of certain organisations is revealed by the way in which they almost automatically have their views included in submissions of evidence to a Royal Commission. Officials should consult all relevant organisations, but in practice not all lobby groups will acquire this official recognition; some will be excluded from the consultative process. Having achieved 'insider status' a lobby group might prefer a strategy of quiet diplomacy to one of 'going public' with issues. Insider groups have a stake in not disrupting cosy relationships with the Government or provoking counter-mobilisation by other groups, which might be awakened by the sound of public controversy.

Finally, access might result from a group's position in a political party, for example as part of the coalition of interests established within the party of government. For years the farming lobby could count on the Minister of Agriculture being part of any Tory Cabinet and have ready access to the department. In similar fashion the TUC could count on the Department of Labour, now the Department of Employment, being more receptive to its overtures during a period of Labour government.

Ideology is a crucial variable determining not only a lobby group's commitments but also its chances of success. Ideology as a system of ideas, which is related to a manner of thinking and practice in a sector of society, can appeal to the wider electorate where it is perceived as consistent with, or even speaking out for, popular latent values. Where a group's ideology is sympathetic to or supportive of party, government or bureaucratic policy then the group will more readily be granted access to, and possible incorporation into, key decision-making bodies.

Some groups gain respectability in the eyes of a government department. M. Ryan in *The Acceptable Pressure Group* contrasts the legitimacy granted to the Howard League by the Home Office, regardless of the party in power, and the outsider status of Radical Alternatives to Prison (RAP).

Lobbying techniques will be directly affected by the system of elections when groups aim their appeal at the electorate. In Britain the lobby group Aims of Industry spends thousands of pounds on advertisements at general election time in the hope of reminding the electorate of the need to promote free enterprise by voting Conservative. In the USA many larger lobby groups single out sympathetic candidates for their endorsement. In California, lobby groups have been able to change the law on the punishment of criminals and alter the level of state taxation through their success at public initiatives – what we would call referendums – which are binding on the state government.

The decline in the relative importance of Parliament has three consequences for lobby groups. Some turned their attention to lobbying the executive; greater complexity and scope of government meant that much of the work of government was hidden from parliamentary scrutiny; it made sense to lobby directly the officials who were making the decisions. Other groups, recognising the importance of the party election manifestos as a source of political initiative for a new Government, sought to influence the decision-making process within a particular party, whether at conference, on the National Executive Committee, or by getting acquiescent candidates endorsed. Both CND and the

274

animal campaigners were successful in the Labour Party; their views were taken up as party policy and included in the election manifestos of 1979 and 1983. The third consequence was that lobby groups adopted a more internationalist strategy and forged links with consumer groups or peace movements in Europe and America.

M. Davies, *Politics of Pressure*, BBC Publications, 1985

Trade Unions

There is little doubt that trade unions are popularly viewed as very powerful pressure groups. A *New Society* survey on people and power in 1975 (29 May), showed that 61 per cent of the respondents believed that major Government decisions were taken with a view to pleasing the trade unions The same survey pointed out that in 1973 an ORC poll found that trade unions at that time were seen as having more effect than the Prime Minister on the way the country was run (respectively rated as the most powerful by 40 per cent and 33 per cent of interviewees). However, the survey in *New Society* did show that, in general, pressure groups were thought to have important influences on decisions by just 37 per cent of all respondents, only a little more than the mass media (33 per cent).

The TUC often claims to exercise influence rather than power – and, of course, it comprises a collection of very different union organisations, lacking the centralised authority of, for instance, the Swedish and Danish LOs or the Austrian AGB. But it did achieve a notable success in indirectly forcing the Labour Government to drop its 1969 Bill on industrial relations (following the Donovan Report in 1968), and it led the determined resistance to the Conservative Industrial Relations Act in 1971, when the TUC's Blackpool Congress instructed unions not to participate in the registration scheme under the Act. The TUC has a budget of millions of pounds; but its staff of about 40 – large perhaps by many pressure groups' standards – is small considering its overall aims and objectives, and in comparison with the resources of the Confederation of British Industry (CBI).

Moreover, since the Conservative Government came into power in 1979, trade union 'powers' have been restricted by legislation in 1980, 1982 and 1984. And 1984–5 saw an ill-fated miners' strike.

Under this legislation unions, notably the NUM in 1984, found themselves the subject of financial penalties in actions brought before the courts.

'The previous Conservative government did initially hold itself aloof from the unions and indeed confront them, but by 1972 Mr Heath was seeking a closer partnership between government and unions than had ever previously occurred. In this he was disappointed, but under Labour a partnership did come to fruition. The very public nature of the close relationship between Labour and the unions

Parliamentary Affairs, Spring 1983

275

between 1974 and 1977 probably rebounded to the disadvantages of both during and after the so-called 'Winter of Discontent' of 1978–9. Those events made it easier for the Conservatives (who, following the manner of their loss of office in 1974, had been nervous of the unions) to embark upon a different kind of relationship after 1979.

This did not involve the government in undertaking the kind of full frontal legislative confrontation with the unions which had occurred in 1971. The 1979 Conservative manifesto had specified three particular areas for reform: to ban secondary picketing, to restrict the closed shop, and to promote wider participation in union affairs. The Employment Act of 1980 introduced by Mr Prior and the Employment Act of 1982 introduced by Mr Tebbit proceeded with reforms along these lines. The unions maintained implacable hostility to this legislation. The TUC encouraged secondary picketing despite this legislation during the health workers dispute in Autumn 1982. It agreed to expel any member union which accepted public money to finance ballots, which meant that the Conservative manifesto commitment to encourage wider use of secret ballots met with no response.

It was this later resistance which led to the passage of further legislation in 1984. The question of accepting Government money for the holding of such ballots remains unresolved and led to a bitter dispute within the TUC in 1986.

The Trade Union Act 1984 makes secret ballots compulsory every five years, for the election of union officers, and every ten years, for the payment of the political levy (to the Labour Party). And those unions which do not ballot their members before mounting industrial action lose legal immunity for damages, in respect of such action. The effects of unemployment and recent legislation have caused a fall in trade union membership to about 10 million by the mid-1980s.

Mr Kinnock and the shadow of the coal strike and Mr Scargill, 1984–5
The Observer, 14 July 1985

Influencing the Government

Trade unions have traditionally used three ways in which to influence the Government, and other pressure groups are no exception: pressure on Parliament and MPs, pressure on Whitehall, and direct action. The latter was seen most dramatically in the 1926 General Strike, and to a lesser extent in the miners' strike in 1973–4. Although the trade union movement is seen as a very significant pressure group today, this position has only been reached in comparatively recent years; the process received its greatest impetus in the 1930s, from increasing Government intervention in the economy and from the determination of trade unionists such as Ernest Bevin and Walter Citrine to have the TUC accepted as a legitimate spokesman for industrial interests, rather in the way that the American AFL-CIO was building up its own organisation at the same time.

Trade unionists now sit on a large number of Government committees and 'ad hoc' bodies. The committees on which the unions are represented are of several types: those whose work affects the specialist interests of one section of workers; advisory committees which need the experience and knowledge of trade unionists; and committees whose work has some bearing upon economic affairs, such as the National Economic Development Council. In addition, there is often direct access to Downing Street and, at times of crisis, tripartite talks between the Government, TUC and CBI, as well as the lobbying of ministers and their departments.

Trade union membership on official committees is usually limited to members of the TUC General Council or their special nominees, although one or two other groups do have direct representation on standing committees which advise the Government. The TUC's relatively enhanced importance is clearly due to the fact that in the 1960s and 1970s governments, of either political complexion, have intervened in collective wage bargaining by various forms of prices and incomes policy. In turn, this process of direct consultation by governments with the TUC has indirectly led to the inclusion of white-collar unions (such as the NUT, the teachers' union, and NALGO, the local government officers' association) within the TUC. The alternative would have been for them to remain outside it, possibly as potential rivals, but more likely in a weakened political position.

Governments, Labour or Conservative, will only entrust more information and confidence to the TUC if the TUC is able to show that it can restrain wage levels and keep the number of strikes down. This was the basis of the 'Social Contract' between 1974 and 1977. But if that type of relationship fails, the alternative may be mass action in the 1920s style, as the shopfloor attitude towards the 1971 Act and the National Industrial Relations Court under the Conservatives amply demonstrated. 'Even more than in the past, the unions will have to operate as a conventional pressure group working through Whitehall if they are to exercise influence on decision making' was a prophetic view in 1973.

T. May and M. Morton, New Society, 6 September 1973

Perhaps the final word on pressure groups can be left with a Member of Parliament, who after all is obliged to hear many points of view from a whole range of interested parties, both organised and disorganised. Paul Rose (the former MP for Manchester Blackley) writing in *The Guardian* in 1977 (27 June) felt that

277

the more deprived sections of the community expected more and better services, even at a time of public spending cuts.

> 'A chiropody service for the elderly or a pharmacy and post office within easy reach of the high rise blocks may mean more to those affected than the tortured Chilean Socialist who now lives in my constituency since the local Young Socialists took his case up with me. . . . Abortion, euthanasia and religious education are the legitimate preoccupation of well organised groups, while the mass lobby has become an expensive way of creating publicity and pressure on everything from pyramid selling to the legalising of cannabis. The deputations that are destined to win, however, are those which temper their request with an understanding of the various, and sometimes conflicting, loyalties of an MP to his constituents, his party, his Whip, and his conscience. They will be well briefed and politically persistent and will feed the Member the material with which to present their case. . . . Paradoxically, those who are frustrated beyond endurance . . . who come without guile . . . but with a genuine case, can turn a complacent or paternal MP into a ferocious fighter . . . on the backbenches at three in the morning urging a tired minister to mend his ways. . . . The deputation today is for the electorate at large, what the first combinations were for the trade unions. Local officials and civil servants who ignore the pleas of MPs on their behalf induce a sense of frustration with the democratic process. What is the result? A bigger and better deputation, and so the pressure grows.'

Summary

Influencing and persuading governments has always been an important political function, but the art of lobbying in the post-war period has become much more sophisticated, and there has been a rapid growth in the number of pressure groups. In the late 1960s and early 1970s it became fashionable to argue that the growth of interest groups posed a threat to the system of representative, parliamentary democracy. This point of view owed much to the existence of industrial unrest and the apparent power of trade union leaders. But there is nothing wrong in a participatory democracy in people having their say through a variety of groups, as long as, of course, this does not conflict with the role of Parliament, and provided also, MPs keep in constant touch with public opinion.

Most of the electorate belong to at least one group, and 10 per cent belong to several or more organisations. The function of political parties must, however, be distinguished from that of interest groups. Parties have national programmes which they wish to implement, they seek political power. Interest groups, on the other hand, do not seek power, their role is to change society, to influence government, to cajole MPs and civil servants, to persuade others, but not to become the State itself. On that last point, however, given at times the close relationship between industry, trade unions and the Government over certain economic issues, such as pay policy, particularly during the period of consensus politics of the 1950s and the 1960s, it might be said that there were elements of a corporate state in operation – the leaders of influential groups, Whitehall and government ministers entered into economic agreements behind the political scenes. Mrs Thatcher, with her vigorous approach to the free market economy, has not pursued the corporatist path. Indeed, both trade union and industrial leaders have, at times, felt deliberately excluded from No. 10 and in some measure from government departments themselves. But some 'corporatist' practices are still in existance, as seen in the close relationship between the NFU (National Farmers' Union) and the Ministry of Agriculture or between the BMA (British Medical Association) and the DHSS. Also, the NEDC has continued since its creation in 1962, to act as a forum for discussion between government ministers, civil servants and the two sides of industry as represented by the CBI and TUC.

Pressure groups are principally divided into two types – the promotional which seek to advance a cause, and the sectional, defending or advancing the interests of a certain section of the community. The latter, like trade unions or the CBI, are likely to be permanent; however, given the nature of such groups, many become bureaucraticised and find other issues to take up, like the Howard League for Penal Reform or Shelter (the campaign for the homeless), whose objectives never seem to be truly realised. Other causal groups become institutionalised over a long period, simply because of an almost total lack of success (for example, CND).

Some, though, are dissolved, since they have fully realised their aims (for instance, the National Campaign for Abolition of Hanging).

As stated earlier, groups do, or at least should, reflect changes in public opinion, such as on abortion or homosexuality in the 1960s, and if legislation is required then governments must be sympathetic. Groups which campaign on issues that run counter to a party's programme or philosophy will achieve nothing. The more members a group has, the more likely it will achieve a ministerial hearing; for the Government votes count. But because the consultative process is deeply imbedded in British politics, minorities, too, will be heard in Whitehall, and that is still very much the position today, notwithstanding the 'anti-corporatist' tendencies since Mrs Thatcher came to power in 1979. And even if some groups are geographically restricted, they may be able to gain a lot of media attention, as was well illustrated in the debate over the route of the Okehampton by-pass in 1985. Moreover, when it does come to influencing the course of legislation, some groups are always much better prepared than others, as seen in the case of Mary Whitehouse and the NVLA (National Viewers' and Listeners' Association), one of the more efficiently organised groups where persuading MPs are concerned, especially those who are fortunate enough to draw a place in the Annual Ballot for Private Members' Bills.

Sometimes, however, the Government rejects the consultative process at its peril, as was well illustrated by the disastrous failure of Mr Heath's Industrial Relations Act of 1971, although admittedly, at that time, trade unions exercised more industrial muscle. The CBI, too, was critical of the Act.

When a group fails to influence MPs or Whitehall or ministers through the 'usual channels', then direct, violent action may be the next step, as seen by the activities of the Welsh Language Society from time to time, the Greenham Common peace movement (1984–5) or Greenpeace, and at the furthest extreme, various Irish organisations since the nineteenth century. But this might be counterproductive, and public opinion may harden against the group's activities. In a similar vein, some industrial groups hesitate to pursue their grievances, partly on grounds of conscience, but partly also because of the fear that public support will be forfeited – for example, the nurses in 1982, and the teachers in 1985–6. Other groups, however, have used all their industrial might and won (the miners in 1972 and 1973–4) and also lost (the firemen in 1977–8, the miners in 1984–5). Most spectacularly, the miners' strike helped bring down the Conservative Government in 1974, when Mr Heath chose unwisely to go to the polls on the question of 'who governs Britain?' The so-called 'Winter of Discontent', which saw a spate of public service strikes, mostly memorable for uncollected rubbish in the streets, contributed towards Mr Callaghan's defeat in the 1979 Election. All governments have tried to 'contain' trade unions, whether by legislation (for example, the 1971 Act), incomes policies, whether statutory or voluntary (for example, Labour's Social Contract in 1974), or through the mechanisms of conciliation (such as ACAS or the NEDC – the National Economic Development Council), or even, since 1979, by means of unemployment.

On the employers' side, governments have not seen the need to worry about the CBI, formed in 1965, since it is even more of a loose organisation than the TUC, and some major companies (for example, Taylor Woodrow) have left it. But the CBI, with its fairly pessimistic predictions about the economy over recent years, can be as much a thorn in the side of a Conservative government as in that of a Labour one. Moreover, the CBI enjoys representation on as many official bodies as members of the TUC.

Questions

1. Which today is more politically powerful – industry or the trade union movement.

2. To what extent are leaders of pressure groups:
(a) responsive to,
(b) representatives of
their members? (AEB specimen question 1986)

3. Make a case for the activities of pressure groups, and a case against them. (London)

4. Are there any limits to the political power of trade unions? (London)

10 Political Parties

Parties as Coalitions of Interests

Party ideology is not usually easy to characterise, and in some countries it is harder than in others. Compare, for example, the wide-ranging policies of the Democratic and Republican parties in the USA with the relatively narrow-based ideals and aims of the parties in the United Kingdom. Moreover, parties will change their tactics and policies – if not always their basic creeds – according to the prevailing political climate.

Labour

In the United Kingdom the Labour Party is traditionally associated with an increase in state ownership and intervention (balanced with a measure of private economic enterprise). The underlying theme is equality in society at home and a minimum of intervention abroad, with perhaps rather more 'loyalty' towards the developing nations of the Commonwealth than to Europe – at least in the shape of the EEC, over which, until recently, the party has been far more divided than its main rival. It is now an anti-nuclear, unilateralist party. While committed to removing nuclear weapons from the country, the party has placed emphasis on strengthening conventional forces. It has also retreated from its opposition to the 'privatisation' of council housing. Unlike the Conservatives it is not opposed to a limited degree of devolution of power to the regions.

Conservatives

The Conservatives, on the other hand, maintain the basic values of free enterprise and the capitalist system, their view being that since 1945 the State has already intervened enough in industry, and that the mixed economy – which the modern Conservative Party initially came to accept as a *fait accompli* – is now too mixed. The Conservatives, as is characteristic of most parties of the right compared to those of the left, have usually been less ideological than Labour, and more pragmatic. They believe the equality of income and wealth – as opposed to equality of opportunity – to be not only impracticable in modern industrial society but also undesirable. Placing more emphasis upon the traditions inherited from the Empire, the Conservatives have always been prepared to assume a more interventionist role in foreign affairs, and, at the same time, they have also generally been more enthusiastic about the UK's role in Europe and the EEC.

Liberals

The Liberals are in agreement with the Conservatives on some fundamental issues, such as Europe and free enterprise; but in its attitudes towards a domestic role for the State (in various areas of social reform), and to defence the party is also close to Labour. As a party which places a great deal of emphasis on social equality and industrial co-partnership, Liberals would generally place themselves left of centre.

Maurice Cranston has remarked that conservatism appeals to reason, liberalism 'to freedom, and socialism to imagination, so that there is nothing absurd about the eclectic individual who subscribes to a party of each of these ideologies, and remains sceptical towards them all. The man of the centre, like the floating voter, is the best friend of democracy: he wants free play for all tendencies, because all are within him.'

Cranston's review of N. O'Sullivan, *Conservatism;* R.N. Berki, *Socialism;* and D.J. Manning, *Liberalism;* Dent, 1977

Social Democrats

It is probably too early to judge what is the SDP philosophy, for the party was founded only in 1981. But as one-half of the electoral Alliance, the SDP is obviously ideologically close to the Liberal Party, though the SDP places less emphasis on 'freedoms of the individual' and decentralisation of government and more emphasis, for example, on the need for economic growth. For many Liberals in recent years the protection of the environment has assumed a greater political significance than economic growth.

Putting Parties on a Left–Right Line

There are always immense difficulties, however, in trying to locate parties on a left–right line. The philosophical similarities (as opposed to historical differences) of the two main parties in the Irish Republic – Fine Gael and Fianna Fail – provide an excellent illustration of this problem, although it should be added that a left–right division began to emerge after the Republic's 1977 General Election.

A given party will appear more left or right to its opponents than to its supporters. Allegorical comparisons put forward by Glenn Wilson suggested that

'Mr Conservative and Mr Labour are both colour-blind, the former preferring very dark colours (as reflected by his house and clothes, for example) while the latter prefers very light colours. Mr Liberal moves in across the road and paints his house in technicolour; to the Conservative this appears like a light house, to Labour like a darkly painted one. In other words we tend to view political "misfits" down the end of the telescope: the emotional telescope bunches all opposition, irrespective of its diverse component parts, at the farthest end, as illustrated by such remarks as "all Chinese look alike," and over-simplistic divisions such as intelligent or dull, Catholic or Protestant.'

New Society,
1 November 1973

Social survey samples are often too small to provide a useful measure of political attitudes. They may also date quickly; people change their opinions, sometimes suddenly, and any survey (even the massive ones conducted by Butler and Stokes, and Särlvik and Crewe) is bound to be incomplete simply because people's political attitudes are so vast a subject. Even more important, we may be judging things in an essentially British/West European context, and our conclusions might be different if the standards of the USA were applied.

See also C. Leeds, *Politics in Action*, Stanley Thornes, 1986, (section K)

But, whatever the statistical facts of the matter, all parties in the UK have faced significant problems since 1945.

Behaviour and Leadership in the Labour Party

Traditional loyalties

The Labour Party has frequently been compelled to face major electoral change and a breakdown in *tradition:* traditional working-class loyalties have often been in danger of being undermined, because of greater mobility, and because old loyalties in remoter regions, once based on religious and political non-conformity (as in rural Wales) are weakening. In respect of rural Wales the failure to recapture Brecon and Radnor in the 1985 by-election was a good example.

One of the main reasons for the overall drop in support at general elections since 1945 has been the steady fall in turn-out in a number of traditionally solid Labour seats in South Wales, the North-East and the Yorkshire mining areas. Changes in inner-city areas have also created major difficulties for Labour: their largely working-class population, displaced by commercial and office development, has become scattered among more Conservative areas on the city fringes. The party has had to adapt to working on new housing estates, especially in the Midlands and Scotland. The redistribution of population has been an important issue for Labour, as shown by the parliamentary row in 1969 when the Labour Government – to insistent Opposition claims of 'gerrymandering' – took the unprecedented step of delaying the implementation of the report of the Boundary Commissioners, on the rather tenuous excuse that any revisions of parliamentary constituency boundaries should coincide with local government reform. The Boundary Commission's proposals were thought by most MPs and experts to be detrimental to the Labour

Party, to the possible loss of 4–6 seats. The 1970 General Election was thus fought on boundaries dating from the revision undertaken in the mid-1950s, and it was not until 1974 that new boundaries came into operation. (Technically there are four Commissions – one for each part of the United Kingdom – as established by Parliament in 1944; they are responsible to the Lord Chancellor's Office, and normally report about every ten years or so.) The Boundary Commission's proposals that took effect just in time for the 1983 General Election, probably cost the Labour Party a further 25 seats.

The influence of history

In addition to the electoral problems of declining tradition and 'population drift', Labour has been more generally handicapped by the past. Psychologically, the party fed on the harsh economic conditions of the earlier part of the century and of the depression years between the wars. Those are not the conditions of the 1980s, despite economic reversals between 1966 and 1969, 1973 and 1976, and since 1979: it can be argued that recently Labour has been living off its political and electoral credit from the 1910s and 1920s. But, as one party worker at the 1973 Annual Conference remarked:

> 'the difference is that the enemy is more subtle and stealthy than before. Capitalism remains the oppressor it has always been, but the inequality and humiliation which used to stare out at you at every street corner is now harder to see, even possible to miss altogether.'

Winning votes

Then, too, there is the problem of living with a radical tradition, but at the same time capturing the middle ground and winning marginal constituencies. The 'middle' ground of politics can, however, be elusive, as American parties have also found, especially in presidential campaigns, as indicated by the humiliating defeats of the conservative Republican, Barry Goldwater, in 1964, of the liberal Democrat, George McGovern, in 1972, and of the centre-liberal Democrat, Walter Mondale in 1984. Thus Labour leaders will never welcome the prospect of a 'red scare' supposedly created by the media about 'extreme' left-wing factions, as seen in the activities of the controlling group on Liverpool City Council in 1985–6.

Far from winning votes, the Labour Party seemed to be intent on losing them after the 1979 General Election, and the results were confirmed by Mrs Thatcher's landslide win in the 1983 General Election. The quarrels within the Party during this period continued unabated, not just over ideological issues but over three key points – the mandatory reselection of MPs, the method for choosing the Leader and Deputy Leader, and the power to draw up the election manifesto. The internal quarrels led to the creation of the SDP in 1981.

Prior to 1981 the parliamentary Labour leader (*de facto* the leader of the whole party as well) was, in Opposition if not in Government, re-elected annually by his parliamentary colleagues – although the election of Mr Callaghan as party Leader, following Sir Harold Wilson's resignation in March 1976, of course revived the question as to how far (if at all) the party in the constituencies should be involved in leader selection. (In Government, the Leader would be re-elected at the beginning of the new Parliament, in other words after the general election which he had just won.)

Harold Wilson, Prime Minister 1964–70, 1974–6

The Deputy Leader of the Labour Party was similarly elected annually by the parliamentary group when in Opposition, as still are other members of the 'shadow Cabinet' – the executive committee, or Parliamentary Committee as it has been called since 1951. The Committee consists of 15 MPs elected by their colleagues in the Commons, and six ex-officio members – the Leader, Deputy Leader, Chief Whips (Commons and Lords), Leader in the Lords and one other peer. Since 1970 the Leader has no longer acted as Chairman.

285

The election of a new Labour leader took place through a series of successive ballots (if there were more than two candidates), using the simple majority method. At the end of each ballot the least successful candidate withdrew. Under the reformed (1981) procedure, each electoral unit can use any method of voting, but the votes are aggregated by the same (exhaustive ballot) system as before.

Choosing the leadership became a much publicised affair, and under pressure from the constituency activists who demanded a greater say in policy-making and a greater degree of answerability of the parliamentary front bench to the annual conference, a special conference was convened in 1981 which agreed to the establishment of an electoral college to elect both the Leader and Deputy Leader. The distribution of votes within the electoral college was to be 40 per cent trade unions (and other affiliated bodies such as the Fabian Society), 30 per cent Parliamentary Labour Party and 30 per cent constituency parties. No one opposed Michael Foot as Leader but the Deputy Leadership was contested in 1981 by Denis Healey and Tony Benn. The campaign was a particularly bitter one and to the press it presented a classic spectacle of the Labour Party tearing itself apart in public between left and right. Mr Healey narrowly won the contest.

See *Parliamentary Affairs*, Summer 1984

After the disastrous performance by Labour in the 1983 General Election, Mr Foot and Mr Healey stood down, and by the same procedure of the electoral college were replaced by Neil Kinnock and Roy Hattersley. The position under the 1981 reforms is that every trade union, constituency party and MP has a right of nomination which may be invoked any year the office holder retires or is challenged.

Sub-groups

The Labour Party's parliamentary groupings are fairly straightforward, the Campaign and Tribune Groups representing the radical left. The party is also associated with the extra-parliamentary Fabian Society, which devotes itself to policy research. In 1974, however, a right-wing group of MPs – the Manifesto Group – was formed, with the aim of keeping the party to the provisions of its election manifestos rather than allowing itself to be side-tracked by further slides towards the more extreme of Tribune's policies.

There have been various extra-parliamentary groups in the Labour Party, some of them constitutionally questionable, such as Militant. The Party, in 1984, decided to expel the members of the board of the newspaper of the same name; further expulsions, of Militant supporters, followed in 1986. Left-wing groups have included the Rank and File Mobilisation Committee for Labour Democracy (1980) and the Labour Co-ordinating Committee (1978) and most of all CLPD – the Campaign for Labour Party Democracy (1973), whose objective has been to consolidate the power of constituency party activists. By 1985 there had emerged 'Labour Left Co-ordination', an umbrella for most of the groups on Labour's so-called 'hard left', outside of Militant.* One right-wing group, the Social Democratic Alliance, was expelled from the Party in early 1981 shortly before the

*How far the Labour Left Co-ordination proceeds is doubtful; certainly (up to 1987) the Labour Co-ordinating Committee is still the most prominent mainstream left-wing group in the party and is supportive of Mr Kinnock. In 1986 the 'LLC' was formally launched as Labour Left Liaison.

formation of the SDP. Similarly, with the creation of the SDP in 1981 the CLV (Campaign for Labour Victory) was disbanded. Those who remained in the Labour Party on the right, such as Roy Hattersley and Denis Healey, formed the Labour Solidarity Campaign. Most centre-right MPs now support the Solidarity group.

It should also be remembered that when the Labour Party is in opposition, the bulk of the Shadow Cabinet (unlike the Conservative case) is elected by the whole PLP. The front-bench team is known as the Parliamentary Committee (15 in number since 1981, 12 before).

See *Parliamentary Affairs*, Autumn 1981

The mass media

For Labour the mass media has always posed a constant problem. Most national newspapers support the Conservatives, and in the 1960s and 1970s the party had an almost paranoic suspicion that the BBC was far too Establishment and Conservative minded. There is little doubt that Harold Wilson's suspicions of the media, and the BBC in particular, increased during his premiership, although the Conservatives harboured equally strong suspicions in the opposite direction during roughly the same period. The Conservatives abolished the committee to enquire into broadcasting which their predecessors in government had set up, but such was the handicap which Labour (particularly at the top) believed itself to be working under that in 1974 another committee to look into the future of broadcasting was established (the Annan Committee). This action was accompanied by threatening background noises from the research unit at Transport House: hints were dropped that the BBC might be broken up, like the French ORTF in 1975. Since 1983 the Conservatives have been less well disposed towards the BBC as Labour was earlier, as shown, for example, by Norman Tebbit's criticisms of BBC news reporting in 1986.

Behaviour and Leadership in the Conservative Party

The influence of external and social change in the UK

If Labour has suffered from an excess of ideology, the Conservatives, at times, have suffered from a traditional stance of avoiding it. Conservative problems have been rather different in character from those of Labour, but no less pressing. Changes in the class structure have affected the Tories too. Perhaps Disraeli foresaw that, as the franchise was inevitably extended, the Conservatives would never get back into government unless some deliberate effort was made to woo the skilled working man's political affections. The party was forced to face political reality, especially at the time of the 1918 Representation of the People Act. As *The Guardian* (1 October 1973) has since commented, 'the knights of the shire have yielded their influence to

287

the knights of industry, and even more to the scrap metal processors, whole-sale fruiterers and works managers.' The loss of influence of the patrician, liberal wing of the Tory Party since 1979 has been clear enough, its chief representatives, the so-called 'wets', having left Mrs Thatcher's Cabinet.

Secondly, Britain's external role has posed an emotional problem – the grudging nature of Tory acceptance of lower international status as a result of imperial and economic decline was reflected in the hostile reaction in 1974 to the Labour Government's proposals to reduce defence spending by some £4700m. over the following ten years. Since 1979, however, the Conservatives, too, have been forced to face the ever escalating costs of defence, not least in terms of new nuclear weapons.

Economic attitudes

Since 1945 the Conservatives have been increasingly torn between, on the one hand strict financial controls, and on the other the belief that governments should steer clear of too much economic intervention and instead favour a 'forces of the market' policy (*laisser-faire*). This can be illustrated by the fact that between 1966 and 1970, when the Labour Government was operating a not very successful statutory prices and incomes policy, the Conservatives pinned their faith in a voluntary system, initially relying on it after winning the 1970 Election. But by 1972 the Tories had moved to a position of statutory control, while almost at the same time Labour had adopted a voluntary, or at least semi-voluntary, position based upon the Social Contract with the TUC. The application of monetarism and other economic theories since 1979 has already been discussed earlier.

Sub-groups

The Conservative Party, like the Labour Party, contains a variety of sub-groups, although by remaining generally 'less ideological' than the Labour Party it has usually presented an image of being more at one with itself. Loyalty is at a high premium in the party, and it has normally managed to conduct disputes internally rather than in public. The Conservatives have marginally fewer intra-party groupings than Labour, but this may account for the party's ability to soak up dissension in the ranks.

Conservative sub-groups became steadily more complicated in the 1970s. Since 1951 the Bow Group has devoted itself to policy research which has usually been of a more progressive kind, and has therefore, technically at least, occupied a centrist position in the party. On the extreme right of the party, the Monday Club has had a chequered, but often successful career, since its foundation in 1961 to keep Macmillan on the true Tory track. Under the chairmanship of Jonathan Guinness in the early 1970s, the Club exercised a more divisive influence within the party; and, perhaps not surprisingly, in 1973 a new group, foreshadowing Labour's Manifesto Group and known as the Selsdon Group was set up, initially outside Parliament.

The Charter Group, formed in 1982, is an organisation attracting support from both left and right wings in the constituencies. It is critical of excessive centralisation of the party and its domination by one person, Mrs Thatcher. It claims that there is too much secrecy and 'feudalism' within the party, and argues that the Party Chairman and other senior officials should be elected by the annual conference, and not selected by the Prime Minister.

The left of the party had been largely dominated since 1960 by PEST (Pressure for Economic and Social Toryism), but in 1975 that merged with another minor group to form the Tory Reform Group, a progressive Conservative body which was viewed with some suspicion by the rest of the party as a refuge for the devotees of Peter Walker, and other former supporters of Mr Heath.

In 1985 Francis Pym, the former Foreign Secretary and dissident 'wet', founded the ill-fated Centre Forward group amongst liberal Tory back-bench MPs.

Electing the leader

The Conservative Party appears, if anything, to like losing elections less than the Labour Party; and that is perhaps understandable in the light of the fact that since 1922 the party has been in office rather more, on average, than the Labour Party. The 13 years of office from 1951 to 1964 created a climate of opinion, right down to constituency level, that the Tories were the natural party of government. Political shell-shock after an election, and with a delayed effect, is a condition from which all political parties suffer, but at times it can be serious. The Conservatives seem somewhat better than Labour in disposing of their leaders after electoral defeats – retribution was swift for Sir Alec Douglas-Home after the 1964 Election and for Mr Heath after 1974. Home, however, an aristocrat, was a political gentleman, the compromise candidate between Hailsham and Butler in 1963. He went in 1965 after a few discreet hints were dropped by the elders. But Heath was a younger political man, and his case was different.

Although public opinion appeared at the end of 1974 to be moving towards the Conservatives, as later confirmed by a by-election win in London (Woolwich West) in the summer of 1975, and by the results of the local government elections in May, the party's spirits remained at a low ebb – perhaps the lowest, for its more ardent followers, since 1945, and something resembling Labour's after 1970. Mr Heath was the first leader of the Conservatives not to 'emerge' but to be popularly elected by his parliamentary colleagues (1965); but, after the disastrous gamble of the February 1974 Election, not compensated for by the October result, the question arose how to rid the party of an unpopular leader.

Mr Heath could hardly have been unaware of criticism in his own party, but decided to brave the storm by offering to submit himself for re-election. A special committee, ironically under the chairmanship of Lord Home, was established, and it came up with some rather involved proposals. Thought had been given to extending the vote to the party outside Parliament, but it was eventually left to MPs to undertake mainly informal consultations in their constituencies. If on the first ballot (if more than two candidates were to stand) one of the contenders received an absolute majority, with the lead over the nearest rival representing 15 per cent of all Tory MPs eligible to vote, he or she would be declared leader. The new system has also provided ground rules for the annual re-election of the Conservative leader, whether the party is in Government or in Opposition. In Heath's case, in 1975, Mrs Thatcher led on the first ballot, but did not reach the magic figure under the formula, which had provisions for second (and third) run-off ballots. On the second ballot, Mr Heath having withdrawn, Mrs Thatcher reached the required figure decisively.

Edward Heath, Prime Minister 1970–4

The Heath–Thatcher division since 1975, is not simply the best example of a serious and continuing rift in the leadership of a political party; it is also important for its demonstration in the 1979 and 1983 Elections that such a division, while it may have a considerable effect on MPs and active supporters, has little direct influence on voting behaviour. The parallel in the Labour Party was the disagreement over policy between Mr Foot and his predecessor, Mr Callaghan, as was very apparent during the 1983 Election campaign. Here the difference of opinion (largely over nuclear weapons) did have some effect upon the voters, whereas the clash between Mr Heath and Mrs Thatcher has been perceived as much to do with the style of government as with policy.

'Mr Callaghan! In your heart you know I'm right – you'd be happier in MY party.'
Daily Express, 18 April 1979

Philosophical variations

The Conservatives were troubled from the 1970 General Election until the mid-1970s by the spectre of 'Selsdon Man'. The term was widely used by the quality newspapers and periodicals to refer to the apparently growing breed of self-made lower middle-class Conservatives. The Conservative leadership had met in Selsdon, south London, shortly before the 1970 Election to discuss strategy. The meeting clearly decided to follow a more *laissez-faire* approach to the economy in general and to the industrial sector in particular – in contrast to the 'progressive' image

291

Macmillan had frequently adopted, much even to the private admiration of the Liberal and Labour parties.

True to Selsdon philosophy, the Secretary for Trade and Industry, John Davies, was responsible for the celebrated statement that the 'lame ducks' of industry would not be given State aid. But during 1971 and 1972 the Conservative Government had to swallow its Selsdon pride and come to the rescue of Upper Clyde Shipbuilders in Glasgow and, perhaps, more seriously for national prestige, Rolls-Royce. The confusion over policy that resulted among Tory back-benchers was reflected in the formation of the Selsdon Group in 1973. The question of 'Selsdon' therefore represented the Conservative Party's struggle with its soul, between past and present. As Lord Blake, the party's principal historian, has remarked, 'if the party speaks too much in the language of its opponents, it incurs the charge of being an echo, rather than a voice. If it speaks too much in its own language it incurs the charge of being a voice from the past.' The renewed economic debate within the Conservative Party, particularly since about 1980, has not yet subsided, as discussed earlier. As early as that year, Mr Heath spoke of the Government's 'ruinous monetarism'; Selsdon Man had returned to haunt the Conservatives – Mrs Thatcher, determined to roll back the frontiers of the State, was truly Selsdonite, while Mr Heath, learning from his earlier painful experience of economic U-turns, took a diametrically opposing view. At the same time a back-bencher, Julian Critchley, spoke of the Prime Minister as 'didatic, tart and obstinate', and later as the 'great she-elephant'. Geoffrey Rippon, who as Environment Secretary under Heath had responsibility for local government affairs, criticised the Government's centralising control over local government finance, saying that 'even the most extreme Labour government would have hesitated to give such draconian powers to a Secretary of State in a measure which a Conservative Party in opposition would fiercely and unanimously resist.' Later, in 1984–5, both he and Mr Heath criticised the abolition of the GLC and the six metropolitan county councils as a constitutional absurdity. From 1981, as seen earlier, Mrs Thatcher started pruning her Cabinet of the economic liberals or 'wets', so that by 1986 the only true 'wet' remaining in the Cabinet was the former supporter of Mr Heath, Peter Walker, whom Mrs Thatcher must have judged as less dangerous inside the Cabinet than without.

The Guardian,
1 October 1973

The Liberal Leadership

In early 1976 the leadership of the Liberal Party was affected by two issues – firstly, a critical Government report about the collapse of a fringe bank (London and Counties) of which Mr Thorpe had been a director, and secondly by the beginning of what became known as the 'Norman Scott Affair'. Discontent within the party grew, and, in extraordinary circumstances, the former leader, Mr Grimond, acted as a caretaker when Thorpe did eventually resign, while the party hastily devised an interesting mechanism for what was the United Kingdom's first primary election.

Jo Grimond and Jeremy Thorpe

Each constituency association that had paid its financial dues (worth 10 votes plus 10 for affiliation the previous year) to headquarters was allocated a number of votes in accordance with whatever number of Liberal votes that constituency had recorded at the previous general election (one vote for every 500 votes received). Most constituencies entitled to participate held meetings (or organised postal ballots) to enable their members to vote for the leadership candidates, the total number of votes in each constituency for each candidate then being counted and entered on a return sheet by a constituency officer, and proportionately 'rendered down' according to the number of votes the constituency had been allocated.

The only other major European examples of such leadership primaries are those operated by the Swedish Social Democrats and the Swiss Socialists. Regrettably, perhaps, the new scheme was not helped by the fact that the ensuing contest between David Steel and John Pardoe was totally devoid of policy discussion and degenerated into a personality struggle of a low order: 'the gradually mounting level of personal abuse in the Liberal leadership campaign is already giving thought to the other big parties and the steaming row about Mr John Pardoe's vanishing bald patch is hardly likely to restore their confidence.' Nomination of candidates was still left in the hands of Liberal MPs themselves, so that although one MP in

The Guardian,
25 July 1976

293

this instance (Russell Johnston of Inverness) had considerable support among the party faithful outside Parliament, he failed to contest the leadership because none of his parliamentary colleagues would nominate him. David Steel won decisively. The Liberal leader no longer faces formal re-election each year. However, the Party's Annual Assembly (Conference) can take steps to set a leadership election into motion. Nevertheless the Liberal experiment, if somewhat sudden and marred by unfortunate circumstances, was a turning point in the history of British political parties.

The SDP

As has already been noted earlier, a new political party was established in 1981 – the Social Democratic Party consisted of a number of breakaway Labour MPs (29 by 1982), and one Conservative MP. It is early days yet to say what its future, after winning six seats in the 1983 General Election, will be, and how close its relationship with the Liberal Party will develop, not least in electoral terms. But it is the most important new political force since the Labour Party itself was founded at the turn of the century.

The method of electing the SDP's leader is quite simple – every member has a postal vote, but nomination lies exclusively with the parliamentary party in the Commons. In 1982 the first such election was held: Mr Jenkins won 26 256 votes (55.7 per cent) over Dr Owen's 20 864 (44.3 per cent) (75.6 per cent turn-out). Dr Owen was unopposed, however, when Mr Jenkins resigned as leader immediately after the 1983 Election.

———— The MP–Party Relationship

Selecting the candidate

There have been no other national primary elections in the United Kingdom, although on one or two occasions similar procedures have been followed in selecting constituency candidates. For example, the Conservatives held a 'closed' primary amongst their own constituency members in Bournemouth East in 1959 (mainly because of local divisions within the constituency party), and in Hampstead in 1949. And in 1968 in Reigate the two finalists, Christopher Chataway and Geoffrey Howe, appeared in a limited public primary which was televised. In some constituencies the Liberals and the SDP are currently holding joint meetings of local members to choose the Alliance candidate.

Choosing a candidate is very much the responsibility of the constituency activists. In all the major parties the final selection has to be made by a full meeting of the membership of the association concerned, but the 'boiling down' process is largely in the hands of the constituency officers and close supporters. In no sense is the general electorate involved, as it is in some American primaries – although there, too, the exact type of primary ('open', or 'closed' – restricted to registered party supporters only) varies from state to state. In 1970, on the retirement of Sir William Teeling, the Brighton Pavilion Conservative Party received 124 applications from parliamentary hopefuls; the final short-list of five which was put to the full local Conservative association was made by the officers of the constituency party and a special committee.

P.G. Richards, *The Backbenchers,* Faber, 1972, p. 157f

Removing a sitting Member

Sometimes the membership of a constituency party changes in terms of political outlook and – particularly in Labour's case – the offices of the local party will pass into the hands of people who may not be of the same political opinions as the parliamentary candidate, or, more seriously, as their MP.

Since 1973 a number of Labour MPs have found themselves at odds with their local party officers, and all Labour MPs since 1980 now have to face a compulsory (mandatory) reselection process between general elections. Their case is slightly different from that of MPs in difficulties with their local party for reasons other than disagreements over policy. For example, S.O. Davies had held Merthyr Tydfil, a South Wales industrial seat, for Labour since 1934. In 1970 he was aged 84, and his local party thought he had served long enough. Mr Davies, however, refused to stand down, and consequently the electorate in the general election of that year had the choice of two Labour candidates, the official one and Davies. Davies won the seat with an impressive 7467 majority and held it for another two years until his death in 1972. In Northumberland, Eddie Milne had held the seat of Blyth since 1960. In 1972 and 1973 he pressed repeatedly for an internal inquiry into the affairs of the Labour Party in the North-East, in the light of local government corruption scandals. This embarrassed the regional party, and in the February 1974 General Election he was dropped as the official Labour candidate; but he retained the seat with a respectable majority until his defeat by a narrow margin in the October 1974 Election.

These episodes have raised the question of how far an MP is responsible to the electorate and how far to his constituency activists, who, though they may appear a small and undemocratic group, nevertheless work to see him elected. Members of Parliament can frequently forget that without their party hacks their political position would be highly precarious. The constituency party officers of today have displaced or rather inherited the position of the great Whig and Tory families in the 'rotten boroughs' of the early nineteenth century. Labour MPs are now obliged to face fresh interviews by their constituency parties before each subsequent general election – the process of 'compulsory reselection'; up to early 1987 there had been few notable casualties, apart from Michael Cocks, the Labour Chief Whip, who was dropped as the Labour candidate for Bristol South. Professor Anthony King has commented:

> 'An important shift in the balance of constituency party/MP power does . . . appear to be taking place. . . . The question of constituency party/MP relations might not matter greatly if only the direct participants were involved. But in practice it has much wider, important ramifications. Everyone who has written about party discipline in the House of Commons agrees that it has a variety of

New Society, 14 March 1974

295

sources: MPs' desire to keep their own side in power (or get the other side out); the desire of some of them to advance themselves politically; MPs' belief that the electorate will punish a divided party at the polls; and the absence, in Britain, of powerful, constituency-based incentives for breaking with the party. Patronage apart, the Whips, despite their name, can only organise party discipline; they cannot enforce it.'

Party Finances

See also
J.R.S. Whiting,
*Politics and
Government*,
Stanley Thornes,
1985, (section A)

For a detailed
concise account of
party revenue see
M. Pinto-
Duschinsky,
*British Political
Funding 1979-83*,
*Parliamentary
Affairs*,
Summer 1985

The Labour Party has two types of parliamentary candidates – those who are sponsored, and therefore financially assisted, by a trade union, and those who are not. About 20 per cent of Labour candidates are sponsored, and 40–50 per cent of Labour MPs (148 out of 268 in 1979 and 123 out of 209 in 1983). In the Conservative Party before the Second World War many constituency parties offered the parliamentary candidacy to the highest bidder. But the shock result for the Conservatives in the 1945 General Election led to many demands for reform, for playing down the 'rich man' image: thus the Maxwell-Fyfe rules of 1949 limited the amount of cash a Conservative MP could give to his local constituency party to £50, £25 per annum for a parliamentary candidate. Democracy is still very cheap in the United Kingdom compared with, say, the USA, although even there proposals were made in 1974 to limit the amount spent in presidential (as opposed to congressional) elections, following Nixon's $80m campaign in the 1972 contest. The Labour Party relies heavily upon the trade unions for financial help (80 per cent of income) and the Conservative Party upon big business (65 per cent), while the SDP and the Liberal Party squeeze in between, relying for 90 per cent of their income upon members including a number of wealthy political philanthropists. The Conservatives can draw upon substantial contributions from their 1¼ million members, four times the Labour membership and six times that of the SDP/Liberal Alliance.

The fact that there were two General Elections in 1974 (and for that matter there were both General and European Elections in 1979) left its mark not just upon the few wealthy Liberals but upon all the other parties too. By 1975 Plaid Cymru was on the verge of bankruptcy and the Labour Party was rumoured to be £500 000 in deficit, while at one point Conservative Central Office was over £1m. in debt, with the result that drastic reorganisation of Central Office staff and services took place after Mrs Thatcher's election as leader.

State aid

Report of the
Committee of
Inquiry on Financial
Aid to Political
Parties,
Cmnd 6601, 1976

It was against this background of party poverty that a Government committee of enquiry (the Houghton Committee) took evidence in 1976 on the question of giving state aid to the political parties according to their electoral support. The subject is always controversial, particularly in times of economic difficulty, precisely when the parties most need the money. Alarmed by declining political activity in the parties, the report suggested a system of public subsidies largely based on the parties' support at the polls. But no action has yet been taken on the recommendations.

The Opposition parties in the Commons had already benefited, in 1975. There had long been criticism among MPs that while the Government (of whatever party affiliation) always had the full weight of the Civil Service behind it, the Opposition had no such support. But suggestions of loaning civil servants to the Opposition parties so that they could undertake adequate research and therefore, by implication, perform their parliamentary functions more effectively were greeted with controversy, since that would have destroyed the traditional nature of the Civil Service as a permanent Government institution.

Instead the Commons approved the making of payments to Opposition parties from public funds to help them in their parliamentary work (including that in the Lords, if the parties so wished). The formula used for these payments (popularly known as the 'Short Money' after the Lord President, Edward Short, who announced the original details) was based both on the number of votes cast at the previous general election and on the number of MPs; it provided £1080 for each seat won and £2.16 for every 200 votes, with a maximum of £325 000 for the biggest Opposition party and a minimum requirement of two MPs, or one MP and 150 000 popular votes. Thus in 1983–4 Labour received £317 056, the Liberals £63 996, the SDP £45 045, the Ulster Unionists £14 685, the SNP £5743, the Democratic Unionists of Northern Ireland £4888 and the Plaid Cymru £3512. Each party is responsible to an accounting officer of the House of Commons for how it deploys the funds given.

Models of Political Parties

Parties play a crucial role in transmitting and reinforcing cultural values and judgements throughout the electorate. The political party demands loyalty not only from its activists and from its publicly elected representatives, but also from the mainstream of its supporters.

In this context four models are noteworthy:

(a) is what we might call the **undeveloped loyalty model,** where a party generally expects its supporters to show a consistently high degree of loyalty and support at every opportunity, whether it be the choosing of the party leader or a parliamentary election. But the political rewards for such support are few and hierarchically organised and the monetary rewards almost non-existent. Most Western European parties come under this heading, especially in the United Kingdom, where loyalty to a party is largely a matter of consistent support at the polls.

(b) In contrast there is the **developed loyalty model,** where loyalty to a party is again high and demands much of the individual, but at the same time there is a well-developed, hierarchical system of promotion and largely covert reward, in terms of either considerable fringe benefits or direct financial payments or enhanced

297

political status. The Communist parties of Eastern Europe are the principal examples here, whereas the Communist Party of China, paradoxically enough, would be more likely to conform to model (a) in some respects – for instance, in the 1950s party membership had to be bought.

(c) is appropriate to large countries with intricate political links between their various geographical parts or even between different states – the **developed non-loyalty model;** this includes a clear, bureaucratised system of promotion, reward and public recognition (as in the USA), but party loyalty is much weaker and switching from one party to another is commonplace, as can be seen in American presidential elections. For example, in the early 1970s the wealthy Annenberg family of Philadelphia had an equally high regard for Mr Rizzo, the Democrat mayor of the city, and for Mr Nixon, a Republican, showing their appreciation 'in both cases by substantial contributions to their campaign funds.' Mexico's parties conform to both model (b) and model (c): the main party (the PRI) operates a mature reward system, which even spreads to members of the opposition parties, where active party loyalty can be of a somewhat tenuous nature; opposition groups can appear to be the 'subsidiary companies' of the principal, Government-directed organisation.

The Observer,
11 July 1976

(d) Finally, we can observe the **undeveloped non-loyalty model,** where parties are weak or non-existent. There may be a system of bureaucratic or financial returns, but it has not penetrated down the social scale. This model is largely applicable to the less developed countries of the Third World. It also fits in with what may be termed **solidaristic corruption** in the Third World, where the party or government office-holder is always under the pressure of constant demands from his extended family. He is expected to share his fortune, give lavish presents and pay for elaborate wedding and funeral ceremonies and perhaps for the education of nephews. Such demands will often exceed his regular income, and the precedence of older loyalties will lead him to put his hand into the political till.

Sometimes the difficulties of political parties in the United Kingdom seem small by comparison (except in Ulster). Universal and recurring, however, are the problems of declining membership and popular participation, of social mobility (both upwards and downwards), of leadership crises and policy quarrels, of friction between representatives and the party organisation at large, and last, but by no means least, of a fractious relationship with the various parts of the mass media.

Summary

Political parties lie at the root of a participatory democracy; they shape choices and encourage political competition and involvement. Of course, for most people parties matter only at election time, in the sense that promises are made and programmes offered. A winning party has a mandate, so-called, to govern, although as under the British system most governments have not been elected with over 50 per cent of the votes, this is perhaps a dubious claim. Moreover, even if governments enact most of their manifesto commitments, few electors are aware of all the details in three or more party documents. Governments are usually voted in or out of office according to their past economic performance. Even if an elector has read a particular manifesto, and does not necessarily agree with all its proposals, he can hardly register his dissent on certain issues on the ballot paper itself.

DOCUMENT

29

The Manifesto as a Mandate

Newly elected ministers invariably regard the election as conferring a mandate on them. The idea of the electoral mandate has changed over the years and even today it has no agreed meaning. Essentially, it refers to the authority of a government to carry out its election promises – which may or may not be enshrined in a manifesto. In some general elections, one issue has predominated and the main parties' positions have been so clearly differentiated on the issue – and recognised as such by many voters – that the outcome is widely regarded as having clear implications for the direction of policy. Free trade in 1906 and reconstruction in 1945 are examples of such elections. A frank acknowledgement of the mandate concept was Stanley Baldwin's election address in 1923 (it also did duty as the Conservative manifesto). It acknowledged that he felt bound by an earlier pledge of his predecessor, Bonar Law, not to introduce a tariff without first consulting the electorate. He wrote: "I am in honour bound to ask the people to release us from this pledge without further prejudicing the situation by any delay. That is the reason, and the only reason, which has made this election necessary."

Since then politicians' views about mandates have changed, as indeed has the nature of manifestos. Before 1945, manifestos were relatively short documents, four or five pages in length. In F.W.S. Craig's recent compilation of party manifestos, only the Conservative one of 1929 and the National Government one of 1935 exceeded five pages. The documents were usually long on rhetoric and short on specific proposals. Conservative and Liberal manifestos were usually addresses from the party leader and did not represent the collective views of the leadership; in 1945 "Mr Churchill's Declaration of Policy to the Electors" served as the Conservative manifesto.

In recent years, however, as S.E. Finer has shown, manifestos have become longer and more detailed. As the central government has extended the range of its activities and responsibilities, and as more specific interests are organised to lobby government, so the number of issues on which parties are expected to take a line has grown. A party's manifesto may ignore an issue at its peril, particularly if its opponents have an attractive policy. It is expected to contain something for consumers, pensioners, immigrants, animal lovers and so on. In 1979, the Labour and Conservative programmes each made nearly 80 pledges covering an incredible range of topics; and the figure would be higher if we included promises to review policy or establish a new policy line.

The various views of the functions of the manifesto have different implications for the conduct of government. The "mandate" view sees the government's actions deriving 299 legitimacy from being foreshadowed in the manifesto. The mandate doctrine is also a theory of consent; a party derives its right to be obeyed from election and from having stated its policies in advance. The "battering-ram" view sees the manifesto as essentially radical, a challenge to the status quo; Crossman sees it as a Labour model, but both Mr Heath in opposition in 1970 and Mrs Thatcher in 1979 have shared the view. (It is tempting to regard this as an opposition view of politics, particularly when there are marked differences between the parties. The only difficulty with this interpretation is that for the past decade Labour's NEC has taken this view even when Labour is in office. It may be that the NEC does regard itself as an opposition to a Labour government!) The "responsible government" view regards the manifesto as a means of judging the faithfulness of a government in carrying through its intentions. Without the manifesto, the voter has no criterion for judging the government. The "inner-party democracy" model sees the manifesto as a link, firstly, between the party leaders and the members, and secondly, between both of these and those who vote for the party. In some measure, the manifesto is a multipurpose document; it is addressed to different audiences and serves different purposes.

It is easy to imagine how these versions may be combined to form a coherent view of the way in which parliamentary democracy does and should work in Britain. Policy is made by the party membership, the resulting manifesto is approved, implicitly or explicitly, by voters who support the party, the manifesto pledges set the agenda for legislation in Parliament (it may or may not be a "battering ram of change") and the government is held responsible at the next election. Ironically, it is the manner in which at least two of the models are combined that prompts criticisms. A policy may be carried by a narrow majority in a party and inserted in the manifesto ("inner-party democracy"). If the party forms a government, then a whipped majority in the House of Commons is able to impose the policy on the country, according to the idea of the "mandate". The disproportional British electoral system, with its propensity to manufacture parliamentary majorities out of voting pluralities, or even minorities, combines with the sovereignty of Parliament to concentrate enormous legislative power in one party government. Hence the practice of inner party democracy (and the party mandate) may be transformed into the electoral mandate.

The record shows that those who claim that a manifesto is important are correct. At election time, candidates look to it for an authoritative statement of party policy, and party leaders invariably take the view that the manifesto is party policy and that any statement or opinion not contained therein is not party policy. Governments do carry out many of the specific or legislative promises in a manifesto, i.e. where the promises may be turned into legislation and the government can carry such a measure through Parliament. And when they introduce policies sharply at variance with those promises or policies not mentioned in the manifesto, then the opposition is fuelled by the cry, "You have not got a mandate!"

D. Kavanagh, *Parliamentary Affairs,* Winter 1981

Two parties are enough for a democracy to operate, but three make political life more interesting, if unpredictable. The 1980s look as if the three-party system of the 1920s is returning, but that does not necessarily mean greater political stability or a return to consensus style politics. In large measure the three-party forum is due to the split in the Labour Party and the formation of the SDP in 1981.

It should, however, be borne in mind that during the last hundred years or so, since the time that modern political parties were developed by Gladstone and Disraeli, it has been the Conservatives who have been the most adept at keeping office: 1874–80, 1885–6, 1886–92, 1895–1905, effectively 1916–22, 1922–4, 1924–9, effectively 1931–45, 1951–64, 1970–4 and since 1979, about 73 years out of 118. The Conservatives, traditionally, at least until the advent of Mrs Thatcher, have been a pragmatic party, uncluttered by the baggage of ideology, but basically committed to free enterprise, limited government intervention and strong defence.

The Labour Party, dating from 1900, is a more recent arrival, and never experienced majority government until 1945. Without the aid of the trade unions, to whom it has been intimately connected to this day, it is doubtful whether the party would ever have succeeded. While it is traditionally more ideological than the Tories, believing in fairness, equality, public ownership, state intervention in the economy and the welfare state, it has been far more pragmatic when in office and less socialist or Marxist orientated than other left-wing parties in Europe. This was particularly noticeable under the stewardship of Harold Wilson, whose tenure in office (1964–70 and 1974–6) many younger Labour activists today would disown as a manifest failure.

In Wales and Scotland, Plaid Cymru and the SNP rose and fell back in the mid-1970s. Of the two, the SNP has always posed the greater political threat to the established, British parties. In Northern Ireland, since the 'troubles' started in 1969, the political parties have grown ever more complicated. The Unionists have been split since 1974, and most notably the DUP (Democratic Unionist Party), led by the Revd Ian Paisley and avowedly Protestant, is again power-sharing with the Catholics. The Catholic SDLP (Social Democratic and Labour Party) favours power-sharing and constitutional change, and in principle a united Ireland. Increasingly, the SDLP has been overshadowed by Sinn Fein, the political wing of the IRA, which favours a united Ireland now rather than later and has not been enthusiastic about constitutional change within the existing political structure. There is also the non-sectarian Alliance Party, which to date has made little headway.

Back on the mainland, the Liberal Party clung on to existence in the 1950s and is now, in conjunction with its SDP allies, a formidable force once more. The Liberal/ SDP ideology is rather more difficult to determine than any of the other parties, but in essence it is centrist orientated, although many Liberals, regarding themselves as 'Radicals', would resent that label. Both parties are committed to the EEC, the mixed economy, some measures of state intervention, electoral reform and industrial co-partnership, as well as decentralisation of power to the regions, although on the latter issue many Social Democrats are noticeably chary and would want the issue tested first in a referendum (the results of the Scottish and Welsh referenda in 1979 not being good omens).

All the main parties have experienced difficulty in recruiting and maintaining membership; perhaps the growth in television since the 1950s has been responsible for the decline in political activity, but the Conservatives must remain easily the largest party. Financially, it also dominates, receiving some £5m. in 1983 from company donations, headed by British & Commonwealth Shipping, Racal Electronics, Plessey, Taylor Woodrow, Allied Lyons, Trusthouse Forte, Marks & Spencer and United Biscuits. (The figure for 1984, not being an election year was £2½m.) But the actual number of companies contributing declined from 470 to 320 over the period 1979–84. The Labour Party depends upon substantial sums from the trade unions (through the political levy), while the Liberals and SDP depend largely on individual members and a few wealthy benefactors, although there has been a small increase in company donations (to £60 000 in 1985).

Of the two principal parties, it is the Labour leadership which always faces the tougher test, since at the annual conference it is dependent upon the block votes of the trade unions, especially the five largest, and, further, Labour activists are far more determined to debate issues and have their say, sometimes to the acute embarrassment of the leader, as with Hugh Gaitskell in 1960 over the vote in favour of unilateral nuclear disarmament, and with Neil Kinnock in 1985 over the coal dispute and overspending by the Liverpool City Council. In contrast, the Conservative Conference is usually carefully stage-managed, with the leadership merely receiving polite advice from the floor, although frequently the issues of law and order and immigration have led to uncharacteristically lively debates. No party leader pays too close attention to conference resolutions because of his sensitivity towards the electorate, especially in the run-up to a general election. But it is not always so easy for the Labour leader to disregard conference policy, nor for that matter the policies of the NEC (National Executive Committee) at other times during the year.

Questions

1. Compare and contrast the roles of the various party conferences.

2. 'In Britain millions vote for a political party but only a few hundred thousand will join one and even fewer will play an active part.' Discuss the reasons why relatively few people actively participate in party politics. (AEB specimen question 1986)

3. Comment on the effectiveness of the Opposition in the House of Commons since 1979. (Joint Matriculation Board)

4. Evaluate the impact upon British politics of the 'Alliance' between the Liberal Party and the Social Democratic Party. (Joint Matriculation Board)

11 Voting Behaviour

'If you are chapel you are Liberal; if you are church you are Conservative. My father was church.'

a 66-year old painter in Carmarthen, quoted in D. Butler and D. Stokes, *Political Change in Britain*, 1969

Political Socialisation

Wide-ranging factors

'Political socialisation' is the process whereby a person learns and develops his political attitudes. Such attitudes are by nature extremely mixed. Socialisation is performed by all agencies which influence the way a person votes. These are, of course, as diverse as the attitudes they produce, and will vary in overall effect from one country to another. In the United Kingdom awareness of social class, via the medium of the family, has had dramatic effects upon voting patterns. Education and work, of course, are also important in giving young people the attitudes which associate party and class. (Elsewhere political divisions may stem from a greater division between industrial and non-industrial areas – for example, the gap between Communists and Christian Democrats in Italy; or there may be religious and ethnic reasons, such as the differences between Malays and Chinese in Malaysia.) Generally speaking, the Labour Party in the UK will receive about one-tenth of the votes of managers, businessmen and professional people. But the Conservative Party (partly for historical reasons stretching back to Disraeli and the second Reform Act in 1867, which gave the urban upper working-class males the vote) will always have to win a greater proportion of working-class votes if it is to stand any chance of forming a Government, simply because the members of the working class are more numerous. The Conservatives, it can be estimated, receive at least one-third to 40 per cent of the votes of the manual workers, while Labour only receives about 20 per cent of the votes of all non-manual workers. The 1979 and 1983 General Elections showed how, relatively speaking, working-class support for the Conservatives increased still further, and to a lesser extent middle-class support for Labour. Richard Rose has commented that political socialisation does not 'determine adult political behaviour, it creates conditions that in later life may be and often are influential upon behaviour.' He went on to say that individuals are always capable of learning new attitudes or altering old ones, since socialisation is a continuous process throughout life. But it is also important to note that what is freshly learned may merely act as a reinforcing influence underlining what has been determined by social factors earlier in life.

R. Rose, *Politics in England*, Faber 1965, p. 59

The family context

Butler and Stokes' classic study of voting behaviour first published in 1969, with revisions published in 1974, found that only one in three respondents to their survey who remembered both parents as interested in politics said that politics were of 'not much' interest to themselves, compared with nearly 60 per cent of respondents who said that neither parent was interested in politics. Similar trends could be seen in respondents' memories of how early in life they first became aware of politics. Of those still in their twenties at the time of the survey (1963–6), and therefore more politically 'plastic', the number who remembered themselves as politically interested by the age of ten was twice as large among those who recalled both parents as interested as among those who recalled neither as interested.

The age 'gap'

The 'plasticity' of the young is an important point. It is a common mistake to imagine that older people are more naturally Conservative voters. More and more older people nowadays have attitudes shaped by the political confusion of the 1920s and 1930s, and Butler and Stokes claimed this would be significant in preserving pro-Labour rather than pro-Conservative attitudes. However, this theory, as discussed below, did not really stand the test of general election results. Old people strengthen social conservatism in the wider sense – although sometimes the older section of the electorate will swing against the national trend, usually when pensions become an important election issue; for example, this appears to have taken place in the 1970 General Election. Old age, in fact, usually confirms and reinforces voting behaviour, strengthening existing ties rather than weakening them, although Himmelweit would dispute this view (see p. 320).

——— The Embourgeoisement Theory

P.G.J. Pulzer,
Political Representa-
tion and Elections
in Britain,
2nd edn.,
Allen and Unwin,
1972, p. 102

However identifiable as all these factors may be, there is clear evidence from parliamentary elections in the 1960s and 1970s and early 1980s that significant parts of the electorate have become increasingly volatile. Despite one comment that 'class is the basis of British party politics, all else is embellishment and detail', the alignments have become less clear. The task of definition has become, if anything, even more difficult, as highlighted by Goldthorpe and Lockwood's research on the 'affluent worker' in the mid-1960s. They postulated three types of working-class sub-cultures – proletarian, deferential, and privatised. The first two were traditionally working class, the former being found in closely-knit and long-established industrial communities surrounding mining, docking, shipbuilding and other heavy industries. The 'deferential' worker would often work in rural areas and service industries and he might have closer contact with employers. But it was the privatised section of the working class which came to be seen as politically the most important in the 1960s. Such workers were likely to be employed in large-scale mass-production industries and live on an equally large-scale suburban housing estate, lacking a sense of involvement in and identification with both work and community. It was the increase in the numbers of this type of worker under the prosperous days of the late 1950s (or in Macmillan's words, the days of 'you've never had it so good') that led to doubts, after the Conservative victory in 1959, that the Labour Party could ever again take power – as Abrams and Rose in 1960 suggested in their work *Must Labour Lose?* The 'embourgeoisement' theory proposed that the upper working-class, 'privatised' worker was adopting middle-class values, including voting Conservative. If this were so the country might be expected to have a long period of Conservative domination at Westminster. However, Goldthorpe and Lockwood, in their studies at Luton found that while the privatised worker might adopt certain middle-class values – a greater confidence in mastering his own environment rather than the usual fatalism associated with the working class, thrift, and considerable involvement in his children's education – he did not necessarily entertain at home, participate in recreational or leisure associations, or vote Conservative, to the extent of his middle-class counterparts. Moreover, the results of the 1964 and 1966 General Elections destroyed the 'embourgeoisement' theory. As Peter Jenkins, writing about these theories in *The Guardian* (16 March) just before the start of the 1979 General Election campaign, remarked:

M. Abrams, R. Rose and R. Hinden, *Must Labour Lose?* Penguin, 1960

J.H. Goldthorpe, D. Lockwood, F. Bechhofer and J. Platt, *The Affluent Worker in the Class Structure,* Cambridge, 1969, p. 96ff

> 'The expansion of the middle class is a secular trend helpful in the long run to the Conservatives, but because it is recruited in large part from the working class it becomes, as a class, less and less reliable. In other words, the most probable explanation of the growing number of middle class Labour supporters, and perhaps also of the upsurge of middle class trade unionism . . . is the influx of working class recruits who do not shed their attitudes and allegiances on admission to the middle class. The phenomenon is similar to one observed in the USA when city Democrats failed to turn into Republicans as a result of migration to the suburbs.'

Yet, for all that, the results of the 1979 and 1983 General Elections have resurrected the embourgeoisement theory, as is discussed below. In both general elections the sale of council and other houses to sitting tenants played a major role.

Butler and Stokes on Class

An alternative theory

The embourgeoisement theory was quickly replaced by the perspective in Butler and Stokes' massive research of the mid-1960s, already referred to. Their basic approach was to trace the progress of 'age-cohorts' (or generations) from the First World War, through the realignment of party politics between the wars, to the relatively stable period after 1945, and to examine how the political attitudes and behaviour of a particular generation affected those of subsequent ones.

Indeed, it could be argued that the return of the Labour Party to office in 1964, after 13 years in Opposition, was greatly helped by younger voters on the register

305

whose parents had been influenced by the Labour Party (maybe negatively rather than positively) in the economically troubled times of the 1920s and 1930s, and by the experiences of the War; this was part of Butler and Stokes' 1969 'age-cohort' theory. Furthermore, a small minority of the middle class began to undergo intellectual conversion to the Labour Party. Butler and Stokes commented:

> 'the reversal of party fortunes suggested that economic expansion had benefited the Conservatives more as the governing party during a prosperous period (the 1950s) than as a party of an expanding middle class. Since the early 1960s the embourgeoisement idea has come under increasingly sharp attack from those who are sceptical whether anything so deeply rooted as identification with class will be transformed merely by changes in consumption. We share this scepticism.'

Another crucial point is that, while in studying political behaviour it is practicable to use mathematical or statistical expressions, even these may not always be precise. Thus Butler and Stokes' own voting behaviour predictions, tentative as they were, were not entirely accurate. Their argument, roughly, was that the older generation of voters, containing a considerable number of pre-1920 working-class Conservatives, would die off through the 1970s and 1980s, leaving the younger Labour generations, and their presumably Labour-inclined children, to dominate the political scene. However, the result of the 1970 General Election came as a profound shock to both politicians and political scientists. As Richard Rose said, the Conservative victory, by a not unreasonable margin, 'surprised pollsters, politicians and those who write electoral laws.'

The Times Guide to the House of Commons, 1970

Criticism of Butler and Stokes

In the light of the 1970 result the Butler and Stokes theory looked flawed, and prompted speculation that perhaps the 'embourgeoisement' idea was not so wrong after all – indeed in that election, it appeared that housewives, more embittered than usual about rising prices, played a significant role. Perhaps political issues, too, played a more direct part (Wilson certainly admitted after the defeat that he should have put more emphasis upon education as well as housing during the election campaign). Possibly the 18-to-21-year-old voters (enfranchised in 1969) were more disaffected with politics than older electors, and Labour would have won if it had made an effort to gain their support. It would, however, be very unfair to overemphasise the weaknesses of Butler and Stokes, in view of the very considerable range of voting behaviour that Butler and Stokes' work covered and in view of the revisions made in their second edition. Nevertheless in 1974 one writer, Crewe, severely criticised their research methods – which, he claimed, were largely based on earlier studies at Michigan in the USA; he disliked their use of 'macro' (nationwide) samples of voting behaviour. He also said that Butler and Stokes ignored the increasing volatility of the electorate. Indeed, it was unfortunate that the second edition of their fundamental piece of research was published in 1974, and did not take into account the two significant general election results of that year. It was the same misfortune which had befallen their first edition in respect of the results of the 1970 Election. The 1974 version had reduced the amount of material devoted to the minority parties, especially the Liberals, who had not done very well in the 1970 Election, but who did much better in 1974. Crewe commented that the problem of why a growing minority should abandon the two parties at elections stubbornly waited for an answer and continued to call the validity of the Butler–Stokes model into question. Crewe also criticised Butler and Stokes for ignoring the question of the falling turn-out at general elections; however, this critique itself was made before the February 1974 Election.

I. Crewe, *European Journal of Political Research*, March 1974

Nevertheless, Butler and Stokes' revised survey, although based on research done from 1963 to 1970, is still a major landmark in British political science, for two fundamental reasons. Firstly, it listed the main factors in political socialisation, and in particular the continuing importance of the family (and through it of social class) from one generation to another. Secondly, it illustrated that dramatic shifts in voting patterns probably only come about through great national occurrences such as war, economic instability or deep-rooted political instability (this last would presumably cover the Scottish situation in the 1970s, as seen earlier).

D. Butler and D. Stokes, *Political Change in Britain*, 2nd edn., Macmillan, 1974, chapters 4, 6 and 11

Class and the Family

Whatever the difficulties of analysing political socialisation in depth, whatever the problems of recent research, the importance of social class in voting behaviour should not be underestimated. As part of social stratification, it also operates not only through the family, but also through work, and through social surroundings. These last include 'peer-groups' – people with whom a voter likes to mix because they are to some extent similar.

Butler and Stokes provide a telling quotation from W.G. Runciman, who in 1963 remarked, 'there is nothing in a sense that needs to be explained about a South Wales miner voting Labour or an executive of General Motors voting Republican. The simplest model of rational self-interest is enough to explain these cases.' But occupational pressures, in particular, vary: the 'traditional' working class is deeply united in its political attitudes through close-knit communities, for example in the coalfields of South Wales or North-East England – yet as many sections of traditional heavy industry decline, and workers move away, political attitudes may soften – if not among the workers themselves, at least among their sons and daughters.

Class and the Liberals

Any class analysis poses the question of where to place Liberal voters, particularly at times such as 1974 when there is a large increase in the party's popular vote. Butler and Stokes found this a difficult problem, concluding that Liberal support was significantly unrelated to 'class self-image' or occupational grade and that in

307

terms of class the Liberals' appeal was broad and even. This appears to have been confirmed by the results of the 1974 and 1979 Elections. And in respect of the 1983 Election Professor Crewe said this about the Liberals and the SDP:

The Guardian, 13 June 1983

'Support for the Alliance was remarkably even across the class spectrum. There was not a trace of evidence that it drew disproportionately from the professions, or the middling, intermediate strata, or that its supposedly middle class image was anathema to the "real" working class. The Alliance's vote was almost exactly the same among the upper middle classes (27 per cent) as among the unemployed (26 per cent).'

—————— Working-class Conservatism

See R.T. McKenzie and A. Silver, Angels in Marble, Heinemann, 1968

The other problem of social class in the context of voting behaviour is the nature of working-class Conservatism. Various attempts have been made to define it, but the supposition of a deferential attitude on the part of some members of the working class, in accepting a particular political élite as a matter of course, must be treated with caution. Butler and Stokes instead offered the following observation:

David Thomas, New Society, 26 May 1983

'we are much more impressed by the fact that the Conservatives attracted working-class support for many of the same reasons they attracted support generally in the country.'

'Since the 1979 election the main shifts among skilled workers have been between Tory and Alliance. Between May 1979 and November 1981, when its support peaked the Alliance increased its C2 share by 31%, 23% from the Conservatives, but only 8% from Labour. By the third quarter of 1982, when we were awash with the Falklands spirit, 21% of the C2s had already deserted the Alliance – 19% to the Conservatives, but only 2% to Labour. Alliance support among skilled workers has been stable for a year at about 25%, hardly enough for a breakthrough. Whatever their worries about unemployment, the skilled workers' worries about Labour may be higher. They are keen on "fairness", less keen, perhaps, on egalitarianism.'

DOCUMENT

30

Electoral Instability

Our conclusion, therefore, is that class differences, whether with respect to objective inequalities, subjective values or support for the political parties, remained at much the same level throughout the postwar period. Whether for better or worse, Britain is still divided by class. On the other hand the shape of the class structure has changed, with important electoral implications particularly for Labour. Its class base is clearly shrinking, and may be expected to continue to do so with the de-industrialisation of Britain. But this can account only for part of Labour's decline at the polls, and for virtually none of the Liberals' rise. Labour has changed from being a rather successful class party in 1964 to being an unsuccessful one in 1983. The Liberals, also a class party, have gained at both Labour and Conservative expense. To explain their modest success, we must look to political explanations, not social ones. The withering away of class is not the answer.

In principle, we would argue, these class inequalities provide a potential for class ideology. The conception of social class which reduces it to income differences and lifestyle suggests that Labour must shift its ground towards the affluent centre. Our conception, which emphasises the more enduring differences of interest suggests that Labour might be able to revive whilst remaining a class party. Just as the petty bourgeoisie was receptive to a free market ideology, so the working class might still be receptive to an egalitarian one. The Labour party does not have to take the existing distribution of values and attitudes as given. Nothing in our evidence indicates that the shift to the right on the class values was an inevitable or irreversible phenomenon. But we would suggest that the language of class struggle is unlikely to be successful in securing an ideological move back to the left. Class inequalities persist but the classes have not been polarised in their values at any time in the postwar period. We doubt if they will become so. An appeal to social justice rather than to class struggle has more hope of success.

For the Alliance, the potentials are of course rather different. As we have shown, their potential recruits are those who tend to the centre or right on the class axis but favour more liberal measures on defence, civil liberties and the welfare state. They have a 'heartland' just like Labour and Conservative, but they have not yet established themselves as the party of the professional and technical worker in the way that Labour and Conservative are *the* parties of the industrial worker and the entrepreneur respectively.

If the Alliance can establish its political identity more firmly, and thus perhaps break down its potential voters' traditional loyalties to the other two parties, it could in principle make the breakthrough in votes that it failed to achieve in 1983. If it secured the same proportion of its heartland as Labour and Conservative do in theirs, it could expect to win an extra 5 per cent to 10 per cent of the vote (largely at Conservative expense).

One of the striking features of the 1983 election was that the Alliance did succeed in establishing itself more securely as a political grouping with a distinctive appeal of its own. But it still falls far short of the other main parties in mobilising its potential supporters. To do so it will probably need to discover some distinctively Alliance principles or to politicise the 'second dimension' of our ideological map. (And perhaps the two will not be unconnected.) As long as the class axis is the primary one around which British politics is organised the Alliance vote will be particularly vulnerable to assaults from the Labour and Conservative parties. A centrist party is vulnerable on both flanks and can expect to have a more volatile vote but by developing an identity as an 'off-centre' party with a distinctive programme of its own, the Liberal (or Social Democratic) party could perhaps move still further from its recent role as a vehicle of protest rather than reform. Its difficulty in doing so is of course that many of the 'non-class' issues – disarmament or the welfare state for example – have already been captured by the Labour party. International cooperation, the environment or local democracy and decentralisation might be better alternatives.

We do not intend this to be prescriptive; rather we wish to illustrate our points that social trends are not inexorable. Potentials exist for both Alliance and Labour but the 309 future will depend on the success of the deliberate political initiatives that the parties can make to shape people's values and mobilise these potentials.

Doubtless potentials exist for the Conservatives too. We have tended to assume that their past success in converting people to the free enterprise ideology means that they have less scope for further advances. It is perhaps in the nature of conversion that initial enthusiasm will tend to wane. Moreover, the very success of the government in the Falklands war and in controlling inflation may bring its own reaction as the raised expectations of government success become harder to live up to. The cyclical nature of political trends suggests that at some point success will be followed by disillusion. But we would be foolish to predict when that point will come.

A. Heath, R. Jowell and J. Curtice, *How Britain Votes,* Pergamon, 1985

Religion

Religion is now generally seen as a minor influence, apart from, of course, in Northern Ireland. In the nineteenth century the Anglican Church, as the established religious institution, was very much identified with the Conservative Party, while religious nonconformity was identified with the Liberal Party – particularly with its more Radical elements, the new, propertied classes born of the Industrial Revolution. Today, with the rapid decline in active religious participation, the connections are much weaker – although they are still there: Rose quoted one MP as saying that he regarded democratic socialism as the political expression of Christianity, and there is little doubt that nonconformity is still linked with the Liberal Party, particularly in Wales and the West Country, although it was further weakened by the rapid growth of the Young Liberal movement in the mid-1960s, whose appeal was not limited to the nonconformist areas of the 'Celtic Fringe'.

The religious feelings of earlier times are encapsulated in the quotation at the beginning of this chapter. But Butler and Stokes concluded, in both 1969 and 1974: 'the religious differences we have found are weak compared with those which an earlier era would have yielded.' They went on to say that this was one of the most interesting facts emerging from their research. Professor Rose has crystallised the situation:

R. Rose,
Politics in England,
Faber, 1965, p. 80

'A London bar-tender, an active Anglican, aptly summed up a point of view in a life history interview; religion, he thought, should play a part in national life, "if not taken so far that it means stopping people doing things." Viewed historically, the chief significance of religion for political socialisation today is its absence of influence.'

Naturally, however, religion plays very different roles in other countries. Perhaps the most dramatic European example is Italy, where the Catholic Church has consistently emphasised the importance of submissiveness to the lawful authorities, which in effect means the Christian Democrat party; but the Catholic Church has also played a variety of other roles, both left-wing and right-wing, particularly in Latin America. The role of Cardinal Sin in the Philippines was crucial in the downfall of President Marcos in 1986.

Education

Educational systems, too, vary from one part of the world to another. In the USA a kind of political education is to be found – under the guise of 'civics', in which values related to the written American constitution are taught. In the UK, however, Rose has emphasised the importance of family influences over educational factors, and drew attention to the fact that at least one survey, comparing Winchester College public school and Taunton Grammar School, found secondary school influences upon political attitudes to be largely unimportant. Of course, in Eastern Europe there is a clear emphasis on the wider political role of schools, while in West Germany, in contrast, their educational and social role is kept rigidly separate from political aims and philosophy. Nevertheless, in every country there arises the question of the conservative influence of ritual in schools; teachers, with their power reinforcing the status quo, are separated and elevated from pupils; each may wear a distinctive uniform. It may be a long way, as Ronald King has pointed out, from the highlands of Burma to the school halls of England, but Edmund Leach in his study of the Kachin reached conclusions broadly similar to King's own survey: 'ritual serves to express the individual's status as a social person in the structure system in which he finds himself.' On the other hand, many university students may vote for non-Conservative parties, despite the Conservative social class of most undergraduates. But even if this is so, and research on the point is lacking, it would amount to a very minimal change in society; the total number of young people becoming eligible to vote annually is about 2 per cent of the electorate, and of that figure university graduates constitute only a tiny proportion. The revolutionary, left-wing student is more fiction than fact.

New Society,
12 July 1973

For an important
analysis of teenagers
see Robert Stradling
(The Hansard
Society), *The Political
Awareness of the
School Leaver,* 1977

Issues

In view of the importance given here to the family and social class, it might be thought that national issues play little part. That, however, would be a gross over-simplification of a complex question. It is national issues, as projected by the political parties through the mass media, or indeed their absence, that help to reinforce or change a family's voting behaviour. Generally in modern times the question of the economy has far outstripped all others in importance, especially those of foreign affairs – except insofar as they too concern the economy (for example, that of membership of the EEC). But usually there is a clear order of priority in the voting mind, which places housing, social services and pensions after the state of the economy. Of course, it should also be added that the Falklands War in 1982 formed an important backdrop to the 1983 General Election.

In Butler and Stokes' 1970 survey (1974 edition) the top three issues were, in order, the state of the economy, welfare and housing; but in their 1963 survey (1969 edition) they were social welfare, followed closely by housing matters, with economic problems third. Certainly foreign relations have lost their nineteenth-century electoral significance: in 1974 the shadow Foreign Secretary, Reginald

311

Maudling, commented that there was virtually no difference between the two major parties in foreign affairs – a statement that later had to be amended in view of the Labour Government's defence cuts in 1975. However, in the 1979 and 1983 General Elections, and particularly in the latter, defence and the question of the retention of the nuclear deterrent became key issues. The increase in the Labour vote in 1966, compared with that in 1964, was undoubtedly due to a feeling in part of the electorate that the Labour Party should be given a chance to prove itself in managing the economy: nine in 20 electors felt the blame for the UK's poor economic position belonged to the Conservatives. As Butler and Stokes said, 'the elector focuses his attention primarily on certain conditions which he values positively or negatively, and simply assumes that past or future governments affect them. The public can call for a team manager's dismissal in a losing season, in each case concluding that causal relationships must exist without knowing in detail what they are.' The same principle can be applied to Mrs Thatcher's win in 1979. Similarly, the Conservative defeat in the February 1974 Election was not due to the three-day working week the Government had introduced as a tactic to beat the miners – indeed, nationalisation and industrial relations issues failed to make much impact on the great majority of the electorate. Rather it was the longer-term overall impression the party had made in relation to economic affairs that counted. Both the Conservative promises to reduce prices in 1970 and to cut taxes in 1979, and the Labour promise in 1974 to restrain soaring inflation by the Social Contract with the trade union movement, made important contributions to the parties'

An election count: counting votes at Barnstaple on the night of 28 February/1 March 1974 – Jeremy Thorpe holds his North Devon seat with an 11 000 majority

respective successes. In 1983 defence and unemployment were major issues, in a way they had not been before in the post-war period. Unemployment was named as the most acute problem facing the country by 72 per cent of the electorate.

The way policies are formulated and then transmitted to the electorate is well practised – a fact which, it might be argued, contributes to the stability of voting behaviour, (although that stability has been seriously questioned by recent general election results). In 1969 Butler and Stokes estimated that only 10 per cent of Conservative and Labour voters made up their mind during the actual election campaign – although for Liberal voters the figure was 34 per cent.

Party Leaders

In the last two decades the growing political use of television has given added immediacy to party leadership. Macmillan appeared skilful at using television and at projecting a general image ('Supermac') through the press. However, this lent only marginal weight to the electoral success that the Conservatives were enjoying at the time for economic reasons. Similarly, Wilson's style of leadership in the late 1960s added a little more difficulty to an already difficult political situation – rather as Sir Alec Douglas-Home's position, after his marginal defeat in 1964, was not aided by poor television appearances. The impact of party leadership may be distinctly less marked than that of the candidates in the USA's presidential races; or indeed than that of the leaders of developing Third World countries, where fostering a sense of national identity through a party leader may take a high priority (for example, with Kenyatta in Kenya and Ne Win in Burma).

Mr Heath's poor standing in public opinion polls did not prevent the considerable increase in Conservative support in 1967–70 which was shown in parliamentary by-elections. It is true that his general lack of political charisma contributed to the crisis in his leadership in 1975 – when, after a series of internal ballots within the parliamentary Conservative Party, he was replaced by Mrs Thatcher – and in the long term affected his party's morale; but it hardly changed the electorate's voting behaviour. Conversely, surveys during the 1979 General Election campaign consistently showed that the electorate thought more highly of Mr Callaghan as a political leader than Mrs Thatcher, yet that did not prevent his Government being decisively rejected at the polls. However, since 1979 Mrs Thatcher's apparently presidential style of premiership has become something of a political phenomenon.

> 'The question which remains moot is whether she has communicated a vision which enough people identify with. Clearly there would be wide support for one aspect of this which David Howell picked out: "She is the anti-bureaucrat in an age of bureaucracy." If Sir Alan Walters, her former economic adviser, is right, the Britain she would like to see may have some attractions: "It's based on solid family moral values . . . an idealised Victorian Society where people did do a great deal of voluntary work for the community, and people were very up-right and honest."'

Hugo Young,
The Listener,
6 June 1985

313

But the picture is harsher than that. Michael Meacher said she wanted a society "in which the rich are cosseted and the poor are penalised, and competitiveness is exalted without any regard for the losers". Jim Prior rather agreed: "The Conservative Party doesn't seem to realise that most of us are ordinary people and we don't aspire to greatness." Roy Jenkins coined a nice epigram which encompasses both her distinctive virtue and its limitations as a tool of political persuasion: "There are some fields in which valour is a great thing, but management of the economy is not one of them."

My interlocuters had little doubt that Mrs Thatcher has changed Britain. Most thought she would leave a permanent mark, for better or worse. What nobody any longer can be sure of is whether she will persuade the British that they must permanently change themselves, From sceptical allies like Sir John Hoskyns, her former policy adviser, to dedicated antagonists like Francis Pym, this is now the message: she has had a long time to show what she can do – the reckoning is at hand.'

'Another large dose and you'll soon be better' *Sunday People,* 22 May 1983

In this context party leadership is probably most important for minority parties, not least the SDP and the Liberals. Jo Grimond's very individual style, and general electoral appeal, must have considerably helped the Liberal Party in its 1962–3 revival. And indeed Jeremy Thorpe's public image was important in the General Elections of 1974 (especially February 1974), although his leadership ended amid scandal in 1976. 'What is beyond doubt is the important boost Thorpe's personal appeal gave to the Liberals. Unlike Heath and Wilson, Thorpe was always more popular than the party he led.' Mr Steel was consistently the most popular leader in the 1983 Election, more popular even than Roy Jenkins, the leader of the SDP and Alliance Prime Minister-designate. Yet as Professor Crewe said:

I. Crewe, B. Särlvik and J. Alt, *New Society*, 12 September 1974

> 'Sifting through the mounds of data, however, one is struck by the way leaders mattered less than policy. The distance between Labour loyalists and Labour defectors was greater on all ten issues in our survey – even on health and unemployment – than on the question of who would make best, or worst, Prime Minister. For example, on the overall, underlying, election issue of which party was more likely to create prosperity, Labour was picked by 83% of its loyalists but a mere 5% of its defectors. The election result turned on issues, on the Government's record, and the opposition's policies, not on Margaret Thatcher's resolve or Michael Foot's walking-stick.'

The Guardian, 14 June 1983

Trade Unions

A further reinforcing agency in the socialisation process is the trade union movement, especially where closed shop agreements operate, although closed shop practices have been in decline over the past few years on account of the pace of technological change and the provisions of the Employment Acts 1980 and 1982. On the 1969 estimates that Butler and Stokes produced, it appeared that in 1964, for example, Labour won some 80 per cent of those votes cast for the major parties by workers in industries where union membership was compulsory. Important traditions live on in mining, shipbuilding, the docks, printing and to a lesser extent the railways. Until recently, there existed a pattern of hereditary recruitment in those industries, and a sense of belonging, of an *esprit de corps,* which was marginally reinforced by memories of the inter-war period; but economic change in all those industries has broken up established patterns.

Thus historical ties will be markedly less influential in the 1980s and 1990s as all those industries become less labour-intensive. Despite the gradual weakening of class alignments, a highly unionised working environment will increase political awareness and indeed activity; but, where union membership is optional, recruitment to the party will be based on existing support of Labour, which is not necessarily stronger than the average in non-union families. Indeed the General Elections of 1979 and 1983 showed that the Conservatives had attracted the votes of a large number of trade unionists. Indeed in 1983 more trade unionists than non-trade unionists voted for the Government. In 1984 the Conservative Government passed legislation which compels trade unions to hold a secret ballot to determine whether their members wish to continue paying a political levy (invariably to the Labour Party). Up to the end of 1986 all such trade unionists had, by a majority, voted for such a levy.

The Media

The influence of the mass media is also generally held to be a reinforcing factor, strengthening voting behaviour that has already been pre-determined by other factors. Again the situation varies from one country to another: in France and the United Kingdom newspapers and television tend to underline voters' prior partisan commitments. But in the USA the position is rather different: its stronger tradition of investigative journalism was dramatically illustrated by the role of *The Washington Post* and *The New York Times* in the fall of President Nixon in 1974. (British newspapers are in any case greatly affected by the *sub-judice* rule, which prevents their reporting on judicial cases pending.) Moreover, American television has little of the careful impartiality of the BBC and IBA. The Liberal and Labour parties, however, have long complained of the Conservative domination of the press. The flirtation of *The Times,* under the editorship of William Rees-Mogg, with the Liberal Party in 1973, and the shift by *The Guardian* from a largely Labour position to a more Liberal one, may have made minor contributions to the Liberals' electoral success in 1974; but they do not appear to have had any lasting effect. Bearing in mind the circulation figures of both those 'quality' newspapers, that is not surprising.

Butler and Stokes have remarked that the press may be just a little more important in forming the opinions of voters whose parents' political allegiance was mixed or relatively weak. But the role of the British press can be almost discounted in comparison with, say, that of *Pravda* or *Izvestia* in the USSR. Conversely, too, it is doubtful whether a party leader being at war with the press (as, for example, Macmillan was at the time of the Vassall spy scandal and Profumo affair in 1962–3) makes the slightest difference to voting intentions. As Butler and Stokes comment, 'a great deal of common information flows out to the mass British electorate through media which are heavily overlapping and which are describing political issues and events that they have seldom done anything to shape.'

This, of course, applies particularly to television and radio, which unlike newspapers are politically neutral. Television and radio merely make political information more readily available. That does not mean, however, that politicians can ignore these two media; intense competition still exists to appear on them, and politicians must adapt constantly in order to project themselves and their parties as agreeably and attractively as possible. And it is probable that a third party – such as the Liberals – will benefit from television exposure in the run-up to an election.

But other minority parties, such as the Scottish Nationalists and Plaid Cymru, argue that they are very harshly treated by the broadcasting authorities. In particular, Plaid Cymru claims to have suffered from the absence of a solely Welsh television channel, a problem supposedly now rectified by the introduction in 1982 of S4C (the variant of Channel 4 in Wales).

Nationalism and Unionism

Two remaining factors in political socialisation deserve to be mentioned. The first is virtually new, namely nationalism. Nationalism has not been an electoral factor for most of this century (apart from the particular problems of Ireland, which, reflected in the composition of the House of Commons, have been present in one form or another since the 1860s). Both it and unionism have cut across traditional party and class lines – to produce 11 Ulster Unionists in the February 1974 Parliament, and three Plaid Cymru and 11 Scottish Nationalist members in

October 1974. (Unionism is included here for convenience, but to most Ulster Protestants 'the nationalists' are Catholic Republicans. But the minority of Protestants who talk of an independent Ulster state could also be classed as nationalists in English eyes, although a very different kind from republicans.) The very nature of nationalist parties tends to disguise the left- or right-wing bias of their supporters and, more to the point, of their activists; to some extent it also disguises their followers' class origins. What remains to be assessed is the voting strength of the nationalist parties after immediate objectives have been achieved (even if long term aims remain). But at any rate British and English voting behaviour are no longer synonymous. Nationalism and the devolution question are examined in more detail in Chapter 7.

Youth Culture

This factor is also difficult to quantify, but it is arguable that any discussion of political socialisation should take account of a separate, if not entirely definable sub-culture of youth. Youth does not of itself persuade people to vote in one particular direction; it cannot be equated with Labour sympathies or 'leftwardness'. Given the importance of family and class, youth movements will largely reflect parental influences.

However, sometimes the politics of the young have had a special quality of their own, especially when reflected by those (albeit few in number) who participate in political youth movements.

Such a generalisation, though, can be very suspect; youth involvement is cyclical. In 1968 there occurred formidable youth protest movements on an international scale, for example the student riots in France, the continual demonstrations in the USA about the Vietnam war. Yet the Young Liberal movement has rapidly declined from being, in the mid-1960s, a potent force, while the Young Conservatives by the early 1970s had retreated, relatively speaking, into concentrating upon the London area, part of a long-term decline since 1950. Peter Hain, the Young Liberal leader in the late 1960s and early 1970s, once claimed that the rejection of party politics by the young was a rejection of its style. But, 'does Hain's performance', one survey asked, 'suggest that the young have a special power to transform politics? That youth politics are, in some way, different in kind from middle-aged or old politics? The weight of psephological evidence is against this. As Butler and Stokes have shown, young voters are unlikely to change voting patterns. They will vote traditionally; with their parents' vote rather than against it.'

D. White,
New Society,
29 March 1973

1983 and Beyond

We might conclude, therefore, that by the time the typical British voter reaches his twenties the pressures of class, kinship and family, possibly reinforced by those of school and work, have set him on a voting course from which it will be increasingly

317

hard to deflect him as time passes by. He may change his vote occasionally in the course of a lifetime, particularly in difficult economic circumstances, and he may try a minority party, perhaps the Liberals, especially if the chance occurs to cast a protest vote in a by-election, rather than in a general election. But, on the whole, the chances of radically altering the voting behaviour of the great majority of Britons are slight indeed. That conclusion, however, would now be faulty, certainly since 1979, if not since 1974. In the 1974 General Elections the Liberals gained nearly a fifth of the total votes cast and in the February election the Conservatives won more votes but fewer seats than Labour. In 1979 the Conservatives won comfortably, although the Liberals fell back somewhat. But by 1983, although Mrs Thatcher won a landslide victory (a 144-seat majority), the total Conservative vote fell a couple of percentage points while the Liberal/SDP Alliance was only a couple of percentage points behind Labour, which achieved its worst result since 1918 (or relative to the number of seats fought the worst since the Party was founded in 1900). It was very clear that while Mrs Thatcher had done well to retain the vote of the skilled working class in the face of mass unemployment, her 'victory' was because the anti-Tory vote was almost equally split between the Labour Party, originally an informal coalition of several political groups, and the Alliance, a formal coalition between a historic party and a newcomer.

A word should be said here about the 1983 General Election in particular. The Conservatives won it resoundingly, and the Alliance did so well in terms of votes cast, if not seats won, because of the mess Labour found itself in. Since it had lost the General Election in 1979 the Labour Party had spent a long time arguing among itself – over the ideological drift towards the Left, and the constitutional position of 'extreme' left groups within the Party – notably Militant, over the compulsory reselection procedure to which Labour MPs had to submit themselves before a general election (the Labour Conference voted for this in 1980), over whether policy-making should be the sole prerogative of the Conference and the National Executive Committee, and in that regard whether the NEC alone should draw up the election manifesto rather than jointly with the Parliamentary Labour Party (Conference voted for this change in 1979 but reversed it in 1980), and over who elected the Party Leader. On the latter point the Conference in 1980 decided on change and this led to the special Wembley Conference in 1981 which established an Electoral College for electing the Party Leader and Deputy Leader, as outlined in the previous chapter. Wembley was the straw that broke the camel's back: it led to the 'Gang of Four' establishing the SDP. Mr Foot, however, had already replaced Mr Callaghan – who appeared to have given up the struggle – under the old rules. Yet although Mr Callaghan had lost the 1979 Election his political standing in the country was high.

If party leadership does matter in terms of elections, then Mr Foot lacked political sex-appeal. In particular he, like Sir Alec Douglas-Home some 20 years before, but probably more so, had not adapted to the television age and his lengthy and vague replies in key interviews did little to convince the electorate that he was of prime ministerial mettle. Yet in the opinion polls Mrs Thatcher in 1981 was shown to be one of the most unpopular Premiers since 1945. But the Falklands War of 1982 changed all that: indeed the Falklands victory was the great unspoken issue of the 1983 campaign.

'The Gang of Four': the founders of the SDP at the launch of the Social Democratic Party in March 1981. (From left to right) Roy Jenkins, David Owen, William Rogers and Shirley Williams

Thus the economic difficulties notwithstanding, the Labour Party remained divided and misjudged the electorate's mood on key issues, such as its non-nuclear defence programme, withdrawal from the EEC, nationalisation, the promises to reduce unemployment quickly, and its opposition to the Conservative 'right to buy' housing programme for public sector tenants. The SDP's fortunes, and those of the Liberals, also fluctuated between 1981–3. So, the Conservative victory of 1983 was not so much a landslide as one that reflected the increasing volatility of the electorate and growing middle-class aspirations among skilled workers in particular. Such features of electoral change have been well documented in two recent major studies of voting behaviour. First, Himmelweit *et al.:*

> 'In our sample, we were looking at the beginning of the men's voting careers, while in the Butler and Stokes panel the elections sampled occurred at different stages on the voting history of the men and women concerned. Even allowing for one abstention, over only four, let alone six elections, voting for the same party throughout was the exception not the rule. The majority were floating voters who had a preferred party to which they returned or from which they deviated, but when and how varied across elections and across individuals. This variation proved so great that the attempt at fine grouping on the basis of the voting history of the respondents, taking account of quantitative, qualitative and chronological aspects, had to be abandoned, as there were so many idiosyncratic pathways. Habit had some effect in that the voter was more likely to vote for a party for which he had voted before, but the consequence of such 'rootedness' or habit was limited and must not be exaggerated. Age made no

319

apparent difference; older people were as volatile as the younger voters and women just as volatile as men.

What markedly distinguished the floating from the confirmed voter in both studies was not apathy, as has been suggested, but their weaker identification with, and liking for, their own party and their attitudes towards the other parties.'

Indeed, some so-called apathetic voters may be highly mature electors, finding it difficult to reconcile themselves to many of the choices offered by the three main parties. Himmelweit continued:

'All the evidence, then, points in favour of a positive decision to move away from a party rather than to a deviation due to apathy leading to a random selection of an alternative party. It has been the practice of pollsters to take recall of vote as an accurate statement of vote cast in previous elections but our data show the size of the error to be considerable. Because errors are not random, but biassed in favour of constituency, they lead to an overestimate of the faithful, especially of the faithful for the two major parties.

The fact that these days floating voters are so numerous, that the consistent voter can so easily become a floating voter, and that the potentially floating voter makes up his or her mind late, puts a particular burden on the election campaign. It may also account for the ever increasing swings in the polls when these are carried out at different stages of a campaign. If fewer voters establish the habit of voting for one party and volatility increases still further, it will place an increasing burden on the timing and conduct of the election campaign.'

However, Himmelweit *et al.*, did warn about certain weaknesses in the nature of Liberal support. They noted that in 1983 only half of the Alliance voters identified themselves with the Alliance (compared with about 85 per cent of both Labour and Conservative voters who identified with their parties) and as many as 33 per cent, while voting for the Alliance, still saw themselves as either Labour or Conservative supporters.

H. Himmelweit,
P. Humphreys and
M. Jaeger, *How
Voters Decide*,
2nd edn., Open
University, 1985,
pp. 46–7, 164–5,
171–2

'Compared with the Conservative and Labour voters, more Liberals voted for the Liberals than identified with it. In 1974, only 42% of our Liberal voters saw themselves as Liberals compared with 74% of Labour and 87% of Conservatives who identified with their parties. Alt *et al.* (1977), analysing the views of the 394 Liberals in their sample, report much the same results for February 1974. Only half the Liberal voters (53%) saw themselves as Liberals compared with 88% of Conservative and 90% of Labour voters who identified with their respective parties. Enthusiastic identification was even rarer, only 14% of the Liberal voters compared with over twice that number among Conservative and Labour voters. Nor was the voter's decision to vote Liberal one of long standing. Only one out of three Liberal voters compared with three out of four Conservative or Labour voters had decided to vote for their party 'a long time ago'.

Even more pertinent were the Liberals' reactions when asked which party they thought would be best at handling particular problems[1]. While the majority of Labour and Conservative voters judged their own party to be best, there was not

[1]The problems referred to were the Common Market, legal control of wages, influence of communists in the trade unions, nationalization and social services.

a single issue on which the Liberal voters preferred the Liberal party. For some issues, they preferred the Conservatives and for others the Labour party. Even amongst the few who had voted Liberal in 1970 as well as in 1974, less than half chose their own party.

Nor was the picture any different in 1979. The Liberal voters did not consider their own party to be best at handling the major problems like inflation, taxation, unemployment, industrial relations or law and order. In 1979 Labour voters were less sure of the superiority of their own party compared with 1974, but, by comparison with the Liberals, they were their party's staunch supporters (Butler and Kavanagh, 1980).

Taken all in all, there is little evidence of a love match between the Liberal voters and the Liberal party, whether in the euphoric climate of the 1974 election or in 1970[2]; more a marriage of convenience.

So far we have considered a variety of factors which explain the special volatility of the Liberal vote. But such volatility does not necessarily mean that an individual who chooses to vote Liberal once, or even twice, might not do so because he has a distinctive set of attitudes which attract him or her, however, fleetingly, to the Liberal party. If so, even though the Liberal voters in one election are not the same individuals in another, they might still share a common set of attitudes and an outlook that would differentiate them from the voters for the two other parties.

Political scientists have tended to dismiss such volatility as short-term fluctuations around a stable party identification. But neither short-term fluctuations nor Butler and Stokes' (1969) concept of homing continue to have much meaning. Fluctuations from what stable pattern? Homing to what nest? Even Casanova returned to the same woman on more than one occasion, but no one would call him either a 'homing' husband or a faithful lover. While the majority of voters still voted for one party more than any other, they varied as to the elections at which they deviated and whether they deviated by abstaining or voting for another party. There is every sign that volatility is here to stay and will increase rather than diminish, not least because the parents of the next generation will provide fewer consistent cues compared with former times. It would be [now] more accurate in the 1980s to describe Labour as a party of a segment of the working class, the segment that is engaged in the declining heavy manufacturing industries in the North and in Scotland.

An increase in the Liberal vote is more likely when:

1 The two main parties indulge in mud slinging and stridency, particularly in the last few days of the election.

2 The Liberals refrain from attacking the main parties on issues which might alienate potential supporters who, as we showed earlier, still hold many of the views of the party from which they intend to defect. That is when the Liberal party remains low key, presenting itself in terms of a general approach rather than in terms of specific proposals. This makes it easier for voters from different parties to project onto the Liberals those features they would wish their own

[2]In 1970 Butler and Stokes found only 25% of Liberal voters willing to identify with the Liberal Party.

party to have, without becoming aware that this choice implies foregoing others which they value.

3 The Liberals emphasize their readiness to collaborate on broad strategy or on specific issues with either Labour or Conservatives. This permits each voter – ex-Labour or ex-Conservative – to think that by voting Liberal he will not desert his own party's policy but add to it a much needed flexibility, since it is the party's rigidity which he or she dislikes.

4 As election day approaches, public opinion polls reflect a rise, or at least not a decline, in the members intending to vote Liberal. This signals to the potential Liberal voter that he is one of many and so reduces his anxiety about a wasted vote, especially important since our studies have shown that Liberals and abstainers make up their minds much later than other voters.

5 The constituency is marginal. The voter's belief that the Liberal candidate has a good chance is important and this may well be affected not only by the opinion polls but also by the level of activity of the candidate and the local party, especially in the last crucial days before the election.'

B. Särlvik and I. Crewe, *Decade of dealignment*, Cambridge, 1983, p. 344

Särlvik and Crewe observe as follows:

'Partisan realignments are only facilitated by significant electoral change. They are created and consolidated by the use politicians make of their newly won support. A breakthrough by the Alliance would only crack the two-party mould. Its leaders could not necessarily secure proportional representation. Even if they did, support at subsequent elections, when they were judged as a party of government not opposition, would not necessarily be enough to create a new multi-party mould in which it held a strategic position. Moreover, multi-party systems are not always conducive to the spirit of consensus-seeking and to the stable, pragmatic, innovatory and adaptable governments sought by the Alliance. Experience shows that multi-party systems which preclude enduring, cohesive majorities in a parliament can be far from desirable. Policies may come to be created in order to sustain a government in office rather than the reverse; and the centre, instead of being a fulcrum of constructive stability, can turn into a deadlock of inertia, the scene of directionless compromise. Moreover, the feasibility of one or other major party forming a stable coalition government with the centre depends not only on the parliamentary strength of the parties, but on the readiness of their leaders and backbenchers to play the new rules, and accept the unfamiliar ethos, of the coalition "game". Thus the prospects for a beneficial as well as permanent change in the party system rest as much on the actions of politicians as on the votes of the electorate. That the 1980s, like the 1970s, will be a decade of dealignment seems fairly certain. Whether it will also be a decade of realignment, and if so a realignment which improves the quality of British government, remains to be seen.'

See also: R. Pinkney, 'Dealignment, Realignment or just Alignment? A Mid-Term Report', *Parliamentary Affairs*, January 1986

A.A. Halsey, *New Society*, 17 March 1983

The Gallup, MORI and Essex University British Election Surveys in 1979 showed the extent of the working-class flight from Labour: 52 per cent of manual workers and their wives voted for non-Labour candidates; in the 1979 Election Labour's share was already the lowest (at 36.9 per cent) since 1931. The percentage of Labour partisans with a very strong identification had fallen from 45 per cent to 27 per cent between 1964 and 1979.

'The swing to the Conservatives was 6.5% among semi-skilled and unskilled workers, 7% among trade unionists, 11% among skilled workers, and as much as 21% among the proletarian newcomers to the electoral rolls – the 18–24 year old manual workers.'

In 1983, the Labour vote, said Professor Crewe, held up best – although still not very well – among council tenants, blacks and the over 65s.

'But there is scant comfort for Labour here. Council tenants are a slowly diminishing group; blacks are a tiny minority; and the over 65s will rapidly depart from the electorate.'

The Guardian,
13 June 1983,
30 April 1984

'The clearest message for the Labour Party [is]: to win an election it needs to capture much more than the industrial working-class heartlands of Scotland, the North and South Wales. By the end of the decade the industrial seat will come to represent as clear a minority interest as agricultural seats did between the wars.'

A further recent study by Heath, Jowell and Curtice (1985) returns to social class investigations in the manner of Butler and Stokes. While emphasising that social class is alive and well, in some contrast to Särlvik and Crewe, the researchers have found that there has occurred a major change in the class structure. In 1983 manual workers accounted for over half Labour's votes (about half the working class voted thus). But the 'salariat' (the managers, administrators and professional classes) had risen to 27 per cent of the electorate – approximately one-third of them voting Alliance (accounting for about one-third also of the Alliance's votes). Support for the Alliance was strongest among those who favoured a mixed economy, the welfare state, civil liberties and 'internationalism'.

The research of Heath *et al.*, concentrating upon the 1983 General Election, emphasised that both the Conservatives and the Alliance drew their support almost evenly from across the classes, while Labour remained a 'much more obviously working-class party . . . a party of the subordinate'. This study played down the Labour 'credibility gap' in 1983, although this was not 'to deny that disunity damaged Labour.' In many ways the gulf between Labour and Conservatives was opened up by the latter: the Tory manifestos of 1979 and 1983 were no more radical than Mr Heath's in 1970; Thatcherism, argue Heath, Jowell and Curtice, was a reincarnation of Selsdon Man.

A. Heath, R. Jowell
and J. Curtice,
*How Britain
Votes,*
Pergamon, 1985,
p. 147

'Mr Heath had long argued for the extension of market forces and the reduction of State interference in the economy. But when unemployment began to rise in 1972 the Heath government decided to change course from a non-interventionist policy to one of wage and price controls, along the lines of previous Labour policies. By 1983, however, Mrs Thatcher had demonstrated her unwillingness to change course as her predecessor had done. . . . The Falklands War established this reputation most powerfully.'

Into the widening gulf between the two main parties stepped the Alliance. While the Alliance was far more of a challenge to Labour and Conservative than the Liberal Party had been earlier, Heath *et al.*, like Himmelweit and Särlvik–Crewe, emphasised that it was the Alliance vote which was the most vulnerable in future campaigns.

323

The volatility of the British electorate has been apparent since 1974; the loyalties to individual parties have been weakened. But if either the Conservative or Labour Party – or both – shows itself to be pragmatic enough to attune to the wishes of the majority, as in the past, the electoral outlook for the third parties might be bleak indeed. That supposition, however, assumes no further deterioration in the economic performance of the nation; a big assumption indeed.

DOCUMENT

31

Voting Behaviour in the 1980s

The task for each party during the 1980s is, of course, different; in the case of the Conservatives it is to hold onto those voters who moved over from Labour; in the case of Labour it is to seek their return and to recruit the first time voters of whom the majority had voted Labour before 1979, and for the SDP/Liberal Alliance to draw in the same first-time voters and also the dissatisfied voters from the two main parties.

The fate of all the parties depends largely on the economic situation and on the degree of strife or harmony in the society, but none more so than the *Conservatives'*. As was discussed earlier, the Conservatives fought the 1979 election around values: a new radicalism which stressed the values of initiative, personal freedom and free enterprise. In 1983, the election was fought on beliefs, on the need to trust the government's direction and competence. That is why the Conservatives' record in office will be so important, given also that re-election for a third term is very rare. There needs to be solid evidence of an upturn in the economy and a reduction in the number of unemployed. A second Falklands factor overriding the effects of continued recession is unlikely to occur.

There are other aspects too which are important. When a particular policy or approach is continued for too long, or pursued too stridently, it may backfire even where initially welcomed. Two such policies initiated by the Conservatives in 1979 fall into this category. The first was the call for reduction in expenditure on welfare services and the second control of the rate of expenditure by local authorities. The impression conveyed was that most of the reduction could be achieved by reducing waste. When real cuts in the services began to make themselves felt in the early 1980s, the public changed their concern about "welfare scroungers" and "spendthrift local authorities" to anxiety about the maintenance of the services themselves. This is why in 1983, 80% said they wanted to preserve the level of the services rather than cut taxes, and was also one of the reasons for the shift in people's views during 1982–1984 about the value of the large metropolitan authorities including the GLC.

The erosion of support for *Labour* during the late 1970s and early 1980s extended beyond lack of approval of its leadership to lack of approval of its programme, ideology and rhetoric. Values and beliefs are involved. This makes the task of revival of such support so difficult. At the level of beliefs, it requires evidence of strong and consistent leadership as well as evidence of the party's ability to work together and agree on a programme of action. Any disagreements will undoubtedly be highlighted and

324

exaggerated by the largely Conservative press and will also be amplified by television.

At the level of values, the Labour party faces two major problems during the 1980s. Unlike the Conservatives whose supporters tend to share a common outlook differing on matters of degree or emphasis, the Labour party contains members who disagree quite fundamentally in their views, not only about the role of the party and that of trade unions in relation to the party, but in their ideology. This disagreement is well illustrated by members' attitudes to the Common Market and the party's attempt in its 1983 election manifesto to arrive at a policy which would encompass these divergent views. To satisfy those who wish to remain in the EEC, the proposal in the manifesto stresses tough negotiation which puts Britain's interests first, and to satisfy those who are opposed to membership it includes the option of withdrawal should the negotiations prove unsatisfactory. "If" statements are neither good for negotiations with the EEC nor for electioneering. Nor are they convincing. On other issues, like defence, the divide is equally wide.

Quite apart from the difficulty of reconciling within the party genuine divergence of views, the party has also to take on board the increased consensus among the electorate for the "middle ground" which in 1984 appears to fall to the right rather than to the left of centre.

Labour fought the 1983 election proposing old remedies and using the old rhetoric associated with these remedies. Regaining support requires working out new specific proposals for particular issues rather than an overarching ideology, and for Labour to convince the public that its objectives are realistic. The claim to be able to effect a large reduction in unemployment which Labour put forward in 1983 did little for the party simply because it was deemed improbable. The party needs to be in closer touch with its potential supporters, especially young voters, to understand better how they see society's problems, how they interpret events, and what they think about possible solutions.

The Labour party might, of course, decide on an alternate strategy and go for an updated, radical approach even if it alienates its supporters, in the hope of attracting young, particularly first-time voters: a risky but perhaps necessary strategy to arrive at a convincing programme of action. Much will depend on whether in the intervening years consensus within society will become less and whether there will be a move away from the right. There are some indications that this is currently beginning to happen (Ashford, 1981; Crewe, 1984).

Of the three parties, the *Alliance's* task is particularly formidable. A new party, it fought its first general election in 1983 with remarkable success. It has inadequate financial backing since it depends primarily on donations from individuals and on the subscriptions of a small number of members. While the Liberals have well established local organizations, the SDP has still to develop theirs. There is also the disadvantage that it is a coalition of two parties with the attendant lack of clarity about how its overall future leadership will be determined. The Alliance's initial campaign built on people's disaffection, on the consensus in the electorate and on the preference for the middle ground to which reference has already been made. It appealed to two sets of values important within British society: a sense of compassion and responsibility for others, wanting liberal rather than repressive solutions, and a preference for pragmatism, as opposed to the rigid, doctrinaire economic ideology of either left or right. But this may also be the Alliance's electoral weakness – it can too easily look as if it wants to be all things to all men, borrowing the policies from left and right, scaling them down and calling them Alliance policies. In the 1960s and 1970s the Liberals had no pretensions about forming a government and so could speak in general terms, offering a convenient resting ground for those disillusioned with the major parties. But the Alliance's hopes are set higher, asking the electorate to consider the party as a potential government. To succeed, their policies (or the packaging of their policies) has to be seen as both distinct from, and more attractive than those offered by either of the other two parties.

The Alliance's campaign, like Labour's, has to be directed at both values and beliefs but with the added task of convincing those inclined to vote for the Alliance that their vote will not be a wasted vote. This is why the emphasis on a change to proportional representation is central to any Alliance campaign. But a massive and extended educational campaign would be needed to bring home to the electorate how inadequately the views of Alliance voters are represented in Parliament given the existing first-past-the-post electoral system. After the 1983 election campaign, 51% of the voters still did not know that the Alliance was in favour of proportional representation (Worcester, 1983); probably few know what proportional representation is. Nor does the electorate fully appreciate that it is not in the interest of the major parties to change the system from which they benefit so much and that therefore the only way to achieve electoral reform is to succeed in strengthening the Alliance share of the vote in such a way that a hung Parliament results with the Alliance holding the balance of power. Under those conditions the Alliance could make electoral reform a precondition of giving its support to one or other of the parties which need it to form a government.

This is, of course, easier said than done given that the Alliance, unlike the major parties, has no regional or social base. On the other hand, the opportunity to create a climate of opinion favourable to change in the electoral system has been strengthened by the results of the 1983 general and the 1984 European elections, each of which highlighted to an unusual degree how little the actual pattern of the public's choices was reflected in the composition of the parliament that was elected.

H.T. Himmelweit, P. Humphreys, M. Jaeger, *How Voters Decide*, 2nd edn., Open University, 1985

32

The Outcome of the 1983 Election

The Conservatives had undoubtedly won a famous victory in 1979. They gained over two million more votes than Labour and enjoyed the largest swing between the two parties recorded since the war – 5.2%. But was it a turning point? Did the election have a longer term significance for the agenda of British politics? The sceptic could point to the Conservative party's share of the vote, 43.9%, which only matched the party's average for post-war general elections; the proportion of voters who still identified with the party had continued to decline – though not as sharply as in the case of the Labour party. It was possible that the context and scale of Labour's defeat disguised the nature of the Conservative victory. Surveys suggested that the election was not a clear mandate for a break with post-war political collectivism: the public continued to welcome the role of the welfare and interventionist state. Many of the 'switchers' to the Conservative party did so because they were attracted by the prospect of lower income tax. Moreover, Labour had been remarkably unsuccessful in 1979 in attracting support for its programme. On six out of eight contentious issues in that election – unemployment, industrial relations, wages, nationalisation, social services, race relations, taxes and the European community – the Conservatives were more representative than Labour of the views of the electorate and also of the working class.

There was some survey evidence to back the proposition that 'Britain is turning right'. The economic recession and unemployment were not radicalising the public. There were criticisms of high levels of taxation and waste in the welfare state. Within the Conservative party and beyond there was concern at the increasingly high cost of existing policies, particularly at a time of no economic growth. Mrs Thatcher led the chorus of complaint against bureaucracy, taxation, and public expenditure. The party's manifesto in 1979 had stated,

> The balance of our society has been increasingly tilted in favour of the State at the expense of individual freedom . . . this election may be the last chance we have to reverse that process.

Yet, there was a paradox. In wanting to undo so many features of the collectivist status quo and reduce the scale of government, the Conservative government found itself having to interfere. Nowhere was this more apparent than in Mr Heseltine's empire at the Department of the Environment. He took measures to force local authorities to sell council houses; he limited their rate rises and he countermanded their spending plans. Similar action was also needed in the field of privatisation: to sell Britoil the government had first to get control of it. The Conservative government was using interventionist means to achieve allegedly non-interventionist goals.

Terms like left and right are not very useful to describe the thinking of the electorate: most do not consider politics in structured or ideological terms. But a majority of people are able to identify correctly the Labour and Conservative parties with the left and right on a political spectrum. A Gallup survey in January 1983 found that 48% of respondents placed themselves on the right, 24% on the left, with 11% in the middle and 19% don't knows. Such information did make sense when related to the unpopularity of many of Labour's actual policies. Yet the welfare state was still popular and Mrs Thatcher frequently proclaimed that the National Health Service was safe in her hands. Over the lifetime of the 1979 parliament, surveys found a reduction in the proportion of voters favouring cuts in taxes and cuts in social programmes. In 1983, 49% of the Gallup sample favoured more spending on the welfare state even if it meant more taxes, while only 23% favoured welfare cuts as a way of lowering taxation.

Social class, another factor which had stabilised the two-party system, continued to weaken. As social structure became 'looser', so Britain became less two-party and two-class. Between 1964 and 1979 manual workers declined from 65% to 56% as a proportion of the work force: by 1983 the figure had fallen to a 50%. Class consciousness was also low: the Essex election study of 1979 indicated that less than half of British voters gave themselves a class identity and only 39% of manual workers called themselves 'working class'. The working class became more fragmented, socially and politically. The spread 327 of home ownership, including council house sales, meant that by 1983 60% of households were privately owned. The working class was evenly divided between those who owned their own homes and those who were council tenants. The spread of other symbols of affluence besides housing – for example, cars and telephones – also weakened working class attachment to the Labour party. Research in 1979 showed that wage-earners who possessed any of these were more likely to vote Conservative than Labour. The leakage of working class support from the Labour party was marked in 1979, when Labour won no more than 45% of the C2/DE vote, compared with 38% for the Conservative party. But there were also some middle class defections from the Conservatives; little more than half of British voters actually voted for the party of their 'natural' class in 1979.

At the same time a sharper geographical distribution of electoral support was developing. The emergence of the 'two Britains', the Conservative south versus the Labour north, was part of a trend which had been going on for twenty years. The Labour party held 36% of English seats in the South and Midlands in 1955; with a very similar total representation in 1979 it held only 27%. Selective class patterns of migration as between north and south, between inner cities and suburbs, and between rural and urban seats accentuated the trends. Of the 100 seats which had the highest rate of unemployment in 1981 the Conservatives held only one. Of the 100 seats which had the lowest rate, Labour held none. The two main parties were probably less able to represent and aggregate the diversity of interests throughout the United Kingdom than at any period since 1918.

There was also much discussion of the abandonment of the post-war political consensus. Changes in social class, in political values and mood, and in the internal dynamics of the two main political parties all helped to accelerate a growing polarisation between them.

Certainly, the advances of Mrs Thatcher on one side and of Mr Foot and Mr Benn on the other were a response by the Conservative and Labour parties to the alleged failures of earlier governments. They also represented the retreat in both parties of formerly dominant groups – in the Conservatives of the 'wets', who favoured a reflation of the economy to boost employment, and the original *One Nation* group, who emphasised social welfare, and in the Labour party of the social democratic revisionists. The two main parties were further apart in their policies and rhetoric than at any time since 1950. But surveys showed that most Conservative and Labour voters, as well as Liberal and SDP supporters, agreed on most issues. It was this 'middle ground' abandoned by the two main parties for much of the Parliament that the Alliance hoped to seize.

Mrs Thatcher certainly did not see herself as a consensus politician. She challenged many of the operating ideas and clichés of the post-war consensus style of political management. Her Conservative predecessors had been accommodating and defensive: they thought it politically necessary to maintain the welfare state and high levels of public expenditure, and to appease the trade unions; she supported individualism, thrift, and self-reliance, and regarded the operation of the free market as not only more efficient but also as morally superior to state socialism. She was not internationalist and not 'communautaire' as EEC ministers discovered. Vernon Bogdanor has noted how she tapped populist and anti-establishment sentiments, not least among the working class.

D. Butler and D. Kavanagh, *The British General Election of 1983,* Macmillan, 1984

Questions

1. Explain the causes and effects of the declining support for the Labour and Conservative parties.

2. Consider the theory of the mandate in relation to the Conservative victories in 1979 and 1983 and show how the government has used this theory in practice. (Joint Matriculation Board)

3. How important is social class in the determination of voting behaviour? (London)

4. How meaningful is the concept of the 'floating voters'?

12 Voting Trends and Electoral Systems

'Four years after she had been elected, all doubt had been erased; no one had any remaining illusion that the lady was for turning. She could only go forward. There appeared to be no one and nothing strong enough to stop her.'

The Times Guide to the House of Commons, 1983

The Results of Political Socialisation

The election campaign rituals

Parliamentary candidates invariably endure a gruelling three weeks or so during a general election campaign, spent on tasks which may sometimes seem totally irrelevant to the real needs of democracy:

The Guardian,
4 June 1970

'Mr Godber interests them in Law and Order. "Are you going to do anything about the BBC?" a questioner asks, finding much of its output full of left-wing bias and "fit for the sewer." On the other hand, a distinctly unhippie young woman pours scorn on this law and order kick, and calls them "weasel words". The candidate soothes them both.'

Not very average voters, rather individual members of the electorate may corner a candidate's time (and patience); but the 'democratic' processes must be preserved – for every politician knows that a small shift in voting behaviour can easily replace one government with another, although it must be said that the 1983 results suggest it will be difficult to dislodge Mrs Thatcher next time. That small shift depends upon the material interests of certain sections of the community; as we have seen, it does not depend particularly upon styles of party leadership, and it is doubtful even if the Thatcher/Foot contest in 1983 was an exception to this 'rule'. (In the USA, by contrast, shifts towards the Democrats or Republicans can depend upon the personal appeal of presidential candidates: compare the landslide win of Johnson over Goldwater in 1964 – completely reversed, in party terms, by Nixon's win over McGovern in 1972 – with the even battle between Nixon and Kennedy in 1960. Similarly, Reagan's homely, old-world charm did much to defeat Carter in

1980 and Mondale in 1984.) But although materialism may move the voter, he is unlikely to be clear about policy issues. It would appear that only one-seventh of the electorate is particularly interested in politics and capable of fully appreciating concepts like 'left' and 'right'. And at most general elections it is hard to persuade much more than 20 per cent of confirmed voters (important though that 20 per cent is) to behave in a different political manner. However, the biggest unknown factor is knowing what emphasis to place upon 'abstainers' (both new non-voters or ex-abstainers now voting for the first time or after a lapse).

Thus Butler and Stokes observe:

> 'Electoral change is due not to a limited group of "floating" voters but to a very broad segment of British electors . . . (Between 1959 and 1970) the percentage moving between voting and non-voting at times reached a quarter of the electorate and never fell below 18%, while the number moving between parties varied from 8% to 13%. Moving to or from the Liberals was always more prevalent than direct switches between the two main parties. The proportion consistently supporting the same party at the beginning and end of these intervals never rose as high as 60%.'

D. Butler and D. Stokes, *Political Change in Britain*, 2nd edn., Macmillan, 1974, pp. 268, 273

But no less than 30 per cent had moved between voting and abstention when 1959 was compared with 1970. Throughout the period 1959–70 less than 40 per cent of the electorate, it appears, held to 'a constant position', but it is extremely important to realise that the figure includes movements towards and away from abstention. Thus:

> 'in our panel of electors who furnished information for the four elections, 1959, 1964, 1966 and 1970 we found a total of 13 per cent who had at one time or another cast their votes both for the Conservatives and for Labour.'

Stability yet Volatility

The stability of electoral behaviour in the United Kingdom is, nevertheless, fairly striking. It is true that some other countries, such as Norway, have experienced greater electoral stability, but many others have not. France has undergone – since the Second World War, and also before it – considerable changes among its political parties, although remaining fundamentally Conservative (Gaullist) for much of the period. Butler and Stokes have commented that few party systems in the world have had such a settled past as Britain's, and that contemporary history has divided itself neatly into the Conservative–Liberal struggle up to the First World War, the party equilibrium and realignment of the 1920s and 1930s, and the Labour–Conservative domination since 1945 – during which there have been three Labour governments (1945–51, 1964–70 and 1974–9) and three Conservative ones (1951–64, 1970–4 and since 1979). But the last of these observations is, at face value, simplistic. The period since the late 1960s witnessed, firstly, massive swings against the Labour Government in by-elections and local government elections, followed by the growing success of parties other than the main two. In the 1970 General Election Labour's share of the vote was the lowest since 1935, dropping by

D. Butler and D. Stokes, *Political Change in Britain*, Macmillan, 1969, p. 247

Professor Ivor
Crewe, *The
Guardian*,
13 June 1983

a greater amount than any of its defeats during the 1950s, while the Conservative share, although rising, was nowhere near its peak of 1955. In 1979 Labour's share was the lowest since 1931. In 1983 it was the lowest since 1918 at 27.6 per cent. The SDP-Liberal Alliance was not far behind at 25.4 per cent of the total vote. The Conservative share of the vote was 1.5 per cent lower than in 1979 at 42.4 per cent, a figure close to that in 1964 when Labour narrowly won. 'The electorate did not embrace the Conservatives; it rebuffed Labour and flirted with the Alliance.' Of 1979 Conservatives 23 per cent switched and of 1979 Liberals 29 per cent switched, 4 per cent and 9 per cent respectively to Labour. Only 63 per cent of 1979 Labour voters stayed loyal, no less than 22 per cent switching to the SDP-Liberal Alliance (13 per cent to Tories). The result of the movement of votes to and from the Alliance was a swing of 1.4 per cent from Labour to Conservative. For every three Labour voters switching to the Alliance one stayed at home and one voted Tory.

DOCUMENT

33

The Decline of Party Loyalties

In the 1970s, as in earlier years, most citizens eligible to vote in Britain did indeed think of themselves as Conservative, Liberal, or Labour. Yet there is a slow but unmistakable downward trend in the proportion who think in this way. In 1964, 92 per cent of the electorate thought of themselves as supporters of one of the three main parties; that percentage went down by a point or so at most of the following elections, to reach 85 in 1979.

A more significant change, however, has occurred in the proportion of the electorate who considered themselves to be 'very strongly' attached to any of the parties. In the 1960s, and as late as in 1970, such voters made up over 40 per cent of the electorate. In this time-series it becomes apparent that the February 1974 election signalled a crisis of confidence in the established party system from which it has not recovered. At the February 1974 election the percentage of 'very strong' party supporters showed a drastic fall to 29 per cent, and since then it has continued to slide – to 26 per cent in October 1974 and to 21 per cent in May 1979. Almost all of this decline reflects a diminution of strongly committed support to the two major parties. The proportion who are very strong supporters of the Liberal party has always been tiny, although it fell from 4 to 2 per cent of the electorate between 1964 and 1979. In 1964, 40 per cent of electors thought of themselves as 'very strong' Conservative or Labour supporters. By 1979, the proportion had fallen to 19 per cent. They are almost equally divided; both of the major parties must now face the fact that their hard core of supporters . . . has shrunk to a tenth of the electorate.

The table shows, for each election, the percentage of each party's identifiers who said they were 'very strong' supporters of their party.

Generally speaking thought of themselves as:	Percentage 'very strong' of each party's identifiers at the election in					
	1979	October 1974	February 1974	1970	1966	1964
Conservative	24%	27%	32%	51%	49%	48%
Liberal	14%	14%	12%	26%	35%	32%
Labour	29%	36%	41%	47%	50%	51%

Data Source: BES May 1979, October 1974 and February 1974 Election Survey.
Butler and Stokes, Election Surveys 1970, 1966, 1964.

B. Särlvik and I. Crewe, *Decade of dealignment,* Cambridge, 1983

Floating Voters

Changes in voting patterns are made up of several different ingredients. The principal ones are **(a) the replacement of the electorate:** the turnover due to death and coming of age of electors is between 1 and 2 per cent per year; **(b) 'differential turn-out'** – decisions on whether to vote at all, including those of former non-voters now exercising their votes: losing political parties invariably conduct election post-mortems to see how far their particular 'supporters' may have stayed at home; **(c) circulation of minor and nationalist party supporters:** this has usually accounted for only about 1 per cent of the voters, excluding Liberal/ SDP support, although in February 1974 the figure was 5.3 per cent, rising to 6.6 per cent in October 1974 but dropping back to 5.4 per cent in 1979 and 4.6 per cent in 1983; **(d) circulation of SDP/Liberals:** the parties' support is remarkably variable; **(e) straight conversion** – direct change between Labour and Conservative (the 'swing' from one to the other).

The concept of the *'floating'* vote is therefore rather wide, and, as H.V. Wiseman has pointed out, is open to much misinterpretation. Wiseman has emphasised that floating voters form a representative cross-section of the whole electorate – and that they are not a static group, since they are mostly people who have moved or registered for the first time and people who have simply had their party loyalties weakened. Over 80 per cent of the electorate, in most post-war elections, have not changed their vote from the previous election, and in fact changes in political allegiance occur between elections, and not during general election campaigns – which, as indicated above, are largely rituals.

H.V. Wiseman, *Politics in Everyday Life,* Blackwell, 1966, p. 93

One study of the floating vote was based upon the 1951 General Election; it was found that 3 per cent of electors had intended to vote for one major party but had in fact voted for the other, 2 per cent had been undecided whether to vote (a category often exaggerated during press coverage of general elections) but had done so, 8 per cent had intended to vote, and did, but were uncertain which party to favour, and 2 per cent had intended to vote but had not; none had voted despite an

R. Rose (ed.),
*Political Studies
in Britain,*
Macmillan, 1969,
p. 175

intention not to. The total thus came to about 15 per cent of the total electorate. The survey concluded that between 4 per cent and 25 per cent might be classed as 'floating in one sense or another', but it also underlined the difficulty or defining the term. It is also possible to distinguish between an 'upper level' of constantly floating voters and a 'potential' group, that is a 'lower level' of voters who merely 'float' at by-elections, returning to their traditional allegiances at general elections. The revival of the Liberal Party's fortunes in the 1960s and, more particularly, between 1972 and 1974 must be seen largely in that perspective, together with that of the support for the Liberal-SDP Alliance in 1981–3. In 1983 the Alliance did least well among the over 65s (19 per cent of the vote); the older generation is less inclined to 'float', since as seen in the previous chapter partisanship ties become stronger with age. Then there is the semi-popular theory, sometimes canvassed in the press, that the Liberal Party is used as a 'half-way house' by voters switching from Labour to Conservative and vice versa. But this appears to be false: it is more common, as the 1974 General Elections demonstrated, for new Liberal voters either to stay or, very possibly, to return to the party allegiance whence they come. There is plenty of evidence to show that Conservative and Labour voters are perfectly capable of straightforward switching. And, as already mentioned, the personal charisma of Liberal leaders (Mr Grimond in the 1960s and Mr Thorpe in the 1970s and Mr Steel in the 1980s) was worth at least several hundred thousand votes.

B. Särlvik and
I. Crewe,
*Decade of
dealignment,*
Cambridge, 1983,
pp. 58–9 and 46

Särlvik and Crewe, in their 1983 study reached this conclusion:

'Our final exploration of voting pathways from 1970 to 1979 focuses on the longer-term impact of the Liberal surge in 1974. How many of its recruits from the major parties did the Liberal party manage to retain five years later – in the midst of the Thorpe trial and after eighteen months of the Lib-Lab pact? Most of the Liberal party's 1974 recruits had deserted it by 1979. For every ten who moved to the Liberals in either February 1974 or in October 1974, seven had moved away again by 1979. Of those who switched to the Liberal party in February 1974, and stayed with it in October 1974, over half had left by 1979. Indeed, even amongst the "core" of thrice-voting Liberals the attrition rate in 1979 was 30 per cent – higher than amongst their Conservative and Labour counterparts (9 per cent and 21 per cent respectively). This is not to deny that the Liberal party's rise in popularity in 1974 produced some enduring gains, but only to suggest that electoral progress for the Liberals takes the slow and frustrating form of three steps forward, two steps back.

Of those who voted Liberal at both 1974 elections, having voted Conservative in 1970, 38 per cent stayed Liberal and 53 per cent returned to the Conservatives; but of those 1974 double-Liberals who had voted Labour in 1970, 45 per cent stayed Liberal and only 25 per cent returned to Labour. These last sets of figures illustrate a second way in which the Liberal surge in 1974 turned out to hurt Labour more than the Conservatives – at least in 1979. Conservative defectors treated the Liberal party as either a permanent resting place or a turn-round point: they either stayed Liberal in 1979 or, more usually, returned home to the Conservatives. But a substantial minority of Labour defectors opted for a third path, using their 1974 move to the Liberals as neither resting place nor turn-round point, but as half-way house on a journey that brought them over to the Conservative party by 1979.

Despite its promotion in 1974 to the status of a major third party, the Liberals continued to distinguish themselves from their two major rivals, and from the major third party north of the Border, by the rapidity with which they could simultaneously win and lose large segments of the electorate.'

The effect of Liberal intervention will vary from region to region. Although some will give their support simply to encourage the Liberal Party to make a good national showing, tactical considerations will immediately bring the 'wasted vote' argument to the fore. This was apparent in the 1983 General Election, the best result for the Liberals in the post-war period: where they won or nearly won was often due to keeping the same candidate who had worked hard on local issues – or 'community politics' – between general elections and where the Labour vote could be squeezed further (as in Yeovil and Chelmsford). Such considerations have weighed heavily against the Liberals since the 1920s, but elsewhere the argument will work in reverse: in areas such as North Cornwall and North Devon (the former in particular) the Labour percentage has, at times, been squeezed far below that in neighbouring seats because the Liberals have demonstrated (often by trading on the history and tradition of the constituency) that they offer the likeliest means of keeping the Tories out, and that it is not therefore a wasted vote to vote for the Liberal candidate. Thus when in 1974, after the result of the Election on 28 February, when Mr Thorpe visited Mr Heath at Downing Street on 3 March at the Prime Minister's invitation, to talk about coalition tactics, he knew full well that many of his supporters might think he was consorting with the political devil. As one newspaper commentator put it,

'the historical reasons for a Liberal tradition in the West are well enough known, they go back to the days when Chapel (traders and labourers) backed Mr Gladstone, and Church (lordling, retainers and farmers) gave its blessing to Disraeli.'

The Guardian,
9 June 1970

Or, as another article in the same paper said,

'the strength of Liberalism in the South-West is that it has long been wedded to nonconformity. Although the marriage is still strong, some say that the connec-tion is dying. If the old radicals are dying, it must be that in some constituencies the Whig squirearchy necessary to offset the Tory squirearchy is disappearing too.'

The Guardian,
4 May 1970

It did at least appear that in both 1974 Elections the Liberals achieved better results, in terms of second places and seats actually won, in Conservative-held seats, with mediocre results only in strong Labour seats. But, in the 1979 Election, voting patterns in the 11 seats held and three lost by the Liberals showed little con-sistency, although in seven constituencies the Labour vote was squeezed still further. In the 1983 Election the Liberals and SDP were able to squeeze the Labour vote dramatically in the South, but not so much in the Midlands and the North. The disaster of 1983 for Labour was very evident in the South where, outside London, Labour won just three seats and in 151 Tory-held seats it came second in only 18, the Alliance being runner-up in the other 133. Moreover, the Labour Party in 1983 suffered from a major redistribution of seats, losing various decaying inner-city constituencies. This had the effect of giving the Tories some 20–30 seats, although the overall effects of redistribution should not be exaggerated, since 30 out of the overall majority of 144 achieved was comparatively small.

335

═══════════ DOCUMENT ═══════════

34

Class and Voting

Apart from the means of political communication, and the substance of political issues, important changes have also been taking place in the wider society. Put briefly, fewer and fewer people in Britain think of themselves as belonging to a social class; and, even among those who still do, it is almost certainly the case that, for most of them, their class membership is no longer freighted with anything like the weight of emotional meaning that it once was. "Class consciousness" has declined in every sense of that term. In 1964, 50 per cent of Butler and Stokes' sample thought of themselves as belonging to a particular social class; according to a study by Market and Opinion Research International (MORI), that figure by May 1981 had fallen to 29 per cent. The proportion of people thinking of themselves as working-class fell during the same period from 32 per cent to a mere 15 per cent. Thus, one of the most powerful ties that had earlier bound both of the major political parties into Britain's social structure was becoming increasingly frayed. Not surprisingly, the statistical correlations between class and voting declined; the gap between the voting preferences of the middle and working classes in May 1979 was the narrowest since the Second World War.

But, above all, both major parties during the 1960s and 1970s signally failed to solve the enduring problems of Britain's economy. Since about 1960, economic issues – unemployment, rising prices, strikes and industrial relations, the balance of payments, the rate of economic growth – have come to matter far more to Britain's voters than any others. In comparison, issues of foreign policy and defence, of social provision, even of law and order have dwindled in insignificance. Voters look to the parties to solve the country's economic problems; the parties in their turn promise that they can, and will, do so. Labour came to power in 1964 claiming to be able to put the economy to rights, then the Conservatives in 1970, then Labour again in 1974, then the Conservatives in 1979. Both major parties have had their specific economic successes, but neither has seemed to most voters to have wrought the looked-for – or at least once looked-for – economic miracles. This is the major single reason why so many voters have turned against both parties.

A. King, 'Whatever is happening to the British Party System?',
Parliamentary Affairs, Summer 1982

Swing, Share and Turn-out

Swing

In 1970 the swing in the General Election from Labour to Conservative was fairly uniform throughout the country, there being little regional variation – not as much, for example, as in 1964. The mean two-party swing was 4.7 per cent to the

Conservatives, the largest since that for Labour's win in 1945. In England all regions produced a swing within 1 per cent of the national average, and all were well within the post-war pattern (although Scotland, Wales and Northern Ireland displayed different patterns, with underlying nationalist or unionist causes).

There are various ways of calculating the shift in votes from Labour to Conservative, or vice versa, or indeed in respect of other parties, but the most common is the 'Butler' swing, and the example given below is self-explanatory.

Example of Swing (Aberavon Constituency)

	1974 (October)	1979	1983
Labour share of vote	62.8%	61.7%	58.8%
Conservative share of vote	16.8%	24.7%	16.3%
Labour majority	46.0%	37.0%	42.5%

Conventional or Butler Swing (1979 and 1983 elections):

$$1979: \frac{(62.8 - 61.7) + (24.7 - 16.8)}{2} = +4.5\% \qquad 1983: \frac{(61.7 - 58.8) + (24.7 - 16.3)}{2} = -5.7\%$$

(A plus sign indicates a swing to the Conservatives, a minus to Labour.)

In contrast, in the General Elections of 1974 the whole idea of swing between the two major parties almost became redundant with the increases in nationalist and Liberal votes. In February 1974 there was a swing away from both main parties; but, since the Labour Party proved better able to hold on to its hard-core support, there was technically a 'swing' to Labour from Conservative of 1.2 per cent. In Wales and Scotland there was in fact a swing towards the Conservatives, since the nationalist groupings appeared to hurt Labour rather more.

In October 1974 the swing towards Labour was rather less in marginal seats. As the national Labour vote increased slightly and the Conservative national total continued to fall, there was a net swing to Labour of 2.25 per cent. Regional variations were less than in February 1974, falling back towards the 1970 pattern. In 1979 Wales and all English regions produced a swing within 1½ per cent of the national average (5.2 per cent to Conservative), the highest since 1945. In contrast, with the dramatic collapse of the SNP vote, in Scotland the swing was only +0.8 per cent. In the 1983 General Election the national swing was 3.9 per cent to the Conservatives, but with the Alliance obtaining almost as many votes as Labour nationally, the concept of 'swing' (between Labour and Tory) once again became difficult to operate. Regionally, the voting pattern achieved a quite remarkable standard of uniformity. Since the election results of 1974, 1979 and 1983, therefore, the idea of 'swing' has become increasingly sophisticated.

Share

The shares of the national vote present an interesting pattern. In 1951 the Conservative and Labour parties combined took 96.8 per cent of the total vote. By 1970 this had fallen to 89.4 per cent, but by February 1974 had dropped to 75.4 per cent (comprising 38.2 per cent Conservative and 37.2 per cent Labour) and in October 1974 it fell to 75 per cent (Labour 39.3 per cent and Conservative 35.7 per cent, the Conservative share being the lowest since 1923). In 1929 the Labour and Conservative parties together took only 75.2 per cent of the national vote; it seemed in 1974 that the inter-war position of the parties was, at least in part, returning, and the question of electoral reform of the voting system became once more a live issue. But in 1979, although the Labour share was the lowest since 1931, at 36.9 per cent, the Tories took 43.9 per cent and the Liberal share fell to 13.8 per cent: had the two-party system returned? Evidently not, judging by the results of the 1983 Election: 42.4 per cent for the Conservatives, 27.6 for Labour, the lowest since 1918, and 25.4 for the SDP-Liberal Alliance.

General Election Results 1945–83

Date	Winning party	Overall majority	Party	No. of seats won	Total vote (%)	Total Electorate	Total Seats	Total Turn-out	Swing (%)
1945 (5 July)	Lab	146	Con	213	39.9	32 836 419	640	76.1	Lab 11.3
			Lab	393	48.0				
			Lib	12	9.0				
			Others	22	3.1				
1950 (20 February)	Lab	5	Con	298	43.5	34 269 770	625	84.0	Con 2.8
			Lab	315	46.1				
			Lib	9	9.1				
			Others	3	1.3				
1951 (25 October)	Con	17	Con	321	48.0	34 645 573	625	82.5	Con 0.9
			Lab	295	48.8				
			Lib	6	2.6				
			Others	3	0.7				
1955 (26 May)	Con	60	Con	345	49.7	34 858 263	630	76.8	Con 2.1
			Lab	277	46.4				
			Lib	6	2.7				
			Others	2	1.2				
1959 (8 October)	Con	100	Con	365	49.3	35 397 080	630	78.8	Con 1.1
			Lab	258	43.8				
			Lib	6	5.9				
			Others	1	1.0				
1964 (15 October)	Lab	4	Con	303	43.4	35 892 572	630	77.0	Lab 3.1
			Lab	317	44.1				
			Lib	9	11.2				
			Others	1	1.3				
1966 (31 March)	Lab	97	Con	253	41.9	35 966 975	630	75.8	Lab 2.6
			Lab	363	47.9				
			Lib	12	8.5				
			Others	2	1.7				
1970 (18 June)	Con	30	Con	330	46.4	39 618 796	630	71.4	Con 4.7
			Lab	287	42.9				
			Lib	6	7.5				
			Others	7	3.2				
1974 (28 February)	Lab	−33	Con	296	38.2	39 752 317	635	78.8	Lab 1.2
			Lab	301	37.2				
			Lib	14	19.3				
			Others	24	5.3				
1974 (10 October)	Lab	3	Con	276	35.8	40 083 286	635	72.8	Lab 2.3
			Lab	319	39.3				
			Lib	13	18.3				
			Others	27	6.5				
1979 (3 May)	Con	43	Con	339	43.9	41 093 264	635	76.0	Con 5.2
			Lab	268	36.9				
			Lib	11	13.8				
			Others	17	5.5				
1983 (9 June)	Con	144	Con	397	42.4	42 197 344	650	72.7	Con 3.9
			Lab	209	27.6				
			Lib/SDP	23	25.4				
			Others	21	4.6				

Turn-out

Turn-out has also attracted attention. The 1970 General Election turn-out of 72 per cent was the lowest since 1935, and continued a general and disturbing decline since 1945 (although there was a rise in 1950 and 1959). It has also been estimated that at least one-quarter of the new young voters (18 to 21-year olds) had failed to register, and that some three-quarters of a million Labour voters abstained. But the fact that the election was held in the unusual month of June must have also been a contributory factor. The February 1974 Election naturally used a much newer register, which may account for some 3 per cent of the extra rise in votes, to 78.7 per cent of the electorate. Interest among the electorate, in view of the situation in the coal-mines and the three-day working week, was also higher. The October Election in 1974 saw a fall again, to 72.8 per cent, but perhaps this is not surprising as it was the second election in just over half a year. It has also been calculated that of the fall of 6 per cent between February and October, 2.2 per cent could be attributed to the ageing of the electoral register. The 1979 turn-out (at 76.0 per cent) appeared to halt, temporarily at least, the downward drift. The turn-out for the EEC membership referendum in June 1975 was 67.2 per cent, higher than predicted by many sections of Parliament and the press. In 1983 the turn-out (72.7 per cent), like others, underlined the fact that Labour supporters (in 1979) did not stay at home more than those of other parties, rather they altered their vote and the Labour Party did not suffer a higher rate of abstention (differential abstention).

The Times Guide to the House of Commons, October 1974

Participation overseas

The question of comparing turn-out in the UK with that in other countries is always a difficult one, particularly as national averages may effectively disguise constituency variations (which may be bizarre: in February 1974, two of the three highest turn-outs were in safe Conservative seats – Shipley at 87.4 per cent and Cardiff NW at 87.1 per cent – and high turn-outs are occasionally recorded in safe Labour mining seats, such as Rhondda at 79.8 per cent in 1979 and in Unionist strongholds in Northern Ireland such as Mid Ulster at 84.3 per cent in 1983). 'For electors thus motivated, voting is like going to church or rooting for the home side at a football match; it may not have any effect, but it makes one feel good'.

Anthony King, *New Society,* 3 October 1974

Some 8 per cent of the UK electorate probably never vote at all, and over half of those who did not vote in 1979 stayed at home in 1983. In Australia voting in parliamentary elections is compulsory. Turn-outs in several Western European countries are distinctly higher than the UK's, Italy, West Germany and Austria consistently exceeding the 90 per cent mark since 1945, Austria being the most notable with a figure of 97 per cent in the parliamentary elections of 1949 and the presidential elections of 1951 and 1957. Technically, voting is compulsory in Italy too; those who fail to vote have their names recorded on a register (*Fedina Penale*), which may be used against them when social assistance of one sort or another is sought from the public authorities. In the USA the picture is more bleak: turn-out in the mid-term Congressional elections in 1986 was 53.8 per cent, at least an improvement on 41.1 per cent in 1982 and 37.7 per cent in 1978. In Austria voting

339

is theoretically compulsory for presidential elections and in some provinces for parliamentary elections. Voting is compulsory, too, in Belgium, but not in West Germany.

One telling point perhaps sums up the very considerable fluctuations in British electoral behaviour during the 1970s: in both 1974 Elections, for the first time since 1929, a majority of MPs were elected by a minority of votes in their constituencies. Enthusiasm for elections to local government and the European Parliament is notably less. For the latter the turn-out was 32.6 per cent in 1979 and 32.4 per cent in 1984, notably the lowest amongst the member states of the EEC. Belgium scored 91.4 per cent and 92.2 per cent respectively.

By-elections

There is still, however, one way in which the electorate can indirectly express its feeling by both deviating from traditional party loyalty and yet ultimately maintaining it. In parliamentary by-elections votes may be used rather differently from the way they are cast at general elections. If the Government has a sizeable majority, the voter who normally supports the governing party may feel much freer to vote for an Opposition party as a timely reminder to the Government that it is failing to meet the aspirations of the electorate.

There have, of course, been some sensational by-election results since 1945, (and some very unremarkable ones as well). The Liberal victory at Orpington in 1962 is probably still the best remembered, occurring, as it did, at a time when the Macmillan Government was attracting considerable unfavourable publicity. Orpington (like Sutton and Cheam in 1972) was a safe Conservative seat in the suburbs of south London, and it was therefore all the more remarkable that it did not pass back into Conservative hands until the 1970 General Election. In 1966 Plaid Cymru gained the seat at Carmarthen and in 1967 the SNP won at Hamilton – victories which led to the establishment of the Kilbrandon Commission. In July 1973, following impressive wins at Sutton and Rochdale in late 1972, the Liberals achieved the distinction – for them very unusual – of winning two by-elections on the same day, at Ripon and the Isle of Ely. They won Ripon by a majority of under 1000 and with a comparatively weak candidate, and the seat subsequently returned safely to the Conservatives in the February 1974 General Election. The presence of a strong, nationally known personality, Clement Freud, in the Isle of Ely was an electoral boost for the Liberals and the seat did not return to the Conservatives at the next general election – indeed the Liberal majority was dramatically increased, and Mr Freud still holds the seat.

Turn-out at by-elections is likely to be lower than at general elections, but it falls less when the seat is seen to be marginal, and particularly when the outcome might make a difference to the Government's fortunes. Volatility often occurs when a Liberal or Nationalist candidate intervenes. One study has shown that from 1945 to 1959 only one in every 16 by-election contests resulted in a change of party representation, and that between 1945 and 1957 the governing party did not lose a

340

seat to the Opposition – that being the period when two-party politics was most dominant. But the same study showed that the situation changed in the 1959–64 Parliament, when one seat changed hands in every seven by-elections. Between 1966 and 1970 Labour lost no less than 15 seats – although nine of those were regained at the 1970 General Election, which underlines the fact that most by-election gains can be expected to be reversed at the subsequent general election.

C. Cook and J. Ramsden, *By-Elections in British Politics*, Macmillan, 1973

Margo MacDonald acknowledges the cheers of supporters after winning the Glasgow Govan by-election in 1973 for the Scottish National Party

341

Electoral volatility at by-elections continued from 1970 to 1979. Until 1974 it was displayed in particular by the fact that a number of seats went to parties other than Conservative and Labour. From 1974–9 it was more a matter of some large (although by no means uniform) swings from the Labour Government to the Conservative Opposition, reminiscent of the period under Wilson from 1966 to 1970. Examples from the 1974–9 period are the by-elections at Ashfield (1977), with a swing of 20.8 per cent to the Tories, and Ilford North (1978) with a swing of 6.9 per cent. The only real exceptions to the trend were Labour's successful holding of Berwick and East Lothian (J.P. Mackintosh's seat), with an increased majority, and of Glasgow Garscadden and Hamilton against the SNP (all in 1978). A few days before the dissolution of Parliament in 1979, the Liberals won the Liverpool Edge Hill by-election with a swing to them from Labour of 32 per cent; however, the issues in that constituency were particularly localised. In the 1979–83 Parliament the pattern was more varied but the chief feature was a return to Liberal gains in alliance with those of its partner, the SDP formed in 1981.

The most remarkable by-election result in the 1979–83 period was in Bermondsey, a run-down working-class Labour stronghold in south-east London. Here in early 1983 there was a swing of 44.2 per cent from Labour to the Liberals, marginally greater than the swing to Dick Taverne at Lincoln in 1973 where he stood as an independent Labour candidate. But here there were special factors, in so far as the Labour Party was split – the election was forced by Bob Mellish, the sitting MP, who had already resigned the Labour whip. An independent Labour candidate took 7.6 per cent of the vote. Moreover, the official Labour candidate, Peter Tatchell, had been disowned by Mr Foot, the Labour Leader, in an unguarded moment in the Commons the year before, although subsequently he endorsed the candidacy. The Liberal triumph at Bermondsey, achieved by years of hard attention to local issues – the community politics character of many Liberal by-election successes since Sutton and Cheam in 1972 – contrasted with Mr Taverne's poor result for the SDP in the neighbouring seat, Peckham, where a by-election was held the previous year. Similarly, one Labour defector to the SDP, Bruce Douglas-Mann, insisted on offering himself to his constituents under his new colours, but in the by-election held in 1982 at the height of the Falklands crisis he lost resoundingly to the Tories, which was the first time a government won a by-election seat from the Opposition since Brighouse and Spenborough in 1960.

The other notable by-election results in the 1979–83 period were Roy Jenkins' victory at Glasgow Hillhead (a Tory seat) in 1982 after a near-win at Warrington in 1981 and Shirley Williams' at Crosby in 1981. Mrs Williams lost her seat at the subsequent 1983 General Election. The Liberals also won Croydon North-West in 1981, but this too was lost in 1983.

During the inter-war period seats at by-elections changed hands on average once in every fifth contest. Perhaps this kind of pattern, characteristic of a period of economic disillusionment, has been appearing again since 1972. Even in the relative stability of the United Kingdom, no party can afford to take everything for granted.

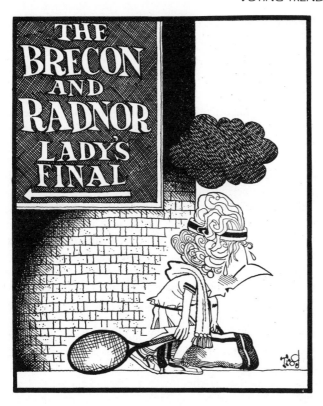

The Observer, 7 July 1985. The Liberals win the Brecon and Radnor by-election from the Conservatives who are pushed into third place. In 1986 the Liberals took Ryedale from the Conservatives. The SDP won Portsmouth South in 1984 and Labour narrowly won Fulham (London) in 1986. The other ten by-elections (1983–6) saw no change in party control.

Electoral Methods

The difficulties of the 1974 and 1983 Elections raised the whole question of how far the British electoral system still serves modern needs. In that system, although the candidate who gains the largest number of crosses on all the ballot papers wins, more people may have voted for others. This system, called 'simple majority', is also to be found in the USA, Canada, New Zealand and South Africa. It has the advantage of being relatively simple to operate, and increases the chance of one-party (and therefore stable?) government. The nature of adversarial government is outlined further at the end of this chapter (Document 35).

However, it also means that minority parties are heavily penalised, and that governments may be elected by a minority of the total votes (as in all of the general elections between 1970 and 1983, discussed above). It can mean that regional representations become heavily favoured (such as the Irish Nationalists before 1918). It usually means that only candidates of the main parties stand a chance – the

343

'wasted vote' argument becomes all-important, that is the voter will not consider supporting a candidate if he judges that the candidate has no real chance of winning, since the first-past-the-post system, with its single member constituencies is, on the face of it, individual rather than party orientated.

(a) Alternative Voting (AV)

A variation on simple majority is the absolute majority in the form of the **alternative vote**. The introduction of this system (and STV) was actively discussed in Britain in 1917, during a period of coalition government, and it was nearly adopted in 1931, at the time of the second minority Labour Government, as a gesture towards the Liberals. However, the Bill concerned was still going through the Lords when the Government fell in August of that year. The subsequent decline of the Liberals caused the matter to be shelved. In this system (which is used for parliamentary elections to the lower house in Australia) voters number the candidates in order of preference, and if no one candidate receives an overall majority of first preference votes over all the other candidates in that constituency, the candidate who has received the fewest first preferences has the second preferences on his ballot paper redistributed to the other candidates accordingly. The process is repeated until one candidate receives an overall majority. Its advantages are that each MP is elected by a majority of votes in his constituency, that it retains the link between each constituency and a single member, and that it gives a somewhat better chance to minority parties. It does, however, mean that the chance of a one-party government majority is reduced and that the result is decided by the most 'worthless' votes, that is the lower preferences of the least successful candidates. Another alternative in 'majority' systems is to institute a second ballot, since again that means most MPs would be elected by a majority vote. The best example of this method has been France; it does, however, mean that horse-trading between the parties between the two polls inevitably takes place, with the result that various candidates or parties decline to enter the run-off ballot. There can, of course, be a succession of run-off ballots, but ideally the final run-off should be between just two surviving candidates, in order to produce a simple majority.*

(b) Proportional Representation (PR)

The other main systems are 'proportional' – although Japan has a quasi-proportional system (or single non-transferable vote) whereby voters have fewer votes than there are seats to be filled; again this is a way of giving special representation to minority parties, but it can encourage some very advanced mathematical risk-taking by the parties concerned in respect of how many candidates to field in the multi-member constituencies. (The system operated in the UK between 1867 and 1884.)

'Proportional' systems are divided principally into 'list' methods and STV ('single transferable vote') methods.

(i) List Systems

In a list system seats are gained by reaching a mathematical quota of votes in multi-member constituencies. This has the advantage of eliminating 'wasted votes', but like STV the list system can be criticised for being technically over-elaborate. It

---

*A system of proportional representation was introduced for the French parliamentary elections in 1986.

moreover destroys the link between constituencies and single members and makes one-party government rare; it also usually helps party candidates, giving virtually no chance to independent (or very small party) candidates.

The vote is cast for a list of party candidates, and seats are distributed proportionally between parties, although many such systems allow the voter to influence the order of each party list by expressing a preference for individual candidates. Countries which employ this method are Israel (with no preference), Belgium and Denmark (with one preference optional), Finland and the Netherlands (with one preference compulsory), Italy (with three or four preferences optional), as well as Norway, Sweden and Switzerland.

In 1977 the Labour Government put forward in its European Assembly Elections Bill a regional list system of voting; this arose from the Lib-Lab Pact. But the Commons rejected it and in its place put the simple majority (Westminster) system for the mainland's 78 European seats However, as indicated below, the UK's other three European seats – covering Northern Ireland – used STV.

(ii) Single Transferable Vote (STV)

The single transferable vote is another system where voters number candidates in order of preference. First preferences are counted and any candidate obtaining the mathematical quota is elected. It necessitates multi-member constituencies, and in a 6-member constituency the quota to reach would be one more vote than one-seventh (where 7 = number of seats plus 1) of the total votes cast (the Droop quota). Any surplus votes are transferred proportionately to his supporters' second choices; but if no candidate has reached the quota, the bottom candidate is eliminated and his votes given to the next candidate, and so on, until all the seats are filled. Of course, huge multi-member constituencies might, in relation to the UK, be electorally unattractive in the vast rural areas of Wales and Scotland, where, if a change in the electoral system on these lines were made, the alternative vote could be the more feasible solution. However, notwithstanding its more uniform topography, Ireland is a more than adequate example of STV. The advantage of STV is that in two-party systems, it gives parties other than the main ones much more accurate representation; hence the Liberal Party unequivocally supports it. At the same time one-party government as in the Republic, is not ruled out – although the Irish Government has twice failed, through referenda, to abandon the STV system. But under STV the only UK Governments this century still to have gained an overall majority would probably have been those of 1918 and 1931 (both coalitions anyway), and possibly those of 1906 and 1945. STV would also encourage cross-voting between candidates of the same party, particularly if one, of whatever party background, had a strong and attractive personality compared to the others on the ballot.

The system, however, has been introduced in Northern Ireland. In order to ensure fair representation of the Catholic minority, and thus break Protestant domination, STV was used for the elections to the Northern Ireland Assembly (Executive) in June 1973. However, the idea of power-sharing was abhorrent to the more extreme Protestants, who proceeded to organise what was practically a general strike in the Province; the new Executive collapsed the following year, and direct rule from Westminster was re-introduced. STV was again employed for

345

electing, in the earlier part of 1975, the abortive consultative Convention whose task was to study various proposals for the political future of Ulster; it is also used for Ulster's EEC and local government elections, as well as for the new Northern Ireland Assembly in 1982, which was subsequently abolished in 1986.

Sometimes it is said the STV system is wide open to the 'gerrymandering' of constituency boundaries, as appears to happen in Ireland from time to time. Where the governing party has just under half the votes in an area, it can establish a constituency with four seats, so that it and the Opposition get two each. But where it is ahead (even by 1 or 2 per cent) it sets up smaller constituencies with three seats, in the hope of gaining two of them in each case. By such means it can guarantee itself a third as many seats again as its opponents, even if the actual first preference votes cast are virtually equal. But this is largely a specious argument – the main point is that any electoral system, STV or otherwise, should be adequately and independently supervised, as is the case with the Boundary Commissions and local registration procedures in the UK.

An interesting hybrid of majority and list systems operates in West Germany. In the Federal Republic each elector votes once for an individual candidate in single-member constituencies as in the UK, and then once for a national party list. Half the lower house (*Bundesrat*) is elected by first votes, but then each party receives an additional share in proportion to its showing in the second votes (with the proviso that it must have secured either three seats on the first vote or 5 per cent on the second – a regulation basically meant to eliminate Nazis and Communists). This means that, although very small parties have little hope, 'third' parties are not necessarily disadvantaged, and that the link between constituencies and individual members is retained. The system became the subject of some attention in the UK in 1976, as described below.

(c) Additional Member System (AMS)

The Report of the Hansard Society Commission on Electoral Reform 1976

In June 1976 the Hansard Society for Parliamentary Government issued a report on the subject of electoral reform. Although it considered STV in some detail, a majority of its committee came down in favour of a system not unlike the German *uberhangsmandaten* called AMS.

The report claimed that while most people were not unhappy with the parliamentary system they were nevertheless dissatisfied with various aspects of its operation. It said that any such system should satisfy four criteria: it should provide effective government, it should represent large minorities adequately, it should be acceptable to the great majority of people and it should ensure that governments do not pursue policies that lack the support of the majority of the electorate. It proposed a House of Commons of 640 MPs, 480 of whom would be elected in single-member constituencies by the first-past-the-post method. The other 160 would be selected from among the losing candidates to compensate parties such as the Liberals which sometimes score a large total of national votes, but gain few seats. To produce a quota, the total votes in each region would be added up and then divided by the number of constituencies within that region. Each party would approach that quota by adding up its regional votes and dividing that by the number of seats it had won plus one. The parties, therefore, that had won few if any seats (provided there was a German-type threshold of, say, 5 per cent) would clearly reach that regional quota first, and allocate the additional seats thus gained to those of its candidates who had come closest to winning directly. A large part of the additional member allocation would thus benefit the Liberals-SDP.

AMS would undoubtedly be more favoured than STV by parliamentarians, since it would largely retain the direct single-member constituency link; it would also be simple to operate, requiring the voter to cast his vote (one cross) in the same way as before. One drawback is that it would reduce the number of candidates fighting constituencies for any one party from 650 to 480; but perhaps a little more competition to get into the Commons is no bad thing. It would also inevitably mean coalition government most of the time.

The debate about electoral reform was generated by such things as the fact that twice since 1945 a party polled most votes but lost the Election (in 1951 and February 1974), that only 29 per cent of the total electorate elected the governing party in October 1974). In the 1966 and 1970 Elections 10 per cent of the votes cast were not for the 'big two' parties; in both 1974 Elections the figure was 25 per cent, in 1979 19 per cent and in 1983 no less than 30 per cent. Moreover, some minority parties suffer more than others; for example, in October 1974 the SNP gained 11 seats with 2.9 per cent of the total UK votes, whereas the Liberals took only 13 seats with 18.3 per cent.

S.E. Finer has argued that since 1964 the major political parties have lost the parliamentary middle ground of 'Butskellism' and consensus, and that perhaps periods of minority or coalition government are not so unwelcome as has been believed.

DOCUMENT

35

Professor Finer's Arguments Against the Adversary System

According to a recent *Observer* poll, 19 out of 20 people in Britain dislike the present parliamentary deadlock and prefer majoritarian party rule. When the outcome of the election became clear, last February, I shared that opinion. After some six months' experience of minority government I have changed my mind. In the present economic climate, and for some years to come, it seems to me that the present parliamentary stalemate is the best of all possible worlds and all its shortcomings necessary evils.

As to the causes of our chronic economic decline and current crisis, all that need be said here is that, as the recent report of the subcommittee of the Commons Expenditure Committee makes plain, there is no consensus: so we can for present purposes get on with the Flood and pass by the Creation of the World – "the Flood," in the present instance, being the social and political turmoil to which the economic crisis will give rise. 347

It is clear that the gross national product will decline next year, and perhaps decline dramatically; and that it may continue to fall for two or three years to come. Sectional groups in our society will continue to compete for shares in this GNP; but since this will be smaller and since the claims will be generously topped up to discount the enormous rate of inflation, this competition will be desperate and ferocious.

National minorities, and notably the Scottish nationalists whose emotional appeal is now laced with the material prospect of turning Scotland into the Kuwait of the north, will press with increased vehemence. The more muscular trade unions will continue to grab their shares at the expense of, among others, the feebler groups like the teachers and postmen. Unemployment will mount, and we may expect some of the unemployed, along with members of a squeezed, tired and demoralised middle class to join populist movements with racialist overtones; and these in their turn will be confronted by leftist counter-movements of students and working class militants.

The scenario will be similar to the thirties – but worse in three ways. Unlike the thirties, today nobody regards mass unemployment as either unavoidable or tolerable; unlike the thirties, world prices are rising, not falling; and unlike the thirties, today some 42 per cent of the labour force is unionised and under radical leadership – a proportion almost double that of 1933.

The "normal" working of our political system is not directly responsible for our economic decline. But, in my view, it has substantially contributed to it; and a return to this "normality" will I believe, make things worse.

This "normal" working is, effectively, the alternation of two majoritarian parties in parliament, and consequentially the alternation of two politically antipodal governments, which could (and did) ram through parliament pretty well everything they had agreed with sectional interests outside the House and with party committees "upstairs" in the House. The conventional wisdom of political scientists from which I now – *mea culpa* – very belatedly dissent, applauds this rather crude arrangement. It affirms that cabinets are stable and durable – which is true. It continues by stating that they can therefore impart a consistent direction to a broad policy which has received general approval at the election – but this has become increasingly false, as may be demonstrated by two observations. First, both the Labour government of 1964–70 and the Conservative government of 1970–74 were forced by external events to make savage U-turns in the policy on which they had been elected. Secondly, both governments found, over the last five years, that their so-called "power" consisted of being able to get the Commons to accept their legislation, but stopped short of getting determined sectional interests to obey it.

The conventional wisdom further affirms that as cabinets tire in office, so they are replaced by another team which, though its ideology or politics may be anathema, is at least endowed with more energy and imagination. Hence the complacent conclusion that the alternating majoritarian party system endows the country with firm and stable government, generating changes which are incremental and evolutionary.

This verdict rests, however, on two unstated or understated presuppositions: that the successor government, though of different political complexion from its predecessor, does on the whole accept the legislation of that predecessor and modifies it but marginally; and that the public on the whole does obey the laws enacted by parliament. Until perhaps the middle sixties, there was much to support both views. The Conservatives preserved the welfare legislation and most of the nationalisation of the Attlee governments; the Labour Party, in its turn, accepted in office much that it had found 348 unpalatable or even immoral in opposition, such as commercial television and the restriction of coloured immigration. Nor, during this period of alternation, did trade unions engineer strikes to secure political objectives, or employers organise currency crises and mass lockouts.

In those lost days of Butskellism and "consensus," the alternation of the two parties in office could well be defended as benign. But since then, the presuppositions have eroded away; and with their erosion that alternation has, in my view, become increasingly destructive. The alternations have become more rapid; the party policies more sharply opposed; and the consequential reversals of policy have generated a climate of such uncertainty as to cripple economic growth.

First, the *alternations*. In the 20 years, 1945–64, there was *one* alternation in party complexion, while in the last ten years, 1964–74, there have been *three*.

Next, the *parties*. These have become increasingly the prisoners of their own clienteles. Organised capital, and those who identify themselves with it, see the Conservatives as "their" party, and they are right. A great proportion of its finances comes from private companies, and its candidates and MPs are overwhelmingly farmers, businessmen or lawyers with business interests. This, however, is mitigated in practice by the fact that, on the average, the socio-economic categories of "working class" and "very poor" account for some 60 per cent of the party's vote, so that the predominantly capitalist leadership has to show a lively concern for their interests. On the other side, the Labour Party, the offspring of the trade unions three quarters of a century ago, has today become increasingly dependent on them; and notably since they bared their fangs over the *In Place of Strife* proposals of 1969. At one time, as Robert McKenzie has showed, the moderate parliamentary leaders could rely on the moderate trade union leaders to defeat the extremists in the party conference. Today there is still this correspondence between the conference platform and the trade unions; but the unions have become highly politicised and radicalised and, willy-nilly, the parliamentary party is pulled along by them. Without their money, militants and members, the Labour Party is not viable. They contribute some two thirds of the party's headquarters income, and about four fifths of their election fund; they outnumber constituency delegates on the conference floor by more than seven to one; and they sponsor about one third of the MPs.

Yet the radicalised leaders of the great unions, which today dictate the party's policy, are far more radical than those who vote for the party. In 1974, the electors (some 31 millions) divided their vote thus: 38 per cent to the Conservatives, 37 per cent to the Labour Party, and some 23 per cent to the Liberals and others. Yet when we turn to the trade unionists (some eleven million), the average distribution of their votes over the last ten years is about 60 per cent to Labour and 40 per cent to other parties. Finally, however, when we reach the decision-making apex that moulds the party's policy, we find the trade union leadership is 100 per cent Labour, or to the left of the Labour Party.

This identification of the respective party leaderships with the trade unions on the one hand, and commerce and industry on the other, has led directly to the recent fluctuation and dislocation of major policy. The philosophy of, first, "Selsdon man" and, subsequently, the statutory incomes policy, have confronted nationalisation and the "social compact." Not only has the alternation of the parties become more rapid, but also the policies have moved away from centre ground and have retreated into ideologies which are usually, more radical (though not, therefore, more progressive) than the views of the electors who voted for them.

This has two serious effects. First, instead of the successor government accepting and building on the work of its predecessor, it has spent an increasing amount of time 349 cancelling their work and substituting something radically opposed. Secondly, civil disobedience and politically motivated strikes have been stimulated among sections of the population who want to "give history a push" – that is to say, to hurry on the day when the government will have to call a general election and so give "their own" party the opportunity to get back into office and do something for them. The paradigm of what we may expect in the future is the present pay-bed dispute, where one numerically insignificant minority in the NHS takes it on itself, by direct and unilateral action, to bring about a change of policy which constitutionally rests with the minister, only to find itself confronted by another section – the consultants – who take direct action to negate their purpose.

In the present conjuncture, with ferocious competition for shares in the diminished GNP, it is easy to foresee that another majoritarian government, whatever its political complexion, will bitterly antagonise supporters of the minority; and, the signals having been set green for direct action, that the militants will no longer wait out their four and a half years in patience to see the return of "their" party to power.

That is not all. Though there's no consensus on the Creation, it *can* fairly be argued that this rapid alternation of political polarised parties in the last decade has substantially contributed to our economic decline by creating a great miasma of incertitude. Working men, exposed to "anti-lame duck" policy, rightly fear for their jobs. Does it help their confidence when a minister takes over one part of Court Line to save the jobs of 9,000 workers, but declines to take over the rest and so throws 3,000 out of work, on the grounds that that part of the company was a "lame duck"? Investors, for their part, do not know which industries will be nationalised; and if they are to be, they do not know when, how, and at what level of compensation. Firms envisaging factory extensions have seen investment-grant arrangements altered no less than 16 times. Savers will not take up shares when it is not the profitability of the company that decides the rate of dividend return but the government – which may restrict it to 5 per cent, raises it to 12 per cent or by the same token freeze it altogether. And so on.

The credulous may believe that such problems would be resolved by taking all enterprises into public ownership. In fact, the public corporations have suffered at least as much, and probably more, from the alternation of union-controlled or employer-controlled cabinets. The coal industry was being run down; now, suddenly it is to be expanded. The railways were to be stripped down to the bare trunk lines; then they were to be maintained and subsidised as a social service. The airways corporation(s) are, first, granted a tight monopoly; and on a change of government find themselves competing with newly licensed independent operators. Pricing policy has been erratic, with governments swithering between subsiding cheap fuel and transport, and charging the full economic cost: until and unless there is a consumer revolt, such as took place over the proposed new tariff for night-storage heaters.

And the damage does not stop at firms and corporations, but stalks in at the front door. Ten years ago, it was the received wisdom in the Labour Party that to permit mortgage holders to set their mortgage payments against tax was a wicked, middle class ramp. Today all three parties, but with Labour in the van, are falling over themselves to make life safer, cheaper, and easier for the house purchaser. As for the constant vagaries in tax law – the ding-dong battle, for instance, over whether a child's investment income shall or shall not be aggregated with its parents' – this has made rational tax planning, and hence rational saving, very hard indeed.

In a climate of uncertainties like this – who will venture either his money or his skills?

The leaders of the two major parties affirm that the present conjuncture demands a "bold" policy. But this is just dogma. The Labour Party started with a bold policy in 1964, and then reversed it for another bold policy; to be succeeded by a bold Conservative policy in 1970, which again was reversed for another bold policy: four bold policies in ten years. Perhaps the time has come for an end to disruption, and a return to a certain predictability; a period of benign neglect of the economy, where some confidence in native skills and resources can revive. But given the nature of our party and electoral system, this requires an end to the alternation of the majoritarian parties; and in turn what this requires is the perpetuation of something very much like what we now have – *stalemate*.

For, of this parliament, something can be said that is difficult to affirm of previous ones: that no major interest has been able to capture it. The parties of nationalist secession are still tiny – but at the next election Scottish nationalists may pick up 20 seats or more. Private enterprise has been able to rely on parliament to reject the government's commitment to nationalisation, but has been in no position to pursue a forward strategy of its own. For their part, the unions have seen parliament snatch away "their" £10 million, and their Trade Union Bill substantially amended. No special interest has been able, as it has in the past, to harness public authority to its own sectional demands, as the result of the hazard of a general election.

Suppose this situation were to be perpetuated, or at least guaranteed, for a decade or more – then the consequences seem more likely to be benign than otherwise. Secessionist minorities would have to accommodate to the United Kingdom as a whole: capital and labour, no longer able to rely on a parliamentary majority to support their causes, would have to carry on their conflict – or their collusion – outside parliament, on the industrial plane to which it belongs. Nothing dramatic would be probable; and for a sectional interest to try to assault and capture parliament would be like trying to sabre a cushion. Finally, we might see an end to the "pianola parliaments," grinding out tunes which have been pre-recorded outside and "upstairs":

The ritual of each party is rehearsed
Dislodging not one vote or prejudice;
The ministers their ministries retain,
And Ins as Ins, and Outs as Outs, remain.

But at the moment, this situation is far from being perpetuated. On the contrary, all parties, and the general public are waiting and preparing for a general election; so the uncertainty is worse than ever. To secure the benefits of minoritarian rule requires certain institutional changes. Whether they will eventuate or not depends on the outcome of the next election. If it returns a majoritarian government, then we are back on the old treadmill indefinitely. But if it should, as I hope, result in another deadlock, then the chance would arise to introduce two changes which would help perpetuate minoritarianism.

The first is a changeover from the present system of election to a more proportional system of representation. It is surely wrong – indeed obscene – that in a mature democracy like ours, two parties each receiving some 38 per cent of the vote should win some 300 seats apiece while another party, receiving some 19 per cent of the vote, should only win 14. But, apart from that, if abrupt change is inimical to the economy (as I have been arguing), it is clearly inexpedient that an electoral swing of what is usually in the order of a mere 3 per cent should suffice to replace one dogmatic cabinet by a counter dogmatic one, especially since neither needs (nor since 1945 has received) over 50 per   351 cent of the popular vote to command a clear majority in the House. Public opinion shifts far less dramatically than do the seats held by the respective parties in the Commons. And, as the experience of West Germany has shown, a proportional representation system does not necessarily multiply parties. Indeed in the West German case it has reduced them to two and a half. Nor does it preclude majoritarian rule: it merely ensures that this requires a majority of the popular vote.

The second change is to alter the system of financing parties; once again, in a way similar to that pursued in West Germany, where the parties receive public funds based on the votes cast for them at the last general election. This would not necessarily free the Conservative and Labour parties from their dependence on capital and the unions respectively: but nothing less would make it possible. And if it occurred, the polarisation of their attitudes could be expected to reverse itself, for common ground.

Taken together, these changes would produce a more subtle, and more parliamentary, form of government. Paradoxically, precisely because this would put an end to the rapid alternations of recriminatory majoritarian parties, social and economic policy would be more continuous, more incremental and more self-consistent than it has been under the hazards of our "normal" political style. It would prove all but impossible for one powerful sectional interest to bully or to capture parliament.

S.E. Finer, 'The present discontents: in defence of deadlock',
New Society, 5 September 1974

Summary

All the major studies of voting behaviour – Butler–Stokes, Crewe–Särlvik, Himmelweit *et al.*, Heath *et al.* – have chronicled the resistance of voters to change party allegiance, such loyalty apparently rooted, between 1945 and 1973, in social class. Equally, this research has recorded the growing electoral volatility in the period since 1974, which has been coupled with some measure of class dealignment, thus giving the Liberal Party renewed vigour, notwithstanding a decline in its overall position in the 1979 General Election. That volatility was reflected, too, in the growth of the nationalist vote from 1973 to 1978 in Scotland and to a lesser extent Wales, and in the formation of the SDP (in electoral alliance with the Liberals) in 1981. Volatility was reflected in a different way in Northern Ireland, with the breakdown of the old Unionist consensus in 1974 and later, at the other end of Ulster's political spectrum, with the rise of Sinn Fein in 1984.

Butler and Stokes (in 1969 and 1974) examined how the essentially two party system was class orientated, but also how the Liberals' small parliamentary presence still represented vigorous support in various parts of the country. Himmelweit *et al.* (1981 and 1985) demonstrated how allegiances were breaking down in the sense that while most electors still identified themselves with one particular party, they were now prepared to cast their votes less loyally than in the past – 'voting for the same party was the exception not the rule'. Särlvik and Crewe (1983) continued this theme, and in a wide-ranging survey showed not just that perceptions of social class were weakening but also that party preferences were becoming detached from membership of any particular class. Särlvik and Crewe therefore emphasised that the arrival of the SDP could, in the longer term, ensure the demise of a system hitherto dominated by two parties (at least since 1945).

The study of Heath, Jowell and Curtice focused upon the 1983 General Election in particular. They concluded that the coherence of the Liberal and Alliance vote was not a wholly new phenomenon in 1983.

> 'There were clear signs of it in 1979, and . . . the formation of the SDP and the perception of Labour's move to the left . . . took place *after* 1979. . . . The Liberal Party has been gradually acquiring a more visible identity and thus has been exerting greater "pull" on the electorate. . . . Doubtless, this increased pull was helped by the Alliance with the Social Democratic Party and the attendant media coverage, but it would also appear to antedate the Alliance.'

See also R. Rose and I. McAllister, *Voters Begin to Choose*, Sage, 1986

But if the Alliance was attracting increasing support amongst the educated middle class, it was not yet proven that that support was permanent, as seen also in earlier studies. Labour and Conservative remained the dominant parties of the industrial worker and the entrepreneur/manager respectively. Heath's figures for 1983 claim that the Conservative vote included 34 per cent from the 'salariat' and 21 per cent from the working-class (the balance of 45 per cent going to routine nonmanual/ petty bourgeoisie/foremen and technicians), the Alliance and Labour figures being respectively 35, 26, 39 and 14, 55, 31.

One route for the Alliance is still through the Liberals' community politics approach, post-1970, whereby local grievances are taken up, thus mobilising mainly working-class support against certain paternalistic Labour councils, but that route is arduous and fraught with dangers. It has worked, however, in some areas, for example, working-class, 'Labour' Bermondsey in south-east London and more rural middle-class Yeovil, both of which returned Liberal MPs at the last election.

If future elections continue to throw up peculiar results under the first-past-the-post system, which the United Kingdom is virtually alone in Western Europe in using, then the Liberal and SDP leaders understandably will continue to cry 'foul', as they did in 1983, when the Alliance finished first or second in nearly as many seats as did Labour. There is limited support from other MPs, more Tory than Labour, for the introduction of some kind of proportional representation. Recently, however, Dr Owen has suggested that the introduction of PR should be subject to a national referendum, a suggestion which did not entirely accord with Mr Steel's views. In the meantime those who favour PR must continue to advertise how well coalition government has succeeded in other countries, most notably West Germany whose post-war political stability has contributed towards its 'economic miracle' since the 1960s, as opposed to other Western European states, it ought to be pointed out, where coalitions have not always proved fruitful, such as in Belgium and Italy.

Meanwhile, also, the Liberal/SDP Alliance needs to keep in the public eye by winning parliamentary by-elections, as and when they occur, and perhaps to bear in mind that the only real peace-time coalition government this century, the National Government in 1931, quickly came to bitter blows and by most historical accounts was a manifest failure.

Questions

1. (a) Explain the circumstances that have led to the holding of referenda in the UK.
(b) Evaluate the case for holding further referenda at the local and national levels. (AEB specimen question 1986)

2. What do the results of the 1979 and 1983 general elections show about the workings of the British electoral system? (Joint Matriculation Board)

3. How do you account for the Conservatives increasing their working-class support and Labour increasing their middle-class support in recent general elections?* (Joint Matriculation Board)

4. What lessons may be learned from by-election results since 1962.

*Note: the writer would consider the second part of the question controversial, in the light of the 1979 and 1983 Election results, and the studies thereon (Särlvik–Crewe for 1979 and Heath *et al.* for 1983). But the question is a challenging one to pose, and perhaps should be related to the period 1966 or 1970 to 1983.

13 The Mass Media

'The [presidential] candidate [Jimmy Carter] had allowed television cameras into his hotel suite to watch him watch television. When you have said that, you have said it all. Politics as it is now written about is no longer about real people, real issues or real life.'

Mr John Pardoe, former MP for north Cornwall, commenting about the American presidential elections in 1976, *The Guardian,* 19 July 1976

Although, as has already been seen from the research findings of Butler and Stokes, the effect of the media upon voting behaviour is limited, the media nevertheless exercise considerable influence on the political system in a variety of other ways.

Parliament and Broadcasting

Members of the British House of Commons have for many years had their own ideas about the powers and bias of the press and television, and many have been more than suspicious that the Westminster Parliament might allow itself to be 'corrupted' by the media – although it is upon the mass media that the very life and soul of politics often depend. Distrust of the instant power of television can be seen in the debates held by the House of Commons about televising its own proceedings. Passionate arguments have been advanced for bringing television to Westminster, apart, that is, from the State opening of Parliament at the beginning of each session, for which coverage has long been allowed. Sir Robin Day, perhaps not surprisingly for a broadcaster, has been one such advocate. 'Parliament', he once said, 'should not be as blind and stubborn towards television as it was in its unhappy struggle with the press.'

The idea was never, as Day himself has said, to broadcast live continuous television of what the Commons was doing or not doing, but rather to provide edited highlights, as in the well-established radio programme *Today in Parliament* on BBC Radio 4. But the power of editing the material has itself sparked off one of the arguments over the proposal.

The attitude of the Commons

In the 1960s, partly because a younger generation of MPs had been brought in by the 1964 and 1966 General Elections, there was a growing trend towards re-examining the case for television in Parliament. In 1965 the Commons, in their

Select Committee on Publications, started their own inquiry. In 1966 the Government proposed a closed-circuit experiment on the lines recommended by the Select Committee. On a free vote in the House the proposal was rejected by one vote. The Commons television experiment thus never took place. However, in 1968 the House of Lords set up a closed-circuit system in their part of Westminster; the episode was inconclusive, except perhaps in so far as it showed that covering the type of work done in the House of Lords was a very different proposition to what would take place in the Commons. The main arguments for television in the Commons were that it would provide the electorate with a better understanding of the political system at a time when the power and authority of traditional parliamentary democracy appeared to be both under attack and in decline.

The arguments

If Parliament is too remote from the electorate, especially the younger generations, television in the Commons might be at least one way of closing that gap. It might also help stimulate Parliament to reform some of the very old and traditional procedures employed in the conduct of its business. More vitally, it could help to maintain legislative control over the Executive, and show pressure groups that Parliament is still the central stage for Western democracy.

Television coverage of Commons' committee hearings might also, the argument goes, educate people in the workings of democracy, as in the television coverage given to Congressional committees of inquiry in the USA – the Fulbright hearings on foreign policy in the 1960s are a good case in point. The difficulty with that claim is that televising the legislature's select committees creates the danger of turning them into entertainment, as rather happened with the US Ervin Committee on the Watergate hearings in 1973–4 (Senate Select Committee on Presidential Campaign Activities). (Watergate was the scandal that led to President Nixon's downfall in 1974.) However, the argument continues, some televising of the Commons at work would at least show the public how the Government has to react to party rebels on its own side of the House, and it would illustrate the tactics of the Opposition. It would show the electorate the process of parliamentary enquiry, of rulers being challenged and questioned by those elected for that very purpose. The extended imagination of television journalists might consequently be dampened.

Parliament will not maintain its prestige and status merely by televising its ritual – in a world where power and political interests are no longer concentrated in one central place, but are diffused throughout society, it should allow coverage of its day-to-day business. How can Parliament, the pro-television lobbyists ask, cut itself off from the country's main medium of mass communication? As a Conservative parliamentarian once put it, 'Parliament must work with the tools of the age or it will sculpt no monuments for the future.'

The Times,
11 November,
1969

In 1985 the Commons voted by a majority of 12 not to allow the televising of its proceedings, the eighth Commons vote on the subject in 19 years. However, where the Commons has feared to tread, the Lords has been bolder. The experimental televising of the upper chamber took place in 1985, and in May 1986 the Lords voted to continue television broadcasting on a permanent basis. It is, of course, too early to say whether the broadcasting is a success, but certainly some of the Lords' debates have attracted large audiences, including some two million viewers on the Local Government Bill 1985.

It must be remembered that only limited broadcasts are shown on television; the sight of many empty benches during the more esoteric debates might not be conducive to public confidence in the House of Lords. But the televising of important, 'set-piece', crowded debates does seem to have performed a valuable educative, if not also entertaining, function. The BBC broadcasts edited highlights in its *The Week in the Lords,* as does ITN in *Their Lordships' House.*

Radio broadcasting

The Commons has remained far more cautious in its approach than some of its European neighbours. (It is quite possible that the American experience of political television has been at the back of many MPs minds.) In 1975 the matter was once more before the House, and again by a narrow margin (275 votes to 263) it rejected a proposal for television coverage. But a British compromise was reached at this stage and the Commons agreed to one month of experimental radio broadcasting, which took place during the summer of the same year.

The experiment attracted a lot of publicity, and no great harm seems to have come to the rather sacrosanct political role that the Commons has traditionally accorded itself. In this period news bulletins frequently used recorded extracts from speeches – extracts which were often muffled by the customary outbursts of Commons 'behaviour'. During this experimental period the broadcasts in BBC radio's *Yesterday/Today in Parliament* series were doubled in length, and it appears their audiences rose by 25 per cent. In addition, question-time was broadcast on several important occasions, as well as two full-length debates. It was estimated that the voices of some 350 MPs were heard, out of about 500 who spoke during the period.

Parliamentary Affairs, Spring 1976

In the following year the Commons considered the merits of the entire experiment and came to the conclusion that it had been worthwhile. Sound broadcasting of their proceedings was therefore made permanent with effect from 1978. But the decision represented only a partial victory for the pro-broadcasting group, and provides another example of the 'gradualist' approach of the British Parliament towards reform and innovation, not least where the conduct of its own affairs is concerned. The compromise has not, however, stifled the still powerful lobby for the use of television inside the Commons. The obviously greater impact of the medium, compared with radio, forms an almost unanswerable argument by itself, but of course that is the very point which most counts against it in MPs' minds.

Objections by MPs to the televising of Parliament have usually centred on the technical difficulties involved in broadcasting (for example, MPs tripping over television cables), the 'threat' to the reputation and stature of the House among voters, the misrepresentation of support for the leading parties in the House, the undermining of procedure and debate in the Commons and the problems of editorial control.

B. Franklin, 'MPs Objections to televising Parliament', Parliamentary Affairs, July 1986

Types and Functions of Political Television

J. Blumler, in
*The Effects of
Television,* ed.
J. Halloran,
Panther, 1970,
pp. 70–102

As Jay Blumler has observed, the makers of political television usually serve one or more of four specific functions. The first is that of acting as a spokesman for the government of the day. This was the role of the French ORTF – but it often found itself at odds with Government policies, so much so that it was disbanded in 1975, and replaced by five different organisations. The first function is usually performed in the one-party countries of Eastern Europe, and in emergent political systems. Yet the French Government's troubles in controlling its radio and television

The Observer, 4 August 1985

The Board of Governors of the BBC agreed to a request from the Prime Minister and Home Secretary not to broadcast a television programme featuring an interview with the alleged Chief of Staff of the Provisional IRA, Martin McGuinness; their decision prompted a national strike by ITV and BBC journalists. Only once before in the BBC's history had Governors seen a film before it was transmitted. This was the occasion of *Yesterday's Men* in 1971, a programme about the former Labour Government which annoyed Harold Wilson but which was nevertheless shown.

Shortly before the IRA row Mrs Thatcher, in a reference to the problems of the Middle East and the hijacking of a TWA aeroplane to Beirut, had spoken of the need to starve terrorists of the oxygen of publicity.

358

channels provide a useful reminder of the ever-present political conflicts in broadcasting under liberal-democratic regimes. The second function is to transmit information to the public centrally but in an uncommitted fashion. BBC and ITN News may be considered examples of this. West German television was almost solely confined to this function in the 1950s and 1960s in all its political productions.

The third function is to provide independent and non-partisan sources of criticism and comment. Blumler, the leading authority on political television, has stated that a good deal of Swedish television, for example, falls into this category; equally a number of Swedish television stations have done the opposite, that is to take a particular theme or point of view and build the programme around it. The political documentary poses special problems, and different European networks will tackle the same problem (coverage of Vietnam was a first-class example) in sometimes alarmingly different ways.

J.G. Blumler and D. McQuail, *Television in Politics*, Faber, 1968, p. 4f and p. 263f

The political documentary has also moved into a more investigative role and away from straight question and answer, simple studio discussion and bland commentary. Today both Government departments and pressure groups may find the spotlight of television upon them – contrast, for example, the style of BBC1's *Panorama* in the 1960s with that of the same programme in the 1970s and 1980s. But whether the political establishment is, on the whole, greatly affected by any significant increase in political television – even of the more truly investigative type – is extremely doubtful. In the United Kingdom investigative journalism may, whether in a newspaper or on television or radio, oust an MP or even, on rare occasions a minister, such as Cecil Parkinson in 1983, but it is unlikely that the Government itself will fall. That, however, is not necessarily the avowed intention of investigative documentaries.

The fourth function of political programme makers is to provide comment on behalf of one particular group or party. In a very commercially orientated network, each political party or group can finance its own television station, as happens on a wide scale in the USA.

DOCUMENT

36

The Government's Powers over Programmes

5.8 The Home Secretary also has some direct powers over programming. The terms of the BBC's Licence and Agreement and the IBA Act 1973 empower the Minister responsible for broadcasting to prescribe in writing the hours during which broadcasting may take place, and, until 1955, for the BBC he did so. In 1955, officials of the Post 359

Office and the two Broadcasting Authorities settled the hours of television broadcasting by agreement and embodied them in a set of "Rules" which were approved by the Postmaster General. In January 1972, the Minister of Posts and Telecommunications announced the end of the restriction on the hours of television and radio broadcasting. But the power to regulate the hours of broadcasting remains, and was used in the winter of 1973–74 to close down broadcasting by 10.30 pm in the interests of fuel economy. Clearly the Government needs such emergency powers, and we recommend that this power should remain and should be applied to all the Broadcasting Authorities in future.

5.9. Any Minister of the Crown may require the Broadcasting Authorities to broadcast on their stations announcements in connection with his functions. They are also required to broadcast any other matter at the request of a Minister in whose opinion an emergency has arisen or continues. The BBC and IBA may announce or not, as they please, that the Minister has required them to do so. In practice, the making of announcements (such as police messages, appeals for blood donors, reports of outbreaks of animal disease and the like) is a matter of day-to-day arrangements rather than of formal requirement. We note that the term "announcements" has always been interpreted very strictly and has not been regarded as covering explanations of Government policies. We recommend that there should be no change in these powers which should be applied to all Authorities. This power should also be extended in future to Ministers with executive powers, comparable to those of Ministers at present in charge of Departments, who may be answerable to Assemblies in Scotland and Wales.

5.10. The Home Secretary's other main power over programmes is the power to veto, by a notice in writing, the broadcasting of any matter or classes of matter. The Broadcasting Authorities can announce that such a direction has been given. This power has always been regarded as a reserve power and only five directions of a general kind have ever been given. Two of these are still in force. In 1927, when the original Licence was granted to the BBC, the Corporation was directed not to broadcast its own opinion on current affairs or on matters of public policy. This direction still stands. A similar prescription for the IBA and its programme contractors, is embodied in the IBA Act so that no direction is necessary. The prescription in the Act is wider than the direction to the BBC: the Authority must also secure exclusion of their opinion and those of their contractors from IBA publications. The BBC was also directed in 1927 not to broadcast matters of political, industrial or religious controversy, but this prohibition was speedily withdrawn in 1928. In July 1955, the BBC and the IBA were directed to refrain from anticipating parliamentary discussions by broadcasting statements or discussions on matters during the fortnight before they were due to be debated in Parliament (the "14 day Rule"). This too was subsequently suspended; initially for a six-months' experimental period and then indefinitely, on assurance from both bodies that they would so act as not to derogate from the primacy of Parliament as the forum for debating the affairs of the nation. In July 1955, the BBC was directed to refrain at all times from broadcasting controversial party political broadcasts other than those arranged in agreement with the leading political parties for broadcasting throughout the United Kingdom. Ten years later this direction too was withdrawn. The IBA was precluded by the Television Act 1954 from including matter designed to serve the interests of any political party, but they were allowed to include relays of the whole BBC series of party political broadcasts, and so include properly balanced discussions and debates on political matters. Parliament now seems to be satisfied by assurances given in correspondence by the BBC and the IBA to the Postmaster General in 1965. In 1964 the BBC and the

IBA were required to refrain at all times from broadcasting matter which uses subliminal techniques.

5.11. Although no direction has ever been made by the Postmaster General or his successors on a particular broadcast this power is, in our view, the one which poses the greatest threat to the independence of the Broadcasting Authorities. We understood that at least on one occasion in recent years the possibility of it being exercised in relation to an individual programme had arisen. This was over the BBC programme *The Question of Ulster*, which was broadcast in January 1972. We discussed this matter at some length with the BBC Chairman and Director-General. They told us that after the Home Secretary, who was then responsible for Northern Ireland but did not have Departmental responsibility for broadcasting, had made representations to the BBC early in December 1971, the Director-General and the then Chairman of the BBC had had a meeting with the Home Secretary. The Chairman had suggested that if the Government wished to stop the programme they should direct the BBC not to transmit it and the BBC would announce that this had been done. In the event, the Government did not exercise their powers of direction and despite further representations from the Home Secretary, the programme was shown. The BBC told us that, while they could not say the Home Secretary was wrong in making the representations he did, they thought they were right to continue with their plans for this programme.

5.12. We also discussed with Sir Michael Swann and Sir Charles Curran the BBC's relationship with Government on programme matters. They gave us detailed instances of how this relationship worked in practice. It is common knowledge that the BBC's relations with Sir Harold Wilson when he was Prime Minister were far from smooth. Sir Charles Curran admitted that since he became Director-General in 1969, the relationship had varied. But the BBC had "far less trouble with the Government than was commonly supposed and, far from being on the up and up, it was actually dropping". They did not feel, and neither did the former Director-General, Sir Hugh Greene, who also gave oral evidence to us, that Government threatened the BBC with the ultimate deterrents of forbidding a programme transmission or of refusing to grant a change in the licence fee. The BBC guessed that Governments were aware that if they destroyed or significantly weakened the broadcasting system, they would bring criticism on themselves. However, if only the top level felt the pressure, it would not be passed on to the programme makers; and in their view "what matters is what the programme makers feel". On the other hand the Association of Directors and Producers told us that as an organisation, the BBC had "failed dismally to resist pressure" and was the primary target for politicians because it was the "softer target". That is not the view of many politicians some of whom resent the fact that they cannot more easily get their point of view accepted by the BBC. Nor was it the view of BBC producers to whom we spoke and who made it clear to us that if pressure was brought to bear from time to time, the BBC's practice was to resist. Such, also, was the view which emerged from discussions we had with a number of civil servants, including Lord Gore-Booth, formerly Permanent Under-Secretary of State at the Foreign and Commonwealth Office.

5.13. The ITCA [Independent Television Companies' Association] acknowledged the representations which Government and other groups make to the broadcasters to be legitimate. But they stressed that, if the Minister responsible for the financing of broadcasting was "responsible for the health and standard of broadcasting", he could not represent "the views of the Government either on programmes or on the way in which a particular part of one of the broadcasting organisations was operating". They had put this 361 to Mr Roy Jenkins, when, as Home Secretary, he assumed responsibility for broadcasting, and he had confirmed that he did not intend to depart from this principle. One representative speaking from the experience of his own company said, however, that "you do get influences from certain government areas – usually very indirect, nothing so direct as a mandate to the IBA and from the IBA to the company, but, as in all forms of media experience, pressure is brought to bear from time to time in subtle ways".

5.14. It is inevitable that Ministers will be tempted to intervene. In the last resort, the Government, not the broadcasters, must make decisions about national security. Moreover, it would be undesirable and impracticable to try to prevent Ministers and Government Departments making representations to the broadcasting organisations about programmes dealing with matters for which they are responsible. Even so, distinctions can, and should, be made. There are on the one hand representations about specific programme matters made through political channels, or by Departments with responsibilities for the subject matter of the programme; these the broadcasting organisations should consider on their merits as they would representations from other individuals and organisations. On the other hand, there are attempts to influence programmes or programme content generally, by Ministers brandishing the threat of using the Home Secretary's powers of direction or, to the BBC, the threat of withholding an increase in the licence fee. Representations of the first kind are inevitable but few allegations of instances of the second have come to us from any source. We consider that if politicians attempt to influence programmes before transmission, they do so at their peril, and broadcasters have every right to make such intervention known. On such matters as the treatment of news and current affairs, the treatment of politicians by journalists and interviewers, on the issues of impartiality and fairness, we shall have more to say in Chapter 17. Here we are solely concerned with the question whether the present powers of Government over programme content are excessive or too slight or should remain unchanged.

5.15. We concluded, paradoxically, that the power of the Minister to veto the transmission of a programme gave the broadcasters greater security from undue pressure than they would have if it were removed. In the last analysis, the Government alone can judge and decide whether a programme (such as *The Question of Ulster*), constitutes a threat to national security, or is likely to lead to riots or other grave disorder. If that responsibility is taken from the Government, it must be transferred to the Broadcasting Authorities: and how much easier it will be for a Minister to paint a picture of the devastating consequences, and how much more difficult for the Authority to stand out against his judgement. In the present system, a Minister can state his grave objections: the Broadcasting Authority can then reject these objections and can inform the Minister that under his powers he is at liberty to ban the programme: but if he does, they will tell the public that he had done so. We believe that this is the best way of reconciling the freedom of the broadcasters with the legitimate concern of the Government and of placing the responsibility for prohibiting programmes in the national interest precisely where it belongs. While we think that the two remaining general directions to the BBC should be incorporated in the Licence and Agreement, we recommend that the Government's power of veto should be retained.

Report of the Committee on the Future of Broadcasting, Cmnd 6753, 1977
(Annan Report)

The Political Effects of Television

Opposing viewpoints

There are two fundamental and opposing points of view about the political effects of television. There are those who view the whole process as one which undermines and trivialises the traditional standards of democracy, as indicated by the quotation at the beginning of this chapter. To some extent these were the fears of those MPs who in the mid-1950s vigorously opposed the introduction of commercial television. Television, in this view, personalises the issue and fails to provide a proper examination of current political affairs.

The other view holds that mass education is anyway bound to improve only gradually, and that television does its best to educate people politically, achieving, on occasion, outstanding successes. However, its adherents admit that such a politically powerful and dynamic instrument as television needs to be carefully monitored. Whether there are adequate channels for that is another matter; most of the political parties began to show quite deep hostility towards the BBC, and to a lesser extent the IBA, during the 1960s and the early 1970s, a situation which the Annan Committee valiantly attempted to resolve in 1977.

Report of the Committee on the Future of Broadcasting, Cmnd 6753, 1977

Question Time on BBC 1 television. Sir Robin Day with his guests (from left to right) David Mellor MP, Lady Ralphs, Joan Maynard MP and David Alton MP

363

Party political broadcasts

In the United Kingdom the duration of party political broadcasts is strictly limited by an inter-broadcasting committee. The ratio between the times allotted to the different parties is based on the numbers of votes cast and seats fought at general elections. (In the USA 'fairness' takes on a different form: any party can claim time provided it can pay for its share at commercial rates – an arrangement which clearly reflects the competitive spirit that imbues American capitalist democracy.)

Britain's Committee on Party Political Broadcasting was established in 1947. Its membership is composed of senior representatives of the broadcasters (the BBC and IBA) and the parliamentary parties.

The basic formula involving the three main parties allows one 10-minute television slot for every two million votes – or larger share thereof – received at the previous general election. Thus for the 1979 Election the ratio was 5:5:3 between the Labour, Conservative and Liberal parties, and this has been the usual ratio, although for October 1974 it was increased to 5:5:4. It was also increased to 5:5:4 in 1983 for the Liberal/SDP Alliance. In Scotland and Wales, a party is entitled to one 10-minute television programme for each 10 per cent – or larger part thereof – of the popular regional vote it has won at the previous election.

As for parties not represented in Parliament they may only qualify for one 5-minute broadcast if they field at least 50 candidates on polling day.

The allocations for radio are based broadly, although not exactly, on these formulae. The ratios are important since they also act as procedural guidance for achieving balanced representation in all other political programmes during an election campaign.

The Committee is self-perpetuating and self-nominating, although the system has served as a model for several other European countries. But whether the system is really democratic, or whether in fact the general significance of party political broadcasts is overrated by the parties and the media themselves, are entirely separate questions.

Colin Munro,
The Times,
12 February 1982

'There is an *ad hoc* flavour about the rules. They have been worked out by the committee itself. The rules in operation at any time are not published. They are regarded by the broadcasting authorities as internal, if not secret, so details of their content and operation have to be gleaned from leaks and hints, although there has been greater openness in recent years.

The committee works like this: the broadcasting authorities, which co-operate amicably for this purpose, offer an amount of time for the use of party broadcasts. The committee, which is chaired by the Prime Minister or another Minister, then decides how it should be allocated. . . . All this means that the broadcasting authorities' handling of political matters is more open to challenge than has previously been thought. There is no detailed statutory regulation of party political broadcasts or election broadcasts. There is, in fact, no obligation to broadcast these at all, and one way out of trouble would be the cessation of the practice. But the BBC and IBA, from motives of public education and service to democracy, continues to hand airtime to the politicians.

In the absence of statutory guidelines, the broadcasting authorities have filled the vacuum with the rules worked out by the Committee on Party Political Broadcasting. Whether in the present situation the committee's arrangements, if unchanged, would be held by a court to satisfy the general obligations of balance and impartiality is at least highly questionable.'

Television and Voting Behaviour

The effects of television upon voting behaviour have already been seen to be somewhat limited, and indeed a major survey conducted at the time of the 1959 General Election concluded that television made no vital difference to the outcome. 'Political change was neither related to the degree of exposure nor to any particular programme or argument put forward.' Parallel surveys specially conducted in other Western European countries at about the same time came forward with similar conclusions, and tended to show that 'floating' voters were no more influenced than 'stable' voters – one theory being that floating voters were in any case less interested in politics.

J. Trenaman and D. McQuail, *Television and the Political Image*, Methuen, 1961

Voters, in fact, are deliberately, if subconsciously, selective – they will choose the broadcasts and material which reinforce their beliefs, already shaped by other factors – a process sociologists call 'selective exposure'. If 'alien' material should be watched, perhaps by mistake or out of curiosity, its political propaganda will be re-interpreted to fit previous experience, loyalties and opinions.

'No one can deny that Mrs Thatcher sold herself very effectively in the 1983 election campaign. What she demonstrated was that performing well on television has now become one of the major measures of a politician's worth.

The Listener, 23 June 1983

The Prime Minister was helped by her opponents' problems. Mr Foot, to his credit, is no Saatchi product, much less a graduate of the Gordon Reece school of charm. David Steel, camera-wise and smooth as silk, eclipsed Roy Jenkins only after the Ettrick Bridge "summit", and then never completely. The scramble to succeed Michael Foot, and Roy Jenkins's replacement by the telegenic David Owen, owes something at least to the older leaders' failure to meet the rapacious demands of television.

However, Mrs Thatcher's performing skills stand up in their own right. While many may recoil from the hectoring style, know-it-all manner and quasi-regal airs and graces, she is undeniably crisp and clear, confident mistress of the facts and figures which underpin her simplistic world view.

Television's professionals have a problem with Mrs Thatcher. It took an ordinary viewer, Mrs Diana Gould of Cirencester, to break one of the toughest moulds in British politics: that of the Prime Minister's expensively nurtured cool. On *Nationwide's* election phone-in (BBC1, 24 May), Mrs Gould harried Mrs Thatcher with questions about why the *General Belgrano* had been sunk when

365

sailing away from the task force and outside the total exclusion zone. Apart from repeatedly saying that the *Belgrano* endangered our ships, Mrs Thatcher wrongly denied that it was sailing away from them. Mrs Gould challenged this and, for the only time during the campaign, Thatcher was unable to correct her questioner. She tried smiles, offered to disclose all in 30 years or so, even assumed an air of heavy authority: "I ask you to accept this . . ." Mrs Gould did not and would not, and said it was not good enough.

Only once more did Mrs Thatcher seem in less than full control. On the BBC tele-radio production *Election Call* (BBC1 and Radio 4, 7 June), as the first call came through she peered around uncertainly and asked Sir Robin Day. "Can you see Mr Crawford? I can only hear him." Sir Robin rather waspishly replied that the questioner was on the other end of a telephone and not in vision.

For Labour, broadcasting was needed more than ever to develop a positive image of its leader, because Michael Foot was scandalously vilified by the press: caricatured as Worzel Gummidge, criticised for his age, his alleged infirmity and poor dress sense, his odd spectacles, his pushy wife, his old-hat rhetoric, even, final straw, his dog.

These banal concerns insinuated their way into radio and television too. At the beginning of the campaign, in *The World at One* (Radio 4, 16 May), Peter Kellner covered the tedious ground of Foot's various tics. Right at the end, on *Election 83* (Radio 4, 9 June) a perfectly self-propelled Foot was said to be "picking his way" along, implying he was an invalid.

But whatever broadcasting's shortcomings, Labour did not help itself too much. Both Jim Mortimer and Mrs Foot made well publicised gaffes about Foot's standing as leader. Besides, the Labour Party failed to exploit the Tories' mistakes. When Tom Finnegan, Conservative candidate for Stockton South, was found to have had fascist connections, television viewers saw Sir Keith Joseph decline to share his platform. However, when Thatcher refused to disown Finnegan, Labour failed to attack far Right infiltration of the Tory Party. Even worse, nor did it defend itself when one of the Tories' new look five-minute *Party Election Broadcasts* (26 May) in effect called the Labour Party a Communist Front. After television viewers had seen Michael Foot share a platform with Militant candidate Pat Wall, he was nicely set up for a hostile question on *TV Eye* (26 May). "Are Militant no longer a pestilential nuisance?" inquired Alastair Burnet. Labour did nothing to force him to ask Mrs Thatcher the following week "Why are ex-Nazis standing for election as Tories?"

The great difference between Labour and the Tories lay in their willingness to pursue arguments in public. When Francis Pym expressed doubts about a landslide victory on BBC1's *Campaign Question Time* he was put down by Thatcher and kept quiet. The same applied to James Prior's dissent on unemployment. Labour's divisions were aired so openly that they inevitably fed broadcast coverage. Once Denis Healey's reservations about phasing out Polaris without a quid pro quo from the Soviet Union became known, Peter Shore expressed similar sentiments on *Election Call* (24 May) and was countered by Frank Allaun on *The World at One* (25 May), who said Polaris would go within five years.'

The Granada Survey and the
Marplan Poll

One survey conducted by Granada TV in the marginal seats of Preston North and Preston South during the February 1974 campaign attempted to formulate some tentative conclusions about the effect of television in closely fought constituencies, and in particular upon undecided voters. Evidence suggested – though only just – that there was truth in the Tory suspicion that opinion polls and television were responsible for the Conservative defeat, by lulling some Tory voters into a sense of false security which encouraged them to defect to the Liberals, while shocking would-be Labour defectors back into their own camp. But the evidence was very limited, and of course, it is always very complicated to disentangle the effects of television from the primary factors of political socialisation.

Another survey (completed the day after polling day in the same general election – the Marplan poll for *Broadcast,* the specialist broadcasting weekly –) suggested that radio and television had a profound effect upon the way people voted at the polls. It claimed that some 7 per cent of people had said that they had actually changed their minds as a result of a television or radio programme. (This figure rose to at least 10 per cent for women voters in the sample, while male voters were almost as low as 3 per cent.) Social class showed up no difference, but the effects of broadcasting were most pronounced upon the young (18–34 year-olds), 9 per cent claiming to have changed their minds for such reasons.

That still left the great bulk of the population in the sample saying that television and radio either had no effect or merely acted to back up what they already believed. Yet the sample also found that 42 per cent of those interviewed had seen seven or more television discussion programmes (apart from the party political broadcasts) over a period of 18 days. One-half of those surveyed said they had found discussion programmes useful; but only 4 per cent found them very helpful, and 14 per cent could not really identify what they thought about such programmes. Those replies seem to indicate that the main purpose of political television, especially at election periods, is to provide information; and that by no means implies that previously conceived political images and attitudes will be abandoned. However, as Mark Twain once said, 'education and soap are deadly in the *long-run.'*

Also interesting was the survey's findings that about the same proportion of people as the national turn-out in the election itself had seen at least one broadcast by each party. One or more of the Conservative broadcasts had been seen by 79 per cent of the sample, compared with 74 per cent for Labour and 76 per cent for Liberal.

An individual will become more interested in political information if he is already involved in politics or if he thinks that political events will affect him personally. But as Blumler has remarked, there is almost a law that the people who follow election campaigns more closely on television – via both straightforward reports and more investigative programmes – are precisely the same ones who are

367

the best informed and who read most about them in newspapers and magazines.

Finally, since 1981 an organisation or a member of the public with a complaint about political bias on radio or television may refer a grievance to the Broadcasting Complaints Commission for adjudication.

The Political Effects of Newspapers

A changing role in the early post-war period

The case of newspapers shows both similarities to and differences from that of broadcasting. Their influence upon voting behaviour is even slighter, yet political impartiality is non-existent – all newspapers on occasion take stands for or against the Government and Opposition. The party system and the newspaper organisations have, historically, been closely related, but that relationship has been very much overshadowed since the Second World War by the importance of broadcasting.

The degree of political partisanship of newspapers changed quite remarkably in the 1960s and 1970s. The custom in the 1940s and 1950s was for each party to enjoy the support of an official or at least quasi-official newspaper. The *Daily Herald,* which ceased publication in 1964, was a prime example; in the 1940s and 1950s its editorial strategy was not so much to question policies and to initiate ideas as to measure and deliver the kind of support the Labour Party required. In the same way *The Daily Telegraph* in the 1950s was much more concerned to maintain a Conservative government in office, in contrast to its more recent independent line. The balance in party political terms has also changed; the spirit of early twentieth-century Liberalism, as far as the newspaper industry was concerned, was buried by the 1960s: the transformation of the *Manchester Guardian* into *The Guardian* in 1959 meant a move away from traditional Liberal Party support towards a more generally left-wing approach, and the absorption of the *News Chronicle* into the *Daily Mail* in 1960 left the Liberals without any newspaper at all.

The days when Lloyd George and Asquith actually tried to buy newspapers – the Conservative Party being almost ruled by Lord Northcliffe and other press barons – had long since passed. But the move away from even a diluted measure of political partisanship was still accelerating in the 1960s, when the more 'popular' parts of the press appeared, in general elections, to adopt a rather more inquiring attitude into the advantages and disadvantages of the policies of the big two parties before eventually recommending their readers to support the party with which they had traditionally sympathised (Labour in the case of the *Daily Mirror,* Tory with the *Daily Mail*). On the other hand, three tabloids, the *Daily Express, The Sun* and *The Star,* have been consistent in their support of the Conservatives.

Since 1959 the prerogative of assessing party strengths at election time has been transferred to opinion polls, whose findings are reported as much by television and radio as by the press, which largely commissions them in the first place. Moreover, in the 1950s 'consensus politics' (Butskellism) seemed a significant notion: the argument was not quite so much about party philosophy and ideology, about political ends, as about political means, the mechanics of achieving a common social aim. To that extent newspapers were deprived of the traditional scale of preferred party loyalties. However, in the late 1960s and in the 1970s the ideological gap between the parties widened again, which, but for the enormous growth of television, might have given newspapers a greater political role.

The way they were: Low represents Churchill's quiet departure from the office of Prime Minister with the Press silenced by a newspaper strike.

Reprinted in *The Observer*, 5 January 1986

The 'Freedoms' of the Press

'Many of the most interesting news stories are ones that someone wants to stop you printing – for example, the revelations about ex-Vice-President Agnew's financial gain from Maryland state contracts or about President Nixon's missing secret tapes', wrote Alistair Hetherington, former editor of *The Guardian* in 1973 (30 November). Hetherington went on to comment that the area of investigative journalism is always a grey one; how far, for instance, should newspapers wait until policy decisions are announced officially before reporting them? Leaks from the Cabinet came ultimately from ministers, and they are almost a standard feature of political life. But newspapers do, of course, run into difficulties in view of the all-embracing effects of D-Notices, Crown privilege and official secrets laws, despite various recommendations for change since the time of Franks and Younger.

Even the 'traditional freedoms' taken for granted in the West may by no means be granted to its correspondents abroad, including those in many developing states. Such a viewpoint was expressed at the Conference of the Commonwealth Press Union in 1977: Dr P.D. Cole, the managing director of the *Daily Times of Nigeria,* said that the tradition of British journalists was to attack their Government whenever possible. He continued:

> 'we think that press people and others throughout the world should accept that the press in different environments often can have different functions and objectives, and we look to fellow journalists for understanding in disseminating this fact.'

Opinion Polls

A final word should be said about that specialised phenomenon in the media – opinion polls. Opinion polls have, in the main, a reasonable record, but there have been one or two memorable upsets, such as the widespread prediction of victory by Dewey over Truman in the 1948 American presidential election. In the United Kingdom nearly all the polls predicted a Labour victory in the 1970 General Election, as well as misjudging the voters' feelings in the by-election at Leyton in 1965, which was to have seen the return to the Commons of Patrick Gordon Walker, the Foreign Secretary. It must be remembered that the British electorate has a healthy scepticism of the pollsters, not least during by-elections as shown in the Brecon and Radnor contest in 1985, Portsmouth South in 1984, and Bermondsey (London) in 1983. The *Daily Mail* is associated with NOP (National Opinion Polls), founded in 1958; NOP in turn has an interest in MORI (Market and Opinion Research International) which carries out polls for the *Daily Mirror, The Sunday Times* and the *Daily Express. The Observer* has been associated with the Harris poll as has ITN. The Conservative Party, on the other hand, with its richer resources, carries out more ambitious and extensive researches privately. Marplan is used by *The Guardian* and Gallup by *The Daily Telegraph* and the BBC. In February 1974 only Business Decisions predicted an actual Labour win, although in such a close contest it was admittedly difficult to predict anything with certainty. In the October 1974 Election it was again Business Decisions (this time followed by Gallup) which came very close to 'predicting' the final result; the other main polls all predicted a Labour win, but were too generous in their assessments. In the mid-1970s it was estimated that about £100 000 a year was being spent on political polling: in an election year the figure would rise to over a quarter of a million pounds. That figure still looks small, however, in comparison with the annual amount committed to political polls and advertising in the USA.

The Observer,
1 September 1974

The failure to predict accurately the 1970 result is no doubt remembered most bitterly by all concerned, not least by Harold Wilson. When the polls conducted their post-mortems they found that their earlier surveys had been largely accurate, but that there had been a large late swing towards the Conservatives in the last four days of the election campaign, perhaps because of the poor trade figures that were issued just before polling day, or, more bizarrely, because of England's defeat in the World Cup. But any suggestion of a last-minute shift in electoral opinion, on a wide scale just before polling day, must remain very much 'not proven' – such an idea risks major conflict with all the fundamental lessons drawn from the studies of voting behaviour.

The opinion polls tried to allow for late swings in their predictions for the 1974 General Elections. But the lessons learned in 1970 and applied in 1974 proved once again that, when it comes to political predictions projected through the media, light does not necessarily follow darkness. But, as underlined above, voting intentions at the February 1974 Election were not easy to analyse, while boundary changes in the constituencies and the increased importance of marginal seats made the polls' life even harder. Opinion research also sometimes has a difficult relationship with the other parts of the media: the newspapers do not particularly want long analyses about the intentions of the voters – they want to be able to print just a few succinct points; complex findings may thus, especially in the more popular press, be reduced to oversimple conclusions which mislead both the electorate and politicians. Furthermore, to be scrupulously fair to the polls, it should be emphasised that their findings are not predictions; they merely relate to the immediate past. It should also be noted that in 1979 all polls (apart from one NOP poll) recorded a Tory lead, although the margins varied substantially. Perhaps polls are more valuable in identifying views rather than intentions, although the results may not be palatable to the parties (for instance, RSL in the 1979 campaign showed that three-quarters of Labour supporters approved of the Tories' policy of selling council houses to their tenants). The polls consistently showed a Conservative lead in the 1983 campaign.

Summary

In various ways the role of the media in British political life is crucial. In the first place the United Kingdom has a large number of daily newspapers and the highest newspaper readership – at least 75 per cent of the adult population claim to read a newspaper. However, to what extent the tabloids can be justly called serious political newspapers is entirely another matter; on the other hand, a greater degree of political comment and reporting may be found in popular daily regional newspapers, such as *The Western Morning News* or *The Scotsman.* The broadcasting authorities (the BBC and the IBA) unlike most newspapers, claim to be politically independent. Nevertheless, that does not prevent fractious relationships developing between the Government and television or radio, most notably the BBC in relation to programmes on Ireland.

The influence of television especially can easily be overrated. About 95 per cent of television programmes are probably instantly forgettable, although that does not mean the viewer experienced no enjoyment. In the political sense, television performs a crucial role of educating and disseminating information. Its function as a moulder of political views is there but it is a strictly limited one. Whatever the political parties at times may claim, both the BBC and IBA do maintain by and large a political balance, in a way that many other Western broadcasting media do not. In the same context newspapers are largely bought to reinforce the voter's predetermined political opinions, not to reshape them fundamentally.

One major difficult area is the annual tussle the BBC has to face over the licence fee, but this has not yet affected the political independence of the BBC as the unsavoury row over the *Real Lives* programme in 1985 illustrated. A less difficult problem, but a problem real enough, is to determine the basis of the coverage the broadcasting authorities give to the political parties at election time. The three main groups receive near equal coverage, currently in the ratio of 5:5:4 (Conservative: Labour: Liberal–SDP).

The most telling criticism of the BBC and IBA is that coverage of industrial disputes is sometimes too Establishment, that is employer-orientated and less favourable in overall tone towards the unions. That does not prevent trade union leaders using television to just as good effect as major politicians. In some cases it may not be in the politicians' best interests to over-use television; poor performances through that medium must have contributed towards certain election defeats, such as that of Sir Alec Douglas-Home in 1964, Mr Heath in 1974 and Mr Foot in 1983.

Questions

1. How valid is the assertion that television's news output 'shows a characteristic anti-union, pro-establishment and anti-left-wing bias'? (Joint Matriculation Board)

2. 'Nowadays newspapers have negligible political influence.' Discuss.

3. What political controls are there over the media in Britain? Should there be more or less control? (London)

4. Discuss the grounds on which public opinion polls on political questions have been criticised. (London)

14   **Culture and Change**

'Mr Attlee's Cabinet had three old Etonians; mine has six – life is twice as good under the Conservatives.'

Harold Macmillan, 1959

The Definition of Culture

The emotional environment

'One day the author of *The Russians* tried to photograph a Soviet petrol station, but was prevented by the workmen in charge. Remembering the way it had been forbidden to photograph the railway station where Tolstoy's coffin was resting in 1910, his wife Ann remarked, "So you see, its nothing new. It was the same under the Tsars. They're the same people".'

Milovan Djilas,
The Sunday Times,
11 July 1976

Political systems come and go, but the basic characteristics of the peoples and races that make up, or help to define, those systems may not change so rapidly. In most developed states, certain fundamental values form a backdrop to the established order.

Political culture is the social part of the constitutional equation; it consists of norms and widely held beliefs, which criss-cross the political process, creating some sense of political unity. For example, Mark Bonham-Carter, the Chairman of the then Community Relations Commission, commented on radio that he was proud of the British tradition that 'we stand by our word'. Similarly, as Richard Hoggart showed in his *Uses of Literacy,* the notions of 'equality of opportunity', 'rags to riches achievement', 'property-owning democracy', are all part of Western society's staple rhetoric. And a variant of the Victorian Protestant ethic (at least in terms of hard work and discipline) can equally be found in Communist states. On the other hand, such cultural and political 'rules' may not be universally accepted, if only because of either the 'horizontal' divisions of social class or the 'vertical' divisions of nationality and regionalism.

BBC Radio 3,
10 July 1976

The term 'political culture', however, is all-embracing; it can also mean the particular type of political system a country has (in contrast to the forces that lie behind the system) or, rather more obviously, the kind of institutions that make up the 'status quo'. In this systems context political culture can be likened to a mathematical game: a problem is set and two countries, indeed two rival parties, philosophies or ideologies, may arrive at roughly the same answer, or rather a similar goal or objective. But the solution – how they get there – is another matter entirely. The working out of the sum may be totally different in each case; different mistakes may be made on the journey, but either way, partly through accident, partly through design, policies will be found.

This approach we might call a macro one that embraces, in part, the methodology of comparative government, and that would include posing root questions about the differences (or indeed similarities) between political systems (for example, totalitarianism versus liberal-democracy) or between political philosophies (for example, Marxism versus Conservatism or Nationalism versus Socialism).

But a more involved approach, in fact a more rewarding and possibly more exciting interpretation of 'political culture', is what we might term the micro method. In other words we should pose detailed questions about the cultural values that underpin each national system. 'Values' would include such things as:

(a) attitudes popularly held about the worth of parliamentary representatives;
(b) attitudes towards local representation;
(c) attitudes towards trade unions, management and interest groups;
(d) respect for the rule of law;
(e) the prevalence of political satire and comment;
(f) the acceptance of bureaucracy or 'red-tape' and official secrecy;
(g) symbolic qualities (such as the monarchy in the UK), perhaps the one feature common, in some way or another, to all political systems;
(h) class and status consciousness;
(i) the recruitment of élites;
(j) attitudes towards corruption and bribery, plus control of the economy;
(k) racial attitudes and attitudes towards other nations (including, presumably in the past, colonialism);
(l) party membership or the like (we should also not forget here the lasting importance of Almond and Verba's work, *The Civic Culture*);
(m) socialisation, including the influence of religion and education, and voting behaviour;
(n) electoral methods, attitudes towards versions of PR, for instance.

There is nothing to prevent us from proceeding to the macro stage, of course, from such micro studies. Indeed, we might well treat the micro output as leading to, in broad terms, the following four-way international model:

(i) similar cultural values, similar political systems (Norway and Sweden, Australia and UK?);
(ii) similar cultural values, different political systems (Indonesia and Malaysia, Afghanistan and Pakistan?);
(iii) different cultural values, similar political systems (UK and India, Bulgaria and Poland?);
(iv) different cultural values, different political systems (UK and China, USA and Iran?).

DOCUMENT

37

Culture and Deference

That brings us to the concept of political culture: the attitudes of a society towards its governmental institutions and its behaviour patterns in relation to them. While constitutional traditions shape the formal arrangements made for the redress of grievances, it is societal values that will determine how individuals actually set about complaints against authority.

In writing about political culture, it is easy to fall into the trap of caricature generalisations about national character. In a recent book the London correspondent of *Pravda* observed that in everyday life, as in sport, the English obey rules because they are "the rules of the game", a rosy picture since we know that many people make false income tax declarations or claim welfare benefits to which they are not entitled. It may be true, however, that there is less inclination than in some countries to think of administrative decisions as the application of laws (much administration, indeed, operates according to procedures that are not fixed in law at all). As a result, the ordinary citizen is less likely to think of "the law" (i.e. the courts) as a natural channel for his complaints.

Perhaps the British are less litigious than other people. This may be because access to the courts is difficult: procedures are almost incomprehensible, delays long and costs prohibitive. There is no free administrative court, as in France, to which the citizen need only submit his complaint, leaving investigation of his case in the court's hand. Moreover, the law itself is usually incomprehensible: scattered in numerous places, the language technical and much depending on earlier judicial decisions impossible for the layman to read up. Most of Europe followed Napoleon in codifying law. The apparent simplicity of codified law may be deceptive, but in so far as the average citizen abroad believes that he can ascertain his rights for himself, legal remedies may appear more attractive to him than they do in Britain. Other cultural factors help explain why certain societies are more prone to litigation than others. Whatever the reason, the British may prefer extra-legal solutions to their problem.

The American authors of the *Civic Culture* saw in Britain a combination of "political competence", i.e. a belief in one's own ability to influence decision-makers, and "political deference", i.e trust of decision-makers based on their superior status. Both are relevant to how grievances are pursued by individuals. Much of the working class, notably the underprivileged of the inner cities, has in fact lacked a sense of competence and – objectively – has not had the competence required to defend its interests against administrators. Deference simply led it to accept their decisions. Deference has declined considerably in recent years, however, and lack of competence is being compensated by the growth of organisations to help the less-educated pursue their claims. On the other hand, the middle classes have long felt competent to deal with public authorities and this may help also to explain the relatively weak development of formal channels for the redress of grievances. Members of the "political class" (those whose voice was heard in debates about administrative reform) have not felt much need for formalised arrangements to protect their individual interests, preferring to rely on their personal influence or the influence of intermediaries to whom they could turn.

Much of decision-making in individual cases is not formalised in Britain but involves the exercise of discretion by officials. Whether trust or deference explains this relationship between administrator and citizen, it is another reason why formalised procedures to challenge decisions have been slow to emerge. The tendency (a declining one, however) has been to accept decisions even if one does not like them. Again, a comparison may be made. Crozier has characterised French culture as one that dislikes personal contacts between power-holders and subordinates (horror of face-to-face relations). Personalised power and discretionary decisions offend because they place the citizen in a dependency relationship with regard to particular officials. The result is a preference for the de-personalised application of general rules to individual cases and the handling of complaints in a similarly impersonal manner. Perhaps the fact that the British are less egalitarian in spirit makes them willing to allow officials discretionary powers. It may also be that there is less fear of partisan bias. Class apart, Britain has had few of the cleavages that divide certain other nations into mutually distrusting camps, though in Northern Ireland, with its Catholic-Protestant division, one finds the same suspicion of bias in decision-making as in other societies with religious or ideological cleavages.

Another comparison is possible. Dahrendorf has stressed the extent to which law is seen as the organising principle of society in Germany. The preference is to regulate all sorts of conflict by law rather than by negotiation, for example in industrial relations. Many institutions of German society are organised on the assumption that disagreements can be solved in a "rational" and "objective" manner by experts, reflecting a certain dislike of politics. The British are more likely to recognise that conflicts of interest and disputes involving value judgements do not allow such solutions: the centrality of politics is accepted. This colours the approach to the redress of grievances.

F.F. Ridley, *Parliamentary Affairs*, Winter 1984

D. Kavanagh,
Political Culture,
Macmillan, 1972,
p. 10

Denis Kavanagh has called 'political culture' a convenient shorthand expression for the 'emotional environment' within which the political process operates. He says – in respect of the micro usage of the term – that political culture may be defined as the 'overall distribution' of people's attitudes towards political objects. Thus, 'political culture' can be interpreted as meaning the psychological and emotional factors that make up the character of a nation and of its various parts. A nation's self-image, however, will not necessarily tally with the image that other nations have of it; this has been illustrated in the UK's relations with other Commonwealth countries.

One country's political institutions, therefore, may be very much the same as another's in basic form and appearance, and indeed in method of operation, but this does not mean that the cultural values associated with them can be assumed to be similar.

Political culture in the UK, however, has come to comprise widely varying values, attitudes and norms. Lord Balfour summed it up thus:

H.V. Wiseman,
*Politics in
Everyday Life,*
Blackwell, 1966,
p. 57

'it is evident that our whole political machinery presupposes a people so fundamentally at one that they can safely afford to bicker, and so sure of their own moderation that they are not disturbed by the never-ending din of political conflict.'

In a lengthy article in 1979 on national attitudes John Cunningham observed:

> 'Traditionally, tolerance, fair-play and fortitude, egalitarianism and individuality are singled out as having a special appeal to the English; all under-pinned and made workable by a consensus stressing reasonableness and non-violence.
>
> These are, of course, moral values, and the great religions lay claim to them as well. They are British because they started to take on special emphasis before the formation of the United Kingdom; they were epitomised particularly in the British Empire. And the over-riding question is whether they are a crumbling relevance now; no longer representing, as they once did, the aspirations of a successful nation.'

The Guardian, 14 November 1979

Cultural Reorientation and Symbolism

In the UK, continuing problems in Ulster, economic recession and the growth of a Scottish consciousness must lead to a reconsideration of the very unity of the United Kingdom. If, for example, what motivates SNP or Plaid Cymru recruitment is a recoil from traditional party politics, with its ritualised factors, it is clear that, even in what is often regarded as a largely static society, English values are changing. Professor Wiseman once remarked that in the United Kingdom modern and traditional attitudes were well combined to produce 'homogeneous culture and traditions', but this may be far more true of the 1950s than of the 1970s and 1980s. He went on to remark that Britain possessed a strong sense of national identity. That may have been true in the past, but after the transition from Empire to Commonwealth in the 1950s and 1960s, and membership of the EEC in 1973, the idea cannot go unquestioned.

However, it is true to say that hitherto there has been no major cleavage along ethnic, linguistic or religious lines; and, with only some 5 per cent of the population employed in agriculture, Britain is predominantly an industrial nation. Moreover, there are still common values about the general rules of politics, let alone about basic constitutional principles such as the idea that, declining turn-outs or not, elections are the most suitable means of choosing governments. Competition among political parties is another fundamental result of the same attitude; parties have the right to grow up as much as to wither away. And the general agreement on what is expected of various political offices, on their functions and on the kinds of aims a government should have – together with a consensus about both the rights and duties of the citizen – also forms part of the political culture, of the political 'rules'. Political symbols are important promoters of political unity. In particular, the monarchy is of key importance where the 'ceremonial' and 'dignified' parts of the system (to take Bagehot's sub-divisions of the constitution) are concerned. The Queen's Speech at the beginning of each parliamentary session is a careful and subtle means of lending to a full and wide-ranging political programme the lawful respectability any government seeks.

377

The many parliamentary traditions – customs, conventions and ceremony – may be thought old-fashioned and time-consuming; nevertheless they provide a reminder of Parliament's long history and, again, serve as an underlying unifying force (even if sometimes only for parliamentarians). As Bagehot said, the 'dignified' parts of the constitution 'excite and preserve the reverence of the population'. And, of course, as Richard Rose has commented, Parliament itself symbolises the British way of politics, since pride in it is stimulated through school (although far less than American pride in the US constitution) and through television.

Popular Attitudes

At the heart of any political culture can be found a whole range of attitudes held by the electorate towards its political masters. That, however, is easy enough to state; it is far more difficult to measure their extent accurately. Popular opinions of politicians, of course, may vary considerably from class to class and from region to region. Members of Parliament nowadays are frequently viewed with distrust, as people seeking personal gain and advancement rather than the common good. But in 1973 two notable rival polls brought forward contradictory evidence on this question.

See also C. Leeds, *Politics in Action*, Stanley Thornes, 1986, (section J)

An ORC poll, conducted for *The Sunday Times* and the BBC, found that MPs were largely distrusted by the electorate. But the NOP surveys for Granada Television's *State of the Nation* series, which were rather more extensive, came to different conclusions. The BBC survey found that 58 per cent of people believed that MPs were at Westminster for personal gain or ambition. The Granada poll found that, while some 39 per cent of their wider sample agreed with a similar proposition, 33 per cent disagreed; and in response to the question, 'why do you think people become MPs?', the most common single answer was 'to serve the country'.

The Granada survey also tended to show that many people thought MPs were not in Parliament to run the country so much as to deal with specific causes, complaints and grievances (an interesting reflection on public knowledge of the Ombudsman machinery). Of the sample 26 per cent thought that MPs were doing a good job, 35 per cent a fair job. It was also noteworthy how MPs were rated in terms of their value and influence. MPs were thought useful by 41 per cent – less so than doctors, judges and, strangely, Government ministers, but more than managing directors of major companies, trade union leaders and senior civil servants. When asked how much influence they thought a Member of Parliament had, only 17 per cent answered 'a great deal' – the lowest figure among the seven categories apart, significantly enough, from the 15 per cent for senior civil servants. 57 per cent agreed that MPs should use their own judgment even if that meant going against public opinion. At least on that sample, a majority seemed to endorse the tradition of representative parliamentary government, and therefore by implication to reject a system of mandated delegates to Parliament.

The other striking finding was that the degree of politicisation was higher in Wales and Scotland (more so in the latter) than in England, in terms of consciousness and knowledge of the workings of Parliament.

In 1979 (29 November) *New Society* produced an extensive survey of the electorate's social, economic and political attitudes. Among its many findings were the following conclusions:

> '[The] judgment of the country's future is *not* due to any feeling that British governments are notably worse than obvious comparisons. In October 1974, as part of his Essex University British Election Study, Ivor Crewe asked voters to say how well they thought we were governed by comparison with other European countries. Then, 52 per cent rated our governments about average, and 33 per cent went so far as to say that they did well. Only 11 per cent gave a definite thumbs-down.
>
> Half a decade later, markedly fewer (26 per cent) think we are governed well, using the same European yardstick. And when we asked people for a forecast how well we would be governed in ten years' time, the total of optimists notched down a little further (to 22 per cent). But, still, the majority stuck with their unflustered estimate that our rulers were no better and no worse than elsewhere.
>
> The survey also found that with regard to British expectations about fair treatment from the police and bureaucrats the position had hardly changed since Almond and Verba's study in 1959. Liberal voters, however, were clearly the most sensitive about the potential growth in government bureaucracy and restrictions.
>
> People are perhaps reflecting the *gains* which Professor Richard Rose pointed to in his recent Strathclyde University survey of the way in which our lives have changed in Britain in recent years. He noted, too, a *narrowing* of regional differences over the years. That may help explain the relative lack of regional distinctions in the replies from our own respondents.
>
> Perhaps the British are whistling in the dark; or perhaps not. You have to assume, in a representative democracy, that people are pretty good judges of how things affect them and their interests. You could say that our survey results add up to a nicely calculated two cheers for the 1980s.'

Élites and Status

Recruitment to a country's political élites is a further important cultural variable. Once British people always deferred to birth and wealth. This picture has been redrawn by developments such as the 1944 Education Act, but socio-political classes in industrialised countries are just as self-perpetuating as in more traditional societies. One survey reinforced the view that the Oxford and Cambridge élite still dominates the corridors of power and strengthens the political culture, if only by continuing it. The survey held that the ancient universities were still associated with the image of a good civil servant, and that civil service selectors (75 per cent of

D. Boyd, *Elites and their Education*, NFER, 1973, chapter 5

whom in 1939 were from Oxford or Cambridge) tended to choose people in their own image: 'within the ancient universities themselves . . . there were corridors to the Civil Service. Many dons and civil servants had been contemporaries at Oxford and Cambridge. The student was therefore exposed to the merits of a civil service career.'

See also *The Times Higher Educational Supplement,* 30 October 1973 and *Social Studies Review,* September 1986, pp. 2–7

The 1973 survey showed that the proportion of people educated at public schools in the upper strata of British society had changed very little since the Second World War. Between 1962 and 1970 there was a slight decrease in the percentage in the Civil Service (at under-secretary level and above): but that still left 62 per cent from public school, while in the Royal Navy, in the Army and among directors of the clearing banks there was a slight increase. Élites breed élites: it was found that for 1970–1 ambassadors were 82 per cent public school educated, judges 80 per cent, major-generals and those of higher rank 86 per cent, bishops 67 per cent and bank directors 80 per cent. As seen earlier in Chapter 4, Oxbridge dominates Administration Trainee recruits to the Civil Service (from 56 per cent in 1977 to 59 per cent in 1985). A recent survey of 465 judges has shown that of ten Law Lords, nine went to public school and eight to Oxford or Cambridge. Of the 23 Court of Appeal judges, 20 attended public school and Oxbridge, while for 79 High Court judges the figures were 42 and 53 respectively.

The Independent, 12 January 1987

The image of an élite: judges in procession

Theories of élitism gained wide currency through the writings of Mosca and Pareto (in inter-war Italy), who both, in their own ways, attempted to demonstrate that Marxism was an ideological myth; for them élitism was something practical and tangible. Pareto concluded that élites invariably got their own way through the use of fraud and force. Of the two it was probably Pareto who made the greater mark on political and sociological literature.

Pareto distinguished between *governing* and *non-governing* élites, the latter enjoying high status in society if not, like the former, day-to-day power and influence. Pareto remarked that history was 'a graveyard of aristocrats'; the non-governing élites were the graveyard's dead.

There have been few studies of British, in contrast to American, élites, and even the 1973 survey mentioned immediately above was conducted by an American academic. Two American works that have also been influential (if controversial) in the academic study of élites are: C.W. Mills s *The Power Elite* (on national élites) and Floyd Hunter's *Community Power Structure* (on local élites). Both were based on research of the 1950s, and both argued that élites resulted from the fact that certain individuals were always joined together by common social and moral values.

Socio-political status

At the other end of the spectrum, groups whose status is challenged (although their property and income are not necessarily threatened) and those who think they should have higher status may turn to politicians who can respond to their feelings and articulate their latent demands. In the 1950s much of the support for Senator Joseph McCarthy in the USA in his violently anti-Communist campaigns came from the *nouveau riche* – from people like the new oil tycoons of Texas or the self-made industrialists of the Mid-West and California. Such people clearly felt that they were not being accorded the higher status they thought they merited. Another American example of those whose status is threatened, is George Wallace who, in the 1960s and early 1970s, was able to capitalise on fears among working-class and lower middle-class whites in the Deep South who not only had real economic grievances but also felt under threat from the rising tide of black consciousness. The Northern Ireland Executive was in effect terminated in 1974 by a general strike – a strike organised by working-class Protestants out of resistance to power-sharing with the Catholics. That resistance was born of status anxiety. Powellism on the United Kingdom mainland falls into much the same category – illustrated, for example, when London dockers marched in support of Mr Powell's anti-immigration policies in 1968.

The *poujadist* element is present, if hidden, in every political society. Cultural norms are adjusted with difficulty; the case of the Englishman who in 1976 refused to sell his house to any but an 'English family', with the resulting legal and political difficulties, was an all too pointed example.

Given such cultural and historical distinctions, the customary routes to occupational advancement, and to the acquisition of wealth and particular life-styles may be wholly or partly blocked, so that there may develop, as Professor

New Society,
2 November 1972

Chinoy has remarked, separate but parallel hierarchies of status within each racial, religious or ethnic group. Prestige and status, in C.W. Mills' phrase, are but 'the shadow of money and power.'

Post-war Change in the UK

British politics have seen some remarkable changes in the last quarter of a century or so, partly because, unlike the 1950s, the 1960s, 1970s and 1980s witnessed recurrent financial difficulties. In such times it is natural to search, perhaps in desperation, for cures to economic problems by embarking upon the systematic reform of political institutions. This will not of itself necessarily solve anything, as many 'revolutionary', totalitarian regimes have found. But it can also serve a distinctly practical purpose, for political sideshows or military adventures may at least attract attention and concern away from daily economic gloom.

The major features of British political change

There have been the devolution proposals of 1968–78; the major reforms of local government from 1973 to 1985; the changes in the Civil Service (after the Fulton Report) in 1968–72 and 1980–4; the reform of the administrative structure of the National Health Service in 1973–4; the 'opening up' of government by the establishment of the central government Ombudsman in 1967 and the extension of the system to local government in 1974; the experiments with specialist committees in the House of Commons after 1966 and the establishment of a more permanent structure in 1979; the extension of the vote to 18–21 year-olds in 1969; the rapid decolonisation of the Empire from 1957; the entry into the European Economic Community in 1973 and the establishment of direct elections to the European Parliament in 1979; a major reform of the courts structure in 1971; and privatisation measures of Mrs Thatcher's Government since 1979. All these have been political changes of a fundamental nature, although in some the electorate has been only marginally interested, as evidenced by the 32 per cent turn-out in the 1979 and 1984 European Elections (in the latter year the Conservative, Labour and Alliance share of the vote was 40.8 per cent, 36.5 per cent and 19.5 per cent and 45, 32 and 0 seats respectively – the figures exclude Northern Ireland).

Secondly, there have been the less noticeable changes that are part of a continuous process; in particular, the seemingly inevitable economic, but not necessarily political, embourgeiosement of society, and the gradual but consistent rise in the influence of interest and pressure groups.

Thirdly, certain changes which appeared to be highly significant at the time were in fact quite ephemeral; examples include the power-sharing arrangements of the Northern Ireland Executive in 1973, the use of a public referendum on the EEC issue in 1975, various prices and incomes policies (statutory under Labour in 1966–9, voluntary under the Conservatives from 1970 to 1972), the National Plan of 1965 and the Ministry of Land and Natural Resources (1964–7), together with the abortive Land Commission (1967–71).

The United Kingdom's entry into Europe: Lord Soames, Edward Heath, Lord Home and Anthony Barber at the negotiations for EEC membership in 1972

So, some forms of political change are clearly more symbolic than real, such as 'voting deviance' at parliamentary by-elections – more protest than change. Also under this heading falls Dick Taverne's success in upsetting the official Labour Party machine in Lincoln in the 1973 by-election and his subsequent attempts to form a more 'moderate' Labour Party until his defeat in the October 1974 General Election. On the other hand, the SDP, formed in 1981, appears to be here to stay. The increase in the number of mainly peaceful protest movements, from the CND (Campaign for Nuclear Disarmament) in the late 1950s and early 1960s, then again in the early 1980s, through to the Vietnam peace movements from 1968 to 1972, is another example, for, in general, the protest march has almost become so commonplace that it is on a level with permanent, institutional change; but individual protests may be noticeably short-lived.

Fourthly, there has been a wide range of legislative change, based on the political parties' programmes but also allied to the subtle, but persuasive, shifts in opinion in society generally.

Lord Croham (Sir Douglas Allen, former head of the Home Civil Service) in the Stockton lecture to the London Business School (January 1978) listed the following political changes that were beginning to affect the British central political process: 1) membership of the EEC; 2) moves to devolution; 3) a tendency to devolve ministerial functions to more and more *ad hoc* agencies (e.g. the Manpower Services Commission); 4) the clawing back of power in Parliament by the back-bencher; 5) the increase in power of interest groups, especially the CBI and TUC; 6) the greater roles of staff consultation and collective bargaining (including civil servants); 7) moves towards greater openness in government; 8) changes in public attitudes towards government and authority. But not all of these 'changes' have been significant – devolution seemed to be killed off in 1979 and under Mrs Thatcher's Government the TUC has lost influence; neither has there been greater openness in Whitehall.

From Tradition to Modernity

For non-revolutionary change to be carried through, a political system must possess the ability to solve problems. However, as well as that capacity, it should also be skilled in political preventative medicine, and in thinking out new policies to replace old ones. In the developing countries there is a dilemma here: the will to modernise is ever present among the political élites, but the quicker the pace the greater the risk of social and political disruption. The irony is that in traditional societies there is often an ingrained respect for the authority and wisdom of government, which provides, at the centre at least, an opportunity of introducing many changes. Steering a course in such situations can be a tricky business, as Saudi Arabia and Iran found when they were caught, in the late 1960s and in the 1970s between the demands of a traditional, 'closed' Islamic world and the problems of what to do with an excess of petro-dollars.

The United Kingdom has faced similar problems: a course had to be steered between the interests of the landed classes of the eighteenth century and the explosion of science and technology in the early 1800s. The new industrial middle classes eventually found a sense of identity in the Liberal Party and in religious non-conformity, although not without civil disturbance and painful social readjustment in the first half of the nineteenth century. Even today, the long tradition of Cabinet government and secrecy tugs at one loyalty, while the fairly widespread and genuine desire for more open government is equally powerful. No political change is achieved without some politician's conscience being wrestled with somewhere.

In the transition from tradition to modernity, it may be that the political culture adopts elements of what might be termed a 'political religion', whereby the belief is developed that a future society will see social order restored at the same time as acquiring material advantages. This is perhaps displayed in recent right-wing movements in the UK, in which the law and order debate has become interlinked (especially in the case of the National Front Party) with status anxiety about immigration. Of course, a charismatic leader will provide an added force for group loyalty, which then overtakes many original beliefs (as with Hitler, and with Perón in Argentina). Here a political trick is performed; old, traditional values are stressed, but at the same time they are combined with the promise of future material gains.

Thus, after the mid-1950s Peronism without Perón was still a vital force in South America. Throughout his first presidency Perón had been obliged (from 1946 to 1955) to rule through an uneasy balance between two or three opposing forces, since it had become clear to him that purely military rule could not be maintained for long. His fall was the result of inability to keep that balance in the much changed economic conditions of the 1950s. Faced with a military coup which was supported by the middle classes, Perón knew that the one remaining possibility was an appeal to the workers. This was a rather bitter pill for him to swallow, but it was not totally indigestible; indeed Peronism survived so well that it staged a second, if shorter, political innings from 1973 to 1976 – first under Perón himself, then under his second wife, María Estella 'Isabelita'.

Equally, there can be change from modernity to tradition, as in the agricultural collectivisation programmes in Vietnam, including the deliberate depopulation of large cities, after the final American withdrawal in 1975, and even more so in those of neighbouring Cambodia from 1975 to 1978. India has also provided us with a good example. As Barrington Moore reminds us, Mahatma Gandhi's love of the village had, with some justification, anti-urban and even anti-capitalist overtones. 'There was a real basis for this outlook in Indian experience. The [alleged] accounts of the destruction of the Indian village handicrafts, especially weaving, by British factory products made a deep impression on Gandhi.' This theme again became prominent in India several decades later, in 1977, when Moraji Desai's Janata alliance party dealt a crushing election defeat to Mrs Indira Gandhi's business-based Congress Government.

Barrington Moore Jr, *Social Origins of Dictatorship and Democracy*, Penguin, 1977, p. 439

A well-established national identity, of course, is no disqualification for experiencing acute problems and dramatic challenges within the political culture. Post-war Japan and Germany are good examples, but in some ways Russia in the twentieth century is the most outstanding. Communist China is another case in point, not just on account of the 1948 revolution but in view of the considerable and almost inevitable periodic upheavals that still take place – Mao's 'Let a hundred flowers blossom and a hundred schools of thought contend' in 1957, his economic 'great leap forward' of 1958–9, the Cultural Revolution and educational changes of 1966–70, and anti-Confucius campaigns in 1974, the disgrace of Deng Xiaoping in 1968 and 1975, of Lin Biao in 1971 and of Madame Mao – Jiang Ging – and the 'Gang of Four' in 1977–8. For many years Ethiopia, to take another instance, maintained strong cultural and religious values, values associated with its long history; but there was considerable internal pressure to modernise them, and they proved impossible to uphold under stress, as was dramatically shown in 1974 by the overthrow of Hailie Selassie. Each of these countries has undergone a traumatic crisis or revolution, economic or military, which has changed the course of its history. Nevertheless it is important to realise the transition from traditional politics to modernity can be made without major disruption. Both Japan (under the Meiji dynasty from 1868 to 1912) and the United Kingdom (after both the Industrial Revolution and the Second World War) managed to achieve dramatic industrial and technological transformation while by and large still leaving intact not only traditional deferential values, but also the existing political system.

At the same time there are also different degrees of confidence in similar political systems, especially in relation to economic prosperity. Until recently

Americans have consistently been more confident about their economic future and their ability to 'advance' society than, say, the British or the French.

In some countries, however, there has often been a lot of dissent in what *appears* to be a very established constitutional order, such as that of Chile until the coup in 1973, and Uruguay before President Bordaberry (1971–6). South American examples are always ready to hand – but the European states can provide plenty as well, such as those of the French Third Republic, established in 1875 by a majority of one vote, and Weimar Germany after 1919.

In all these cases very powerful and active forces have wished, and often worked, for different constitutional structures. And even in those stable democracies in which there has been no real pressure for *fundamental* political change for a long time, such as the UK, the 'older' ex-British dominions, the USA and the Scandinavian countries, there have been occasions when constitutional controversies have become highly active political issues. The crises in Britain over the House of Lords in 1909–11, with 'the Peers versus the People' General Elections of 1910, and in the USA over Roosevelt's proposal to change the political balance among the judges of the Supreme Court illustrate the point.

In most of the established Western-type democracies, what is needed to cause a significant part of the community to look afresh at its usual acceptance of the fundamental organisation of the political system is a major upset in the economy, or some other drastic disturbance of accepted social patterns. Perhaps in the United Kingdom those factors (in the shape of economic difficulties combined with a considerable reorganisation of class boundaries) were most forcefully present this century in 1926, the year of the General Strike.

Summary

'Political culture' as a piece of terminology in political science is capable of wide meaning. However, in the British context it is usually taken to mean the background to, and the values within, the parliamentary system.

Firstly, the British state has not had to face violent challenges to its overall authority. In that sense attitudes among the populace are deferential – the system is widely accepted and respected, if not beloved. The parliamentary process with its constitutional monarchy is here to stay. That does not mean that there have not been violent disorders and protests in the past, such as the suffragette movement in the early part of the twentieth century, or the Chartists in the 1840s, or certain industrial disputes in the 1970s. But as always, we must remember to add the exception – Northern Ireland, hardly a model of political unity.

Politicians may not be held in high esteem, compared with certain professions, but whichever party wins a general election, in the short term its leaders enjoy political legitimacy, even if, as is usual, that party has been elected by less than half those voting, and by even less a proportion of those entitled to vote.

By and large the 'rule of law' operates. Whatever parliamentary legislation is enacted, the electorate obeys. But on occasion well-organised groups, often expressing the deeply held hostility of a wider audience, will oppose a law by unlawful means. In recent years this has mainly occurred in the area of industrial relations, and most notably in respect of Mr Heath's Industrial Relations Act of 1971.

Another aspect of the political culture is that although support for the two largest parties has declined, the electorate is deeply conservative. Only three parties since 1918 have dominated the political scene – Liberal, Labour and Conservative; the nationalist parties, Plaid Cymru and the SNP, have, of course, been restricted to their own geographical areas, as have the nationalist or unionist parties of Ulster. Only the SDP has made an impact since 1981, but had the Liberal Party opposed it, it would never have retained its six seats in the 1983 General Election; and like other political ventures before, it would have sunk without trace.

The Monarchy as a symbol: the Queen on a visit to the Cayman Islands

Then, too, there is the element of political symbolism; that is part of the culture just as the parties themselves are. Symbolism can take various forms, including flags and motifs. But the most notable political symbol is the monarchy itself.

A further aspect of political culture can be seen in what has frequently, and often, misleadingly, been termed political consensus. If there is agreement about fundamentals, then there is political stability, and arising from that little challenge to authority. But in recent years consensus about the economic future has appeared to break down. If Labour has moved leftwards, the Conservatives, as Sir Keith Joseph and Mrs Thatcher spotted, should move to the right to arrest the trend and to stop the party, as they saw it, being pulled increasingly, if imperceptibly, towards socialism. Mrs Thatcher is a conviction, not a consensus politician. But it is a mistake to over emphasise the changes. In the post-war period there have always been considerable disagreements between the two leading parties over nationalisation; Mrs Thatcher's programme of privatisation has deepened this division, and placed the Labour Party in a dilemma as precisely how to respond. The 'mixed economy' appears to be an idea no longer acceptable to both sides. And on other issues the divisions have been no less severe since 1945 – on the NHS, the EEC, nuclear weapons, independence of India. But attitudes change, and the approach has often become a bipartisan one – in the case of the NHS, the EEC and decolonisation, but not yet in respect of nuclear weapons. Moreover, a large proportion of the legislation that Parliament passes each year is not the subject of party differences.

Equally, any British Prime Minister knows that the bulk of the electorate supports entrepreneurial activity and individual initiative, as well illustrated by the popularity of Sir Freddie Laker, at least before the demise of Skytrain. Yet, by the same token, there are very few who wish to see the National Health Service or the Social Security system or state education dismantled or radically altered. Most voters want more services and less taxes, not an easy task for any government, and little wonder that governments frequently reverse themselves on economic policy one in office – Mr Heath's interventionism in 1971 (for example, to save Upper Clyde Shipbuilders and Rolls-Royce), Mr Callaghan in 1976 (the cuts in expenditure following the visit of the IMF), and even Mrs Thatcher, since the first real cuts in public expenditure, as opposed to cuts in planned expenditure, do not take effect until 1988–9, notwithstanding her aim to 'roll back the frontiers of the State, following the £10 billion increase announced in late 1986.

Autumn Statement
1986, Cmnd 14

Mrs Thatcher may not be a universally popular leader; her ratings were low in 1981, but much higher from the time of the Falklands episode in 1982. Yet history plays its part in political culture; neither Lloyd George nor Winston Churchill were consistently popular figures, but the popular view has given a romantic edge to their memory, and to others, too, most notably Harold Macmillan, if not to Eden or Chamberlain, the architects of Suez and Munich. Mrs Thatcher's place in history is assured – one way or the other. The popular sense of history, of parliamentary traditions and political events, subtly reinforces the mass acceptance of the constitutional status quo.

Further aspects of political culture include the way in which power is distributed, among interest groups, the parties, the Civil Service and other organisations, as well as the way in which people participate in the political process, whether by voting, working for a party, standing for local office or for Parliament. The last point begs the question – what kind of people become MPs? As we have seen, they are increasingly middle-class on both sides of the House, and, of course, still male. Many are university educated and have political connections through their families, this being even more true of those MPs who eventually become ministers.

The political élite, however, is wider than just MPs. Apart from peers, bishops, judges and influential broadcasters, financiers, businessmen and trade unionists, the political élite, a notoriously vague term, can be said to include all those subject to ministerial patronage, such as those nominated as members of administrative tribunals, as well as the several thousand on the Whitehall list of the 'Great and the Good' prepared to serve on government appointed committees and inquiries. It is not easy to say precisely what the Establishment or the political élite is. But it is certainly arguable that many of those who exercise power are linked by marriage and family and a public school/Oxbridge background, at least in terms of the City, the Conservative Party and the judiciary. Equally, it can be argued, that although such élites exist, political power is still diffuse – society is pluralist, at least up to a point. There is plenty of opportunity to participate politically, and not just in elections, but also through the parties, pressure groups, local government, the magistracy and quangos.

Questions

1. Discuss the view that the British political system rests on a deferential political culture. (AEB specimen question 1986)

2. To what extent have attitudes to the Rule of Law changed in recent years? (Joint Matriculation Board)

3. What do you understand by either
(a) political culture or (b) political power?

4. What justifications can there be, if any, for ever denying people political rights? (London)

15 Political Systems

Pointers for the Future

Dr David Butler, writing in *The Sunday Times* in 1977 (17 April), suggested eight ways in which the traditional stability and gradualism of British politics, referred to in the opening chapter of this book, has been disturbed in recent years. Those points have already been considered in more detail in previous chapters, but it is worth recapitulating them here. In the first place he suggested that while, alone amongst major nations, we had had a largely unwritten constitution, pressures had been building up (hastened by membership of the EEC) for some form of codification, embracing a Bill of Rights. Secondly, the doctrine of the absolute supremacy of Parliament, in the sense that no Parliament could bind its successors, seemed *de facto* to have been curtailed by EEC law. Thirdly, the idea of 'responsible' government was shown to have been much amended of late, in the sense that ministers appeared not to be responsible, as at one time they had been, for the actions of their own departments. More dramatically, the principle of collective ministerial responsibility at Cabinet level appeared to have been gradually weakened: more ministers nowadays were ready to disagree politically with each other in public, and there were more deliberate 'leaks' to the press. In 1975 the EEC referendum allowed ministers to take a line against the Government of which they were a member, and that permission was repeated in 1977 in connection with the voting system proposed in the European Assembly Elections Bill; while in the same year the Liberal Party was allowed, through the circumstances of minority government, a limited influence over ministerial actions.

In the fourth place, Butler argued that the UK used to seem to have a stable electorate – combined with an overwhelmingly two-party system: his fifth point was that from 1950 to 1970 some 92 per cent of all votes cast were for Labour or Tory candidates, but this had shrunk to 75 per cent by 1974, and, it might be added, to 70 per cent by 1983. The electorate had shown increasing volatility at by-elections in the late 1960s and in the 1970s, and in 1974 there had been an upsurge in Liberal and SNP support, and in 1983 of Liberal–SDP support. His sixth, and related, point was that the electoral system, and the possibilities of proportional representation, were now under closer scrutiny than ever before, especially in the context of elections in Northern Ireland, and, perhaps most important of all, the new European Parliament.

His seventh point was that the traditional picture (notwithstanding Northern Ireland's rather special status) of the UK as a centralised, unitary state was now beginning to disintegrate, not just because of demands for a strong local government service, but also on account of the very significant implications of domestic

Assemblies in Wales and Scotland. By 1987 however, this point looks decidedly weaker, with the failure of devolution in 1979 and the Thatcher Government's strict control of local government spending since 1980. And lastly, Butler argued, the notion of the separation of powers, of the 'independence' of the judiciary was being questioned, as, for example, the Tameside dispute in 1976 showed. Butler's comment on this was that unless Parliament took drastic action, further loopholes would be found; 'citizens aggrieved by some action of an ever-more complex state machine will discover legal objections which the judges will sustain.'

In addition, the separation of powers set the stage for another battle – between Commons back-benchers and Government ministers. Minority Labour administrations from 1974 found this all too true.

Butler concluded his article as follows:

> 'Each one of the trends detected here may stop dead in its tracks. I am not here predicting a multi-party, proportional representation Britain, with a written federal constitution enshrining the separation of powers, governed by a coalition answerable to an assertive Parliament and an ever-more fickle electorate. But some of these developments are at least on the cards. In the rules of government, as in so many other things, the pace of change has increased faster than we have realised. We must be prepared for future shocks.'

In a way what Butler was saying was that the taken-for-granted, unchanging nature of the British political system was now under test in the 1970s in the same way that those of many other parts of Western Europe, not least France and Germany, had been under great political pressures in the 1940s and 1950s.

Butler might have increased his points to a dozen: in the first place, the UK's external relations underwent immense change from the late 1940s to the early 1960s, in the transition from Empire to Commonwealth (during which the gradualist method gave way to a certain amount of indecent haste). Secondly, there is the UK's growing experience of a European role. Thirdly and fourthly, the quality of government and, as government becomes big business, the general liberty and freedom of the electorate, both seemed to be increasingly talked about in the 1970s and 1980s. It is pertinent that, since the Second World War, government – central even more than local – has become increasingly large and bureaucratic. To say that the UK, or indeed any other modern industrial society, is governed worse as a result is probably to miss the point – but governed differently, yes; that is hardly a matter for dispute.

Professor Peter Self, also writing in 1977, commented:

> 'twenty-five years ago, the doctrine of "majoritorian representative democracy" dominated political beliefs'.

New Society,
19 May 1977

This had now gradually been eroded by the growth of interest and pressure groups, by the decrease of 'stable' voting behaviour, and by the slow but steady upsurge in 'populism', as manifested in the holding of the 1975 EEC referendum.

> 'Changes in beliefs about political legitimacy and acceptability have thus considerably influenced the workings of government. They have required government decisions to take account of many more factors and interests than

391

> previously. . . . Possibly the [arguments for decentralisation] are mere eddies against the strong tide of organisational and professional specialisation and scale. But if they are more than eddies, we must think more realistically about *bureaucratic,* as well as *political,* decentralisation. . . . The tides of pluralism and population have far from run their course.'

Writing at the same time, Professor Claude Lévi-Strauss elaborated upon that point in the context of the freedoms of the electorate generally. He remarked that, as a political solution, pluralism cannot be defined in the abstract, that it loses all solidity unless applied to positive content drawn from liberties consisting of 'inheritances, habits and beliefs which existed before laws and which it is the business of laws to protect.'

Professor Lévi-Strauss observed that it had been the custom in political thought since the eighteenth century to make a distinction between freedom in the 'English' and the 'French' senses. He recalled that a century before in 1871, Renan, in *La Réforme intellectuelle en France,* had made the following observations:

New Society,
26 May 1977

> 'England has attained the most liberal conditions that the world has so far seen by developing her medieval institutions. . . . Freedom in England . . . stems from the country's entire history and from the respect equally accorded to the rights of the King, the rights of the Lords and those of the Commons and corporations of every kind. France took the opposite path. The King had long before abolished the rights of the nobility and the commons. France adopted a philosophical approach to a matter that required a historical one.'

And that observation about the strength of tradition and history in the United Kingdom just about brings us, as the saying goes, to where we came in. For the moment, the dozen or so 'pointers for the future' outlined above remain largely academic stepping-stones into a British political future which is admittedly somewhat uncertain. Ten years later, in 1987, what Butler, Self and Lévi-Strauss observed about the British political scene still holds very true. British politics over the next decade could well be entering its most dynamic phase in the whole of the post-war period, at the very least on two fronts – the continuing search for a solution to economic ills and allied to that a possible return to the three-party politics of the inter-war period.

As stated in the opening chapter, brief consideration would be given to other political systems, and it is on that point that this study concludes.

Political Systems

S.E. Finer,
*Comparative
Government,*
Allen Lane, 1970,
p. 96ff

It could be said that the one major alternative to the liberal-democratic model of the United Kingdom and other Western states, is the totalitarian state, and in the economically developed world that is largely, although certainly not totally, true. Professor S.E. Finer, however, in his concise study of comparative government in 1970, has remarked that the 'Third World' largely comprises states that are not unambiguously liberal-democratic nor unambiguously communist/totalitarian. They often share certain characteristics, such as being ex-colonies still subject to outside diplomatic pressures, from either their former colonial masters or the super-powers of the USA and USSR. In addition, there exist traditions of dynasty and (especially in Asia) rule by divine right, and predominance of military forces, as well as economic underdevelopment. Third World countries, according to Finer's classification, are frequently **facade democracies,** in which Western liberal institutions are outwardly adopted, but in practice a manipulating élite is assured of continued power (as in Nepal, Morocco, Burma, South Africa, and Saudi Arabia). Others can be classed as **quasi-democracies,** nearer in the real sense to the Western model but where, because of the cultural background of the country or the nature of the 'rules of the game', one party or political group invariably stays in office (as in Kenya, Mexico, Tanzania and Thailand).

Thirdly, there is the **military regime,** in which the armed forces are constantly present and politically active, as opposed to intervening on isolated occasions – as in France in 1958 and in Turkey in 1971–3. But military regimes vary considerably when placed on a left-right line – compare, for instance, the regime of President Velasco in Peru between 1969 and 1975 (on its position on land reform, in particular) with the Chilean government of General Pinochet which replaced that of Salvador Allende in 1973.

However, a study of Finer's classification reveals how, even since the late 1960s, the 'Third' world itself has changed. It is probably no longer appropriate politically, socially or economically to speak of 'Third World' states; one should refer to the third, fourth and fifth worlds, or to states that are military (left)/military (right), theocratic, dominant one-party, or nihilistic (as in Cambodia between 1975 and 1979). Many countries no longer occupy the same categories in Finer's table. Some nations have even travelled full circle, such as Thailand via its relatively short-lived experiment with parliamentary democracy from 1973 to 1976.

The Eastern bloc

The main alternative to the Western approach, totalitarianism, is best displayed in the Communist countries of Eastern Europe. It can be argued that totalitarianism embraces both fascism (and Nazism) on the right as well as Marxism (in various forms) on the left. But, strictly speaking, fascism is dead, at least in its original Italian context, just as German Nazism no longer exists in terms of major political significance.

The main feature of the Russian totalitarian model is that there is one 'agreed' aim in society, especially in the economic sphere, about which little or no disagreement is tolerated. One party has a monopoly of power, and the power structure is shaped in a very hierarchical way around a formal creed and ideology.

It is only in the last decade or so, however, that Western political scientists have come to appreciate, and to analyse, even if superficially, the differences in Communism within the Eastern European bloc, not all of which is totally Russian in outlook or practice. These are illustrated by, for example, the individualistic foreign policies of Yugoslavia and Romania, the occasional multi-candidate elections in Romania, the periods of literary 'freedom' and economic decentralisation in Hungary since 1956 under Kadar and the tolerance of opposition groups,

393

including a powerful Roman Catholic Church, in Poland. On the other hand, the fate of Dubček in Czechoslovakia in 1968–9 is an equally important reminder of what happens when the liberalisation process 'gets out of hand', as with the Polish 'Solidarity' movement in 1981–2.

One of the USSR's most distinctive features is the extent of the State's direct control over society. For instance, C.J. Friedrich in 1954 enumerated five features of totalitarianism: official ideology, one mass party organised in a hierarchical manner, control over mass communications, terroristic police control and State bureaucracy. In 1956 he added (with Z. Brzezinski) an all-important sixth point: central direction by the State of the entire economy.

L. Schapiro,
Totalitarianism,
Macmillan, 1972,
pp. 18–20

However, it should also be recorded that the term 'totalitarian' lacks precision and is often used very broadly by political scientists and journalists alike; Tsarist Russia before 1917 equally qualified for the label, just as various regimes and dynasties in China have done. Liberal-democratic regimes, too, can be called totalitarian when their policies prove to be highly unpopular, as the USA's Vietnam strategy did in the 1960s. And it is not just states and regimes who bear the label: so do groups and 'movements' – even religious organisations, as the Roman Catholic Church knows only too well. The term is notoriously imprecise.

Totalitarian leadership

The totalitarian leader, it may be said, can hardly permit the existence of any kind of serious opposition group; thus, Schapiro says, normal, recognisable law and morality must be replaced by a new order – as he pointed out, Mussolini remarked that the 'crowd loves strong men, the crowd is like a woman.' However, legitimacy and morality raise further philosophical problems in the definition of a new order. Professor Schapiro has claimed that the leader's rule is based on three essential instruments: an ideology, a party and an administrative machine.

With regard to ideology there is something of a paradox. Communist regimes, from the Western, liberal-democratic point of view, are usually viewed as being rigidly based upon Marxist ideology. However, Marx himself was suspicious of ideology in the nineteenth-century bourgeois sense, since, he said, the very existence of competing but similar ideologies (among different elements of the middle and upper classes) was itself a capitalist trick, almost designed to confuse the proletariat. Mussolini himself only too readily admitted that fascism was more concerned with political tactics than ideological warfare, although it can be strongly argued that, in contrast to German Nazism, the fascist regime of inter-war Italy did possess a quasi-ideology, especially with regard to economic matters.

Communist China since the Second World War has also furnished us with some interesting examples of totalitarian ideology. The events following Chairman Mao's death in 1976 provided textbook examples, within the Marxist framework, of conflicts between the *ideologists,* the permanent revolutionaries (including Mao's wife) and the economic *pragmatists,* who included the then new Party Chairman, Hua Guo-feng, and the leadership that has succeeded Hua.

Leonard Schapiro has observed that the tendency for one-party government to become leadership government could also be seen in nationalist China under the Kuomintang. Indeed Ch'ien Tuan Sheng had noted that the government of inter-war China was merely a group of men who had called themselves 'Kuomintang' and who had 'all revolved around the Leader of the Kuomintang in the person of Chiang Kai-Shek.'

Finally, the administrative apparatus that any such leader is bound to require, whether in party or government, cannot be allowed to mushroom to such an extent that it overshadows or threatens his own position and personality; Mussolini was not very successful in this respect, while Stalin and Hitler manifestly were. Indeed, Hitler pursued the tactic of divide and rule; the various bureaucratic parts of the German political system were frequently in competition with each other, often unconsciously so.

'Totalitarianism' is a blanket term, and its imprecision is indicative of the fact that for a long time political science has suffered from the over-use of generalisations. But noble attempts to make the science more mathematically precise, to apply on a wide scale what we now call 'quantitative methods' have not been without their difficulties; for as long as politics remains the 'art of the possible', some of its aspects can be quantified only loosely at best. That applies equally to the United Kingdom's political system.

We can conclude that there is an enormous range of political systems throughout the world, just as of the cultures which support them. Much to do with political systems is a matter of interpretation and value-judgement; nevertheless, it is possible to note a few theoretical macro-models.

All these models, described originally in 1968 by the American social scientist, David E. Apter, contain features which are relevant to the various types of Western political cultures, but in broader outline they denote, in order, the liberal-democratic (Western) political system, the communist (Eastern) bloc, and developing (Third World) systems.

D.E. Apter,
Political Change,
Cass, 1973
p. 75ff

Theoretical models

The **mechanistic** political system emphasises the fact that society is composed of various competing and interacting elements and groups, which generate conflict as well as social attitudes (or norms). Government is viewed as the means whereby such conflicts are resolved into acceptable solutions. In this model the free exchange of information is crucial; thus it is the social system as a whole which determines governmental activity.

The **organic** model, in contrast, implies a very positive role for government, which has the task of directing society towards a higher end. It stresses the role of the community over that of the individual, and is thus appropriate for revolutionary cultures. It is the government's policy decisions which determine both the nature of and changes in the social system.

However, **newly established** governments may be based on quite different and contrasting forms of political culture – particularly those in Africa and parts of

Asia, where there are clear attachments to 'primitive' forms of government, which sometimes compete with central government and administration for district loyalties. Examples include India, even in the post-war period of parliamentary rule, where the various states have often been engaged in powerful conflicts with the political centre. The very special development of Tanzania under Julius Nyerere is another telling example, for the manner of its socialisation and collectivisation of rural areas; so, for rather different reasons, were Algeria under Ben Bella and Egypt under Nasser in the 1950s.

In practice there is much political diversity: no political process or culture can ever be adequately defined, but we must at least try to understand a little more closely the subtle but pervasive forces which affect the way any political system functions – and, in particular, to identify influences which are more than purely national or regional. And, most important of all to remember, the success or otherwise of a political system will depend upon human practicalities at any given moment. Who better to have the last word on that point than Machiavelli, in *The Prince:*

> 'I also believe that the one who adapts his policy to the times prospers, and likewise that the one whose policy clashes with the demands of the times does not. It can be observed that men use various methods in pursuing their own personal objectives, namely, glory and riches. One man proceeds with circumspection, another impetuously; one uses violence, another stratagem; one man goes about things patiently, another does the opposite; and yet everyone, for all this diversity of method, can reach his objective.'

Niccolò
Machiavelli,
The Prince,
translated by
G. Bull, Penguin,
1961, p. 131

Each British Prime Minister would recognise the wisdom of Machiavelli's observations, but nevertheless unlike leaders in other parts of the world, the occupants of Downing Street face the threat of the ballot box at least every five years and in practice earlier than that. 'Elections? Such beastly affairs!' Harold Macmillan is alleged once to have said.

The USA: The Presidential System

The differences between the United Kingdom and the USA are most important. While the latter's system is based upon a very distinct separation of powers, a written constitution, and the Supreme Court as final political arbiter, the United Kingdom's is steeped in custom and convention – and in the notional supremacy of Parliament, with the Executive and Judiciary as an integral part of that essentially parliamentary system. The UK also possesses a Cabinet, whereas the American system is more presidential- than Cabinet-orientated.

With the growing debate in the United Kingdom about the need for a Bill of Rights and possibly for a written constitution, and with the growth of presidential power and the effects of the Nixon administration, a comparison between the two countries has become especially pertinent. Churchill was supposed to have remarked to Franklin D. Roosevelt that, whereas American Presidents always had the difficulty of finding a suitable rapport with Congress but had little to worry about in relation to their Cabinets, in the case of British Prime Ministers Cabinet members had to be cultivated carefully whereas party support in the Commons was usually assured.

More telling than that, however, are the differences in cultures; the attitudes of the mass electorate towards the institutions of government are quite different – the office of the American President (as opposed to some of its incumbents, such as President Nixon) is widely revered, while Congress is held in less respect (Mark Twain once remarked, 'there is no distinctly native American criminal class except Congress'). Yet in the United Kingdom attitudes towards Parliament and the Queen's First Minister are more complicated, since the Prime Minister is the embodiment of government, and the Government resides within Parliament.

Presidents and political parties

R.S. Hirschfield has said that the power of the American Presidency is complex. 'It cannot be determined simply by reviewing the various roles and functions assigned to the President by the Constitution or by custom.' Despite the written constitution and the role of the Supreme Court in interpreting its various ramifications in accordance, roughly, with shifts in public opinion, there are still grey areas in the American system.

Parliamentary Affairs, Autumn 1968

Presidents are only authorised to conclude treaties with the advice and consent of two-thirds of the Senate, but it is questionable whether that means real power-sharing in foreign policy and international relations generally. President Nixon, in regard to the transcripts of the secret Watergate tapes, claimed 'executive privilege', although many constitutional lawyers denied that any such thing existed under the constitution.

In America the separation of executive and legislative powers and the less ideological nature of the political parties themselves both mean that, in stark contrast to the UK, party government is only a vague idea: party organisation is not particularly national, except at convention time, and even conventions play little part in formulating policy compared with British annual party conferences.

Nor indeed is party organisation disciplined. (It could be argued, however, that the recent experience of minority government in the UK has made party discipline more flexible and more 'American', at least in Parliament.) And, by the nature of the electoral system, one party may be represented in the White House while the other controls one or both of the Congressional chambers. Indeed a President who wishes to pursue a policy of active domestic change (such as Kennedy's New Frontier programme or Johnson's New Society campaign), may find that his majority in Congress is on paper only, and not workable. The major parties in America represent even more disparate interests than those in the United Kingdom. The most notable example for many years of intra-party division in the USA has been the great difference in cultural and political outlooks between southern Democrats and their northern (majority) counterparts. In the 1970s, however, the political rivalries of the two wings of the party declined.

USA and UK – some basic political differences

	USA	UK
A. Political culture/ geography	Large country, full of ethnic and cultural contrasts.	Ireland apart, more homogenous, and generally less sharp cultural and ethnic differences (although Welsh and Scottish identities more important nowadays).
B. Federalism	A large amount of legal and legislative independence in each state (more than in British counties). Certain large local governments authorities enjoy a considerable degree of political autonomy too.	A centralist/unitary state, only possibly a quasi-federal one with devolution to Wales and Scotland; and a formal relationship does exist between central and local government; UK is less 'unitary' than France or, at the other extreme, the USSR, which by its constitution is a 'federal' country.
C. Separation of powers	Reasonably clear and distinct. President elected separately from Congress, and vital revising role vested in Supreme Court.	'Overlapping separation': one election to produce both a Government (Executive) and a Parliament; House of Lords has both *legal* and *legislative* role.
D. Nature of the Constitution	Written, 200 years old and without large-scale modification. State and federal Supreme Courts will interpret the constitution in the light of public opinion and political developments.	Partly unwritten, and dependent on customs and convention as well as on the laws Parliament passes. No supreme court as such, House of Lords only final court of appeal. No Bill of Rights (in USA part of the written constitution). (France's latest written constitution dates from 1958; the USSR's from 1977.)
E. The nature of the political parties	Democratic and Republican both loose, flexible organisations. Considerable amount of common ground – people changing their voting behaviour more easily, especially in presidential elections. But also public differences between different sections of the same party more apparent. Turn-out fairly low – presidential elections barely 60%; mid-term Congressional elections usually around 40%.	Party loyalty amongst the activists, and even the mass electorate, quite high, and slightly more so among the Tories. Internal party differences of opinion, especially in the 1945–81 period, kept more private, and party philosophies usually more polarised. Turn-out higher (although lower than most other Western European countries), generally about 75%.

On the other hand, a weak President is not so much one afraid to act as one who interprets his role as a custodial, moderating one, mainly concerned with foreign affairs, leaving Congress, the States and local government to fulfil their own wide domestic functions. Such a President may be in some ways a 'moral' leader, but he is invariably a non-innovator, merely seeking efficiency in government. In contrast, the strong President, whether a Democrat or a Republican, will be far more of an innovator, seeking to expand presidential power (often to the concern of Congress, as in the late 1960s and early 1970s), and perhaps possessing national and international vision. Under such men efficient administration will usually take second place to an attempt to change American society radically.

Thus, there is more scope for the American President than the British Prime Minister to create a personal as opposed to a party image in a crisis. President Hoover's 'wait and see' approach in the economically depressed inter-war years was far removed from President Roosevelt's New Deal measures, and in the same way President Eisenhower's reluctance to act over racial matters was in marked contrast to the attitude of his successor, President Kennedy, in the early 1960s (in fact it was the Supreme Court which in 1954 set the standard for future generations in its judgment in the case of *Brown* v. *Topeka Board of Education*, Kansas).

M.J.C. Vile, *Politics in the USA*, 3rd edn., Hutchinson, 1983, chapters 3, 6 and 9

President Kennedy

The USA: The Supreme Court and Congress

The Supreme Court, like all American courts, and especially the Supreme Courts in each State, is more overtly political than any British court, since it is the final arbiter in the political system. There is no such thing as Congressional (parliamentary) supremacy either in theory or in practice. Moreover, the presidential power of appointing its members gives it an even more definite political complexion. Thus the American Civil Liberties Union won 90 per cent of its cases in 1968–9, the last year in which the progressive Earl Warren was Chief Justice, but with the advent of President Nixon its composition was changed. (Nixon did experience difficulty, however, in getting his proposed Chief Justice, Warren Burger, approved by Congress, and President Reagan experienced similar difficulties in 1986, with regard to Chief Justice William Rhenquist.)

The Guardian,
12 October 1973

As Charles Morgan, one of the South's leading civil liberties lawyers, said in 1973, 'with Nixon's appointees controlling the Supreme Court, and some of the lower courts as well, we're back to where we were before 1954', the year that the Court, in the *Brown* case, outlawed racial segregation in schools.* It should be noted that the contemporary power of the Supreme Court in acting as a political (as well as purely legal) referee by the process of judicial review, in other words by interpreting the Constitution and applying that interpretation to a particular case, whether at State or Federal level, has only been acquired through a series of test-cases. The Constitution itself, almost deliberately, does not lend total clarity to the precise powers of the Court.

Nevertheless the Supreme Court, with its various interpretations and reinterpretations of the written constitution, is in essence a mechanism, just as the Presidency usually is, of binding together not 50 different states but 50 different nations. Federal flexibility, as both the Supreme Court and the President realise, is virtually the only way of overcoming ethnic disparity on a large scale, even after two hundred years; as Simon Winchester commented in *The Guardian* (2 July) in the USA's bi-centennial year of 1976:

> 'It must seem incredible to an outsider that flags will flutter from the sides of houses in Polish Cleveland and in Italian Chicago and in Chinese San Francisco. Or that Sioux Indians will join hands with black South Dakotans in Rapid City, or that Catholic Irish will drink celebratory German beers in Brooklyn taverns beside Scottish presbyterian welders from the navy yard, or that Spanish-speaking and Greek-speaking and Basque-speaking Americans will watch it all on television together on Sunday night. That is surely one of the major achievements of the incredible experiment that is the United States. *E Pluribus Unum* we are reminded on the coinage – and really, how very well they have forged that *unum* out of that amazingly disparate *pluribus.*'

---

*But it was not until 1969 that the Supreme Court, faced with Southern intransigence, ordered immediate desegregation; see David McKay, *American Politics and Society,* Martin Robertson, 1983.

The Presidential–Congressional Relationship

Alistair Cooke has called the Supreme Court 'a monumental institution', and its importance in the American political system must never be underrated. However, it was the relationship between Congress and the President that was particularly highlighted in the 1970s. The Nixon era, culminating in the Watergate Affair, saw a reawakening of Congressional consciousness.

See Ronald Dworkin, *Taking Rights Seriously*, Duckworth, 1978, chapter 5

President Nixon addresses his White House staff on the eve of his resignation and departure from office

The parties between the wars were even more amorphous in their philosophies and organisation than they are now, and, whatever the merits and demerits of Roosevelt's social policies, it was from the 1930s that presidential power, in relation to the authority of Congress, grew in real terms. It is true that Roosevelt had to take account of very powerful interests in Congress, especially powerful members

401

of the Senate, and various legislative measures, like the 1935 National Labor Relations Act, restricted some aspects of the New Deal programme. But in the period from 1935 to 1972 Congress was generally willing to uphold presidential wishes, and even most vetoes from the White House.

The early 1970s, however, saw a significant shift in the relationship, one that has relevance to the apparent decline of parliamentary power at Westminster. The importance of this shift can be seen when it is appreciated that it has occurred mainly in the economic field. The 1974 'Budget Reform' Act established a budget committee of the Senate and a parallel committee in the House of Representatives, and it set a timetable for their work programme. Its purpose was to give Congress better machinery for assessing the general social and economic effect of its legislation. These measures had the backing of President Ford's administration. President Reagan's difficulties with Congress in 1985–6 on the economic front illustrate how permanent that shift in power has become since Nixon's period of office, notwithstanding Reagan's general popularity within the country.

Congressional
Budget and
Impoundment
Control Act of
1974

If back-bench MPs often complain that the British House of Commons has lost effective control of Government spending, a similar cry has been heard on Capitol Hill. The limits Congress set on departmental programmes were rarely observed, especially under Nixon. Matters reached a head in 1972 when, conversely, the President refused to spend money on authorised programmes of which he did not particularly approve. Under the 1974 legislation, Congress is also assisted in its monitoring by a Congressional Budget Office (CBO) with a staff of more than 250.

Nowadays, once Congress agrees its budget (and 'budget' means the equivalent of estimates in Britain, not of the Westminster-kind budget, which merely refers to the fiscal devices used for raising the right amount of revenue for previously agreed estimates), any money bill which breaches it can be vetoed on the motion of a single member. This is similar to the growing practice in the House of Commons (under pressure from Select Committees such as the PAC) of applying 'cash limits' to Government spending in each department; this now applies to most supply expenditure (i.e. estimates as originally approved by MPs) and it means that by and large the Government must adhere to the financial allocations originally made for major projects, and rely less upon the House agreeing to vote supplementary monies. (The Lords are largely irrelevant in this context as they cannot alter the financial provisions eventually agreed by the Commons as a whole, except by a one-month 'delay'.)

In the USA it is the House of Representatives which must *initiate* all financial legislation, but the Senate has powers of amendment and rejection.

At the beginning of each year, the President submits his 'current services' budget, outlining what it will cost to maintain existing public services at the same standard, and a presidential budget which suggests new possibilities. Both budgets are scrutinised by the CBO, which then reports on them to Congress, putting them into the broader social and economic context. In the space of a short time Congress had 'firmly established an effective means of controlling the overall scale of public spending', something the chairmen of the Commons Public Accounts and the former Expenditure Committees had long demanded. Previously the President had enjoyed immense power, 'irrespective of his party political affiliation and the party

F. Vogl,
The Times,
23 September 1976

Federal Government structure in the USA after reorganisations by Presidents Nixon, Carter and Reagan

THE CONSTITUTION

EXECUTIVE

JUDICIARY

including Federal
Supreme Court

THE PRESIDENT

Executive Office of the President

White House Office

Office of Management & Budget

Council of Economic Advisers

National Security Council

Office of the United States
Trade Representative

Office of Administration

Regulatory Information
Service Center

Council on
Environmental Quality

Office of Science &
Technology Policy

Office of Policy
Development

DEPARTMENTS OF

STATE	TREASURY	DEFENSE	JUSTICE	THE INTERIOR	ENERGY
AGRICULTURE	COMMERCE	LABOR	HEALTH AND HUMAN SERVICES	HOUSING AND URBAN DEVELOPMENT	TRANSPORTATION
					EDUCATION

403

colours of the majority of Congressmen. The President alone proposed a rounded public spending and tax generating programme. By means of lobbying individual committees and by dividing his opponents by all manner of acceptable Washington trickery, he could expect to see his basic budget plan accepted by Congress.' The traditional, historic indiscipline and flexibility within the two main American political parties, whose ideologies are more overlapping than competitive, far more pragmatic than truly philosophical, coupled with the strength of presidential influence, results in a great deal of cross-party voting in Congress, especially in committee – far more than in either House of the British Parliament.

Frank Vogl also pointed out that Congress had now established methods to monitor public expenditure performance and force quick changes in spending plans if it appeared that levels were not consistent with the terms of the final budget resolutions. Brock Adams, chairman of the House Budget Committee, commented in 1975: 'This is a historic turning point for our nation which has laboured for almost 200 years with no structured budget process of its own.' Vogl concluded: 'Congress has indeed gained control of the Budget. It will now fight to maintain control.'

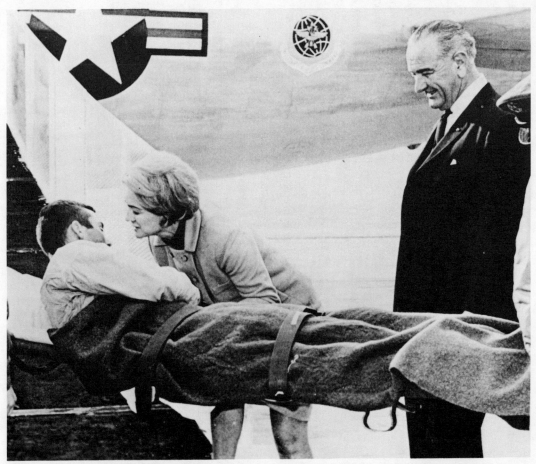

404   President Johnson greets an American marine returning wounded from the Vietnam war

The move towards greater economic control by Congress, developing through the 1960s, was accelerated by the Watergate Affair, by Nixon's large-scale administrative reorganisation of federal government, by inflation and also, ironically, by the manifestation of presidential power in foreign affairs – first in Vietnam under Johnson, then in Nixon's early days as President with the 'short-term' occupation of Cambodia (and the establishment of the Lon Nol regime in 1970). In addition, the War Powers Act of 1973 was, in one way, an attempt by Congress to limit the President's power to commit the armed forces to hostilities, a power which had grown through the 1950s (via the situations in Korea in 1950 and the Lebanon in 1958), reaching a climax during the Cambodian episode. It was, however, an ambiguous Act: liberals were disturbed that it formally gave the President 90 days to disengage militarily, so that a *de facto* situation was liable to turn into a *de jure* one, while conservatives saw it as an intolerable restriction of presidential authority.

For an excellent account of the growth of Congressional power in the 1970s, see M. Shaw, *Parliamentary Affairs*, Summer 1981

These, then, have been the main developments over the past 20 years in the American political system, different from, yet in some respects similar to the British parliamentary process. If, in recent times, both government and legislature in the United Kingdom have faced acute pressures, so, too, have the American institutions, especially at the time of Nixon, Watergate and the USA's withdrawal from South-East Asia. We have also observed the variety and complexity of political systems, from totalitarian regimes to quasi-democracies, from enlightened autocracies to military dictatorships. But the shifting political sands across most of the continents ensure that the academic classification of political states is fraught with danger.

Summary

Whatever the current difficulties about the British political system, and as has been seen there are many, it is important to remember that the United Kingdom is a liberal democracy, and there are all too few such states around the world. Britain has the oldest, continuous democracy, whereby both official and unofficial opposition to the state is tolerated, although it is equally true to point out that many political reformers in the eighteenth and nineteenth centuries would hardly have viewed this system, with its grossly restricted franchise, as anything but un-democratic. Moreover, Britain's sense of liberal democracy is strengthened because of its geographical insularity from Europe; its boundaries have not been under threat, but that very insularity, in European terms if not in imperial or Commonwealth terms, has perhaps meant a high national economic price has been paid in return.

Within the United Kingdom boundaries have posed a problem, most notably and tragically with Ireland; it is Ireland that gives the lie to any claim that the United Kingdom is a homogeneous and politically united society. Even on the mainland, the socio-economic gap between the traditionally industrialised north and the service economy and high technology south has widened in recent years. Overall, the United Kingdom over the last quarter of a century has consistently lagged behind other major Western nations, in terms of inflation, declining productivity, and unemployment. Despite those major economic blemishes, however, its political values remain intact; what is in doubt is not those values as such – free speech, the right to criticise a government, the exercise of voting, but whether the institutions, the adversarial two-party system, the divisions of social class, the anti-industrial culture of the educational system and an Oxbridge dominated Civil Service, plus the laws of official secrecy, can survive the current pressures for economic and political change. Political change is constant, but whether it will be radical is altogether another matter: Britain at heart is a cautious, pragmatic, conservative society, but if there is a real economic downturn by the early 1990s, fundamental reappraisal will clearly be on the political agenda.

Meanwhile, in that pragmatic tradition, the British political system operates via an 'unwritten' constitution. In fact, legislation, including constitutional statutes like the Representation of the People Act 1983, the European Communities Act 1972 and the Government of Ireland Act 1920, is a written source of law. Of course, there are established unwritten conventions, such as an annual meeting of Parliament, the Royal Assent, and the Prime Minister's right to seek a dissolution. Whether the political system would be improved by the enactment of a written constitution or a Bill of Rights or both is another matter; clearer, no doubt, but better, probably unproven. As long as the advocates of one party parliamentary majorities win the day (principally Labour and Conservative MPs) the advocates of a written Constitution, a Bill of Rights, proportional representation and decentralisation of power to the regions (largely Liberals and Social Democrats) will have their ideas untested. Those who advocate such reforms see it as a way of breaking down the two party system, the class structure, the Establishment and the dominance of London, all of which will not only improve democracy but also, so it is claimed, develop an otherwise ailing economy.

It has to be said, however, that Britain's record in inventing or amending constitutions does not fall into the first division, as the experiences of Ireland and the Commonwealth amply illustrate, as well as the costly failure of the 1977–9 devolution programme in Scotland and Wales. The realisation of a written constitution is still a distant prospect, although the enactment of a Bill of Rights (probably the European Convention on Human Rights) is perhaps more likely. In the meantime the novel use of the referendum, in 1975 over membership of the EEC and in 1979 over Scottish and Welsh devolution, has acted as a political safety-valve, even though many MPs and the two respective Prime Ministers (Harold Wilson and James Callaghan) were not overwhelmed by such a development.

For a note on a Bill of Rights and the European Convention, see M. Zander, *New Society,* 6 December 1985

Questions

1. Describe and account for the developments in extra-parliamentary forms of protest since the 1960s. (AEB specimen question 1986)

2. Consider the claims of some one-party states to be called democratic. (London)

3. To what extent is political change in the United Kingdom non-violent?

4. Some people believe that parliamentary government actually restrains democracy. State the case for and against this view.

Appendix A

The Armstrong Note, 1985

(1) During the last few months a number of my colleagues have suggested to me that it would be timely to restate the general duties and responsibilities of civil servants in relation to ministers. Recent events, and the public discussion to which they have given rise, have led me to conclude that the time has come when it would be right for me, as Head of the Home Civil Service, to respond to these suggestions. I am accordingly putting out the guidance in this note. It is issued after consultation with Permanent Secretaries in charge of departments, and with their agreement.

(2) Civil servants are servants of the Crown. For all practical purposes the Crown in this context means and is represented by the government of the day. There are special cases in which certain functions are conferred by law upon particular members or groups of members of the public service; but in general the executive powers of the Crown are exercised by and on the advice of Her Majesty's ministers, who are in turn answerable to Parliament. The Civil Service as such has no constitutional personality or responsibility separate from the duly elected government of the day. It is there to provide the government of the day with advice on the formulation of the policies of the government, to assist in carrying out the decisions of the government, and to manage and deliver the services for which the government is responsible. Some civil servants are also involved, as a proper part of their duties, in the processes of presentation of government policies and decisions.

(3) The Civil Service serves the government of the day as a whole, that is to say Her Majesty's ministers collectively, and the Prime Minister is the minister for the Civil Service. The duty of the individual civil servant is first and foremost to the minister of the Crown who is in charge of the department in which he or she is serving. It is the minister who is responsible, and answerable in Parliament, for the conduct of the department's affairs and the management of its business. It is the duty of civil servants to serve their ministers with integrity and to the best of their ability.

(4) The British Civil Service is a non-political and disciplined career service. Civil servants are required to serve the duly elected government of the day, of whatever political complexion. It is of the first importance that civil servants should conduct themselves in such a way as to deserve and retain the confidence of ministers, and as to be able to establish the same relationship with those whom they may be required to serve in some future administration. That confidence is the indispensable foundation of a good relationship between ministers and civil servants. The conduct of civil servants should at all times be such that ministers and potential future ministers can be sure that confidence

can be freely given, and that the Civil Service will at all times conscientiously fulfil its duties and obligations to, and impartially assist, advise and carry out the policies of, the duly elected government of the day.

(5) The determination of policy is the responsibility of the minister (within the convention of collective responsibility of the whole government for the decisions and actions of every member of it). In the determination of policy the civil servant has no constitutional responsibility or role, distinct from that of the minister. Subject to the conventions limiting the access of ministers to papers of previous administrations, it is the duty of the civil servant to make available to the minister all the information and experience at his or her disposal which may have a bearing on the policy decisions to which the minister is committed or which he is preparing to make, and to give to the minister honest and impartial advice, without fear or favour, and whether the advice accords with the minister's view or not. Civil servants are in breach of their duty, and damage their integrity as servants of the Crown, if they deliberately withhold relevant information from their minister, or if they give their minister other advice than the best they believe they can give, or if they seek to obstruct or delay a decision simply because they do not agree with it. When, having been given all the relevant information and advice, the minister has taken a decision, it is the duty of civil servants loyally to carry out that decision with precisely the same energy and good will, whether they agree with it or not.

(6) Civil servants are under an obligation to keep the confidences to which they become privy in the course of their official duties; not only the maintenance of trust between ministers and civil servants but also the efficiency of government depend on their doing so. There is and must be a general duty upon every civil servant, serving or retired, not to disclose, in breach of that obligation, any document or information or detail about the course of business, which has come his or her way in the course of duty as a civil servant. Whether such disclosure is done from political or personal motives, or for pecuniary gain, and quite apart from liability to prosecution under the Official Secrets Acts, the civil servant concerned forfeits the trust that is put in him or her as a servant of the Crown, and may well forfeit the right to continue in the Service. He or she also undermines the confidence that ought to subsist between ministers and civil servants and thus damages colleagues and the Service as well as him or herself.

(7) The previous paragraphs have set out the basic principles which govern civil servants' relations with ministers. The rest of this note deals with particular aspects of conduct which derive from them, where it may be felt that more detailed guidance would be helpful.

(8) A civil servant should not be required to do anything unlawful. In the very unlikely event of a civil servant being asked to do something which he or she believes would put him or her in clear breach of the law, the matter should be reported to a superior officer or to the Principal Establishment Officer, who should if necessary seek the advice of the legal adviser to the department. If legal advice confirms that the action would be likely to be held to be unlawful, the matter should be reported in writing to the Permanent Head of the department.

(9) Civil servants often find themselves in situations where they are required or expected to give information to a parliamentary select committee, to the media, or to individuals. In doing so they should be guided by the general policy

of the government on evidence to select committees and on the disclosure of information, by any specifically departmental policies in relation to departmental information, and by the requirements of security and confidentiality. In this respect, however, as in other respects, the civil servant's first duty is to his or her minister. Ultimately the responsibility lies with ministers, and not with civil servants, to decide what information should be made available, and how and when it should be released, whether it is to Parliament, to select committees, to the media or to individuals. It is not acceptable for a serving or former civil servant to seek to frustrate policies or decisions of ministers by the disclosure outside the government, in breach of confidence, of information to which he or she has had access as a civil servant.

(10) It is ministers and not civil servants who bear political responsibility. Civil servants should not decline to take, or abstain from taking, an action merely because to do so would conflict with their personal opinions on matters of political choice or judgment between alternative or competing objectives and benefits; they should consider the possibility of declining only if taking or abstaining from the action in question is felt to be directly contrary to deeply held personal conviction on a fundamental issue of conscience.

(11) A civil servant who feels that to act or to abstain from acting in a particular way, or to acquiesce in a particular decision or course of action, would raise for him or her a fundamental issue of conscience, or is so profoundly opposed to a policy as to feel unable conscientiously to administer it in accordance with the standards described in this note, should consult a superior officer, who can and should if necessary consult the Head of the Home Civil Service. If that does not enable the matter to be resolved on a basis which the civil servant concerned is able to accept, he or she must either carry out his or her instructions or resign from the public service – though even after resignation he or she will still be bound to keep the confidences to which he or she has become privy as a civil servant.

The Duties and Responsibilities of Civil Servants in Relation to Ministers

A note of guidance issued by the Head of the Home Civil Service (Sir Robert Armstrong) and part of a written answer by the Prime Minister to the House of Commons in February 1985, following the prosecutions of Tisdall in 1984 and Clive Ponting in 1985 under the Official Secrets Act. The Ponting acquittal, together with an apparently harsh sentence of six months in the Tisdall case, led to further public demands for reform of the Act. (Sarah Tisdall, a MOD clerk, had sent a secret document to *The Guardian* about the arrival of nuclear missiles in Berkshire.)

Appendix B

Local Government Politics

The Widdicombe Report 1986: The Conduct of Local Authority Business (Cmnd 9797)

The state of local government

In addition to variations in structure and functions of local authorities, there were also differences in size and population. For example, in Birmingham there was one councillor to every 8600 people, while in Powys the ratio was 1::590. Elections also varied. All county and Scottish regional councils were elected once every four years, whilst 129 of 333 districts in England and Wales had opted for elections by thirds, rather than whole council elections.

As the Robinson Committee showed, in 1976 there were 26 per cent of councillors aged under 45, the same figure for 1986 (9 per cent and 7 per cent respectively for those aged under 35). But in the big cities there had been a significant increase in younger councillors.

Scottish councillors represented more people, devoted more time to council duties, and received more remuneration. Scotland also had differences in law on several matters. Wales had nearly the same legislation and structure of local government as in England, but it had more councillors per head of population, a higher percentage of independent councillors and a tradition of detailed involvement by elected members in staff appointments. But by international standards British local government could be seen as ordered and homogeneous.

In 1967 the Maud Committee had found 39 per cent of councillors were 'independents'. Widdicombe in 1986 put the figure at 15 per cent, with the proportion of councils in political control rising from 50 to 84 per cent.

It was not unusual for the majority party to take a greater share of seats on committees than they had on the council as a whole. 94 per cent of all party controlled authorities took all the committee chairmanships. Widdicombe noted that with only 20 of the 47 county councils in England and Wales having an overall majority after the 1985 elections the old two-party conventions based on an administration and opposition had broken down. Complaints about minority party rights often came from Alliance councillors (resulting in three successful High Court actions) and Plaid Cymru. Ideological polarisation had increased on issues such as contracting-out, privatisation, the housing 'right to buy', assisted school places and most of all over spending generally.

Widdicombe found that while in law chairmen of committees had no powers in their own right, in practice they often acted like a central government minister, working closely with chief officers and taking routine decisions between committee meetings, a point underlined by Maud in 1967. But chairmen were increasingly initiating policy, or acting as advocates for policies initiated in the party group.

Despite increasing politicisation of local authorities and larger units since re-organisation in 1974, public enthusiasm remained low, turn-out in local elections being about 40 per cent (41 per cent in English county elections in 1985). (In the USA the comparable figure was 25 per cent, in New Zealand 53 per cent, in Sweden 90 per cent.) People over 55 were twice as likely to use their local vote as those under 35, while 80 per cent of electors thought county councils ran services well (95 per cent at the time of Maud).

The role and purpose of local government

Local government employs almost 3 million people and accounts for 28% of public expenditure. This sheer scale determines that it cannot be insulated from the macro-economic policies of central government. Where central government is pursuing a policy of economic expansion, it can achieve such expansion by loosening the reins on local government and enabling it to spend at its discretion. Since the IMF crisis of 1976, however, the climate has been one of public expenditure retrenchment.

It is pointless to debate whether or not such centralising forces should exist, in much the same way as it is pointless to debate whether politics should exist. They do exist and will continue to do so, and the more realism about this the better. What does, however, need to be considered is whether the cumulative affect of centralism is eroding local government to such an extent that it no longer possesses the attributes on which its case depends. The Redcliffe-Maud Report, in a statement which we endorsed in our Interim Report said that

'Local government is more than the sum of the particular services provided. It is an essential part of English democratic government.'

That, however, is a statement of the ideal. It might be argued that the reality is now that local government has become, or is in danger of becoming, less than the sum of its parts – ie that it lacks sufficient financial and political discretion to reflect local choice even in the basic statutory services which it delivers.

If therefore local government is strong on the delivery of services but weak in the extent to which it provides for local democratic self expression, it ceases to be sufficiently distinct from local administration. If on the other hand it is strong on democratic self-expression, but weak on service delivery the danger is that it will in the long term become only a means of democratic expression, and that services will be administered by other means. These are the Scylla and Charybdis between which local government must steer if it is to continue to be viable.

The political framework

Although there has been a general growth in the geographical spread of politics, and in its intensity, it is important to distinguish between the differing ways in

411

which this has manifested itself. From the research, and our own observations, we would highlight the following manifestations, all of which are separable and do not necessarily flow from each other:

a) elections being contested on party lines;

b) formal council offices (membership of committees, chairmanship, etc) being allocated on party lines;

c) party groups determining an agreed policy line in advance of meetings of the council or its committees;

d) services being delivered according to party political policies (privatisation, direct labour organisations, etc);

e) party political policies being set out in election manifestos and subsequently regarded as committing the majority party;

f) councillors playing a fuller role vis a vis officers in decision taking;

g) councillors taking a fuller role vis a vis officers in day to day management;

h) appointment of officers as a means of political patronage;

i) use of council services and funds as a resource for political patronage;

j) use of local government as a platform for national political issues and ambitions.

Moreover local government has to an extent become more 'political' independently of the impact of councillors. Over the last decade the climate of financial retrenchment has increasingly required decisions as to priorities between and within services. At the same time local communities have become less prepared to accept professional approaches to service delivery, notably in relation to housing, planning, and – most recently – social services, and have sought direct participation through consultation. Lastly local government's internal management has become more corporate and less based on the old service professions. All these factors have contributed to a greater stress on 'political' approaches to decision taking. The organisation of councillors on party lines creates an appropriate framework of accountability in which such increasingly political decisions can be taken.

At the same time strains have developed between majority and minority parties. Their relationships depend on a balance whereby the majority party is able to pursue the policies for which it was elected, but within a corporate framework where decisions are formally taken by the council as a whole (either directly or through delegation). This relationship can break down where the majority party, or their leaders, operate as if they hold executive power in their own right – in the manner of central government Ministers. It can also break down if minority parties do not recognise political realities, and fail to accept that their most effective role will often be one of scrutiny and constructive criticism rather than a direct impact on the formulation of decisions. Strains have also developed within majority parties, most notably over differing views as to their proper relationship with the local party organisation.

The decision taking process

The corporate nature of the current system does not recognise the existence of adversarial party politics. This creates particular difficulties in those authorities which are effectively controlled by the majority party, with the minority party acting as an opposition rather than contributing to the formulation of decisions. In such authorities the political parties have created arrangements of their own, outside and alongside the formal statutory framework, whereby they can develop their policies in a one-party setting. Often policies will be developed in meetings of the full party group, although in other authorities informal meetings of the leader and committee chairmen will be more influential. Ultimately decisions must still be taken formally within the council structure, but this formal process can become a hollow ritual devoid of substance if the issue has been pre-determined elsewhere. This is undesirable for four reasons. First, the formal system is brought into disrepute if it is seen to lack substance. Second, the public cannot see where, or by whom, or on what grounds decisions are formulated. Third, it is wasteful of time and resources to have two systems operating in parallel. Fourth, officers are placed in an ambiguous position: the law requires them to serve the council as a whole through its formal machinery, but political reality – and the need to ensure that decisions take account of their advice – requires them to work closely with the majority party through the informal machinery.

Local government is open to the public view. The legislation in this respect was strengthened during the course of our Inquiry by the Local Government (Access to Information) Act 1985.* Except in certain specified exceptions, meetings of the council, its committees and sub-committees are open to the public and the public are entitled to see copies of agenda and minutes of the meetings and of reports which form the basis for discussion. This provides a guarantee of open-ness in the formal taking of decisions. In this country such open-ness is unique to local government with no parallel among other public sector institutions. It is particularly important given the immediacy of local government decisions to people's lives. It may be argued that the process of debate at the formal decision taking stage will often be very limited because it is known that the majority party have pre-determined their position and cannot be outvoted. Although this might sometimes be true of debate, it is not so of the documentation on which decisions are based. Local authorities need, as a matter of law, to show that in taking decisions they have taken into account all relevant considerations. They will therefore have before them the advice of officers, given on the open record; this not only enables the public to see the basis on which decisions are taken but ensures that the council as a whole – not just the majority – has the benefit of the assessment of officers.

We therefore recommend that:

the system of decision taking in local government should continue to be one in which:

(i)   the council is a corporate body;

(ii) decisions are taken openly by, or on behalf of, the whole council, without any separate source of executive authority;

(iii) officers serve the council as a whole;

local authorities should be statutorily required to include provisions in their standing orders governing the composition of committees and sub-committees with delegated powers to take decisions on behalf of the council. These provisions should provide:

413

(i)   for the composition of such committees and sub-committees to reflect, as far as practicable, the composition of the council as a whole, except in so far as individual parties or councillors might waive their rights;

(ii)   for the chief executive to be responsible for the detailed application of this rule;

the legislation* should be amended so that the rights of members of the public and the press to attend meetings and inspect documents do not apply to meetings of committees and sub-committees which are purely deliberative with no powers to take decisions on behalf of the council; the law in respect of councillors' rights to inspect documents and attend meetings should be amended so that:

(i)   these rights are all contained in statute, with no reliance on common law;

(ii)   these rights do not apply to committees and sub-committees which are purely deliberative with no powers to take decisions on behalf of the council;

(iii) the chief executive is responsible for deciding whether councillors have a need to inspect a document or attend a meeting in order to carry out their duties;

(iv)   councillors do not have a right to inspect documents in which they have a pecuniary interest if those documents are not open to public inspection.

Councillors and officers: roles and relationships

We consider that, after some 15 years of experience of the post of chief executive, there is now a need for it to be clarified and formalised. This is for three reasons.

First, the developments outlined above show that there is a stronger need than ever before to ensure that local authorities are organised corporately (rather than on the basis of service departments), and this would be assisted by vesting clearer responsibility in the chief executive for the overall performance of a local authority's staff.

Second, the increasing frictions between councillors and officers will tend to be exacerbated where there is no clear management authority within the officer hierarchy. The chief executive has an important pivotal role in ensuring that officers understand, and are sensitive to, the political aspirations of councillors; and in ensuring that councillors recognise, and do not encroach on, the day-to-day management responsibilities of officers. We have been concerned by suggestions that where there is no chief executive, or a weak one, this has been accompanied by poor relations between councillors and senior officers and a tendency for their roles to merge.

Third, management problems tend to arise where formal legal responsibilities are vested in an officer who is not the chief executive.

In summary we recommend that:

chief executives should be given the following new statutory functions in relation to the propriety of council business:

(i)   to decide on the detailed application of the rules for party balance on committees;

(ii) to decide whether a councillor has a need to inspect a document or attend a meeting;

(iii) to agree that a matter is urgent before the chairman of a committee may take a decision on it;

(iv) to act as the registrar responsible for the upkeep of the register of councillors' interests;

(v) without prejudice to their general duty to advise the council, to provide advice at the request of any councillor as to the legality of any proposed action or inaction by the council;

(a) local authorities should be able, if they wish, to attach staff to the party groups or their leaders;

(b) such arrangements should be subject to the following safeguards:

(i) the officers should be clearly differentiated from officers serving the council as a whole: they should not carry out or be involved in executive functions and should report direct to councillors, not through the chief executive;

(ii) they should be strictly limited in number and seniority;

(iii) the facility should be made available to minority parties;

(iv) it should be made clear whether or not the appointment is being made on political criteria.

Public challenge

Widdicombe pointed out that under s19 of the Local Government Finance Act 1982 the *court* may order a councillor to be disqualified, for a discretionary period, for unlawful expenditure in excess of £2000, if that person was responsible and acted unreasonably or in the belief that the expenditure was illegal. Under s20 a local authority member is automatically disqualified for five years if the *auditor* certifies the loss of over £2000 has been incurred by wilful misconduct. Widdicombe recommended that disqualification be extended to the office of chief executive where his statutory responsibilities were knowingly and wilfully abused and to councillors in non-expenditure cases of unlawful action.

As for surcharge, 'the incidence of cases has continued to decline.' Since Clay Cross in 1973 the major cases of surcharge were those against 49 Liverpool councillors (£106 123) and 32 Lambeth (London) councillors (£126 947) in 1985. The surcharge powers are under ss19–20 again of the 1982 Act and apply to officers as well as councillors. Under s19 the court may order the repayment of unlawful expenditure in whole or in part; under s20, on the issue of the auditor's certificate, the individual is liable to repay the amount in full. Widdicombe recommended that the procedure leading to surcharge and disqualification in s20 of the 1982 Act (wilful misconduct leading to financial loss) should be brought in line with those in s19 of that Act (illegal expenditure) except that in both cases there should be a duty rather than a discretion to apply to the court.

Further Reading

Below are listed the author's suggestions for building up a small Politics library; many of the works have already been referred to earlier in the text. In addition, much useful information can be gleaned from the quality press, that is *The Guardian, Financial Times, The Independent, The Times, The Sunday Times* and *The Observer,* but particularly the first three publications. Useful weeklies are *New Society* and *The Listener.* Valuable periodicals include the *British Journal of Political Science, Public Administration* and particularly *Parliamentary Affairs.*

Cabinet, Government and Prime Ministers

R.H.S. Crossman, *The Diaries of a Cabinet Minister,* Hamish Hamilton and Jonathan Cape, 1977
R. Hennessy, *Cabinet,* Blackwell, 1986
A. King (ed.), *The British Prime Minister,* Macmillan, 1969
J. Mackintosh, *The British Cabinet,* Stevens, 1968
R. Rose, *The Problem of Party Government,* Macmillan, 1974
R. Rose, *Understanding Big Government,* Sage, 1984

Civil Service

R.G.S. Brown and D.R. Steel, *The Administrative Process in Britain,* 2nd edn., Methuen, 1979
J. Garrett, *Managing the Civil Service,* Heinemann, 1980
A. Gray and W.I. Jenkins, *Administrative Politics in British Government,* Wheatsheaf Books, 1985
J. Greenwood and D. Wilson, *Public Administration in Britain,* Allen and Unwin, 1984
P Kellner and Lord Crowther-Hunt, *The Civil Servants,* Macdonald, 1980
H. Young and A. Sloman, *No, Minister,* BBC, 1982

Culture and Media

G. Almond and S. Verba, *Civic Culture Revisited,* Little Brown, 1979
G. Almond and S. Verba, *The Civic Culture,* Princeton, 1963
J. Blumler and D. McQuail, *Television in Politics,* Faber, 1968
C.H. Dodd, *Political Development,* Macmillan, 1972
D. Kavanagh, *Political Culture,* Macmillan, 1972
L.J. Macfarlane, *Political Disobedience,* Macmillan, 1971
C. Seymour-Ure, *The Political Impact of the Mass Media,* Constable, 1974

Local Government and Regionalism

A. Alexander, *The Politics of Local Government in the United Kingdom,* Longman, 1982
A.H. Birch, *Political Integration and Disintegration in the British Isles,* Allen and Unwin, 1977
V. Bogdanor, *Devolution,* Oxford, 1979
J. Brand, *The National Movement in Scotland,* RKP, 1978
T. Byrne, *Local Government in Britain,* 3rd edn., Penguin, 1985

J. Gyford, *Local Politics in Britain*, 2nd edn., Croom Helm, 1984
G.W. Jones and J.D. Stewart, *The Case for Local Government*, Allen and Unwin, 1983
J. Osmond, *Creative Conflict: the Politics of Welsh Devolution*, RKP, 1977
Lord Redcliffe-Maud and B. Wood, *English Local Government Reformed*, Oxford, 1974
R. Rose, *Understanding the United Kingdom*, Longman, 1982

Parliament

A.H. Birch, *Representative and Responsible Government*, Allen and Unwin, 1964
P. Norton, *The Commons in Perspective*, Martin Robertson, 1981
P. Norton (ed.), *Parliament in the 1980s*, Blackwell, 1985
M. Punnett, *Front-Bench Opposition*, Heinemann, 1973
P.G. Richards, *The Backbenchers*, Faber, 1972
M. Rush, *Parliamentary Government in Britain*, Pitman, 1981

Parties and Pressure Groups

S. Beer, *Modern British Politics: a study of parties and pressure groups in the collectivist age*, Faber, 1982
V. Bogdanor, *Multi-party politics and the Constitution*, Cambridge, 1983
D. Butler and A.H. Halsey (eds.), *Policy and Politics*, Macmillan, 1978
M. Davies, *Politics of Pressure*, BBC, 1985
H. Drucker (ed.), *Multi-Party Britain*, Macmillan, 1979
R. Kimber and J. Richardson (eds.), *Pressure Groups in Britain*, Dent, 1974
R.T. McKenzie, *British Political Parties*, Heinemann, 1963
M. Pinto-Duschinsky, *British Political Finance 1830–1980*, American Enterprise Institute, 1981
R. Rose, *Do Parties Make a Difference?* 2nd edn., Macmillan, 1984

Voting Behaviour

D. Butler, *Governing without a majority*, Collins, 1983
D. Butler and D. Stokes, *Political Change in Britain*, 2nd edn., Macmillan, 1974
S.E. Finer (ed.), *Adversary Politics and Electoral Reform*, Anthony Wigram, 1975
J. Goldthorpe and D. Lockwood *et al., The Affluent Worker,* Cambridge, 1969
A. Heath, R. Jowell and J. Curtice, *How Britain Votes*, Pergamon, 1985
H.T. Himmelweit, P. Humphreys and M. Jaeger, *How Voters Decide*, 2nd edn., Open University, 1985
R.T. McKenzie, *Angels in Marble*, Heinemann, 1968
W.L. Millar, *Electoral Dynamics in Britain since 1918*, Macmillan, 1977
R. Rose and I. McAllister, *Voters Begin to Choose*, Sage, 1986
B. Sarlvik and I. Crewe, *Decade of dealignment*, Cambridge, 1983

General

S. Beer, *Modern British Politics*, Faber, 1969
H. Drucker *et al.* (ed.) *Developments in British Politics,* Macmillan, 1984
M. Duverger, *The Study of Politics*, Nelson, 1972
D. Kavanagh and R. Rose (eds.), *New Trends in British Politics*, Sage 1977
A. King (ed.), *British Politics*, Heath, 1966

D. McKay, *American Politics and Society*, Martin Robertson, 1983

R. Rose, *Politics in England*, 4th edn., Faber, 1985

R. Rose (ed.), *Studies in British Politics*, 3rd edn., Macmillan, 1976

H. Street, *Freedom, the Individual and the Law*, 3rd edn., Penguin, 1972

M.J.C. Vile, *Politics in the USA*, 3rd edn., Hutchinson, 1983

P. Whitehead, *The Writing on the Wall: Britain in the Seventies*, Michael Joseph, 1985

Index

419

Local Commissioner for Administration, 94
local government, 197f.
 finance, 202
 functions, 213
 internal management, 215
 party politics, 221, 223
 reform, 211
 structure, 212
Local Government Act 1933, 199
Local Government Act 1963, 199
Local Government Act 1972, 199
Local Government Act 1974, 94
Local Government Act 1978, 95
Local Government Finance Act 1982, 206, 415
Local Government, Planning and Land Act 1980, 203
Lohan, S., 88
Longford, Lord, 41
Luce, R., 44
Lygo, Sir Raymond, 64

MacDonald, Margo, 231, 266
MacDonald, Ramsay, 192, 235
McCarthy, J., 381
McKenzie, R.T., 39, 40, 266, 271
Mackenzie, W.J.M., 22, 265
McGovern, G., 284
Mackintosh, J.P., 6, 23, 26, 28, 30, 40, 68, 121
Macmillan, Harold (Lord Stockton), 23, 29, 60, 61, 190, 340, 388, 396
maladministration, 89
Malaysia, 9, 19, 150, 303
Mallaby Report, 120, 216
mandate, doctrine of, 299
manifestos, 299
Marre, Sir Alan, 90
Marsh, Sir Richard (Lord Marsh), 42, 117, 250
Marshall, Sir Robert, 110
Marx, Karl, 394
Marxism, 374, 381, 393
mass media, 316, 355f.
Maud Report 1967, 200, 212, 216, 222, 410, 411
Maud Report 1969, 200, 211, 230
Maudling, Reginald, 59, 312
Maxwell-Fyfe, Sir David, 296
Maxwell-Hyslop, Robin, 160
Mayhew, Christopher (Lord Mayhew), 41
Mayhew, Sir Patrick, 65
Mellish, Bob (Lord Mellish), 169
Merthyr Tydfil, 295
Mexico, 271, 298

Miki, T., 22
Militant, 318
Mill, J.S., 4, 200
Milne, E., 295
Mills, C.W., 381, 382
MINIS (management information systems for ministers), 146
ministers, 56
ministerial responsibility, 58
minority government, 172
Mitcham and Morden, 342
mixed economy, 243
Monarchy, 191f.
Mondale, Walter, 330
money Bills, 178
Moore, Jr, B., 385
Moore Report, 123
Mosca, G., 138, 381
Mountbatten, Lord, 239
MTFS (Medium Term Financial Strategy), 243
Mulley, Fred, 54, 208

NCCL, 12
Namibia, 152
National Audit Act 1983, 158
National Bus Company, 13, 228
National Coal Board, 254
National Economic Development Council, 277, 280
National Enterprise Board, 255
National Farmers' Union, 268, 271
National Freight Corporation, 258
National Front, 384
National Health Service, 198
National Health Service Reorganisation Act 1973, 227
National Plan, 255, 382
National Union of Mineworkers, 25, 271
nationalised industries, 245
nationalist parties and nationalism, 236, 316, 374
Netherlands, 191, 193, 345
New Society, 116, 275, 379
New Zealand, 5, 184, 343, 411
Newcastle-under-Lyme, 265
Newham North-East, 265
newspapers, 368
Nicaragua, 152
Nicolson, Nigel, 265
Nigeria, 153
Nixon, Richard, M., 58, 270, 296, 298, 330, 356, 369, 397, 400, 401, 402, 405
North Atlantic Treaty Organisation (NATO), 14, 19, 68

North Cornwall, 335
North Devon, 335
Northcliffe, Lord, 368
Northern Ireland, 4, 237f., 310, 339, 345, 381, 390
Northern Ireland Office, 228, 238
Northern Ireland Act 1982, 239
Northern Ireland (Border Poll) Act 1972, 69
Norton-Taylor, R., 110
Norway, 173, 184, 331
Nott, Sir John, 60
Nyerere, J., 396

Official Secrets Act 1911, 67, 74, 129, 409
Ombudsman, see Parliamentary Commissioner for Administration
opinion polls, 370
Opposition, Her Majesty's, 176
Orpington, 340
Owen, David, 1, 104, 294, 353

PAR, 111
Paisley, I., 301
Palliser, Sir Michael, 113
Pardoe, John, 104, 293, 355
Pareto, V., 381
Parker, Sir Peter, 256
Parkinson, Cecil, 29, 59, 359
Parliament, see also the House of Commons and House of Lords, 30, 149f., 178f.
Parliament Act 1911, 178
Parliament Act 1949, 178
Parliamentary Commissioner for Administration, 54, 60, 89f., 161, 382
participation in politics, 1, 263
party leaders, 313
party organisation, 263f., 281f.
party system, 263f., 281f.
Peckham, 342
Pentagon Papers, 99
Perón, Gen. Juan, 384
Peronism, 385
Peru, 393
Philippines, 227, 310
Plaid Cymru, 230, 296, 301, 316, 340, 377, 410
planning agreements, 255
Plowden Report, 155
pluralism, 1, 3, 4, 389
police, 95
Police Act 1964, 198
Police and Criminal Evidence Act 1984, 95
policy making, 103